VENETIAN ARCHITECTURE OF THE EARLY RENAISSANCE

The MIT Press
Cambridge, Massachusetts,
and London, England

VENETIAN ARCHITECTURE OF THE EARLY RENAISSANCE

John McAndrew

This book was set in VIP Trump Mediaeval
by DEKR Corporation and printed by
Nimrod Press and bound by Halliday
Lithograph in the United States of America.

Library of Congress Cataloging in
Publication Data

McAndrew, John.
   Venetian architecture of the early
Renaissance.

   Bibliography: p.
   Includes index.
   1. Architecture, Renaissance—Italy—
Venice. 2. Architecture—Italy—Venice.
3. Venice—Buildings.
I. Title.
NA1121.V4M32 720'.945'31 80-17045
ISBN 0-262-13157-9

For Alfred and Margaret Barr who, for
many happy years, were my family

CONTENTS

FOREWORD

My husband, John McAndrew, who died in February 1978, had intended at least two more chapters in this book; however, it is complete in itself as it stands. The only work on the manuscript that remained to be done was some straightforward editing and the collecting of about fifty photographs not yet in hand but all on his list. For the work on the manuscript, Laurance and Isabel Roberts gave several weeks of their time, and their help was invaluable. Having read and discussed much of the text with my husband a month before his death, they made it possible for me to present the text to the publisher in its present form.

The missing photographs could not have been procured without the knowledge and generous assistance of Dottore Architetto Renato Padoan, superintendant of the Soprintendenza per i Beni Architettonici e Ambientali di Venezia, who both donated and himself took many of the required photographs. Of course my husband had intended to spend more time polishing, rechecking, photographing, and above all taking yet another searching look at the buildings discussed, but I hope that not too many avoidable errors will be found.

My most grateful thanks are due to the many people who have helped in the preparation of this book for publication. Since it was accepted by The MIT Press in November 1978, I have been most fortunate in having the able assistance of Professor Anthony Kurneta in the detailed work involved in the publishing process. His knowledge, judgment, and patience are deeply appreciated. He has also done the bibliography and the index—no small task under the circumstances.

The first person to read parts of the manuscript was Anne Ferry, and her suggestions and enthusiasm were of great value to the author, as was the early reading by Robert Whittlesey. A great deal of useful research was carried out over several years by Teodora Sissa Sammartini. Count Lodovico Donà dalle Rose did some important work, and Eleanor Garvey, Anna Valcanover, and Sabina Vianello contributed some necessary information.

Some particularly hard-to-get photographs were taken by Dr. David Ashdown. Robert Birnbaum gave his photographs of S Maria Maggiore. Professor Robert Munman, Patricia Peck, and Julia Keydel gave photographs taken by themselves. Thanks must go to Mr. Robert Cecil for arranging for our reproduction of a Canaletto in the Wallace Collection. I am extremely indebted to Dottoressa Ileana Chiappini for assistance in identifying or confirming the credits for all the photographs from the Museo Correr. Professore Architetto Giorgio Bellavitis generously supplied the plan of the Palazzo Zorzi. Monsignore Bortolan solved a difficult problem, as did Dottoressa Colasanti of the Archivio di Stato di Venezia. Dottoressa Bianca Lanfranchi of the Archivio gave me invaluable assistance, and Professore Architetto Giorgia Scattolin kindly found some missing credits. Professors Peter Fergusson, Sydney Freedberg, Henry Millon, and Terisio Pignatti have given support, encouragement, and concrete assistance for which my gratitude knows no bounds. Many other friends of the author also helped; to them I extend my warm thanks.

The retyping of the manuscript was accomplished in record time by Signorina Anna Maria Franco, and Signora Maria Luisa Weston typed all the copies of the photograph captions.

Finally, I want to give very special thanks to Professor Wolfgang Lotz for all his kindness and to Professor James Ackerman for writing the appendix on the cloisters of S Zaccaria.

Betty Bartlett McAndrew

PREFACE

One summer afternoon some years ago I was sitting at Florian's in the Piazza S Marco, having coffee with two German professors distinguished for both their works and their years. Suddenly one announced, "Too bad no one can work on the later architecture of Venice." The other nodded, and then asked why. "Because there are no photographs of it in the Cini Library." (Happily, there are now, and at the Soprintendenza ai Monumenti, and the Correr Library, easy and pleasant places to work, all in Venice and regularly open; and some can be found at a few fine professional photographers.)

That exchange was disturbing not because it pointed out an obstacle—quite imaginary—to work in a rewarding and neglected province of art but because it exposed a sinister belief, that work with photographs is essential and work with actual buildings is not. Most of the Renaissance and Baroque buildings of Venice are still splendidly there and not hard to see. My mind went back with growing awe to Crowe and Cavalcaselle and other great critics or scholars of the last century, who had to do much of their work by looking at real monuments, printing pictures in the mind, and printing them well enough for sound comparison with works hundreds of miles away, with no more help than perhaps a few sketches and sometimes daguerreotypes.

I walked around in Venice without a camera for several summers after this conversation, looking, trying to learn to remember accurately, and determined to write something based mainly on direct ocular experience. But then there came an interruption that crowded out time for writing—efforts to hold up some of the buildings after the unthinkable storm and flood of November 1966. Only lately has it become possible to go back to the original project, with the results that fill the following pages.

We know how histories of Italian painting can suffer if written mainly from photographs; for sculpture it is worse; for architecture, impossible. Studying only views or diagrams flat on paper does not allow us to experience the hollow or solid effects of mass and of void and the shifting play of light and shade. I began, therefore, to inspect at first hand—and several times—every work considered in the following pages (except those no longer standing). I used photographs only as reminders or for comparison, and this I have continued to the end. Immediate visual contact cannot be replaced by any book, but text and illustrations can sometimes half-reanimate a building, particularly if they are so tied together that the eye keeps going from one to the other. Although authors ought not to beg readers for special treatment, it does seem permissible here to urge that the text be read only in constant alternation with the pictures, for it was written in an effort to help people to see as much as possible in the monuments themselves, rather than to trail docilely along after the musings of one observer-writer, like captives of a guide-conductor on a processed and packaged tour.

Is yet another book on the buildings of Venice justifiable, even if limited to the first years of the "later" or Renaissance ones? If so, it is only because for some generations no ample account of her Renaissance architecture has appeared in English. Although scattered bits—some of them precious—have been studied in the sharp light of modern scholarship, few have been fitted into a sequence of ideas approaching the length of a book. Even if justifiable as a filling for some of this gap, what follows cannot claim much new material or daringly new points of view for several reasons. From the mid-XVc to the XVIIIc, architecture did not develop in Venice as it did in other places. No new needs called for new types. Like the plan of the city—a city for boats,

pedestrians, and horses, but nothing with wheels—the scheme of the Venetian dwelling had long been fixed; there were few innovations in the schemes of churches; no important new structural or decorative materials were introduced; no novelties appeared in construction or the manipulation of space. Political and economic events had less effect than elsewhere, for although less might be built during wars or financial depressions, after recovery work was picked up where it had been left off, little altered; and furthermore, the interruptions were short. Change barely showed in monolithic Venetian social life or in the buildings made to house it, and what changes there were came at the speed of a lava flow. It is almost as though when the Golden Book, a short and very strict sort of early Social Register, was closed in the XIVc and new families were excluded, new ideas were shut out too. One cannot, then, dwell on any great developments in Venetian architecture contingent on technical, historical, or economic changes.

One element that did develop or change was style. A history of post-mediaeval building in Venice will have to be concerned chiefly with its morphology. But even the succession of styles was peculiar. Here Venice is oddly akin to Spain; she invented little and borrowed much, but once taken across the Lagoon, as over the Pyrenees, the borrowed forms or concepts underwent such transmutations that they soon became thoroughly and unmistakably Venetian or Spanish. Evident in mediaeval times, this local peculiarity continued as strong if not stronger in the Renaissance and Baroque periods.

Extended discussions of style cannot be made without considerable detailed description of the monuments whose style is being studied. Analysis demands it. Illustrations can reduce description, but even in illustrations certain features or qualities have to be pointed out. There is some danger that the descriptions will duplicate what is already shown in a photograph and that the text may slip away from dealing with ideas and lose itself in a repetitious kind of slide talk.

Although some of the differences between this and older studies come from changed ways of dealing with style or styles, another comes from the correcting of a few no longer reliable old "facts" and the adding of some more reliable new ones. I cannot claim to have made major discoveries in documents. The Venetian archives, largest in the world after those of the Vatican, could be an inexhaustible mine for a book of great value, a book that would take an inexhaustible lifetime. I have spent less time in the Archives than some of my colleagues, partly because for the Early Renaissance they have already been so deeply mined by such scholars as Pietro Paoletti, and only occasionally yield bonanzas to a handful of distinguished Italians or young foreigners. In good weather, I make daily forays to work from the buildings themselves; in bad, or away from Venice, I work mainly from printed sources, old and new, less as a search for new facts than to take a fresh look at the old monuments. There will be, then, emphasis not only on what is there but also on how it appears to the eye, how it works visually, and sometimes even empathetically. This cannot be wholly objective, of course, but has to be tinged by the individual viewer's gestalt. Assessments of artistic merit may follow and they too have to be personal. Thus some of what follows may appear old-fashioned, more characteristic of a time between Ruskin and Wölfflin than of works written in our lifetime.

Dealing with appearances above everything else can lead to certain special kinds of emphasis, in a way less common now than it once was. For example, in considering how the orders are used, I have to return over and over to an "as if" tectonic quality—whether the orders seem inadequate or hypertrophied in performing their apparent structural role. This would seem to be how most of the architects thought of them at the time, a way of thinking they must have conveyed also to their clients, usually well-educated men. Empathy will have to be forced on a great many working parts, whether they are really doing what they appear to or not (cf. Scott, 1924, ch. VIII).

Other attitudes that might seem unusual may come from particular ways of handling problems. For example, anyone trained and practiced as an architect may deal with the conditions behind the planning, construction, and design of a building differently from a pure art historian and consequently may approach discussion of it by a different route. When confronted by a professional problem, even an obsolete one, he may be able to draw on parallel past experience that could bring him closer to how the mind of another architect might have worked on it; and this may be different from the ideas arrived at by a historian, whether theoretical, aesthetic, social, economic, or whatever—usually a mixture. He will feel more poignantly than any historian how many decisions, minor and major, may have been made less by the architect than the client, who was in a position to impose his will. All clients have not been docile; some have had aggressively independent taste or have been subservient to what they took to be the good taste of the time. Every building was commissioned by someone or, often in Venice, by some group who wanted it enough to pay for it; not one was a free creation by an artist aiming only to please himself. He could rarely create as independently as he might have liked, as freely as a Picasso who could ignore clients or a Frank Lloyd Wright who could dominate them.

Critical histories of architecture can be arranged chronologically, building by building, which gives a rigid logic to the whole, but at a price, for it will separate some monuments that could be better illuminated if examined together. Or a history can be arranged by categories: all the churches together, all the palaces, all the chapels, and so on, which makes chronology choppy but often helps analysis of style. Necessarily this splits up the work of an architect disturbingly. And, of course, the complete oeuvre of one architect after another can be set down in approximate chronological order. Alone, none of these methods works well for the material that follows, and I have shifted about among them, mostly from the last two, choosing for each case whichever seemed to fit best. This also has its price, and one master (such as Codussi) may have to appear scores of pages after an important contemporary (such as Pietro Lombardo). It is hoped that a few reminding phrases here and there can help avoid major misunderstanding.

This book is concerned with Venice only, with little reference to related buildings elsewhere. That exclusionary policy is less arbitrary than it might at first seem, for with few exceptions the chief architects of the city built their chief works there. Sansovino, for example, was not a major architect when he fled Rome for Venice, and Venice so changed his architecture that his works there can be understood without giving his earlier efforts more than a glance. What Pietro Lombardo built outside Venice, for example, could add facts to our knowledge of him but almost no new ideas.

Some of what this book is not may thus be explained. What it is need not be explained here, for the pages that follow ought to do that; there is, in fact, no hiding it.

There are few footnotes, for information already printed in two or three standard sources may be considered in the public domain and in no need of justification by notes. Notes to less obvious sources merely refer to the author and the page, with the date if more than one of his works is listed in the bibliography. Anything I believed worth saying is included in the text, and if it did not deserve space there, it was tossed out. Nearly all the facts (such as dates) come from the researches of my predecessors and, when repeated by several writers, need no footnote justification. Recent discoveries by individuals are, of course, credited. The interpretation of facts, such as the design or function of the actual buildings, is nearly always my own.

Dimensions were mainly measured, paced, or approximated by myself, or come from the Soprintendenza ai Monumenti.

Names are sometimes given in Italian, sometimes in Venetian, whichever is heard most often today. When needed, there are cross-references in the index.

A glossary for the use of readers not familiar with some of the architectural terms and the few uniquely Venetian ones will be found at the end of the book. Terms that have to be used frequently are explained in the text the first time they are used, then adopted and naturalized and used like standard architectural terms.

John McAndrew

Venys round, rich and stout,
And Venys stands all in the sea,
And Isles about it great plenty.
And Lords they been of divers places.
To tell their lordship I have no space,
But I dare it so descry,
It is a rich town of spicery,
And of all other merchandise also,
And rightewell victualled thereto . . .

Purchase, his Pilgrimes, 1422

I EARLIEST WORK

I | FIRST EARLY RENAISSANCE WORK

Long ago we were taught that Renaissance architecture began suddenly in the work of one genius in Florence, and soon matured in the ideas and rare buildings of another. Brunelleschi and Alberti, however, had little to do with the buildings of the Early Renaissance in Venice. In Northern Italy, nearby, a sort of classicizing patois was taken up after the more properly classical ideas were first formulated and then followed in Florence for a generation. More parvenu than the Florentines, Lombard patrons began to enjoy showing off newly learned bits of the classical vocabulary, not realizing that it had been developed along with a new syntax based on Roman forms, and that one could not be counted on to be coherent without the other. The results were wayward, sometimes charming, sometimes close to gibberish.

Since ideas often took time to cross the lagoon, a long generation passed before Venice tried the new style. Michelangelo was born and the Florentine pioneers of the Renaissance were dead before it took firm root in Venice. Moreover, there was little cultural interchange with Florence, for all Florentines had been expelled from Venetian territory in 1440, and the two states were often at war (like a feud, though luckily no one was killed). When the first Renaissance importations did come, they were brought by men from Milan, Como, Bergamo, or the region of Lugano, remote from Florence and closer to Venice—closer in more ways than one, since Venice then held North Italy to within twenty miles of Milan. So many North Italians came to work in the city that they engendered resentment; by 1486 native craftsmen complained of discrimination against them in their own city—the immigrants must have been well entrenched—and in 1491 the masons again protested poaching by foreign labor. But however

North Italian their manner when they arrived, in a decade it took on enough Venetian flavor to set it well apart from what it had been. Not one of the inaugurators of the Renaissance in Venice was born there. No battle of the styles had to be fought, for the native Gothic slowly faded away without any nationalistic last stand.

These early visitors were not what we would now call architects; some were masons and some were sculptors. The use of sculptors as architects may give a clue to the ornamental extravagance of many Early Renaissance buildings—that and perhaps some envy of the Byzantine and Gothic richnesses still there in such abundance. The architectural compositions were largely in low relief; and enthusiasm for surface decoration was often combined with ignorance or innocence of such architectural fundamentals as coherence, consistency, balance, or emphasis. New words and phrases were freely arranged, sometimes with the old Gothic grammar or what was left of it—with one exception, almost nothing Byzantine was still active—or even with no discernible grammar at all. Renaissance ideas began to bud here and there on almost any part of a building, but they did not sprout or unfold consistently as though from organic growth.

The quality of craftsmanship was unusually high, highest of all in the decorative carving. This was executed not only with great technical skill but very often also with exquisite taste (if that term can be used in so absolute a sense and not merely for comparison or chronological identification). The new designers were not, on the other hand, notably inventive; no new kind of building or new kinds of design were developed. Yet somehow the borrowed finery and its general arrangement could add up to something original, something recognizably Venetian, something that was not to be found elsewhere in Italy.

Historians of art with an innate sense of order or a compulsive wish to impose one have tried to classify these early developments in Venice systematically, working them into a pattern easier to grasp than the elusive and all-too-random truth. The visits of the Florentine architects Michelozzo (1433) and Filarete (1458) could be conveniently revealing—if only there were specific knowledge of something they had built, and what it looked like. No results of their visits can be pulled out of limbo. Vasari (1963, I, 316) said that Michelozzo made many models and drawings for Venetian friends of Cosimo de' Medici, but Vasari may have made up the tale to give more standing to Florentine Michelozzo. Filarete may have had less effect on Venice than Venice had on him. Michelozzo's famous library at S Giorgio Maggiore, destroyed in the XVIIc, may have been all or partly Gothic; the one view of it, on Jacopo de' Barbari's bird's-eye view of 1500, seems to show Gothic windows.

Since the Middle Ages in Venice did not stop neatly when the Renaissance began—that never happened anywhere —buildings in the two styles could and did go up side by side at the same time. Gothic work might sometimes be built later than its Renaissance neighbors. No conflict was felt. When, in the same building, isolated episodes in the new style appear in old-style contexts, it is clear that such episodes must have been made by men with ideas more advanced than were known to their less adventurous fellow workers.

For example, on the large late Gothic Ca' Foscari, the man who carved the winged *putti* on the front—a new-style motif surely brought by someone lately in Florence—was more advanced than the men who controlled the main design all around it (fig. 1.1). How else explain the side-canal entrance of the Palazzo Contarini dagli Scrigni, a rectangle formed by a rope, flat band, and

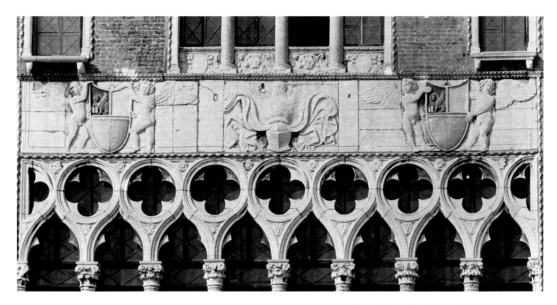

1.1 Ca' Foscari. Frieze with *putti.*

billet molding, like dozens of Gothic portals in the city, but crowned by a classical frieze and cornice, and standing only a few feet from an arrantly late Gothic window (fig. 1.2) ? How else account for the exquisite Ca' Morolin (fig. 1.3)? (Arslan 1971 gives additional examples, some doubtful.)

An overorderly historian might insist that there had been remodeling in these samples, but a look at the jointing of the masonry would confute such a simplistic explanation. Sometimes elements seemingly built together, yet stylistically far apart, cannot be dated convincingly together or apart. When, for example, were the small Renaissance cornices and Ionic pilasters filled with square panels put on the front of the late Gothic Palazzo Pisani-Moretta on the Grand Canal (fig. 1.4)? Were they part of the original work? Or, more likely, put on during some early remodeling, ca. 1480–1500? Why alter a palace still so new (unless to show unity with relatives just moved in next door)? Or was the exterior remodeling done along with the interior, when Renaissance traceried windows were put in the grand central hall indoors? Or did some member of the family admire the similarly compartmented pilasters on the front of S Petronio at Bologna (with uncopiable reliefs by Jacopo della Quercia)? There are more possible answers than the question merits.

At this time, more or less coincident with the thirty-four-year term of Doge Francesco Foscari (1423–57), many of the handsomest of Venetian late Gothic works were being built, several commissioned by the doge himself, such as the vast Ca' Foscari, or the Arco Foscari of the Ducal Palace, major monuments of social and political propaganda as well as of artistic value. Under the next two doges, Pasquale Malipiero (1457–62) and Cristoforo Moro (1462–72), and for a few years more, late Gothic continued little

changed, though at the same time the Renaissance was already announcing itself in such works as the remodeling of S Giobbe promoted by Doge Moro. Uncontaminated Gothic persisted, nevertheless, for decades more, as in the handsome Palazzo Van Axel (1470s?) and scores of more modest buildings.

1.2 Palazzo Contarini degli Scrigni. Side portal.

1.3 Ca' Morolin, Rio S Polo. Gothic windows with ogee arches flank a Renaissance loggia with four round arches set under a classical cornice. The top cornice (later raised in the middle) must have been the last part to be built, as it is thoroughly Gothic and chronologically perverse. The balconies and the windows on the side may be slightly later additions.

1.4 Palazzo Pisani-Moretta on the Grand Canal. The open-work rail and top floors are modern. Note the pilasters filled with square panels.

2 | TRANSITIONAL WORKS

A whole group of monuments with Gothic and Renaissance elements set side by side but not amalgamated may be classified as a family and called Transitional. They may so blend or blur Gothic and Renaissance episodes that they cannot rightly be called one or the other. For example, the funerary monument of Doge Francesco Foscari (d.1457) in the chancel of the Franciscan Church of the Frari has a composition here Gothic and there Renaissance, and in some places both inextricably merged (fig. 2.1). Some of the most classicizing parts were once brightly painted and gilded, in a tradition more Gothic than classical—now by the accidents of time left with no more than a wonderfully dusky glitter.

Some may find it odd that such a decorative and sculptural composition as the Foscari tomb is put here among works of architecture; but since Venetian wall tombs grew into major creations of sculpture and architecture conceived together on a scale unmatched elsewhere in Italy, they claim legitimate place as architecture. More in the nature of monumental epitaphs, often they did not include a real tomb or grave; the body might be buried under the pavement in front, or in the sacristy, cloister, or chapter house, or even in another building. Interment inside churches required a special permit, not easily given. Usually the monuments were an expression less of piety or grief than of the virtues claimed for the deceased, with less concern for the salvation of his soul than for the perpetuation of his fame. On the whole, grand monuments in churches were made only for important members of families with money, men who had held high office. Similar but lesser works for men of intellectual or professional distinction also appeared, but less often. Funds were commonly set apart in the will and sometimes, to make sure that it would be satisfactory, the monument would be begun in the lifetime of the dedicatee. A reclining effigy might be made while he was alive, but other poses were banned except in very special cases, typically for doges, who might be shown kneeling (before they died), usually in front of the Lion of S Mark. Only a dead doge or military hero could be shown standing.

The Foscari monument is now given to the Bregno brothers, originally called Rigesio, from Righeggia on Lake Lugano. Trained somewhere in Lombardy, they carried out their mature work in Venice. This tomb can hardly have been begun before ca. 1466, for although Doge Foscari had died in 1457, the end of the church where his monument stands was not finished until 1468. The tomb could have been started at the bottom while the final touches were being given to the architecture at the top of the chancel, though not during any of the heavy construction. The tomb was probably finished in about four years, ca. 1470. Paolo Bregno, who was more of an architect than his sculptor brother Antonio, must have been responsible for most of it. The whole monument was gone over in 1940 and given summary cleaning and reinforcing.

The monument fills the center of the south chancel wall. The general scheme, with its proxy sarcophagus held up by brackets under a swooping tentlike canopy, follows Venetian and North Italian traditions (cf. the monument of Tommaso Mocenigo, 1423, SS Giovanni e Paolo). At the same time, it shows some new motifs in the columns and pilasters above them. Still novel in such a context, the columns boost the main part so high as to give the whole an unconventional long-legged look. The shafts are not canonically classical, since they show no entasis and lack the little curved flare of apophyge at the top and bottom. No one in Venice had yet observed this last regular Roman refinement, but

Brunelleschi had, and had dutifully respected it from the beginning. At this date Venetian workmen would not have known that classical shafts should have entasis and curve out in apophyges at top and bottom, and they would have shaped their shafts routinely without them, like the Byzantine or Gothic models all about; or they could have appropriated shafts from some late classical or Byzantine building, no longer useful or usable. The bases, made new for this monument, sprout flat leaves at the corners, far from antique, and clearly Gothic *griffes*. Some of the workmen in Venice did learn quickly, however, for soon after 1473 the columns on the florid Gothic Madonna dell' Orto flex into a sort of timid entasis and also have classical pedestals, simplified and a little clumsy, but showing a conscious wish to be properly classical (Clarke-Rylands, 11).

An effort was made to carve capitals that would be classically correct. Though clumsy, these must have been copied from legitimate Corinthian antiques, for they have two rows of would-be acanthus leaves under almost correct corner spirals, unlike most Early Renaissance capitals that are really of a restyled Gothic type only one leaf high (fig. 2.2). But such an archaeological effort was short-winded, and the capitals of the columns carry no entablature; atavistically following a mediaeval custom, they are topped by brackets big enough to support a figure. One might say that the almost classical columns, grammatically put together on a pedestal and with a base, shaft, and capital, were unable to keep on in the same Latin syntax after that brave beginning.

Classicizing pilasters run on upward from these capitals, but begin abruptly without bases; they are among the first classical pilasters to appear in Venice, possibly the very first. Unlike the capitals below, they support a proper entablature with an identifiable architrave,

2.1 Paolo and Antonio
Bregno. Monument of Doge
Francesco Foscari in the
Frari. The pedestals and
Corinthian columns are
completely in the new classicizing style, which has
also affected, somewhat less,
the pilasters above them.

2.2 Foscari Monument. Detail of center part, showing the would-be pilasters with their panels of near-*rinceaux,* Corinthian capitals, and would-be entablature.

frieze, and cornice. Undeveloped as it is, this simple arrangement must refer consciously to standard Roman precedents. Old photographs in the Fototeca of the Correr Museum show that it once ran beyond the body of the monument on each side and continued along the wall, somewhat simplified but still respecting the main divisions—until some antisepticizing restorer scraped it off the wall about seventy years ago. Such blended classical and mediaeval features as the fluttering zigzag of foliage in the panels of the pilasters and the row of little leaves (or could they be brackets?) under the architrave soon disappeared from Venice, and the Transition period was then almost over. This last moment may be equated to the stage of the three-toed horse in evolution.

Among the churches of Venice there is no full representative of the short years of Transition. The nearest might be S Zaccaria, begun Gothic and finished in a spectacular Renaissance manner, but it is not really halfway so much as half-and-half in style. The later parts embodied far-from-Transitional ideas in the 1480s and 1490s, and it is logical to consider them only later. The earlier parts will be examined in the next chapter.

Parts of two unique palaces stand out in the limbo between Gothic and Renaissance: the so-called Ca' del Duca on the Grand Canal and the back wing of the Palazzo Contarini del Bovolo deep in the city behind. They are unlike each other and neither is like anything else. Their uncertain quasi-Gothic quasi-Renaissance status, their freakish independence, and the fact that they are parts of palaces is all they have in common. Not typical, but so striking in their individual ways, they demand inclusion here.

Much of the history of the Ca' del Duca is hard to unravel. Work on a house for the Cornaro family was begun about 1453, from designs by Bartolomeo Buon. Though the site had been cleared and building materials gathered, there was little to show in the winter of 1460/61, when the property was bought by the ambitious Duke Francesco Sforza of Milan (who had served as a condottiere for Venice) for an embassy and occasional residence. New ideas were brought or transmitted by Benedetto Ferrini, a Florentine sent to Venice by the duke in 1461 to make models and drawings for it. Old Buon had refused to turn over his designs for the site to this intruder with newfangled ideas. After six months, during which he sent back more than one proposal, Ferrini was recalled, but some scheme must already have been accepted, at least in part, for difficult-to-find extra-long timbers for the job had already been cut (Beltrami 1900, 30, 36). A facade of 166' was being planned, with a central hall running back an incredible 178' between two courtyards. Not even for the Palace of the Doges had anything been envisaged in Venice on such a scale. It is an outstanding example of how the client rather than the architect could dominate a building.

Another Florentine, Antonio Averlino, known as Filarete, a sculptor beginning to try architecture, had been consulted and may have been commissioned to make the design Ferrini was to carry out. Illustrations in Filarete's then unpublished but already well circulated *Treatise* (1460–65) reveal him as a fantasist, given to free-and-easy use of classical details but still uncomfortable with them, despite his offhand references to Alberti and Vitruvius and his association with learned men at the Milanese court. One illustration, "A Palace on a Marshy Site," may reflect some stage of his Ca' del Duca ideas (fig. 2.3). He wrote that it was "a building that was built in a swampy and boggy place . . . . The water was brackish and emptied into the sea in

2.3 Filarete. "A Palace on a
Marshy Site" (Book XXI,
170, Biblioteca Nazionale
Centrale di Firenze).

2.4 Corner of the Ca' del
Duca on the Grand Canal.
The base is rusticated with
alternating square and oblong blocks with joints sunk
in shallow channels. Above,
diamond-faceted blocks are
laid up in the same header
and stretcher pattern. (The
diagonal screenlike hatching
at the bottom of the Filarete
drawing may refer to this.)

many places, but there were many no-ble buildings here" (Filarete XXI, 1965, 169v, 170r). This shows that it was imagined as in Venice, which Filarete had already visited in 1449, 1458, and 1459, and perhaps oftener; but it is far from clear how many of his ideas were incorporated in the actual building for the duke if, indeed, any were. A copy of the *Treatise* came from Hungary to Venice in 1490 and became part of the library of the friars of SS Giovanni e Paolo (now in the Biblioteca Marciana), but it is unlikely that his ideas were known locally before the palace was begun.

Work was going on in 1462, but not smoothly; the duke pawned his jewels in 1465 to pay his Venetian debts (Newett, in Casola, 356n16); and all work must have stopped when he died in 1466. The building had not yet emerged very far above ground or water level. In the next decade it was several times noted on the canal bank as an abandoned behemoth.

Already in 1461 the duke had specified that the canal front be "in the Venetian style" and the rest "modern" (Renaissance), and had it gone ahead that way, it would have been the first Renaissance palace in the city. The surviving fragment is modern in its extravagant—not to say exhibition-ist—rustication (fig. 2.4). The faceted, square, smaller stones stick out like sharp little pyramids, as similar ones already had on the corner towers of the Castello at Milan in what may have been their Renaissance debut in Italy, arranged there perhaps by Filarete in 1455-57 (Heydenreich-Lotz, 97; 343n8). The resulting effect is less one of deep stones in a thick wall than of a decorative metaphor for them. In-spired by Milan, reinforced perhaps by palaces seen in Florence, these arrogant surfaces are the earliest examples of rustication known in Venice.

There are elements here of both old and new styles. The big column mark-ing the corner could have been con-ceived as classical; the proper torus-scotia-torus base might suggest this, although the same convex-concave-convex conjunction can equally well be mediaeval; but inasmuch as leaves be-low it run out to the corners of the square plinth, they demand to be read as Gothic *griffes*, which would cer-tainly be rejected in a consciously clas-sicizing work. Furthermore, the col-umn is unclassically half-sunk in a nichelike recess, like many of the By-zantine and Gothic columns in various churches in the city, or the more slen-der shafts marking the corners of local mediaeval palaces. The column shaft is so thick that it may have been in-tended to rise through two stories, which would have made it the first co-lossal or giant order of the Renaissance, an amazingly sophisticated idea for anyone to have stumbled on here. The Filarete drawing shows no such pro-phetic novelty, but only columns at the corners, one to a floor, novelty enough at this date. The main central feature, the Gothic loggia, is far from prophetic. Nothing of the existing building is identifiably Venetian; both it and Fila-rete's palace could as well be in some other city with enough water for it to stand in—Mantua, for example.

The most plausible history for it is that some of the plan and some of the foundations go back to Buon's project for the Cornaros; that Ferrini, perhaps under Filarete's direction, working with what was there at hand, contrived a modern elevation with a loggia in the center and towers at the corners in the then usual Venetian style (confined perhaps only to the *parti*). The new fea-tures were, then, all imported. The building would not have been really Venetian. Though it is impossible now to reconstruct just what the duke fi-nally intended to build, it was too big and too important a commission his-torically to be ignored, shadowy though it must remain.

Not so clearly Transitional—if anything Transitional can be classed as clearly so—but contemporary with that shifting nonstyle, was a loose body of domestic architecture, largely retardataire, or styleless, or a bit of both. A spectacular example appears on the Ca' Contarini del Bovolo ("of the snail," in Venetian) (fig. 2.5).

Just before 1500 a remarkable addition was pinned to the back of the unremarkable late Gothic palace of the senators Marco, Nicolo, and Giovanni Battista Contarini. Half the addition, facing a *campiello* off the Calle della Vida, was made by piling up triple loggias, and half by a round tower enclosing a circular staircase. Toward the garden and *campiello*, the tower was opened out with arcades running uphill to join the top story of the loggia, where everything was crowned by a domed belvedere open with arches almost all the way around. The windowless other side of the tower is attached to the older Gothic palace. The tower and the flat plane of stacked loggias beside it, are not comfortably joined, nor are the loggias happily attached to the wall on the other end. The most unsettling feature may be the scale, for the whole seems to have been built bigger than the number and size of its components ask, so that it comes to suggest an overenlarged photograph of some smaller scheme. It is not so much the rarity of its type as the scale and unique openness that make the Bobolo so striking. Helical stairways (not spiral, which would expand in developing), were not rare in Gothic Venice; there is another, for example, built earlier by Contarini cousins in the Palazzo Contarini dagli Scrigni (now partly rebuilt).

Everything betrays the determined but untrained hand of a tyro rather than an experienced architect, and most likely a provincial. He can be identified by name as Giovanni Candi (d.1506), a carpenter who had worked on the Scuola di S Marco from 1487 or 1488 onward. At the Scuola he might have seen what was left of a notable circular stairway built by Antonio Rizzo from sketches by the painter Gentile Bellini—if any of it had survived the fire of 1485 that had ruined most of the building. He may have gained some architectural experience of a sort in Belluno in the 1490s, unless the notices there refer to someone else named Candi, which is not impossible. (The plaque on the ground floor of the loggia, inscribed MDXXXVIII, was put up later, perhaps having been taken from some other building.)

The outer end of the block of each limestone step runs through the brick wall of the cylinder, and shows itself on the outer surface, finished like a small panel. On these step ends stand the classical bases of the columns that, in turn, carry on their simple, half-Gothic capitals a ramping or climbing series of round arches, each stilted on one side in order to come out right on the other, at the top of the next column, set one step higher. The stone handrail, the only diagonal line allowed to show, all else being stepped, runs above regular Gothic dwarf columns working as balusters.

Only the ground floor of the loggia shows anything that is in no way Gothic, and it shows that only equivocally. Slender, square piers, their faces sunk with the plainest of panels, are topped by severe and vaguely Tuscan capitals carrying slender, stilted archivolts of the same coarse one-molding profile as those of the stairway. Arcades on square piers had a great vogue ca. 1490–1520, and these may be early examples. They are the only elements that might place this freakish and retardataire tower and loggia in relation to distinguished company.

The adjacent loggia has similar detail, with columns more widely spaced, and reduced in height for the two upper stories. Those at the top, beside the

2.5 Palazzo Contarini del
Bovolo. Stair tower and
loggias.

belvedere at the top of the tower, are only half as high as those at the bottom, and are thus so short as to seem heavy; they carry segmental arches (always a heavy-looking form) and the combination here, with them set above airier lower stories, cannot escape looking top-heavy. The stories seem to have been stacked upside down, and this, the strongest and heaviest, seems to ask to be put at the bottom. The only concession to the load is that the bottom has square piers instead of columns. Structural imperatives must have controlled the choice.

The stairway was such an eye-catching sight that the whole palace became known as the Ca' Contarini del Bovolo, and the same name was attached to the line of the ramiferous Contarini family who lived in it. In 1717 it went by marriage to the wealthy and unpopular Minellis—who had sold sausages so successfully in Bergamo that by 1711 they could buy themselves into the Venetian patriciate. In the XIXc it became the Inn of the Man from Malta, then the Inn of the Stair, and again a private house. In the XXc it has been repaired and restored, with new interiors, and it now houses the offices of the Ente Comunale di Assistenza and other municipal charities, who keep up its pretty garden.

Transitional works such as these cannot be accepted as typical of the Early Renaissance, for that would ask for a stronger will to be classical and a stronger rejection of Gothic. In Venice the Early Renaissance did not have an orderly early growth but, rather, an abruptly irregular one. To deal with it handily, one must separate it into parts. First would have to come a few adventurous, improvised, and exploratory works, each of markedly individual or unique character, not wholly free from confusion. The earliest is surely the gateway to the Arsenal (fig. 2.6).

The grand gateway of Venice's Arsenal is the first and most assertive work of genuine antiquarianism, breaking abruptly with Gothic tradition. Already the largest industrial complex in Europe, the Arsenal was being enlarged from 1456 on, and soon dominated sixty acres of land and water. The news that the Turks had begun a huge new arsenal in Constantinople right after they had taken the city in 1453, must have given a push to Venice's project. The name *Arsenal* antedates the Turkish threat, however, by over two centuries, from a time when the threat came from the Arabs. The word *arsenale* itself was the Venetian version of the Arab *dar sina'a*, or "place for construction." (The Spaniards, more of whom spoke Arabic, took the term over as *darsena*.)

In Venice a new main portal was begun ca. 1457, so early in the campaign of expansion that it must have been considered something of major importance; it was pushed ahead so quickly that it was finished and inscribed with the date in 1460. The design has often been given to Antonio Gambello, but no documents implicate him, and no work known to be his looks like it or approaches its overt imitation of the antique. Gambello's certain work is sometimes Gothic, sometimes in part Transitional, but never like this. In fact nothing else being built in Venice or Venetian lands at the time was so thoroughly Roman. By the end of the XVc it was already being mistaken for a legitimately antique monument. Small wonder it was misunderstood and banished from the familiar Venetian world of the time; it was an oddity without influence, an exotic hybrid, an infertile flower or fruit without seeds.

Unprecedented in its obeisance to antiquity, it has long been heralded as the first Venetian work of the Renaissance entirely free of mediaeval reminiscences. The rich cornice could be a copy of some Roman model, despite

2.6 The Arch at the Arsenal.

the uncommon heaviness of the entablature in proportion to the columns that hold it up, nearer a third of their height than the classic Roman fifth.

A specific Roman model can be identified for the lower half, the Arch of the Sergii at Pola (now Pula), a Venetian port on the tip of Istria, eighty miles across the Adriatic (fig. 2.7). Once a Roman naval base and still active, thanks to its excellent harbor, its strategic location, and its trade in sand for the best Murano glass, it was a town of importance to Venetian merchants and to the naval officials who were in charge of it. Its monuments must have been known to many of the men concerned with the development of the Arsenal. To some of them, the idea of a grand entrance that echoed a Roman arch of triumph might have seemed attractive and wonderfully suitable—not at all the same as the better known humanistic interest in antique architecture fashionable in Florence and Rome. Classical forms were brought in through a military side door, as it were. No one since the Emperor Frederick II had thought of using antique architecture for vainglory, except King Alfonso of Naples in just these same years; but no connection suggests itself here, unless—improbably—through the Dalmatian Laurana, working in Naples for the king.

Vasari wrote that Brunelleschi had a "Slavonian" (Dalmatian or Istrian) pupil "who did a lot of things in Venice" (Vasari II, 1963, 300), and if that is so, this portal could be his work. The names of other Slav builders are known, but none surely enough active in Venice to be safely associated with this. Since Venice attracted Lombards, she may have drawn men from the opposite direction also, for she was as easy to reach by sea from the east as by land from Lombardy, and the chances of making money were better than at home. Later architects made the trip to Istria to the sights of Pula, Fra Giocondo, for example, and Falconetto,

who drew the arch without noticing the inclined fascias (Temanza 1778, 142; Zorzi, G.G. 1959, pl. 69–71, 74). If these men went later, others may have gone sooner. A specific connection with any traveler from either direction can now be no more than guesswork, but connections of some sort there surely were, for enough details of the provincial Roman architecture of Istria crop up in Venice in the late XVc to assure occasional contacts.

The freestanding pairs of Greek marble columns—silvery *cipollino* ("onionskin")—and their Byzantine capitals must have been taken from some building of the XIc or XIIc, perhaps on Torcello, the nearby mainland, or Istria, all with plenty of conveniently unused architectural elements and miscellaneous marbles to spare (fig. 2.8). To XVc eyes these columns might count as antique. Although they may have wanted to recall a Roman triumphal arch for its associational value, the entrepreneurs of the Arsenal would not have been scholarly in such matters. The marble shafts are undoubtedly mediaeval, typically Byzantine, with no entasis. Such architectural cannibalism had been found a handy means of saving money in Venice for centuries, and would continue as long as there were tempting bits left to devour. (It continues in duller form today, as bricks and roof tiles are pilfered from ruins on the lesser and remoter islands.) All the rest of the gateway is of white Istrian limestone except for one tender pink Verona marble molding in the shadow of the cornice, a delicate and subtle polychromy unseen at Pula, less antique than contemporary, similar to that being used by Alberti on the Malatesta Church at Rimini, built in the same years as this arch.

Transmitted by sketches reinforced by a bit of memory, the disposition and proportions follow Pula about as closely as would be expected. The spacing of the columns and their relation to

2.7 The Arch at Pula.

the arch—in no way unusual for republican Rome—are nearly all the same. Many details, such as the leaf-covered brackets and the bold flowers between them, are as would be anticipated in a XVc copy. The evidence makes plain that this *is* in good part a copy, but with a few variations; the Arsenal is richer in ornamented moldings, Venetian opulence advancing over republican purity? The Istrian peculiarity of an architrave with sloping fascias was ignored, although found on the Arch of the Sergii, the Temple of Augustus at Pula, and the arch at Trieste, all republican or Augustan. Perhaps it had not been noted on the transmitter's sketch. All the Arsenal ornament is severely antique, really academic, and more in amount than in detail like the rich Venetian ornament made in the decades just before and after the gate was built.

One item more advanced than the model at Pula is the keystone. It does not quite perform its expected duty, that of linking the archivolt to the architrave, the arch to the beam. They miss contact, but by only 5″ or 6″. Keystones in this, their normal, context are the result of educated habit based on sophisticated pseudostructural thinking, and they had not yet often been used in this proper context when the Pula arch was built in early republican times (ca. 30 BC), before the traditional Greek trabeated system had been closely integrated with Roman arched construction. Occasionally there was equivalent fumbling in Early Renaissance times.

This particular keystone could have been added to the gateway when the figures of Victories were crowded into the spandrels in 1578, to commemorate the great victory at Lepanto of 1571. By this time literate architects understood very well that an ornamental keystone, structurally a working voussoir, had to reach the architrave and seem to support it, just as most Roman architects knew it a generation after the

2.8 The Arsenal Arch. Greek marble shaft without apophyge; spiny acanthus Byzantine capital; architrave with vertical fascias and carved moldings, unlike Pula; plain frieze, unlike Pula; corner bracket set on mediaeval and un-Roman diagonal.

2.9 The Arsenal Arch. Note the uncertainty of the joint with the architrave.

2.10 The Arsenal Arch. Details of lower and upper orders (from Cicognara-Diedo-Selva).

Pula arch. But something went wrong at the Arsenal gateway and the remodeling—if there was one—could not quite come out right. The keystone cuts the leaves of the outer edge of the archivolt in an unplanned way, with a whole leaf on one side and only half a leaf on the other, and the joints between keystone and archivolt are wider and coarser than the joints in the original masonry all around, telltales of breaking in on earlier work (fig. 2.9).

The upper section of the gateway is less correct, and ill coordinated with what is below (fig. 2.10). It may have been built after some short delay and under different direction, with Pula no longer the model. The stubby pilasters have crude flat capitals with leaves of the more succulent Roman acanthus, invitingly ready to be pulled off like the leaves of a boiled artichoke. Without the requisite architrave, these capitals ungrammatically carry only a cornice, its bumpy profile a diagonal piling-up of ornamental moldings, perhaps like some late provincial pieces of cornice lying about on the mainland. Stylistically it looks earlier than the entablature below it, but here there is no question of date—only one of knowledge. By this time Florentine and Roman masters already understood the sanctioned form, with bed molding and a shelflike corona, but the Venetians were not to learn it for some time. The upper cornice of the gateway lacks the overhanging corona entirely, as had a few antique provincial ones, and comes to an end instead with an improvised swollen quarter-round of laurel garland, antique, it is true, but uncomfortably misplaced.

In Jacopo de' Barbari's woodcut city view, published in 1500, the gateway is shown at the end of its original drawbridge, free of such accretions as the present forecourt with its pagan allegorical figures and pilfered Roman and Greek lions, or the Victories in the spandrels, or the figure at the top of the pediment. Luckily the gate was unhurt by the big Arsenal fires of 1509 and 1569, or in either world war. The flood and hurricane of 1966 were more damaging, but now the whole has been handsomely restored and strengthened (1972–74) by the Dante Alighieri Society. (Dante had referred to the Arsenal in the *Inferno,* XXI.) Much of the girdle of high brick walls, a work of super-Piranesian scale, almost three miles long, may date back to the period of the portal. Inside, as the types of ships built and repaired kept developing, the many buildings, basins, drydocks, and workshops for making ropes, oars, sails, and dozens more necessities, plus a few official residences, were remodeled over and over again, and no picture of the early Arsenal except the grand portal can be regained.

It is with a jolt that one remembers that the gateway was going up at the same time as the splendid late Gothic Arco Foscari leading into the courtyard of the Doges' Palace. The peaceful coexistence of the two styles had begun.

3 | ANTONIO GAMBELLO

A fugitive and unstable intermezzo, the Transition was not able to create any large complete church, which would have taken decades, but it did dominate the interior of one of the principal churches of the city, S Zaccaria, unequaled except by S Mark's in its accumulation of age, prestige, and wealth. In the IXc the *Participazio* Doges had established a convent beside the church, legendarily founded in the Dark Ages. Its importance grew, particularly after the Emperor Leo V, the Armenian, presented it with the body of S Zacharias. Other relics soon poured in as gifts. To the popular mind it was not clear whether the principal saint was Zacharias, husband of S Elizabeth and father of the Baptist; or Pope Zacharias (741–52), a Greek who had favored the Lombards; or a lesser Greek saint of the same name, whom Constantinople could easily spare. The first was preferred. Visited more and more, the church and convent buildings had to be enlarged or rebuilt several times. After the Benedictine nuns had profitably transferred their orchard—now half the Piazza S Marco—to Doge Ziani in 1170 and the dowries of noble novices kept accumulating steadily and substantially, S Zaccaria must, after S Mark's, have been the richest foundation in the city.

A new brick Gothic church was built in the XIVc and early XVc, but in the 1450s it was ravaged by a fire that also destroyed much of the convent, killing, it was said, a hundred nuns. Inasmuch as the Emperor Frederick III was received in what was called a new church in 1458, built mainly under Doge Francesco Foscari, the damage to the church, the dates, and the suspiciously round number of just a hundred nuns must be questioned (Bozzoni, 73, 74; Cornaro, 131). What is certain is that a large church building was begun beside the old one in the 1450s, appropriating its north aisle (perhaps damaged in the fire) as space for the south aisle of the new building. Parts of the older church, such as the late Gothic chapel of S Tarasio, are still extant, but once the new church was in use, most of the older one was taken over, downgraded, and remodeled into such practical adjuncts as a sacristy and a reception room for visitors.

The new church was begun under the direction of Antonio di Marco Gambello, who had submitted a wood model in 1458 (Franzoi–DiStefano, 397). Gambello has often been mentioned in connection with the gateway of the Arsenal, though he probably had nothing to do with it. He is named in the will of Doge Cristoforo Moro, Foscari's successor, for work on the church of S Giobbe, work not now traceable and perhaps never done. The unfinished lower part of the vast Dominican Church of SS Giovanni e Paolo (1458–ca. 1470) is often associated with him too, but again without documentation. Both his oeuvre and his background are obscure.

The last big Gothic church built in Venice, S Zaccaria is also the most Gothic, the first, last, and only one to be fully vaulted. The nave has three 25′-square bays, covered with ribless groin vaults rising 78′ from the floor, and aisles with similar vaults, oblongs running lengthwise (fig. 3.1). These rise almost as high, so that the effect from many places in the church would be that of a level-topped hall-church, were it not for a glimpse of clerestory windows on the south, in the narrow space between the nave vaults and aisle arcade. Except for S Mark's, this was the only church in Venice where high vaults had been risked; the weight of masonry vaults, even when of brick and kept thin, as here, put an alarming strain on the semisubmarine foundations. The last part of the structure to go up, these vaults were probably made after Gambello's death, but he must have planned them or something very like them.

The new church is also a product of the Transition, since some parts look forward to the classical style (shafts, capitals, frieze with coiling *rinceau*, cornice, door frames) while others contradict by remaining Gothic (bases with *griffes*, multiplied jambs, pointed arches). What might have been a conflict must come from unlettered eagerness for the new (the antique) not backed up with enough knowledge. Several hands must have been at work here, including Bartolomeo Bon (dealt with in chapter 32). Gambello *may* have directed the whole work, and probably did direct 80 percent of it.

The five-sided apse is enclosed by an ambulatory, with each of its bays radiating a semicircular apsidiole except at the extreme right, where the older church blocks it (fig. 3.2). The ambulatory, rare in Italy, is unique in Venice, but had long been common in France, and had come to Italy with the buildings of international monastic orders. How it happened to be chosen for S Zaccaria cannot now be explained.

Except for later modifications and details, and the execution of most of the vaulting, the scheme must go back to Gambello and his model. He was in charge for twenty-three years—from 1458 to his early death in 1481. By then he was no longer the thoroughgoing Gothic practitioner he had been at the beginning, but one of the most daring and original masters of the Transition, either from his own new ideas or from some advanced by members of the team he had assembled for the work. His development is not clear and it may not have been consistent, nor is it clear what can be properly included in his oeuvre; the chips of fact and probability do not fit into one clear shape. Neither his typical style—if he had one—nor that of his helper, Buora, can now be consistently isolated and defined. When the nuns accepted his appointment, they can have had no notion of what he would be giving

3.1 S Zaccaria. Nave.

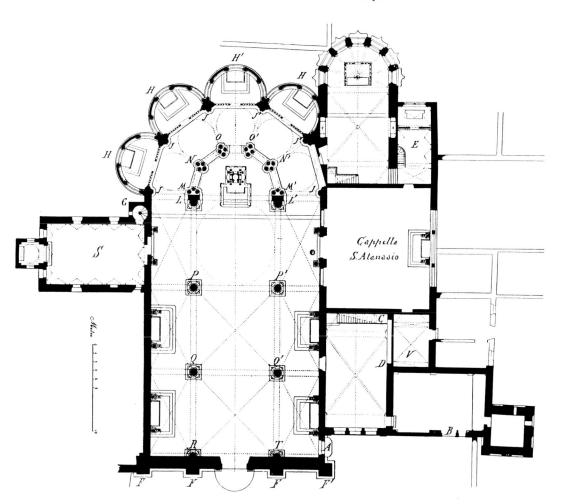

3.2 S Zaccaria. Plan. The
right aisle has absorbed
the left aisle of the earlier
church, whose choir and
apse are still preserved, and
also a piece of its right aisle,
now transformed into a
small chapel.

Cappella
S Atanasio

them—nor yet perhaps did he. One has a sensation of growth, or at least change, in the church as it rose. Doge Cristoforo Moro and the Patriarch Maffeo Gerardo, humanists and enthusiasts for the new art, may have had the decisive voices here—certainly more than the nuns.

It is known that twenty-two columns from the monastery on the now submerged island of Ammiana and two more from Istria were received ca. 1460—a documented proof of cannibalism—and that more came later. It is not possible to locate them in the parts of the church built first, as the date suggests, but perhaps they were bought hastily, as bargains too good to be missed. To add to the confusion surrounding Gambello's doings, he was often not on the spot, being repeatedly called off to work for the republic in outlying posts as a military engineer. So many people wanted his services, both artistic and practical, that he must have had a sound reputation.

After he died, assistants went ahead, supposedly following his model, which may have been revised and updated, until 1483, when Codussi was named *protomagister* and commissioned to finish the church. The lower part of the facade and all the exterior walls were up, at least in the raw. Only some of the nave columns were in place, and none of their arches; consequently, neither the nave nor the aisles could yet have received their vaults. What had been done shows that Gambello had, in his way, welcomed the Renaissance with gusto. Condemned by ignorance of its more sophisticated rules, he tried free inventions in ways unmatched by his contemporaries.

The nave supports, for example, show unwonted originality (fig. 3.3). They begin inconspicuously, with 4' of two layers of big square plinths paneled in little squares, an arrangement familiar neither in Gothic nor Renaissance

architecture, but with some resemblance to Gambello's socle on the facade; they too may have been put in place by Gambello. On them stand bases of singular novelty, octagonal (for the octagonal pedestals they support), coaxed toward the corners of the square plinth by mediaeval *griffes* translated into an unmistakable Renaissance form like elaborate Roman scrolled keystones laid flat (fig. 3.4). There is doubt that they were devised for the occasion by Gambello, though their position near the bottom favors it. The details, which make use of Renaissance forms not only different in style but also different from anything in Gambello's earlier parts of the church, may be Buora's (cf. chapter 31). *Griffes* were an old motif; coiled S-curve keystones were older; their happy conjunction here comes from a rare creative architectural imagination of the highest quality.

The actual base of the pier is put together in a sequence of bulgy, reeded, and concave fluted moldings (convex trimming on convex, concave trimming on concave), big, rugged, and ideal for where they are, for what they do or express, and in their relation to the fat but taut keystone *griffes*. This can hardly have been conceived first by Gambello (for Buora to execute), for he did not care to mix Renaissance and Gothic parts in this way. But here, with keystones working in a new role, there is more of a synthesis than a mixture or mere juxtaposition.

The octagonal pedestals are plain, about 9' tall, or 13' with their plinths. Worshippers standing in the church do not come even halfway up to the bases of the columns on the pedestals, and there is something about this unexpected dimension that makes the church seem grander, deliberately and dramatically out of scale with human visitors, who are there only on kindly sufferance in a building made for something greater, more suitable to be the consecrated house of God.

3.3 S Zaccaria. Lower part of nave supports.

3.4 S Zaccaria. Base of octagonal pedestal. Detail.

Between the top of the pedestals and the base of the columns comes a special band, so vigorous in profile that it is a fitting stop to the 13' of support, and rugged enough to assert its adequacy as the main element in the underpinning of the columns above. An unorthodox and unnamable element, it can be seen either as part of the column base or as a cap for the pier; the form is so original that the classic divisions cannot be applied convincingly—yet the actual elements convince that they are able to do what they are meant to do. In other words, they express their function with immediate and legible vigor.

The shafts alone are heavy by classical canons—about seven diameters high—and obviously robust and easily able to carry their sweeping arches and vaults (fig. 3.5). But if considered together with their pedestals as one continuous support—both ways seem natural—they do not look heavy, but like typical fairly slender Gothic piers. (Transitional work often asks to be looked at twice, once as Gothic and once as classical.) The shafts come to an end without the usual neat little flare of apophyge at the top and bottom, but neither do they substitute the common wider mediaeval flat band. There is no telltale sign of when they may have been cut, or where, but it must have been some place of fair sophistication; the slightness of the entasis, expertly handled, could indicate a late antique or early Byzantine origin. The stocky proportions may come from cutting them down a bit on each end to make them fit here.

If no arches were up when Gambello died, neither were any capitals, although some preparatory work, such as cutting stones for both shafts and capitals, may have been begun on the ground. It is likely that this and most of the last work on the walls was done by assistants, including Buora (cf. chapter 31), guided by the wooden model that may by this time have been altered or even replaced. They probably did not, however, get around to putting vaults over the nave until Codussi was put in charge in 1483.

Semicircular arches run down the nave and pointed arches cross the aisles as boundaries of the humped-up vaults there. On the walls above the nave arcade a straight entablature is carried all around, normal in proportion but heavy-looking where it is, and asserting a strong horizontal where none is wanted. It seems a classicizing intrusion in a church still Gothic in space and linearity. The cornice is knowingly a little interrupted in a classic way above each column and at each corner over a console bracket shaped like a Roman keystone, having the unpleasant effect of hanging down more than supporting, and helping the spark of vertical force to jump from the columns below to the arches of the vaults. The consoles are particularly ineffectual, since the movement has been interrupted—if not stopped—by the intrusive horizontal of the cornice. Most of this, near the top, must be post-Gambello, perhaps clumsily adapted from his model by his confused assistants before Codussi took charge in 1483.

The combination of big plain vaults, surely intended (but not built) by Gambello, with nave and aisles set at almost the same height, and borne on widely spaced slender supports that leave a large open space bounded by flat walls, is typical of Italian late Gothic in interiors such as the cathedral of Florence or S Petronio at Bologna. (The effect at S Zaccaria has been diminished by the huge XVIIc pictures covering almost every inch of the upper walls.) The character of the resulting all-but-continuous space is closer to Roman ideals of mass and void than to the all-but-massless linearity of French Gothic. That may be why the space here can be so masterfully combined with classicizing detail

3.5 S Zaccaria. East end of nave.

that could run into trouble in a more Gothic, more linear ensemble. A glance at non-Italian Transitional churches, such as S Etienne-du-Mont or S Eustache in Paris, shows late Gothic disrupted by classical columns and entablatures that cannot adapt themselves to such busy, highly characterized, complex systems of ribs and multiplied shafts. In contrast, much of the Italian Transitional seems natural and easy, hybrid though it is. In S Zaccaria, only the entablature at the top of the nave space balks at cooperating.

The chancel, ambulatory, and radiating chapels presented more complicated problems. A church building was usually begun at the east end, so that it could be finished first and services could be held there while the rest was still building; but here at S Zaccaria, since the older church was preserved next door and could and was being used, the pressure to finish the new one was less. It was possible to linger over the intricacies entailed in adjusting ambulatory to apse and to apsidioles.

To modern eyes, the screen between the apse and ambulatory and what is beyond it are the strangest part of the church, rivaled in their ingenious, unexpected, and probably improvised mixture of Gothic and Renaissance only by the freakish and beautiful cathedral of Šibenik (Sebenico) on the Dalmatian coast. This cathedral was made just a few years later by Giorgio "Orsini" of Šibenik (who had worked on the palace at Urbino in the 1450s) and Nicholas of Florence (Deverak, *passim*). There is no warrantable reason to make any connection between the cathedral and the church, although it has been tried.

After a small slice of wall and a nondescript entablature, comes the more-or-less half-dome of the apse, creased by a bit of polygonality below, but soon sliding into the suitable sphericity of the traditional half-dome above. At

least some of the apsidal chapels were recorded as completed before Gambello died, perhaps with their semidomes and little round arched arcades with windows, where he had left Gothic entirely behind. The vaults of the actual ambulatory and apse were not, however, put up until Codussi took over. This whole complex of apse, two-story screen to the ambulatory, then ambulatory and chapels, as worked out with shafts, capitals, and vaults, is surely the most complicated bit of building of the late XVc in Venice, but not, alas, as resolved as it is complicated.

The lowest stages of the supports between the five sides of the polygonal apse and the ambulatory corridor bent around it consist of clusters of free-standing columns, three against the last nave support, to which a slice of pier has been added to ease the transition, and then clusters of four shafts for the other piers dividing apse and ambulatory (fig. 3.6). All the shafts are almost the same height, about 14', as the octagonal piers of the nave. There are twenty-two of them, and quite possibly these are the twenty-two shafts brought from the former establishment on the Island of Ammiana (which had sunk into the lagoon in an earthquake on Christmas Day of 1223). They vary in thickness, as not unexpected in antique sets. Some have the proper apophyge at both ends, some at only one, some at neither; these last must have been cut at each end to fit their new duties. Entasis is slight or lacking, indicating either provincialism or a late date. All are of a particularly fine *cipollino* marble. Although the bases match, the capitals do not and show a great freshness, even capriciousness. As Buora was under contract to supply capitals by 1474 (Hubala 1974, 354), these may be the ones (cf. chapter 31).

The clusters support arches and lengths of octagonal piers, corresponding to the Gothic shafts from which

3.6 S Zaccaria. Ambulatory.

they derive, rising through the next story, open to the ambulatory with traceried windows under pointed arches, thoroughly Gothic yet placed above Early Renaissance column clusters. All this too must be either by Gambello or supervised by him and carried out by assistants with conflicting ideas, more advanced below, less above. Though Gambello had to be away on official business a number of times, he is credited with having put up the lower part of the chapels (Puppi-Puppi, 1977, 191), compound piers, arches, and perhaps the small chapel vaults, but he did not put on the ambulatory vaults. The confusion may come from too many cooks.

The apsidioles, semicircular and not truly Gothic in plan, seem as overmembered as the ambulatory, with an asparagus-bunch profusion of marble columns in tiers like the facade of S Mark's, where columns were hung like trophies, a difficult and unsuitable model for a would-be-classical scheme. Unpedantic Gambello would not have known that and he invented a fanciful new scheme of his own.

Antonio Gambello must have been designer and supervisor of the lowest zone of the facade, as large as any in Venice (begun ca. 1460). Its busy socle consists of a proliferation of moldings arranged in a bold nonclassical sequence (fig. 3.7). Above this comes a pattern of sharp moldings enclosing inlaid marbles akin to the decorative squares on the plinths inside; some are squares inside squares inside other squares, while others are squares inside diamonds inside squares, their Verona marble, tawny and faded now, played against cream and a pewter color. This flattish ornamental profusion is articulated but not really interrupted by three big flat buttresses over 4' wide, sheathed in the same marble patterns. The buttresses mark the walls at the edges of the building and the divisions

between nave and aisles, a traditional disciplinary arrangement. All this is thoroughly Gothic, notable more for its quality than for any novelty.

Each of the side bays, in front of the aisles, has one larger rectangle inset in the middle, designed perhaps a bit later because more Renaissance in character—monochrome, carved in relief with classical garlands and arabesques, and with circles enframing busts of prophets (fig. 3.8). The middle bay has an Early Renaissance doorway different from everything else on the same story (fig. 3.9). The busy arabesques in its pilasters show less blank background than usual, and are crowded with fine-scale carving in relief higher and sharper than in equivalent situations elsewhere. The work must have been made by a well-trained sculptor not used to making parts of such big outdoor ensembles. Giovanni Buora was paid for carving a frieze for a doorway in 1483, but this door has a plain frieze. If he did any work on the door—which is not likely—it was on the pilasters, cornice or pediment, though they are not like what is presumed to be his other work here in the church. Gambello was already dead in 1483, and supervision—if any—must have been by an assistant. Documentation is thin, perhaps partly because Buora could not write.

The zone above the square panels, different from the squares below, used to be given to Gambello's successor, Codussi, who was surely responsible for everything above it, but the attribution of this intermediate zone will not stand up when compared with what Codussi had already done or was about to do. Gambello, we know, changed his style more radically than Codussi ever did, and his greatest change, from Gothic to Renaissance, took place while he was working here on S Zaccaria. This intermediate story could, then, be a later design made after he had rejected

3.7 S Zaccaria. Lower part of
facade.

3.8 S Zaccaria. Lower left
part of facade.

3.9 S Zaccaria. Center part
of facade.

Gothic and absorbed some of the Renaissance idiom (Hubala 1965, 950; but not Hubala 1974). It could have been carried out under his supervision or, more likely, during the interregnum, by his faithful but occasionally stumbling assistants. The work may have come from the same campaign that produced the doorway paid for in 1483, by then almost surely completed—but these two parts need not have been made by the same hands.

This story is made by repeating a tall narrow arch nineteen times, once on each of the buttresses, four times to make the two double windows at the end of the aisles (with mediaeval proportions but timid classical details), and eleven times more as flattened niches on the church wall, with their shell heads pulled downward in the middle as though in false perspective to make the niches appear deeper. They do not succeed in this, nor would anyone have thought of making them try at this date. The motif goes back to antiquity, but not with serious illusionistic intent. Though a traditional element, they are less suited to a big church front outdoors than to decorative work inside, such as reliquaries or tombs; for instance, Pietro Lombardo's tomb for Doge Mocenigo in SS Giovanni e Paolo, finished in 1481, just before the niches here were begun. The little fluted pilasters, the pipe-thin colonnettes dividing the windows, and the foliate carving in the spandrels seem overdainty in scale for this front 75′ wide and 95′ high. As with the doorway, the designer cannot have been used to such a large scale.

Gambello's work, or the work dependent on the design he left at his death, stops abruptly here, and so, therefore, does discussion of it here. Gambello is thoroughly Transitional, but in his own special way. The whole big building of S Zaccaria, with its abnormal high vaults and abnormal radiating chapels and ambulatory bent around the apse, is characteristically Gothic, but in no way Venetian Gothic. The carved detail enhancing these forms is fully of the Renaissance. Either Gambello developed into a new person while working for the noble nuns here in his last years, or he left most of the detailing of the great church to helpers—certainly on the inside more than the outside—and the principal assistant would have been Buora. The latter hypothesis is the more probable.

4 | EARLY RENAISSANCE CHAPELS

At the same time as the work already discussed, a great deal more was being built in Venice, a city nearly always prosperous and active despite a few shortlived distractions and one big break for the War of Cambrai. Although this work does not conform to any one clear evolutionary development, it does have to be considered.

The city must have had over thirty churches of the traditional scheme of nave with two aisles, and perhaps the same number of smaller, aisleless churches that were like a box with an altar and perhaps an apse at one end. These were all Gothic—or older. There was also a handful of provincial Byzantinizing churches with a central dome, a special group that will be considered later. (S Mark's is not, of course, being counted here.) No new aisled churches seem to have been put up in the Early Renaissance except S Zaccaria, which was planned as Gothic, S Maria Maggiore (to be discussed in chapter 30), S Croce (now in a jail and altered to an aisleless, uninformative, and characterless box; cf. chapter 33), and a much remodeled S Sofia (cf. chapter 33). These four refuse to be joined into a coherent group. They are related only by their three-aisled plans, and not by the buildings raised on those plans. Altogether there must have been about 120 churches of one kind or another, a dozen monasteries and nunneries in some 75 parishes served by 350 to 400 priests—all in a city of about 100,000. Most parishes and churches were small.

When Canon Casola wrote in 1494, "I have not found in any city so many beautiful and ornate churches as there are in Venice. . . . The poorest parish church there is more ornate than the finest in Milan" (Casola, 137, 138), he cannot have been referring to newly built churches. Of the important examples known from the end of the XVc, all but S Maria dei Miracoli and S Zaccaria were either still unfinished or else close to the anti-ornate school of Mauro Codussi, far from what Casola, with his Milanese nouveau-riche taste, would admire. With these two exceptions, none was ornate in its architecture, though some had splendid paintings and rich fittings, eclipsing anything in Milan.

There is no convenient continuum, then, of churches showing the phases of a maturing style, such as can be seen intermittently and imperfectly, but still seen in the courtyard of the Palazzo Ducale or in the sequence of Early Renaissance tombs. In church building, the Early Renaissance begins with a clear break, that made by Mauro Codussi. Family chapels were another matter, less pretentious, formal, or costly, and more subject to the individual taste of the donor.

To the right of the main apse of the Church of S Lio, a small square chapel was built in the 1480s or 1490s for Senator Jacopo Gussoni (Sansovino, 41), whose small palace was close by (fig. 4.1). The commission must have come before he died in 1501, though it cannot be said whether a year or a decade before. The design used often to be given to Pietro Lombardo, although no documents name him. A relief of the Pietà above the altar was given to Tullio, also without documentation. Neither attribution wins much acceptance today, though the work—architecture and sculpture—must come from the crowded near-neighborhood of the Lombardo workshop. Despite the wealth of Early Renaissance ornament and the several victories of decoration over the discipline of expressed structure, there is something behind the architectural scheme that comes from a rational, genuinely architectonic way of thinking.

Strong pilasters at the corners, set well out from the walls, lead to well-marked arches that bound a set of pendentives and help support a dome, a scheme of four legs carrying an upward-swelling canopylike top. Varieties of such a baldacchino scheme are found in mediaeval architecture in and around Venice; this may be the first Renaissance translation of it.

The dome is gored like a melon. Because this shape is close to Brunelleschi but to few others, one might think it the first Early Renaissance dome in Venice with borrowings from Florence; but that cannot be maintained, since in other respects this chapel is less Brunelleschian than Codussi's dome in S Michele or Pietro's in S Giobbe. It refuses to be fitted into any early evolutionary slot, as it would have to do to be closer to Brunelleschi. Stylistically, the Gussoni Chapel cannot be Transitional, a work of the late 1460s, as it would have to be if the first, and the link between the other early domes and Brunelleschi. It looks like a creation of ca. 1480 or later. While it must have taken ideas from Florence, the odd idea of the melon dome need not have come to Venice by a direct route.

It need not have, for it could have come roundabout by way of the chapel that the Medici banker, Pigello Portinari, had had added to S Eustorgio in Milan ca. 1462–68, from designs presumably by Michelozzo, on a basic scheme taken from Brunelleschi's Old Sacristy of S Lorenzo. Since that chapel has Lombard decoration spread over most of its surfaces in a manner more Milanese than Brunelleschian, as does the Gussoni Chapel in a similar but not identical way, the connection gains probability. A sketch of the Portinari could have been brought to Venice by one of the emigrating craftsmen. It was the kind of fresh architectural news in Milan that might have attracted a practical young sketcher and an ambitious client and, if so, when it took material form in Venice, the chapel would have been lavishly embellished as a matter of course. The putative sketch need not have shown all the trimming in detail, only the underlying scheme and some

4.1 S Lio. Gussoni Chapel.

indication that it was heavily ornamented. Not unexpectedly, then, the
vines on the Gussoni piers and friezes
are not of the same family as the Portinari vines, nor of a species or by a hand
familiar from typical Lombardo work.
The freshly invented capitals, for example, are unique, with their thin,
graceful palmettes—first a half, then a
whole, then another half—instead of
the long-sanctioned leaves (fig. 4.2).

Much of the charming carved ornament seems overassertive in its context, attracting attention to itself and
away from what it trims. The arabesques on pilaster and archivolt are
too lively to be securely held in by the
tapelike edging. The cornice is a piled-
up succession of bands of carving,
seemingly bought by the random yard
rather than an organized sequence.
Also, there are a few ill-controlled intersections: the moldings framing the
gilded (now regilded) roundels of the
Evangelists are sheared off by the
arches of the pendentives; both the pediments (on the altar, on the chapel
front) touch, but lack the normal
spliced connection with the cornices
below them and, as a result, seem to be
drifting unanchored; the less than semicircular arches bounding the pendentives have the disturbing look of having
been chopped off at the bottom (fig.
4.3).

The materials are rich: tan limestone
membering, with walls of fine creamy
marble, well polished, as is also the
marble semidome of the apse, a rare
and technically difficult extravagance.
The disposition of parts is carefully
worked out. For example, the two windows on the right wall have been made
to correlate neatly with the paneling
system, and the panel between them,
as well as the three matching panels on
the opposite side, was made particularly deep in order to correspond better
to the deep sinkages of the adjacent
windows. All these are conceived as

4.2 Gussoni Chapel.
Capitals.

4.3 Gussoni Chapel. Pen-
dentive with roundel of
S John.

equivalent parts of one whole. The plan of the little apse is also carefully worked out, with a flat stretch in the middle to take the flat marble slab of the relief of the altarpiece and its frame, while in compensation the bits of wall on each side sweep forward in taut quarter-circles to meet the corner piers of the chapel proper, a slight dislocation that gives a particular liveliness and distinction to the whole.

An endeavor was made to absorb the altarpiece, today still in its original frame in its original place, into the overall architectural scheme. While altarpiece and architecture never quite jibe, the compressed entablature of the frame is similar to that of the main order, and some of the lines are carried through. Above little pilasters half as high as the big ones, the lesser entablature could not suitably match the main one, yet the two are kept in close relation—not always an easy feat.

The overall design seems knowing, but as the working out of some details does not, the chief author may not have been thoroughly experienced. The waywardnesses of the Palazzetto Gussoni nearby make it clear that the commissioning members of the family were not architecturally literate enough to know or care. It is unusual, nevertheless, to find, as here, greater control of the whole than of so many of the parts, the opposite of what would be expected so early.

The outer front of the chapel, facing the boxlike nave of the church, is finished at the top in a different way. Above the entrance arch there are spandrels of cool gray marble, inset with black marble discs. The fine curvy keystone interrupts the archivolt and reaches the cornice above, but without having any steadying effect; it seems, rather, a fulcrum on which the cornice could seesaw, an effect implied by the tangent relation of cornice and arch. The cornice is thin and shallow, more like a frame than a crowning element. A figure of the Risen Christ once stood on the peak of the pediment (Selvatico-Lazari, 115).

In the tympanum, a fancy elliptical frame encloses an inscription S MA-RIAE DOLOROSAE EXEMPLAR, referring to the dedication of the chapel and the Pietà of the altarpiece. The chapel had a going-over in the XVIIc and thorough repairs in 1783, when the plaster gores in the dome were painted with arabesques typical of the late XVIIIc; the ellipse must have been put in then. A new altar frontal was made in the XIXc, with the now familiar porphyry and serpentine discs, possibly copying the original one, but made when the floor of the chapel was raised 6″. This cut the ornamental plinths under the rear pilasters in half, with the result that each now shows a smiling *putto* head with its chubby chin set right on the floor.

In 1483 Giorgio Cornaro won permission to have a chapel built at the SS Apostoli "with several tombs" (Puppi-Puppi, 230). The already old church was often tampered with, and finally replaced by the existing characterless building in the mid–XVIIIc. Work on the chapel must have begun within a few years, for it was finished long enough before 1500 to be shown clearly on the Barbari map view, firmly attached to the right side of the old church much as it is to the new. Its floor is now two steps down from that of the nave, and lower than the campo outside, which became higher when paved. Once attributed to Pietro Lombardo, that favorite wasteyard of uncertain early writers, this chapel seems farther from his now better defined style than the Gussoni Chapel, a work of the same genus but of different species (fig. 4.4). Money never raised any problems here, for the Cornaros were the richest family in Venice, thanks to their attentiveness to the cultivation of sugar on Cyprus.

4.4 SS Apostoli. Cornaro
Chapel.

The core has a dome on pendentives springing from well-defined supports in the corners of a square (here 17' on a side), a baldacchino scheme like that of the Gussoni Chapel, with a few important variants. Instead of a furrowed dome on salient pilasters, here a smooth near hemisphere is borne by freestanding corner columns (fig. 4.5). Columns tucked into the angles of a square below a dome were no novelty, but a common late Byzantine practice, familiar in Venice, for example, from the presbytery of S Mark's, and probably also from some of the small Byzantinizing churches no longer standing. The novelty here was in translating the old scheme into the new architecture.

The features that led to the attribution to Pietro are the columns on round pedestals, with shafts of two kinds of fluting separated by a bandage-like band, so much like the columns of Pietro's Marcello monument of fifteen years before as to suggest that those were taken as models (fig. 4.6). Being so foreign to the firm logic and severe style that control everything else in the chapel, they suggest that a Cornaro rather than the architect may have chosen them. The entasis bulge of the lower shaft was not repeated, and the more restrained architect may have corrected it consciously, just as he rationally reversed the two types of fluting, putting the seemingly stronger vertical below, where strength is called for, and the less stable spiral above, where license is more acceptable.

Apart from additions, almost nothing in the chapel has any carved ornament except a fluted band used for discreet emphasis in a few telling places, stiff flowers in standard coffers, and what carving was mandatory on capitals and brackets, unthinkable as plain blocks. The leaves of these capitals are deeply serrated and ridged, yet kept more abstract and architectural than naturalistic, impossible to classify botanically.

These capitals and brackets underpin the architrave that, since it overhangs the walls by a foot, is particularly prominent, a vigorous structural component and not just a few bands of tapelike ornament. From capital to capital, or corner to corner, it would have had too long a span for a stone beam by itself, and some intermediate support or seeming support was called for. This was supplied by three brackets, like those Brunelleschi put under his long architraves in the Old Sacristy at S Lorenzo, shaped like Roman keystones, seeming less to be holding up than just hanging down. Here in the Cornaro Chapel, they are made to play their role with more vigor.

Joining the columns, with minor assistance from the brackets, the architrave is a major component of the armature from which the arches of the pendentives spring, to become the next element of the baldacchino. The intersection of the thin archivolts is still unresolved; they cut each other off, and would destroy the strength of the arches were it not immediately recovered by their foot-deep soffits corresponding to the foot-deep overhang of the architrave. A strong armature is thus established, with all its members of strong-looking limestone, contrasting with the inert smooth white plaster of the nonworking surfaces all around, such as the pendentives, which seem suitably weightless. Although of stone, the slender columns on their high pedestals seem to belong to a weaker order of being than the rest of the baldacchino armature. They symbolize the support they do not seem quite capable of effectuating.

The plaster dome does not float serenely, partly because it is narrowed on each side by the overhang of the architrave and the arches (it is reduced to only 15'), and it seems small, low, dark, and somehow anticlimactic after the ablebodied preparation below. The chapel is tall, and asserts itself as tall,

4.5 Cornaro Chapel. Section.

4.6 Cornaro Chapel. Detail.

4.7 Cornaro Chapel. Detail.

making the eye travel upward; but the dome, less than a hemisphere and rather dark, does not continue the upward sensation, seeming instead to act like a shadowy lid, shutting the chapel firmly down.

The arch that opens the chapel out to the nave has square coffers sunk in its soffit, and they reappear on the opposite side of the chapel under a similar arch that continues inward a couple of feet as a barrel vault to roof the small flatbacked apse (fig. 4.7). This apse is just deep enough to allow two narrow arched windows in the side walls that, though they show little on the outside, provide a particularly beautiful and quietly dramatic light on the altar (thanks partly to chamfering) and on the superb Tiepolo altarpiece. Such a subtle and appropriate use of light for dramatic emphasis is rare before the Baroque. More light comes from an *oculus* in the arch above the altar, and from *oculi* centered in the pendentive arches, all somehow adding to the feeling of order that pervades the chapel.

A stone bench along the side walls breaks out under the cylindrical pedestals and gives more stable support, helping also to relate the columns to the rest of the chapel. A band taking over from the line of the bands around the middle of the columns runs across the side walls, linking the columns to the other elements. Above the band is plaster; below, marble paneling.

The upper part of the side walls now serves as background for two wall tombs for members of the Cornaro family (Marco, d.1511, Zorzi, d.1540), fitted in after the main architectural scheme had been completed. Minor alterations were made for laudatory inscriptions later. These additions have diluted the pure late Quattrocento quality of the ensemble only a little.

Uncorrupted by showy ornaments— the tombs are discreet—the chapel speaks with both clarity and strength, achieved by logic refined by keen sensibility. The architecture is both too simple and too bold for Pietro Lombardo, certainly in the 1490s when it was built. But if it will not fit into his oeuvre because it is too architectural, neither can it be made to fit easily into the other principal stylistic group of the late 1400s, that of Mauro Codussi and his satellites (Lewis 1973, 364, disagrees), though it is surely nearer to them. It has to be the work of someone who drew from both currents, or who created naturally in one but was given orders to accept something from the other.

The outside is even more severe, less from any particular choice of the designer's than from the fact that the outsides of family chapels had not yet come to assert themselves as small architectural entities linked to larger ones (fig. 4.8). It does, nonetheless, have a special character from its little lead-leafed dome, higher than the plastered brick dome it encloses, like S Mark's or the recent Miracoli, and also from the flat apse, with its *oculus* near the top and its slits of side windows for lighting the altar, windows of typical early form with round heads and no marking of the imposts. It is not quite trustworthy, however, because the apse was so much rebuilt in the XVIIIc, perhaps at the time the Tiepolo altarpiece was installed. Even so, the plain little ensemble is unique.

In a different relation to the Lombardos in its architectural design is the chapel of the Giustiniani family in S Francesco della Vigna (fig. 4.9). Its walls are covered with friezes filled with figures at small scale, a rich stone altarpiece, and most notably a series of relief panels with busts of twelve prophets by Pietro Lombardo, to which Tullio and Antonio (according to most scholars) later added the four Evangelists. All or most of this was commissioned and executed before 1500 for a chapel in the older and more modest

4.8 Cornaro Chapel.
Exterior.

S Francesco, which was pulled down in the 1530s to make way for the present building by Sansovino.

In the late 1530s or soon after, a new Giustiniani Chapel was arranged in the new church, using again much of the material of the older one. The barrel vault must date from this campaign, but it may recall an earlier one. If Tullio and Antonio added figures, some new arrangement was most likely considered and perhaps carried out before the new building was begun, for Antonio left Venice ca. 1506, and Tullio died in 1532. Their not quite integrated figures may have been worked into some remodeling at the last minute. Whatever happened, it seems unlikely that much of the original work was eliminated when the existing chapel was built, for the Giustiniani would hardly have let their family chapel be made smaller when it was being incorporated into a larger and more princely church. The new version may not yet have been fully finished in 1552 (Howard 1975, passim, and 173n37). Perhaps the pieces were not all from the same source, and were fitted into the new space bit by bit, though only the altarpiece and the friezes are distinct from the rest (fig. 4.10).

In spite of being made up largely of figure sculpture, the present composition is severe, based on wall-covering rows of rectangles in plain, strong, deep frames (fig. 4.11). This is far from Florentine or Lombard models, and perhaps closer to Rizzo's and Spavento's uncompromising paneled compositions on the back of S Mark's and the Palazzo Ducale, possibly contemporary with the first scheme of the chapel, or the ingenious panel and window organization of the Gussoni Chapel. But Rizzo and Spavento had been dead for over a generation when the present scheme was set up. All of these examples may stem from one minor tradition, quite different from the arabesque-dominated Lombardo style. Such coincidences can

4.9 S Francesco della Vigna.
Giustinian Chapel. Frieze,
two Evangelists and six
Prophets.

4.10 Giustinian Chapel. Altar of XVc with XVIc frame.

4.11 Giustinian Chapel.
Typical moldings.

occur in early phases of a developing style, when the repertory of forms and compositional ideas is still limited, and occasional unrelated works turn out to look rather like one another.

Another possible explanation for the similarity of the present chapel to work of fifty years before might be that the new chapel was intended to look like the old one. The family that decided to preserve the old sculpture may have decided to preserve the old form as well. Unfortunately, although so much of the old chapel is still here in pieces, the original whole cannot be recovered as more than a guess. One change is clear: the old altarpiece, small and with smallscale details, not being either big or authoritative enough, was newly framed, perhaps by Sansovino, with robust columns and entablature at much larger scale, able to fill the east end. Another explanation could be that the second-hand material is not from one earlier ensemble but from several, and they were well reconciled, with a severity that is either Codussian—chronologically difficult to explain—or Sansovinian. The latter would be equally difficult to justify because although there are only a few carved moldings and some surprisingly pure details (both quite conceivably either ca. 1485 or ca. 1550), there are also decidedly Quattrocento architraves with inclined fascias.

Even less related to the work of the Lombardos is a displaced islet of purest Tuscan, the small chapel of S John the Baptist, attached to S Giobbe in 1471–76, while the Lombardos were still working in the church. It was made for the Martini family, wealthy members of a colony of silk merchants from Lucca then living in Venice. Just before 1581, Francesco Sansovino, son of the sculptor-architect, wrote in his wonderful *Venezia, Città Nobilissima*, of the "marble relief altarpiece in the chapel of Pietro Grimani . . . made by the Florentine Antonio Rosselli" (Sansovino, 155). This includes a double error: Antonio Rosselli for Antonio Rossellino (1427–ca. 1478) and Grimani Chapel for Martini Chapel. Although a Domenico Roselli had been working at Urbino (Heydenreich-Lotz, 76), there is no reason to connect either him or a relative with this chapel. The Grimanis bought the chapel next to the Martini in 1529, and it has an altar with a marble S Luke by Lorenzo Bregno made ten years later. Like the Martini chapel, it is a separate little building and, except for the vault, its architecture is a copy of the Martini. Sansovino must have mixed his notes.

A uniquely un-Venetian feature of the Martini Chapel is its dome, not a dome on pendentives like that at the chancel of S Giobbe but a pendentive dome. This, too, is a Byzantine type, formed from a hemisphere sliced off on all four sides so that it will fit over a square. The model for this example, however, was not local or Byzantine.

The inside is covered not with plaster or mosaic but with glazed terracotta, in diamond shapes—green, ochre, cream—in a trompe l'oeil pattern of what appear to be cubes, now sticking out, now in (fig. 4.12). Since such glazed tiles were not being made in Venice at this time, the dome must have been fabricated in Florence. When it was assembled in Venice, it must have been a novelty, not alone for its glistening surface but even more as the first dome of the Renaissance in the city, earlier than Pietro's at the other end of the church or Codussi's at S Michele. It is a different kind of dome, too different to have inspired Pietro's: all one continuous surface, all part of one sphere, and not the compound of parts of two spheres that makes up a dome on pendentives.

Novel for Venice, the design and material were not absolutely novel, for they follow closely Luca della Robbia's dome over the chapel of the Cardinal of Portugal at S Miniato in Florence,

4.12 S Giobbe. Martini
Chapel. Glazed terra-cotta
dome.

4.13 S Giobbe. Grimani
Chapel. Scheme repeating
that of the Martini Chapel,
including its pendentive
dome.

made just ten years earlier (1461–66). The tomb of the young royal cardinal was designed and carved by Antonio Rossellino (with assistants), and he presumably also supervised the architecture, from designs by Antonio Manetti (Pope-Hennessy 1958, 49), who had just died (1460). A pupil of Brunelleschi, Manetti may have taken over the form of the pendentive dome from his master, who had used it often. The reintroduction of this kind of dome into monumental architecture may go back to Brunelleschi, as does the dome on pendentives. The Martinis must have admired the exquisite chapel in S Miniato enough to commission the same workshop for the chapel they proposed building in Venice. Vasari, always a patriotic Tuscan, gave the chapel in S Giobbe a Tuscan artistic parent, quite rightly, but when he foisted Antonio Rossellino on it, he made a wrong guess.

The tiles must have been brought over the Apennines on donkeyback. Somewhere, something must have slipped in the measurements, for the edge of the dome and the edges of the carved marble frames had to be sliced off to make the dome fit over the square of the chapel. The arches on the walls and the arch opening into the church, marking the edges of the dome, are of gray stone, as are the cornice and fluted pilasters; and all are carved with a sharpness and firmness that suggest Florentine workmen imported for the job. The darkish stone, where white *pietra d'Istria* would have been expected, also looks more Florentine than Venetian, and adds to the pervasive air of foreignness. Even the apparent simplicity of structure, particularly at the corners, seems Florentine. The scheme of folded pilasters, arches with deep soffits to make up for the strength lost where they intersect, and the dome itself make a baldacchino structure as logical as at the Gussoni and Cornaro chapels, both later, both thoroughly

Venetian, and both less intellectual. The Martini design is more clearly and simply stated and flatter and simpler than the other two: it accomplishes more with less. Its imitation in the Grimani Chapel next door does the same (fig. 4.13).

An Austrian bomb, lobbed over from Mestre during the abortive revolution of 1848–49, cracked the Martini dome; the outer wall, now cut for better light by a *finestra termale* or Diocletian window, has sunk a couple of inches more than the rest. Despite the consequent deformation and a few cracks, the chapel is stable according to a recent diagnosis (1975–76). Only minor repairs have been needed. The S John on the marble altar, sometimes still given to Antonio Rossellino himself but more often now to an assistant, is still in place along with the whole altarpiece, and the chapel remains a handsome visitor from the Florentine Quattrocento.

5 | COROS AND ALTARS

It seems suitable to pause here and look at some small works that already make full use of the Renaissance vocabulary. They have found the old rules and have been able to apply them, but to problems so slight that they are not quite comfortably classed with real buildings—architectural though their language is—for they are not more than choir enclosures and altar frames.

Within the Transition period there are hybrids that resist classification; one such is the provision made for the choir at the Frari. Large churches of the mendicant orders, particularly if attached to monasteries with over a score of friars, were often equipped with a permanent stone or wood choir: a U of seats near the east end of the nave. This blocked the view of the main altar for most of the congregation, but that was held incidental, for the church had not been built for them—it was not a parish church—but for the friars. Public Masses were extracurricular, but the friars' uses of the *coro* were mandatory; it was there that they met for their regular daily and nightly offices sung in plainsong; matins, lauds, prime, sext, nones, vespers, and compline. The music was not intended as a social concert for the delectation of the faithful, or even to inspire them, but as a form of prescribed ritual. No response from the people—if any were present—was required. Still seen in monasteries or a few cathedrals or collegiate churches in Spain or Latin America, such choirs, once far more common, could be large and lavish. The choir stalls inside were treated as furniture; while the outside could occasionally also be so treated, it was more often designed as a piece of architecture, a small church inside the big one.

The one in the Frari is, on the outside, a large rectangular block of carved stone, known as the Septo Marmoreo (fig. 5.1). The inside, with its 124 seats and wealth of carved and inlaid wood,

5.1 *Coro* or Septo Marmoreo
of the Frari.

was finished by the workshop of the Gozzi family in 1468 (carved inscription), one of several similar choirs they made for other Venetian churches, all now destroyed. Within a few years, Bartolomeo Buon, the first designer of the Ca' del Duca and by now one of the old masters of the florid late Gothic, famous for the Porta della Carta and the Arco Foscari, was enclosing the woodwork perhaps not yet completed in an outer wall of marble and Istrian limestone, a gift from the wealthy Morosini family.

Some time before 1475, the supervision was shifted to the sculptor-architect Pietro Lombardo. The workmen hired for Buon would not all have been dismissed when Pietro was put in charge, though he may have brought with him a small team of men attuned to his own taste. Most of the work must already have been planned, and pieces already carved would have been put up as Buon intended. The outside, then, would embody more of Buon's late Gothic than of Pietro's already Transitional preferences, which could have been introduced only among the last architectural items and some of the sculpture.

Lengthy discussion of a work by Pietro Lombardo here might lead to the idea that he was the first of Venice's Early Renaissance architects, which is not so. His work began with some glances toward the Venetian past and more to the beginnings of the Renaissance in Florence and Padua. Contemporary with his activities, however, are those of Mauro Codussi, an architect who looked more steadily at the Renaissance present and even divined some of its future. For the arrangement of the material in this book, it works out better—despite the violation of timetable chronology—to consider Pietro first, even though some of his oeuvre postdates Codussi's, and also to consider his early Transitional work on the *coro,* then going on to the mature main body of his oeuvre.

The whole *coro* of the Frari looks like an orderly small building, 45' wide and twice as long, set inside a roomy church. Its marble walls, 15' high, once glittering with gilding, are marked off evenly by not yet quite classical pilasters with leafy capitals, also not yet quite classical, both less advanced in form than those of the Foscari Monument, close to them in date and forty yards away. Most of the architectural details are indeterminate, but, where namable, more late Gothic than antique. On the other hand, a regular row of pilasters carrying a straight cornice, even if not a classical one, may at first seem more antique than Gothic; but the original idea of pilasters and trabeation as representatives of a possible or ideal structure has largely dissolved here into not more than a surface pattern like the edges of the panels of a long screen. It must be remembered that the Gothic, too, could use evenly spaced pseudosupports under a level cornice, often on the walls of a vaulted space where the verticals were part of the movement about to spray out as the ribs of the vaults above. Buon must have seen an example of this every day as he walked to work through the passage from his Porta della Carta to his Arco Foscari in the Ducal Palace. Little classicizing information would have been needed to adapt this to the pilasters and rather Gothic capitals and cornice in the Frari, and a little classical flavor was all he gave them.

The main entrance from the nave to the inside of the *coro* is between two of these pilasters. They hold up a round arch with a Renaissance archivolt ornamented by a curly vine growing out of a basket at each end. The outer edges of the arch are hemmed in by dwarf pilasters, half as high as those below, and unable to continue in the line above them—as would be expected—because shouldered aside by the archivolt. The book-carrying lion of the Evangelist

S Mark and the book-carrying ox of the Evangelist S Luke curl cosily in roundels whose scale and location in the mottled gray and yellow marble spandrels are like direct classical quotations. At either end are the polygonal pulpits for the Gospel and Epistle, concessions to Masses for a lay congregation.

If anything in the architecture shows the ideas of Pietro, it would be in this upper section—perhaps the arch (with its classical rosettes in coffers on the soffit), the dwarf pilasters with arabesques, and the dentils in the cornice. But even these are not as different from the rest as Pietro might have chosen to make them had he been free to follow his own modern ideas. The beginning of the two sides of the *Septo* facing the aisles is more classical in detail, as are also the pilasters of the reveals of the doorway, and it is hard to see why they would have been made later than what is next to them, unless there was some special condition caused by the way the scaffolding was taken down.

The miscellany of florid late Gothic with touches of Transitional Early Renaissance is worked into an all-over pattern of embroiderylike richness, less like other Venetian architectural works of the time than like contemporary big-scale furniture—and this is by no means inappropriate. As in Spanish Plateresque, which at first glance the *coro* may seem to resemble, there is no hostility between the juxtaposed Gothic and near Renaissance parts, for both have been denatured, flattened, reduced to patterns, leaving neither one strongly enough characterized to assert itself over the other. Thus they are able to cooperate in peaceful coexistence, a condition traditional works do not always achieve.

Inasmuch as the ensemble or end product looks like no sure work of his, Pietro Lombardo's role here can hardly have gone beyond that of administrator or supervisor for architecture, and carver of some of the figures in the octagonal panels or freestanding on top. The only part with real Renaissance character is the center arch. Pietro could not yet be called an architect on the strength of that—slim strength—and at this date he ought not to be called architect at all.

The *coro* set up in the late Gothic Church of S Stefano of the Augustinians (ca. 1488) was so large that it ran a third of the way down the nave. Although of the same type as that in the Frari, a screen wall of panels and reliefs marked off by evenly spaced columns or pilasters, in style it went a step beyond (fig. 5.2). Some of its sculpture may be documented as by Vittorio Gambello (ca. 1460–1535), a son of Antonio of S Zaccaria, or perhaps by Pietro Lombardo, but it is most convincingly given to someone else in or near the Lombardo atelier. The architecture may have been independently designed. When it was taken down in 1613 (Bortolan, 31; Hubala 1974, 344), some parts were thriftily saved to ornament the side walls of the chancel (now more exposed), perhaps with additions of decorative material from the original altar, pulled down at the same time.

The lower part is paneled between old-fashioned polygonal piers which carry a miniature but self-consciously classical entablature. Above are small *cipollino* columns with Early Renaissance capitals of several types—the use of nonmatching capitals is mediaeval—supporting another entablature with another convincingly classical cornice (despite its flaring cyma where the corona should be). At the top, aligned with the columns, stand life-size marble Apostles. The composition was probably inspired by the striking iconostasis of S Mark's, made by the Dalle Masegne brothers a century earlier, and here freshly translated into the new language.

5.2 S Stefano. Part of the old *coro* rearranged in the chancel.

5.3 Sebastiano Mariani da Lugano. S Giovanni in Bragora. Fragments of old *coro* rearranged against wall.

The most unusual episodes are now in the intercolumniations. Small free-standing figures occupy two niches whose arches are squeezed between the shafts of the columns in a way that suggests an adaptation of old material more than a new creation. Alternating with these niches are marble panels of dove gray and peach from Vicenza, set in pink Verona frames in the lower part; above them are squares with reliefs of saints fitted into outsize cockleshells now sadly gray with dirt. (The chancel was not cleaned with the rest of the church by the Comitato Italiano per Venezia, 1973–74, a particularly successful effort in bringing a wealth of colored marbles in the nave back to life.)

Changes made at the time of the moving show under the columns and above the niches. Under the bases of the columns are plain square blocks of a different stone, disproportionate to the shafts above and awkward in relation to the cornice below. A band with cherubs' heads in high relief comes above the niches, and between it and the capitals fruity swags are hanging, also in high relief and of a different stone. These are unlike any of the rest of the carving, but like work of the XVIIc, when the rearrangements were carried out. If the blocks and band of swags were eliminated, the columns and niche bays would fit together and reach the same height, though they would not then fit properly with the superposed panels in the other bays. Such an arrangement cannot have been the original one, unless the panels now set one above the other had then been placed differently—there must have been plenty of room when the coro was so large—perhaps alternating, or perhaps with some outside and some inside the coro wall. The plaster background to the swags, the plaster strips fitting the column shafts to the adjacent stone, and the bad joints in some

panels cannot be original XVc work, but could well be part of a makeshift XVIIc remodeling.

At about the same time, shortly before or after 1490, a decade or so after the Church of S Giovanni in Bragora was repaired and largely rebuilt, it too was given a coro. But this, and whatever was left of the early high altar, both designed by Sebastiano Mariani da Lugano (d. before 1518), were dismembered in 1728. As at S Stefano, some pieces were worked into ornamental panels behind marble seats on either side of the chancel, an area not at all prominent when screened by the coro (fig. 5.3). The fine quality of the materials and execution can still be made out, but not the original arrangement (fig. 5.4). The Frari is now the only place in Venice to see a large coro intact in situ.

As S Giovanni was a parish church, the coro must have been made for the large body of subordinate priests. Many parishes in Venice had a special corps of lesser priests, like canons, who were in charge at night and at other off hours, performed a variety of duties, and were supported by parish funds, not a practice common in other cities. Though not made for a group as large as that in a monastic church, this coro could surely once seat more than its remains can now. It may not have been entirely freestanding, but may have projected one bay into the nave, for the two nearest piers of the nave arcade are treated like those separating the marble panels on the chancel wall. More color is still visible here than on any other coro: cream, lemon, pink, silver gray, and slate gray marbles. The arabesques are gilded, and the carving, exceptionally fine, is of an unfamiliar type, not close to the work of the Lombardo group.

Sebastiano Mariani had redesigned the chancel and its altar, but only fragments of this work, other than the coro, have survived, such as the exceptionally fine main cornice. The rest

5.4 Sebastiano Mariani da Lugano. S Giovanni in Bragora. Pier of *coro*.

5.5 Giovanni Bellini. Altarpiece in the Pesaro Chapel of the sacristy of the Frari.

was soon completed, redesigned, or re-modeled for the installation of Cima's *Baptism* (1492–95), perhaps his master-piece, set in a stone frame of only slightly later date than the *coro*. Sebas-tiano, who had probably begun as a sculptor, worked later at the Church of the Carmini and at S Antonio Abate, in each case in a manner different from what is left of the *coro* of S Giovanni.

The carved wood frames of large al-tarpieces may have affected the design of some stone architecture at the be-ginning of the Renaissance. By the end of the XVc, influence was also running the other way. Several important altar-pieces by Giovanni Bellini whose origi-nal frames survive are thoroughly ar-chitectural: for example, that at SS Giovanni e Paolo (ca. 1475?, picture de-stroyed by fire 1867), that at S Giobbe (ca. 1480–85?, picture now in the Acca-demia), and above all that in the Pesaro Chapel of the sacristy of the Frari, where the painting (signed, 1488) and frame are still together (fig. 5.5), and one can see the architecture of the frame continued in the painting (as also at S Giobbe). The Frari altar made ad-vances on its model, Mantegna's at S Zeno, Verona (1459).

The frame is a sophisticated work by Jacopo da Faenza, with fairly standard contemporary vocabulary and a few ad-vanced features, such as the pilasters planted on the front of other pilasters, a strip of which shows behind on either side. A woodworker might be less in-hibited by classical precedent than a would-be classicizing architect, even though he was restricting himself to the classical vocabulary and following directions from a highly educated painter. The pagan-looking sirens hold-ing flaming vases on the top will reap-pear a decade later holding medallions of the Infant Jesus on the Vendramin tomb in SS Giovanni e Paolo. The new gold glistening everywhere shows how

a great many arabesque pilasters must originally have been intended to look. They glitter so much that their details are hard to read in many places. Such bright reflections are almost always an-titectonic, if not out-and-out antiarchi-tectural. The capitals, for example, can be understood more clearly as they ap-pear in the painted version on the wings of the triptych, which continues in two dimensions the harder-to-perceive three-dimensional realities on the frame.

6 | ANTONIO RIZZO: THE TRON AND BARBARIGO TOMBS

Three important architects emerged at the beginning of the Early Renaissance in Venice and began building there around the end of the 1460s. Trained as sculptors, Antonio Rizzo (ca. 1430–98 or '99) and Pietro Lombardo (ca. 1440–1515) kept on working as sculptors while also accepting building and decorating commissions. As far as we know, Mauro Codussi (ca. 1440–1504) was trained in the crafts of building from the beginning, and of the three he is the most advanced and architectural. All left Transitional oddities behind, and all welcomed the Renaissance openheartedly, each with a different and quite personal understanding.

Antonio Rizzo, once confusingly known also as Antonio Dentone, was born in Verona (or Como?) and early won esteem as a sculptor in marble. Most of his building, which came later, was determined from a stonecutter's point of view, as was that of most of his contemporaries in the city. As an architect, he is now a puzzle and may have to remain one; his taste in architecture, unlike his sculpture, was less for the simple and clear, more for the elaborate and hard to read. Yet in a few works, not easily reconciled with the rest, he showed a more severe mastery. The artistic predispositions of his clients might elucidate some of the differences, but there is no evidence here to help. Stylistically he can be seen as gently schizoid, or merely inexperienced, but with some fine flashes of originality.

In 1465–66 he was working at the Certosa di Pavia, making columns and capitals, almost certainly ornate. The earliest records of him in Venice, where he must have come in the early 1460s, are as sculptor for the tomb of Orsato Giustinian in a chapel of the Church of S Andrea of the Carthusians, on their island at the edge of the city (fig. 6.1). He may have been recommended by the Carthusians of Pavia. Now dismembered, with only a few of its figures preserved, the tomb's design is known only from a drawing of the XVIIIc, but this drawing shows that he was using nothing but Renaissance ornament, which he would have to have learned before he came to Venice.

He helped on the final touches to the Arco Foscari, in association with Antonio Bregno, with whom he was confused for a couple of centuries. He surely worked with Bregno a number of times, though the records do not show whether as pupil, assistant, or partner. By 1467 or soon after, he had begun the portal of the Church of S Elena, unpartnered though perhaps assisted (Munman 1971, 141; Hubala 1974, 265).

About 1469 he was paid for the elaborate small twin altars of S Paolo and S Giacomo in S Mark's, given by that early patron of the Renaissance in Venice, Doge Cristoforo Moro (fig. 6.2). They are backed up against stout pairs of Byzantine columns similar to those of the Arsenal gateway, but here a working part of the architecture of the church. Everything is in the Renaissance vocabulary, but not quite coordinated. The lower parts are sheathed in relief so low and fine that from more than a yard away it looks like dark lace, while the tops are heavy with bold-scale cresting of creatures from another world: fleshy sirens, chubby *putti*, and rank floral scrolls seemingly jungle grown. Both tops and bottoms are beautifully carved, and handsome in their opposing ways, but the architectural discipline needed to make them cohere is lacking.

Solidly settled in Venice, Rizzo married there in 1477. After the decorative works already mentioned, he carved for the Scuola di S Marco a five-sided pulpit and worked out a circular stairway from drawings made by Gentile Bellini, both now destroyed. Before being chosen for his first big commission, the monument of Doge Tron, he must already have made influential friends, some of whom would then have helped

him win the even bigger commission to rebuild or repair the Doges' Palace after the fire of 1483.

When his patron, Doge Agostino Barbarigo, was disgraced (but not deposed) in 1495, Rizzo began to be in trouble also, and so he began to try other kinds of work on the side. He invented some sort of new mill and tried designing forts. Caught embezzling palace funds in 1498, he fled to Foligno and very soon died. Venice revengefully reduced him to a nonperson; his name was suppressed and his works ascribed to others, most often to Antonio Bregno.

His first major commission was for the memorial monument of Doge Nicolò Tron (1471–73), the largest yet made in the city (fig. 6.3). On the evidence of some of its sculpture, the architecture is now accepted also as Rizzo's work, with the help of many subordinates.

Although physically impressive, Doge Tron was politically inconsequential, save for contriving an alliance with the Muslim Persians against the Muslim Turks. For an imposing memorial to him, his son Filippo won concession in 1476 for the whole north wall of the chancel of the Church of the Frari, directly across from the Foscari monument. Neither the plague of 1478 nor the on and off financial troubles of the republic hampered the progress of the work, already largely complete by 1479 (Dienstfrey-Pincus 1969, 247nl), because the Tron family, thanks to what they had managed to extract from Rhodes, had ample funds to build when and what they wanted. Everything must have been finished by the very early 1480s.

In only twenty years, the Gothic features of the Foscari monument have been so purged that none is readily seen in the Tron composition. All the details come from the repertory of the Renaissance; the way they are put together does not. In other words, while the vocabulary is classical, the syntax

6.1 Tomb of Orsato Gius-
tinian (d.1464). Once at the
destroyed Certosa di S Andrea (drawing by Jan II van
Grevenbroeck, Museo Cor-
rer, Cod. Gradenigo 228,
I/12).

6.2 Altarino di S Giacomo
in the right transept of
S Mark's.

6.3 Tron Monument in the
Frari. The cascade of red
drapery frescoed on the wall
and the multiplication of
moldings at the bottom
still have Gothic character,
though the latter counts for
little under the big panels of
yellow marble streaked with
grey. The idea of tiers of
niches stacked up on each
side also has Gothic antecedents, though their details
here are entirely Renais-
sance.

is not—but neither is it something held over from Gothic. The combination is new, not macaronic, and new also is the portentous scale, 65' high and 25' wide, twice as wide as the Foscari tomb.

The general idea appears to have been taken from another art, the frames of painted polyptychs or carved reredos, and not from some facadelike bit of freestanding architecture. With few exceptions, such frames were set against walls, like the showy tombs that had already become one of the admired sights of the city. Although almost wholly made up of little parts, the whole Tron tomb proclaims a majesty and grandeur more often found in real architecture than in the altarpiece frames—so often finicky—that seem to have been one of its chief begetters.

The crowning entablature and arch are the only elements not at small scale; such all-over preponderance of little parts is not to be expected in a work of such size. At either end, for example, the tall pierlike verticals bounding the whole, which might be expected to be authoritatively large in conception, are instead compounded of small bits: first, a pair of dwarf pilasters on a disproportionately high pedestal that makes them look even more dwarfed, then three superposed niches containing statues, all stopped at the top by a block of the entablature. Somehow this busy miscellany manages to weld itself on each side into an effective substitute for a more normal frame and support. Without being the product of ordinary architectural thinking—far from it—the compound works as architecture—or instead of it.

Parenthetically, one curious counterpart may be pointed out, the Cappella di Piazza on the Campo in Siena (fig. 6.4). Between the corner piers of three superposed niches, one arch rises the full height of the composition, and the whole is topped by a big-scale Early Renaissance entablature of the mid-XVc, well before any idea of a Tron monument in Venice. Singly, none of these elements is unusual, but all three in combination occur only here and on the Tron tomb. This is a good example of how resemblances in architecture can be as fortuitous as resemblances between unrelated people. Here there is no more reason to claim consanguinity than between the prince and the pauper, or the harassed doubles making *The Comedy of Errors*.

The lowest zone of the Tron tomb could be a stone version of the frame of some painted polyptych, such as that of the S Vincent altarpiece in SS Giovanni e Paolo, made about a decade earlier (Robertson, 43-46). Like most, this frame is of wood, and the lower part of the Tron monument implies an origin in something carved in wood rather than stone (fig. 6.5). It looks as much like furniture as architecture—and as for the frame, vice versa. Furthermore, parts of the stone of the tomb were gilded, and more color came from the marbles in some of the panels (fig. 6.6).

The details of the arabesques, though fairly standard, do not appear to have been archaeologically derived, nor to have descended directly from the usual antique sources in Rome widely circulated in artists' pattern books. There is little resemblance either to the offbeat late antique examples lying about nearer by, more of them then than now. All the arabesques have the common long straight center stem, here standing in a vase, with a botanically hybrid miscellany sprouting in neat symmetry on either side.

Not everything in this lowest story, however, is attuned in unflawed harmony. The three archways against backgrounds of blue gray stone make an arrangement not only curious in itself, but also foreign to what comes above. The archivolts spring from piers that have bases and near capitals, almost like pilasters. Their surfaces, as

6.4 The Cappella di Piazza
at the foot of the Torre di
Mangia of the Palazzo Pubblico, Siena, built mainly in
the mid-XIVc.

6.5 Part of the Altarpiece of S Vincent Ferrer in SS Giovanni e Paolo. The gilded wood frame, now set inside another of stone, is more architectural than most and has been thought by some to have been designed by Giovanni Bellini himself (if the picture is accepted as an early work of his).

6.6 Tron Monument in the Frari. Center of lowest zone with a standing effigy of the Doge and two of his Virtues, between varied piers covered with unvaried relief.

well as those of the spandrels above, are lightly ruffled by arabesques, so that from a short distance the exquisite carving so blurs the definition of some parts that only a few can keep any strong identity. The strips supporting the middle arch, for example, stand so little in advance of their neighbors, which are supporting a strip reaching as high as the arch, that the shallow difference in plane is lost in the overall shimmer. But, taken together (as they almost have to be) their combination announces a readying for something above; at first there is nothing but a flat epitaph nearly a whole story high, needing no support, and only above that comes something calling for support, the jutting pseudosarcophagus, held up with no trouble by four strong brackets. The preparation at the bottom is clearly inadequate to hold up whatever is going to hold up the sarcophagus, but it does not have to, since the brackets can do it by themselves. The lower layer is left, then, at the bottom of an inert blank, all ready for something but with nothing to do.

The paired pilasters at the bottom of the side piers show off their daintily decorated surfaces so much more than they can show their role as supports, that they too seem ill-prepared to carry as much as is asked of them. The tall, projecting pier above them might be expected to be fairly substantial in order to look able to carry its load, yet its three superposed niches cut away more than three-quarters of its substance; but somehow, the emphatic shadows and the standing stone figures take over and make the lack of continuous solid irrelevant. Something other than the traditional belief in expressed stability has been substituted and has turned this assortment to unforeseen account. Perhaps enough strength is offered by the projection of the side verticals, varied and cut away as their individual elements are. However the final

effect is brought about, the result is more vigorous and less flimsy than the old rules would allow.

The proxy sarcophagus in the third zone—the doge and his family are buried under the chancel floor—is similar to what must have been its model, the tomb of Orsato Giustinian. The similarity of the two sarcophagi is one of the reasons for attributing the Tron monument to Rizzo (fig. 6.7).

The doge's head rests on a pillow arranged on one end of a bier, as though he might be asleep and able to rise from the sleep of death to a new life in heaven. Surprisingly, he appears again under the arch at the bottom, standing in his robes of office, erect like a living man, the first occurrence in almost a century of the animated effigy that was soon again to become a familiar feature of Venetian memorials. The importance of the standing figure of the commemorated doge might lead one to assume that Rizzo himself would have carved it, as the heirs might have asked, but a look at the dull figure denies that, though the master may have touched the head.

Even more striking is the zone above, with its row of five niches in the center set only a little apart from two more, one in each of the outer piers. Statues stand in all seven, lined up like jars in an old-fashioned apothecary's shop. Of once white polished Carrara marble, these figures were discreetly played up by contrast with the duller matte Istrian stone all around them. The row of niches, seemingly so novel, was not so, for a like scheme had been used about fifty years earlier at smaller scale for the tomb of Doge Tommaso Mocenigo in SS Giovanni e Paolo, with far less authority (fig. 6.8). There it may have been a transfer from a familiar type of late Gothic altarpiece, such as that in the Emiliani chapel in the Frari. While the Tron niches have a traceable Venetian pedigree, it is only here that the motif reached full maturity.

6.7 Tron Monument. The lid of the sarcophagus carries an effigy of the deceased, as on the Tomb of Orsato Giustinian, and, as often earlier, on other tombs in Venice and in Florence.

6.8 The late Gothic tomb of
Doge Tommaso Mocenigo
in SS Giovanni e Paolo.
Comparable to that of Doge
Tron in its great curtain,
rows of niches, and personi-
fications of Virtues. Some of
the work was done at least a
generation later than its
beginning in the 1420s.

The tops of these niches are less than semicircular, and are carved inside with fluted cockleshells, an ornament never out of the repertory since Roman times. Half-a-dozen are on the Tommaso Mocenigo monument, tucked under Gothic gables. They had appeared just before the Tron tomb in a more developed form on the Arco Foscari, where Rizzo had been working with Antonio Bregno while the salaries were still being paid by Doge Tron. What Rizzo may have had to do with them there—more than seeing them every day—cannot be determined, for he is recognizable on the Arco only in sculpture, and not in architecture.

The tiers of niches are plainly separated into stories by a few carved moldings stacked up along lumpy diagonals, like so many of equally early date. But then, suddenly, the horizontal above the top niches comes on fortissimo, more resoundingly than any of the lesser cornices below. That big entablature is not only imposing in its size (more than half as high as the figures in the niches), but manages at the same time to be in harmony with the whole it so compellingly crowns. Those below, when seen in relation to it, lose their identities as cornices, and retreat as no more than sets of moldings to mark the divisions into stories. Nothing else in the monument is more antique, more learned, or stronger.

The last entablature supports an arch spanning the tomb, gathering, enclosing, and stopping the restless impulses below. Its forms follow those of the arch over the doorway of the Church of S Elena, made by Rizzo in 1467 or soon after (fig. 6.9). While nearly all the architectural elements of both arches come from the classical vocabulary, they are freely used for new needs, uncurbed by standardized Roman practice that Rizzo could not have mastered very well in Verona or Pavia. The cornice at S Elena has no shelf of projecting, shadow-casting corona. The Tron arch does not match the cornice on

which it stands, as a pediment would, but compresses everything into a simple diagonal profile as at S Elena. Late antique equivalents may have been lying about nearby, in Altino or other Roman sites, or there may have been mediaeval fragments already old enough to have been mythologized into antiques, pieces like the cornices on the capitals of the great granite columns of S Mark and S Theodore at the end of the Piazzetta.

One difference shows that Rizzo went ahead unevenly in learning the correct syntax of classical elements: at S Elena the capitals do not support an architrave, but have a cornice laid directly on their tops, more as in a Gothic procedure. One step has been taken here—the moldings of the misplaced cornice are classical individually, and in a fairly proper sequence—but it is not a giant step, not the full stride to an entablature with a beam-like architrave. The full stride was taken later, at the top of the Tron monument, and the bowed cornice arch stands on a full entablature with all its three elements, though it is not borne on columns, as at S Elena. Rizzo seems to have been learning, not just stumbling ahead.

The arch at S Elena, framing the more than life-size Parian marble figure of General Vittore Cappello on his knees before his patroness, S Helena (carved, perhaps, by another hand; Munman, in conversation), is the first instance in the Renaissance of using a church front for a monument to a recently deceased personage, a practice soon taken up more enthusiastically in Venice than in any other city. The main part of the usual grand monument above a sarcophagus has here been transposed from its normal place on an interior wall to the exterior front. It is set under an arch not unlike those of plainer older tombs attached to the outside of churches, usually along the flanks though sometimes on

6.9 Portal of S Elena. Earlier
and more transitional than
the Tron Tomb in some features, such as the cornices
of diagonally stepped-out
moldings, but more "cor-
rect" in others, such as the
Composite capitals and the
rosette-filled coffers, probably both copied directly
from antique models. The
portal was taken down in
the XIXc, used again for the
church of S Polo, and put
back where it had been only
in 1929.

6.10 Tron Monument in the Frari. Upper left side showing the main, crowning entablature, the pediment-arch, its coffered soffit, the Angel Gabriel, and, on the wall behind, traces of the frescoed red drapery canopy.

either side of the main doorway. Perhaps the big portrait of the nonrecumbent donor here was thought unsuitable for a church interior. Although sarcophagi had been fastened to church walls, never before had one been part of a monument like this, with big sculptured figures. (A simulacrum of a sarcophagus has been slipped in behind them here.)

As the tympanum or background has been sunk over a foot behind the wall plane of the front of the church, the soffit of the enclosing arch is deep, with space for two rows of square coffers framing deep-throated stone flowers, once gilded, an antique motif soon repeated many times in Venice.

The enframing arch at S Elena can be read as a sort of pediment, put together with the same moldings as the cornice serving as its floor, a profile more proper for pediments than arches. The arch itself is almost semicircular, a shape more proper for arches than pediments. Furthermore, it starts up almost vertically above the columns, as though supported by them, an association proper for arches, but impossible for pediments.

Outside, at its ends, are rosettes joined to half an anthemion, a classical ornament like a honeysuckle flower, already common in Florence on the curved type of pediment invented by Donatello for his *Annunciation* in S Croce (ca. 1435) and soon made familiar on many tombs, tabernacles, and other decorative works.

The pediment-arch at S Elena was repeated and refined for the monument at the Frari. The rosettes and half-honeysuckle were left off, sparing room at the top of the piers for a gliding Gabriel on one side and a receptive Mary standing on the other (fig. 6.10). Closed off from the everyday world by the embracing arch and its deep shadow—the one strong line neither predominantly vertical nor horizontal— the figure of the Risen Christ gains great impressiveness as he stands tall in his tomb, alone, isolated in the largest area of empty, quiet space anywhere in the monument.

This does not, however, seem at first to be the climax of the composition. One's eye goes earlier to the standing doge at the bottom, or to the protuberant sarcophagus in the middle, both competing for attention. Resolution is reached only at the top, where the standing figure and the horizontal tomb recall them in a harmony independent of any but a formal relation, with no symbolism or iconographic connection—yet a quiet power is somehow added to the coda of the composition.

Not preclusively arch or pediment and not antique, the motif, called a "Florentine pediment," must have been borrowed at first- or secondhand from Florence. After S Elena (1467), the arch-as-pediment with side rosettes appeared again: in grander, more original, and more dramatic form on Codussi's facade of S Michele in Isola (1468–ca. 1470?); and also, probably before its use on the Tron tomb, in Pietro Lombardo's Malipiero tomb in SS Giovanni e Paolo (early 1470s?), if, as is probable, their tops were finished first. The Tron composition is closer, however, to S Elena, very close, and the author is the same; and as S Elena is the earliest, it must be the source for Rizzo's monument. By 1500, the motif was common property all over Italy.

The ensemble is effective enough in its unconventional assemblage of forms to govern a dense sculptural population: twenty-six figures of four different scales—two portraits, fourteen allegorical statues, four children in relief, two shield bearers, plus only four religious figures—twenty confined to the upper zones, with an absurdly small God the Father above and outside. The subjects show that the top of a tomb was often equated with the heavenly regions. It is, in fact, the one part of tomb monuments where the themes are regularly religious, and often the only part. Doge Tron, below, seems less to be awaiting his resurrection and salvation than presiding over an orderly meeting of his own virtues, all embodied as thinly-clad pretty girls, almost Greuze-like in their modest demeanor and immodest exposure. The dominance of worldly subject matter may come not only from the temper of the time and place but also from the fact that it seems easier to express civic rectitude in architecture than yearning for redemption; sculpture has the wider range of expression.

The whole work is largely an original organization, affected only in minor ways by Venetian altarpieces or non-Venetian tombs. The monument looks little like its contemporaries or predecessors in Florence or Rome, with the exception of the arched top and, in the two lowest niches, the youths carrying shields with the family arms, called *reggiscudi*. Here they are more grown-up than their baby brothers in Florence, but it is the younger and more Florentine boys rather than the Tron adolescents who will be more popular on Venetian monuments for some years to come.

The primacy and self-determination of the Tron monument is not absolutely secure, for possibly in the same year, 1476, Pietro Lombardo designed his memorial for Doge Pietro Mocenigo in SS Giovanni e Paolo. Several features beside the Florentine pediment—some of them new—appear on both works. The two sculptors would surely have known about each other's current work. What is certain is that whether the actual work was begun earlier or not, in style the Tron tomb belongs to an earlier phase. The Mocenigo fits more easily into a sequence of handsome later memorials, many of them from the Lombardo family shop.

It is still uncertain whether the Tron design goes back to Rizzo or even whether it all goes back to only one artist. The sculpture is by several hands, and so might be the architecture (though that is less likely). A difference can be seen between the oldest part, the mediaeval overmembered socle at the bottom and the suddenly more classical entablature and Florentine pediment on an unanticipated scale at the top. While these and the intermediate changes could come from successive ideas of successive designers, they more probably result from successive steps in Rizzo's uncertain maturing in architecture. His other work can give little support to either hypothesis, for his secure productions are in sculpture, and what is thought to be his in architecture is confused by other conditions, and surely by having helpers who had their own ideas. But without new information to the contrary, the whole design had best remain credited to him.

The peculiarities and inconsistencies do not come from a clinging to Gothic so much as from an innocence of the antique, and from fresh inventions, improvisations prompted in part perhaps by that very ignorance. There is not enough of the classical vocabulary in either quantity or purity for one to be bothered by the lack of the niceties of Roman grammar in putting it together. This is not bad Latin, but something in a different tongue, and it is not rightly judged by the rules of the older tongue any more than is the spoken Venetian of the time.

Rizzo had not been trained as an architect, and many of the quirks here, if looked at as architecture, come from the treatment of a large composition not in its own terms alone but also as a frame for a quantity of sculpture; it was not conceived as a sort of facade for a little building, such as a mausoleum. But even so, its relation to its antecedents is equivocal, whether to tombs, mausoleums, frames, or whatever. Its peculiarity must be recognized—and even respected.

If wholly or mainly conceived by Rizzo, this is not only his first major architectural work but his best worked-out combination of architecture and sculpture. Despite the finicalness that might come from the juxtaposing of so many small parts, despite the feeling of composition by an agglomeration of items with little weight, evading the discipline of support, emphasis, and even logic, and despite Rizzo's greenness in classical syntax—despite all this, the total effect is stable, monumental, and though unconforming, not bizarre. The relief, though varied, is controlled. The repetitions of vertical and horizontal do not give the feeling that something is being constantly cut up, for they work instead so that something else happens, and a convincing whole is created. Mysteriously the whole Tron monument proclaims itself a near masterpiece of near architecture by a near architect.

Although the works considered so far as the first of the Renaissance in Venice are all in the city, it could not be claimed that they are all in a truly and uniquely Venetian style. The first Transitional works—Gothic perhaps with a faint bit of Byzantine dressed up with a few Renaissance novelties— need not be Venetian. The gateway of the Arsenal is truly a *rarissima avis* and could have come to earth almost anywhere; it is not of any local species. Nor do the oddities of the Renaissance Tron monument call Venice compellingly to mind, for one can imagine it elsewhere—say in Verona.

Only two tomb monuments have usually been associated with Rizzo, that of Orsato Giustinian, and that of Nicolò Tron. There are, nevertheless, two more, now destroyed, that of Giovanni Emo and that of the Barbarigo brother doges, Marco (1485–86) and Agostino (1486–1501). The latter has sometimes been tentatively associated with Codussi, but the likeness is thin, based on elements that can be found not only in genuine works by Codussi, but also in works by a number of others (fig. 6.11).

6.11 Tomb of the Barbarigo
Doges, once in the church of
the Carità. Its appearance is
known now only from this
accurate-looking engraving
made by Sister Isabella Pic-
cini in 1682 (Museo Correr,
Coll. Cicogna, stampe 1551).

Rizzo had worked for both of the Barbarigos on the Palazzo Ducale—he was, in a way, the family architect—and an attribution to him (with heavy participation of helpers) has lately been strengthened (Munman 1968, 267; 1977, 89 ff; Muraro 1961, 357).

As soon as Marco was elected in 1485, the Barbarigos had begun promoting Renaissance rebuilding work on the Palazzo after the fire of 1483, and they had been consistently concerned with architecture right along. They must have been impressed by the Tron memorial, already finished (and very visible), above all by its size, and they must have decided to outdo it. Their choice for a designer would naturally have been its author, whom they already knew well from his operations at the Palazzo. From their wishes, affected by both palace and tomb, may come the peculiar nature and scale of their monument.

This ran along the north wall of the new Gothic Church of the Carità, larger than any other tomb and larger than all but the largest palace fronts, for it was over 40′ high and 60′ long. Adapting itself to the architecture of the church building, which naturally had not been planned to shelter any such mammoth, it absorbed one high round window and two lower vertical ones. There can have been little choice where it could go, for the length of the side walls had already been cut by a singing gallery like a bridge across the nave (Franzoi-DiStefano, 219). It may never have been fully finished; Rizzo had had to flee, and perhaps Barbarigo funds were not available (or not willingly sacrificed) to complete it with anything like the sculptural population of the Tron monument. Work stopped in the middle of the XVIc. It was demolished in 1807 when the church was deconsecrated, and the nave drastically remodeled into two stories to accommodate part of the new galleries of the Accademia. No remains of it show under the new floor (as examined by Professor Valcanover).

Its three huge arches along the wall must have dominated the whole church. The ones at the ends framed the usual effigies lying on biers atop raised sarcophagi on brackets, and the middle arch, equipped as a functioning chapel, had an elaborate altar flanked by kneeling figures of the two doges. Three pieces of the sculpture survive, but nothing tangible of the surrounding architecture.

It is not only that it is so enormous and double that sets it apart, but also the architecture, largely a veneer of veined marbles, is peculiar in itself. For example, the piers supporting the three arches are strikingly chopped into three sections: first a high pedestal, then a pair of small columns under an abnormally high entablature, and last, round-headed niches eating into the face of the pier, all of this crowned by another big entablature. Both cornices have shelflike coronas with cymas projecting so far that they aggravate the disjunction of the three piled-up sections. The arches, with weak, narrow archivolts, rest on the cornice above the niches, leaving room at the extreme outer edges for a tall, thin pilaster, whose impossible duty it is to act as a visual sustainer for the long, heavy top entablature (incomplete in Sister Isabella's engraving and perhaps also in the monument itself). This runs uninterrupted from one pilaster to its mate at the far other end, equivocally buoyed up a bit along the way by the bounding tops of the arches. Such an arrangement cannot have been worked out in detail by an experienced architect. Could it be some idea of Rizzo's botched by the assistants who carried it out after he had had to leave town?

Doge Marco died in 1486; Marin Sanudo (IV, 261) saw his tomb in 1494; Rizzo fled Venice in 1498; the whole tomb was not yet finished in 1499 when the doge's son added a codicil to his will to pay for continuing the work. Doge Marco, meanwhile, was buried temporarily in the family chapel in the Certosa di S Andrea (Da Mosto, 259). The big composition in the Carità was probably begun in the late 1480s, after the death of Doge Marco and the election of his brother, and from the beginning it must have been planned as a grand double monument for them both.

Already distinguished as a sculptor, Rizzo had been called to work as an architect by both doges as *proto* of the Palazzo. If he designed the Barbarigos' monument, it would have been discussed first during Marco's term, nine months in 1485-86. It was finished enough by 1494 for Sanudo to call it Doge Marco's tomb. It would still have been under Rizzo's close supervision when he came under suspicion—along with his employer Doge Agostino—in 1495, and probably remained so until just before he fled in 1498, for this private work had nothing to do with his embezzlement of public funds. Work continued after 1498 without Rizzo, but no doubt it was handled by the same crew who had been working on it before his defection. Funds from the codicil and gifts from relatives were enough to have it finished as much as it ever was—no doubt in a simplified way—though not until the middle of the XVIc.

Two of the surviving pieces of sculpture are in Rizzo's style, probably as diluted through shop assistants: the kneeling Doge Agostino in the sacristy of the Salute, and the bronze relief of the Resurrection in the Scuola di S Giovanni Evangelista. These and the miscellany of facts just listed all point toward Rizzo, but an attribution of the architecture ought to rest on the nature of the architecture of the monument. If his, it would have been begun soon after 1486 while he was busy on the Palazzo. While it might, then, be expected to correspond stylistically more to that than to the Tron tomb begun a decade earlier, still the style of one tomb might more naturally stem from the style of another tomb than from part of a palace. Here neither tomb nor Palace seems obviously close, at least not at first glance; but something akin to the Tron design can be discovered in a number of features, enough to propose a good possibility, though not enough to claim a certainty. Much of the apparent difference comes from the difference in *parti*, in each case determined largely by the location.

The contriving of a large ensemble by putting many small parts together is obvious in both, particularly in the building-up in small layers often not closely interrelated. The piers, above all, starting out with paired small columns with every quality needed to express support except that of size and strength, are contradictorily followed by niches that eat away the whole face of the pier, the very part expected to take over the task of supporting. There are equivalencies in the Tron monument, but there the piers have to carry only a single less ponderous arch and, being closer together, seem better able to support it and to bound its varied inner episodes; whereas here, in the large work, the arches are heavier not only individually but cumulatively (since there are three of them), and the piers are not only farther apart in both fact and proportion, but also more dismembered by slicing cornices. Although there are more superposed sections on the Tron tomb, they are smaller, project less, and slice less. The top zone of the Barbarigo, with its three huge arches, is on a grander scale than anything below, as is also true, of course, of the earlier Tron arch, but to a far lesser degree; and there the shift is on a scale to make a suitable strong crowning rather than just a top-heavy addition.

6.12 Monuments of the
humanist Alvise Trevisan
(d.1528) and Doge Steno
(d.1414) in SS Giovanni e
Paolo, removed from S
Marina.

6.13 Tomb of the Senator
Giovanni Emo, once in the
church of the Servi (drawing
by Jan II van Grevenbroeck,
Museo Correr, Cod. Gradenigo 228, III/25).

The amount of sculpture on the Barbarigo work is small for such a large expanse, and for an architect who was an important sculptor. That it was finished posthumously may explain this, as has been suggested, though that would be rare at this date, and common only later. The many paneled areas on the back wall are not able to mitigate this bareness despite the vein patterns in the marble, as carefully shown in the engraving. The windows in the center section, already fixed, no doubt, by the church building, have been awkwardly worked into the overall design; the tall windows were pushed to the edges of the blank wall of their bay, though nothing is there that seems capable of pushing, and the bull's-eye was worked awkwardly into the semicircular molding that ran into its frame. As in many parts of the composition, control seems weak.

Little more than the wealth of colored marbles suggests anything of Rizzo's contemporary work on the Doges' Palace, unless it be the 60' of a straight unbroken entablature, superficially similar to long stretches in the court. Unlike Rizzo is the scattered profusion of single discs in six different sizes, particularly the set of five wheeling between two semicircles at the top of each outer bay, reminiscent of the semicircular gable ornaments of Pietro Lombardo's recently finished Church of the Miracoli rather than of anything known in Rizzo's oeuvre. Perhaps the showy Miracoli was admired by the clients. The recumbent effigies on biers on sarcophagi on brackets could, on the other hand, be seen as like Rizzo's Tron tomb, but such arrangements can be seen on a score of tombs by others. Inasmuch as this large and important monument no longer exists, further discussion of it here might be of doubtful value.

The one funeral monument that shows likeness of *parti* to the Barbarigo tomb is really two tombs, adventitiously linked: the Gothic tomb of Doge Steno and the Early Renaissance tomb of the young humanist Alvise Trevisan, on the wall of SS Giovanni e Paolo. These tombs are set under two arches formerly part of the church's cloister (Hubala 1965, 795); but this arrangement, more orderly and orthodox, was made long after the scheme of the Barbarigo monument was fixed. If related, the Barbarigo is the parent, not the offspring (fig. 6.12).

The monument to Giovanni Emo (1485) was once in the Servi but is now destroyed, like most of the others there (fig. 6.13). The Emo family, as often, was buried under a floor slab in front of the monument. This must be the last tomb Rizzo made in Venice; it is the least original and, at the same time, the most sophisticated.

It takes two identical socles set against other, wider socles to raise the sarcophagus to an acceptable height, a more simpleminded way of accomplishing this than usual. The *reggiscudi* were by now standard, but here, as a novelty, they are clothed. The fluted columns on fancy round pedestals were no longer a rarity either. The strikingly placed effigy, in gilded robes, stands in front of more blank open space than any before, adding dramatically to its impressiveness. The paucity of sculpture may show that the spareness in the Barbarigo tomb was willed, an idea of Rizzo's last phase, not the result of hurried finishing or short funds (A. Zorzi, 133, 135, 353). Or it may show that both monuments were completed after Rizzo's defection. The *reggiscudi* are now in the Louvre, and the standing figure and its sarcophagus are in the Vicenza Museum.

7 | ANTONIO RIZZO AND OTHERS: THE PALAZZO DUCALE

The Doges' Palace, with its various parts built and rebuilt at different times, had recently suffered several fires: one in 1474 and another in 1479, when the doge had had to move to a private palace on the opposite side of the Rio di Palazzo, to which there was, providentially, a private covered bridge. The blaze of 1483 was still worse; it wrecked the old living quarters and some of the state rooms nearby. Damage was done to the walls of the three or four small courts within the building and to most of the back walls along the rio. In other words, most of the east or back range of the palace was left unusable. Nothing is known of the appearance here before the fires except that behind the Molo and Piazzetta fronts there was little homogeneity; the whole most have been a stone and brick chimera, pieced from parts of three old buildings: the residence of the doges; a block which would be remodeled into a Palace of Justice; and an older Treasury tower in the southeast corner, surviving from an older fortress-palace (Bassi 1964, VI, 182).

The interior walls of these older structures had been spliced in different ways at different times to gain space for expanding government activities. Many had survived the fires structurally sound, and only some stretches of the outer walls needed repairing or replacing. While the palace was ripped up and workmen were at hand, new designs could be developed to pull the three old buildings together into what would seem one new one. The possibilities were discussed in detail until the summer and autumn of 1484. For the interiors, the problems were simpler, little more than redecorating.

No obvious candidate stood out for this important commission, but some powerful or persuasive person must have promoted the idea that the new work ought to be in the new style. No native Venetian had yet made a name by building in the new manner; any older master would doubtless have been set in his Gothic ways. The special committee of the Collegio would have needed clairvoyance to put their collective finger on Mauro Codussi, a Bergamasque in his early thirties whose first Venetian work was not yet completed, or Pietro Lombardo, a recently arrived Ticinese Lombard already admired for his handsome tombs and his ornamentation of the Church of S Giobbe, but not yet for any substantial building. Neither man would have come naturally to the mind of anyone looking for someone to entrust with the design and construction of the capitol building of a powerful, rich, and proud state. As Panofsky suggested in another connection, it might have been as shocking as asking Frank Lloyd Wright to remodel the White House (Panofsky, in conversation).

As a competition could be a means of getting around many of the difficul-·ties, the design for a public building was often chosen thus. Soon something of the sort was organized for the new parts of the palace. Rizzo, who already in 1483 had been ordering stone for the rebuilding from the best quarries in Istria—presumably as no more than a good sideline business—won the commission for the design and supervision of the palace on the virtues of a model chosen over a number of others in May 1484. Unfortunately, nothing is known of the other submissions, nor who made them. Most would have been Gothic.

Soon after Rizzo was named *Proto di Palazzo*, protomaestro, or chief architect, the long east wall of the back (along the canal) and the shorter wall at the north end of the court (by S Mark's) were begun under his supervision. By 1485 about half were up, at least in the raw, and the long east wall of the court must have been begun, or about to be. Work went quickly, with a few temporary delays from shortages of funds or

labor. Little more than extensions, repetitions, and a few incidentals on the upper floors can have been needed after the first intensive campaign, and after Rizzo left in 1498 few of his ideas can have been drastically altered. They had to be carried out by others, most of whom were former assistants likely to be faithful to his ideas, particularly at the beginning.

The largest section of the palace that can surely be given to him is the lower part of the back facade, along the Rio di Palazzo (or della Canonica). The north end, under the doges' apartments, had been given priority, and Rizzo had been commissioned for it by Doge Giovanni Mocenigo (1478-85). The facade is not uniform for its full length, for part of what looks like one long facade turns out not even to be part of the palace: north of the doges' quarters and in line with them, a stretch of nine windows and four panels makes the back wall of the chapel of S Theodore and the sacristy of S Mark's (fig. 7.1). A close look makes the division clear. Though on the outside associated more with the palace, on the inside these windows are functionally associated only with the adjuncts of the church. Giorgio Spavento, who had done some work under Rizzo in the courtyard, was commissioned for the new sacristy in 1486, and must have completed it, or most of it, before he died in 1509. As a work of his, it will be considered later. The entire rio facade went through restoration from 1873 to 1889.

The north end of Rizzo's design begins at the south end of Spavento's. The division is marked by a plain pier and a pilaster above with the arms of Doge Mocenigo, establishing an earlier date for the beginning of Rizzo's operations than Spavento's, since the doge died in November 1485, before Spavento was commissioned. The two

7.1 Palazzo Ducale. Rio facade. At the right are four
bays of Spavento's rear elevation of some adjuncts of
S Mark's.

7.2 Palazzo Ducale. Rio facade. The socle is rusticated
with square stones, one
sticking out like a small,
sharp pyramid and the next
sticking in as though for an
identical pyramid of air.

parts were under two different committees, and the preparation of the two designs and the actual work on the two
parts cannot be exactly dated; but
Rizzo's must have come first. His
scheme runs along for about 130'
southward and then displays the arms
of his next important patron, Doge
Agostino Barbarigo (1486–1501). Beyond
this, on the old part of the building
known as the Palace of Justice, the
work continues little changed up to
where there was an old stair, stopping
where there was still a corner tower of
the old fortress-castle beside the quay
of the Molo. (This was pulled down in
1507 and replaced by an unsightly
lower element of raw brick, presumably not intended as the final surface.)

Rizzo's scheme is both innovative
and harmonious. Ruskin (III, 16) found
it "the noblest" work of what he quirkily chose to call "the Byzantine Renaissance." Set on a few bold moldings,
now above, now below the tide, the
socle is truculently rusticated (fig. 7.2).
Some suggestions may have come from
the Ca' del Duca, but hypertrophied
into a near-Brobdingnagian nutmeg
grater. Thomas Coryat (I, 246), who
saw it in 1608, found it "exceedingly
beautifull. . . . The lower part is mar-
veilous faire. . . . There is very curious
worke made in the form of pointed diamonds, like that of the two formost
bulwarks of the Citadel of Milan"—
true, but not likely to have been the
source here.

This is interrupted once by a modest
doorway; then by a loggia of four high-
arched water entrances; and once again
by a loggia of two *cavanas,* or indoor
boathouses like wet garages (fig. 7.3).
Their openings run up through the next
story, a mezzanine with nearly square
windows more or less alternating with
panels of almost the same size, all
framed by simple, bold moldings. Services and kitchens, among other miscellaneous necessities, are in the lower
parts.

7.3 Palazzo Ducale. Rio
facade. *Cavana* entrance,
mezzanine, windows, and
panels above rusticated socle, pseudo-pediments, and
stiff foliage-framed discs alternating in the zone above.

Above these two low stories comes a taller one, with a loose alternation of tall panels and arched windows. Although everywhere paneled, this wall does not hint at carpentry, but is only a strong pattern of windows and panels with ridges between. All this is brought to an end at the top by the long lines of a larger entablature, with a wide frieze ornamented with plain circles, clearly part of the wall and not a strip pasted on, and a cornice not projecting enough to slice the building here. The entablature is part of the building, not trimming affixed to it.

Since temporary lack of money brought much work to a halt in 1493 and again in 1495, the rio front may have been stopped for a while at the level of the first big cornice or, more likely, after part of the next story had been begun. The section under the doges' apartments and part of the wall of the apartments themselves—the parts being rushed to completion—must have been directed by Rizzo personally and carried out by his immediate team. That much can be kept as a hard fact, separate from the necessary conjectures for the rest. The section south of this may be a few years later, but still close to Rizzo; the *cavanas* may be later interpolations; the two long balconies were added in the XVIc.

The total effect so far is bold, vivid, orderly, and grand. The slight irregularities in the alternation of windows and panels make an enlivening rubato, but the basic beat is strong enough to keep everything in one long sustained phrase. The entire stretch is flat, without the openness and shadowy recesses of the arcades of the other exterior facades on the Piazzetta and the Molo. The problem was different, for this new work can only be seen in swiftly receding perspective from one end or the other, or in short sections from a boat passing along the rio. It is clearly a back wall, not called on to be impressive and monumental, as are the other

two showpieces. Seen from some ideal distance, it might look monotonous; seen close and obliquely, as it has to be, it does not, for the varied rustication, the strong paneling, and its synthesis with the fenestration all keep it artistically alive. Rizzo used only a small vocabulary, but he used it with force and elegance.

Like the Tron monument, the lower third of the facade has been put together mainly out of small parts, and like it, achieves an effect of some grandeur. But here, more is done with less. One is an early and the other a mature work of a semiprofessional architect of uneven—not to say intermittent—talent. Even Ruskin, so easily outraged by Renaissance work, had to admire this "as an example of finished masonry one of the finest things not only in Venice but in the whole world" (Ruskin III, 38). So near the commanding Gothic facades on the Molo and the Piazzetta, and the overstated splendors of the courtyard, the rio front hardly ever is granted the admiration its understated virtues deserve. Even most visitors crossing the bridges over the Rio di Palazzo pay more heed to the fictitiously romantic but architecturally feeble Prison or the Bridge of Sighs.

While the irregularities in the courts of the three old buildings—whatever they were—might have been coaxed into some sort of asymmetrical but balanced Gothic composition in one big new court, to do so might have been harder to bring off in Venice than elsewhere, for the local ideal for Gothic palaces was the most symmetrical in Europe. The Piazzetta and Molo facades of the palazzo, each over 300' long, were aggressively symmetrical, glaringly unsuitable for a picturesquely random court inside.

A daring choice was made by the building committee of the Collegio; although Early Renaissance was being accepted as a suitable style by a few cultured patricians and clergy, the decision to use the modern style to reface two sides of the court of the most important and largest government building—the heart and stronghold of the government and its ceremonials—was not only bold (if knowingly made), but also may have given the new movement its most effective backing yet. The rio facade was less important, less useful to display the power and pride of the republic; furthermore it was being designed with little that was specifically identifiable with the new style.

Once the detritus had been cleared out of the old courts—in three quick months—and determination had been made to salvage everything usable of what was left standing, a new problem began to show itself more vexingly: how to achieve a uniform design. Could this be done by deducing it from the leftover miscellany, or better by procrustean ruthlessness in imposing a new design on what was still there? As the building rose, the problem grew and its resolution retreated; hope for a single coherent scheme was defeated.

Giovanni Mocenigo, doge at the time of the fire of 1483, can have seen little of the work finished before he died in November 1485, though there must have been some selective overhauling of old structural parts and substituting of a few new ones at the north end, still almost a separate building (Bassi, *Boll Pall* 1964 VI, 181–87). His arms have already been noted on a pilaster at the bottom. His reign was not favorable for major official building, with the plagues of 1478–79 and 1485, a series of short wars with the Turks (to whom Venice had been paying a galling annual tribute), and short wars with Milan, Ferrara, Naples, and the Holy See. In 1482 a sort of lend-lease bond issue had to be floated. But shortly before he died, conditions began to look better; the Treaty of Bognolo (1484) left Venice at peace on the mainland, with

her lands there a bit increased. Work on the palace cannot have been difficult to push ahead.

His successor, Doge Marco Barbarigo, lived only nine months in office (1485–86), but he kept the work going. His arms were carved on the palace twice, presumably where the underlying rough work had been well advanced under his predecessor. Under his unpopular but efficient brother, Doge Agostino Barbarigo (1486–1501), enough of the exterior on court and canal was finished to show what the new full scheme was going to be like, and so to fix much of what would be carried on after he died. These were the decisive years.

Times now favored building. By 1500, 120,000 people were living in the city (more than today) and nearly all paid taxes, direct or indirect. Some 2,500 adult males were nobles, most of them educated and rich, many of them officeholders and hence potential patrons of the arts, including architecture.

Sir Richard Guylforde put it well in 1506:

The rychesse, the sumptous buyldynge, the relygyoys houses, and the stablys-shynge of their justyces and councylles, with all other thynges y^t maketh a cytie glorious, surmounteth in Venyse aboue all other places y^t euer I saw. (Pylgrymage of Sir Richard Guylforde)

Venice had gained profitable Cyprus in 1489 by a contrived inheritance from its widowed dummy queen, a Venetian. At least one fleet sailed every year to Alexandria, and one to Beirut, the two main outlets for Eastern trade, and another almost every year to Byzantium. Venice was the busiest marketplace of Europe. Furthermore, she was already gaining almost twice as much from her lands in Italy as from her holdings overseas. After many years as a sea creature, she had become an amphibian (Hale, in Toynbee 1967, 65). Expert and efficient management of her money was the chief secret of her wealth, and her income was the largest of any state in Italy. A steady 10 percent of it could be counted on from the salt monopoly, and salt tax money was often allotted to public building.

All of this benefited the building of the palace in one way or another. The idea of unifying the cluster of half-wrecked courts into one open space in scale with the arcaded facades on the outside, though obviously attractive, may have been slow in developing; now it was pushed. Because the rehabilitation of the private apartments of the doge had priority, activity had to begin there, but much of it must have been no more than work for decorators—woodcarvers, weavers, plasterers, and such. The lower arcade of the court was started where the main floor of the domestic quarters adjoined S Mark's at the end of its south transept, in what is now called the Cortiletto dei Senatori, as confirmed by two carvings of the arms of Doge Marco Barbarigo.

Once the decision to run an arcade in front of the odds and ends of old walls had been taken, the lower zone of the court would have posed few problems, for an arcade could mask the random spacing of the openings of the two low stories behind without calling for any relocation of walls or openings. In the northwest corner, by the transept of S Mark's, running along the short side there, and then down the long east side of the court, rows of octagonal piers were set up, carrying round arches splayed so that the diagonal band of their archivolts would continue from the diagonal faces of the piers (fig. 7.4). Octagonal columns were not rare in Italian Gothic; splayed arches to fit them were less familiar. The piers, which had to be stout to support three upper stories, understate their real heaviness by presenting only one face

to the court, those adjacent being in diagonal retreat. The four main faces—front, back, and sides—are extruded a little from the eight-sided core, and count visually more than the diagonals, which are slightly pulled in, but not too far to be able to add to the sense of strength without apparent heaviness. Each face is carved with a cascade of acanthus and oakleaves, peapods, flowers, *putti*, dolphins, lions, torches, helmets, and other conceits then becoming fashionable, and surely with no hidden symbolic meaning.

Circular holes, ornamental *oculi*, were set above these arches, with some of their outermost moldings folded or bent to merge into those immediately above and below, in mediaeval, non-classical fashion. The archivolt moldings meet; both give in, and they slice one another above the capitals. Above a corner pier, where arches have to meet at right angles, their archivolts cut each other off completely, leaving only a sharp point hanging unsupported in midair. Common in mediaeval North Italy, such unclassical vagaries cannot have been found any more disturbing in Venice.

Although the round openings mask no separate story and are there only to let in more light—less than their models in the Gothic tracery on the outer facades—they do add up to a long horizontal in tomtom rhythm. Under Rizzo and his patron, Agostino Barbarigo, this scheme of round arches and *oculi* was carried along the east side for over 100' (with one interruption for a stairway). While this may look more Renaissance than Gothic at first glance, that impression must come from the serene, classical proportions, since the simple geometrical forms generated by arcs and straight lines have few classical details except the pilasters on the piers, even though the piers themselves are put together more like some mediaeval compound than anything classical.

Above this calm arcade the court facade grows livelier. The next story, the piano nobile, is also arcaded, in order to provide a broad open corridor with access to all the principal rooms. This new arcade was designed in reference to the one below, as well as to the two stories of arcades on the two outer facades; and for a more immediate and detailed model, a short Gothic loggiato at the same level on the opposite side of the courtyard. (The arcades now on both stories of the west side had not yet been built or even planned.)

Instead of the round arches that might have been predicted here, in view of those below, pointed arches were chosen, and made a superposition of shapes less familiar and more disturbing to tutored modern eyes than to XVc eyes quite used to seeing them together, both being staples in the late Gothic repertory. The pointed arches had been chosen to go with the similar pointed ones of the loggiato at the same level across the court, and the round arches below to go with the big round opening of the Arco Foscari, just across from them.

The piers, fundamentally more Gothic on this upper level, are more compound and more restless than the octagonal ones below. Rizzo felt no awkwardness in juxtaposing the Gothic and Renaissance styles, considered successive if not hostile in most histories of architecture, but here in Venice untroubled contemporaries for over a generation. No awkwardness shows, though the serene equipoise of the design of the rio facade was not recaptured.

The front colonnettes are arranged so that one of each pair has room on its abacus to receive one complete archivolt with all its fat Gothic moldings. Since one capital can take one full archivolt, two can take two without any collision. Everything fits, and there is even a little breathing space left between. Roundels of purple porphyry slipped into the spandrels beat out

a quiet syncopation to the more emphatic beat of the round shadows of the *oculi* over the arches below.

These two lower stories must have been designed by Rizzo, and their construction supervised by him. Together they correspond in height to his work on the rio facade. Except for the limitations called for by the remains of the old buildings—minimal here—his hand would have been free, or ought to have been. But this may not have been the case everywhere; it is harder to cope with a corporate client than an individual one, and the building committee of the Collegio that had hired him could have forced him to accede to some of their preferences here and there. But once the standard arcades had been accepted, this cannot have happened often.

During the construction of the lower floors, few problems were recorded beyond the recurrent ones of not enough money nor enough skilled labor. Rizzo was bold, effective, and perhaps ruthless in clearing these up; he demanded and got additional Lombard craftsmen in 1486, perhaps coaxed from other local jobs, and he probably managed to win more later. In 1486 there were 126 "foreign" (North Italian) mastermasons and carvers at work, plus some fifty young apprentice helpers, also non-Venetian. When strong objections were raised by local workmen, some young Venetians were engaged to help, and incidentally to learn (Moretti, in Fontana 1967 I, 6).

The east side of the court had one threat to the regularity of the arcades, where the grand stairway leads up to the halls of state on the principal floor. A stairway, perhaps of wood, may have been here for a few years before the building campaign following the big fire of 1483. A new stairway may already have been envisioned by Doge Moro before he died in 1473. He was an eager builder, and was just then

7.4 Palazzo Ducale. Court, lower arcades of east wall.

7.5 Jacopo Bellini. A stairway, possibly in the Palazzo Ducale (drawing in the British Museum).

having the Arco Foscari finished; a stairway might well have been imagined as the last development in the sequence of the Portego and Arco. If anything was built before the fire, it would hardly have had time to be finished.

To get onto the covered stairway, then running back westward along the outside wall of the Portego Foscari at the end of the court, officials going up to the main story for state meetings had to make a complete turn of one-hundred and eighty degrees. This would land these dignitaries on the side of the court opposite the main meeting halls and they would have had to walk through many rooms to reach them. (There was not yet any arcaded walk on the west side of the court.) A couple of simpler, smaller, old stairways were still somewhere in the fire-damaged wing, perhaps usable, perhaps not, but until now there had been neither a convenient nor a suitably impressive access to the piano nobile and its grand rooms, where the most important business of the republic was transacted, as well as the obsessively formal ceremonials.

In addition to a stairway, a special area was needed for one particular semipublic spectacle, open to those invited from a select list. This was the climax of the celebrations at the installation of a new doge, after he had completed the religious rites in S Mark's and the popular rites in the Piazza, where he was carried on show and acclaimed by the people—all that was left of the "popular" election of a doge—preceded by eight banners, white when the republic was at peace, green during a truce, and red when at war. Some striking raised place was needed for the administration of the solemn oath of office, as he intoned, "Accipe coronam ducalem ducatus Venetiarum," and for the crowning with his principal emblem of office, the unique hat or bonnet the nuns of S Zaccaria had made for him, the jeweled cloth-of-gold *corno*

or *zoia*. And then some easy means was needed to carry him down again to be borne around the Piazza for the still more popular rite of flinging coins to the crowd.

A possible space could have been contrived in any of several ways if the line of procession could turn a corner, or if the ceremonies could take place on some sort of temporary platform in the court, or even behind some of the arches of the lower story. But no such scheme seemed satisfactory. Just how much had been worked out before the existing stairway was begun—if anything—is not known. Two drawings in Jacopo Bellini's sketchbooks of the 1450s (Louvre 57; London, BM 49) give insubstantial hints, but they may be his inventions, or hints of some old and perhaps temporary arrangements, rather than hints of what was soon to develop (fig. 7.5). It has been claimed that Rizzo had made a stairway in wood that was an anticipation of his postfire one in stone (Muraro 1961, I, 364).

A major stairway not fixed to a wall on one side, but rather reared in space free on both sides, was a daring novelty in Venice in 1484, probably revolutionary and perhaps unique. For centuries grand exposed freestanding stairways had not been welcomed in monumental architecture, nor would they be again until Bramante designed the great court of the Vatican. Few suggestions could have come to Rizzo from monumental examples outside Venice, such as that in front of the cathedral of Salerno—but Salerno would have been known to very few Venetians. Aleppo, doubtless known to more (who had done business there from their local trading post), has a spectacular flight leading up to its citadel. The other major trading centers of the Venetians were flat Alexandria, rolling Cairo, and hilly Constantinople; perhaps there were impressive exterior

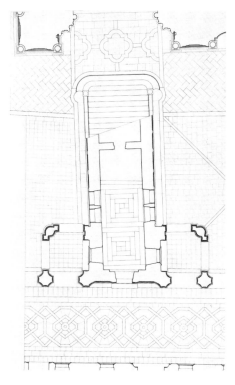

7.6 Palazzo Ducale. Scala dei Giganti. Plan of lower level.

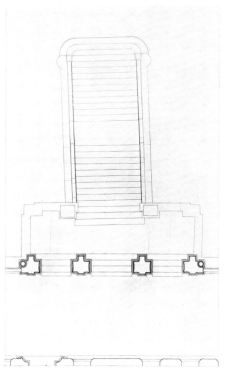

7.7 Scala dei Giganti. Plan of upper level.

stairways in the last two. Wherever they came from, the main suggestions can hardly have come from the Christian West, less familiar to many important Venetians than the infidel East. But all such suggestions seem weak. No outside stimulus need have come into play for two reasons: first, there may have been a wood predecessor (and it could have been the one to have accepted extraneous ideas): and second, the nature of the problem and the layout could have led to the solution with nothing more than good architectural sense and some inventiveness. Whatever the source or sources or lack of them, the result is astonishing for the date, and aesthetically rewarding regardless of the date.

There must have been a conviction that the cortège ought to come into the Palace through the main doorway, the painted and gilded Porta della Carta, open to the Piazza and the Piazzetta, and monumentally on axis with the Campanile. It would proceed under the five shadowy vaults of the Portego Foscari and out through the Arco Foscari into the bright courtyard, and then go directly up the stairway, a sequence unsurpassed in the city and little rivaled in contemporary Europe. This conviction, then, determined what was to be built, and precisely where.

In order to make the axis of the stair coordinate with the regular meter of the arcades on both stories of the court and, at the same time, coordinate it with the processional way through the Portego and Arco (which are not quite on the center line of the elements opposite), the whole stairway was cunningly skewed to the left, and stretched a little wider as it rose, but so subtly that, in order to find the warping, a visitor has to get himself into one of the few spots where it can be made out, and then hold his camera just where the refinement can be caught and made to show (figs. 7.6 and 7.7).

The all-but-imperative straight route through Porta, Portego, and Arco was hampered by another circumstance: the court is narrow here (only 44') and could afford only minimal space for a stairway that not only must not look cramped but must instead have an air of grandeur. This threat was avoided with such frictionless ingenuity that the solution looks easy—which it cannot have been. The necessary air of calm solemnity was achieved; in fact it is inescapable.

The first three steps were pushed out as close to the Arco Foscari as they could be without crowding or blocking anyone the moment he walked into the court. These three steps are low and unemphasized; they count more as part of the pavement than of the stair, not yet asserted as a volume in the court. By sharing the space of the court and of the wide Arco so unobtrusively, this beginning seems to allow the rest of the stairway more space than it actually has, and this seeming amplitude comes right where it is particularly needed.

Once the steps continue beyond these three, and rise between the handrails, they demand and get attention. Twelve climb to a landing some 14' wide but only a third as deep, with barely space enough not to seem pinched when several senators would pause there in their billowing saillike velvet robes, with prodigious spinnaker sleeves and an equally overblown jib of a stole. The tourists we sometimes see there now are no substitute, but occasionally on summer evenings a handsome counterpart appears, when that end of the court is put to use for a performance of Verdi's *Otello*, in splendid Carpaccesque costumes (fig. 7.8).

After the steps have reached up some 9' to the level of the landing, ten similar steps run up to the platform where the ceremonies took place (fig. 7.9). One by one the senators had to walk up to this, and kneel before their new doge. The axis of the *via triumphalis* stopped here, for no opening to the palace was on the axis, just a blank wall. Appropriately, the doge on his throne was the end of the long vista. Their homage done, the senators would have to turn aside and walk less ceremoniously along the upper loggia and then come down some other way, where they would not crowd the senators still ascending, largo maestoso (fig. 7.10). (It cannot be, as sometimes claimed, that every adult male patrician, all the members of the Great Council, had to do all this, for there were over 2,000 of them, and no one could have stood or even sat through the hours of their successive genuflections.)

To get themselves out of the way for the next in the procession, the senators must have taken a small stair by the doges' apartments, leading them down to the small Court of the Two Wells behind the main apse of S Mark's, whence they could make their way to the Cortiletto dei Senatori, an annex of the main court. (All these are still there, but not all accessible or communicating.)

Rizzo's grand stairway contributed still another visual asset by separating this subordinate area, the cortiletto, from the large main area of the court that, though half-severed from it by the stairway, would be sensed in most eye-level views as having absorbed it into one grand, clear rectangle of space. Its decoration may have been fancy—and increasingly so as the building rose—but the simple form of the whole court was made clear, monumental, and somehow authoritative—not so difficult for the combination of an unimpeded space 200' long plus 50' more for the stairway and cortiletto beyond it. The fact that the cortiletto is seen as something added to the main court after having been briefly cut off from it, makes the whole space more animated than it would be if it were just 250' of emptiness, the same length as the empty hollow of the street in a New York block.

7.8 Scala dei Giganti. Painting by Canaletto (private collection, Mexico City).

7.9 Scala dei Giganti.
Pierced marble parapet,
transparent and bulk-
defying.

7.10 Scala dei Giganti. *The Crowning of the Doge* (painting by Gabriele Bella in the picture gallery of the Querini Stampalia Foundation).

7.11 Scala dei Giganti. Under the lengthened top platform, the supporting arches have to meet at right angles. The L-shaped pier at the inner corner leads to trouble with the archivolts. The outer pier is enlarged by a quarter of a cylinder of wall, against which the pilasters of the arches are engaged.

The ceremonial stage at the top is narrower, less than twice as deep as the narrow landing below (fig. 7.11). The stairs themselves, the width of only two bays of the lower arcade, are inadequate for the consummation of the ceremony, too short for a seated doge, a kneeling senator, and several standing high-office-holding supernumeraries. To augment this space, the stage is expanded by appropriating one more bay of the arcades on each side, doubling the area, and making it more emphatic, not alone by its greater size but equally by its power to interrupt the long regular rhythm of the two stories of arcades.

At a slightly later date, as work went ahead, the whole stage-platform was emphasized again by varying the arches behind it, making a shift in the regular chiaroscuro and in the center, a powerful concentration of shadow sensed as a visual counterpart to the dark hole of the Arco Foscari across and below (fig. 7.12). More than anything contrivable on solid wall, the dark hollow behind him must have been the most fitting and dramatic background for the single figure of the enthroned doge, glittering in his cloth of gold and silver below the bright white of his ermine cape.

A bit more room, and a sense of still more, comes from making practical use of the space between the piers of the upper loggia behind the upper platform. The last four steps were cut between them, where officials on the stage went up to the level of the loggia floor of the piano nobile. There was space to fit these last steps here because of the extra depth of these piers. The stage thus came to be emphasized in yet another way by being alone on its own level, four steps below the long level of the floor of the arcade, an entity in itself and not a subordinate part of any other element.

The stairway is as unusual in detail and construction as it is in design; in many ways it is a virtuoso performance (fig. 7.13). The stone is fitted together like wood in fine cabinetmaking, with many joints hardly visible because made to coincide with the crease caused by a change of plane or material. (A few, originally all but hidden, are now all too clear, after centuries of weathering.) The construction could have been contrived by a fine woodworker, for much of it is put together with little posts and beams, like the vertical styles (or muntins) and horizontal rails framing the larger areas of normal wood paneling. These small working members are of white marble, perhaps Greek, so fine that Thomas Coryat (I, 249), who examined the stairway with awe in 1608, mistook it for alabaster.

An air of stability was given the whole stairway by setting it on a base or stone bench that continues the topmost plane of the three steps that flowed out beyond the confines of the side parapets. The side walls standing on this base have flat panels of sumptuous mottled white, silver, cream, peach, and pale violet *breccia*, a marble equivalent of wood burl, framed here in white Carrara moldings. The *breccia* adds nothing to the stability because it is more liable to cracking and flaking than most marbles—as time and weather have disturbingly shown—and also because it is used only in thin plates like rare wood panels in similar kinds of construction. The entire stairway can easily be imagined as a petrification of cabinet work. Other samples of equivalent character can be pictured in the same way: the choir of the Frari, for example, or half-a-dozen Early Renaissance stone pulpits. Perhaps the suggestion of carpentry comes from their furniturelike functions and from the construction of their many wood forerunners.

Even the vertical little styles of the side walls and of the parapet, edging the panels of those areas, are themselves delicately paneled, and carved with arabesques nowhere raised more

7.12 Scala dei Giganti. Behind the top platform different openings are used, interrupting the long pointed arcade by three arches, wider, higher, richer, and round, with the middle one expanded more than the other two. Some of the work is post-Rizzo, including Sansovino's giants.

7.13 Scala dei Giganti. Carrara posts and *breccia* panels at the lower end.

than half an inch above the background, carving now as suggestive of fine metalwork as of carved wood. The crisp outlines and subtle inflection of planes, the swelling or gently hollowed surfaces, all make a major effect with minimal means, in a bravura exhibition of *rilievo schiacciato* ("squashed relief"). The patterns are everywhere varied, not identifiably repeated, inside or out.

Still more like carpentry and less like stone construction are the parapets running diagonally up each side of the steps. Having to be so high, the walls of the upper platform-stage, where it extends outward in front of the last two bays of the arcade, might have looked heavy, had their integrity as walls not been devalued in the middle by being cut by windows, denying heavy mass. (As these grilled windows light no more than a storeroom under the steps, it is clear that their purpose is aesthetic, not practical.)

The underlying scheme and its overall forms are simple, and this adds greatly to the effect of stability. But the surfaces are never plain; the flat panels are of multicolored *breccia*; the structural members are ornamented with carving; almost every molding is carved with some classical pattern such as the then still novel bead and reel, or egg and dart; and the risers of the steps, which one is almost forced to notice in this tight composition, are of white marble inlaid with gilded lead (niello) in another virtuoso display with a non-repeating prodigality of arabesque patterns.

As has already been said, the chronology of the early work in the courtyard is beset by riddles. Giovanni Mocenigo was crowned here in 1478, before the big fire, and the ceremony may have been on something intended to be permanent—or it may not. For Doge Marco Barbarigo, crowned in 1485, after the fire, something similar must have been contrived. Documents attest that a stairway, probably of stone, was being considered in 1484, and that the commission to build it was issued in 1485. It was then that Rizzo asked for a raise and for a number of Lombards to help him. There must have been pressure from above to get the work done quickly but, notwithstanding, the stairway was not entirely finished for at least another ten years—probably more—though it must have been well enough along to have been usable somewhat sooner, though how much sooner cannot be ventured.

It was surely under way in 1491. The doges' apartments, to which it was the main access, were occupied by Agostino Barbarigo by 1492 or before. He could have reached them circuitously, if it was made plain that that would not be for long. When stopping in Venice en route to the Holy Land in May 1494, Canon Casola wrote that he saw "a new flight of steps . . . being built . . . a stupendous and costly work." It must, then, have been still incomplete, perhaps temporarily stopped when work came to a halt in 1493 from a shortage of funds. But at the end of May, on Corpus Domini, the canon saw the doge standing "at the head of the staircase until all the gentlemen had mounted . . . and then he went into the Palace to his own Apartments" (Casola, 126, 153). Finished or not, it was then usable. Most of the work must have been done near the beginning, and less near the end, probably just details of the decorative finish.

By 1495 it had begun to seem unreasonably expensive, along with the rest of the work, and redundant workmen were dismissed. In 1496 the account books were impounded and audited. The cost of reconditioning the Palace, first estimated at 6,000 ducats, had been wildly exceeded, in part because additional work had been undertaken; 80,000 ducats had already been paid out; and in 1498 it was discovered that Rizzo had filched at least 12,000, possibly more. He fled to Foligno, out of Venetian territory, was never heard of again, and probably soon died. The work on the Palace was at least half complete and the stairway more than half. It was first used for the coronation ceremonies in 1521, for Doge Antonio Grimani, after the twenty-year reign of Leonardo Loredan, which might indicate that all was not ready for Loredan's crowning in 1501. Despite the disruptions that must have followed Rizzo's flight, his designs would have been followed for a number of years, continuing parts already begun and making use of materials already gathered. The crew of skilled craftsmen would have stayed predominantly the same.

For example, after his flight but probably according to his designs, came the execution of the special arches that come forward as underpinning for the widened ends of the ceremonial stage. Unlike the others, they have large high-relief figures of Victories in the spandrels. The Barbarigo arms must have been put here before Doge Agostino died in 1501, but probably after the lapses in activity of 1493 and 1495–98. The three arches at the back of the stage may also follow Rizzo's ideas, but they differ in ornament and relief—denser, more deeply carved, and in a more patently Renaissance vocabulary. The grand panoply of shields, helmets, torches, ewers, and antique bric-a-brac, like the loot carried in a Roman triumph, was probably thought suitably symbolic here for the office of doge. After everything on the stairway was finished, it came to be known as the Scala dei Giganti, still its usual name, from the addition in 1556 of Sansovino's ungainly Mars and Neptune at the top.

The Scala dei Giganti, the least architectural of the work at the Palace ascribed to Rizzo, seems the most Venetian, everywhere incrusted with low carving and colored marbles organized as surface pattern with little concern for structure (which could have been of only minor interest here). Like the Tron monument, it stands outside any charted evolution. The Renaissance had arrived in Venice, or some items of it had, but had they yet rooted and put out identifiably Venetian fruit? Or were they still transplanted Florentine? The best Chianti grapes can be transplanted to the Veneto, but the wine they give will not taste like Chianti; it will be just like other local wines.

The general form of the Scala and the organization of lesser shapes within it have not, of course, changed, but time has dimmed the color of most of the marbles as they have slowly lost their polish, or actually changed color as the iron oxide in some has rusted and added warm yellow orange in uneven streaks. As monuments of the period go it is, happily, in better than average condition.

Once he had the commission to renew the palace, Rizzo must have been oppressively busy. Undoubtedly he called for that group of Lombard stone craftsmen in 1486 because he really needed trained help. He would have made the main designs himself, based on the model that had won him the job. Additional detailed models may have been demanded, and many drawings. Most of his architecture, like that of most of his contemporaries, is fairly flat, and could have been shown on drawings as satisfactorily as on more expensive and more slowly produced models. Models were, however, often used; perhaps they were easier for clients to understand. Models, if any, and preliminary drawings would have been turned over to a top cadre of assistants, who might develop and coordinate them as necessary. Many more drawings than models are preserved from the XVIc—presentation drawings with shadings and no dimensions, drawings of a door, a window, etc.

No working drawings are extant, naturally, for they had to be hard-used and were made on any kind of paper at hand, or on board, or on the stone to be cut. There is nothing tangible now to show what were the routines of transmitting designs from mind to solid. But these procedures may not have been so different from what happens in a big office today, not so different as most of the other pieces of work have become. The master prepared the main design and detailed its main parts—and that was probably what was presented to win the commission. But as the atelier grew, this had to change. From the mid–1480s on, Rizzo's atelier would have been what today would be known as "Antonio Rizzo and Associates." Pietro Lombardo may have been the top associate, the chief designer, for some years Rizzo's Gordon Bunshaft. In a few years he would be running a big atelier himself, bigger than Rizzo's, and with a hierarchy of more helpers. And always, there were the changeable preferences of the all-powerful clients.

For the oeuvre of a single architect, the unsteady framework of facts, probabilities, and possibilities does not extricate itself from a subjunctive into an affirmative sequence. Rizzo's works that can reasonably be classed as architecture—the Tron monument, the lower part of the rio facade and the lower part of the east wall of the court of the Palace, and the Scala dei Giganti—do not look compellingly like the work of one artist with one style, nor of one man developing sequentially in what may to him have been only an auxiliary art, an art not sculpture at least until the later part of his life. But such uncertainties may be only because so much is missing, both of buildings and of facts.

All that is left in Venice from the last quarter of the XVc cannot reasonably be seen as a consistent whole. In Rizzo's day, the city had not accepted any uniform style, old or new, or even any family of closely related styles; it

had no special look of its own that could quickly be recognized and dated if met in a stray building in Beirut, or Dubrovnik, or anywhere else where someone might have wanted a Venetian building put up. The same is true of what is left of the oeuvre of Rizzo. It would still be hard or impossible to identify an unrecorded building of his, or a tomb, unless by its figure sculpture. There is only one way that his work can be put into a sequence that shows any architectural development or, more accurately, a progress into architecture: first, the tomb of Orsato Giustinian—architecture only as an incidental, with moldings of proper architectural profile used as dividers or containers; second, the portal of S Elena—architecture as a strong frame, but subordinate to the sculpture it frames; third, the Tron monument—architecture and sculpture of equal importance, happily wed, with neither dominant; and last, the rio facade and the arcades of the court of the Palazzo Ducale—completely architectural with only minor sculptural trimming. The Scala dei Giganti was the solution to such a special problem that it cannot be forced into line with the works just named; it has to stand as a unique masterpiece.

The largest and richest demonstration of the Early Renaissance in Venice, the upper parts of the court and rio facades are far from the most consistent or successful. Some of the evident conflicts must come from thriftily wishing to adapt old work, and some from having too many cooks—architects, master carvers, and perhaps interfering officials. But these parts must have been based mainly on Rizzo's accepted ideas, perhaps gradually modified and given more trimming under Pietro Lombardo, who had been associated with the work since about 1495 (Zanotto 1847, VII, 346).

There was a slowing down after 1495, when the soaring expenses had to be investigated, and suspicion lit on

Rizzo. Pietro Lombardo, his chief assistant, was put in charge as *proto* in 1498 when Rizzo had gone, and he demanded and got Rizzo's full salary. He promised to give up all other work—which he did not do any more than Rizzo had after making the same promise.

Most of the north stretch of the long court facade, the model for the rest, must have been finished all the way the top by the time Pietro withdrew in 1511—he died in 1515—and work was being concentrated on the remaining interiors, where Pietro was responsible for half-a-dozen fancy fireplaces. The south end went more slowly, as the carvings of the datable arms of later doges prove. Since the palazzo was probably all roofed by 1503, the various later activities must have been mainly decorative finishing. Different masters were in charge at different times, but none left traces of an individual style. Attributions are not dependable or even always possible.

Perhaps it was only in the 1520s that the decision was reached to go ahead with refacing the old Palace of Justice on the south end, to balance Rizzo's section for the doges' apartments at the north (fig. 7.14). The old Palace of Justice had been almost a separate building, about which little is known before the rebuilding. Everything south of the seventh bay beyond the stairway is a generation later than the main section at the north, and since the arcades on the court were made to match, they need not take our time here. Some work on the upper stories had to be done over after the fires in 1574 and 1577, transforming some of the already confused facade into a copy of a copy. Dates of decision and execution are not clear in many parts, nor are they of great consequence.

The arcades which form the two lower stories in the court show everywhere twice as much open as solid; the two upper stories and their attics together show three times more solid than open. The lower stories count as dark from the deep shadows behind their arches; the upper count as light from the areas of pale Istrian stone (now unpleasantly blotched) in a solid-above-open distribution that looks back, no doubt deliberately, to the fronts on the Piazzetta and the Molo.

Nearly everything above the entablature that skims the points of the arches of the piano nobile must have been put up after Rizzo's flight in 1498. The cornice here, and the next one above, both incidental markers between stories, revert to that Transitional line of moldings with no projecting corona. Since they cling close enough to the clifflike wall not to threaten to divide it, as Rizzo had demonstrated already on the rio facade, but were clearly no more than the outward sign of something inside (the different floors), they seem to be properly subordinate episodes on the wall, well shaped to show their role. The topmost cornice is equally suited to its greater role, and shows it by crowning all with a bold, shelflike, overhanging corona.

The result, which is what we see today, was unified in some parts, confused in more. Unified—because the bay system, established by Rizzo's lower arcades, varies little; if scanned horizontally, as it demands to be, there is only a rubato in the long beating of short measures. Unified—because three entablatures run unbroken for the full 250' length of the court, again leading the eye along on one level. Unified—because the whole is kept to the same low limits of relief and of small scale in an endless (and soon tiresome) profusion of ornament.

The effort—conscious or unconscious—may have been to keep the entire surface busy in a sort of Brobdingnagian lacework, busy enough to distract attention from the lack of order in the spacing of the openings; but they look all too like holes poked irregularly in the lace, vitiating its power to hold

7.14 Palazzo Ducale. East
wall of courtyard.

the surface together. Even the best of lace curtains between windows cannot hide the big black shadows made by the windows themselves. Furthermore, lace looks weightless, while window openings in masonry reveal some thickness of wall, and hence some mass and concomitant sense of weight. The whole is undeniably and inescapably confused.

It is confused because the irregular spacing of the windows insists on being noticed, noticed as something unclear, particularly when the eye manages to travel vertically (neither natural nor easy here). Some of the irregularity could not be avoided because it was cheaper to keep old walls, but often—despite what has been repeatedly claimed—the plan shows that many old interior walls did not have to affect the spacing of the windows. That could very often have been readjusted, but to save money it may have been decided to use even the old window openings again and give them new trim to go with the new all-over decoration. (Decoration won again over discipline.) Even when windows were left where they had been, the accident of their old placing was not turned to advantage; they were not accepted as given conditions for a fresh design but grudgingly accommodated into some sort of rhythm where they could be, or ignored when their unavoidable emphasis could not come near the regular beat.

Any funds saved by leaving walls or openings where they had been were squandered on the ornament pullulating over every square yard. All surfaces are decorated; no plain walls, no large plain panels, nothing like Rizzo's chaste front along the rio. The many little shadows made by colonnettes, pilasters, moldings, or arabesques may reduce apparent differences between a light panel and a dark hole next to it, but only a little; they cannot hide the difference in effect of overall light or

dark. A decorator can rarely solve architectural problems with nothing more than surface trimming.

On the lower of the two closed floors, the vertical impulse of the pilasters that stop at the impost of the window arches is transmitted by an unorthodox and unnamable little strip on each side, which then goes up to a frieze (which may also be an architrave) and a sharp one-molding cornice (fig. 7.15). Such strips began to appear soon after the start of the Early Renaissance in Venice and long remained in the repertory. The big entablature above them runs the full 250′ of the court and is its last unifying element.

While the parts are classical, the way they are used runs from orthodox to chaotic. For example, the upper of the two superposed friezes of the south half of the top story has *oculi* alternating with lions' heads, sometimes on the beat, sometimes off; the jumpy result cannot be scanned rhythmically (fig. 7.16). At the north end, porphyry circles alternate with the lions at double the tempo. But while the *oculi* and lions have real existence in three dimensions, the flat discs have only two, and yet the *oculi* and the dark discs count as equal accents, and the jutting lions count less. Physical fact is subordinate to optical effect, three dimensions to two. The confusion seems to have no purpose, tricky or dramatic or even fanciful, but just to be an example of the irresolute order run riot in the upper stories.

Half-ordered and half-disordered bewilders more than all one or all the other, for expectations are raised only to be ignored or contradicted. Venetians could poke about fragments of Roman work in a few ruins on the nearby mainland in once great but now dead cities, or look at notebook sketches of normal Roman work—no useful manuals had yet been printed—but they would rarely if ever see an ancient building with a full set of its parts working properly together. Few

7.16 Palazzo Ducale. North end of the top floor of the east wall of the court. The alternating lions' heads and porphyry circles are set twice as close together as at the south end and are repeatedly out of phase with the windows below.

7.15 Palazzo Ducale. First story above the pointed open arcade. Above some windows, such as that at the extreme right, curved pediments are squeezed into a narrow band which, further on, reads as a frieze with inlaid discs. But it can as well be read as an architrave, for above it runs a long, richly carved frieze, with larger porphyry discs in molded frames, and a proper cornice in its proper place above.

Venetians ever set foot in Rome, and only the exceptional highly educated humanist or artist would have much sympathy for what ancient works were to be seen there.

The detail in the court probably comes primarily from whatever Rizzo had left, drawings, models, or stone already cut or even carved. Although much of the execution may have been by or under the Lombardos, they did not supplant his manner with their own—or not at first—and when his intentions had not been specified they seem to have improvised as much in his style as in theirs. But if the design of his upper stories had the same quality as his lower ones, its coherence was lost as the Lombardos added their exuberant richnesses. The relief becomes bolder story by story, and not just in the ornamental panels but also in the members enframing the windows, reaching its extreme projection in the topmost cornice, which thus brings the dizzying cliff to a full stop. All this does not seem so much a conscious sequence as something that just happened with the passing of time, increased technical skill, and greater familiarity with the ever-growing vocabulary of Renaissance forms.

Could any Renaissance design have made the face of this congeries coherent? Probably not, for regularity was unobtainable, and no rational Renaissance front could do without underlying regularity. A picturesque irregular Gothic front might have been coaxed from what was there, but for a Renaissance design it was intractable, even for the unintellectual, free-and-easy North Italians who had directed it. It must be kept in mind that the courtyard was the work of foreigners, not of Venetians.

It took a later Venetian to give it a coherent look. Canaletto, in his view of the court now in the Fitzwilliam Museum (Cambridge University, 194),

managed to make it look like an orderly and rational facade, by putting it in sharp perspective from the south end, a trick carried off with bravura by an expert (fig. 7.17). (The southwest corner is still the station from which it looks best.) More innocent eyes have had little trouble with it. Eupeptic Thomas Coryat found it in 1608 "the beautifullest that ever I saw" (Coryat, I, 245).

Since the upper part of the court looks little like anything else in Venice, it might be thought un-Venetian, and in a limited way it may be. But although Rizzo and many of his helpers were Lombards, it does not look North Italian either. The Lombards may have learned the new vocabulary; the first Venetian workmen may not have known it. Working side by side they could produce chaos, much as later Italian designers and Russian workers sometimes did at S Petersburg, and for the same reasons: more enthusiasm than understanding of a new style, and reliance for execution on workmen unlettered in it. The court of the palazzo is more confused than the Certosa di Pavia, the prime example of the North Italian Early Renaissance (where, incidentally, young Rizzo had once worked), for although that had an equal or greater abundance of ornament, it was laid over something noncompetitive and passive, not actively disorderly in itself. Here at the palazzo, the ornament may be more rational, with no colonnettes imitating candelabra stems as they do at Pavia, and it is carved with less exaggeration and flinty sharpness than equivalent ornament on the Certosa, but this somewhat more orderly system of ornament is laid over obtrusive disorder. Disorder naturally results.

The ensemble is unique, and though pretty in many passages, too disorganized to call for an autopsy here. Although unique, it is so only from its largely adventitious combinations, for it offers no new architectural ideas. To

7.17 Palazzo Ducale. Court
from the upper covered walk
at the south end (painting
by Canaletto in the Fitzwilliam Museum, Cambridge).

7.18 Palazzo Ducale. Capitals under arches at the top of the Scala dei Giganti. An example of the variety and virtuoso technical skill in the carving of ornament. The undercutting approaches fine Byzantine work. All the moldings are deeply cut and give a sparkle of maximum light and shade, while strictly following antique patterns.

7.19 Palazzo Ducale. Rio facade.

the nearsighted, it might look better in closeups than to those who can back away enough to see long stretches in focus at once (fig. 7.18). If a quake shook it down, it could make a fascinating ruin, and most of the pieces would be not only rich but delightful in their fine carving, samples of Early Renaissance ornament at its peak, with each piece providentially dissociated from every other. Mies van der Rohe's immediately notorious dictum, "Less is more," may well apply to the rio facade of the palace. But equally true, then, would be its antithesis displayed in the courtyard, "More is less."

Much of what was said of the upper stories of the court can be said of the upper parts of the rio facade, which becomes a bit disorderly as it rises, but never to the same degree as the court (fig. 7.19). Above the spare zones of rustication, windows, wreaths, and the long entablature already discussed, comes a development of the simple elements in the stories below; the panels, windows, pediments, and circles are reassembled into a larger but still fairly easy harmony. It is still everywhere discreetly accepted that this wall is not a showpiece, but just the back of a very grand building.

Above the first cornice, and corresponding to the second piano nobile of the court, panels and windows alternate appropriately in an antiphon or modification of the story below. For example, the little curved pediments have opened up and become the open tops of arched windows. The second major cornice in the clifflike wall has the most antique look of all, with its series of modillions tucked under a properly projecting corona. Most of the design may still be Rizzo's, but the execution is probably posthumous.

On the floor corresponding to the upper stories of the courtyard, the windows are not always on axis with those below But they give the impression

that they submit where possible to the same overall rhythm, now and then a little faster or slower, or with an enlivening episode of three over two, which disrupts the pulsing rhythmical drive no more than it does in a habanera. Nothing in these upper parts can be seen head on, but only at an angle steep enough to tone them down.

The disorganization of the design, particularly in the courtyard, has been aggravated by time, for the stone of which it is built—like so much else in Venice—is no longer uniform in tone. No longer all white, the range of tones has shifted through extreme light and dark, and has turned as dappled as a Dalmatian.

The Doges' Palace is a unique work in a unique city, and aside from its aesthetic vagaries and occasional vulgarities, it managed to proclaim fortissimo the power, pride, and wealth of the self-confident government it housed, a government untroubled by revolts or political assassinations. The building blazoned forth the republic's official view of itself by deliberate choice.

The Early Renaissance had started in a city with palaces and churches of brick, exposed or stuccoed, and the Early Renaissance left it, as here, a city with its best buildings apparently of stone, though nearly all the stone walls, like those of much of the Palazzo Ducale, were brick inside and stone only outside where it would make a show. Three major architects, Rizzo, Codussi, and Pietro Lombardo, were largely responsible for the change.

II | PIETRO LOMBARDO

8 | BIOGRAPHY

After the tentative forward steps and occasional leaps of Rizzo, a clear division comes into Venetian building, separating the contemporary Renaissance masters from one another. The first great architect of the Venetian Early Renaissance was surely Mauro Codussi, early rivaled in success by the attractive but less advanced Pietro Lombardo. But inasmuch as Pietro looked backward and sideways as well as forward, preserving much of the expert craftsmanship of late Gothic decoration while adapting it to the Renaissance, or holding to the overwhelming and little understood Renaissance ornament of his native North Italy, he can better be discussed here, before the more revolutionary Codussi, who looked more steadily forward and, like Brunelleschi and Alberti—artistically his two foster fathers—rejected the wealth of Renaissance ornament being exuberantly applied with late Gothic taste by many contemporaries.

Much of what was said of Rizzo could be said for the first years of Pietro Lombardo (b. ca. 1430–35, d.1515). Like Rizzo, he had been trained as a sculptor. There were no guilds in Venice, no guilds of architects in Italy, no specialized training for young men who wanted to become architects. In the organization of trades, architecture was not yet classed as a separate art. Architects usually began as sculptors or stonemasons, and gradually picked up specialized architectural knowledge on their various jobs.

Even after they had arrived as architects, they did not perform in that role as it is now understood, for the masons' association responsible for a building was not a group of workmen following the orders of a master but a group (or groups) of individual craftsmen, who might have some say in the work that was finally coordinated by the chief—or should have been. They had considerable freedom in carrying out details and even in their design. Below them were, of course, the simple manual laborers. The man we would now call the architect was recognized as the leader in some matters but not all; it was he who dealt with the client, and had the model of the work prepared. He might at the same time be engaged in businesses on the side, such as dealing in stone or other building materials. In partnership with his son Tullio, Pietro Lombardo kept up a profitable sideline of supplying stone, not only for his own commissions but also for others. Rizzo may have run a similar business. Both men were regularly busy as sculptors at the same time they were actively practicing architecture.

Pietro's early prestige as a sculptor and decorator created a demand for his work, and as this began to run beyond what he himself could carry out, he called on his two gifted sons, Antonio (who left Venice 1505–6) and Tullio (who outlived his father and was active in Venice until 1532). They helped him early and kept on helping him as middle-aged men in what had become a sort of family firm. There were other skilled assistants, many of them Venetians, and some kept on for years as important members of the workshop. When he was a successful, well-established master in his fifties, Pietro still worked regularly as an assistant or collaborator for Rizzo on the Palace.

The problem of the extent of Pietro's participation in any work is complicated by the persistent riddle of the role of the client. All works were commissioned by someone or some group; no work was an independent creation of an artist aiming only to please himself. Self-expression was incidental and subordinate. An individual or corporate client with specially favored ideas was in a position to have them heeded. There is no way of knowing now how much or where a client may have intervened. If the architect was unusually lucky, he might have a docile client who never spoke up. It is clear, however, that Pietro had troubles with some of his corporate clients.

Although his first identifiable work, the tomb of the humanist Antonio Roselli, made for S Antonio in Padua in the middle 1460s, is patently Florentine, Pietro himself was no Florentine. Like the Bregnos, he came from Carona on the Lake of Lugano, a town that for a few generations bred sculptors and builders in a profusion comparable to Cremona's later violin makers. He was born between 1430 and 1435 in a family called Solari. After at least one visit to Florence and probably a stay in Bologna, he went to Padua, where he was surely settled from 1464 to 1467. About 1467 he arrived in Venice, where he was not known as Solari but always as Pietro Lombardo. By 1474 he had his own workshop, which shows that he had already achieved some success. About 1475 he finished his work on the *coro* of the Frari.

While his work in Padua, where he had come to know the work of Donatello, had been in a displaced Florentine idiom, in Venice his reliance on Florence became less, and he gradually created one of the main branches of the Venetian Early Renaissance style, at first contemporaneously with Rizzo, whom he surely knew. (He shows no signs of contact with the other great master of Early Renaissance architecture in the city, Mauro Codussi.) How much Pietro owed to Rizzo or Rizzo to Pietro cannot now be measured, nor how much each contributed to the formation of the new decorative style (distinct from Codussi's); the probabilities lean toward Pietro as the dominant influence. His style is the more decorative, the more consistent despite the novelties he introduced, and the more limited despite the exuberance of his decorative vocabulary. Rizzo's may be more varied, but in a far more limited language.

Although not a Florentine, Pietro had mastered what interested him there, though he never went so far as to try to impose the Florentine manner in toto on any of his buildings in Venice. He had his own preferences and, making fastidious use of what he had been attracted to pick up (no doubt in a sketchbook), he created his own somewhat hybrid style. It was such an immediate success and spread so fast that it soon became typical of Venice. The Venetians, with no classical past to look back to, had no compulsion toward or particular taste for research into Roman antiquity. Venice began its Renaissance late, with considerable familiarity with Florentine models, matched by a kind of patriotic indifference to them. Pietro, in spite of not being a native Venetian, fitted into the local gestalt better than rivals born there.

No architect of the Renaissance surpassed him as a decorative carver, either in his refinement and dexterity in stonecutting or in his invention of forms within a clearly bounded repertory. His arabesques, for example, abstract in general composition and easily assimilable into an architectural context, are at the same time fresh and naturalistic in details. Some have a ramrod-straight center stem, like a materialized axis line, from which botanically identifiable leaves and flowers sprout in strict bilateral symmetry, while others climb or run along in undulating coils derived from Roman *rinceaux*, but animated by a new springiness. Fauna may perch on flora—small birds of many kinds, lizards, and other small creatures, and wonderful miscegenations of scaly and feathered, of man and fish or bird, or man and plant. For seaborne Venice there are surprisingly few marine creatures, only a rare dolphin or mermaid. The ornament is not thick, but is kept transparent enough for the plane of the background to show through in over half the area.

The vines range from what would win blue ribbons at any horticultural show to exuberant vegetation, something like lace vines, kudzos, that grow with inconvenient speed and commonplace patterns. Examples vary, of course, in quality, having either been improvised by the master or some expert assistants with delicacy and gusto, or hurriedly turned out by helpers in a sort of high-grade mass production.

Capitals are generally of that Early Renaissance species that is really a continuation of a plain and widespread mediaeval type, picked up from a less plain and less widespread but still genuine Roman type (figs. 8.1–8.4). The simplest examples are no more than an upside-down bell sheathed in four leaves, coiled back under the corners of the abacus—usually there is no echinus—to form substitutes for the corner volutes of regular Corinthian. Pietro's leaves are usually more serrated and specific than the plain, pad-like Gothic or Romanesque. In the middle of each side, instead of the Corinthian tendrillike *caulicoli* springing from a pair of leaves like a calyx or auricle, themselves sprouting from a stalk growing up from the bottom, Pietro (and others) would try some original ornament, formal or naturalistic, but always symmetrical. This rarely runs down to the bottom of the capital, like the regular Corinthian stalk, but may instead turn inward in little leaves or curls no more than halfway down; it may be shaped more like a lyre than a plant; and at the top, this new ornament may spread suddenly outward to coil into pseudovolutes, under the corners of the abacus, winding indifferently either clockwise or counterclockwise. Many of the variations that look fresh and newly invented turn out to have some sort of Roman precedent, genuinely antique but in one sense unclassical. The abacus may be a square, but more usually has concave sides, and swoops out at the corners in memory of the stock of Corinthian models.

8.1 Typical Lombardo capital, Scuola di S Marco.

8.2 Typical Lombardo capital, Scuola di S Marco.

8.3 Typical Lombardo capital, Scuola di S Marco.

8.4 Typical Lombardo capital, Scuola di S Rocco.

There is less originality or vitality in Pietro's moldings, for his interest flagged when he had to move away from free or naturalistic decoration to stricter architectural and abstract concerns. To make up for the loss, he fell into a *horror vacui* that led him to extravagant indulgence in standard egg and darts, bead and reels, and a wealth of leaf moldings.

If he were to be singled out for one architectural accomplishment, it would be for his ornament, and here he might well triumph as the creator of the greatest variety of arabesques carved with the greatest and seemingly most effortless skill of anyone in the Italian Renaissance, perhaps not quite a major accomplishment, but still notable and unusually engaging.

In Lombardo's work and in similar work by others, the fine Gothic craftsmanship in decorative carving was easily taken over into the Renaissance. The main group in Florence, that of Brunelleschi and Alberti in particular, had cut down the abundant growth of naturalistic ornament of late Gothic for the more austere classic forms and the fastidious proportioning of bare areas and plain moldings. But the Venetians, particularly the Lombardos and Lombardeschi, wary of the potential coldness of bare panels, pilasters, or moldings, outdid their Gothic fathers by spreading their light ornament all over. Another impetus may have come from the wish for rich decorative displays of light and shade, always important in Venice, which tended to value color (including shade) over form. The Gothic style had done this with slightly deeper three-dimensional effects that the flatter Early Renaissance could rival only with its more linear carving. Such luxuriance of decoration in Pietro's output, shallow decoration everywhere, exerts so little force—a few darting volts but no foot-pounds—that it causes little or no tension. Conflict is avoided as much by indifference to the expression of structure, real or imagined, as by the sensibility controlling the distribution of ornament.

Pietro made no mark in larger architectural matters; he thought through no problems that had come up with the use of the new vocabulary, and discovered no new way of organizing a facade, no new plan, no new way of composing space. Instead he refined and invented variations on the classical vocabulary, enriching it with engaging conceits. He applied it ingeniously to familiar old forms or, more rarely, to new forms borrowed from someone else. In other words, he was little concerned with the most purely architectural aspects.

For convenience, his work in architecture—which cannot be comfortably fitted into any neat chronology—may be divided into three parts of unequal importance: first, decorative works such as the well-known tombs, most of them early; second, a few complete buildings or additions to existing buildings, mainly from midcareer; and third, his not always identifiable contributions to works for which he was only partly responsible, such as the Scuola di S Marco or the Palazzo Ducale, work that did not end with his death in 1515, thanks to his sons and other faithful helpers. His sculpture, of equal if not greater importance, must be ignored here.

9 | TOMBS

The first work in Venice generally accepted, though not documented, as Pietro's, begun by him to his own design, and the last to follow Florentine models closely, is the monument of the doge who followed Foscari, Pasquale Malipiero (1457–62). In his reign of only five fainéant years, he must be credited with two important and quite different architectural accomplishments: he continued the work being done on the Arco Foscari by the Bregnos and Rizzo in florid late Gothic, and he put up the gateway of the Arsenal, which must have looked not just exotic but out-and-out revolutionary when it was new. He can also be given one posthumous accomplishment, his handsome tomb (fig. 9.1).

When Doge Malipiero died in 1462, William Wey of Eton wrote down some of the elaborate ceremonials of the funeral he had just seen. After lying in state in the Palazzo Ducale for three days, the corpse, dressed entirely in gold and laid out on cloth of gold, was carried "to the Church of the Preaching Friars" (Dominican SS Giovanni e Paolo) to his tomb (Wey, 85). What is now his tomb monument cannot have been built, yet the doge was buried here, probably in the brick wall in front of which Pietro would soon erect the monument, or else under the floor just in front. The lavishness of the funeral arrangements was a fit prelude to the lavish monument to come.

The Malipiero family's choice of Pietro was bold, for he had not yet earned the renown that would ordinarily have won him a commission to make a doge's tomb. It was the family and not the state who paid for such monuments. At times they were built well after a doge's death, occasionally some years before, ordered by the doge himself so that he could see what he would have. Some have thought that this one was begun even before Pietro appeared in Padua in 1464, on the grounds that it is not strikingly advanced—and Pietro developed rapidly—and that it still shows so much Lombard and Florentine character. But many writers now postpone this one until some time after 1467 or the early 1470s; some time, that is, after Pietro had arrived in Venice. Whatever its precise date, stylistically it fits best between the Foscari and Tron memorials.

Here, among the huddled memorials of SS Giovanni e Paolo, Pietro was able to work with his own ideas and not on a scheme begun by someone else, as in the Frari *coro*. His own particular manner begins to show itself, mainly in details, always the principal bearers of his style. Already in 1475 he was extolled as a "famous sculptor" who "made the city resplendent," but by a Paduan poet, not a Venetian, and in reference to his work in Padua, not in Venice (cited in Pope-Hennessy 1958, 109). "Famous sculptor" and his work in Padua have little to do with architecture, except that they are concerned with carved ornament, and this fine praise is no help in arranging his work in Venice in any fully satisfactory chronological order.

He must recently have visited Florence, perhaps more than once, and must have kept a sketchbook on his travels. Artists made notebooks with ideas for possible later use, as one can see, for example, from those of Jacopo Bellini. Sketches are the most reasonable explanation for the resemblance of some parts of this tomb to two in S Croce in Florence, still famous now and already famous and novel then: Rossellini's Bruni and Desiderio's Marsuppini monuments (fig. 9.2). These were just what an eager young visitor would have studied; they must have been even more arresting to him then than they are to us now. Odd motifs, such as the winged cockleshell under the Malipiero sarcophagus, are specifically Florentine and surely not a spontaneous reinvention by a young

sculptor 150 miles away from the Marsuppini monument, where they had appeared some years before.

The Florentine tomb, imitated all over Italy, consisted of a widely-spaced pair of pilasters standing on a common element, together carrying an arch, with a sarcophagus and effigy enclosed in the resulting niche. A religious relief might be in the upper part of the niche, and sometimes another above it, outside. A few allegorical figures might stand in suitable places. Some surfaces might be lightly covered by foliate ornament in low relief, such as arabesques or *rinceaux*. Many surfaces were left plain.

Most of this appears on the Malipiero monument, and consequently it seems quite Florentine, except that instead of standing on the floor, it is supported on wall brackets in the old-fashioned Venetian way, more like a big tabernacle than a self-sufficient piece of architecture (fig. 9.3). The canopy is more like a tent than ever, or like bed curtains shutting the bier off from its surroundings, but without seeming to protect or enshrine it. The Malipiero family may have specified that they wanted this traditional Gothic feature, long more common in Venice than Florence. The drapery is heavy—furlined in fact—and although meant to represent hanging curtains, its long lively curves can be read as working the opposite way, swooping upward like a waterspout.

Yet the top of the curtains never touches the lintel above, as one would expect, for they run in behind it and hang from a barely visible crown on the strip of ceiling between the lintel and the back wall. The lintel is a long beam, supported only at the ends by freestanding piers that might seem weak; and the architrave is so long for a heavily-loaded stone beam that one might be made empathetically uncomfortable. But one is not, for the pretty

9.1 Malipiero Monument in
SS Giovanni e Paolo.

9.2 Desiderio da Settignano.
Marsuppini Monument,
S Croce, Florence.

9.3 Malipiero Monument. The oblique view shows the freestanding piers and the architrave beam, with the curtain rising to the slice of ceiling behind it.

9.4 Malipiero Monument. The *rinceaux* run along on the soffit of the cornice, which is made entirely of moldings of antique pattern. The arch repeats the cornice, leaving just enough room for a flower with whirling leaves, not a very steady support for the figure.

carving keeps the eye on the surface and pulls everything together optically, so that structural implications cannot ever come effectively into the open.

The carving is exquisite, and everywhere rather Florentine. All its details are correct. The freestanding piers and their frieze have half-naturalistic *rinceaux*, by now almost standard, and every molding is carved at a very fine scale (fig. 9.4).

Handsome though the monument is in its general lines and the quality of the carving, it cannot compete with its models in Florence. While it can easily be interpolated into an evolutionary series of tombs in Venice, it earns prominence less by architectural imagination than by the delicacy of its carving and its pervasive taste. In a way it is akin to some lesser composition by someone like d'Indy or Saint-Saëns, where everything is correct, well worked out, distinguished in detail, but not—alas—very interesting. While still in small part Transitional, it is well on its way into the blossoming Early Renaissance, and has sometimes been put on that side of the indefinable boundary as the first Renaissance tomb in Venice (Rambaldi 1913, 30, for example).

The next tomb by Pietro Lombardo and his sons is also in SS Giovanni e Paolo, which was becoming the most desired church for ducal monuments, even though the body might be buried elsewhere. It commemorates Doge Pietro Mocenigo (1474–76), and has been praised ever since it was finished—or almost finished—in 1481 (fig. 9.5). As usual, the sons' share cannot be measured, but the whole was surely dominated by the father. The lighting, from a large, high-set window on the left, is ideal on all counts, and shows the tomb at its best, in unhappy contrast to the Malipiero monument, subjected to dim, vague, directionless light that blurs and half dissolves its forms. The Mocenigo monument, furthermore, has recently been admirably cleaned.

The Mocenigo heirs commissioned the work in 1476, soon after the doge had died, in the same year that the Tron heirs commissioned their monument to their doge. The Mocenigos seem to have been particularly anxious to make an impressive showing of the prowess of their hero, who had won more distinction as a captain in wars with the Turks than in his fourteen months as doge. Imperious, alert, and ready to move, not lying supine on his bier, he stands in full armor, well displayed because of the gesture of his right hand (once carrying a banner) that flings back his doge's robe. The figure was once brightly colored, as many small traces still attest. Though his air is that of a *triumphator* in a chariot, he is only standing on the lid of his sarcophagus, inscribed in a laurel wreath, EX HOSTIAM MANUBIIS ("from the booty of the enemy") to make it plain that state funds had not been spent on a family tomb. On either side of the inscription are reliefs: of the entry into wrecked Scutari (1471), and of the handing of the keys of Famagusta to Venice's adopted daughter, Queen Caterina Cornaro of Cyprus (1472), events that had happened before he was chosen doge.

He is larger than any of the other figures (fourteen now, two having been transferred to a later Mocenigo tomb nearby), standing between two nearly naked youths who, not coming up to his waist, make him seem to tower taller and stronger. One carries his general's baton and the other a shield with the family arms, the first of the *reggiscudi* in Venice, unless anticipated by Rizzo on his tomb for the Trons. The motif is a borrowing from Florence. Pietro made use of what he had seen in such a variety of sites that it comes close to certainty that he kept a sketchbook. The sarcophagus, which, exceptionally, holds the bones of several members of the family, is carried

9.5 Tomb of Doge Pietro
Mocenigo in SS Giovanni e
Paolo.

effortlessly by three soldiers in Roman costume, the first of such figures in Venice. On the socle are reliefs of military trophies and two of the labors of Hercules alluding to his masculine virtues, too pagan and exotic on a Christian tomb to have been welcomed by all. To correct the ignorantly pious who took Hercules for Samson, Friar Fabri, who saw the tomb still new in 1484, expounded their proper symbolic meaning (Fabri 1881, 72).

The doge and his five attendants stand within an arch of new and grandiose character. Its vine-covered piers do not end in capitals but in blocks of the beamlike band that runs across the whole monument. These blocks serve as imposts for an archivolt, wider than the piers implicitly supporting it, so wide that it slices the bottom corners of the panel above the arch to knifelike points, making it seem to hang rather than stand. The entablature above is the first normal architectural member so far.

Beyond the piers three niches are stacked up on either side to house more adolescents, not representing allegories or virtues but just a junior guard of honor, got up as Roman soldiers as though for a school play (fig. 9.6). Neither these nor any other figures pay one another any heed. Derived, one supposes, from Rizzo's stronger tiers of niches on the Tron monument, which have to look like elements of support, the niches here are set back and divorced from the adjacent piers; they are no more than ornamental wings, and can justifiably look weaker. They show only a brittle thin rim at the outer edge. Because of its size and long uninterrupted lines, the center archway, rising effortlessly through all three tiers, holds everything together, whereas the several stories of niches on the Tron monument, similarly placed, can seem potential threats, ready to divide it into horizontal layers.

9.6 Mocenigo Tomb. The two guardian figures at the top are older than those in the lower tiers. The delicacy and crispness of Lombardo ornament here is unsurpassed.

Both ensembles are fresh combinations of inventions and borrowings, and they stand at the beginning of a long line of Venetian Renaissance tomb monuments. Such niches, for example, will be recurrent features of Lombardo and other tombs from now on. Neither the Tron nor the Mocenigo tomb is, of course, really classical. That of Doge Mocenigo is no more convincingly antique than the young Italians dressed up in golden cuirasses are convincingly Roman—charming, but not believable.

A century later (1572) the Mocenigo family commissioned a redesigning of the whole west wall of the church as one grand family memorial, and the monument of Doge Pietro had to be homologized with those of later Mocenigos. Two figures, the Venetian patron Saints Mark and Theodore, originally standing on top of the stacked niches, were shifted to a huge new adjacent tomb. Since all the other figures had been placed with adroit compositional strategy, these may have been telling in the overall impact when placed where they were first intended. In their relation to the architecture and in their quality as sculpture, Pietro's figures count as superior to the general quality of the ensemble if it be judged as an architectural composition. They are of marble of a particularly fine white, distinguished from the slightly cooler and stronger-looking Istrian limestone of the architectural membering, with an effective though barely perceptible shift of tone.

The composition is not just architecture with sculpture but innately architecture *and* sculpture, and of a particular kind: not self-sufficient architecture with self-sufficient sculpture, as on a classical temple; nor architecture that would be inadequate alone combined with sculpture that would be inadequate alone, as on many Romanesque facades; but self-sufficient sculpture combined with architecture insufficient by itself. The small niches, if emptied

of their figures, would seem flimsier than an altarpiece frame (as may be seen by a glance to the left, where a Lombardesque frame holds the S Vincent Ferrer polyptych and is dependent on it, being a frame and nothing else). Even the center arch and entablature of the tomb here, more like parts of a stable structure, might seem incomplete alone. Deprived of the figures, the architecture would not hold togther; but it does not have to, for the figures are there and were planned to be there from the beginning.

On the little attic story, the dwarf pilasters carry a thin cornice but no architrave (a Gothic custom), topped by a curved pediment not correlated with the pilasters and seemingly easy to slide left or right. The lovely relief of the Marys at the tomb, crowded and inadequately framed, comes as an abrupt religious intrusion into an otherwise lay monument. The three figures at the top, Christ and two angels, are the least effective of all. Possibly when the SS Mark and Theodore (sometimes wrongly called Peter and George) were in their places on either side, the upper parts of the tomb would have seemed less adrift.

This monument was a favorite for centuries, and was cited with special admiration as early as the 1480s (Fabri 1881, 72; Sabellico 1502, 24), when other tombs were not often singled out; and it was still being praised in the XIXc, when many critics were sharp-eyed toward sculptural detail but myopic toward the coherence of an architectural ensemble seen at a distance. It has held up well for those who look at architecture as sculpture, less well for those whose interest is primarily architectural; either limitation misses half the point.

The third tomb by Pietro Lombardo in SS Giovanni e Paolo is that of Doge Nicolò Marcello, whose term was ended by his death on December 1 1474, after fifteen uneventful months in office (fig. 9.7). Ignoring his inconsequence, Pietro's monument is the richest of the three and the most coherent. Although stylistically the latest, its date cannot be fixed more firmly than some time after ca. 1475, most likely ca. 1481–85 (Munman 1968, 138), while Rizzo was getting the Palazzo Ducale under way. As so often, Pietro's reliance on assistants complicates the fixing of attribution and date. The monument must follow that of Pietro Mocenigo, who had followed Marcello as doge; the chronologies of tombs and terms of office do not always correlate. After Doge Marcello's funeral in SS Giovanni e Paolo in December 1474, his body was temporarily interred at the Certosa di S Andrea (the Carthusians' Masses for the Dead were specially prized), until the existing monument was ready to receive him in S Marina, as intended from the first. The direct involvement of three churches in the burial of a doge is typical. At S Marina there was some sort of restoration in 1753. Sometime between 1808, when S Marina was deconsecrated, and 1818, when it was demolished, the tomb was disassembled stone by stone, along with that of Doge Michele Steno, and both were set up again on the north wall of SS Giovanni e Paolo, by now almost an official pantheon. Modifications may have been made in the reconstruction.

It is both a synthesis and a critique of the two earlier works, more elaborate yet more ordered, more in the main evolutionary line yet with new independent elements. Above a long bottom molding, a flat floral band breaks forward twice for brackets that foretell something to come: two squatting half-human, half-gryphon creatures who, with effort, make still more of a break to carry the cornice that is also the floor of the center niche. In comparison with the meager projection of the Mocenigo tomb, the center here

springs out a foot, and its background sinks in almost as much, forming an effective deep recess. The total depth of the Mocenigo tomb is only a little less, but it counts as less since it comes almost entirely from the recess in the wall; the projection of the center there seems weak at only 3 or 4 inches.

The brackets and the young satyrs prepare for one of Pietro's ornamental oddities, the columns above them. These stand on round pedestals draped with garlands, more like Roman altars than classical pedestals. He may have seen and sketched a round statue base or part of one, and have adapted it without knowing what it had been made for. The lower part of the columns has twisted fluting (a Roman and mediaeval fantasticality picked up perhaps from the idiosyncratic Arco dei Borsari in Verona, or some simpler columns with twisted flutes in Florence). Swelling as it rises, this bit of shaft seems to have been stood upside down. After a bandagelike band, the upper part continues normally with diminishing entasis and standard fluting. Like so much else, this shows a typical attitude of Pietro's toward structural members or members with mimetic structural implications. When there was rivalry between tectonic expression and nontectonic decoration, decoration won. (We must remember that the authoritative texts of Alberti and Vitruvius were printed—in Latin—only in 1485 and 1486, and that Pietro would not have been a reader of Latin.)

He avoided columns, perhaps because their clear structural statement was uncongenial to him, but when he did use them, he found he could modulate them more to his taste by sheathing them with ornament. Only in that they are fancy do the columns here resemble those at the Certosa di Pavia, where Pietro had served some early apprenticeship, and those at the Certosa are derived from candelabra stems and are not, like these, true columns tricked out with prankish trimming. (Columns

9.7 Marcello Monument in
SS Giovanni e Paolo, moved
from S Marina.

derived from candelabra, favored in Lombardy, were rejected in Venice.) Here, the columns are ineffective in one of their main tasks; they look weak as elements to enclose the big projecting blocks of sarcophagus and bier that, when looked at together with the columns, seem brought in from another, larger composition.

The big arch has become the most authoritative feature, closing the top of the essential recess containing the tomb proper. In passing, it knifes off the lower corners of the panel above, but that does not disturb since the panel is a neutral non-weight-bearing surface, acceptable as something that could be hanging. The panel attracts no attention from the size, shape, or color of the spandrels, but serves only as an inert background for two classical profile heads framed in laurel wreaths, like enlarged coins of Roman emperors, which may have been their models, though similar ones had already appeared in Venice on Rizzo's tomb of Orsato Giustiniani. They are the only items that could be quotations from the Certosa di Pavia, which Pietro had of course known well as a young apprentice.

At the top, a low stone roof covers everything in a slowly swelling concave-convex-concave curve, imbricated in a fish-scale or tile-edge pattern like the top of a sarcophagus. The tomb is set so high now, beginning 8' above the floor, that the roof is visible only from the opposite side of the church. In S Marina it would presumably have been lower. A half-length figure of God the Father, hand raised in benediction —an idea borrowed perhaps from the Tron monument—tops the whole, or was intended to; but now, sunk back in a small niche, perhaps from some change made when the tomb was repaired or moved it is visually ineffectual. The niche is clumsily cut into one of the brick wall-piers of the XIVc

church, a pier largely hidden now by the tomb. The figure cannot be accepted as a work of any major Lombardo master (Munman 1968, 159n19).

The flanking niches are semicircular in plan, the lower ones with the common cockleshell heads, the upper with less common straight tops. The four cardinal virtues stand in them, a little less than life-size, uncomfortably boxed in, but managing to push out here and there with body or gesture so that they seem able to move like human figures and even communicate with our space and, by implication, with us—something new for tomb sculpture (fig. 9.8). Surely among Pietro's most attractive figures, as pure sculpture they cannot be discussed here any more than can the various reliefs on the tomb. Both, nevertheless, are essential in the organization of the whole.

The figure of the doge lies in sleeplike death or deathlike sleep. His pillowed bier, ornately carved in bolder relief than most of the rest, has cramped baby lions with heraldic shields helping to support it (or trying to keep from being crushed by it). The lower element is so much larger and more sober than the upper one on which the doge lies in state, that it and not the upper one is understood as the sarcophagus proper—though there may be misunderstanding at first glance.

The two panels of yellowish veined marble on the front of this sarcophagus attract attention by their flatness among so much busy carving. Reliefs may have been here until the tampering repairing of 1753, for although the flat marble appears in one of Grevenbroeck's graceless sketches of tombs made between 1752 and 1754, he could have skipped recording some carved details, though this is unlikely (fig. 9.9). In the detailed early engravings from drawings made ca. 1812–18, in Cicognara-Diedo-Selva's two usually reliable volumes (Cicognara-Diedo-Selva, II, 35), the sarcophagus was shown with the panels filled with reliefs of genii

9.8 Marcello Monument. The figure of Charity, with typical Lombardo ornamental carving on everything possible except the inside of the niche, the cyma, and the spandrel. The head in a wreath probably echoes a Roman coin.

amid whorls of foliage (fig. 9.10). While S Marina and its storerooms were being emptied, Cicognara's draftsman may have seen something still on the sarcophagus that was not recorded sixty years before, or something he thought might once have been on it; it would not be like these faithful recorders to invent. Now flat, the panels tend to exaggerate the bulk behind, and the box looms large and crowds its neighbors.

While busy on these tombs in the first and most formative years of his Venetian career—from ca. 1468 to 1485—Pietro was also taking on other work and running an ever larger workshop. Everything that came out of it would have to have agreed with his own ideas, should have been approved by him in early sketch form, and should have been given his final acceptance when finished. Unfortunately, little is known of shop procedures at this time, or of the extent of the use of sketches, finished drawings, or models—except that all were used.

A particularly difficult example is the monument of Doge Andrea Vendramin (1476–78) in SS Giovanni e Paolo. It was almost surely begun under Pietro's supervision and surely embellished and probably finished by his son Tullio. By that time, Tullio's style had developed, not by continuing that of his father but by moving in a new direction into a new field. Since so much of the monument, perhaps the major part, seems to embody ideals of Tullio, it will be discussed later (cf. chapter 30), along with his other work.

An architect can never be related to his finished work in the same intimate way as a painter or sculptor can. Unlike them, he does not leave traces of his original handwriting or touch. There are a few grand exceptions, but only a few; Michelangelo or Borromini controlled not only the general designs

9.9 Marcello Monument
when it was in S Marina
(drawing by Jan II van Grevenbroeck, Museo Correr,
Cod. Gradenigo 228, III/33).

9.10 Marcello Monument.
Engraving in Cicognara-
Diedo-Selva made ca. 1818–
20, when the monument
was already in SS Giovanni
e Paolo, but from a drawing
made a few years earlier.

but also the exact formation of the details, often of distinctive nonstandard character. These men were as far from usual practice in this as in many other ways. They are like composers who play or conduct their own works, whereas the common run of architects have to submit to performers who show their own ideas, sometimes in their own transcriptions. In addition, a swallowing-up of ideas originated by subordinates must also be supposed in the accredited works of major architects; such a general practice now, it must also have been general then. An architect, then as now, had to be able to act as a sort of chairman, and some parts of his work may really have been the work of some officer, assistant, or subcommittee, adapted or reconciled to an overall scheme.

In early Renaissance work it may not be possible, then, to detach and identify what was exclusively the work of the master, but it is possible and convenient to assemble a cluster of works alike enough to be labeled "under the direct domination of Pietro Lombardo," and a looser group "strongly influenced by Pietro Lombardo, perhaps from his *bottega* or else by a close imitator." The latter could be called "Lombardesque."

But is it really essential to know every time just what was thought up first by the master or what was merely approved by him after having been thought up by a helper trained by him? What is certain here is that from the Malipiero tomb (which in general design might as well be in Florence, except for the extravagance of the curtains)—from this work onward, Pietro developed along his own lines into his own artistic identity, and took along a small horde of helpers who did their best to keep up.

A number of decorative works, such as tombs and coros, are in an equivocal relation to the Lombardo *bottega* as well as to the master. They use characteristic Lombardo features, but along

with others so different in nature that they cannot be accepted as from the regular workshop—yet they cannot be put far from it. They could be the work of alumni or secessionists. It would be impossible to define the typical Lombardo kind of composition, much harder to classify than its ornament. But it is possible to make a group of peripheral contemporary compositions that cannot be accepted as legitimate works of anyone of the Lombardo family. They can best be thought of as cognates.

IO | S GIOBBE

Not counting tombs, the first architectural undertaking attached to the name of Pietro Lombardo is the Church of S Giobbe, near the outer end of the Cannaregio Canal. In Venice, as in the Christian East, but only very rarely in the rest of Italy, Job and a few other Old Testament prophets or heroes could be ranked as saints and have churches dedicated to them. In Constantinople, Job had twice been chosen for churches, each connected with a hospital. Venice's S Giobbe had been first a hospital chapel, then a modest hermitage of Franciscan Observants. In the 1450s it took on new prestige when a Gothic church was begun, probably as a result of the canonization of S Bernardino of Siena (1450), who had preached there earlier and to whom the new church was dedicated. The impulse and most of the funds for building came from Senator Cristoforo Moro, who had known S Bernardino well (the correct name of this new church is SS Giobbe e Bernardino).

After he was crowned doge in 1462, Moro made more of the church. He gave it some controversial relics of S Luke, and began improvements to the not yet finished building still identified by his arms, now adorned with the ducal *corno*. In his will (1470, with a codicil of 1471) he left it a large bequest, stipulating that the church be enlarged and beautified by Antonio Gambello, then working at S Zaccaria, or by Lorenzo di Gian Francesco, then working at S Severo. Both may already have been employed on the unfinished Gothic church. Although Gambello did not die until 1481, both he and Lorenzo quickly disappeared from consideration, and by 1471 Pietro Lombardo seems to have become established on the project. Some have believed that he had already been working there in the 1460s, while Doge Moro was still alive, but the naming of others in the codicil without mention of Pietro makes that unlikely.

While no document connects him with the architecture, a letter of 1486 refers to figures carved by him already in the church (Collaccio, cited by Pope-Hennessy 1958, 351).

Doge Moro, an eager patron of the arts and a friend of such powerful patrons as popes Nicholas V, Paul II, and Pius II, may at the end of his life have come to feel that a young Lombardo and the young and still radically modern Renaissance style—which he had seen beginning to flower in Rome—were what he ought to have for his church, rather than the old-fashioned Gothic of Gambello. The commission had become even more important to him since he had chosen it as a burying place for himself and his dogaressa. The result, which he never saw, may be close to what he wanted: a handsome affirmation of the intellectually fashionable new style.

The first demonstration was probably the front doorway (fig. 10.1). This is an early essay in the soon to be typical Lombardo style, above all in the ornamental carving deployed over a scheme based on Florentine models. The whole shows signs that the imported ideas were already becoming naturalized, and beginning to turn into what was to be the regular Lombardo manner for another generation: a simplicity in the fundamental disposition combined with an elaboration of carved moldings, arabesques, one-leaf capitals, and an entablature with every possible component carved at small scale, and the relief everywhere kept low.

The panels on the pilasters are enlivened by a vine springing from a prickly calyx and sprouting buds, shoots, and flowers on the way up before ending as a perch for a bird with prettily flared wings. The capitals have flowers wrapped in the tendrils, which act as their volutes, above a would-be antique ox skull. Everything is ornamented except the fascias of the architrave and the final cyma, items protected perhaps by their once-functional past. Free and even inventive use is made of the Roman vocabulary, yet without distorting Roman precepts (except in the Florentine pediment, by now, like the baluster, accepted into the classical repertory all over Italy).

The rest of the facade has been very much changed, raised, cut with two big new windows, and finished off with a stock pediment in place of the livelier curved Gothic skyline (cf. Barbari map of 1500).

Inside the church, the east end had still to be finished. (The retrochoir behind the chancel is a late addition made by the friars when they became so numerous that they had to have more space.) The doge gave funds for a chancel, a square flanked by semicircular nichelike chapels. Though flickering everywhere with delicate, sharp chiaroscuro, there is no color and little contrast of tone—only between the white Istrian stone and the still whiter plaster. The church, including the new chancel, should have been finished or very well along when it was consecrated in 1493.

Here early Lombardo decoration is shown off at its best (fig. 10.2). Pietro himself must have carved much of the big arch at the end of the nave, as well as the figures that go with it. Admired by our grandparents for its author's skill in making marble "look just like wax," now it is often frowned on for that same accomplishment. The ornament, exquisite by itself, lessens what little structural role some of the architectural members might have been able to offer. Pietro was sensitive to the perfection of individual parts, but less to what could be done in relating them, and less still to their role in effect at large scale.

The capitals of the side chapels, for instance, are snipped off where the stronger main pilasters have to pass by them. And though the archivolts start out properly above their pilasters, that

10.1 S Giobbe. Main portal.
The stone frame of the
wood doors, of architrave-
like profile, turns in at right
angles at the bottom, an antique practice already used
by Brunelleschi (S Lorenzo),
from whom Pietro is more
likely to have taken it than
directly from any ancient
example.

10.2 S Giobbe. Apse and flanking chapels.

of the main arch, less a normal archivolt than a bowed cornice, is wider
than its pilasters can take comfortably.
It is not linked to the principal cornice
above by its keystone in the structurally logical way, for the keystone is
only a pretty punctuation on the archivolt, and not a minor support for the
architrave above.

Work was going ahead by 1472, and
Pietro's hand has been distinguished in
some of the earlier parts. As he became
busier elsewhere, he would have had
less time to work here, perhaps even
none by 1493 when the chancel was
consecrated. Nearly everything must
have been entrusted to helpers. Besides
his sons Antonio and Tullio, he had
others of uncommon distinction,
among them perhaps Ambrogio
d'Urbino, who had done decorative
work for Codussi, and Giovanni Buora,
who had worked for Pietro elsewhere
and would soon emerge as an architect
on his own. It is hard to think of any
comparable *bottega* in the early Renaissance except at Urbino. The quality
of the work at S Giobbe shows how su-
perbly the helpers had been trained,
and how skillful and lucky Pietro had
been in choosing them. One feels that
they could all have gourmandized over
their ornament every day.

The presbytery, behind the lavish
archway from the nave, is a square covered by a dome on pendentives, unlike
anything else in the church and unlike
anything made before by Pietro, foreign
to what we know of his earlier artistic
gestalt (fig. 10.3). Hitherto he had been
less an architect than a maker of ensembles of sculpture in architectural
settings. But this dome and its pendentives are essentially architecture before
they are decoration, concerned with
such fundamental architectural matters
as vault construction, the shape and effect of enclosed space, or the control of
lighting as an element in composition.
So far as is known, Pietro had not

shown interest in these before. Perhaps
he had never had the opportunity—but
that does not seem to be a convincing
explanation.

If it was begun in the early 1470s,
along with work on the entrance arch,
this would be as early as any surviving
dome on pendentives in Renaissance
Venice—if not the earliest—with serious competition only from Codussi's
similar dome at S Michele in Isola (cf.
chapter 17), a church begun earlier
(1468), though the chancel may have
been built a few years later. While the
precedent for the dome of S Giobbe
could just possibly, then, have been
Codussi's, made familiar from a model
or drawings, more likely the archetype
was not in Venice. Doge Moro's taste
and Pietro's experience favor Florence.
Pietro could, of course, have drawn on
both cities, but Florence alone is more
likely. There is no reason to connect
Doge Moro with young Codussi, only
recently arrived in Venice, or to assume that Codussi gave the idea to
Moro who gave it to Pietro, though art-
historically and morphologically that
would be the smoothest and neatest
sequence.

As a young man, Pietro could have
looked at the Brunelleschian pendentive scheme in the Old Sacristy of
S Lorenzo or at the Pazzi Chapel in
Florence, and these could be the
models for his white plaster pendentives outlined by slender stone moldings, and for the roundels with relief
sculpture in each pendentive (fig. 10.4).
The reliefs in the roundels at S Lorenzo
are by Donatello, and could be what
first drew young Pietro, still only a
sculptor, to that church; they are the
most likely source for the idea of putting roundels in pendentives here,
without Roman or clear Byzantine pre-
cursors. (The Evangelists in the roundels in S Giobbe are generally thought
to be by Pietro's own hand.) The round
medallions of mosaic on some of the
pendentives at S Mark's, smooth and
without relief, seem too different to be

10.3 S Giobbe. Interior of presbytery dome.

10.4 S Giobbe. Looking up at soffit of main arch of presbytery, showing also one pendentive with its roundel of S Luke held up by a *putto* below.

a possible inspiration, though everything in S Mark's would have been known to any Venetian; Pietro, a Lombard, might have been less susceptible to their prestige, and clearly he revered Florence more than "foreign" Venice. He was not yet quite at home with the motif of a circle in a pendentive, however, for his are so tightly fitted between the curving moldings at the edges that they seem in danger of being squeezed out of shape. One original idea was filling the little triangles at the bottom with reliefs of children, who hold up the roundels on their heads and hands.

Except for the dome on the cathedral, largely designed before Pietro was born, Brunelleschi's main domes are of an umbrella or half-melon shape. That on S Giobbe is not gored like these but is an approximate hemisphere, more like those at S Mark's or later Florentine domes; simpler, easier to build, and far easier to read as one part of an organization of confluent curved spaces. It is less surprising that Pietro used it than that Brunelleschi quirkily did not, at least not for a major space. (He could make hemispherical domes, and did—for the altar recesses at S Lorenzo and the Pazzi Chapel, though on a much smaller scale.)

The essential compound, a dome on pendentives over a cube of space, would soon appear in a handful of small churches in Venice (McAndrew 1969, 15-17), and by Pietro himself in an addition to S Maria dei Miracoli soon after 1485. In less than a decade it became such a favored item in the Venetian monumental stock that its acceptance must surely have been eased by the unforgettable, never remote domes of S Mark's. Its popularity was not limited to real buildings, for it became a means of making an impressive feature of the settings devised in painted altarpieces; it was also used to provide relief setting around a door in a small tabernacle relief (T. Lombardo, sacristy of the Frari, ca. 1480).

In addition to the largest and most conspicuous, at S Mark's, there must have been a dozen other Byzantine domes in Venice at the time, and most of them must have risen from pendentives. The Byzantines had found the smooth surfaces of a dome and its pendentives rewardingly suited to gold-backed glass mosaics, since light would always gleam from some part of their curves. Surfaces were not cut off by moldings where different areas met, but were smoothly rounded as though by wear or aerial erosion, so that mosaic could flow over them without interruption. Yet, while still easy to see in local examples in his day, such Byzantine formations are not likely to have been the prototypes for Pietro's domes. Familiarity with them may have made it easier to adopt the idea of putting a dome on a church, but the type he used was not the Byzanto-Venetian scheme but the Florentine, derived from Roman vaulting, and the pendentives were specifically Brunelleschian. The boundaries where two surfaces met were not softened, but stiffened by stone moldings emphasizing the edges as much as the areas. Pietro Lombardo, no inventor of spaces or structures, presumably borrowed the whole arrangement—Rome to Brunelleschi to Pietro to Venice.

Un-Roman but more Brunelleschian are the eight small windows cut into the lower part of the dome of S Giobbe, with their sills on the ring at the base. The arrangement is not close to the windows around the lower part of the domes in S Mark's, without sills and unconnected with any ring of molding, but more like the integrated arrangements in Florence; but the arrangement is so simple and easy for anyone to think up that it need not be connected to either. These windows and those under the side arches bounding the pendentives bathe the chapel in a singularly beautiful light, which must have been even more rewarding and dramatic before half of them were walled up, and glaring competition was made by larger windows added nearby in the higher nave.

Neither an interest in a form so essentially architectural (as opposed to a decorative form) nor concern for the spatial feeling it engenders fits with Pietro's other work. This sudden flyer in a new direction might have been his own idea, but more probably it comes as a suggestion from some stimulating friend or professional connection, such as his experienced and well-traveled client, Cristoforo Moro. Even if Pietro's, prompted by a recent look into his Florentine sketchbook, it was surely an idea that Moro could have welcomed. The doge would never have chosen the old S Giobbe as his burial place for its beauty or impressiveness. More likely, he would have discussed with his architect, his new architect, how to make it handsomer and more impressive, and the novel idea of a crowning dome could then have been proposed. The doge could thus dramatically honor both himself and his wife and also S Bernardino, the friend to whom he had had the church dedicated and a saint not yet formally honored anywhere in Venice.

The dome is at the center of another problem. It has usually been thought to have been built or at least to have been begun in the early or mid-1470s, and when the church was consecrated in 1493 it should have been complete. Only in extraordinary circumstances—none is noted here—were churches consecrated before they were finished. Yet Jacopo de' Barbari, in his bird's-eye view map, published in 1500, showed S Giobbe with a semicircular apse attached to the end of the nave (fig. 10.5), and without any trace of a dome (first noted by Franzoi–DiStefano, 109).

The map is a nearly faultless source of information, almost like Holy Writ; a few items not visible from the church towers from which the draftsmen took

the observations collated on the final map—such as the cloisters of S Zaccaria—were left out, but nowhere was anything shown that was not there, and all was shown as it was. The half-cylindrical apse is not there now, but it should have been then, before being demolished for the XVIIc retrochoir. The pitched roof leading to the apse that is set against the back wall of the building is clearly shown, but there is no dome. If there was one, it would presumably have been conspicuous, too conspicuous to overlook. The chancel up to the springing of the dome might somehow have fitted under a continuation of the pitched roof of the nave (now altered and raised), but the chancel is only half as wide and would not have had a roof as wide as that of the nave (unless there were some improbable closetlike chambers behind the small side apses). Something is not right. There is no tall building nearby to hide anything from the draftsmen gathering data for the map. It is hard to believe that the whole new chancel was there but disregarded. It is equally hard to believe that it was not. There does not appear to be anything in the bonding of the masonry now visible that could favor one guess over the other.

There are three possible explanations. First, the church could have been consecrated for some special reason before it was complete, left with a temporary flat ceiling on the ring made by the tops of the pendentives of the early 1470s, like the flat ceiling still on the ring of pendentives at S Ignazio in Rome. A little later, perhaps when funds had been replenished, the masonry dome was built, too late for the Barbari map, but still accounting for sculpture in pendentives earlier than the dome above them.

Or second, the mapmakers were careless here, and the dome and high choir were there all along but somehow—inexplicably—ignored. There are

10.5 S Giobbe. Exterior of
apse (from the de' Barbari
map).

several hypotheses as to whose idea the dome was in the first place, and just when that idea was carried out, but none wins unshakable confidence. The dome was most likely the idea of Doge Moro and went up in the 1470s, the work on the chancel having proceeded without interruption; but then the mapmakers—and this is the hardest to accept—did not bother to record this remote church accurately. (To be sure, they had slipped occasionally in other places: Bellavitis 1976, ill.n11.)

Or third, the last hypothesis, also not easily accepted, is that the dome was there all along, but it was so low, set directly on the pendentive ring with no drum, that its saucerlike, less-than-semicircular section did not rise high enough to interrupt the ridge line of the roof. This could happen, and did almost certainly, for example, in the church of the Certosa, if the only evidence we have, XVIIIc drawings and engravings (McAndrew 1969, 16; 1974, 35), is to be trusted; of the three domes on the central axis, only one emerged above the long roof. If this could happen at the Certosa, it could happen at S Giobbe at more or less the same time. This might be acceptable if it were not for the ring of windows around the base of the dome. They cannot have opened into the dark space under the roof, and the whole hypothesis must be discarded unless it can be shown that the windows were cut later and the roof rebuilt; neither operation seems probable.

In view of all this, none of the theories proposed for the dome can reach its QED.

If the dome is contemporary with Codussi's main dome on S Michele in Isola, as it seems to be, the idea of reviving the impressive form of a dome on pendentives could have originated with (or first been executed by) either master. It is far more in tune with Codussi's thinking than with Pietro's.

Codussi, too, had patrons, patrons as learned, humanistic, and aware of modern architecture as Doge Moro. The Patriarch Maffeo Gerardo (1466-92), for example, was a former abbott of S Michele, a church he continued to visit and to favor. Beyond a doubt interested in the building of the new church, he would have come to know the architect. The doge and the patriarch may both have been attracted to the idea of a domed chancel, and have discussed it with one another, and then with the architects. Or one of the architects may have thought of it first and proposed it; the idea could have caught on and spread. We cannot be sure of the originator.

I I | SCUOLA DI S GIOVANNI EVANGELISTA

In the late 1470s a more fitting entrance to the Church and Scuola (men's religious confraternity) of S Giovanni Evangelista was begun, and an inscription carved on an architrave shows that the work was finished by 1481. The lunette above it has been spirited away to the Berlin Museum (Mariacher 1955, 48). The church, in a crowded part of the city, lacked the pleasant and useful oasis of a campo, or small square, usually found beside a parish church, though some minor area here may have offered meager lebensraum. A small atrium or forecourt was contrived off the busy Calle del Caffetier, a trim harbor of space soon known as the Campiello S Zuanne (fig. 11.1). A doorway in the middle of its back wall led into an oblong area between the side of the church and the scuola; a minor vein of traffic ran on between the two buildings and then expanded into the Calle della Laca. This haven of orderly city planning was unique: no atrium, no campo, not even the Piazza S Marco, as it was then, had been made so orderly and so symmetrical. The only rival would have been in the area of arcaded streets at the business end of the wooden Rialto Bridge, all soon to be destroyed by fire. (Only their plan is still known, nothing of their elevations.) All other campi were irregular, stopped at the edges by the walls of buildings of varying heights. Here alone was a true city square, a regular shape defined by walls of regular height. Whose farsighted idea it first was is not known.

Long attributed to Pietro Lombardo, like so much else given to him, more by passive repetition of old guesses than from active investigation of documents or the work itself, this forecourt shows some parts close to his manner, and other parts not. No documents record him here. The one definite fact is of no real use: in 1514 he was *gastaldo* or "steward" of the scuola, thirty-three years after his putative work here was done, and he was an old man with only a year to live. Yet much here can be called Lombardesque and could have come from a design that originated in the family workshop. Begun later and finished earlier than the chancel at S Giobbe, it is not close in style to anything there.

Advantage was taken of the walls of the two parallel buildings, between which the court was laid out, by having them count as its side boundaries (fig. 11.2). They were measured off into three equal lengths by pilasters with a straight entablature that breaks above each one, out and then back in—as though the order of the Septo Marmoreo had been folded around the hollow inside of a court rather than folded around the solid outside of a *coro.* But none of the Gothic lingering on the Septo is to be seen here. The proportions and most of the details show a knowledge of antique procedure, sometimes with unexpected sophistication.

Arranging the three sides similarly into three bays each, hinting at an equivalent imaginary fourth, may evoke a spatial scheme for the whole little composition: a square divided into nine smaller squares like a big tic-tac-toe. But any idea like this, too, is foreign to anything known in the secure works of Pietro, and probably exists only as a private game in the imagination of an occasional beholder. The composition is more reasonably read as nothing more than a surface continuum echoing itself along three adjoining walls.

The lowest member of the socle is a guilloche of rolling and intertwining ribbons that enclose deep-throated flowers, overrefined for a position down by the pavement, vulnerable to kicking by man and horse—there were still many horses in the city then—more suited to some safer place indoors (fig. 11.3). The capitals show off a little Latin learning with a squash blossom

poking out from the middle of each abacus (fig. 11.4). They do not, however, conform on the whole to specific Lombardesque types.

The fascias of the architrave are slightly inclined, for if each were vertical, the one below would force the next one to stand out, and the next after that in the same way, like steep steps, and the total projection would accumulate to a clumsy overhang, as had happened at the Arsenal gate. This subtle adjustment by inclining the fascia faces was not a Lombardo practice. The frieze is the most Lombardesque item so far. The small dentils hang over it like so much blocky machine-made fringe, awkwardly out of scale with the big egg and dart above. The corona is notable only for the little flutes of just the size to suggest that the dentils had recently been extracted from them. The crowning cyma, shown already battered in XIXc photographs, though the court had been repaired in 1732, must have been replaced in the restoration of 1881. Despite these lesser vagaries, this is on the whole an orthodox classical entablature, made to look passably Lombardesque mainly by having everything carvable carved.

The wall across the back has its middle bay spread wider than the others to make room for a doorway for through traffic. In compensation, the side bays are narrowed, so that together the three will equal the total of the three on either side. The doorway is topped by a Florentine pediment, with its ends rising directly above the mimetically supporting pilasters, respecting structural sense, and appropriately shoving the usual rosettes to the side. Another example of sophisticated structural sense, also minor, is given by the architrave over the doorway, not breaking back to wall level on each side as it does everywhere else, but running in an unbroken span from capital to capital, acknowledging that it is a working beam. These

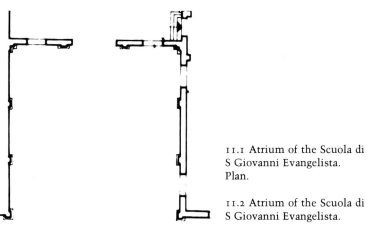

11.1 Atrium of the Scuola di
S Giovanni Evangelista.
Plan.

11.2 Atrium of the Scuola di
S Giovanni Evangelista.

are small samples, but taken together they show a respect for structural integrity rare in Venice at this date, particularly for the Lombardo *bottega*. Pointing out such minor structural proprieties—a sort of good behavior—would be trifling were it not in such clear contrast to non- or antistructural behavior in other works by Pietro Lombardo.

The angels at either end of the cross wall kneel above blank areas and appear unsupported, in spite of the obvious weight of their stony bulk. (Perhaps angels have no need of material props?) The corner pilasters are formed in a notably logical way new for Venice (already tried by Brunelleschi in the Old Sacristy of S Lorenzo): two half-pilasters at right angles, one on each wall, together adding up to one full pilaster, are folded down the middle (fig. 11.5).

This is unlike Pietro's usual light-hearted indifference to structural decorum and his avidity for ornament for its own sake rather than as a suitable enhancement for what underlies it. The folded pilasters are unlike his handling of inner corners in anything he did earlier or—more significantly—later. The idea has more to do with architectural grammar than trimming. They could of course have been suggested by one of his assistants and, if so, none more likely than Tullio, who would soon be developing ideas clearly different from his father's. But was he developing them so early? Would he have had such sophisticated ideas, while he was still probably under thirty? And if he did, would he have relinquished them for a decade until he came into his own? He is not quite a convincing candidate, but he is the best we have.

The bays on either side of the doorway are pierced by windows with grilles (modern?) that have no raison d'être, since the doorway is wide open and probably always was, there being no

11.3 Atrium of the Scuola di S Giovanni Evangelista. Socle with carved guilloche.

11.4 Atrium of the Scuola di S Giovanni Evangelista. Typical Early Renaissance capital one leaf high, architrave with oblique fascias.

11.5 Atrium of the Scuola di S Giovanni Evangelista. Folded corner pilaster, in difficulty only where the squash blossoms collide.

11.6 Atrium of the Scuola di
S Giovanni Evangelista.
Window in back wall.

trace of hinges or pivots (fig. 11.6). No
ornamental feature was needed where
the windows are, for the similar bays
on the side walls are blank and are satisfactory that way. Windows are so explicitly practical that they become disturbing when miscast in merely
decorative roles. Foreign to the elegance of the rest, the fussy frames,
seeming like dowdy country cousins,
are the least successful elements in the
ensemble. Their cornice peaks into a
steep gable more like a dormer than a
pediment. These details might be the
contribution of an ill-trained new assistant or an insensitive old one. The
marble-faced wall that the windows
pierce is, on the other hand, laid up
with most elegant discretion, its Carrara facing edged with a band of pale
gray (matching the silvery striations of
the veneer), and punctuated by two
rings of gray, quietly enlivening the
blank areas above the pediment slopes.

As it is undocumented, reasons for
the assignment to Pietro must be
drawn from internal evidence only. Except for the windows, the carving is
consistently refined and Lombardesque,
and typical also in quantity, for almost
every molding is chattering with ornament. Pietro, as far as is known, had
never yet built a real building, only
decorative ensembles such as tombs
and the additions to S Giobbe. Only
the dome on pendentives there is really
architectural, and it may have been
built later than the atrium. Here at
S Giovanni there was no serious problem, nothing more than how to deco-
rate three walls, but the kind of decoration is soberly architectural with little
free sculpture, only a sober pilaster order handled with special tact in the
corners and over the doorway.

It is not, therefore, easy to accept the
repeated assignment to Pietro without
question. Aside from the rational de-
ployment of the order, unapproached in
his earlier work, there is the general
spareness, discreet in its modest respect for tectonic discipline and in its

knowledge of antique proportions. A first look weakens the attribution, but a better informed second look may strengthen it. The fluted pilasters, still uncommon in Venice, appeared also on Pietro's tomb for Nicolò Marcello at about the same time. The simple handling of the pilaster order, so unlike his previous uses, will appear again almost immediately in the lower part of the nave of S Maria dei Miracoli, surely executed by him or closely under his direction.

While it was building, from 1478 to 1481, Pietro had his sons as junior partners, and perhaps they were becoming less junior since both had qualified as masters in 1475. Because of the conscious classicism of the general scheme, the fluted pilasters, the conventionally overhanging corona, and other such details, a case could be made out for Tullio, soon to become the most orthodox in the whole Lombardo group, as designer or part-designer. A few of the freewheeling deviations could have been brought in by some subordinate who worked a bit independently on the windows. There is no proof, however, of such an hypothesis. Some of the general character and a few specific details reappear on the Ca' Gussoni of about the same date, Lombardesque too, but half a step farther away from the mainstream, farther from Pietro, and farther from Tullio. The atrium of S Giovanni is halfway between the Ca' Gussoni and headquarters.

If, except for the windows, it has to be fitted into Pietro's oeuvre, it would have to be as something designed under his direction but carried out independently, too independently for us to believe that what we see everywhere was designed by him. The difficulty is that it is the general design that seems unlike him, not the execution. The great XIXc scholar Piero Paoletti proposed Giovanni Buora several times as chief designer and executant (P Paoletti 1893-1897, 222), but today Buora's style is more elusive than Pietro's, and what we know of it is not like this. Others have suggested Codussi (Hubala 1974, 357), who would soon be working on the scuola behind this atrium, but while the general design might be fitted into his oeuvre with some dating trouble, much of the execution is foreign to him. The Florentine sculptor Leopardi has been proposed also, but no one knows what his architectural style was, or even if he had one. The reasonable conclusion is that there are too many unknowns for a secure attribution—there may have been a change in supervisors or in crews of workmen—but whatever it turns out to be, it will be near though perhaps not in the Lombardo group.

As has already been said, attribution cannot be sure when a composition and details may have been affected by the hands of so many men working on the same building: the client, the chief designer, the carvers of this or that. Such a work can come to be like those so-called autobiographies of Mme. X "as told to B." The whole handsome little court had best be left in the limbo of the Lombardesque miscellany, but in a good position near the top, and possibly a bit on Tullio's side of it. Or could it be the progeny of a brief Lombardo-Codussi shotgun wedding?

12 | S MARIA DEI MIRACOLI

The building most often called to mind by the name of Pietro Lombardo is one of the most famous in Venice, S Maria dei Miracoli. Friar Felix Fabri of Ulm saw it on his return from the Holy Land, where he had admired many splendid sights; it was still unfinished (1484), but already "with such magnificence that to see it is something wonderful. No prince in Germany could afford such a building." Sabellico, at the same time, found it "a magnificent work that except for the Church of Gold [S Mark's] surpasses all in workmanship, cost of materials, and beauty." An English traveler, Fynes Moryson, saw it just completed in 1494 as "the fairest of any Nunnery, for the beauty and rare stones, the walls covered with marble" (Fabri, 75; Sabellico 1502, 23; Moryson, I, 180). On through the centuries praises accumulated, for the exquisiteness of the craftsmanship and the preciousness of the marbles, but never a word for the novelty of the style. XIXc guidebooks and the accounts of XIXc travelers made pause to admire it. It took Renaissance-deploring but still sensitive Ruskin to speak out in a different tone: "All its sculpture should be examined with great care as the best possible example of a bad style" (Ruskin, Stones, III, 311). Until recently, its architecture has been considered mainly as a support for decoration, little for itself (most recent study of its *architecture*: Lieberman, *Dissertation*, 1972).

Along with many other churches, the Miracoli was suppressed in 1810, but it was reopened by the end of the year. After the nuns had been sent away, windows were broken and birds began to nest inside. The covered bridge by which unseen sisters in *clausura* crossed the street to their screened balcony was pulled down as useless in 1865, though the half-derelict old building was still in use as an oratory, subject to the Church of S Canciano (fig. 12.1). When there were no more nuns attending the daily and nightly celebrations of their prescribed offices—at the end there were about seventy of them—the organ was moved up to their now useless screened balcony. The organ shutters, with an Annunciation by Giovanni Bellini, the earliest commissioned from a major Italian painter (ca. 1490), went to the new gallery of the Accademia, where they still are. The wings of the triptych of the Madonna, for which the church had been built, had already disappeared. The two marble panels of youths, brought from Ravenna soon after the church was finished, and vaingloriously claimed as works by Praxiteles, are now in the Archaeological Museum of Venice, with more modest labeling.

The Austrians undertook to restore the building in 1865, in a manner that was conscientious for the time. Funds were stopped in 1873, after the exterior had been largely refaced, as well as much of the interior. After Venice became Italian, Queen Margherita became interested in the Miracoli, and government funds were obtained through her intercession for repairs from 1883 until the building could be reopened as a church in 1887 (Bernardi 1887, 20-21). Post-Renaissance work was destroyed by purist restorers: four Baroque side altars, the high altar of 1602, and a number of tombs. Large areas of deteriorated marble, inside and out, and battered limestone moldings, bases, and such, were replaced; but, although supposedly from the same old quarries, much of the new stone was inferior, and has since cracked, chipped, and flaked. Little of the original facing can still be in place. The dwelling of the nuns had been converted into ordinary houses for laymen, though recently a part has again been occupied by sisters, who run a nursery school there, with a pretty playground and garden ornamented by one side of the original little cloister, much patched. A pair of the original windows still looks out on the street.

The flood and storm of 1966 penetrated the church in a particularly destructive way: salt water rose above the top of the limestone base and worked into the brick core of the marble-faced walls, where it slowly rose as in a wick. After the storm, as part of the precautionary repairs, a damp-course of metal and plastic plates was slid in above the stone base and below the now damp brick core. Months later, the water that had been soaked up began to come down and, unable to pass the damp-course, began to find its way out through the mortar joints, through the thin marble facing, and through some blocks of inferior limestone, crystallizing on the surface and then flaking off. The lower 6' of the facade, for example, has turned yellow on the surface, and is now pitted with white where the marble has blistered off. A number of small elements have had to be replaced. The carvings of the lower parts of the main doorway have deteriorated to the consistency of brown sugar, and have crumbled beyond saving. This was probably unavoidable. The restoration, one of the most difficult of all, was undertaken by the Stifterbund für die deutsche Wissenschaft, several generous Germans, and firms who made gifts of equipment and materials. The defaced but restored church, still one of the prettiest sights in the city, is much favored for weddings, ideal in its size, its cheerful charm, and the ease with which a bride can arrive and leave by gondola. Small wonder a photographer is established across the street.

Its origin goes back to the 1470s and the growing popular devotion to a miracle-working image of a Madonna and Child with two saints, said to have been painted in 1408 by Master Nicolò di Pietro or di Paradiso (Bortolan, 85; Chechia, 4), and kept in a niche on an old house in the parish of S Marina. Neighbors kept wreathing it with flowers; they kept a votive lamp burning

12.1 S Maria dei Miracoli.
View showing now de-
stroyed bridge from west
end of church to convent
building (XIXc lithograph by
Tosini-Lazzari).

below it; and once a week they lit candles beside it—customs still continued at little shrines in some parts of the city. The reputation for beneficent miracles grew so quickly that several local families wanted to appropriate the picture and house it more worthily—preferably in their own houses. The devotions had increased so by 1480 "that the image at the entrance to the Corte Nuova . . . because of the crush of people in the narrow street, had to be taken away and put in the courtyard of the Ca' Amai. . . : There was such an offering of wax candles, ex-votos, pennies, and silver, that it came to as much as 400 ducats a month. . . . In time the gifts mounted to 3,000 ducats, and the Corte Nuova was bought for it" (Malipiero, 672, written 1457–1500). A splendid procession, with the patriarch, procurators, senators, and citizens, with drums, trumpets, pipes and candles, carried it to a temporary wooden chapel or shrine draped in cloth of gold and silver, put up to serve until some suitable more permanent housing could be built (Bernardi, 11).

The history after this is less clear. A *Cronichetta* of 1664, written 180 years later but convincingly said to be "based on old documents," and *Chroniche* based on it by Pietro Chechia in 1742, are tiresomely filled with some details and exasperatingly empty of others. A competition for a new building was held in 1480, after several striking cures and other miracles; one model, kept in the house of Pier Francesco Zeno, was preferred by everyone. In Renaissance Venice several models were often commissioned or invited for a building to be put up by a committee, or council, or other group (here, five procurators), and a scheme would be chosen by majority vote. After the choice had been made in this case, Pietro Lombardo was contracted for the building operations, and told that he "must follow the model," but there is

no record of whose model it was (Bernardi, 13; Chechia, 22ff; Cicognara-Diedo-Selva, II, 53; Zanotto 1847, II, ii, 181).

If he won the competition, it is odd that no mention was made of the design as his, odd that he was ordered to follow the model, and odd that he was not allowed to keep it himself. If not his, whose was it? There is no answer, and the *Chronichetta* and *Chroniche* are not wholly to be trusted. In 1480, having not yet built anything more than tombs and decorative works, Pietro would hardly have been considered an architect; Rizzo was older and established, and so were the Bregno brothers, Codussi, Gambello, and others. Pietro's cannot have been the only project in the new Renaissance style. It is not possible to know what the others were, nor whose design was chosen. Almost always given to Pietro, this first design need not have been his. Early work on the building shows nothing that is identifiably like anything he had done before, nor is there anything recognizably from the hand of anyone else. Had Rizzo or Codussi or someone else equally well established made the winning model, he almost surely would have been awarded the commission.

As the contractor or supervisor, Pietro would have been responsible for most of the detail—which could not have been specific on the small model—and it is only the detail that is in his recognizable manner. While he may not have created the basic design on which the first work was done, surely he was responsible for building it from the beginning, and for controlling the ornamentation.

At the end of 1480 or the beginning of 1481, work was begun under Pietro's direction, first with the clearing of the site. Pietro was called *maestro*, which does not necessarily mean "architect," and could as well mean "foreman." In January 1481, the building permit came from the pope, Sixtus IV, and the patriarch laid the first stone in February. Clearly, the undertaking was important.

The pope specified that it should be dedicated to Mary of the Immaculate Conception, a suggestion made earlier by the patriarch. Only five years before, Sixtus had proclaimed this feast, which he chose to promote many times, to celebrate the miracle that Mary was mystically purged of Original Sin while still a young girl, in order to become the spotless vessel from which the Savior was to be born. (Conception in the more modern sense was known as the Incarnation, the moment when the Word became flesh, as Gabriel pronounced the Annunciation to Mary.) Franciscans approved this doctrine, while Dominicans maintained that Mary had been born already free of Original Sin. (The Immaculate Conception was not declared dogma until 1854.) Pope Sixtus was a Franciscan, and the sisters chosen for S Maria dei Miracoli, when its program was expanded to include nuns to venerate and watch over the precious picture, were Franciscans, twelve Poor Clares from S Chiara in Murano.

The contract of 1481 specified the marbles to be used, but only "up to the first cornice." The working core of the wall was to be of brick, as usual, but sheathed everywhere with marble, specifically with Carrara, Parian (Greek, from the Island of Paros, one of the finest and whitest), *cipollino* (onion skin), black and red Veronas "of the best quality." Rumor said that stones of great sumptuousness were given from surplus accumulated at S Mark's (Zanotto (1847) II, ii, 183). A ship was sent to Pisa, or to the Genoese coast, or both, to buy special materials, and it picked up a bit extra by piracy. It cannot now be determined where many stones in which parts of the building originated—and furthermore many of the flat plates of the facing, inside and out, have been replaced. All structural parts, or pseudo-structural—pilasters, cornices, door and window frames, etc.—are of Istrian limestone.

Like S Giobbe, many churches had walls of bare brick even for their main facades; others were stuccoed; and the front of Codussi's S Michele was just then being covered entirely with limestone. But no church other than the Miracoli was completely clad in marble, except S Mark's, where the sheathing had been added gradually to a Byzantine building that had originally been considered finished when it was still mostly bare brick. XIXc writers, seeing its difference from its contemporaries, presumed a Byzantine influence on the Miracoli, or even saw what they imagined to be a "Byzantine Renaissance" there, although it resembles nothing in Byzantine lands, and its marble veneer recalls nothing except S Mark's. It was only in the XIVc and XVc that S Mark's got its splendid sheathing, after its connections with Byzantine art had already become weak and it was welcoming new Gothic ideas and, at the same time, becoming ever more independent, more truly Venetian. Such sheathing is really a Venetian feature, more suitably classified with the XVc Ca' d'Oro and the fanciful buildings painted by Carpaccio and Gentile Bellini than with anything in the Byzantine cities with which Venice was in contact—and where Pietro Lombardo had never set foot.

It must be remembered that colored buildings change with time, much as colored paintings do. The balancing of color, held important in the Early Renaissance, and particularly by Pietro Lombardo, is probably no longer as it was first intended, for no stone can escape the effects of continued exposure to weather. The strange shifts of Istrian limestone from light to dark are particularly striking here at the Miracoli, where the south side is lighter than the north, and black blotches are almost everywhere violent.

The streaked and striated varieties of stone with color from impurities were specially esteemed, particularly the opalescent *cipollino* that is found in several zones of Italy and Greece. The slabs sheathing most of the Miracoli that so dazzled the early writers are (or were) some kind of *cipollino* or *zebrino* ("little zebra"—an exaggeration) or *paonazzetto* ("little purple," but here more yellow, cream, and gray), probably from Carrara or nearby. (Identification by eye alone, without chemical analysis, is uncertain.)

Work on the Miracoli must have been carried on from the beginning of 1481 with many workmen and great speed. A new contract, made in March 1481, confirmed Pietro as contractor, again without naming him as architect, competition winner, or designer, but identifying him only as the man who had made the tomb of Doge Pietro Mocenigo, thus seeming to imply that he was not yet recognized as an important architect, one who might have been given the charge of designing such a precious new building.

Although the State, which generally paid for churches, was beginning to run behind in payments on loans and interest, there was plenty of money for the Miracoli. There was, in fact, more than usual, for although they had given permission to build it, neither the State nor the Church had commissioned it; the funds came from the unprecedented donations made by the local gentry and devotees of the miraculous picture. For years past and years to come, no other church in Venice would be able to draw on such generous sources, or be so independent of the economic realities distressing the State.

There was so much money on hand by the end of 1484 that the procurators had to meet several times to decide what to do with it. They voted to buy land and build a nunnery on it, and to add to the new little church. Another contract was signed in February 1485,

and it too is puzzling. Pietro Lombardo was retained, now specifically named *proto*, which means "architect," and contracted to vault the building (was it yet covered?) and design and build a *cappella maggiore,* or chancel (Chechia, 25). The model that had won approbation in 1481 must either have been for a simple box of a building without a separately shaped element for a chancel, or have been still incomplete at the east end. Those in control must for some reason no longer have been content with the old scheme and, perhaps because it was now to be a convent church, have changed their minds as to how they wanted it finished. A new model was probably made (Bernardi, 14). In the beginning a normally equipped church may not have been envisioned (despite permission for one in Sixtus's Bull of Foundation); the scheme may instead have been for a sort of votive chapel to care for the crowds wishing to venerate the image. But now something more was needed for bigger crowds whose contributions could pay for building such an addition (convincingly argued by Lieberman, 58 and passim).

Although it was made clear that the new east end was to be designed by Pietro, it was not said whether the first part had also been his. It becomes harder to believe that he had made the competition-winning model for a little box of an oratory that could easily have been the effort of a tyro; he may have modified its design a bit to conform to his own taste, professional or at least semiprofessional by now. What gives the nave its character is not the basic scheme, nondescript and commonplace, but the decorative covering inside and out, and this is easily in agreement with the taste of Pietro Lombardo.

By 1488 the augmented church building was complete; it had to be left for some months to let the mortar dry out, and by the beginning of 1489 it was

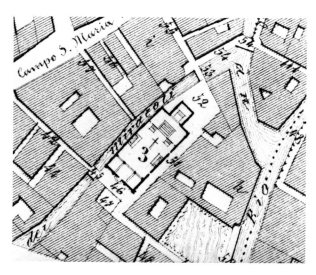

12.2 S Maria dei Miracoli.
Site plan (from the Combatti map of 1847).

ready, except for a few details of decoration finished later. Part of the convent building was already habitable. (Some of this may have been an adaptation of existing houses, but most was new, though not fully finished until 1513.) The patriarch, Cardinal Maffeo Ghirardi, was asked when the twelve nuns might move in and begin their *clausura*. For their first abbess he had already chosen his own sister. On December 30, 1489, the famous triptych was carried in a grand procession around the parish, and then placed on the high altar. Veiled in black to the ground, the nuns from Murano arrived by gondola on the thirty-first, moved into their new convent, and heard their first Mass in their new church at midnight on New Year's Eve (Chechia, 33). For "Poor" Clares the new church must have been almost alarmingly dazzling.

The site has special advantages (fig. 12.2). A small irregular campo opens in front, and a street runs along the right side, almost wide enough to count as an arm of the campo. An essential pedestrian artery in the circulatory system of the city, a street had to be maintained here. The space behind the church was then dominated by the back of the Church of S Maria Nova (destroyed in the XIXc) across the canal, yet made to feel ampler by the bigger campo there. The narrow canal flows along the left side of the Miracoli, spanned by bridges near each end, that at the back having been added to help accommodate the crowds drawn to the miraculous image (Chechia, 12). (Both bridges now provide much admired views and provoke an endless clicking of tourist cameras. How fortunate that the physical substance of a subject cannot be eroded by snapshots!) The church thus stands free on all sides, not a rare advantage in many cities but enjoyed in Venice by only two others, S Zulian and the Angelo Raffaele, and turned to account by neither.

Very few campos have any clear geo-metrical shape, and often a church can offer no more than a flank or part of a flank to even what unshaped space it adjoins. Pietro, or the unnamed author of the first model, made a good thing of the site by treating all four sides as of almost equal importance.

The site has no grandeur, but except for that of S Mark's at the end of the Piazza, no church site in Venice has; no church is at the end of an avenue or even in the center of one side of a regu-lar space. In this regard Venice is the very opposite of Rome, but it has one unique asset, the water. Interest is added to the site of the Miracoli by the canal; at a different level, and with a different surface from the stone paving on the other three sides, it makes an irregularity that enhances the general picturesqueness of the ensemble (fig. 12.3). The church is not clearly re-flected in the water, almost never smooth enough for that here or else-where, but light reflected from its gently lapping waves often plays on the side wall.

The limestone socle, or continuous base, underlies the whole church wall to a little above the level of the pave-ment of the campo and street and, car-ried higher, forms a pedestal all around the building. Originally, before the pavement was made over and raised, more of the socle could be seen. The organic parts, structural or pseudo-structural—pilasters, entablatures, ar-chivolts, window and door frames—are also of this stone, now grayed or black-ened in sheltered parts except for dis-turbing paler replacements. Even so, chipped, faded, and smudged, the whole manages to show much of its original quality to our first glances.

The pilasters frame tall rectangles proportioned about two to three. The original pale caramel marble streaked with soft gray, now dull and badly

flaked or else replaced, must once have looked so much lighter that Thomas Coryat (in Venice in 1608) could write, "all the outward walles round about were built of pure milke-white alabas-ter" (Coryat, I, 289). The bays flanking the main doorway gain particular em-phasis from plaques of still glistening porphyry. Nowhere else in Europe at the time were outdoor walls so richly colored unless from paint, or made of such sumptuous materials (fig. 12.4).

The pilaster capitals are of the typi-cal form, with single acanthoid leaves curling under convoluted shoots below the thin, swoopingly curved abacus, a type so often repeated that exemplars must have been common in copybooks (fig. 12.5). Its popularity endured for over a generation, until more orthodox antique models took over. The chang-ing of the pattern from capital to capi-tal is a mediaeval survival, also soon to be rejected. Possibly mediaeval, but more likely no more than a conve-nience, are the slight variations in the widths of the bays, stretched here to accommodate doorways and compressed there to compensate, or squeezed at the east end where there was not quite enough space left. Like the deviation from a pure rectangle in the plan (a little narrower at the east end) and a few other slight deforma-tions, these give a lively handmade or freehand drawing freshness to the whole.

The three doorways are triumphs of Lombardo decoration. The order fram-ing them is an enrichment of that run-ning around the rest of the building, with the *rinceaux* in the pilaster panels sprouting from a spiky acanthus calyx and growing upward with wheat, flow-ers, peapods, and birds—at once live-lier and more delicate than those at S Giobbe. Florentine pediments—the first on the side is largely XIXc—float above a break in the frieze, and the ro-settes at its ends offer no guarantee of pinning them in place. Since the top of

12.3 S Maria dei Miracoli.
Facade.

each pediment slices a piece of the pedestal of the pilaster above, the lesser or weaker is allowed to damage the greater or stronger. This is a belittling of structural logic through subordinating it to what is only trimming, but in this context such behavior is not very disturbing. While Pietro used many elements decoratively, they were most successful when made to surrender much of their old meaning.

The marble panels on the canal side are of a different stone, silver gray without yellow veins. Here the pilasters above the water brought a special problem for, since the water is below the level of the street, there is a space below their pedestals that does not exist on the other side (fig. 12.6). They cannot be left hanging in the air, and to make a satisfactory ending without extending them down into the water, Pietro improvised a support by stretching (or deforming) an Ionic capital (fig. 12.7). As so often, his use of the classical vocabulary in a new context veers from tradition without finding a convincing form for a new use. What is done with the antique vocabulary is incorrect or ungrammatical, but while some artists in Florence could modify Latin into elegant Tuscan, a language with a grammar of its own, the work of the Lombardos is more often like a patois. Venetians claim that true Venetian speech is—or was, for it is disappearing—a language as old, authentic, and respectable as Tuscan. Whether this is true or not, its architectural equivalent appears at its happiest in the local late Gothic or in a few developments of the Early Renaissance rather than in the output of the hybrid Lombardo school; that is an incomplete entity, a kind of decoration and no more, a dialect or accent rather than a developed language, a vocabulary with no syntax of its own.

The entablature of the lower order has a peculiarity found also at the Scuola di S Giovanni, inclined fascias in the architrave. Barely noticeable here,

12.4 S Maria dei Miracoli. Lower story. The large panels between the pilasters are of pewtery *bardiglio*, subdivided by crosses of mottled and faded red orange, both from Verona.

12.5 S Maria dei Miracoli. Capital of main doorway.

12.6 S Maria dei Miracoli.
Rio side pilasters with
brackets.

12.7 S Maria dei Miracoli.
Rio side pilasters with
brackets.

the slope in some places is too slight to count at all. The beads in the molding below the upper fascia are so fat that to give them enough space to nestle comfortably underneath, the fascia had to have its bottom flipped out. This unorthodox detail, found also in provincial Roman work in Istria, was used much more often, more vigorously, and more consistently by Codussi and his circle, and rarely by anyone in the Lombardo circle (three times in thirty years), except Tullio as he became more independent. It could be seen here as a sign of a possible early intervention by him, as it could be also in the court of the Scuola di S Giovanni, which is in several ways more correct. Or possibly there was some nameless assistant who strayed a couple of times from the Lombardo line in this one detail.

The interior of the nave, just under 40' wide, is also sheathed in marble, pale and pewtery gray measured off by red gold bands (fig. 12.8). A frieze and a shallow cornice of limestone, partway up, is followed by more sheets of veined yellow and dove gray, divided by slightly deeper gray strips, and above that, another carved entablature, again kept suitably close to the wall. These two tiers of panels together reach about the same height as the cornice of the lower order outside, which must be the top of the work specified in the first contract. Up to this point, the work must have been carried out between early 1481 and late 1484 or early 1485.

The so-called vault of painted and gilded wood, commissioned early in 1485, is not structurally a vault at all, but a curved wood ceiling, with a compound of extruded frames and recessed panels in quarter-circles, oblongs, and squares (fig. 12.9). The squares, framing pictures of prophets, more subordinate in the whole effect than one would expect, are traditionally given to Piermaria Pennacchi and assistants (fig.

12.10). The ceiling has appeared advanced for the 1480s to some writers, who have suggested that it was put in later, perhaps as some sort of replacement, in the 1520s (Paoletti 1893–1897, II, 219; Schulz 1968, pl 4). But it is not easy to see why this would have been done so soon after the church had been complete enough to have been in regular use for years. It must have had some kind of ceiling, and it is hard to think that it was not a rich one. There could not have been a delay for lack of money. A new ceiling or new paintings to fit into the old one could perhaps have come through the unending bonanza of offerings or through some special gift, thus altering the normal chronological sequence for making ceilings containing paintings.

Under ordinary circumstances, Pennacchi would probably not have won the commission when the church was being finished in the 1480s—the ceiling has been dated as early as 1485 (Mariacher)—for he was only in his early twenties (b.1464). Nor could he have been assisted then by his son (b.1498), nor have done it in the 1520s, as also suggested, for he died in 1514 or 1515, after spending his last years in Treviso (Tramontin 1959, 26). The ceiling must be earlier than that, or the paintings must have been done by Pennacchi almost at the end of his life, or else they must have been done by his brother Gerolamo Pennacchi, or someone not even in the Pennacchi family. The best guess is that the wood ceiling was put up in the late 1480s under the supervision of Pietro Lombardo, and that the paintings were added to it, slipped into the ornamental frames that may have been made without a definite plan for future paintings.

The pattern of the ceiling frames might seem advanced in comparison with contemporary works in Florence or Rome, where the patterns were determined mainly by the structure: by the beams and coffers between them or, if based on Roman precedents, by

12.8 S Maria dei Miracoli.
Interior (lithograph by Moro
and Kier).

12.9 S Maria dei Miracoli.
Ceiling.

12.10 S Maria dei Miracoli.
Ceiling, detail.

the wood forms into which the concrete had been poured and bricks laid. Here in the Miracoli the pattern is a free conceit, unaffected by basic structure, and it shows what it is: an ornamental framework hung from wood trusses, dependent on them for support only, not for design. Nothing, then, would keep it from being an unstructural fancy of Pietro's, for it shows no details that would have to be of later date. Its freedom from structural behest need not date it after the years when such freedom had developed in Florence, for Pietro had from the beginning been indifferent to such strictures.

The "vault" has ten identical bays set on eleven wall arches that evade any rhythmical relation to them (fig. 12.11). The arches spring from brackets worked into the upper cornice and are out of phase with the windows and marble panels below (a regular meter of window, two panels, window, two panels, and so on, beginning and ending with a window). The smaller marble panels of the lower story are out of phase with the panels above them. In other words, there is no coinciding beat, and no vertical continuity except where the two side doors come directly under the windows. Everything seems as though bought by the yard, piecemeal, and then laid up haphazard, in rhythmically unrelated layers, much as in the court of the Doges' Palace. But this does not become disturbing, for there is so little sense of structure, weight, or even stability effective in the interior anyway, based as it is on ornamental surfaces of handsome materials and carving in suitable places.

The upper part may not have been foreseen when the lower part was being made. The decorative scheme may have changed partway up, and the upper zone may have been planned for something else, perhaps plain plaster for frescoes, or gilded leather, much admired at the time (Mariacher 1967, 240). The brackets for the arches that prepare for the ceiling appear to have

been afterthoughts, not normally adjusted to the marble facing. The carpenters making the ten-bay "vault" may not have been aware that it was going to rest on eleven arches put up by stonemasons operating out of a different shop; this suggests that they were being made at the same time and not that the "vault" was designed later, when what it was to rest on was there for its designer to see. Each layer comes out right at each end after running the whole length at its own independent speed. The one safe deduction is that what is there now was not all planned at once. Some change may have come as a result of the accumulated funds and new contract of 1485, when Pietro's design for a proper church may have superseded that of the model for a chapel; or, as suggested, different parts may have been worked out in different workshops.

Another possibility is that the upper decoration of the wall is quite a bit later, perhaps contemporary with the little choir balcony at the west end, which appears to be work of the late XVIc, perhaps all new then, or perhaps replaced or remodeled. If these elements are part of an otherwise unrecorded later campaign, the later date for the ceiling would offer no problem, though some reason would have to be found for its incorporation of earlier painted panels. That so much could be done at one time to an otherwise well-documented church is, however, doubtful. The *Chronichetta* of 1664 was chronologically close, and would presumably have mentioned it.

In the original model, the top of the nave must have been missing, fairly simple, or somehow unsatisfactory; otherwise there would not have been a clause in the 1485 contract commissioning Pietro to add a vault. By making a pseudo-vault of wood, he avoided the statical problems of supporting and buttressing a masonry vault on high walls no more than 2' thick, walls clearly not built to carry one. Masonry vaults were generally avoided in Venice where the weight on foundations had to be a major concern.

If a semicircle or part of a semicircle in section, the Miracoli ceiling could have been a simple carpenter's construction. Pietro chose instead to make it 2' less than half an ellipse. Probably no more than an artistic whim, this may show his airy innocence of structural procedures. More than an average carpenter's skill would have been needed to lay out this curve and cut the timbers for it; but Venice was then a city where legions of shipbuilding carpenters were used to more sophisticated curves as everyday matters. There is nothing here comparable to cutting a keel and then fitting to it ribs of ever-changing curve and length.

Above this ceiling and under the roof, which in section is slightly less than a semicircle, the arching wood trusses could absorb much of the light outward push of the ceiling and the heavier push of the lead-covered roof (fig. 12.12). As a precaution against this sideways thrust, the nave was spanned by ten iron rods that tied the side walls to one another and kept them from being shoved outward. Of course the rods show, but so did scores of others; they were so familiar in the Quattrocento that painters would show them as an everyday feature of interiors. In its 500 years, the Miracoli has had no record of threatened bulge.

Had the wood "vault" been strong enough, a roof of lead plates could have been laid on it directly. This would have been an exceptional way of covering a large wooden pseudo-vault, and would have introduced problems of statics, support, and waterproofing. A normal gable of tiles on roof rafters could not have served well here, as commonly over other vaults, because its straight rafters would have made it rise above the arched gable of the facade, and it would have had to begin

on the sides above the cornices already located at the top of the existing walls and at the bottom of the ceiling curve. A two-slope gambrel might have fitted better, though not really well; furthermore, the form was then scarcely used in Venice.

Originally there was a gutter in the top of the cornice, the normal place for one, and it sent rainwater to *glass* downspouts, made of slightly conical tubes fitted into one another and imbedded in the walls behind the marble facing (Lieberman, 230). The gutter was buried in the edge of the roof after some subsequent repairs, and the roof now sends water over the edge of the cornice in the way that is commonplace for cheaper buildings. Some of this spill runs back on the underside of the cornice and slides over the marble facing, speeding its disintegration.

Slightly docked geometric shapes, such as the not quite semicircular roof, can look incomplete to eyes conditioned to imagine regular and easily commensurable shapes, particularly in classical Renaissance architecture, where the eye is ever aware of an ideal geometry, visible or strongly implied. Much of the vocabulary of the Miracoli is classical enough to guide one's vision with that gestalt. To avoid such a threat, perhaps, Pietro hid the imperfect curve of his roof behind a perfect semicircular gable (fig. 12.13).

Around at the side of the building, it becomes clear that the new walls above those built on the first contract are based on them, both physically and artistically. Superposed orders, commonplace later, appeared here momentarily (and imperfectly) for the first time in Venice. Antiquity offered many memorable precedents, some close at Verona or Pula. There was one more distant but more relevant example, then believed to be antique: the Romanesque baptistery of Florence, with its glistening carapace of colored marble confined by two tiers of pilasters. Pietro would

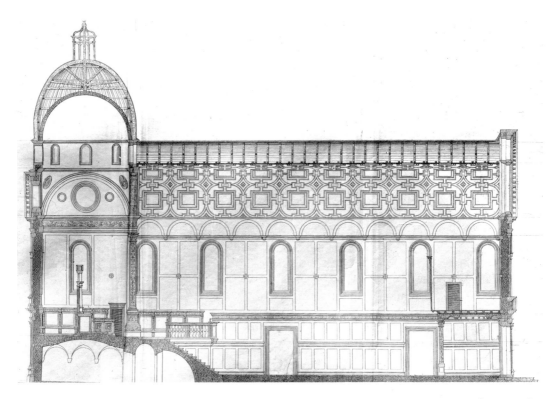

12.11 S Maria dei Miracoli.
Longitudinal section, showing lack of relation of ceiling pattern, wall arches,
windows, and marble
panels.

12.12 S Maria dei Miracoli.
Cross section, showing relation of "vault" and roof.

12.13 S Maria dei Miracoli.
Air view.

12.14 S Maria dei Miracoli.
Flank (from Cicognara-
Diedo-Selva).

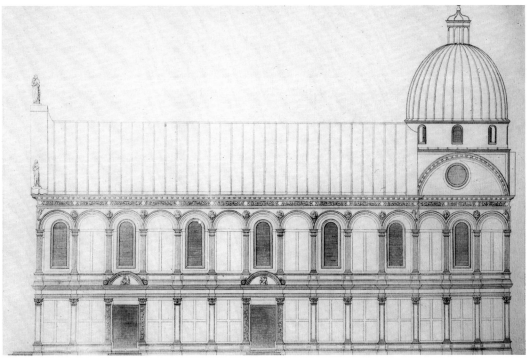

have known it well, also the showy marble veneer of the front of S Miniato, and probably that of other Florentine Romanesque monuments as well.

The new upper zone of the wall does not repeat the lower exactly, for its pilasters, with awkward capitals uncanonically Ionic above Corinthian, do not carry an entablature but a row of arches, recalling specifically and perhaps deliberately the arrangement on the baptistery of Florence. The upper entablature has to hover above these rippling arches without any apparent support; Lombardo indifference again to making parts look as though they might be working together, unshackling them instead from their structural duties or any symbolic portrayal of them (fig. 12.14).

There is not enough space at the top of the capitals for the arches swinging in to them from each side to land there complete. Hence, as so often, the outermost moldings, scaly boa-like quarter-rounds without legitimate antique parentage (but similar to earlier efforts such as the top of the Arsenal Gate) cut each other off, and end in an unsupported stiletto point (fig. 12.15). The archivolts, therefore, seem not so much to be supported as to be hanging. Circles with angels in relief are shoved into the spandrel clefts above this collision.

Since the front door called for a bay wider than the others, on this upper tier the middle bay called for an arch wider than its neighbors, and was given half an ellipse. To reach the same height, that established by the normal semicircular arches elsewhere, the narrower bays on either side had to have their slightly narrower semicircular arches stilted. This stretching and shrinking of adjacent arches instinctively expected to match gives a bouncy vitality to the sequence, much as wilder variations had animated many Romanesque facades, or the arches across the front of S Mark's.

At the two front corners, the pilasters have to meet a special condition. Since each story has a full pilaster at the end, two pilasters have to touch at each corner, one on each face (fig. 12.16). Together these are naturally read as two sides of a stout square pier whose other two sides must be embedded in the wall. This imagined pier counts as much stronger than the ordinary pilasters along each side that, since they stand out only 4″, seem much less solid, stuck on rather than sunk in. No depth greater than the 4″ is implied. Having nothing to do but look nice, they seem quite up to their task. The duality, working vs. non-working, makes neither confusion nor tension here, as structural vs. antistructural contradictions sometimes can. There is no rule, only an instinctive judgment by the eye, variable from case to case. Here the difference is so clear that it is accepted without even being thought over. There is no more than a pianissimo clash that in no way disturbs, but instead subtly energizes the whole.

Because the row of arches stops at the corner, only one archivolt lands on the pilaster capital there, and leaves half of the top of the abacus unoccupied. On each free face of the building, a sliver of blank wall is thus left beyond the arch, and it grows wider as the archivolt curves away. The reliefs of Gabriel and Mary applied to the corner spandrels on the main facade do not distract the eye from the seeming weakness, just above the pseudo-powerful two-pilaster corner piers. The seeming loss of strength comes from the lack of any structural or effective pseudo-structural member where—having been so clearly prepared for—such a conductor of force would be expected.

In this context, the exposed thin marble veneer, all there is at this crucial area, looks feeble. The oblong slabs are laid up vertically in what may be a deliberately antistructural way, to demonstrate that they are no more than a veneer, as Ruskin believed had been done at S Mark's. It is doubtful that he was right, and more doubtful that any such sophisticated idea controlled the thoughts of the sheathers of the Miracoli who, more likely, were just following the precedent of S Mark's without troubling their heads as to whether it had any such logical principle behind it. Pietro Lombardo and Ruskin did not think of architecture in the same way.

The semicircular gable—its top is about 38' above the campo—brings a new character to the facade, and must come from the second phase, along with the curved ceiling. The semicircle is fancifully garnished with circles: a large non-Gothic rose window which lets light into the end of the nave, plus what look like three smaller windows (fig 12.17). Only one of these lets light into the space between the ceiling and the roof, for the other two are glazed dummies. There are also two discs of porphyry surrounded by eleven smaller ones of different colored stones, entwined in a snaking band of mosaic of a kind much admired and long repeated in Venice. Eleven is an odd number to have chosen—it cannot have been easy to lay out—and the reason for it may be that small discs of just that size were available from slicing antique shafts, and eleven was the number that fitted best.

Although the rose seems as low as a sinking sun, it is not low enough in the semicircle to keep from crowding the circles above it into the arching cornice. This last gives no sense of getting support from below. The feeling of instability is aggravated by the rosettes, shoved out to the very ends of the main cornice, where they have to overhang the solid block of the building and yet support more than life-size stone angels (perhaps by Tullio). Furthermore, the relation of the ends of the big bowed cornice to the corner piers is not an integrated or a stable one; they do not jibe.

The whole facade has been seen as directly inspired by S Mark's, but directly is far too strong a word here. Only the veneer and perhaps the curved gable could be directly related, and either one could have been thought up independently, whether S Mark's was there or not. Arching gables were familiar locally; old maps show a similar semicircular-fronted church nestled next to the Frari, though without the Miracoli's semicylindrical roof; there are several more in the Veneto, such as the cathedral at Oderzo; and a score in Dalmatia and its islands, such as S Josep at Hvar.

Below the half-circle of extravagance at the top, the facade is almost square, in one of the scattered instances suggesting that Pietro might have been guided by ideal proportions in laying out his designs. He did not carry such ideas very far (Lieberman, 158ff, disagrees), and there is no easy awareness here of a set of harmonic proportions underlying the whole. No such ideal dominates the form of the exterior of the nave; a longitudinal slice of cylinder laid like a lid on a long block. The block is proportioned approximately five to two, about 90' by 36', and cannot be perceived as an ideal ratio since the five and the two cannot be seen together except in steep and deforming perspective amid a host of distracting details. That need not be a conclusive argument, however, since some Renaissance designers could be fascinated by ratios as beautiful and even virtuous in themselves, regardless of whether it was easy or even possible to perceive them with the eye. Pietro Lombardo, if he be rightly understood here, would not have been concerned with such an abstract intellectual conceit.

The decisions of 1484–85 covered not only the building of the upper half of the nave but also the whole chancel. A difficult problem came with the planning of the latter, for the site so suited to a narrow nave left only one tightly limited direction in which the church

12.15 S Maria dei Miracoli. Window of upper zone, not fitted concentrically to the arch above, which is higher like a raised eyebrow. The extra space is shaped like a sickle. The window jambs, ornamented with long stalks of laurel, are splayed outward, like many mediaeval windows, to let in more light.

12.16 S Maria dei Miracoli. Condition at upper front corner.

12.17 S Maria dei Miracoli. Upper facade.

might grow—toward the space in back—and without even the narrowest of sacristies beside or behind, there was room for only a small chancel two-thirds as wide as the nave (fig. 12.18).

The solution lay in an ingenious and unfamiliar arrangement, a chancel on top of a sacristy. The sacristy could not be put in an ordinary basement story because it was a sacristy, a consecrated part of a building, a part by long tradition not underground; and also because Venice was a city on wet foundations and had no basements. Since the sacristy could not be sunk, the chancel would have to be raised. Since no projection at the east seems to have been planned in the original model, the new arrangement must be entirely Pietro's; it was ordered by the building committee in late 1484 because of the unforeseen increases in attendance and in funds, and the decision to expand the oratory to a complete convent church (fig. 12.19).

In other parts of Italy chancels had sometimes been raised above the level of the nave and this had been done at S Mark's, though not conspicuously. Chancels raised more than three steps (traditionally always an odd number) are found in only a few other churches in the city. Crypts below them, even fewer, were low, dark, damp, and unimportant, again with the semiexception of S Mark's. Such crypts were not sacristies, and when the Miracoli was going up few crypts were being built anywhere, while sacristies were taking on greater importance. Making the space below the chancel a sacristy was an original idea, either Pietro's or his committee's. Those concerned with the planning must have known mainland churches with chancels dramatically raised, such as S Zeno at Verona, the cathedral at Modena, or perhaps S Miniato at Florence, a richly polychrome building that might have been to Pietro's taste. Not a Venetian, not brought

up in Venice, when faced with the problem of contriving a small church where a picture had to be given an impressive setting, he had several examples to look to, and none could have offered anything more inspiring than the memory of Mantegna's Madonna looming high at the end of S Zeno at Verona.

To set the chancel on top of a low sacristy, it had to be raised only 8' above the nave, which was already three steps above the street. The floor of the sacristy was dropped about 2', four steps below the nave but still safely above the water level (then, less safely now). Instead of with an ordinary beamed ceiling, Pietro covered the sacristy with a flattish vault, not easy to build, but expertly done. Perhaps it was not thought suitable either statically or monumentally in this idealized little building to put the altar and other marble furnishings, as well as the marble floor of the chancel, on ordinary wooden beams.

For the new chancel he may have thought back to a monument surely familiar to him in Florence: Brunelleschi's Old Sacristy at S Lorenzo, a small square with a high dome on pendentives, that may already have inspired him or his patron at S Giobbe. The new chancel is nearly square, about 25' wide, some 12' narrower than the nave from which it opens. Its lightweight brick dome rises from a low drum with seven small windows—the campanile blocks the space where the eighth would be—easier to build and geometrically neater than the dome-cutting windows of S Giobbe or some of the Byzantinesque examples. The drum rests on pendentives that are once again ornamented with round reliefs of the Evangelists.

The outside of the masonry dome is hidden under a dummy dome of lead plates on wood framing, pulled up 6' higher and capped with a little lantern or *cupolino* in homage to the domes of S Mark's (fig. 12.20). Without this

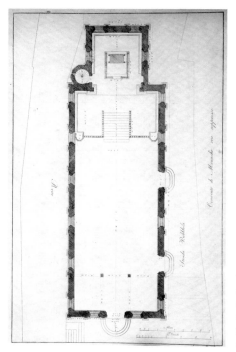

12.18 S Maria dei Miracoli. Plan, nave, and chancel, with indication of narrow boundaries of site.

12.19 S Maria dei Miracoli. East end. The drum stands on what appears to be part of a marble-faced cube whose exposed corners contain and conceal the pendentives. The arches bounding the pendentives reappear outside as moldings and enclose 4′ *oculi* once filled with stained glass (now replaced). Because of the thickness of the wall, and the wide splay of their jambs, the windows on the east end miss the center of their arches and consequently, in the rear view of the church, they look oddly cross-eyed.

12.20 S Maria dei Miracoli. Chancel exterior and campanile.

steeper false dome, the true dome would have looked low, and undramatic if not insignificant, when it ought to be the climax of the exterior, emphasizing the altar and the miracle-working picture below, the heart of the entire work.

The back outer corners of the nave block are treated like those at the front, with a full pilaster on each face. In the tight corner where the side of the chancel meets the back wall of the nave, a new problem appeared: the arch of the upper story is sliced down to a mere vestige at its springing, and the pilaster is no more than a sliver, barely emerging from the corner. This sliver can be seen as part of a solid square pier buried deep in the wall, unlike the other pilasters which are thin members applied to the surface. A square pier sunk in a wall is anomalous and this problem of a pilaster in the tight quarters of an inner corner had been bothering Italian architects, beginning with Brunelleschi. It is not well solved here, not nearly as well as it had been earlier in the corners of the atrium of S Giovanni Evangelista where, there being more space, each wall was given half a pilaster of the same thickness as all the others. There the effect is of a full pilaster folded to fit into an inner corner; here at the Miracoli, it is of a heavy pier imprisoned in the walls.

The solution or, rather, the avoidance of a real solution of this problem is so different from the kind of architectural thinking that chose the folded pilasters for the inner corners at S Giovanni Evangelista, with their strong, discreet, structural decorum, that it raises difficult questions, largely concerning the putative role of Tullio. It would seem perverse of Pietro, had he been the one to arrive at the corner solution at S Giovanni, to regress to the awkward illiteracy here less than ten years later. He was a man of about fifty, successful and kept busy, no longer an amateur but not yet senile,

merely indifferent to structural decorum. But he could not be ignorant of one solution if he had already used it at S Giovanni. Someone there and someone here at the Miracoli must have had the responsibility, and it is hard to believe they were the same person. It is not hard to believe that Pietro did not care much; though the Miracoli was a wonderful commission, his interest in it was perhaps confined to the surface sheathing and reliefs—and they are indeed superb.

The little campanile is covered with the same marbles arranged in the same sort of panels, measured off and bound to the rest by similar strips and cornices. But, not absorbed into the otherwise compact composition of geometrical shapes, it speaks with a different character and is so picturesque from the water and the bridge in back that it dominates the more temperate composition of the rear of the church. The campanile's performance is one of mediaeval irregularity and surprise, certainly not one of Renaissance equilibration. Compositionally it is the least classic and most mediaeval element in the ensemble.

Nowhere can the quintessence of the art of the Lombardos be seen to such advantage as in the decoration of the presbytery, for nowhere else is the workmanship more deft or finer; nowhere is the ornament such a happy mingling of abstract form, fresh invention, and charmingly observed flora and fauna; and nowhere was the replacing of implied structural facts by carefree decoration less hampered. In every way in this church there is a ripening and a refining of that other similar chancel Pietro had added to S Giobbe ten to twelve years before.

In the nave, the eye can slide along easily over the smooth marble, more polished then than now, a surface that reflects glossily outward without implying any mass behind. In contrast, the painted, gilded, and far from flat ceiling insistently shows itself as something of quite another kind—here sunk in, there pushed out—equivocal as to implicit mass and depth. Visually, one senses a jolt between it and the wall. To find that some think the ceiling an afterthought is no surprise, though probably it comes from contemporary but uncoordinated ideas. Different though they are, less dichotomy is sensed between nave and chancel, the latter known to be an afterthought, but a better harmonized one. Still, once one is aware that the nave had been conceived as an oratory, complete in itself, and that the sanctuary was an addition not foreseen (Lieberman's deduction of this is surely right), one senses them as two entities, ingeniously joined—but still two.

The simple cubical space in the chancel is immediately clear, and above it and continuous with it comes part of another cube sheared off at the corners by parts of a big sphere (forming the pendentives); above that there is a low cylinder, capped by a neatly fitting hemisphere. Together these join in a sequence of straight and curved, simple, clear, geometrical, and comprehensible shapes in an age-old combination familiar from S Mark's and small Byzantinizing churches in Venice (without the drum), and Brunelleschi's Old Sacristy at S Lorenzo (with a different dome). Surely it is one of the most satisfying of all the compound spaces in the repertory of monumental architecture. Here it quietly asserts its power and grace without effort, and marshals an endless interplay of ornament—man-made carving and nature's veining in the marble—into an accompaniment in perfect tune, varied only by the different timbres of the different materials and kinds of decoration.

The walls, again of polished brass- and pewter-colored marbles, are set mirror flat. Silvery gray veins shimmer through them, as through most of the marbles everywhere. The pendentives,

flexed triangles on the surface of a sphere, cannot take their completely true shape when made with flat slabs, and here their sphericity is only approximated by a sequence of moderate-size flat planes of the same marble (fig. 12.21). It matters little, for with curves of the moldings arching up their sides and across their tops to mark the defining edges, and with deep-set circles filling most of the center of each pendentive, no big stretches of flat surface that should be curved are left, and furthermore, small areas, with or without such curvature, cannot easily be checked by eyes 30' below.

The drum is faced more easily because it has only the simple curve of a cylinder, and flat stone plates set around the rim lend themselves to it with less trouble. The dome, alone with a seamless finish of plain matte white plaster, takes the light differently, and comes almost as a hushed resolution to so much busy richness, floating weightlessly above its ring of windows (fig. 12.22).

The steps leading up to the sanctuary were once fewer and steeper, though not the fourteen the young Virgin was traditionally said to have climbed to be presented in the Temple, as sometimes claimed for this church dedicated to her (fig. 12.23). More than a third as wide as the nave, they lead to a zone still part of the nave space but functionally already part of the presbytery. The officiating priest, sometimes with two deacons, and members of the important patrician families who had paid for the church or had relatives among the nuns, would have been seated in this privileged section.

The pale gray and white paneling here is edged with bands of soft pink Verona framed in white styles and rails, and so are the small polygonal pulpits of dappled *breccia*, protruding at either end above the low doors to the sacristy (fig. 12.24). This front area

12.21 S Maria dei Miracoli.
Chancel. Marble-faced pendentive bounded by richly
carved moldings that also
bound the roundel with
S John the Evangelist.

12.22 S Maria dei Miracoli.
View up into chancel dome.

12.23 S Maria dei Miracoli.
The wide steps lead up to
the platform in front of the
chancel. The low doors in
the corners lead down to the
sacristy.

12.24 S Maria dei Miracoli. Rail of raised end of nave, with spindle balusters and pulpit on bracket over sacristy door.

12.25 S Maria dei Miracoli. A double baluster.

12.26 S Maria dei Miracoli. Part of parapet around altar.

is closed off by a railing of slender balusters of spindle shape, one of the earliest uses of this Early Renaissance invention first popularized in Venice (fig. 12.25). The marble floor at the top of the steps is worked with a millimeter-deep fine-scale pattern in pseudo-niello. The new altar (1887) is enclosed by an elegant, lightly pierced parapet, part of the original furnishing of white marble with colored inlays (fig. 12.26).

From the forespace, the sanctuary proper is entered through a grand arch twice as high (36') as wide, outshining its model at S Giobbe. The archivolt, flushed with fruit, flowers, and foliage, swings up until it is tangent to the curve of the ceiling. The arch and the entablature from which it springs are borne on capitals so deeply undercut that the single leaves stand out white against deep shadow, a contrast familiar from Byzantine work and here possibly inspired by it, quite unlike the more sculptural and more Florentine capitals at S Giobbe (figs. 12.27 and 12.28). The pilasters, with their symmetrical arabesques entwining eagles, flaming urns, ribbons, garlands, foliate sprays, flowers, and much more, are bolder and crisper than usual, and catch sharp lights and cast small shadows affirming special importance for what they ornament. But busy though moldings and panels are with yards of fine-scale carving, making thousands of little highlights and shadows, these are almost always played off against broad areas of smooth marble veneer, ornamented only by its soft veining.

Unaided, neither the first high altar nor the second (by Girolamo Campagna, after 1602) could have dominated the visual ensemble amid so much busy all-over splendor; but when it was essential that it should do so, the symbolic and liturgical heart of the church would become its visual climax through the color of the flowers, the sumptuous vestments, the glittering

12.27 S Maria dei Miracoli. Capital.

12.28 S Giobbe. Capital.

12.29 S Maria dei Miracoli.
Bottom of support of chancel arch—base with plinth,
pedestal, band of figure
sculpture, and cushion.

gold of the chalice, cruets, monstrance,
and candlesticks, the brightness of the
flames, and of course the miracle-working picture with its frame and background of gold (now dark and dirty).

The sanctuary is more complex in its
ornament than in its form, and this
shows nowhere more than on the pilasters of the grand arch where the Lombardos' gourmandizing of ornament became most intense. The richest part is
at the bottom, nearest the altar, where
most eyes would most often be looking
(fig. 12.29). Classical bases are worked
with garland and guilloche. The pedestals below them frame panels with
whorls of leafage in medium relief. Below the pedestals comes the most original and extravagant of all, a gently
flaring and somehow soft-seeming wide
band, only half-seen behind a throng of
putti, little dragons, mermaids, and
merboys sitting on their tails, all
among sprays of oak and of greenery
nature has not yet got around to evolv-
ing—all standing on a fat marble cushion that bulges out between the fastenings of its once gilded and bronzed
silky slipcover now sadly damaged.
(Inside Alberti's church at Rimini
Agostino di Duccio had already stood
piers on soft baskets bulging with
grapes.) Neither here at the Miracoli
nor elsewhere does the ornament have
iconographical meaning. Its extravagant
repertory must come from the untram-
meled exuberance of a few virtuoso
carvers, one of whom is distinguishable
by his outstandingly odd and personal
forms not yet identified in any other
work.

Classically impure, this is, moreover,
architecturally absurd; those playful
creatures may be only incidental applied trimming but the cushions are
there as structural support. To a mind
limited by logic they are outrageous,
but their appeal is away from logic and
toward fantasy, as proper a province of
art as reason, less often found and even

less often accepted in architecture than in the other arts. Familiarity with the creations of the Lombardos will show that an undercurrent of quirkiness quite often rises to the surface, routing reason for a moment or two (Frankl, 188). In this carefree context, only a little effort is needed to bring about a brief suspension of common sense. The mass between the pedestal of the pilaster and the nonrigid cushion is so big and so much wider on every side than the pedestal it carries, that any notions of strain or instability are not empathetically felt; any objection would have to come from reason alone, and reason alone is not comfortable here.

Whoever planned the Miracoli's dome on pendentives was a serious architect, or someone closely following the ideas of a serious architect, or even an enlightened amateur. The same can hardly be said for the designer of the piers of the chancel arch; he was a decorator with engaging inventiveness, but architecturally ignorant, innocent, or uninterested. Can the same man have done both? Or were there two men? The work that stands farthest from the greater part of Pietro's output is this dome. As it is almost a duplication of the dome at S Giobbe, except for the drum, the explanation of the architect-decorator duality—if there is one—must be sought there. One possibility has already been proposed, that the idea for the dome of S Giobbe may have originated not with Pietro but with Doge Moro, Pietro merely carrying it out. If he could build a dome on pendentives there, he could do it here.

Another possibility is a bit stronger: both Pietro's domes could follow another model, that which Mauro Codussi put on his church at S Michele in Isola. If the date of the dome of S Giobbe could be fixed, the others might fall into line, but the date is cloaked in doubt. The Miracoli dome was begun after 1485 and finished before 1489. The dome of Codussi's S

Michele was made almost exactly ten years earlier. Were it not for S Giobbe, there could be no doubt about precedence and influence, but S Giobbe *is* there. The most consistent sequence is S Michele, S Giobbe, S Maria dei Miracoli, but the known facts suggest a shift to S Giobbe, S Michele, the Miracoli.

When Canon Casola wrote in 1494, "I have not found in any city so many beautiful and ornate churches as there are in Venice. . . . The poorest parish church there is more ornate than the finest in Milan" (Casola, 137, 138), he not only put into words the nouveau-riche taste of the Milanese and other North Italians for ornateness as the highest good, but also showed that he cannot have visited most of the really newest churches in Venice, for most of the churches surviving from the end of the XVc were either still unfinished or else belonged to the sober, anti-Lombardo school of Codussi and his followers, far from what Casola and his compatriots would have admired as ornate. Some churches had splendid paintings and rich fittings, but with the exception of the Miracoli, none was ornate in its architecture—or not yet. Casola may not have distinguished between architecture and nonarchitectural enrichments. He would probably not have been concerned with the fact that the Miracoli was not a *parish* church, though as a churchman he might have found that out. Surely he would have seen it, for it must already have been one of the sights of the town shown off to visitors, and surely it would have been just what he admired.

13 | SCUOLA DI S MARCO

By 1489 or shortly before, the important tombs, the atrium of S Giovanni, and the Miracoli were finished. Pietro was intermittently busy supervising work under Rizzo at the Palazzo Ducale when an important new commission came to him, the Scuola Grande di S Marco. The circumstances under which he undertook it are not clear, and the strange and often altered building does not supply many clues.

There were two classes of men's religious confraternities: the scuole grandi, and the many scuole piccole. The first consisted of a few hundred solid citizens, such as tradesmen and lawyers, and a few of the nobility and clergy (not allowed to be officers or serve on committees). Manual workers were not accepted as members. Less restricted as to class, a scuola piccola could be as small as thirty men, usually in the same trade, rather like a guild; or men in the same foreign colony, Albanians, Armenians, Greeks, or other non-Catholic Christians. The treasury of a scuola grande paid for funerals for the poorer members, dowries for their daughters, or endowments if they chose to become nuns, aid to widows, and other good works, particularly in times of war, famine, or plague. A few scuolas accumulated notable funds from initiation fees, annual dues, bequests, and gifts, and all this was almost always meticulously administered. Some came into possession of considerable real estate, and some became important corporate patrons of the arts, not spending all their money on good works but some on a grand building and appropriate cycles of paintings for its walls.

In general, the layout of the Scuola di S Marco follows that of the older building on the site, at right angles to the Church of SS Giovanni e Paolo, which had burned down on Holy Thursday 1485. Since it was consumed in four hours (Malipiero, II, ii, 675), it must have been mostly of wood, like much of mediaeval Venice. Founded in 1437, the scuola had had a late Gothic building begun by Giovanni Buon and finished by his son Bartolomeo. Some refurbishing, perhaps by Rizzo, was begun before the fire, and scaffolding or piled lumber may have fueled the flames. Now it matters little what had been the Buons' and what Rizzo's, though it is deplorable that the latter's pentagonal pulpit and helical stairway, made from drawings by Gentile Bellini, burned with everything else. Friar Fabri, writing in 1488 from notes taken in 1484, said, "they are doing it over and on new and very fine foundations" (Fabri, 77). Either he had heard of the fire after he left, or else some work, maybe Rizzo's, had already been begun on the foundations before the fire (or some dates have been misrecorded?). There is little reason to believe that the foundations for the new building were all new, for foundations in Venice are always wet and do not burn. Tommaso Temanza, a conscientious architectural historian writing in the mid-XVIIIc, said that the new building was built "on the remains of the old" (Temanza 1778, 93), which implies reuse of its foundations. Unreliable Sabellico, writing hurriedly in 1489-90, said that the scuola had been rebuilt "of more expensive material" (Sabellico 1502, 237v). It might have been more accurate to say that it was *being* rebuilt, or being completed.

In 1487 and 1488, Gregorio Antonio da Padova, a horde of assistants, and Giovanni Candi (for carpentry) were engaged to adapt what could be mended of the Scuola di S Marco, to save walls worth saving, put up new side and back walls where needed, and set foundations for some new columns. When he had to provide additional interior space, Gregorio Antonio may have added a bay or two in front of what was—or had been—already there, but just what happened is not clear.

The fire would not have damaged the old foundations seriously, and many yards of them must have been used again. (Both the older foundations and the newer ones presumably added in front are, so far as is known, typical, and in good condition today, after holding up their building for some 500 years.) The governors of the scuola must have been in a hurry to have something usable soon. For two years the city made a monthly grant (perhaps more like a loan) to help pay for the work and keep it going (Puppi-Puppi, 196). The scuola, though considered wealthy, did not always have enough funds to meet its payroll.

Gregorio Antonio cannot have done much more than repair the walls and add to the foundations, for he was active only from 1487 to 1489, when Pietro Lombardo, who had been called on the year before to supply stone, was given a contract, together with his sons and Giovanni Buora, presumably to complete the building by putting up the walls and roof. Pietro must have just completed his work at the Miracoli, and must have been enjoying a very high reputation. Buora may have been important here too, but just how is not clear.

Since the scheme is so simple—a main hall with two rows of columns supporting a hall above, next to a smaller room (the *albergo*) for smaller business meetings—it need not be attributed to Gregorio Antonio or Pietro Lombardo or some combination of the two (fig. 13.1). It could have been produced at almost any time by almost anyone, architect or officer of the scuola. The same scheme served for hundreds of years. The only nonstandard features were an old Chapel of Peace (Martinelli, 157; drawing by A Visentini, BM, AUV III, 116–17), somehow merged into the lower floor of the *albergo* wing, and, somewhere, that circular stairway of Rizzo's.

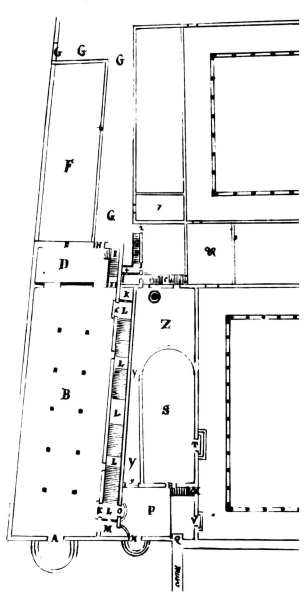

13.1 Scuola di S Marco. Plan of ground floor of entire complex, with stairway (destroyed and now rebuilt) between main block and *albergo*, and Cappella della Pace under the *albergo* proper on the floor above.

Work was well along—surely the governors of the scuola were pressing—when the contract with Pietro was signed in 1489; it may have been a second contract (not unusual). Pietro's columns for the great hall were finished, but not in place. By 1490, just as the room was about to be covered, trouble broke out. After having been ordered to finish the job in one month—perhaps impossible, and perhaps deliberately impossible—the Lombardos were abruptly dropped. Neither their names nor that of their principal assistant, almost a partner-carver, Giovanni Buora, were ever mentioned in the scuola's papers again. They may have been too extravagant, having just left the prodigal Miracoli, or they may have strayed too far from the prescribed scheme—the contract had specified that the model must be respected—or else they were too busy elsewhere to give as much attention here as the governors wanted. Mauro Codussi was called in to examine the work, and probably also Rizzo, a member of the scuola. A change of architects resulted, and the commission now went to Codussi. He may have intervened in the upper part of the facade, but it is so out of tune with the rest of his work that it seems likely that some model was left that the directors wanted followed, and that Codussi was obliging.

Asymmetry naturally resulted, since the two adjacent parts of the front reflected the two parts inside, the large hall on the left and the smaller *albergo* on the right. The Cappella della Pace was back some yards and did not show on the facade. Each part is symmetrical in itself and makes use of repetitions, variations, and miscellaneous relationships with the other. The whole is as rich and as confused as the court of the Palazzo Ducale, to which it is, however, little related in style.

One novelty is the frieze-like band that runs between the capitals; coils of foliage at the end of each section turn out to be flourishes of the tails of two gryphons snarling at one another across a porphyry circle that each steadies with one paw. Pietro had already used the same motif for the upper frieze of the Miracoli exterior. That they echo the frieze of the Temple of Antoninus and Faustina in the Roman Forum is clear, but does not prove that any of the carvers had ever seen it, for even in antiquity the motif was popular and spread quickly. (The ever-closed museum of the Seminario in Venice has a IIc provincial quotation of this motif "of unknown provenance.") The entablature above it at the scuola is almost identical to that of S Giovanni Evangelista, even in its ornamental moldings, but here more refined, perhaps a later work from the same shop. Like those of S Giovanni and the Miracoli, the fascias of the architrave are lightly inclined, a non-Lombardo trace in a Lombardo context.

The bay with the main doorway won particular emphasis: it is wider, it frames a deep-shadowed recess, it projects farther, not only upward with its pediment pushing into the next story but also outward with its freestanding columns (fig. 13.2). Their shafts suggest that they were old ones put to new use, for they reach only a little more than a third of the height needed, the rest being pieced out by a cylindrical pedestal on top of a square one (fig. 13.3). Columns taken from Torcello were used on the adjacent front of the church (Zava Bocazzi, 30), and one can see that the facade of the scuola was intended to match it in the height of the cornices. But nothing shows a common origin for the shafts.

Another peculiarity comes from their exaggerated entasis: they bulge before becoming slimmer. This is more like an unsure imitation of an antique model than an antique shaft reused. Furthermore, a dozen columns made in 1489, used inside, have the same cigar-shaped shafts. The facade shafts could

have survived from before the fire, and those inside could have copied their form, but that has the ring of an over-contrived hypothesis. Those outside were probably made the way they are to go where they are. (In Roman times, provincials sometimes made the same mistake.) When, in another generation, architects in Venice knew and used the correct Roman shape, often learned from books (Krinsky 1967, 38; lst Vitruvius, 1486; *ms* copy of Vitruvius known in Venice by 1474), columns with the double entasis bulge were still made, and not only in amateur, provincial, or wayward work, but intermittently in the most respectable surroundings until the Neoclassic purifiers took over in the late XVIIIc.

The arch-pediment over the door flexes not only a length of cornice but a length of frieze, and it frames an earlier work not at home in such surroundings, a relief of S Mark venerated by a dozen cowled members of the scuola. The newest feature is the marble crest rimming the arch, an adaptation of the frothy Gothic cresting on S Mark's, a suitable quotation for a scuola dedicated to the same saint (fig. 13.4). Gryphons take the place of the usual rosette and honeysuckle at the ends, and support figures a few sizes too small, perhaps also leftovers from an earlier scheme. Winged leaf-children clasp a pedestal at the top for a figure of Charity known to have been saved from the old building of Bartolomeo Buon. (Erosion from polluted air has damaged it more in the last 30 years than anything in the preceding 450.)

The doorway is complicated, even prolix, with its two arches (pediment and overdoor) and its orders in three different sizes. The keystone, with scroll and a particularly engaging cornucopia-carrying cherub, larger than life, carved by Giovanni Buora (Munman 1976, 49), misses the architrave it should appear to uphold by half a foot. Most extravagant of all are the freestanding columns, whose separateness

13.2 Scuola di S Marco.
Main doorway.

is stressed by their difference—shaft plus two pedestals—from the pilasters just behind them, here (and only here) of yellow marble, with purple discs at a level conspicuously different from all the others.

Superposed pedestals would be redundant if understood simply as two pedestals, one on top of the other. The upper, however, can shift its role and be taken as the lower component of a column shaft, despite what can be seen as the base of the smooth section above. Though not common, such a division of plain and carved column was no novelty in antiquity or in early Mediaeval or Early Renaissance Venice; Pietro himself had used something similar for his Marcello tomb inside the adjacent church. Since the pilaster behind continues on through the combined height of sure shaft and putative round pedestal, it reinforces the possibility of accepting shaft and pedestal as one continuous unit.

Prolix may be the best word, and prolixity pushed to this extreme seems farther than Pietro would go. Some have seen the hard-to-trace hand of Buora here, but he is more easily seen as sculptor than as architect (Munman 1976, 49, 58n21). Such extravagance is not found in other works that can be given to him, and it is probably a mistake to try to force this doorway on any one designer. Since the entire front is a passementerie of the ideas of several men, the doorway too can ask for mixed authorship. In contrast, the doorway to the space before the *albergo*, carved by 1490 but not yet set in place, is not only simpler, but more appropriate for its lesser function and, above all, much clearer (fig. 13.5).

What insistently calls for comment is the set of large reliefs in the four bays without doors: paired perspective pictures, two of lions on the left, and two of scenes from the story of S Mark on the right. The latter must have been

13.3 Scuola di S Marco. Right, pilaster of door frame. Left, bottom of shaft, base, round pedestal, and square pedestal.

13.4 Scuola di S Marco. Cresting of main doorway.

13.5 Scuola di S Marco. Lower half of *albergo* wing with relief pictures by Tullio Lombardo.

begun before November 1489, since they are mentioned then in a contract. Each pair is worked out with a common vanishing point on the center line of the doors, between the two panels, and the simultaneous presence of these two separate axes, one of the main hall, one of the *albergo,* splits any comprehensive view of the whole, and insists on the individuality of the two parts of the facade. All four panels show deeply receding halls of non-Lombardesque architecture.

The lions stand on steps at the back of a barrel-vaulted hall flanked by bare piers. Everything fits under an arch which itself fits into the wall space left between the pilasters of the main order, an area matching the arched recess around the main doorway. A plain background of atmospheric blue-gray marble suggests undefined distance.

The scenes from the legend of S Mark, his baptism, and his healing of S Anianus, on the *albergo* front, are set in arcaded halls with flat ceilings, different from those for the lions. Their frames of pilasters and architraves do not fit neatly into their bays, and there is a band of leftover space at the top that tends to be read as a frieze, although not followed by the requisite cornice; the band with the gryphons is there instead, and above that, redundantly, another architrave. Somewhere, someone's mind must have been changed, or new circumstances must have led to a hasty ungrammatical improvisation.

The groups of figures, by Tullio or a close follower, are composed to face in toward the door, complementing the convergence of perspective lines. The figures are carved on squares of marble only a quarter as high as the space available. The figures seem inadequate in scale, drowned in their excess lebensraum. The squares, whiter than anything else on the facade, may first have been intended for some other

place, in some other scheme begun perhaps before the fire of 1485, and only later made to serve in this imperfect arrangement as a second choice.

The accurate perspective construction of the settings, particularly those of the lions, invites our eyes back some 20′. The real light and shade play over the imagined and flattened architecture, and cannot act as they would were they playing over real architecture 20′ deep. Also, there is no escaping the refusal of our two eyes to move as they would in readjusting the axes of their separate lines of sight in the normal binocular way to focus successively on elements some feet nearer or farther off. They cannot, since everything *is* near, and all in focus at once, the focus needed for one thing at one distance. These phenomena destroy any illusion of real depth. While the intellect has been cleverly invited to go in deep, the senses will not be fooled into judging more than the couple of inches they know to be the true depth. The fine situation of the front of the scuola at the end of a big campo allows one to try looking at the reliefs from a variety of distances; but no distance here can lend enchantment. The failed illusionism is ingenious and playfully enjoyable, and the fact that it cannot fool adds to the enjoyment.

A typical example of non–trompe l'oeil perspective relief had already been tried by Tullio Lombardo. He had been commissioned to make a tabernacle-reliquary for a phial of the Precious Blood brought from Constantinople, where it was once carried in processions only by the emperor himself. It was given to the friars of the Frari in 1480 and they decided to have it enshrined in a tabernacle affixed to the wall of the sacristy. Not itself a work of architecture, the tabernacle is a low relief depicting architecture, an imaginary building with ample empty space covered with a dome on pendentives based on Tullio's father's S

13.6 Tullio Lombardo. Tabernacle of the Precious Blood in the sacristy of the Frari.

Giobbe or one by Codussi (fig. 13.6). What makes it relevant here is not the representation of the dome but the deep architectural interior below it, shown in accurate perspective in low relief and emphasized spatially by showing some back elements partly hidden by overlapping nearer ones. The idea is not far from the perspective relief pictures at the Scuola di S Marco. The small tabernacle is properly like a picture on a wall; the big facade reliefs do not seem to be in their right place.

In contrast to Florentine, Venetian architecture had long had a pictorial quality, variously ill-defined but always accepted as one of its prime traits. Never had "pictorial" been so literally true as here at the scuola, where pictures of architecture are worked into real architecture. Though it is often found beguiling today, another century found this would-be trompe l'oeil outrageous. G. E. Street, mediaevalist, architect, and respected writer on architecture pronounced it vile, "the lowest depth to which architecture has ever reached" (Street, cited in Honour 1965, 85). Neither he nor any other Victorian critic castigated S Mark's for the mosaic pictures worked into its architecture, though they sometimes berated the later ones as too realistic for mosaic. Nor did they see that S Mark's pictures must have inspired those on the scuola just as S Mark's has inspired much of the design of the facade. (There is no reason to look for any relation to trompe l'oeil relief architecture elsewhere, such as the famous example expainter Bramante contrived at huge scale in Milan—after Pietro and Tullio had left the region.)

On the front of the scuola, it is not only the reliefs that are flat. Except for the arrangement around the doorway, with its freestanding columns, jutting cornices, and deep recess, everything on the facade was kept to low relief. As a result, the architectural membering, though busy, looks thin. The loss of shadow, and hence of sculpturesque emphasis, drains away the potential organic character of those members and some of the discipline they could have given the design. This might be the mark of Pietro Lombardo, despite the several details that cannot be his. Contradictorily, while the membering has lost its ability to look structurally effective, the way it is disposed is more rational than in much of the earlier Lombardo work, and much more rational than the upper wall of the court of the Doges' Palace. No standard way of handling the classical orders had yet been established in Venice.

Who did what is an unsolved and probably insoluble puzzle. Many of the peculiarities of the court of the Palazzo Ducale appear again, perhaps because some men were shuttled from one job to the other by Pietro, who was overseeing both at the same time. Such workmen would have been carvers rather than designers of architectural ensembles. The new direction of the work, after Pietro was dropped in 1490, may have kept on with his design or bits of it (which may have incorporated bits of the prefire design), whether it was sympathetic or not. The whole front may early have become a palimpsest, and have become an even more complicated one as new layers of ideas were imposed by new bosses. It came out at the end like a sheet from the drawing game of "Consequences" (or *Le Cadavre Exquis*), where head, thorax, hips, and legs are each drawn by a different person who, because the paper is folded back, does not see what has gone before.

Chronologically, the upper parts do not belong here with the work of Pietro, although he may have had quite a lot to do with them; but they are so peculiar that they do not fit comfortably among the works of Codussi either, even though he was supervising the top half as it went up. The design may not have been thought out afresh, certainly not all of it, and the top must have

been put up quickly, for Canon Casola, always with an eye for fancy finery, found it in 1494 "very beautiful and recently adorned with marbles and gold" (Casola, 138).

No church or palace front had been as intemperately trimmed as this facade, and the reason may be that churches and palaces were built by clergymen and patricians with more education (and educated friends with whom they could discuss their building projects) than the worthy, little-lettered, but often rich governing boards of the scuolas. They may have been more like the nouveaux-riches Milanese, unable to resist what their money could buy. The taste is that of old Hollywood (though the Venetian materials are better) or the Moscow subway stations.

The flank along the Rio dei Mendicanti follows the normal scheme for enlivening an important length of blank wall by punctuating it with evenly spaced pilasters, more or less as Pietro had already done on the sides of the Miracoli and at the Scuola di S Giovanni, if it was he who did it there. Here the detailing is simpler, a toned-down version of that on the facade. Here, as also on the front, part of the socle is no longer visible, having been sunk into later paving and repaving.

On Jacopo de' Barbari's view-map of 1500, the building of the scuola is shown backing into the lagoon, much closer to it before several hundred feet of new-made land were gained by filling in the Fondamenta Nuova (1546–50) along the north edge of the city. Some change must have been made in the building here earlier than that, for a single capital is carved with the date 1533, which must mark either the end or the beginning of a building campaign, certainly not the middle of one. Some construction and interior finishing had dragged on to that year, and

13.7 Scuola di S Marco.
Main hall on ground floor.
The capitals of the columns
carry wood brackets spreading out fore and aft to give
more area for bearing the big
beams that, in turn, carry
the closely spaced cross-
beams, in typical Venetian
wood construction.

some sort of new work went on from 1533 to 1546. This flank, of little intrinsic interest, has been attributed to Jacopo Sansovino on uncertain grounds. If involved at all, which is unlikely, he could be responsible only for some extension following the already established bay system, or some repairs.

With the columns separating its three lanes like the aisles and nave of a church, the ground floor hall is typical of the larger scuolas (fig. 13.7). Finished, but not yet set up by 1489, the columns were in place by 1490, but not covered. They stand on abnormally high square pedestals, a peculiarity not inaugurated here but soon widespread in Venice, particularly at scuolas. They end in a deep-cut egg and dart, chippable where an experienced craftsman would have put something plainer and stronger; but Lombard helpers more than once favored trimming over reasonable maintenance. The whole interior must have been finished enough to be visible and probably usable by May 1494, when Canon Casola found that "the decoration inside is worthy of the outside" (Casola, 138).

Pietro had taken full charge of the Palace only in 1498, and he left the scuola in 1490. Even if many of his late ideas came after he had left the scuola, still they could not safely be counted as expressions of his last ideas, partly because they do not agree among themselves, and partly because it is not possible to be sure just what was his. He was born ca. 1430–35, and would have been in his mid-sixties when in charge of the Palace. "Late style" is a phenomenon well-known in the work of a number of great masters who lived to a ripe age—Titian, Rembrandt, Cézanne, Renoir—as an exceptionally exalted kind of expression. A similar phenomenon sometimes appears, but not so clearly, in the late architecture of Michelangelo, Le Corbusier, and Wright. Possibly, more like the case of Cranach or De Chirico, the genius that vivified Pietro's early work had leaked away by his late middle age.

As has already been said, except for some fireplaces and designs for ceilings, Pietro's last work at the Palazzo Ducale is unidentifiable, inseparable from that of his well-trained shop; yet it might have been expected to be a sort of summation, or a quintessential statement. But his career does not follow a development leading to a final maturity, since his identifiable late works are as improvisational as his early ones. It is not a progress so much as an amble from this to that to the other. The evolution that might have been expected is to be found, rather, in the later works of his son Tullio, who went beyond his father's Early Renaissance manner to something more sober, more mature, and a step nearer to Venice's equivalent of the High Renaissance.

14 EARLY RENAISSANCE PALACES

"I never saw palaces anywhere but at Venice. Those at Rome are dungeons to them," wrote William Hazlitt in 1824 (II, 170–71). Has any other city as many palaces as Venice or, rather, fine houses we now indiscriminately call palaces? The XIVc and the beginning of the XVc had been a busy time for building in Venice, as a trip down the Grand Canal still shows. Many of the wealthy families then built and rebuilt palaces or fine houses in the late Gothic style; close to 200 of them are still extant, whole or in good part. Their singularity is paraded down the Grand Canal with such assurance that many foreigners agree with Venetians that their city is unique beyond arguing, and part of Italy only by a geographic accident.

Dwellings for patrician families inscribed in the Golden Book and the better houses of prosperous merchants were not called "palazzos" in the XVc and XVIc; only the Palazzo Ducale was then regularly spoken of as a "palazzo," and it is still known as *The* Palazzo." With counterfeited modesty the others were called "Ca' So-and-so," "Ca'" being short for "casa" or, more fully, "casa di stazio" ("principal dwelling," as distinguished from country house or seat). "Palazzo," which came into common use in the XVIIc, has now generally taken the place of "Ca'," and smaller dwellings of important people may be known as "palazzettos" or "palazzinas." There is no test for the proper term, but size and richness are the chief clues, and in some border cases, the pretentiousness of owners insistent on their status, or the architectural pretentiousness of the building.

There are no big palaces of the beginning of the Early Renaissance typical of what we might imagine the Bregnos or Rizzo might have built—if what we know of their style could be shifted to palace design. And there are none by Pietro Lombardo. There are instead miscellaneous examples, unattributed or unattributable, only a few of major interest, and many more bits of early work here or there on buildings since remodeled.

Changing social or economic conditions might be expected to influence architecture enough so that one decade of Early Renaissance building could easily be distinguished from another; but style developed almost independently of economic conditions, and so unsystematically that in the absence of dated documents it is often impossible to know whether something was built around 1480, 1490, or 1500. Such independence of cause and effect in these matters is rare in architecture after the early Middle Ages. Even state enterprises followed practical needs more than fluctuations in the level of the treasury, melodramatic as those might be. Work on the Ducal Palace was more the result of the big fires of 1474, 1479, and 1483 than of anything to do with money. Palaces were conservative in their own way, and the changes that came over them—they were forever being remodeled—were superficial. In churches, not only did functions not change but the clientele (priests, donors, and congregations) and the senate (which usually paid for them) were not often desirous of change; even less change of style to be in style than occurred in private palaces. Renaissance palaces are no bigger or showier than the preceding late Gothic ones that are equally proclamations of the glory and wealth of a family. They look different mainly because their owners wanted them to look different, and the difference is only skin-deep.

There was, nevertheless, a temporary decline in building in the last years of the XVc, from a depression worse than most. Sixteen years of costly wars with the Turks came to an end in 1479, but Venice then had to begin paying a yearly tribute of 10,000 ducats. In 1485 there was a plague. But then the Republic began to win profitable trading privileges (because of paying the tribute); in 1489 she "inherited" Cyprus; she still had Crete; both were worth more than Negroponte (Euboea), which she had had to give up. Conditions, though discouraging, were by no means disastrous. Half-a-dozen private banks failed around 1500 and some fortunes shrank, but that did not stop other private fortunes—less affected—from financing grand tombs, family chapels, and a few palaces. This temporary and never more than partial drop in building activity kept on until ca. 1520.

Most palaces were rectangular blocks, then often freestanding on all sides. Party walls were not yet common (Fabri, 29). Although never as independent of their neighbors as their Florentine contemporaries, such as the pugnacious and independent Palazzo Strozzi, in Venice all but rent-producing, low-cost housing schemes generally showed themselves as a row of individual units. Alterations have now filled in many of the individual gaps, but the individuality remains.

Having to be fitted into the peculiar Venetian net of canals and streets, houses were usually narrow in front, and deep (fig. 14.1). Rooms ran along either side of a long hall down the middle of the building. On the ground floor this led from a water entrance on the front to a land entrance in back. This typical Ventian *androne* or *portego* was unlike anything in Florence, Rome, or Milan. In late mediaeval times it had often been T-shaped, with the head of the T toward the water, or L-shaped, with one arm beside a small court with an outside stairway and perhaps a well and cistern (the only item except foundations put underground in cellarless Venice). In the Early Renaissance, the simpler, regular schemes were preferred, with a plain *androne* running straight through the building. The stairway, on one or, more usually, two

14.1 Plans of typical Venetian palaces of ca. 1500 (from the Combatti map of 1847).

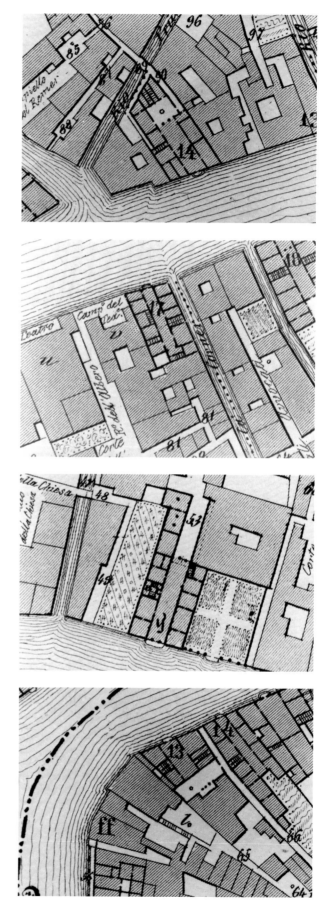

straight flights between straight supporting walls, was moved indoors, to open off the *androne* near the middle of the house.

Since the gentry did not walk from door to door, but went about by gondola, the main entrance was on the water. A land entrance was necessary for the humbler functions of service and business, entered either from an alley in back or on one side—there were not yet half-a-dozen wide streets in the city—or from a campo. The land door, less important than that on the water, was narrower and square-headed, while the latter was regularly more monumental, wider, and arched, perhaps as a memory of the open fronts of late Byzantine and occasional Gothic palaces arcaded all the way across. All this made it grander for the entrances and exits of the resident grandees and their visitors, and also made it easier to get bulky goods, in which many of the owners might be dealing, in and out. A good part might be stored on the bottom floor. Although after the mid-XVc courtyards were rarely laid out, sometimes there might be a small walled garden in back (not a service yard) above a cistern that took rainwater filtered through sand under the greenery and paving. But as time passed, less and less space could be spared for big gardens except for the palaces and pleasure pavilions on the island of the Giudecca or on Murano (fig. 14.2). (The growth of the city has now destroyed nearly all gardens, large and small.)

The ground floor rooms toward the front of the palace, flanking the *androne,* were for offices and storage. The *androne* had a way of filling up with boats, old family armor, and a jumble of bulky effects, as well as merchandise in transit that had to be stored close to the water door. Although that entrance might look monumental from the outside, the impression inside must have been quite different until the XVIc, when nearly everything was forced into

greater formality, including the daily life of the occupants. Doge Leonardo Loredan (1501–21) criticized the luxurious new customs, confessing that he himself had been among the first to transform the traditional role of the *androne* (Gilbert, in Hale 1973, 277). This change was not made just by the great nobles, but by any family with a medium social rank to keep up. But behind doors on the ground floor, kept more discreetly out of sight, there were still generous spaces for the family business, an office, and storerooms.

The stories above, usually two in the Early Renaissance, followed similar plans, and the center hall, here called the *sala,* opened to suites of rooms on either side and became a hall for entertainments on the now ever more recurrent grand occasions. Bedrooms would be on the floor above, though one or more corners on the main floor, the piano nobile, might be saved for bedrooms for the heads of the family. Tradition set the pattern so fixedly that it is not easy now to trace what each room once was, for size, shape, and location were little affected by function, and interiors have been rearranged, remodeled and re-remodeled so often— easy to do when one room was so much like another. Even the original kitchens, in spite of the needs for special equipment, are hard to distinguish. Sometimes they were banished to a corner of the top floor to avoid percolation of the house by smoke and smell. It is said that in the late XVc and early XVIc at least a quarter of the houses in the city were more or less basically altered (Pignatti 1971, 135). This may be a corollary of the reduction in the number of new palaces built during those years.

It comes as a surprise that in the houses of the grander nobles space was very rarely developed for a family chapel, but the regulations of the Venetian Church, virtually a state institution, did not allow them except by special permission of the patriarch, rarely

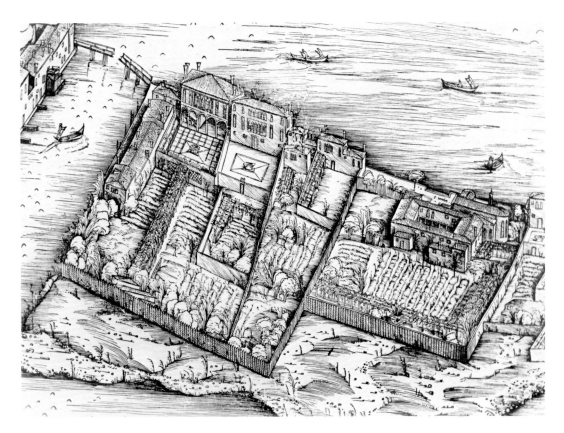

14.2 The Giudecca. End with gardens (from the de' Barbari map of 1500).

14.3 Interior showing windows. From *The Dream of S Ursula* by Carpaccio (Gallerie dell'Accademia, Venice).

given. After the XVc, sometimes a little oratory was slipped into a closetlike space behind a double door in one of the large rooms that could be opened wide to reveal an altar that might be used for a semi-surreptitious Mass when some ordained relative was visiting (with a portable altar stone?). Private prayers or other individual devotions could, or course, take place there at any time. It was properly more of a private oratory than a chapel, and never, so far as we know, fully consecrated. Mass was not to be celebrated except on very special occasions, and then only by special permit.

The houses were often large; several generations and the families of several brothers might be living under one roof. This often proved a convenience, for several of the same household might be involved in some joint business venture, foreign commerce, or the development of estates on the mainland. Some of the servants on the ground floor might be quartered there or else in small rooms under the roof.

Except for those of the corner rooms, the windows along the sides almost always had to give on a narrow canal or alley. Finding light only at its ends, the *sala* had to let in all it could there. Hence the walls at each end were pierced as much as possible by openings linked into loggias. The *androne* below might be left open, occasionally without a protective screen of windows or doors or even gates, but this must have been rare. There do not often seem to have been metal grilles that could have given good security. The loggias above may once have been open too, but by the Early Renaissance some sort of screen of windows was more usually set behind their arches. Glass had been made in Murano since the XIVc, and XVc paintings show windows of considerable size filled by casements of bottle-end glass (fig. 14.3). Nothing was attached to the column shafts, difficult, expensive, and leaky at

best, but a few traces still show fastenings for french doors or grilles on the more tractable flat sides of bases and abaci (Ruskin, Stones, I, 93). Often the screen of windows was set a yard or so in back, leaving a pleasant outdoor space behind the loggia.

Single windows were often outfitted with grilles like a box, with an iron-barred crisscross set a foot or so out in front of the plane of the wall, almost always on the ground floor where the windows were small and plain. Naturally there were no shops, unlike Florence or Rome.

A long hall with rooms down each side brought about a three-part facade, the open loggia of the *sala* flanked by walled wings, each cut by two windows. Already by the XIVc such a triptych arrangement in three stories had become standard. (By the late XVc, the occasional low corner towers had disappeared entirely, leaving no trace but the name *torreselle* applied to the wings from which they once rose.) There might be an occasional mezzanine, but this was not really established until later. Small houses had only two divisions, a loggia with *androne* and *sala* behind, and a single wing. Triple and duple schemes persisted little changed for centuries. What determined the facade was always the traditional pattern, derived long ago from the interior arrangement, but not now always organically related to any particular needs or any specialized rooms except the central hall. There seems to have been no fear of repetitiousness.

Only the main front was developed architecturally, as a showpiece on one face of a plain block, making maximum effect with minimum effort and expense. The sides and back left flat and plain, were usually hard to see well, and design could be skimped, without any formal scheme. The front was organized mainly with what had to be there: the set pattern of the openings, the cornice, and the frames for windows, loggias, and doors, all flattish. Simple surface decoration sometimes enlivened the wall spaces between. In spite of the obvious invitation, the middle or loggia section was never recessed or advanced to give more relief to the facade. As the main front was on the water, it was advantageous to push everything out to the edge of the canal to give more light and air and more interesting views, and also to make use of every square foot of the plot.

The front wall had less actual work to do than the longer side walls or even the walls lining the central halls, for these had to support the ends of the beams of the floors and roof. The front facade was pierced so much by the loggias that it did not look like a working structural wall. No matter how diaphanous, one continuous plane dominated the facade, as it had in the past and would in the future. The ornamentation of windows, doors, or applied stone coats of arms did not often project as much as a foot. The resulting flatness was suitable because, standing in the water and not on visible firm land, the fronts were conceived more as big decorative patterns than as tectonically stable and weighty walls calling for stout underpinning.

Nearly all, as has been said, were symmetrical in three parts, unvaried save in slight stretching or squeezing of the flat wall space between the windows of the wings, for they did not always quite match; or occasionally the main doorway might be displaced a little to one side of the central axis. Shifts in the loggias, such as running one window more to one side than that below it, can sometimes be found, but rarely, and so subtly worked into the all-over surface pattern—for the design is no more than a surface pattern—that they go all but unnoticed. Even the smaller palaces with only one wing beside the loggia are symmetrical in each of those parts and give the impression of being elements of a symmetrical whole momentarily not all there.

None is composed as a balanced asymmetry, that "occult balance" found in North European Gothic town houses, and none uses a small projecting element or recess as a balancing visual weight in a more complicated asymmetrical scheme. Flatness and an air of symmetry pervade everything, and none of the rare exceptions is consequential in amount or in effect.

As a happy consequence, although the facades may vary in size, material, and style, they line up to the canal edge more or less in one unending and sometimes unfolding plane, following one another like panels in a mile-long screen, separated only a little here and there by an alley or side canal. Long stretches of palace fronts on the Grand Canal or the Cannaregio have a rippling rhythm of three beats with accent on the second, only enlivened here and there by minor irregularities. The result is the urban opposite of the relentless rat-a-tat-tat of uniform window spacing on the avenues of Milan, Paris, or New York.

The construction was sound and thoroughly standardized. The dimensions of the rooms were commonly determined by the lengths available in ready-cut timbers, easier to bring down from the forests than tree-length logs. Some of the elements of planning and disposition of the separate rooms became so typical as later to seem time-sanctioned essentials. There seems never to have been any call for experiment. There is more variety in early Gothic palaces, from the trial and error that led to the standard plan. The resulting sound structure and practical plan of the late Gothic palaces explain why relatively few Early Renaissance palaces were built; they were not needed.

The base or socle (called the *basamento*) was regularly of Istrian stone, heavily molded and sloped slightly inward, the heaviest and most rugged-looking part of a building otherwise flat and light-looking. For the walls above, brick was preferred to stone: it weighed less; it was cheaper; made on nearby islands or the mainland, it was closer to hand than any building stone and easier to transport by boat; furthermore, it could be used over and over again (fig. 14.4). Much of mediaeval Torcello was swallowed in new walls in Venice, and so many bricks were taken from late Roman Altinum that they were commonly called *altinelle*, as soon were also new ones of the same size. (Older Roman bricks of the sort familiar in Rome were larger, about 2' square, but because they were not common in the neighborhood of Venice they were not often reused there.) Common new bricks were about 9" by 5" by 2½"; old ones were usually a little longer.

Sometimes the main areas of a facade were of exposed brick, new and baked harder than that in the core of the walls. Sometimes they were stuccoed, and from the XVc on the stucco was sometimes painted. The painted patterns, often bold and vividly colored, have now been erased by weather or replastering, but the effect is still shown in old pictures of the city (fig. 14.5). The frescoes between the windows might be of large figures, but more often they were of lively patterns (fig. 14.6). Only a few fronts were grandly faced with fine stone before the end of the XVc.

No city in Europe could boast more color, now sadly reduced by modern tan or gray stucco. The palaces along the Grand Canal so dazzled foreigners that they took painted imitation for real marble. Aeneas Sylvius Piccolomini, before he became pope (Pius II, 1458-64), thought he saw the city "all of marble, where the houses of the patricians are almost all covered with marble and gold." Yet when he was there, other than the Doges' Palace and the Ca' d'Oro, few had marble or limestone fronts. Istrian stone was unlike

anything he had seen in Rome or in the North for, when fresh, it can be eggshell white. Little wonder he was dazzled. In 1484 Father Fabri, who thought he saw palaces "of choice marbles, beautiful with gold . . . not of common stone," must also have been taken in by trompe l'oeil paint. Philippe de Commines recorded dwellings in 1495, "strong and tall, built of stone, and the old ones all painted; those of the last hundred years have fronts of white marble from Istria a hundred miles away, and inlaid with porphyry and serpentine." Instead of a hundred years he should have claimed fifty, and instead of claiming that all the new palaces were of marble, he should have limited them to a few. Thomas Coryat, in Venice a century later, in 1608, noted palaces more accurately, "most being built with bricke, and some few with fair free stone." The palace was more than just a place to live: it was a proclamation of family pride and "honor." As Venice was a city without dust, palaces looked fresh and bright for generations; in no other city in Europe were they so clean (Diehl, 133; Fabri, 28; Commines, xviii, lvii; Coryat, I, 203).

More strictly architectural ornament came from the stone window frames, especially when there was late Gothic openwork tracery in the loggias. Early Renaissance loggias had to be far more sober (fig. 14.7). Two windows were usually put on each floor of each wing, one directly above the other, and in the center one loggia was now almost always precisely above another. Void predominated over solid here. Stone bands sometimes marked the different stories, and the facade plane was capped by another unbroken horizontal—a low, shallow cornice with widely spaced stone brackets, never under a deep overhang (like Florence) that would have darkened the little streets and alleys.

14.4 Maffeo da Verona. *The Building of Troy* (painting in the Fitzwilliam Museum, Cambridge) showing typical inclined socle and wall.

14.5 Gentile Bellini. *Miracle of the Cross at S Lorenzo*, showing stucco with checkerboard grills (Gallerie dell'Accademia, Venice).

14.6 Carpaccio. *Return of the British Ambassadors*, showing painted walls (Gallerie dell'Accademia, Venice).

14.7 Palazzo Giustinian-
Persico on the Grand Canal
at the Rio S Tomà. Simple
moldings marking the floor
levels and the minimal cornice are both typical, as is
the four-window loggia and
the two small windows in
each more solid wing.

The composition was an ordering of rectangles; some were plain wall (perhaps with an occasional panel of colored stone), some were of arched windows set into rectangles by spandrels of different material or color, and the largest and most elaborate were the loggias, rich in play of light stone against dark openings—but all kept flat. Balconies began to appear in the late XVc or early XVIc, short for single windows, longer for loggias. They were pleasant for taking the air, and compensated a bit for the lack of gardens or open courts. Soon Venice had more balconies than any other city in Europe (figs. 14.8, 14.9, 14.10). Miniature marble columns served for balusters to carry the handrail at first, but they soon gave way to spindle balusters of a form invented by Donatello for his Annunciation relief in S Croce in Florence (1452), taken over as a standard part of the balcony rail more by Venice than any other city (Wittkower 1968, 332). They were made up of identical, long, tear-shaped halves, set upside down and downside up, bulge to bulge.

The general horizontality made it easier to remodel a Gothic facade into a Renaissance one in Venice than in more northern cities, for in Venice neither style made much use of strong verticals. Until shortly after 1500, at the corners there might be a long, slender, unassertive, polelike vertical of stone, sometimes carved like a twisted rope, set on alternating layers of long and short quoins laid flat with the wall. Although small, this could be effective in closing off the facade and tying it together. In good work, corners or projecting angles were of stone, never of chippable plaster or brick. As only the balconies projected more than a few inches, and that only on the upper floors, safely out of danger, little stone suffered damage. Unless badly eroded by weather or pollution in the air, or by a rare fire, many late Gothic fronts are in excellent condition today.

The roofs were usually hipped to a low pyramid, little seen from most points of view. In a city famous for its virtuoso shipwrights, it is a surprise that nothing but the simplest carpenter's framing was tried here. The pyramid might be capped by an *altana*, a belvedere or mirador of wood, the only feature taken over from the architecture of the Near East, which many palace owners must have known well. Here the ladies of the family would take the air on warm afternoons or evenings. Big terraces were unknown in the Early Renaissance. Even the grandest palaces had their laundry dried on the *altana* during the day, and still do.

Chimneys (*fumaioli*) would animate the silhouette further, punctuating the skyline more often along the sides than the front, since fireplaces were most often set in the outside walls of rooms on the piano nobile, walls with no doors and usually without such large or closely set windows as those on the front or back. Where they emerged from the roof, the chimneys were usually cylindrical, with large conical caps to catch any stray sparks, vitally important in a city still so largely of wood (fig. 14.11). They took many fanciful forms, and were painted in even more extravagant designs.

All this building was accomplished with the simplest kind of construction; with foundations like those already described, and with supporting brick walls only 15″ to 20″ thick on the exterior, and 12″ to 15″ on the inside. Both brick and mortar were weak by modern standards and would not be allowed by many cities' building codes today.

The floors were usually surfaced with terrazzo, a lightweight layer of terra cotta sherds and chips of brick covered with a special mortar often dyed with cinnabar (natural mercuric sulphide); then garnished with bits of marble to make a border or more extended pattern, rubbed down,

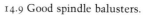
14.9 Good spindle balusters.

14.8 Typical use of colonnettes as balusters.

14.10 Typical corner balcony with typical early spindle balusters, brackets, and ornamented rail and archivolts. Palace at the corner of the Campo S Polo and the Calle della Madonna.

14.11 "Carpaccio" chimneys
(detail from Carpaccio's *Miracle of the Cross at the Rialto*, Gallerie dell'Accademia).

smoothed, and polished many times with oil. This was spread on planks laid on the close-spaced wood joists, usually left exposed for the ceilings of the rooms below, painted, gilded, and perhaps carved. An astonishing number of these are still performing their original work. The roof was carried on similar joists or rafters left plain. Vaults were not used in houses because they were so much heavier than ordinary wood-supported floors. There was no need for defensive solidity, as in Florence, Milan, or most other Italian cities. The tricky lagoon, impenetrable to those who did not know or were not guided through its shallow channels was defense enough. (The city was never captured until Napoleon took it.)

Smaller palaces from the end of the XVc may still be found here and there, but most are too modest to be datable or assignable to any special class in the Early Renaissance. An example is the small and once semi-elegant Ca' Zen di S Paternian (ca. 1500?) on the Rio di S Luca opposite the end of the Rio Terà dei Assassini (Venetian spelling). There is only one wing, with one window normally placed beside the loggia and one at the end beside a square corner pier. Another window is just around the corner—together they make a Renaissance version of the old Gothic corner window—and one balcony folds around to serve both. This pleasant *palazzetto* has no importance beyond that of a good work of its time and, as so often with minor examples, it may have been put up a generation later than when the style was at its peak. One supposes a minor architect who could follow fashion but neither quite control everything nor invent anything really new.

Although the preceding pages may have fostered the notion that all dwellings in Venice were palaces, this was of course far from true. Three-quarters of

the population was of the working class, and lived in very different quarters. The palaces almost always had more architectural interest than the humbler homes; they profited from the ideas of the best architects, have been better kept up, and are, consequently, more today as they were when built.

The modest houses were, on the whole, of exposed brick and were no wider than the ready-cut timbers that held them up, about 13' to 17', cheaper than any special lengths. The ground floor often had a little shop in front, under an arch or a stock wood beam running the width of the house. Rooms were not specialized for any definite use, and might be for a variety of uses in a one-family house, or a family flat, or they might be rented out singly. The houses were low, and their stairways steep. They were scattered all over the city, except along the Grand Canal and the Cannaregio, and usually would get their water from the municipal well in the nearest campo.

Many were built as part of what today would be called "developments," row houses for the poor (and for what their rents would bring in), or charitable undertakings for sailors' widows or other deserving unfortunates. Two identical blocks would often face one another across a little street, or one up to 30' wide if provided with a couple of communal walls. Sometimes adjacent houses would share a stairway, and some even had a single semiprivate well for both.

Few of these complexes are in acceptable condition today, but quite a number could be ideal for the urban renewal so much talked of and practiced almost not at all.

There are other buildings outside the Venetian Early Renaissance norms, varied though those are, that, while exotic to Venice, are not eccentric. For example, a house that will not fit into the usual local type is the Rocca Bianca (end of XVc) near the Navy Depot on the east end of the island of the Giudecca (fig. 14.12). Built for the Visconti of Milan, it has no Milanese features. Although its piano nobile has the common wing-loggia-wing, the house looks more as if it had been brought intact from Florence, partly because of its high ground floor with large square-headed windows, partly from the non-Venetian but elegant proportioning of blank stone wall and simple openings, and more from the exquisite detailing of the doorway, with its very Florentine arch-pediment with superb flourishes of honeysuckle (fig. 14.13). This door did not give on the water, often too rough to be navigable by gondola on the wide Giudecca Canal, too rough for guests to debark or inmates embark. It gave instead on to the *fondamenta* or wide quay. The ground floor, set safely back a few yards and above the water, was dry, well-lighted and lofty, and generously open to the famous garden in back (Puppi in *The Italian Garden*, 1972, 92n30), now vanished. This garden must have been as important as the house, which was not an everyday dwelling but a casino for entertaining, much of it feasting, dancing, and hearing music in the garden.

One example of a nondomestic building following palace design to a surprising degree is the harbor office of Venice, or Capitaneria del Porto (since 1810), begun in 1492 as the wholesale office of the huge public granaries next door (where the small park behind the ex–Royal Palace is now). Used for a while by the Department of Health of the Venetian navy, from 1774 onward the building was ceded room by room to the Academy of Painting, Sculpture, and Architecture, under the presidency of Giovanni Battista Tiepolo. It is typical of most Venetian planning that the layout of the building was so simple that it could be used virtually unchanged for such a variety of functions,

and nothing could epitomize the Venice of today better than a Quattrocento building associated with Tiepolo lodged between the ex–air depot (Padiglione del Selva) and Harry's Bar (fig. 14.14).

The lower story has an open arcade of five bays, one bay deep, with its arches springing from square piers, those at each end suitably a little heavier. Normal now, these square piers were a comparative novelty in Venice in 1492 (fig. 14.15). They are not pilasters, which by definition must be attached to a wall, but isolated supports—in other words, piers. A number of public buildings, for example the Doges' Palace, had arcades on columns, but only a few had arcades on square piers, such as the mediaeval Orseolo Hospital in the Piazza (now destroyed, but still known from Gentile Bellini's big procession picture in the Accademia).

The upper story follows the triple division of a small palace: two-window wing, three-arch loggia, another two-window wing. The windowsills are part of a continuous stringcourse and, together with another at floor level, they form a continuous parapet or parapet-band, like those already noted on several palaces. The simple window frames are continued down below the sills into this parapet-band, and thus they add to the interweaving of vertical and horizontal lines of white stone against tinted plaster that is (or was) such a striking feature of the design at least until 1977, when the whole building was covered with paint the color of mashed bananas. Everything is plain, but knowingly worked together (fig. 14.16). The result is simple, businesslike, and curiously sophisticated (McAndrew 1974, 27). The Loggia del Consiglio in Padua (1496–1509 and 1516–33) resembles it and may have been affected by it.

14.12 The "Rocca Bianca."

14.13 The "Rocca Bianca."
Detail of door.

14.14 Capitaneria del Porto.

14.15 Capitaneria del Porto.
Detail.

14.16 Capitaneria del Porto.
Detail.

15 | EXCEPTIONAL EARLY RENAISSANCE PALACES

Since there are no palaces fully showing the type or norm that controlled most of the better houses of the city, ca. 1480–ca. 1500, and since the type has, in the preceding chapter, been illustrated only by apposite fragments, for complete buildings of the period we have to look at exceptional ones—of which Venice can show quite a few, from mildly unusual to wildly outlandish. Some owe their oddity only to an odd site, some to the odd taste of the designer, and some to that of the client.

The front of the Ca' Cocco-Molin on the Rio dei Barcaroli is extraordinarily long because the oblong lot had its main side there, and was shallow in depth, around the corner on the Piscina della Frezzeria (then a long narrow pool, but now paved, and an important street). The rio facade is the only important part left, for most of the rest has been altered out of recognition, the principal volume having been distended to become the Cinema Centrale. The preserved arrangement of the windows (ca. 1490s?) is still individual without crossing over into eccentricity, atypical overall, yet typical in all its parts (fig. 15.1).

The windows of the bottom story are coordinated with those above, but in a peculiar way. The two outermost light mezzanines, above smaller openings for low (and doubtless damp) storerooms. Having no storerooms below, the innermost windows of the wings can be larger. The water entrance comes in the middle, normally, under the middle of the loggia of the piano nobile. But it is duplicated on its left, perhaps as the entrance to a *cavana*, or built-in boathouse, but just as possibly not, for *cavanas* were rarely put in private palaces. Jacopo de' Barbari showed no sure examples in the hundreds of palaces he recorded, nor even gondolas moored in front of palaces. Where gondolas went at night or in the rain cannot have been of much concern then any more than it is now (unlike the provision for carriages in more normal cities—and gondolas cost as much, if not more). The second big water door here could conceivably have been a secondary entrance for a secondary branch of the family—if there were then two sets of stairs, which seems unlikely. Big twin entrances exist in a number of late Gothic palaces, and appear in the middle of the front (not off center like these), both opening into the same *androne.* The gutting of the inside has destroyed the evidence that might perhaps explain this peculiar arrangement.

The rest of the main front follows the regular three-part division, but pulls it out to a rare length because of the shape of the lot. On the main floor, the widened wings have three windows instead of the usual two, and the six openings of the loggia seem to have spread to eight, since the inner windows of the wing trios are divided from the six by the slivers of wall hardly wider than the loggia columns. All eight are equipped with short balustrades (not balconies), as though eight and not six was the real division. Six and eight then coexist. The handrail, on fine Early Renaissance spindle balusters, is cut only by a little when it encounters a column, and it continues as a molding across the whole front. The stringcourse at floor level also runs uninterrupted from corner to corner and, together with the handrail molding, forms a parapet-band, effective as a strong disciplinary divider and guarantor of continuity (fig. 15.2).

The piano nobile is unusually high, and made to seem higher by the eight french windows in the middle coming right down to the floor, and also by the unexpectedly low story above, locally called a "mezzanine under the roof" (*mezzanino sotto tetto*). Its almost square windows align with the tall ones below (a correspondence since

confused by the blocking of several when the inside of the palace was wrenched to serve as a theatre). The lower rooms here at the top were probably for servants, children, or lesser relatives.

There has been a subtle interlayering of rhythm at different levels of the facade, rare for the Renaissance though not for the not yet dead local Gothic. The lower part, having introduced a mezzanine for the outer end of each wing, suddenly shifts to one story. The main axis in the center is abruptly displaced and temporarily starts to make another, but that is promptly canceled by the floor above. Vertical continuity is maintained, then, only in the wings. But all is kept in order, otherwise, not only by the rhythm of the openings everywhere (except for the shift made by the two biggest) but also and even more by the repeated long horizontals: the cornice; the lintels and sills of the attic windows; the isolated stringcourse above the piano nobile; the parapet-band and the unexpected stringcourse generated by the imposts of the lower mezzanine windows; the almost continuous band made by the lengths of cornice capping the arched entrances and flanking windows and tied down to them by framelike strips; and finally at the bottom by a strong socle. The moldings embodying these disciplinary lines are simple and strong; flat fillets, convex or concave quarter-circles, or simple cymas, all plain and severe.

The avoidance of carved ornament is not so much ascetic as elegant. Ornament is allowed only where unavoidable: on the capitals, reduced to almost nothing, on the jambs, and on the simple fluted bands for balustrades and archivolts; all else depends on the harmonious proportions of the shapes. The walls are of smooth stuccoed brick, once apparently a good Venetian red. The articulating members are of white Istrian stone, including the vulnerable corner shaft (a direct Gothic survival),

15.1 Ca' Cocco-Molin.
Facade.

15.2 Ca' Cocco-Molin. Window of piano nobile.

rounded from socle to cornice like an embedded pole, with the stringcourses gently curled around it instead of making sharp corners. The spare grace and authority of the whole come from the sensitive spacing and scansion, from the harmonious, varied, yet unanalyzable proportions. A knowing and subtle hand was in control, a hand to which nothing else can be assigned with any confidence.

Even within the three-part, three-story format, some houses might have one startling nonconforming feature; the Ca' Cappello-Memmo (ca. 1500?), for example, on the Rio dei Greci behind the Church of the Pietà, now part of its orphanage (figs. 15.3 and 15.4). Like that of the Ca' Cocco, the plan is long and narrow, limited by a big courtyard in back. The eye-catching novelty is not in the general arrangement, which may once have been close to that of the Ca' Cocco, but in the decoration. It is the row of twenty-two circles above the piano nobile, once inlaid with colored marbles, and also four elliptical porphyry plaques, still intact. Ellipses were rare before the mid-XVIc—there cannot be half-a-dozen others left in the city—probably because of the trickiness involved in laying them out, unless that were sidestepped, as here, by slicing an old stone shaft diagonally. Geometrically learned Alberti had shown how at Rimini, or any housewife could have shown how by slicing a long sausage or loaf of French bread on the bias. Since about the XIIc, discs made of straight cuts of old shafts had enlivened the fronts of Venetian palaces as an ornamental device, as they had floors in several other parts of Italy. They are now often said to have been borrowed in Venice from the East—Cairo, Aleppo, or Byzantium— but no such provenance can be established; the feature is as Venetian in ancestry as in frequency. Nowhere else that we know was it used with such gusto as here.

In general, the design of this front seems loose, with only two continuous horizontal moldings to divide it up and tie it together at the same time. The windows seem to float or drift on an undefined surface. Some have now been walled up; others perhaps moved. The doorway is a later alteration, perhaps not in the original location. The general condition is lamentable, both from the insensitive alterations and from years of neglect.

Since the Lombardo style is limited to decoration, there being no typical Lombardo plan or elevation, older houses could easily be brought up to date by altering no more than a doorway and a few windows. Two such remodelings used to be assigned to Pietro Lombardo and still show some likeness to his manner insofar as we can define it in ornament only: the well-known Ca' Dario on the Grand Canal, and the less-known Ca' Gussoni-Algarotti on the Rio della Fava near the Church of S Lio. In both cases, sharper looks will move them farther from him, but not necessarily out of range of some frequenter of his *bottega*. Neither is quite of the standard type; both are remodelings; both are on narrow lots and lack the full triple facade.

The Ca' Dario, seemingly an exotic on the Grand Canal, has an exotic background, but that has nothing directly to do with its architecture. Giovanni Dario, born in Crete, once a *bailo* or high-ranking diplomatic councillor at Constantinople, was acclaimed after his return to Venice in 1484 for having coaxed the Turks to ratify a treaty. The next year the republic rewarded him with a fat purse and he soon began to build a palace. Land had first to be bought and designs worked out, and construction would probably not have been begun before about 1487. Early in the building campaign he had an inscription put on the lower story, URBIS GENIO JOANNES DARIUS.

15.3 Ca' Cappello-Memmo.
Facade with original loggia
when walled up.

15.4 Ca' Cappello-Memmo.
Facade with loggia as subsequently reopened.

(Ruskin, whose friend Rawdon Brown lived there from 1837 to 1842, had the inscription renewed, no doubt correctly.)

No house front is richer in colored stones, and this has often been pointed out as a consequence of Dario's years in Byzantium. But no such polychrome facades are known there, and dwellings had no more than an occasional marble plaque on an interior wall (UNESCO, *Rapporto* 1969, 170). Rather than Byzantium, it may instead reflect Dario's ego. If he wanted to make a pretty show, he succeeded. What may be the most arresting is its air of gaiety; if any palace among those on the Grand Canal could ever be said to have developed into a scherzo, it is this. Only one other building, the Miracoli, has a like character, and enough of it had already been built to provide direct inspiration; the arrangements of some of the porphyry, *verde antico,* and polished granite discs of different sizes—there must originally have been about seventy all together—look like quotations. The fine materials, workmanship, and decorative treatment of the surface were matched only by the Miracoli, parts of S Mark's, and some of the wonderful buildings made up by Carpaccio and other painters (fig. 15.5). Older writers often saw the Ca' Dario as the fullest realization of the Lombardo style, but there is nothing specifically Lombardo-like in the details.

In height, the top and bottom floors are alike, and the two taller piani nobili between also match each other (fig. 15.6). The whole front is shorter than an ordinary gondola (33'), as can be seen when one is moored in front. The alley and canal at the sides make the plot unalterably narrow, and must always have done so, so that the omission of one wing here must date back before the present facade. One side wall still has windows left from an earlier Gothic building, much of the other side and back are recycled Gothic, and a few Gothic columns are still at work

15.5 Cima da Conegliano. *The Healing of Anianus* (Stattliche Museen Gemäldegalerie, Berlin).

15.6 Ca' Dario. Grand Canal front.

15.7 Ca' Dario. Facade (lithograph by Moro and Kier).

inside. Entirely freestanding, then, as few Venetian palaces still are, it enjoys access to daylight from all four sides and all the rooms can be so easily lighted that the *sala,* put here from habit rather than from need, could do without its pretty facade loggia.

But neither the plan nor the walls can now be trusted fully, because there were such ruthless repairs in the XIXc; and in rescuing the whole from near collapse in 1904, the bluestocking, literary-lion-hunting French lady-owner had it overhauled, replacing piles, reinforcing outside walls to preserve the tilt time had pressed on them, fitting a new skeleton inside (helped by iron chains), and taking down the facade, stone by stone, to reinforce what was behind. There were additional repairs in the 1960s, said by some to be of doubtful value, but considered efficacious by others (Zuccolo, 87, 147). Little is now uncontaminated.

Except for the late XIXc iron balcony and the addition of some discs, the front above the ground floor is a dutiful reconstruction. Old photographs show a terrace set into the roof, clearly a late interpolation, and a mid-XIXc lithograph shows an earlier plain hipped roof, presumably like the original (fig. 15.7). Today there is again a plain hipped roof of standard tile. The chimneys of the so-called "Carpaccio" type are overstyled picturesque inventions, punctuating the skyline on the front and wherever they would show most, independent of any fireplaces below. Something is disturbingly familiar, something evokes Williamsburg or Pierrefonds.

The socle or base is richly molded, as so often at this date. The comparatively solid ground floor front, of extra-fine Istrian stone, has an arched doorway in the center, with a XIXc arched window between *oculi* on either side—inventions of the rebuilder (Fontana, 221). The original arrangement is not known.

Without warning, the next story shifts back to the original and abandons symmetry for a loggia on the left and a wing on the right. The openings are alike—there is no room for variations—and the left-hand window of the wing is scarcely to be told apart from the three of the adjacent loggia. The second window of the wing comes at the edge of the facade, and another is around the corner. Most of the windows near the corner are now filled in, for stability, but they were shown still open in the XIXc (Fontana, pl. 52). The two almost joining here could have made a corner window, a type often favored in Gothic, but the design was not developed for that. Except for the marble-faced square in the middle of the wing at each story, there is no solid wall on the front, unless one counts the small parapet-band below the windows. Void predominates over solid as much as on any Gothic front.

The two stories above the first piano nobile, also piani nobili in their own right, repeat the scheme, and as a result the upper three-quarters of the front are made mainly of verticals and horizontals framing curved decorative elements (arches, discs), a late Gothic principle of design persisting while it turns into one of the Early Renaissance. The two lower floors are marked by thin, shallow entablatures that still aim to conform to classical norms. Although the whole *parti* is older Venetian, the detail is already of the Early Renaissance. As so often, the words follow the new style, but the grammar does not.

Above the altered lower story, the front is kept coherent by a recurrent rhythm, for although the only stone surfaces are the square panels in the center of each wing, together with the moldings and frames of the void, all manage to work as one balanced asymmetrical design, as though a patterned marble floor had been stood up vertically (most apparent where the binding around the circles makes Cosmatesque loops). Streaks in the milky marble of the upper stories have now oxidized to a rich butter color, with their striations juxtaposed in matching halves like pages in an opened book, an age-old patterning trick familiar from grander displays on the walls of S Mark's. The marble may be largely a replacement, doubtless accurate. Varying kinds and amounts of damp in the air make the appearance change far more than on a normal building with a normal amount of relief. Here there is almost no modeling above the socle; the facade is flat and depends for its design and what visual coherence it has on the arrangement of color areas.

Since the Ca' Dario correlates with nothing except the Miracoli, it could be thought that it stemmed from the same source, Pietro Lombardo, or a major partner, or, more likely, someone else in the shop (not Tullio). Nothing denies this, but it can be no more than an unbuttressed guess. If the execution were to be attributed to someone who had worked on the outside of the Miracoli—less specifically Lombardesque in detail than the inside—it would be seen that what is Lombardesque there, the limestone membering, is not close to the membering of the Ca' Dario. The supposition of a common master craftsman turns out to be weak. The Miracoli can still somehow have been a forebear, but the relation may not have been direct or even legitimate.

Marin Sanudo, who wrote the fifty-eight volumes of his diaries in Venice between 1496 and 1533, mentioned the Ca' Dario so often as a place for entertaining distinguished visitors (XX, 543, 550; XXII, 454, 455; XXIII, 361—for example) that one wonders if it had been singled out not only as particularly luxurious and impressive but also as conveniently central without being too close to government offices. (It may have been a sort of Blair House.) Its XIXc and XXc history, except as it involved building and remodeling—the little palace now contains a bathroom tricked out in the style of the Alhambra—is less rewarding: a *pensione,* a pretentious literary salon, residence for a motley series of foreigners, English, German, Hungarian, Armenian, French, and the scene of an exceptionally unpleasant murder.

While the Ca' Dario is uniquely outside the norm, the other major small palace of the period, the Ca' Gussoni, is frankly aberrant. It stands on the east side of the Rio della Fava, near the Church of S Lio. Some resemblance can be found to the work of the Lombardos, but this is hardly more than superficial. (Mariacher 1955, 36, and others disagree.) As so often, a remodeling of something on the site accounts for the peculiarities of the plan, but almost solely of the plan. Money must have been saved by appropriating not only the old foundations, but also some of the old walls (fig. 15.8).

The water front, exceptionally, is narrower than the back. On one side, space had to be given up for an alley, to let foot traffic through to the water, and on the other side, a larger piece was cut off halfway between the front and back; near the middle, space was squeezed out for a courtyard 24' square, unexpected in so small a house. Where it has any identifiable character, the plan is Gothic, having come ready-made to the designer with little need for change.

The most striking part is the canal front, a playful encounter between the not very strong forces of tradition and those of an innocent improviser. Disregarding the later top story, one sees the designer's most trying problem: an upper floor that hangs a yard over the left edge of the bottom floor to leave space for the egress from the alley (fig. 15.9). The easygoing designer ignored this as far as he could, and began with a traditional trio of arched doorway between

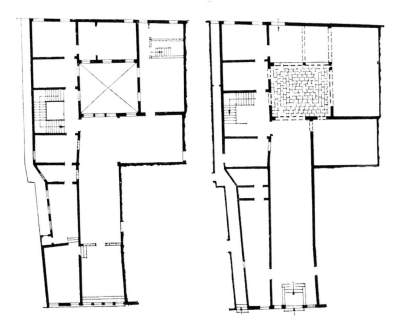

15.8 Ca' Gussoni. Plan. Piano nobile and pian terreno.

15.9 Ca' Gussoni. Canal front.

arched windows, under a normal four-part loggia. The usual two-window wing is on the left. (There is no space for a wing on the right.) But while the inner window of this wing is over the solid wall of the lower story, its mate is out over the void of the alley. The inner window has a further difficulty, being not quite in the center of the square windows under it.

The asymmetry and irregularities that could have been manipulated in a Gothic design here push through and try to disrupt the formal Renaissance scheme imposed on them (if one can accept it as a scheme planned in advance). The owner may have wanted something in the newest fashion, and wanted it quickly; perhaps he had come into money or was marrying it—and he had a stylish new slipcover put over the old front. The new scheme is all on the surface. The date and some of the details seem close to the Cappella Gussoni nearby, but neither close enough nor far enough away to assure or refute a common authorship. It is the way these details are assembled that is unlike, and that makes it hard to imagine one author for both.

The details are at the same time wayward and refined. The socle, for example, has a band of tender pink Verona marble, and then three strips of carving, all so often under water that they are regularly green and slippery with slime (fig. 15.10). On this socle stand three pilasters, a pair for the normal jambs of the entrance and one standing alone beside the alley. The accompanying windows also have pilasters, to enframe them; and they look curiously insubstantial, most likely from the weakness of the shelf-like windowsills on which they have to stand.

On the extreme right, a sliver of blank wall runs up along one side of the window pilaster, while pinched on the other by the weakest molding of all (and the longest), a strip that runs to

the top of the building, turns, runs across the frieze, and then turns once again to run halfway down the other side, not like a tectonic member but like a weak picture frame or tape edging. The logically weaker parts do not submit to the logically stronger; both go their own heedless way, a behavior not found in the Cappella Gussoni.

The other window beside the door also has trouble: its outer pilaster is crowded by a square window of a different type, with a papery ornament on the top and bottom, unrelated to its neighbor. Above this comes another like it. Here and elsewhere, the several collisions and near misses can be seen as structurally outrageous unless the whole front be taken as something no more substantial than a big piece of embroidery—which may be more or less the way it had been conceived.

The indiscretions do not stop here, for the pilaster on the left edge of the building, which begins as though it had more of a function than merely to end a short bit of wall, loses any raison d'être at the top; the capital, in essence a supporting member, stops dead below a blank bit of wall (fig. 15.11).

Then immediately to the left a new problem comes up, how to reach over the alley in order to make a piano nobile wider than the story underneath it. The use of pilasters and archivolts has established a modified classical state of things that has no resources for the needed cantilever. The intrepid improviser has contrived otherwise, with three fancy brackets, one above and beyond the other. While they do manage to get there, it is a way unsanctioned and locally unprecedented in classicizing stone construction, though not—significantly—in Gothic carpentry. One side of the courtyard still shows an equivalent extension made by Gothic wood brackets. Possibly there had once been a series of similar wood brackets above the alley, and the ingenious and uninhibited designer chose simply to petrify them.

15.10 Ca' Gussoni. Water entrance.

15.11 Ca' Gussoni. Left side of facade.

The top of the lower floor is marked by a stringcourse and a band of wall and a continuous windowsill, forming a parapet-band. These tie together the newly increased width of the piano nobile. The four openings of the loggia and the pairs of windows of the wing are spaced in a way that might like to be both logical and orderly, possible where the quartet of loggia windows comes neatly over the equivalent width of the trio of window-doorway-window, but troublesome where one of the windows abuts the loggia. To make the division between loggia and wing visible without interrupting the calming regular rhythm would not be possible, and so the wing window has to edge a bit off the axis of the awkwardly placed square window underneath (which could more easily have been moved to be on axis with the more important window above; the wrong one was moved). The other wing window is freer, adrift in the space above the triply stepped brackets.

Where they have to work as supports, the window pilasters in the loggia are a skinny 10′ tall and 10″ wide, piers as much as pilasters, or posts, pilasters planted on posts of the same width. Where they serve only as trimming, for the jambs of the wing windows, they are even narrower, strips clearly not intended to look capable of being supports. The rubato rhythm that these beat out across the front is reasserted in the long parapet-band below them by small vertical strips like dwarf piers. Although their location suggests it—even demands it—these last do not seem even mimetically capable of holding up much of anything, certainly not the 10′ pilasters standing on top of them. (The loggia, in a reduction to three arches, is repeated in the courtyard as the back window of the big main room whose front window is the loggia on the water side of the house.)

The limited architectural notions of a decorator are everywhere evident. Everything that could be ornamented

has been, except the small areas of blank upper wall, and they were faced with smooth Carrara. Some sense of order, independent of structural implications, was imposed by the repeated underlining by the horizontals of socle, parapet-band, and cornice, and this emphasis was needed in view of the waywardness of so many verticals and the haphazard nature of their placing.

The lower wall and the piers, pilasters, and moldings are of Istrian stone, and the details are everywhere beautifully carved, and adapted individually to their immediate decorative roles. The archivolts, for example, are kept narrow enough to come down on the capitals without jostling one another, and the assertiveness lost by their lack of bulk is won back by the sparkle of their tiny repeated flutes. The arches of the piano nobile carry urns on their crests, with flames that shoot up into the red marble frieze, linking it to the luxuriance of ornament elsewhere. This would seem to be a translation of the leafy topknots on the points of late Gothic windows. The cornice has brackets with leaves carved on the bottom, and deep-throated flowers catch light and cast dark shadows in the spaces between.

Could this be the work of Pietro Lombardo? The delight in decoration and indifference to the logic of structure are not alien to him, but both are pushed beyond his usual bounds. The rosettes in the socle repeat the form and perverse placing of those at S Giovanni Evangelista, but the latter is not surely by Pietro, and the rest of the ornamentation of the palace has no specific details that have to be his. While the details may imply a connection with his atelier, which must have been large, they cannot establish a connection with its master, though highly respected scholars have given the facade to him, accounting for the incongruities by suggesting it as his first work in

Venice, ca. 1474–80. But these incongruities are hard to accept as Pietro's, for even in 1474 he was no tyro but a successful artist some forty years old, though not yet experienced as an architect. He did countenance surprising inconsistencies at the Miracoli, but of another kind; there the difficulties are not primary, but more the result of a lack of foresight or of a change in the program, while here the incongruities are in the very bones of the design and must have been there in good part from the beginning. The design cannot be assigned to an experienced master, or even to one only as half-experienced as Pietro was then, and it cannot be assumed to be an early design among Renaissance palaces, almost pioneering. A date near the end of the XVc is more defensible.

Was there an architect at all? His first task for the front would have been to decide on an underlying scheme, and the decorative details would have to be brought to it later. Any discipline from the old Gothic facade was lost, and no new one imposed. It is impossible to picture a preparatory drawing or model, for the lower parts do not prepare for what comes above them, and it is hard to think that anyone as educated as a Gussoni would have accepted such a design if he had had a chance to study it and discuss it with his peers. Other palace patrons regularly knew more—from the evidence of what they built in the same years. This building may have been commissioned by the same Senator Jacopo Gussoni (1422–1501) who commissioned the family chapel in S Lio; there is no solid proof for either, though the chapel is a little less uncertain (Mariacher 1955, 36). If he commissioned the palace, something must have kept him from studying the elevations as he should have (assuming that any were made), or watching the execution. Perhaps he was out of town.

The front seems just to have happened to come out that way, the end product of continuous improvisation by some carefree, unintellectual ornamentalist, intent on what he was doing at the moment and heedless of what he had done before or might do later. The strongest probability would be that a few decorative carvers from the Lombardo or perhaps a related shop were called in to put a stylish new dress on an old body, trimming it as they went along without planning ahead. The normally serious, antique-derived vocabulary has been used with what must be called triviality, lots of spice but little substance and even less coherence. The result has a wry and wayward charm—particularly for the myopic—and it is an extreme example of one of the recurrent tendencies of the Early Renaissance in Venice. It would have shocked a contemporary Florentine, but probably not a Milanese.

Almost every generation produced a few buildings so impromptu or eccentric as to be out-and-out freakish. Two examples from around 1500 that follow cannot but owe much of their outlandishness to the notions of their owners, abetted by their hiring of maverick masons and carvers, certainly not anyone who could presume to be thought an architect.

All that is left of the Ca' Magno on the Barbaria delle Tole (number 6687-89) near the Ospedaletto, is a small dilapidated court with an open-air stairway that climbs to an upper walk leading into the piano nobile through an elegant pedimented doorway (fig. 15.12). The arched double window beside it, and the reliefs over the arches that hold up the stairs must have been carved by a different man from the carver of the rest, for he was much less skilled and much bolder in his ignorance. The work, unlike anything else in Venice, with its flat, plain leaves, is spaced to show more blank background than usual. The jambs of the double window look like stalks of Indian corn in full leaf, with that on the center pier

15.12 Ca' Magno.

15.13 Ca' Magno. Detail of window.

growing incongruously out of a pot (fig. 15.13). The reliefs above the arches stepping up under the zigzag of the stairs are less like normal architectural ornament than like chintz cut to left-over shapes. They make a jolting contrast to the suave foliage and tendrils coiling in the spandrels of the big arch that carries the walkway to the piano nobile on its long back and to the thoroughly conventional pedimented doorway. It is hard to imagine that the two carvers ever spoke to each other.

The other exception is even odder: the Ca' Mastelli, on the Campo dei Mori and the Rio della Madonna dell' Orto. From a famous relief on the water side, it is known also as "the House of the Camel" (fig. 15.14). The plan is more normal than the rest, in its old-fashioned way, with a courtyard with an open stairway, originally late Gothic but now half remodeled and half ruined. The whole is a jumble of Roman (a round altar, that may instead be a pedestal), of Gothic (windows and capitals, later set on dropsical globes instead of shafts), and of Early Renaissance (spindle balusters). The main remodeling was probably done around 1500, with indiscriminate cannibalizing of old bits from here and there jumbled into a magpie's ensemble—an unexpected whiff of Hearst's San Simeon (fig. 15.15).

15.14 Ca' Mastelli.

15.15 Ca' Mastelli. Detail.

III | MAURO CODUSSI

. . . this most beautiful Queene, this unstained virgine, this Paradise, this Temple, this rich Diademe and most flourishing garland of Christendome. . . . The sight whereof hath yeelded unto me such infinite and unspeakeable contentment . . . .

Coryat, II, 73, 74

16 | BIOGRAPHY

At the very beginning of the Renaissance, one architect appeared in Venice as suddenly and brilliantly as a comet: Mauro Codussi (or Moro, Moreto da Bergamo, Mauro di Martino, Codussis, Coduxis, or other variants, even the misleading Moro Lombardo). He reappeared just as meteorically at the end of the last century, for until then the history of art had lost him; his work was ignored, confused, or dissipated into that of various contemporaries. Since his work is so different, to our eyes, from that of his contemporaries in Venice, and so radically unlike earlier work there, the tardiness of its recognition still astonishes. He was the victim of the same frown of fortune that had called down oblivion on El Greco, Vermeer, and Georges de la Tour.

His virtual disappearance may be a consequence of the rather obscure places where early references to him are found, and to their scarcity and confusion. Francesco Sansovino, writing mainly in the 1570s, mentioned a Moro whom he associated with the family of the Lombardos; and so did the first real architectural historian of Venice, Tommaso Temanza, writing in the 1770s. Some sixty years later, Francesco Zanotto was conscious enough of Mauro's particular quality to venture one attribution to him, but he could not isolate his style consistently nor be sure of his right name. Not until 1893-97 did the thorough and perceptive Pietro Paoletti rescue Codussi from this murky limbo by piecing together the miscellany of notices about him, making an acceptable biography and—most important—assembling a catalog of his main buildings, arranging them in a chronological order, and defining their style. (Sansovino, 154; Temanza 1777, 96; Zanotto 1847, II, 185; P. Paoletti 1893-1897, 162 ff.)

Now it is known that he was born ca. 1440 in the village of Lenna in the Val Brembana, twenty miles north of Bergamo. About ten years younger than

Rizzo, he would have been of an age with Pietro Lombardo. While still young, he was working south of Venice, for the Camaldolesians at Classe just outside Ravenna, and was sent to lesser jobs in the neighborhood—for example, to Cesenatico. He must have been aware of the progress of Alberti's Tempio Malatestiano at Rimini, and probably more than merely aware, even intensely interested. It would be convenient to find that he actually worked on the building, but there is not a shred of evidence that he did so. He could have heard of Alberti's theories, not yet codified in *De Re Aedificatoria,* in Classe or at Rimini; someone in Classe must have been enlarging his outlook with humanist ideas. It was not so much the grand Roman massive and spatial interests of Alberti that he picked up as Alberti's simplicity, clarity, and archaeologically more accurate classicism.

On the recommendation of the Camaldolesians of Classe, he was sent to Venice in 1468, where the local Camaldolesians contracted him for what was probably his first independent commission, or surely the first of any size. He would have been twenty-eight or twenty-nine. Up to this age, his activities are too clouded to admit light. His first known work is already avant-garde. His earlier career has to be worked out backward by magnetic induction, and this tends to pull toward Alberti, and at the same time to Brunelleschi. At least one early trip to Florence has to be assumed.

When the young man arrived in the beautiful late Gothic city of Venice, there were still some monuments in the local Byzantinesque style, and nothing of importance yet dominated by the Renaissance. The Arsenal gate was finished, or almost; the Bregnos were completing the Foscari Monument; Pietro Lombardo was beginning the Malipiero Monument; and Rizzo, having finished the doorway at S Elena, was making two little altars for S

Mark's; the exotic tile dome was already on the Martini Chapel at S Giobbe. There were, then, no important Renaissance *buildings* in the city, only a few decorative ensembles. Mauro became one of the pioneers. For several decades his rather strict art had less effect on his contemporaries than that of the flashier and more improvisational Pietro. With the Lombardos and their followers, the superb skills of late Gothic craftsmanship in the carving of ornament passed easily into the Venetian Early Renaissance, whereas Codussi, closer to Brunelleschi and Alberti, eliminated much of it for more severe interest in the purer elements of architecture. Most clients attracted to the new fashion preferred the elaborately trimmed creations of the Lombardos, more easily seen as artistic and right up to the minute by those of unsophisticated taste.

One formative condition of his early career can be assumed: unlike Rizzo and Pietro, he had not been trained as a sculptor. His feeling and thinking, as revealed by his buildings, are intrinsically those of an architect and an architect only, not a sculptor-architect or an architect-decorator. His early experience has to have been as a stonemason, a conjecture that can be strengthened by early references to him always as *murer, lapicida,* or *tajapietra* until 1492, when for the first time he was recorded as "tajapietra architetto" (Malipiero, VII, 11); he was then already over fifty. He understood the procedures of building, whereas most of his contemporaries made effective episodes of new trimming but left the actual building to crews of masons who knew their work better and must have been given considerable freedom, having no guide with superior knowledge. He was more akin to Palladio, also trained as a stonemason, first assisting in actual building and later advanced and educated in Renaissance forms by humanist patrons; in other words, craft first, followed by refinement of design based on fundamental practical knowledge. The architect had no place in the social hierarchy. Alberti, alone, saw him as a gentleman; not a craftsman but an aloof artist-intellectual with humanistic knowledge. Though illegitimate, Alberti was well-born. Codussi—we assume—would not have had pretensions to aristocracy.

Other than this, Codussi's preparation in architecture can only be surmised. His knowledge of Alberti's temple-church of S Francesco at Rimini seems close to certain. Time and again the works of Codussi show some relation to Alberti, definite but not imitative, and only to Alberti's buildings, not to his theories as later adumbrated in writing—in Latin—which Mauro almost certainly would not have been able to read. Alberti's architecture was based not merely on observation of the antique, but strongly on theory, as his letters to his subordinates show. He would never have got his hands dirty on a building going up—assistants could always care for that—whereas Codussi, we feel sure, must have been right there with his workmen nearly every day. He made trips to Verona and to Istria to select suitable stone, of which he must have had knowledge based on experience. His buildings show a steady reliance on a mason's experience, along with a fastidious, simple, and spare humanist's taste. The last must have been partly inherent, partly learned from distinguished associates who were not architects and partly from observation of the best works of older Florentines.

Although he mastered the regular grammar of the classical orders (as well as his humanist friends mastered the regular grammar of Latin), he does not appear to have known at first hand any of the most important antique monuments later to be part of the regular stock of knowledge of reputable architects. He must have seen the few in

Verona many times when going back and forth for the winter from Venice to Lenna. He must have seen the rather "corrupt" arch at Rimini. But there is no reason to suppose that he, any more than Rizzo or Pietro, had ever been to Rome.

He may not have known the work of the Florentine contemporaries of his most active years, or not well, but he did know what he wanted of the work of Brunelleschi of a generation earlier. Haunting correspondences to episodes in Brunelleschi keep coming to light: in the emphatic clarity of forms, particularly the plain membering and moldings which underline those forms rather than just ornamenting them and, above all in his later work, in the felicity of his handling of geometrized space, something he may also have sensed in Alberti. Although not provable, it is all but certain that he had visited Florence profitably, which has already been implied, either on a youthful study trip or, more modestly but more nourishingly, as a mason's helper. Although there is no circumstantial evidence, he must have drawn items that interested him, which would prove of practical value later, sometimes decades later. Architectural drawings, sketches, or notes of the period are now of the greatest rarity, but he must have made a working packet of them while he was learning. They would, on the whole, have been of classical details and some felicities in combining them, not of grand plans or spatial schemes.

While Rizzo, Pietro, and Codussi were all working in the last three decades of the XVc, they were contemporary only in the strict measure of elapsed time. Their work is not closely related and will not coalesce into one Early Renaissance style typical of Venice and nowhere else. It pulls apart into three different personal manners that hardly need be contemporary: Rizzo, an improvising explorer; Pietro, a sculptor with a gift for decoration who got into architecture without having planned to; and Mauro, a born architect of genius. The venerable and encyclopedic historian of Italian art, Adolfo Venturi, once pointed out sharply (VIII, ii, 549), "While the Lombardos were printing the same textile patterns over and over in Venice and its neighborhood, Mauro Codussi of Bergamo practised architecture."

He was more the equivalent of Giovanni Bellini, who was born a decade before Mauro and died a dozen years after. Both discarded the florid Gothic being elaborated all around them in their youth; both found a new harmony, past that of their fellows; both welcomed the Renaissance and educed from it a personal, congenial, and unevenly classic language of form without ever becoming subservient or academic—Mauro with the fervor of a neophyte (Fiocco, 1930/31, 1203).

Working among Venetians from 1468-69 onward, he showed his different artistic credo clearly. From the first, for example, his exteriors have a certain relief, fairly low but not as flat as the facades of most of his contemporaries; his moldings are of geometrically pure profiles unlike anything else in Venice. They stand out clearly even in the softest light (and no city has more hours of soft light than Venice, not alone from drifting haze blown in from the sea but also from the pull of the sun on the water in every channel in the archipelagic city). A section cut through one of his examples of the genus cornice is plainly of quite a different species from anyone else's—until he began to be imitated.

He must have had to use the workmen he could find available in the city, some attracted there from outside, from Lombardy or Istria, surprisingly many (Puppi-Puppi, 181), already practiced in either the local or some more provincial manner, and sometimes a few from the sophisticated atelier at Urbino. Still, he managed to materialize his own ideals of form, at first with enough of the Venetian idiom not to alarm his clients—or perhaps because he was still finding his way. From the beginning it is clear that he was very much in charge, and gave less freedom to decorative carvers than did his predecessors or contemporaries. Locally unprecedented, his intellectual, elegant, but not austere style became acceptable to a widening circle, largely of humanistic ecclesiastics and aristocrats, and after a score of years detached elements from it began to appear in the work of others. Within a generation he had a few followers, including—surely to everyone's surprise—Tullio Lombardo. One could not say, however, that like the Lombardos he founded a Venetian school; his followers were not close imitators (he was not easy to imitate) and there were too few of them. Some followed his principles insofar as they could understand them—that was difficult—and some borrowed, not always comprehendingly, from his restricted but specific repertory of forms—and that was easier.

He died in 1504. Save for the work of a few serious followers, some of great distinction, and for a score of works still unattributed, some of equal distinction, his pure style barely survived him. His oeuvre thus stands apart from what is considered typical of his time in much the same way as would Palladio a couple of generations later. More accessible to local tastes, the Lombardo bequest outlasted Codussi's for decades, sometimes little altered, now flavored by personal idiosyncrasies, or weakened by old age, or mixed with a dilution of the heritage of Codussi. The real Lombardo heritage never really died, but slowly mutated into a more generalized kind of ornament, easily learned and adapted.

17 | S MICHELE IN ISOLA

The Island of S Michele Arcangelo, just north of Venice proper and halfway to Murano, was once called the *cavana*, or boathouse, of Murano, since it could serve as refuge for boats caught in squalls on the way there. Geographically peripheral and of no use economically or socially, it was given to the monks of the Camaldolesian order in 1212. Separated from both cities, the little island was thought ideal for the brothers' hermitlike regimen; also, legend claimed that S Romualdo (ca. 950-1027), the founder of the order, had stayed with a hermit on the island, where there was already a modest church of S Michele. (The Island of S Francesco del Deserto would later be given to the Franciscans because of a similar legend.) The first Camaldolesians had lived in colonies like hermits and called their monasteries "deserts," but by the XIIIc, here at S Michele, their life had become less eremitic and more cenobitic; a small, substantial monastery and brick church were built, probably not very different from small monasteries elsewhere.

By the 1460s the church had begun to crumble so that a new building was needed, and needed soon. After consultation with the superior Camaldolesian house at Classe, approval of its abbot was won, and work was begun late in 1468. Little more than a few lengths of foundation and an old wall on the cloister side proved worth saving, though other bits of foundation and walls may have been strengthened enough to have been used also.

It is not recorded whether Codussi had yet designed and built anything anywhere on his own. Although they fail to say that he made the first designs, the few documents about the beginnings of S Michele do say that he was already directing the work in 1469. A model would have been prepared and accepted earlier, say in 1468, and some preparation of the site would have begun then also, and probably some work on the foundations. The principal witness for Codussi's early presence is the church itself, which proclaims loud and clear that he certainly did design most of it.

Mauro must quickly have won enthusiastic confidence by his ability—later it was said that workmen did twice as much when he was there as when he was not—and as those in charge were eager to replace their time-worn old church, they had him go ahead as supervisor or architect or both. Their choice was bold, for there was not even one complete Renaissance building in Venice. Some influential Camaldolesians, as well as Mauro, must have known and admired Renaissance work elsewhere. Secure in their position, dependent on no public and little committee approval, the prior and his supporters dared appoint a revolutionary young architect (who must have offered mesmeric persuasions), quite the antithesis of those in charge of the Palazzo Ducale, who played safer and delayed longer before deciding on Rizzo, older, locally better known, and even so a bold choice.

Work would naturally have begun with whatever footings and foundations were needed, new ones or old ones repaired, and then with the outer walls of the church, nearly all new. Much must have been done quickly, for the new front doorway was already finished in 1470. The east end was built toward the last, perhaps so that services could be conducted in the old chancel as long as possible.

No other church had so spectacular a site. None rose straight out of the lagoon, or was so dramatically visible from so far. The front can rarely, despite poetic claims, be doubled by its reflection in mirror-smooth water, for the stretches of the lagoon between it, Venice proper, and Murano, can hardly ever be free of waves or ripples. But even so, the vast flat of shiny water, smooth or ruffled, cannot but lend dramatic impact to the elegant white front looming out of it, curbing it suddenly; surely Codussi took account of that.

The facade must have made a sensation as soon as the scaffold came down and the all stone white front was revealed, for there was nothing like it in Venice. No other church in Lombardy, the Veneto, Emilia or the Romagna, seen by Codussi or anyone else, can have prepared people for what they would see. In Venice there was no awareness of what Renaissance work could be like at large scale; only the unpredictable Arsenal gate, and some few decorative frontispieces, small, and not really quite architecture.

In 1469, Prior Delfin wrote his superior in Classe, with his typical hyperbole, "In the space of not even a year there has been completed what others could not have managed to do in many. And so I cannot fail already to see that a work of marvellous beauty and elegance has been begun, and if the part still to be built conforms to what has already been made, it will be considered among the noblest churches of our time" (Meneghin, I, 298).

Only the general outline of the facade is traditional, a tall center section with a half-round gable set between lower quarter-rounds at the ends of the aisles. Seeming original now, this outline was not rare then, and a few Gothic examples can be seen in Venice.*

There are or were other examples not far away, in Bologna, Concordia, Ferrara, and Vicenza. Soon there would be more in Venice, prompted by Codussi's authoritative reinterpretation of the old form, and then over a score of echoes in Friuli and the Istrian and Dalmatian coasts and islands.

* S Andrea della Zirada, S Aponal, S Giovanni in Bragora, S Giobbe (before it was reroofed), the Trinità (before it was demolished for the Salute), S Giorgio in Alga (before it burned in 1716), and others (fig. 17.1).

17.1 S Giovanni in Bragora.
Facade with typical late
Gothic three-part quarter-,
half-, and quarter-circular
skyline.

The three-part silhouette is an exterior projection of a basilican interior, especially in those churches where the nave had the much-esteemed boatlike wooden ceiling of bravura carpentry known as a *carena di nave* ("keel"), with a half-cylinder in the center sometimes abutted by quarter-cylinders over the aisles. (One of the finest, at S Caterina, was destroyed by flames on Christmas morning, 1977; the most splendid one now left is at S Stefano.) The curves of these tripartite facades, including S Michele, are not, however, immediate images of what is just behind, for they are usually in front of roofs set on straight rafters, a gable over the nave and lean-tos over the aisles (fig. 17.2). The late Gothic type of tripartite outline is probably not the sole source for S Michele. None of those Codussi would have seen had the full Renaissance vocabulary that S Michele shows as an integral part of its translation of the old Gothic shape. There was another model.

For that combination there was only one example, or rather part of one, the unfinished front of Alberti's S Francesco at Rimini (fig. 17.3). Its final design was known then from a model and drawings (now lost) and the compressed representation on the foundation medal by Matteo de' Pasti, 1450 (Heydenreich-Lotz, 32, 335n20, n23). To an eager architect-to-be in his twenties, working thirty miles away, this building must have been by far the most stimulating sight in the neighborhood, and he may have been watching it go up for years. He would have known of the wooden barrel vault proposed for the nave, theoretically justifying the half-round gable (even though the vault would have been covered by a pitched roof). Something between quadrants and scrolls would have screened the straight roofs over the side chapels of the aisleless S Francesco. The columns of the lower story would have offered visual support where it was needed for the heavy cornices of the semicircles and quarter-circles. The likenesses are too strong and the differences from other work too great to be only coincidence; S Francesco has to stand behind S Michele. Details, however, are not the same, and could not be expected to be, for the front of S Francesco was unfinished, and presumably few of its surprisingly unantique details can have been in place.

A dimmer but still powerful source was nearer by. The inspiration for the arched gable may have been nourished by the unforgettable front of S Mark's, where arched gables on the outside echo vaults on the inside (as in other Byzantine churches Codussi would not have known).

The later reflections in Venice, the Veneto, Emilia, and Dalmatia may make one fail now to recognize Codussi's daring in this first synthesis of the Renaissance vocabulary with the late Gothic and slightly Byzantine facade form. Inspired in large part by the unbuilt design for Rimini, he accepted Alberti's basic premises, but refined and reinterpreted them in simpler and more legible terms (fig. 17.4). The Renaissance elements have been so adroitly manipulated to function within the old shapes that their coordination looks natural and unforced, almost inevitable. Their combination on the front of S Michele is the clearest expression of the Renaissance yet carried out in Venice, as well as one of the very first, begun, it may be, before the Arsenal gateway was entirely finished. Here Codussi made a spectacular leap into the future.

In the upper half of the facade, pilasters carry a full entablature running the full width of the middle section. Its correct cornice is repeated as a rim for both the swinging quadrants and the arched gable-pediment, calling attention to itself by its scale and projection as well as the strong shadow it casts.

17.2 S Michele in Isola.
Church and surroundings in
1856 (lithograph by Moro
and Kier).

17.3 Rimini, S Francesco.
Medal (by Matteo de' Pasti)
showing the unbuilt facade
(Staatliche Museum, Berlin).

17.4 S Michele in Isola.
Facade. (The chapel at the
left is later, and the late
Gothic doorway at the right,
earlier.)

While unquestionably they enrich, the yards of egg and dart, dentils, and flutes are not allowed enough interest in themselves to arrest the eye anywhere; they reinforce without interrupting the shapes to which they adhere, more a small-scale pitter-patter than a rhythmical beat that might mark off the main lengths in recognizable measures. Punctiliously architectural in the strictest sense, they are far from the make-up of Rizzo's arch-pediment at S Elena, a bending of three rich moldings into a semicircle and not, as here, a bending of a real cornice; and both are a world away from the tumbles of flora and fauna of the Lombardos that keep inviting us to stop, examine, and enjoy.

As a sliver less than a semicircle, the middle arch is tied more to the wall below than a perfect autonomous semicircle would be. In the same way each quadrant is sliced at the bottom to less than a quarter-circle, which increases its call for apparent support, and also adds to its centralizing push inward. While none of the curves is easily sensed as incomplete, all are sensed as dependent on something else; none is self-sufficient. If detached, and no longer part of the walls they top, they would show their incompleteness. They work interdependently: the truncated quadrants together act like the ends of a giant bow; and the quiet but taut relations of the areas to one another may be sensed like the relations in a good Mondrian (in whose paintings, although at first glance there may seem to be a perfect square, there never is, nor are the rectangles in such simple apprehensible proportions as 1:2, 1:3, 2:3). While nothing, then, is geometrically ideal, all depends instead on push, pull, or counterweight as neighbors to come at last to that Olympian equipoise.

The fragmentary tympanums are edged with a band of silver-gray marble, and the rest is filled with cockleshell fluting, ideally suited to the curved spaces it has to fill. It develops into that space by the nature of its flutes, expanding as they radiate, fanlike, from one unemphasized source. Within the cornice of the big gable, more fluting wheels around in an equally appropriate way, and since one flute is like another, again the eye is not tempted to stop, but travels on to take in the complete set. All this ornament works in such an inevitable way in its place that one has to be reminded how original some of it was when it was made. Similar flutes wheeling around inside a curve were imitated in the portal of the Church of the Madonna dell' Orto (fig. 17.5, also with a big *oculus* above and a smaller circle above that) begun only a few years later, in 1473 (Clarke-Rylands, 11).

At the ends, the juncture of curved gable and level cornice is enlivened by a rosette, as so often on "Florentine" pediments. The rose is neatly rolled in the top fillet-band of the cornice, and enriched somewhat exclamatorily by a big openwork half-honeysuckle above. Similar openwork, doubled, supports a figure of the Redeemer at the top (a reworking after the 1819 hurricane?), standing out alone against the sky in the many fine views of the church across the water, even from as far as Murano or Venice. Even though not repetitive like the flutes and dentils, these accents are allowed to play only a small part in the whole. Prepared for, even expected, they come at strategic points in the currents of implied movement that are important in tying the composition together: the whole dominates everything.

The pediment-gable stands on a full entablature whose frieze is plain except for the elegant incised inscription, DOMVS MEA DOMVS ORATIONIS. Lettering on a frieze and even the very Roman formation of the individual letters must come straight from Alberti's Tempio Malatestiano at Rimini, or from the palace at Urbino. (This is before Aldus Manutius set up his famous printing shop in Venice. He did design one inscription at S Michele, but later, and inside the church.)

The two fascias of the architrave are sloped so that each will catch more light than if it were vertical. Inclined fascias are so habitual with Codussi as to be almost an autograph. The examples noted earlier, at the atrium of S Giovanni and at the Miracoli, were made later than these at S Michele, and could come from the intervention of Tullio, who underwent a conversion to the tenets of Codussi. Such fascias remained a Venetian peculiarity for decades, until they were spontaneously (?) reinvented by Michelangelo at the Palazzo Farnese in Rome, although antique examples had been recorded in the city, for example in the *Codex Coner*, 83, 89, 92, 98, 106, 110 (fig. 17.6). Without knowing antique samples, Codussi could have reinvented them, or he could have seen drawings showing them in Rome or Istria (trips thither cannot be assumed), but more probably he had seen some antique example nearby, maybe at Verona on the Arco dei Leoni, the Arch of Jupiter Ammon, or the Porta dei Borsari (G G Zorzi 1959, 1, 16, 18, 22, 23, 27), which he may have noticed on his annual winter trips to and from Lenna.

The rectangle between the upper and lower entablatures is faced with white Greek marble, pierced by a large bull's-eye window framed by plain moldings and one carved like a chain. Rectangle and *oculus* are bordered by the same pale gray marble as the quadrants and gable. Circles of porphyry and serpentine in the corners may derive from the same old Venetian custom already taken over by Alberti for Rimini, which might have sanctified it for Codussi. While the *oculus* and discs are perfect geometric shapes, in the all-over design only the *oculus* counts forcefully. But the centralizing pull it might be expected to exert is lessened by its not being in the true center of the rectangle, not the same distance from top and bottom of the rectangle; and the distance from the sides is still greater. The lack of exact centrality is pointed up by the relation to the cornices of the quadrants, which push intrusively into the oblong wall, but evade any relation to discs or *oculus.* The small porphyry ellipse set into the arched gable, just below the flutes, is correspondingly raised above its expected center position, and adds another (though small) lift to the facade. (The ellipse, rare at this date, may have been copied from Alberti at Rimini.)

The strongest motif to compete with the cornices and *oculus* in this upper half is the pair of paneled pilasters that carry the breaks in the upper cornice supporting the ends of the arched gable. Their Composite capitals (nothing like Rimini), one leaf high, are repeated around the corner on the sides, with the corner volutes merging "properly" to project at 45°, probably in a sophisticated show of conscious antiquarianism. By Vitruvian standards the form is a hybrid, but Vitruvian standards are as irrelevant at this date as Linnaean botanical standards would be for the leaves. A short length of pilaster runs down under these capitals on the sides of the building, but is soon stopped dead by the top of the quadrant.

An abrupt chop is made in these pilasters by the piece of cornice that breaks around them, at once continuing and bringing to an end the sweep of the quadrants. This is not only non-Vitruvian, but out-and-out anticlassical. As symbols of support, pilasters are not to be interrupted by anything, certainly not by a piece of heavy cornice. Below this intrusion, the shaft reappears for a short length as though nothing had happened, with an all but unnoticeable acknowledgment only by the small molding of its paneling, returned below the break.

17.5 Madonna dell'Orto.
Main portal, 1473.

17.6 Antique architraves
with inclined fascias (sheet
98 of the Codex Coner,
Soane Museum, London).

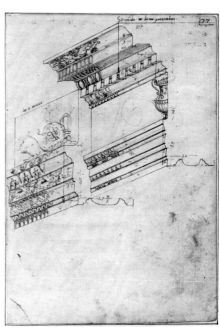

The reason that the pilasters are cut by the cornices is easy to see. Pilasters had been thought suitable for the upper part of the wall here, to give visual underpinning for the ends of the arched gable. Also, the cornices of the quadrants had to have some justification for being brought to a quick stop, and what could do this as well as breaking them around the pilasters in the ordinary way for cornices above engaged supports? (But neither pilasters nor supports could, of course, be quite normal here.) At the top, a similar break was made in the full entablature, under normal conditions; below, in the middle of the pilaster, conditions could not be normal, but the breaking out of the cornice manages to offer a solution or near solution to a new problem with no classical precedent. The solution must have seemed the best one to Codussi, for he used it later when confronted with the same problem.

One difference from Alberti can be seen in the greater animation worked into the composition to guide our eyes along the directions controlled by the main sequences of the membering on the facade. Implications of movement, or channels along which our glances are enticed, meet at right angles where the horizontal end at the top of the quadrant crosses the vertical pilaster. The quadrant has considerable force, yet the pilaster, seemingly weaker, is not cut off by it, but merely gives in for a moment and then goes on again to carry out its duty of seeming to support the round gable by transmitting the upward movement begun by the pilasters of the ground story. The gable accepts this thrust at its springing and then swings the kinetic impulse around to a close. The quadrants do their part by bending the upward impulse of the pilasters that lead to them inward toward the middle of the composition, where it can be easily contained.

The shock of all this impropriety of cutting through pilasters and such comes to us now only as a second thought. The first impact of the upper half of the front is one of equipoise, not simple, but achieved by sensitive maneuvering of strict architectural elements into a new order that balances but does not annihilate inherent implications of movement. The few clumsy details count for little. There is a strong harmony that comes from an equilibration of forces as much as from equilibrium of shapes. There is something assertive, even affirmative about the arrangement, and it is therefore markedly different from the quiescent decorativeness of the upper part of the Miracoli, whose large number of circles and larger gable are all complete, all fairly inactive, with none intimately related to another. The implicit movements at S Michele are greater than those in Alberti's serene and static facade, and the composition is therefore less stable and more animated, less Roman and in this one respect newer, perhaps from a much transformed retention of mediaeval kinetics.

The frieze of the entablature running across the front between the upper and lower stories is inscribed, HOC IN TEMPLOS VMME DEVS EXORATVS ADVENIET CLEMEN BON PR VOSVECIPE. The wall below, of Istrian limestone, must be the second example of rustication in the city, made in the same decade as the Ca' del Duca—one at the beginning, the other at the end (fig. 17.7). The effect is more delicate, and so much flatter that in the strictest sense it might be denied the term "rusticated," for the surfaces of the blocks are smooth and the sunk channels are narrow. The effect is less staccato and more continuous, like the second story of Michelozzo's Medici Palace (after 1444) or like Alberti's Rucellai (ca. 1455-60) in Florence (fig. 17.8). The origin of Mauro's idea may well be Florentine—he might have recalled the upper floors of the Medici Palace while

17.7 S Michele in Isola.
Lower half of facade.

17.8 Alberti and Bernardo
Rossellino. Palazzo Rucellai,
Florence. *Bifora* of piano
nobile.

ignoring the rougher and more truly rusticated floor below—unless there were antique Roman examples, now vanished, in regions he knew in his early years. He would not have known, as Michelozzo and Alberti did, the beautiful channeled ashlar of the tomb of Cecilia Metella on the Appian Way, the outstanding Roman prototype.

There appear to be only two lengths of stone blocks, squares and rectangles twice as long; but while this appears to be so, actually there are stretchings and compressions to make the stone joints come out in agreement with the pilasters. Without showing themselves unless deliberately hunted, these irregularities give a stimulating and insinuating animation to the overall rhythm.

At the ends of the rusticated wall, under the breaks in the entablature from which the quadrants spring, and also under the stubby pilasters that carry the breaks from which the gable springs, there are strong visual supports in the form of pilasters. Ten times higher than wide, they gain needed ruggedness from their rustication. This seems a leap into some of the future tricks of Mannerism, but even bolder rusticated pilasters had been used in Roman work, perhaps unknown to Mauro, and less extreme ones may have been seen by him on the Piccolomini Palace at Pienza (1460-62), by Bernardo Rossellino following designs by Alberti, who may not, however, have intended to have them rusticated (fig. 17.9).

The whole front is vivid white, for it is always being washed by sun, rain, and wind. In spite of the strong projection of the cornice and capitals, little black has formed on the stone below them, and that only on the lower parts of the building. Even the channels of the rustication of the building stay clean, for the sides of the blocks that run between are so sloped that rainwater runs off and sunlight bathes them

easily. The front is boldly modeled, and unlike the flattish background for flattish ornament favored by the Lombardos. It shows a feeling for the structure of the wall, and it makes that an essential of the design. Although the whole has strong monumentality, no part is at large scale; the monumental quality is inherent, not just something acted out by a few grandiose parts.

The rustication is interrupted by the doorway and by two Brunelleschian windows three squares high, with round tops, a staple form beginning to go out of fashion in Florence and Rome. The moldings of the frames run continuously around them in the Brunelleschian way, uncut by sill or impost. The form may have been a favorite in Venice so long because it was so familiar as an echo of the tall, narrow, arched windows long used on Gothic churches and palaces.

To receive the rods of an iron grille, a band with holes runs up the inner part of each window jamb and unexpectedly ends in its own little capital at the base of the arch. Unlike this un-Brunelleschian improvisation, inexperience allows the tops of the arched heads to cut the network pattern of the rustication without being made to coordinate with its channels. No voussoirs or other elements are worked into the pattern; instead, the regularity of the alternating blocks is simply bitten into, leaving those over the windows looking brittle and weak.

To make a suitable portal on rather standard lines, jamb-pilasters carry an entablature (the architrave with non-Codussian vertical fascias and the frieze lettered, DIVI MICHAELIS AR TEMPLUM) ending in a pediment (its cyma set correctly on the slopes only). The little tympanum and the narrow slices between the door frame and the pilasters are faced with sumptuous purple onyx streaked with cream (fig. 17.10). So discreetly introduced—almost furtively—these come as surprises

17.9 Palazzo Piccolomini, Pienza.

17.10 S Michele in Isola. Main doorway.

when first noticed in what had seemed a wholly white facade, despite its pianissimo of silvery gray bands and piano of four small colored discs, drowned out by the surrounding areas of strong white.

The frame enclosing the door turns inward on itself at the bottom in an antique manner, probably taken over secondhand from Brunelleschi rather than from any antique example. Everything carvable is carved, yet this must be earlier than nearly all Lombardo work in Venice, and certainly earlier than the separation of the Lombardo and Codussi streams. The profiles of the moldings, the appropriateness of the carved patterns to the profiles they overlay, and the suitable shape of each molding to its particular place are all closer to the antique via Florence than to everyday Lombardo practice. Still, the portal, probably made in 1469-70 (at more or less the same time as Pietro's at S Giobbe) is closer to typical Lombardo work than anything else on the facade. As such, it asks for special explanation.

The date comes so early in the building campaign that it shows that the doorway must have been carved independently in the shop before half the front was up. One notice (1470) gave it to Ambrogio da Milano (Sansovino, 235), a Lombard but not necessarily a Lombardo, perhaps the man known as Ambrogio da Urbino after he began working there in 1474. Recent study now favors instead Lorenzo da Venezia, with a contract of 1469 for windows and a "doorway of his own design" (Meneghin, I, 300). Whichever of them did what—both may have been involved—the product was not yet in tune with Mauro's still developing style. The carver is known for no other comparable work and his exact identity is of little importance. But the fact that Lorenzo may have been allowed to use "his own design" is, as far as we know,

unique for Codussi. It shows that at the beginning he did not command the complete authority that would be his from then on (except for insistent clients), and also that there was still some Gothic freedom for the carver, soon to disappear into the complete control of the architect in charge. Soon he would plan every bit of his creation in advance—the role proclaimed and practiced by Alberti. Anyone who was able to impose a new style as quickly and as thoroughly as Alberti or Codussi must have had a remarkably winning or intimidating character.

Not only the carving but the whole portal is overdainty for the size of the facade and for the scale of its other openings. This could come from the ingrained habits of the professional carver, unused to Codussi and unused to such monumentality, or it could be evidence of Mauro's inexperience at the start of his Venetian career. Only the height of the Madonna standing on a tall base at the top of the pediment pulls the whole composition of the doorway up into an acceptable relation in scale with the rest of the front. Perhaps, furthermore, it had a bit more importance and dignity when it rose higher, as shown in old prints, before half the flight of semicircular steps leading up to it was buried when the pavement was raised (E Paoletti, I, 161. Since the pavement area in front of the church is narrow, one cannot see the front except at a sharp angle; the doorway hence looms more than it would if seen in a good all-over view, possible only from a boat. (The scale of the florid Gothic portal to the cloister, on the right, does not help the door by contrast, nor does the chapel added on the left ca. 1530.)

Codussi must have chosen to ignore the possibilities for a composition made up of masses—or never have thought of it. The left side of the church, now separated from the front by the hexagonal chapel, could undoubtedly have been worked into some sort of three-dimensional composition with the facade; and the entrance to the cloister, arranged with the old Gothic portal, could have been set somewhat farther back, throwing the main facade into relief. For a building that could be seen from such a wide variety of views from the water, left and right, near and far, a composition of organized masses might have been rewarding. But Venice was not then, any more than it had been or would be, a city sensitive to such complex solid compositions; and Codussi, only a little more three-dimensional than everyone else, designed an essentially flat facade, one that could as well have been made to go on a canal or a street.

Prior Delfin's enthusiasm never flagged, and the finished front inspired him to a spate of praise. In 1476 he wrote, "Every day the elegance of the building invites more admiration; it is praised by everyone." And in 1477, "it not only recalls antiquity, but surpasses it. Come hither, then to see something great and singular, with enrichment and decorousness that bring credit not only to our Order but also to our city. . . . Excepting only, of course, the Church of S Mark, I prefer our facade to all others. It has already been brought to perfection and splendor, with such beauty that it attracts the gaze of all who go by" (Meneghin, I, 305, 308, 309). He cannot have been bothered at all that the Istrian stone front made it cost far more than the stuccoed or raw brick on its immediate forebears and contemporaries. He wanted the best and he got it.

Although S Michele is the first church of the Renaissance in Venice, its plan is not uniquely of the Renaissance, nor really unusual; it may not even be all new, for some of the south wall was used again, and since the underpinning must be old there, it may be in other parts too. The three east bays of the present five-bay nave may stand where the old church was and may perhaps stand on the old foundations if those were good enough to be used again. The body of the old church would, then, have been almost square, only a couple of feet longer than wide (Angelini 1945, fig 2, inaccurate plan; Meneghin, I, fig 27, accurate plan). The new nave is longer than the old, and the new east end is probably quite different but, taken together, they show little novelty. The Renaissance qualities must be sought elsewhere.

The arcades separating the nave from the aisles would not have been spaced the same way, for the new arrangement has lofty and wide arches, unlike XIIIc work and more like something late Gothic or Brunelleschian (figs. 17.11 and 17.12). There are now only three arches on each side of the area the early church supposedly occupied; there would probably have been five or six in the original. The foundations for the new columns would have to be larger, and specially made. The new arrangement makes the nave and aisles almost one continuous space, punctuated by four slender columns, and varied in only a minor way by the different levels in their flat ceilings.

Some of the columns were made in 1475, but probably not erected; more were being made in 1476. They stand on low, wide pedestals, typical of Codussi (as his later work will show). Neither classical nor Gothic in proportion, they were classicized a bit by discreet moldings top and bottom. The bases of the columns are properly orthodox: square plinth under convex-concave-convex moldings more geometrically explicit than the variants of Mauro's contemporaries. The shafts, six to seven diameters high, flare a little at top and bottom with what may be the first classical apophyges of the Renaissance in the city, a small thing, but indicative. They must come from good observation of a good antique

17.11 S Michele in Isola.
View from nave into chancel and apse.

17.12 S Michele in Isola.
View from aisle into nave
and chancel.

example, for neither Byzantine nor Gothic shafts were finished off in this way; they usually had no more than a wider flat band, as on the appropriated mediaeval shafts at the Arsenal or the Foscari Monument.

Codussi's interests were not slavishly antiquarian; these same shafts show a barely perceptible swelling before they begin tapering, in a double entasis not rare at the time, and soon—surprisingly—sanctioned by Alberti (Alberti, II, bk VII, ch iv, fig 13). The columns carry the nave arches directly, which was not done by the Romans in anything Mauro would have seen (with the semi-exception of the baptistery of Florence, then thought an ex-temple of Mars); this is a scheme at variance with the precepts soon to be set down by Alberti (II, bk VII, ch V, 560 for example). The capitals vary from bay to bay, unclassically but mediaevally, with each matching its mate across the aisle. The carved details are varied, more or less classical but put together in a far from classical way. The proper echinus is a square with concave sides over volutes springing out radially under the cut-off corners, interrupting a fat echinus trimmed with an egg and dart, a braid, and a wreath. But the bell below is left oddly bare, sometimes transparently sheathed in lily leaves, spiral flutes, or draped beads, nonstandard designs Mauro or one of his assistants (Buora?) would use for variations at S Zaccaria. The details must have been carved by men used to working in the old way, but now at work under a nonsculptor architect designing in a new way unfamiliar to them.

Some arches were reported as being carved in 1473, and if they were not for the nave, they were probably destined for the heads of windows (Guida artistica . . . 1889, 24). What were more surely the nave archivolts must have been made later, and they were kept narrow so that the abacus of each capital could receive one arch from each side, with only their outermost moldings having to merge where they met a foot above the capital, then to come straight down in a modest stilt. The slenderness and spareness of columns and archivolts, and the lightness given by the stilting would not look out of place in a work of Brunelleschi.

The flat wooden ceiling is arranged with square coffers, three across the nave, two across the aisles. Brunelleschi's S Lorenzo (which keeps recurring as a possible model for various parts of the church) may have suggested this, though by the late XVc, such coffered ceilings were not rare. Money for the roof timbers was given in 1476; the prior was desperate to get the roof on in 1477; and after building activity was slowed down by an epidemic in 1478, the church was considered all but completed in 1479. Once the roof was up, the ceiling, not a structural element, could have been fitted in under it at any time. There probably was a delay, for a fragment survives painted with the date 1499. The original ceiling was wrecked in a hurricane in 1819 and quickly patched somehow. The existing ceiling is a replacement of 1899, probably accurate. The entire church underwent minor alterations and restorations in 1546 and again in 1690, both of unknown extent.

The old church may have been covered by only three bays of the new one, ending where the bridgelike *barco, cantoria,* or singing gallery crosses the nave, setting off what is left of the fourth bay and all of the fifth into a sort of forechurch or pseudo-narthex. There were a few similar galleries in other monastic churches in Venice and more on the mainland. Other Camaldolesian churches gave them sanction. But the pseudo-forechurch at S Michele may have been unique. Except for S Mark's and the Carthusian Church of S Andrea, narthexes were not used in XVc Venice, as far as is known.

The narthex-like space, the nave, and then the deep east end add up to a fairly large and complex church to serve a few dozen monks on an island with no parish. The equivalent case of the Carthusians on their island of S Andrea called for only a small fore-church for occasional visitors and the score of workmen helping on the monks' farm (McAndrew 1969, 20). The Camaldolesians were not, apparently, such farmers, but they had more visitors from the city; relatives and distinguished intellectuals attracted by the fine library of the monastery, certain scholarly monks, and famous eloquent preachers.

The nave leads to a rectangular presbytery, flat-walled on both sides, semicircular in back, and covered by a barrel vault and a shallow dome on pendentives, the whole flanked on each side by smaller chapels of similar formation. As has been said, vaulting had been little used in Venice since the building of S Mark's. Since S Michele was about complete in 1479, and one of the flanking chapels had already been dedicated, if the main dome was not up in 1479—as is most likely—it was well foreseen and prepared for; the side chapels could provide adequate buttressing.

The scheme of a nave and aisles with flat wood ceilings leading to an east end with barrel vaults, semidomes, and three full domes on pendentives seems to imply some sort of contradiction, some change of ideas. Work had begun at the west end so that the old nave could be used for services as long as possible—at least until 1475; the old chancel was pulled down in 1476 (Puppi-Puppi, 177, 181). These vaults and domes may not have been on the original model but have been conceived in the late 1470s, in a situation somewhat like that at S Giobbe. The monks and the Venetian patrons of the church were notably intellectual, humanistic,

unafraid of new ideas, and delightfully rich. It has been suggested that the new idea came from some unused scheme of Alberti's for the east end at Rimini (Puppi-Puppi, 28), which Codussi might have known, but there is no evidence for this.

The main dome could then anticipate S Giobbe's in conception and execution. Codussi's ought to be the first fair-sized dome on pendentives of the Venetian Renaissance (ignoring the small, non-Venetian, imported Florentine pendentive domes of the Martini Chapel at S Giobbe, begun about 1471), a claim that would fit well with what is known of Codussi's career. It does not fit well with Pietro Lombardo's, whose puzzling dome at S Giobbe may be earlier—from the early 1470s or possibly the late 1470s or, less probably, from a generation later. Typical of Pietro's other work, his composition is lavishly introduced by a grand carved arch, and the pendentives are filled with sculpture; typical of Codussi is his scheme, relying on architectural forms almost alone, with no carved ornament except the obligatory capitals.

No chronological parade of domes up to about 1505 can be kept in satisfactory order; they cannot be arranged with documented certainty, but only by induction. Moreover, before such a sequence could be worked out, one strange monument that could have some relation to S Michele ought to be considered: the destroyed Carthusian Church of S Andrea, on its own island just east of the main part of the city. A recently found XVIIc plan (McAndrew 1969, 20n20, fig 13) shows a square chancel with a dome on pendentives and a semicircular apse, flanked by similar chapels with similar domes. These alone are not enough to set the two churches together, and apart from the general run. For one thing, the rest of S Andrea was vaulted. What they have in common is the trio of three domed chapels at the east end found nowhere else. Those at S Andrea were probably begun only in the 1480s, when enough of S Michele was built to make clear how it was going to be finished. The author of S Andrea is nowhere reliably named, but he has been seen as close to Codussi, or as Codussi himself (Timofiewitsch 1964, 282n7); though not impossible, this can be neither proved nor disproved. Since the construction is presumably later, however, it may be no more than a Carthusian borrowing from the Camaldolesians, not a sibling but an offspring. Yet the same arrangement of domed chancel flanked by domed chapels was not uncommon in Byzantine architecture in the Xc and XIc. Similar though the arrangements are, there does not seem to be any clear connection and there need be no copying, for the same design could have been thought up more than once.

With all this in mind, the following chronology might be suggested. S Michele may claim to be the first real dome on pendentives of the Renaissance in Venice, though some argue that Pietro Lombardo's dome at S Giobbe should be declared at least a tie for first place, if not the first. The next would be the small one on the Cappella Gussoni (ca. 1480?), also carried by engaged pilaster-piers. But the gored Gussoni dome is so different that it probably stems from another antecedent. Next would come Codussi's larger dome on S Zaccaria (1483), and Pietro Lombardo's on the Miracoli (ca. 1485–89?). Perhaps later in the 1480s would come that on the Certosa di S Andrea. Then that on the Cornaro Chapel (ca. 1490), tentatively ascribed by some to Mauro, like that on the Certosa (P. Paoletti, 234; Franzoi Di-Stefano 156; Lewis 1973, 364). And after all these comes one surely by him, on S Maria Formosa (1492–1502), rebuilt in the Baroque but now rebuilt again on the probable original lines.

After all of these might come Pietro's dome at S Giobbe, if it does not come at the beginning. It is clear that Codussi, whose name comes up in connection with five—three times securely—is the major figure in the development of the Renaissance dome in Venice. His inspiration would have come from Brunelleschi, just as for the facade it had come from Alberti. He chose the best tutors!

Bold arches span the chancel of S Michele with archivolts as wide as the depth of the piers. The plain north and south arches are carried by flattish capitals that might be expected to come at the top of pilasters, but are simply hung on blank wall instead, like the corbel capitals Brunelleschi had used on the Hospital of the Innocents in Florence (a possible inspiration for these, which may be the first in Venice). Tangent to the crowns of all four of these arches is the circle of molding that marks the tops of the pendentives of which the arches mark the sides.

On this circle rests the low, blind dome, dark in spite of the light from the windows under the side arches between the pendentives (taking light from above the roofs of the side chapels). More light comes from the five dramatic, tall, narrow, arched windows cut in the apse, shaped like those in the facade. The flanking Zorzi and Donà family chapels, with arches level with those of the nave arcade, are handled in the same way except that their arches spring from capitals on unusual corbels with cherubs' heads, and also that everything is at smaller scale.

S Michele's vaulted east end seems like a different kind of building from the nave, which is thin, linear, airy, and closer to Brunelleschi. The nave is divided by a rift from the walled and vaulted east end, which is heavier, more concerned with mass, and even more with commensurable enclosed space. Had Mauro been eyeing antique or Byzantine vaulting somewhere? He may have had to be persuasive to have his new, grand, and more costly ideas accepted by the Camaldolesians, who had surely never before had a church like this. Many of the brothers came from the greatest Venetian families and may have maintained some taste for unmonastic luxury; many of them and of the generous patrons were humanistically educated enough not to draw back from a proposal which was patently so new in being so classical.

The prior, D Pietro Delfin, a dedicated humanist, was obsessively ambitious for his new building (Letters to his superior, Abbot D Pietro Donà, in *Epistolarum . . . Epistole inedite . . . ,* cited by Meneghin 1962, passim). He might well have been enthusiastic over the proposal to add three domes to a scheme otherwise unusual only in detail. He never stopped asking for more and more money, even when he must have known that little was available. There were several work stoppages, some while waiting for money, one for the epidemic of 1478, and one every winter when all building operations ordinarily shut down in Venice. If the decoration was done last, as is probable, it may have had less supervision directly by Mauro, who was beginning to be busy elsewhere; but the basic idea of a walled and vaulted east end, whether originally envisaged or added later, is certainly his.

Father Delfin's begging was sometimes generously rewarded. As early as 1475, the patrician Marco Zorzi, soon to commission a palace from Mauro, gave handsomely for the lesser chapel at the right of the chancel, and most of the work, including vaults and dome, was finished in two years. First dedicated to the Madonna, a change was made when Giovanni Bellini's wonderful altarpiece of the Resurrection (now in Berlin) was installed in 1479. Another Pietro Donà, not the abbot in Ravenna but probably a relative, must have commissioned the twin chapel on the left soon after, and his wife's tomb

was already in place there by 1493. The domed chancel was probably designed before work was begun in 1475 on the adjoining Zorzi chapel, which helps buttress it. The nave was not yet finished, for columns for it were still being made in 1476. If this vaulted east end shows an advance in Mauro's style, that must have come about in a very few years, for by 1480 everything must have been well along, and much as it is now, including the vaults. The brothers Tommaso and Bernardo Loredan gave money and goods, probably for the furnishings of the finished but empty chancel. In his will of 1482, Pietro Donà left money for its paving; it must already have been fully vaulted. Their kinsman, Andrea Loredan, for whom Mauro would build his last palace, also made generous contributions. The whole east end, then, was made from ca. 1475-76 to ca. 1480-82.

In the chancel, the pilasters stand on tall pedestals ornamented with arabesques more Lombardo-like than anything yet seen in the nave, yet stricter and less fanciful than genuine Lombardo work. Above them, the deep pilasters or engaged square piers carry a full entablature, not Lombardesque at all but Codussi-like in its lack of fancy carving.

The dome at S Michele was half-disguised on the outside, encased in a low cylindrical wall like a drum, under a low cone of roof. The curved brick walls of the apse and apsidioles, lower down, are entirely traditional, with pilaster strips and arched corbel tables at the top, with a corbel above each apse window. They look like work of any time after ca. 1000, all in brick, but undoubtedly they were made in the 1470s. Not expected to show much, they were not given monumental or modern treatment. The whole arrangement is shown clearly in Jacopo de' Barbari's map of 1500. It is little changed today, still with its low tiled cone over the dome, and plain brick side walls, now with a few added chapels (fig. 17.13). It is and always must have been unrelated to the design of the facade.

In 1513, in the middle of the war with the League of Cambrai, the worst threat in Venice's history, Andrea Loredan was killed. He had been a patron of the church and of Codussi, whom he probably knew well. More funds for the presbytery came from his estate; marble seats were built along the sides, a new pavement of colored marbles was laid, and Loredan and his wife were buried there. Sets of sumptuous dorsals (hangings to go behind the altar) were specially made in the major liturgical colors. In the donor's honor, the engaged piers were decorated with reliefs (in round panels already there?) with the six roses of the Loredan arms. Henceforth the chancel was often called the Cappella Loredana.

At the same time, a new arrangement was made, with funds from the same gift, for sheathing the dome with a much higher dummy dome of lead plates on wood framing, like those of S Mark's, SS Giovanni e Paolo, and the Miracoli. To the striking facade this now added a striking silhouette in distant views. It was hit by lightning in 1671 and 1738, and ordered taken down and replaced in 1774, but it can still be seen on a number of drawings and engravings looking much as it does at present. (Vavassore (Vadagnino) woodcut map ca. 1525, and others, one copying another, v. Cassini 35–37 and passim; pen drawing 1734 originally in library of S Michele, Cod Vat Lit 13691; engraving by A Visentini in Giucciardini, *Istoria d'Italia* in his 1777 *Isolario*.)

Conceived at about the same time as the nave and chancel, but realized a little later, are two dependencies on the left. Money was given for a sacristy by Pietro Boldù in 1483; work was begun

in 1485, finished in 1500. His tomb is there, dated 1495, and his arms are carved on the pilasters. The architecture is a simpler version of that of the chapels beside the chancel, with the special refinement that the little apse here has two windows, one near each edge, so that light can flood the altar and altarpiece in the middle without shining in anyone's eyes. (The similar arrangement at the Cappella Corner in the SS Apostoli was made at about the same time, but for a rectangular apse.) The once much praised lavabo is carved with fine-scale ornament on every molding and bracket, and the flat areas are of slabs of the most richly striated marble. It is not like an idea of Codussi's or even of an architect's, but of some specialist in rich church furniture. No other piece from the Quattrocento in Venice is more luxurious.

The Cappella della Croce, finished by 1480 but surely a somewhat sudden addition not planned in the original scheme, is entered from the left aisle through a particularly fine and noticeably Florentine doorway. Its apse, polygonal outside, an old Adriatic tradition, has a pair of windows placed like those of the sacristy, and once they gave light to a triptych by Giovanni Bellini, finished in 1507 (now in the Düsseldorf Gallery). Most of the interior has been remodeled at one time or another, but the basic form must go back to Codussi. The space was long used as a family chapel by the Priuli family.

Beyond any question, the most important addition to the nave was the *barco*, bridging it near the west end (fig. 17.14). This could hardly have been begun before 1480, but something of the sort must have been foreseen, since an extra yard was given to the last bay of the nave to assure room for it. *Barcos* were rare in Venice, as has been said, and this is the only survivor of the *pontile* or bridgelike type, though once there were others in S Antonio, the Carità, and the Servi (McAndrew 1974, 27, 34; Meneghin, I,

17.13 S Michele in Isola.
Exterior of apse and dome.

17.14 S Michele in Isola.
Barco. East side, facing
nave.

327n94). The raised space for the monks was handily entered through an upstairs doorway from the corridor beside their cells, so that they could come easily into the church to sing or recite their obligatory offices, day and night.

The whole marble and limestone construction, half the height of the nave, consists of five arched square bays, all alike. While its function, location, and scale are those of a large piece of furniture, its design and material are not, but are thoroughly architectural. The nave probably had no other furniture—no chairs, no confessionals, not even a pulpit—for there was no lay congregation to hear sermons. The rituals performed by the monks here in their own monastery church were in a number of ways different from the Masses said or sung in parish churches.

Arches set on piers and enriched with pilasters on pedestals face the main part of the nave, and make a rich effect with many arabesques of conventional design. The soffits of the arches are restless with many rosettes, and at their springing, the arches are idiosyncratically enlivened with heads in semicircular panels, probably unique (figs. 17.15, 17.16). Everything is as rich as if it had been made by Pietro Lombardo, not unsuitably since the *barco* is as much furniture as architecture, but the details are not Pietro's. They are as refined as his in execution, but more classical and less individual in design, with a few odd exceptions. Above the standard architrave, instead of a standard frieze, a big quarter-circle swings suddenly forward, reinforced by paired brackets set among calicolike dozens of rosettes. The stone parapet at the top is almost massless in its effect because pierced all over with a fish-scale pattern like a Roman bronze grille. Except for the marble spandrels and a pair of circles, there is no color. The only color in the entire nave is on the ceiling, the marble floor, and a few discs set here and there in the wall.

The side of the *barco* facing the door must be the work of another team of craftsmen. Not only is the design (slender, garlanded, and engaged columns in a standard Roman arch order) different in character but so are the details of the carving and the exuberance of color. The spandrels are of rich peach and plum marbles, and the parapet has slabs of five other kinds and one of onyx (fig. 17.17). All this is close to the current idiom of the Lombardos seen at the Miracoli, including an inlaid cross and circles of serpentine and porphyry, but not close enough in specific details to assign anything here to the same craftsman. Lombardesque episodes appear occasionally in the oeuvre of Codussi, presumably from workmen trained in the Lombardo manner, but no Codussi-type episodes show themselves in the certain works of Pietro Lombardo. As Codussi was occupied elsewhere from 1482 on, much of the *barco* may have been made without his close supervision. In all the church it is the least like what will come to be his identifiable personal style. It could depend here more on the taste of the ambitious prior.

The elaborately inlaid wood seats have nothing to do with Mauro, for they were made after he died, in 1532-34, by Alessandro Bigno. In the heyday of the monastery, they may have had to hold quite a crowd, for forty monks, seven priests, seven choristers, eight novices, six lay brothers, and four servitors lived there, and sometimes nearly all of them, except the servants and the few officiating at Mass or other monastic functions would have been on the *pontile* at the same time.

The spatial effect of the nave crossed by the *pontile* cannot be found in any other Venetian church today, and probably the bridgelike affairs at the Gothic Carità and the Gothic Servi, being in higher naves, seemed even more furniturelike, and made less of an effect on

17.16 S Michele in Isola. *Barco* Capital and head at springing of arch on west side.

17.15 S Michele in Isola. *Barco.* Coffered soffit of overhang on east side.

17.17 S Michele in Isola. *Barco* from west side.

18.1 S Pietro di Castello.
Belltower.

as satisfactory. Sabellico, writing in 1489-90, noted it as "recently finished" (Sabellico, 26). It stood intact for nearly 200 years, but then in 1670 a thunderbolt destroyed the bell chamber. Codussi's original is known only from fingernail-size depictions on printed panoramas, such as Jacopo de' Barbari's of 1500 (fig. 18.2), or Vavassore's (Vadagnino's) of ca. 1525 (Cassini, 35; Schulz 1970, 42), based on Jacopo's, but with an engaging onion dome that must be only fanciful. A new all-stone belfry of different design was put in its place. In 1975, as a memorial to her husband, a generous lady from Los Angeles had this repaired, the shaft of the white tower cleaned, and the bells put back into harmonious working order.

The general form is traditional and plain, a square tower with flat walls indented by long panels between slightly projecting strips (or *lesenas*), arched together at the top, not unlike the XIVc brick towers of the Frari and S Polo. S Pietro's, however, is all of brilliant white *pietra d'Istria*, an idea new for Venice, perhaps following the tower Alberti had begun for the cathedral of Ferrara. The idea was surely Mauro's, Mauro who had just created the bold white front of S Michele, and Mauro who had gone to Istria more than once to select the best stone. The tower shows plainly that it is built of thick blocks of stone in rugged construction, and not just surfaced like most stone-faced buildings (mostly later). The inner part of the walls is brick, strong, and lighter in weight; this is where any that was usable from the collapsed earlier tower might have been used again. From a 30'-square base, the shaft rears up 150', and still stands almost straight (rare in Venice). It was one of the first grand sights to greet those coming to Venice the only proper way, by ship (fig. 18.3).

Codussi kept the standard old scheme from seeming trite; his hand shows not only in the striking color but also in modifications of the standard proportions and in some novel details. For one, he made the tower stand on a prominent base, almost 9' high, formed of two benchlike steps and a row of four flat bands, stopped by a cyma that swoops out nearly a foot. (Some of this, perhaps the steps, could be left over from the earlier tower.) The sinkage of the paired vertical panels is marked by an even curvier cyma, cut into the masonry on an even more daring scale, a foot deep and a foot and a half wide. The soaring panels are arched at the top, a simplified memory of age-old practice (fig. 18.4). The lower set of them is stopped by a cornice with huge dentils and even bigger egg and darts, and the section between the base and this cornice is twice as high as wide, probably by calculation (fig. 18.5). The division by a big classical cornice seems to be a new idea, possibly picked up from Alberti's campanile at Ferrara. The panels of the upper and slightly higher half of the shaft are stopped by a full entablature, simple and bold: flipped fascias, giant dentils, flaring cornice—full of stony strength when seen from over 100' below. Above that comes the XVIIc bell chamber, a free (and perhaps reduced) adaptation of Mauro's, prettily detailed and bold enough for most places, but seeming slight here, a little fussy, a bit insubstantial above Mauro's vigorous shaft. The little octagon above, even less substantial, is of XVIIIc design and construction.

The campanile (*campaniel* in Venetian) is one of the most vigorous and surely the most elegant in the city, not just from the superb moldings of pure geometric profiles but also from the simple yet subtle spacing of the few elements used in the design. Contrary to common practice, the strips are wider than the sunk panels, so that what is symbolically miming support looks stronger than the apparently less structural space between. The corner

18.2 S Pietro di Castello
(from the de' Barbari map of
1500).

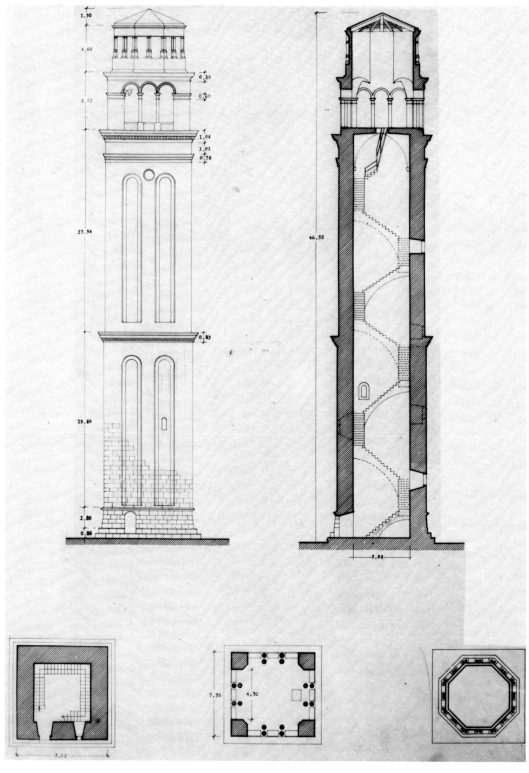

18.3 S Pietro di Castello. Belltower. Elevations and plans.

strips are the widest, and look un-
budgeably stable. The space between
the heads of the arches and the horizontals above them is twice what
might be expected, so that there is a
strong girdle to hold in the tops of the
long piers, which otherwise might
seem planklike and weak, rather than
thick and strong. The whole is fastidi-
ously tapered, but so little that this is
sensed rather than consciously noted.
Also, the upper half, above the middle
cornice, starts out a bit narrower than
the top of the lower half on which it
rests—another refinement felt rather
than recognized, though here more easily discernible if looked for. The one
obvious effort to capture elegance
comes from the medallions of saints
set in the spandrels between the twin
arches at the top of each face, ineffective from below and from any distance;
they were additions made when the
new belfry and top were put on in
place of Codussi's.

18.4 S Pietro di Castello.
Belltower. Detail of lower
cornice.

18.5 S Pietro di Castello.
Belltower. Detail of lower
cornice.

19 | S ZACCARIA

While still supervising the last touches at S Michele, Codussi must have been offered other jobs. Because of the novelty of his style, his reputation must have soared—proportionately to the amount of enlightened humanism in the possible employers. From the early 1480s until he died in 1504, he was always kept busy and, as far as we can tell, usually managed to have his way, thanks to sympathetic clients.

After S Pietro, his next known commission was to finish Gambello's S Zaccaria. Gambello had died in 1481, and in his place, Mauro was named *protomagister*, chief architect, or builder in charge. This was in the year after he had taken on the tower of S Pietro, in June of 1483. Except for the last touches at S Michele and the first work at the Miracoli, no other Renaissance churches were then being built in the city. Most of Gambello's scheme was already up in the raw, and some of it had been clothed in his original Renaissance details, such as the bases and the capitals of the nave arcade, carved (and designed?) by Buora. The walls must have been finished up to the level of the vaults, which had probably already been designed, and some could even have already been put in place by Gambello's assistants—though that is not likely. Just below the wall arches of the vaults, each bay of the aisle walls is pierced by a 5' round window with an elaborately molded frame, more in Gambello's taste than Codussi's. These are the principal source of light for much of the main body of the church, though a bit more comes in at the ends through the windows in the facade and the choir, all probably placed by Gambello, at least in the rough. The facade windows have minimal moldings, most likely put in by Codussi, while the windows of the apsidioles, slipped between engaged columns, have no moldings at all; they do not resemble typical details by either architect.

The three windows of the clerestory
proper, each in a bay on the south side
of the nave, were cut into the lunettes
of wall over the cornice, above the aisle
arcade and under the wall arches of the
nave vaults, a position that renders
them not only unnoticeable but even
hard to see. They are set so high that,
though they are larger, they give less
light than the *oculi* in the aisles. Their
importance comes from their form,
novel at this date, possibly worked out
by Gambello before he died, but more
probably by Codussi. These are variants
of a standard Gothic two-light traceried
window, modestly beginning to be done
in Renaissance terms (fig. 19.1). Still
tentative, it was later developed by
Codussi in two important palaces,
and handled there with such success
that others copied it for a generation.
These first traceried *bifore* (paired windows) would have been installed a bit
after 1483, when Codussi was put in
charge of S Zaccaria (assuming that
they are not Gambello's), perhaps by
1486 when the interior of the chancel
was finished, and surely before 1500
when they were well shown in Jacopo
de' Barbari's bird's-eye view. The
church was entirely finished by 1515.

It is surprising that together these
varied small openings bring adequate
light into so large a church, but less
was needed then than would be wanted
now, because most of the congregation
at Mass could not read—though the
nuns must have been literate—and
there were not yet any printed prayerbooks. By the turn of the century, however, Venice was printing more books
than any city in Italy. By then, most of
the lay congregation would have been
going to S Provolo, which functioned as
the parish church, S Zaccaria being
fundamentally conventual.

The linear quality of the upper parts
of the nave—slender stone arches and
windows with frames set against matte
white plaster—would have been typical

19.1 S Zaccaria. Clerestory
window. Heavy frame of
simple Codussian moldings
with no marking of imposts.
Two arches on octagonal
colonnettes act as tracery of
a similar octagonal section;
these curl upward to make
an opening like a teardrop
upside down, leaving an
open triangle on each side.

of the Early Renaissance almost any-where in Italy (fig. 19.2). By 1515 these upper walls had been frescoed, again typically, and the effect must have been different from what it is now with the big, dark canvases of the XVIIc masking the walls completely (restored soon after 1966 by the Committee to Rescue Italian Art). The lower walls have been transformed by the addition of tombs and a set of handsome match-ing altarpiece frames of marble, probably made soon after the death of Codussi, to set off—among others—Giovanni Bellini's famous Madonna of 1505 (recently cleaned by the Soprinten-denza per i Beni Artistici e Storici di Venezia), which had to have its shape changed to fit. Otherwise, the appear-ance of the nave has changed less than in most churches of its period, allowing a discount for time's darkening and dulling. The spaciousness of the funda-mental scheme and the surprises of the fantastic east end remain powerful in spite of the radical surface changes.

The last bay of the nave before the apse is covered by a dome, less than hemispherical in section and not quite circular in plan (fig. 19.3). The result looks provisional or handmade, but is not disturbing because the dome does not loom importantly or even look very different from the high groin vaults in front. It sits on normal pendentives, their plain plaster areas bounded by stone moldings as spidery as their Bru-nelleschian equivalents at S Michele. Outside, above this true dome, rises a false one of wood, over twice as high, lead-covered, and topped with a *cupo-letto* and fancy metal cross, clearly an offspring of S Mark's. Since it is shown in Reuwich's early woodcut view of Venice, it must have been finished by 1486, the year Codussi was paid for the vaults (fig. 19.4). It appears again in the 1493 Nürnberg Chronicle and, of course, on the Barbari map. These also tell that the body of the church must have been finished under Codussi, and with considerable speed. Sabellico

wrote ca. 1489 of the church as though it was already finished (Sabellico, 27). Someone in authority must have doubted the building's stability, for in 1487 iron bars were put under the nave arches, but not across the nave itself where—though they would have been more prominent—they would have done more good. Someone must have cared enough about appearance to take risks, an unusual preference at this time. There is no way of knowing whether it was Codussi.

The five trapezoidal bays of Gam-bello's ambulatory had been left un-vaulted at his death, and are now marked off by strong ribs of necessarily varied arches (fig. 19.5). To reach as high as the wider ones, the narrower ones are stilted, so that all of them to-gether can manage to get a set of only slightly warped pendentives up to the same height to carry a ring on which the only slightly deformed dome over each bay of the ambulatory can rest. It is no easy feat to erect arches on the unmatching sides of a trapezoid and then fit a ring on top of them, and it would have been far easier if the work had been frankly Gothic (as it must have been conceived by Gambello in the beginning), where trapezoidal am-bulatory vaults are commonplace and easily worked out. But Gothic was rejected and a willful, ingenious and somewhat wayward Renaissance scheme was imposed—surely by Co-dussi. As the apsidal chapels were given their vaults—lower down—in 1487, the ambulatory vaults must have come soon after.

Codussi's most prominent work here was on the facade that Gambello had already begun with the paneled and marble-inlaid bottom zone. The next, a row of niches with two pairs of win-dows worked into it, presents problems because it does not look like either Co-dussi's or Gambello's style (fig. 19.6).

19.2 S Zaccaria. Nave, with
apse and ambulatory.

19.3 S Zaccaria. Vaults of nave and aisles, dome of chancel, and semi-dome of apse.

19.4 S Zaccaria. View, including dome (detail of woodcut by Reuwich in Bernhard von Breydenbach, *Peregrinatio in Terram Sanctam*, 1486).

19.5 S Zaccaria. Ambulatory, looking upward.

19.6 S Zaccaria. Main portal.

But, as has been pointed out earlier, Gambello's manner could vary from standard late Gothic to an improvised Early Renaissance, and this row of niches could represent a late and unfamiliar phase of it, whereas no similar phase can be assumed for Codussi. Only two bare and weak facts associate the work with Codussi: first, unlike Gambello's lower zone, the zone of niches is all of white Istrian stone, which Codussi had innovatively used for the church front at S Michele a dozen years before; and second, he had had his brother Bernardo in Istria much of the time from 1484 to 1490 selecting stone for S Zaccaria. Even taken together, these facts bring no conviction. Work here was probably under way well before 1484, and anyone could have decided to use limestone above marble, since limestone from Istrian quarries had been on the market in Venice for centuries. If the niches have to be attributed to someone, they can better be proposed for Gambello, perhaps carried out after he died, for stylistically they are alien to Codussi.

They could more conveniently be given to the assistants, Venier and Lazzaro di Nicolo, who worked in the interim between the two masters, and the Lombard workmen who were still busy there in 1485 and most probably longer (Franzoi-DiStefano, 397, 398). The little pilasters between the niches do not line up with the divisions of the panels below as one designer for both would normally have insisted. Nothing of the niche zone recalls anything in the panel zone; nothing below prepares for what will come above. There seems to have been a pause, not just in building but also in thinking. Since a great deal of stone was ordered in 1483, it may be that a new burst of activity was about to begin under Codussi. He may have had to finish the tops of the niches, already started, and then gone ahead on his own above.

Furthermore, the weak entablature, weakest of the four on the front, between the niche story and the panel story under it, while adequate for the doorway—clearly from a design by a different man—is far from adequate for the whole 65' stretch of the front (fig. 19.7). Although without any carved moldings, which might seem to coincide with Codussi's strict taste, the proportions are not convincingly like any of his. While the cornice has a modestly projecting corona, it is uncomfortably narrow and ends in a tiny cyma.

In contrast, the entablature above the niches is almost twice as high, although the story it tops is a third lower. The proportions are properly classical; the profiles are geometrically definite and gratefully clear to the eye; the ornament is restricted to a minor molding like dwarf dentils at the top of the architrave, proper dentils in their proper place low in the cornice, and an egg and dart where it belongs in the bed molding, in the shadow of the well proportioned overhanging corona; a sharp full-size cyma brings it to a strong ending. There has been a change from everything below, and a new character controls the facade from here up. That must be the result of Codussi's arrival.

Instead of only an ornamental wall, the next story, the tallest, is a three-dimensional composition, more tectonic and more rational architecturally than that below. Pairs of freestanding columns have taken the place of the massive inert buttresses (fig. 19.8). Standing on a low, strong pedestal, they are topped by elegant, crisp, one-leaf capitals. The sections between the pairs of columns—the actual front wall of the church—ignore the monotonous rhythm made by the niches below for larger, less repetitious divisions, resulting from the spacing fixed by the immediate needs, the windows and the buttresses. One big arched window comes logically in the center of each aisle, and three in the center of the

19.7 S Zaccaria. Facade.

nave. These openings are three times as high as wide, and are far less pinched than the mediaeval ones below, where each of the twin windows is four widths high. Pilasters flank the larger windows, and leave slightly narrower panels of wall beside the columns, quietly assuring a look of stability just where it might be needed because of the shift from the solid mass of the buttresses to the much lighter octet of columns. But these columns, while transforming the buttresses and making them lighter, also increase their visual emphasis and their disciplinary power to organize the design, mainly from the sudden increase in plasticity and resulting increase in strong light and shade. The facade has become as three-dimensional as any in Venice (except for S Mark's), and unlike not only contemporary facades by other architects but also unlike anything by Codussi. The reason is clear; he was not entirely free, but continuing and bringing into order a work begun by others.

The columns and pilasters carry an entablature as severe as the one just below, but larger, mainly because of its wide frieze. The break forward around the column buttresses has become narrower than on Gambello's lower story, and subtly narrower than that over the niches, because pulled in naturally by the difference in the width of the plinths of the column bases and the width of the abaci of the capitals immediately underneath. The effect of this story is grander and simpler than anything below, and that difference is one of the chief characteristics separating cerebral Codussi from instinctive Gambello.

Above this, the idea ruling the top of the front of S Michele takes over; quadrants spring over the aisles and an arch-pediment rises high over the nave. Each quadrant springs from the middle of the outside buttress, leaving room at the outer edge for a giant rosette, a yard across, ample support for one

19.8 S Zaccaria. Facade. Detail of order of third zone. (The dark beams at the top are part of temporary scaffolding.)

end of the base of a 7' angel. As at S Michele, the quadrants start out on a slope, being here again an arc of less than a quarter-circle. Then, after arching up, they go on straight and horizontal for about a quarter of their length before breaking out around the projecting buttresses, and thence on between them across the whole wall of the nave. Any impulse of upward movement on the facade is cut across and almost canceled here, as it has already been by the several cornices below. The long horizontals do individually tie the facade together at their different levels, but they do not act in concert as an organizing force, since they do not show any relation to one another beyond the rudimentary one of marking successive layers. Nothing affects them but the four buttresses that force each one to give way by making each break out around the vertical projection. The effect is not that of controlled and easily reconciled forces as it is at S Michele. There is friction.

In this zone paneled piers with pedestals but no bases or capitals take the place of the columns and pilasters below, two for the line of the buttresses and then pairs between the two blank arches and the two windows in the nave wall. All this is out of phase with the divisions on the story below, with its three central windows flanked by panels; and the shift in rhythm adds to the shift already there from a single window above a double or three windows over a fluttery repetition of blind niches. The little piers do not line up with the pilasters under them; nothing in this whole story lines up except the transformed buttresses. The shrinking of the story height, furthermore, to almost half that of the one below is disturbing. There is no complete entablature, only a cornice continuing naturally from the quadrants (where a full entablature would have been unmanageably crowded).

Clearly the problem here and below was how to be monumental with only small membering to work with, a problem more easily handled in the Tron monument, smaller, and only a decorative arrangement on a wall, not the real architecture of the front of a real building. Here the classical stock of parts cannot be made to work with all the new variations demanded of it.

The next and last story is a little taller than the squashed one under it, whose general divisions it nevertheless follows. Carried out partly with the same forms as the story below that, this top story fails to reconcile the two schemes from which it borrows. Small freestanding paired columns reappear for the buttresses and continue up also from the little paired piers just below. These colonnettes, the shortest on the facade, carry an overwhelming entablature, half their height. This entablature suddenly introduces a new character, again not prepared for: carving on the ribbon-narrow architrave, colored inlays and panels of carving on the abnormally wide frieze. Where one might expect a resolution at the end, one senses instead a new confusion.

At S Michele, the problems were simpler; the church was smaller and arcades were not run across the front. Romanesque and Gothic churches in Italy had often managed to clothe themselves with small arcades, tiers of them, but with a different and more flexible vocabulary. Some have thought that the arcades here might have been derived from mediaeval prototypes, but it would be hard to think that Codussi's eye strayed so far afield—unless his building committee had ideas of their own, possibly based on some favored feature of the older church here. While possible, this does not seem probable.

The many strong horizontals and the discontinuity of the weak little verticals or the stronger accents of the dark holes of the windows ensure that any sense of upward movement—if there was to be any—would have to rely almost entirely on the buttresses, with questionable assistance from the general proportions of the tall front. And neither is quite adequate to take over any such control. It is as though several basic schemes coexist, with no one dominant.

Perhaps the cornice of the top story was made so big to prepare for the climactic sweep of the crowning arch: a cornice, a frieze with similar colored inlays and bouquets, then a curious deeply fluted S-curve molding, anticipated at S Michele (fig. 19.9). All this wheels around a marble tympanum with a round window ringed by many deep moldings and stabilized by touching the fluting above and a sort of paneling or pedestal below. Possibly the blank bands at the beginning of each upper story were put there to keep the bottoms of pilasters or panels or whatever from being hidden in the sharp perspective view from below, which—if consciously done—would be an astonishing performance for this date, when parts were made to be perfect in the absolute, not as they might appear to a spectator who happened to see them from some point where perspective or overlapping would deform them. Thanks to these blank bottom bands, little of the round window is sliced off in normal views.

The expected rosettes appear at the edges of the arch-pediment, and on them stand two more angels with the instruments of the Passion. At the very top, two more rosettes, giant podlike anthemia, and a special pedestal, support a figure of the Risen Christ holding the traditional banner of the Resurrection. These acroterial figures give animation to the skyline, as lively as Gothic, livelier than at the smaller S Michele or the still smaller S Maria dei Miracoli, which may have demonstrated to Mauro the effectiveness of such skyline figures in contexts more related than those of the huge acroterial population of S Mark's.

The whole center section of the front can be seen as bearing a curious resemblance to the Tron monument, with its stacked-up pairs of small columns making piers to carry a large-scale arch-pediment. Many stories with unequal and shifting numbers of bays between the piers are superposed in each case. It is difficult to think that Mauro, with the most advanced Renaissance thinking of any architect in Venice, might have turned for an idea to Rizzo's primitive effort, successful as it was. To Mauro, it must have seemed full of mistakes. Any resemblance is accidental.

In three ways the facade stands outside Mauro's style as it might be defined today. First, it is a huge whole made of many little pieces that call attention to themselves individually more than to the whole. Without the enclosing power of the swooping skyline, the composition would fall apart even more, despite the efforts of the buttresses to hold it in and of the many entablatures to hold it down. No continuous currents carry our glances over the vast restless area and our eyes are left to wander. Second, the front is not easy or even clear to read as an expression of structure, idealized or even partly imaginary, for the busy modeling of the tiers of colonnettes, pilasters, and piers catches lights and throws shadows that deny the validity of the structural wall behind, which is really doing the work; Codussi normally tended not to stray far from structural truths. Third, save possibly his last palaces, no other work of his is as three-dimensional as the upper parts of this composition. There is an unexpected gradation upward, from Gambello's flattish lower story (or stories) to the zone with the screen of freestanding pairs of colonnettes, then to the deep scoop of concave fluting and the final

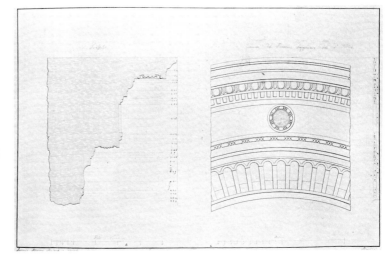

19.9 S Zaccaria. Section and elevation of semicircular gable cornice (drawing by A. Mezzani, Museo Correr).

19.10 S Zaccaria. Air view of campo, church, and cloisters.

flare of the cyma; the sequence—planar
to plastic, or papery to ponderous—
sometimes seems to be upside down.

The facade must have been finished
by 1500 or a bit before, for it is fully
shown on Jacopo de' Barbari's view of
the city. Although patched here and
there, as would be expected after 500
years, the general appearance can have
changed little. The front still towers
about 7' above the ridge of the roof behind, more yet over everything else in
the neighborhood (fig. 19.10). Once it
towered a foot more above its campo,
for that has been raised by paving and
repaving, burying two of the three
semicircular steps shown by Jacopo de'
Barbari as leading up to the entrance—
the same fate that has befallen the
front of S Michele. The irregular-
shaped campo is large and must once
have been locked at night (Franzoi-Di-
Stefano, 404). It has only two entrances
and must have been considered a private precinct by the nuns, always jeal-
ous of their rights and perquisites.

In the Napoleonic ordinance of 1806,
cutting the number of religious houses,
S Zaccaria—big, rich, noble—was put
into the first class, not closed but made
to serve as a receptacle for the surplus
of nuns from other convents being shut
down. Then in 1810 it too was ordered
closed, and the nuns were given two
months to move out. The church
building was reopened as a parish
church, a function largely handled before by S Provolo (demolished). The
convent buildings were given to the
carabinieri for barracks and offices.
Thus they passed from female religious
clausura without a break to male polit-
ico-military *clausura,* and what was inside, including the two splendid cloisters, was known to almost no one on
the outside. (See appendix C.)

Codussi's first mature masterpiece, and
one of the most original churches of
the Early Renaissance, was the rebuilding or, rather, replacement of S Maria
Formosa, the first church in Venice
dedicated to the Virgin, who, in a leg-
endary vision to Bishop Magno, had
shown him the site where she wished
her church to be built—by sending
down a small white cloud to hover
over it. She appeared so wonderfully
beautiful (formosa) that the church became known as S Maria Formosa instead of its original title of S Maria
della Purificazione.

After several extensions and patch-
ings, the first enfeebled church was replaced early in the XIIc by a new brick
building, almost surely Byzantine in
style. After some 350 years, this had
become so decrepit that another new
church was needed. A legacy came in
1487 from Antonio Bragadin, of the
neighboring parish of S Marina, who
had such devotion to the Madonna that
he left the new church the bulk of
his fortune (Puppi-Puppi, 111, 206).
To add to this bonanza, a loan was
floated—with delicious success. A
commission was awarded to the muraro ("mason") Mauro Codussi on
November 15, 1491 (archives of the
church, kindness of Mgr. Bortolan). At
the time, S Maria dei Miracoli must
have been almost finished, and S Zaccaria well along; save in unimportant
details, neither shows similarities to S
Maria Formosa, which was about to
take shape as something new and fresh.
The first stone was laid on June 1,
1492, after the church had been laid
out and tidied up for the ceremony, as
was customary. In June, the annalist
Malipiero (689) saw work under way,
and he referred to Mauro as tajapietra
architetto ("stonemason architect")
in the first notice calling him an
architect.

The kernel of his new church was
pretty surely a Greek cross, like several
city churches of the XIIc but none between then and the late XVc. It serves

less well for the Roman rite than for the Greek or Patriarchal rite, which Venice was relinquishing only in the XVc (Bortolan, 9). There may have been some special reason for using it here. Perhaps, as in Florence, Early Renaissance men searching for an antiquity still half-veiled reached back behind the Gothic, but not very far, only to the XIIc proto-Renaissance in Florence and the Veneto-Byzantine here. Or Codussi might have picked up ideas from a Greek refugee, many of whom were then coming to Venice from Crete (whence many intellectuals had fled after the fall of Constantinople); or from a Greek from one of the other islands or coastal cities that Venetians knew well, for it was these that sent most immigrants to Venice. (After the loss of the capital and the limited massacres that followed more or less automatically, many Christians stayed on there, tolerated and doing business; only a few left for Venice.) But Codussi would have tended to take more from what he could see right where he was about to build. He did not take what would have been easiest to copy, typical Byzantine decorative details, but instead followed much of the fundamental plan and spatial composition, perhaps because he had been given them by the old walls and foundations.

Whatever its source, the result is superb, and historically of prime importance as the first church in Venice conceived and all carried out in accord with Renaissance ideals. Here Codussi created a unified architectural scheme; S Giobbe had been only a set of additions; the Miracoli had not been planned as a unit; S Michele was new in some parts, but too traditional and not unified enough to count as a developed creation of a new kind. But here at S Maria Formosa is what must be counted a new plan (in comparison with those of the three preceding centuries), and a newer idea of space, clothed in an elegant set of new forms, both large and small. All that is missing is an exterior of the same nature. Mauro died in 1504 when the west and north facades were no more than rough walls waiting to be clad. Only the east end with its towering apses, and much of the outer face of the south transept, could go back to what he had imagined. After he died, his sons were retained to finish the work, but only for a couple of years, and they would not have been likely to alter his scheme.

The plan shows the Greek cross immediately and soon reveals that it varies a bit from the strict geometrical figure (fig. 20.1). Including the apse, the interior measures about 100' long and 93' across the transepts. The nave arm is longer than the others, the north transept next, then the south; the chancel is the shortest, if the curved apse is not counted, but equal to the west arm if it is. The nave has three bays and its extra length comes from an extra yard at the west end, perhaps added by Codussi to the Byzantine nave or perhaps made in the 1540s when a new facade was being made. The difference in the length of the two transepts may follow the old foundations, or come from the inviting fullness of space outside on the north and the paucity of it on the south.

At the east, the chancel and apse are flanked by side chapels, narrower than the chancel but as deep. Beyond, flanking the north chapel, a wider chapel, still unfinished in 1526 (Pavanello, 8), opens off the transept and runs back as far as the three main chapels. On the other side, in an equivalent place, is a narrower chapel, only 4' deep, hardly more than a recess, but roomy enough to display Palma's famous S Barbara altarpiece from 1509 to 1823 (replaced in 1921—Pavanello, 7). The sacristy behind it, accessible only from the chancel, fills out the space to match the north side. The chapter room is above it. On both sides, then, the walls come

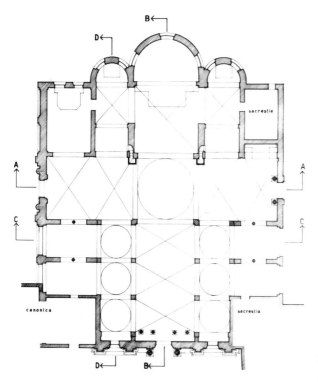

20.1 S Maria Formosa. Plan.

out flush with the ends of the transepts, making each outside wall run in one straight plane.

The west half is more complicated; the three oblong bays of the nave are bordered by three square bays in the aisles, picking up and prolonging the east-west corridor-like space begun with the flanking chapels across the transepts from them, but unexpectedly shrunk slightly narrower when no more than aisles. Except for the westernmost pair, each of the aisle bays opens out not only to the nave but also fully on the other side to a deep chapel.

The body of the church would compose into a near square except for the projection of the three apses and two asymmetrical blocks running out from the front corners, already shown in 1500 by Jacopo de' Barbari. At the northwest corner, a block for a scuola joins church and campanile (presumably once freestanding). This block had been built chiefly for a Confraternity of the Purification of the Virgin, but with space also for the patron of grocers, Jehosaphat. When the scuolas were suppressed by Napoleon, and when the nearby Church of S Marina was pulled down, her relics, a onetime gift from the Byzantine emperor, were moved here, and the ex-scuola became a popular oratory for this virgin-martyr, long one of the chief patronesses of the city.

A subordinate sacristy and a house extend from the other front corner, the southwest, probably then as now the residence of the parish priest (fig. 20.2). The lower story was the hall of the Confraternity of the Bombardiers, an exuberant group rather like present-day carabinieri, who delighted in dressing up and marching in processions, and who had commissioned Palma's S Barbara for their altar in the church. Except for these two protuberances at the west end, the church would have been freestanding (rare in Venice) and square (also rare). The interior asks to be filled out to simple geometric perfection, and the exterior asks to be cut down to it.

20.2 S Maria Formosa. Air
view.

Now, though eccentrically set in it, the church dominates one of the largest campos in Venice, with ample space all around except on half the south side, where a neighboring house stands too close to leave easy space between it and the wall of the transept and chapels. At the southwest corner, the priest's house runs forward from the body of the church to the canal in front, shutting off one end of the forecourt-like space between the facade and the Rio S Maria Formosa. There may have been a portico here before the present front was built in 1542 (Pavanello, 2).

The largest area spreads hundreds of feet to the north, with space for a couple of markets, two cafes, a newspaper kiosk, and miscellaneous stands. There is more space to the southeast; two or three hundred people do not crowd it. Nothing is regular, parallel, or at right angles, but the informal and indefinable roominess does not seem uncontrolled, for it is disciplined by the long straight lines of houses along the sides, by the block of the church, and pinned down somewhere near the middle by the campanile. There is a kind of hidden equilibrium, implicit rather than explicit. Even so, when one comes at last into the church after walking through the planless maze of narrow streets, and then through some of the pleasant, humane, but incomprehensible campo, one feels that finally one has come into the Promised Land, where all is calm, right, and beneficent.

It is uncertain how much of the plan may have been inherited from the earlier church and how much invented by Codussi, but the assumption that the Greek cross was already there and a determinant is so persuasive that it can be taken as a working hypothesis, nearly as a fact. The burden of disproof is on the doubter. The apses, too, may observe earlier lines. Economical use would sensibly have been made of old foundations, for in Venice, despite its uncertain soil, these could be remarkably rugged, as buildings as heavy as vaulted S Mark's and its massive campanile attest. There is no sure way of knowing the history of the aisles of S Maria or of the end of the nave or the transepts—whether something was there or something was added—for a XIIc church might or might not have these features. The extensions of the northeast and southeast corners, however, eking the whole out to a near-square, might have been conceived by Mauro, given his recognizable love of neat shapes. The geometrically less assimilable extrusions at the northwest and southwest corners would probably have been dictated by imperatives of use rather than formal preference.

To suit their various shapes, the bays were covered by vaults of several different kinds. The nave, chancel, transepts, and the bays in front of the three apses have ribless groined vaults, all normal. The flanking chapels add a length of barrel vault in front of their groin vaults. The chapels off the side aisles are also under barrel vaults, fitting perfectly over their plain oblong form, as at earlier works, the Cappella dei Mascoli in S Mark's and many others. Running out at right angles to the aisles, they come as minor but lively surprises after the compelling sweep to the east declared by the nave and affirmed intermittently by the aisles, interweaving with them in a subordinate weft.

The most original part of the vaulting is over the aisles, still presumably intact after a quake in the XVIIc. Small saucerlike domes are so flattened as to make them, along with their pendentives, read almost like continuous parts of the surface of one hemisphere (fig. 20.3). They are, therefore, almost pendentive domes, but that is denied by a thin circle of stone demarcating the pendentives from the edge of the dome. Consistent with this, the sides of the pendentives are bounded by slender limestone arches, in contrast to the vault surfaces of matte white plaster.

20.3 S Maria Formosa. South
aisle looking west.

Although the forms are similar, the effect is less like those Byzantine domes of the saucer-on-pendentive type in the narthex of S Mark's than like something Florentine, even like Brunelleschi; though for his aisles he did not use such flattened domes on pendentives but, rather, little pendentive domes, as at S Lorenzo and S Spirito. The adjustments that Codussi had had to make earlier in order to fit similar saucers to the trapezoidal bays of the ambulatory of S Zaccaria seem a hard-pressed rehearsal for these natural-looking little constructions. Their apparent strength was at some time doubted, for every one of their supporting arches is now safeguarded by an iron tie-rod.

The crossing is now covered by a low dome on a low drum on pendentives, where its Byzantine predecessor had doubtless had some kind of dome of now uncertain form. For a model Codussi might naturally have used his dome at S Michele rather than the old Byzantine dome he must have had to pull down.

There is one obstacle, however: no dome shows on the Barbari bird's-eye view of 1500 or on the Vavassore of ca. 1525 (Cassini, 35–37), yet it is hard to believe that it was not already there in 1500, or at least begun, or at the very least intended and already somehow defined. It may not have been done enough to be visible above the surrounding roofs at the end of the 1490s, when Barbari's helpers were making their visual notes; and Vavassore, like everybody else for generations, cribbed from Barbari, with a few scattered tokens of fresh architectural news.

Another explanation could be that Codussi's dome had no drum, and was less than hemispherical, and thus able to fit under the same gable roof that covered the nave, like two of the domes at the Certosa di S Andrea. Francesco Sansovino (I, 39), writing ca. 1580, said that the church was "like

the middle of S Mark's," which sounds more like the XIIc church he could never have seen than like Codussi's, which he had. Whatever the case, he must have seen a dome at the intersection. A dome was there by 1580 and probably by 1500; the doubt is not whether it was there so much as whether it was hidden, and how, or whether Jacopo de' Barbari made one of his very few mistakes here. (Still it is odd that among his potential omissions, two should be of domes.) The domes of St Mark's are without drums, and most are less than hemispherical, a fact which can add a bit of probability to the proposal of a drumless dome under the roof here, in which case it would not be so much like S Michele. Like S Michele and S Mark's, and unlike the domes of Brunelleschi and Pietro Lombardo, the pendentives were almost surely left plain, without sculpture and probably without even empty roundels.

The dome could have been finished by Codussi before he died in 1504, or by his sons still on the payroll two years later. The dogged diarist Marin Sanudo went to many official ceremonies in the church without noting whether it was finished or not (XIII, 428; XIV, 253; XV, 90; XVII, 625, etc.). Probably it was, and not cluttered with even the light Venetian scaffolding for a dome still in construction, since from the early XVIc onward there were important baptisms, weddings, funerals, and grand vespers for the doge's annual visits to the church. The panoramic view of Venice once in the castle at Trent (Corret Museum), painted probably between 1615 and 1635, shows a dome above the roof; this is the oldest view of a dome here, but the painting, full of approximations and omissions, is not trustworthy. The Barbari view is a synthesized transcription of evidence recorded on the spot, and is astonishingly accurate, while the Trent panorama, less dependent on direct information and less accurate even in what it borrowed, has many faulty bits of guesswork. In this case, however, showing a dome is almost certainly correct.

Whatever it was, a quake brought it down on Palm Sunday of 1688. The *oculi* in the wall arches of the groin vaults of the nave and transepts were walled up when it became clear that the upper parts of the building were seriously weakened. Soon the dome was rebuilt, but in a different form; higher, on a drum, and octagonal (fig. 20.4). Extra windows were cut in the drum in the 1840s, enfeebling the construction. In 1844 the dome and broad wall areas in the church were covered with murals in the typical taste of the time, enfeebling it in a new way—aesthetically. There was some restoration in 1890. But then in 1916 an Austrian hydroplane from Trieste dropped an incendiary bomb, doubtless intended for the Arsenal, destroying the vaults of the nave and some neighboring parts (fig. 20.5). Photographs of the wrecked church show the walls intact not only below but also above where the vaults had been, making it clear that the vaults, whether XVc or XVIIc, must have been light and scarcely if at all integrated into the walls, which otherwise could not have survived upright with hardly a scar. The XVIIc dome, astonishingly, was still standing.

These vaults must, therefore, have been either thin brick shells (photographs in the Soprintendenza ai Monumenti show the rubble on the floor with bits of brick in it) or else only plaster on laths of wood or reeds held up from above, as was often done later to make vault shapes without vault weight or vault thrust. (There appears to be much more plaster than brick in the rubble on the church floor.) Independence of vault and wall, both kept as light as possible, is specially suited to Venice, with its unstable soil. A thin brick shell might owe something to the

example of the XIIc Byzantine model, which Codussi knew, since he pulled it down, and while such a debt could be possible for the dome, the nave vaults are another problem. It is not possible to see how Codussi's vaults here could have been shaken down without pulling some of the side walls with them or pushing some of them over. His vaults cannot have been slipped in with no structural connection with what was beside them, specially near the corbels. Photographs of the bombed church show that the pendentives at the crossing were of brick, but without any indication of whether they might be of the XVc or of the XVIIc. At the time of the bombing, they must have carried an octagonal sill of wood for the drum and dome. It is extraordinary that this did not burn along with the roof of the nave. It was, however, so weakened that it soon had to be pulled down. The most acceptable conclusion to all this, probable but not provable, is that the nave vaults were of XVIIc construction, replacing Codussi's, and probably not of brick masonry but of plaster on lath.

It is not only possible that they were not his, but probable that both walls and vaults had been rebuilt after the crash of 1688, along with the dome— the quake is known to have been severe (Corner 1758, 42)—and then the vaults would have been made without traditional masonry construction but with the new technique of suspended almost weightless pseudo-vaults of plaster. There is no information beyond the inferences from the photographs taken between 1916 and 1919 (in the Correr Library Fototeca and the Soprintendenza ai Monumenti), and comparison with other works in the city. The vaults one sees in S Maria today are plaster, and hang from the larch rafters of the roof.

An exemplary restoration was carried out mainly between 1919 and 1921, strengthening, patching, cleaning off over-scale frescoes, opening the clerestory *oculi* in each bay of the nave and

20.4 S Maria Formosa. Looking down nave, through crossing and chancel to apse (lithograph by G. P. Cecchini and Kier soon after 1844).

20.5 S Maria Formosa. Nave after bombing of 1916, looking west.

recreating the dome in a presumed likeness of Codussi's other domes, earlier and later (fig. 20.6). Since there were no traces of his original dome here, that was the wisest choice. The authorization for the rebuilding, urged by the parish priest and the engineer and accepted by Rome, was as exemplary as the work that was done "to bring the church back to the type of the beginning of the XVIc—arches, vaults, and *oculi*" and to make a new round dome in place of the octagon (copy in Soprintendenza ai Monumenti, Castello, S Maria Formosa, 687). The dome may not be a replica of Codussi's, for it rises well above the roofs, and even the pendentives are indicated on the outside by blocks like the corners of a cube, well above where the real pendentives are. Whatever its accuracy, the result is a success—and convincing. Except for the problematic dome, there must have been enough of Codussi's church left, remodeled and touched up, to assure a reconstruction more reliable than many. The groin vaults are most likely of the XVIIc, but probably of the same shape as Mauro's.

The church now has the most interesting—not to say rewarding—interior of any yet built in the Early Renaissance in Venice, particularly admired today by the informed coterie of historians of architecture, discriminating architects, and amateurs, rivaled only by S Salvatore if that can be considered a work of the Early Renaissance. Its quality cannot, of course, be measured or captured in words, but it is strongly sensed by most of the visitors who are responsive to such architectural virtues as clarity, refinement, and vigor—and imagination.

The various interior spaces, only lightly differentiated, are too multifarious to survey as a whole from any one point of view, or even to assimilate after a single walk through the church from end to end. But complex as they are, they are not confused. Some, such as the chapels running out from the sides, reveal themselves from only a few viewpoints (fig. 20.7). Only one component, the basic Greek cross, emerges at once from almost everywhere—clear, authoritative, and dominant. The idea that all parts add up to a near square came basically from an intellectual captivation with geometrical neatness, espoused because it could be clearly demonstrated—in the flat, on a piece of paper, statically. But definite though it is, it could not be sensed three-dimensionally by the exploring eyes of a visitor (figs. 20.8 and 20.9). It can be clearly and perhaps rewardingly understood only as an abstract diagram, but can never take on the compelling conviction of a sensory experience.

Not rising as high and not as well lighted, the aisles and chapels flanking the main apse, though contiguous, accept their secondary role. Still more subordinate and complicated (but not confused), the chapels off the aisles take an even lower position in the hierarchy, there being no real competition and no near equals. The extraordinary double windows cutting through the walls between these chapels link them lightly into one subordinate and multiform entity, the last one to reveal itself. Something, however, is still held back here—suitably perhaps, to help keep so minor a part always minor.

In the end, after a few moments to assimilate vistas from several points of view, the visitor's impressions begin to coalesce—but never quite completely. His perception is mainly clear, but always a little elusive; specific in the main, but in some parts no more than implied.

Clearest and first comes a big, bright Greek-cross church (assuming that Codussi had used groin vaults of much the same shape as those there now, and that good-size *oculi* were in the wall arches, as they are now). The cross-shaped core stands inside another

20.6 S Maria Formosa.
Dome in the course of re-
building, 1920–21.

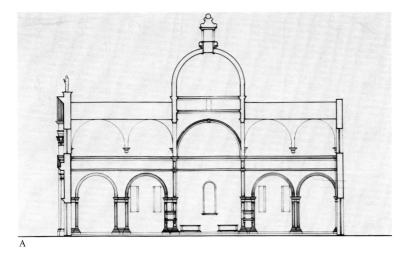

A

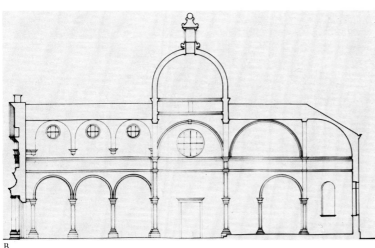

B

20.7 S Maria Formosa. Section drawings. A: cross section through transept; B: longitudinal section down center axis; C: cross section through nave; D: longitudinal section down aisle.

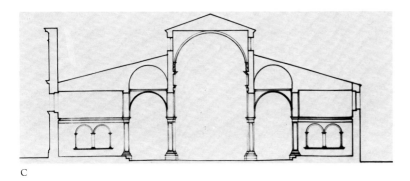

C

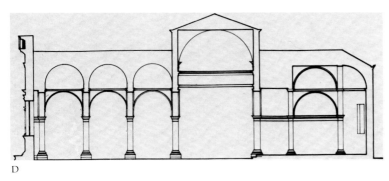

D

20.8 S Maria Formosa. Looking northwest into side
aisle, nave, and north
transept.

20.9 S Maria Formosa. Looking east up north aisle.

space, a lower and dimmer church revealed by the aisles and their continuation in the deep chapels beside the main apse (fig 20.10). When this secondary space has to cross the high transept, its longitudinal continuity is arrested for a moment, but not stopped. Twin currents, one lengthwise, one crosswise, interweave without interrupting. The parts of this second complex of space retain more individual autonomy than do the bays of the uninterruptedly sweeping nave and transepts, sweeping themselves into one major dominating central space. The secondary space is more like an imaginary basilica, enclosing the longitudinal parts of the cross while pierced by its transverse transepts (fig. 20.11).

Outside this lesser and lower volume and dependent on it, a fragmentary third is implied, lower, darker, and more elusive—made up of the lateral chapels running out at right angles from the aisles. This outer jacket of space is less complete and has less independence; from some angles it seems to have none, but to exist only as a set of protrusions off the aisles. Its very nature is equivocal. But from some places it does show itself, and cannot be ignored, and so in time the visitor comes to sense a polyphonic composition of a space within a space within a space.

Not only concentrically, these three space systems are interrelated in other ways as well. The supports between the nave and aisles, for example, are so slender and wide apart that they mark the frontier only lightly. Most of the spatial cubicles are confluent, thanks to the shaping and disposition of these piers, and also to such novelties as the pierced walls between the chapels beyond the aisles. Because of the different formations of the varied intervening supports, the flow of space is easier in some places, while in others it can be momentarily half-blocked. But even when one cannot see beyond, one

knows that the space does go on, and is confident that what is not yet revealed, and hence might hold some mystery or surprise, will when exposed be as orderly and clear as everything else.

It is only later that what had confidently been seen as rooted in reason, clarity, and regularity slowly refuses to be fully apprehensible by reason, to be in some fugitive way neither quite clear nor quite regular. Something has its own life and refuses the rationale of pure geometry.

Until the restorations of the 1840s when a new floor was laid, destroying all the old tomb slabs, this feeling of a space within a space and equivocally within parts of another was further underlined by differences in the floor-levels, a quiet prelude to something that was going to be played out fully in the air above. The aisles are said once to have been a step above the nave (Tramontin 1962, 26n2), and the side chapels are still two steps above the aisles off which they open. The chancel and its adjacent chapels, everything east of the transept in fact, are still set two steps above it. Such slight lifting of some areas above others to clarify certain functional distinctions by marking them out visually was made in a few other churches, such as S Felice (until twenty years ago—now no longer visible). It is most apparent at the Ognissanti, where the cross form of the nave plus transepts plus chancel, all on the same main level, is marked off by the large rectangles pushed up a little under the blocks of seats in the four corners. Brunelleschi had pioneered this scheme, and had lifted his aisle chapels three steps at S Lorenzo, with an effectiveness young Mauro might well have noticed. It recurs vividly on the edge of Florence at the Badia Fiesolana (1461), a beautiful and mysterious building, hauntingly Albertian in some ways yet Brunelleschian in detail (Saalman 1978, 30). It is

20.10 S Maria Formosa. Upper part of nave, with *oculus* and vault; crossing beyond, with pendentive and dark dome.

20.11 S Maria Formosa. West end of nave. The groin vaults are carried on corbels floating a yard above the main cornice. The round windows in the lunettes below the vaults may not be Codussi's originally.

brought to mind often enough by Codussi to place it among the works he admired in Florence.

Everywhere in the restored S Maria, the spare stone membering, limited to verticals, horizontals, and arcs of circles, is set off in a Brunelleschian way against smooth areas of plaster, flat below and curved above in sections of cylinders or spheres. The stone parts combine to form a delicate but firm, cagelike armature, while the plaster does no more than bound the interior volumes of air, showing where they come to their ends. They do not show themselves as the face of massive masonry (which, of course, is what they actually are). The vaults of the nave and transepts, resting apparently on small corbels, appear to float weightlessly, not like lids but only as surfaces lightly indicating the top of the interior air. The profiles of the various moldings are everywhere immediately clear and geometrically pure and, like the larger forms, they are generated only by straight lines or perfect arcs, never irregular curves or angles. The delicate armature could never really hold anything up—and the weightless vaults pretend that they do not have to—for they just act out in pantomime what the supporting forces would be doing if we could somehow see them.

The openings are everywhere soberly framed; the *oculi* of the nave clerestory have only a flat fillet and a simple cyma, now restored, but supposedly on the basis of preserved telltales. These openings had been walled to strengthen the upper fabric after the shaking of 1688, and this must have made the church darker; maybe then the similar and smaller *oculi* at the end of the aisle chapels were replaced by the large and distracting semicircles now there. Lighting by highly placed *oculi*, as planned at the beginning, recalls Brunelleschi's at S Lorenzo.

The main apse windows are of the tall, arched, Brunelleschian type, like those of S Michele. Once there were three, but the middle one was blocked in 1592 for a large new altarpiece, which made use of *verde antico* colonnettes from the old one. Codussi's original altar had been freestanding on the chord of the curve of the apse (Pavanello, 3). The windows of the flanking chapels have been more drastically altered.

The double windows between the aisle chapels are framed like the others. The colonnettes have simple one-leaf capitals (of less Latin lineage) and a shaft with marked double entasis, both a bit old-fashioned now for Codussi. Above them the archivolt folds back on itself at right angles, and then folds upward again to start the other arch. On the outer sides, the archivolt, having swept around the arch, runs down straight, with no marking at the impost, and at the bottom, where it hits the sill, it folds at a right angle and then turns in to the wall in antique Roman or Brunelleschian fashion, or like the Badia Fiesolana. Codussi had become very conscious of finding the best precedents for such details.

The vertical members expressing support are also spare, less Brunelleschian, more uniquely Codussian. Those at the end of the side chapels are paneled like piers or pilasters, and stand on proper bases, set on a pair of square plinths. Without capitals at the top, they display instead a combination of another narrow flat band and a cyma bent around the four sides of the pier to make something like an entablature block, a minimal abridgment of an order, not just an arbitrary set of bare blocks and bands. The same is repeated for the square piers of the arcade between aisles and nave. The four piers at the crossing are a compound made by merging two unequal square posts, with two strips to take the two arches, east and west, of the aisle vaults and two more, north and south, for the arches that cross the nave and transepts—again a reminder of S Lorenzo in Florence.

From the lower impost on these compound corner piers, slightly narrower strips climb to another modified entablature, larger than anything below; a narrow cyma where an architrave might have been expected, an unusually wide frieze, and a reduced cornice to mark the springing of the crossing arches. This does not mark the impost of the nave vaults, as it might have been expected to, if there were a barrel vault over the nave, but since there are groin vaults, there is no continuous impost to mark; and the vaults are borne at their corners on small corbels a bay apart, oddly set a yard above the top of this entablature, floating, and neither quite adequate nor consistent with the rest. (Their shortcomings may not date back to the XVc originals but only to the XVIIc.) It is conceivable that Codussi planned or even built barrel vaults, simpler and more like S Mark's, to which Francesco Sansovino compared them in 1581 (Sansovino, 39). But, though conceivable, it is not probable, for barrel vaults, without lunettes with windows, would have made a dark church. There may have been a conflict between aesthetic and practical preferences, and this time the practical won.

Everywhere the moldings cling close to the wall, delimiting or linking adjacent areas or mimetic structural elements, and never pushing out enough to divide or seriously dissociate one part from another. The items of the stone pseudo-armature—it does no real work—are separated more widely than usual, leaving open spaces or wall areas unencumbered. Even the arches bounding the crossing and generating the pendentives for the dome, and likewise those for the domes of the aisles, are kept close to the wall; protruding only a couple of inches, they could look papery and weak if not for their ample width. The membering seems to be halfway between diagrammatic drawing and a real working armature, and this may be one of the hard to catch factors that give the ideal look to the interior.

When the church was restored between 1919 and 1921, thanks largely to Count Venier and architect Scolari, a number of post-Codussian accretions were swept away: the frescoes, and miscellaneous later decorations and monuments. One tomb of the late XVIc still covers the end of the south transept; the doorway at the end of the north transept and that of the sacristy are later than their surroundings, but not enough to make discords. Facing the transept on either side of the chancel are two raised pulpits, like little balconies, late XVc in style but of modern manufacture. Stone pulpits had been put in in the beginning and had unaccountably been replaced by wooden ones (Pavanello, 2, 4).

The balcony for the organ has become a puzzle, compounded of bits made at different times. The oldest could be the supports, round pedestals with Codussian moldings under marble columns made taller by added drums; the shafts could be all or in part antique or could come from the XIIc church as a borrowing of something already borrowed there. An organ was here by 1526, rebuilt or altered in 1542 when extensive but undefinable changes were made in much of the west end to contrive a facade that would be a monument to Admiral Vincenzo Cappello. Whatever the age of the shafts, the timid Ionic capitals cannot be forced into any era other than late XVc to early XVIc. The whole organ loft could be an adaptation of something there earlier, made over when a new organ was installed or an old one enlarged. Some work was going on here in 1563, and again after the quake, and again in 1766, and finally there was a major revision after the bombing of 1916 (Pavanello, 9).

20.12 S Maria Formosa. East end from the campo.

20.13 S Maria Formosa. Doorway to south transept. The niche and bust at top are later additions.

There are a few irregularities in the general fabric, mainly as a result of the plan. Because the north transept is longer than the south, spaces north of the aisle (or chapel alongside the chancel) are wider than those corresponding on the south. The chapel at the north end of the transept, for example, is a quarter again wider than the south chapel (with Palma's S Barbara), and as a result its arch is wider and higher; also there is more wall between the chapel openings here than on the south. Unless hunted out, none of these irregularities is normally noticed, nor are any of them of importance. If anything, they give a freehand or fresh look to the long transept wall.

Little of the outside goes back to Codussi except the facade of the south transept and the whole east end (fig. 20.12). Here the merged half-cylinders of the apses are backed up against the long flat wall of the square block of the church. Later modifications in height and in the windows luckily matter little in the all-over monumental effect. The center apse is the least altered, with only the middle window walled in. The south apse is proportionately lower, and is linked to its taller neighbor by a stucco band carrying the line of the lower cornice around the higher apse. The north apse has been made taller. Despite obvious additions and subtractions, the rectangular windows of these side apses may be largely original. A new story has been put on top of the sacristy and chapter room, but the original scheme of three towerlike apses backed up against a clifflike flat wall is strong enough to make all these contaminations seem inconsequential. The only surely original details surviving are on the socle, two convex and one concave quarter-circles and two flat bands, running not only around the curves of the apses but across the straight walls at the ends, tying them all firmly together at the bottom. The

window frames, where original, are unmolded. The cornice is a postbomb restoration, probably correct in scale and projection.

The original stucco and subsequent coats having fallen off in many places, the bricks are now exposed, and they are mostly of the type common since the XIVc (Trincanato 1948, 94), about 10½" to 11" long and 2½" high, set in thick mortar beds of ¼" or more. The bricks are porous, lightly fired, uneven in color and shape, and look decidedly handmade. Except for replacements, they must have been newly made, not secondhand. Elsewhere, bricks of different sizes may be older, perhaps reused from the XIIc church, but in most places such shifts are probably in part the result of miscellaneous later patching.

The outside of the south transept is virtually complete, much as seen by Jacopo de' Barbari and, as expected, plain and rather grand. The ends of the restored thin cornice of the gable are tied by a band at the bottom to make a simplified pediment. The blank area of wall below is interrupted only by a big round window high up and a correct doorway below, with pediment and pilasters (fig. 20.13). The architrave is made of two fascias, both markedly inclined in the usual Codussi fashion. The inner frame around the actual door turns inward horizontally at the bottom, as in Roman or Brunelleschian prototypes. One of Codussi's most severe, this south front is suitable for a secondary entrance on a narrow space. The execution may be posthumous, by the sons or other faithful followers.

21 | S GIOVANNI GRISOSTOMO

S John Chrysostom ("golden mouth") was an eloquent and cantankerous Greek from Antioch whose learning and preaching won him the post of Patriarch of Constantinople in 398, and posthumously lifted him higher to become one of the great Doctors of the Greek church. Few Western churches were dedicated to him, but there was one in Venice in the early XIc (Candiano-M et al., 118) when the city was still half Byzantine. A gift of relics from Constantinople later in the XIc gave it more prestige, and increased both attendance and income. Venetian speech soon softened the name to S Giovanni Grisostomo, and in the near neighborhood of the church it dwindled to Zangrisostomo.

Sadly deteriorated, the old church building caught fire in 1475, and was such a wreck by 1488 that a ten-year indulgence was offered by the pope to those who would contribute to the rebuilding. The testament of a donor, dated 1494, made provision for a chapel, and that would have been either for a church already under way or about to be begun. By 1496 enough funds had accumulated for official authorization to pull down whatever was left of the old church; and in 1497 a contract was signed to go ahead with a new one. The builder was Codussi. He was paid for another chapel in 1499, enough to show that considerable work on it had already been done. The building was very well along, nearly finished by 1500, for Jacopo de' Barbari had it shown from the outside, with a low conical roof for a dome, and the other parts of the roof all there, but as equivocal in spatial relations as the roofs in Picasso's proto-Cubist Horta landscapes of 1909. Mauro died in 1504, and a document of that year referred to him here as *M Morus lapicida* ('stonemason') *et architectus.*

Suddenly thus deprived of their architect, the procurators in charge consulted Giovanni Buora, who had already worked for Codussi at S Michele and S Zaccaria and had been working with him again here; he proposed that the building be turned over to Mauro's son Domenico, already familiar with this project, as he was also with the unfinished S Maria Formosa, turned over to him at the same time. He is thought to have carried out the two exterior doorways and to have finished a few details. The church must have been completed by ca. 1513, and it was consecrated in 1525. (Consecration in Venice often lagged some years or decades behind the completion of the church.) On the saint's feast day, Mass is still said in his church in the Greek rite of the Roman church.

Despite the contract, records of payment, and papers transferring responsibility to Domenico, Mauro's authorship of this church, as of his other certain works, was never clearly stated by writers or even understood by historians until the 1890s, when he was "reconstructed" by Pietro Paoletti. Before that, the church was credited to various Lombardos: to Tullio (who did work there, but only on a chapel, under Mauro), to a "Moro Lombardo" (right first name, wrong last), or to Sebastiano Mariani da Lugano (who probably had nothing to do with it). The rapid disappearance of Codussi from written architectural history has not yet been rationally explained.

It is no surprise that S Giovanni is a late work of Codussi's, for in it are found the solutions to problems he had faced before. While at S Michele and S Maria Formosa he had tried out new ideas, and while in several ways these churches are architecturally adventurous and in others unique, here in his last church he shows himself grandly severe and Epicurean, in a sort of Summa of his art. Like the others, S Giovanni is personal in expression, but less exploratory, and far more easily contained within an ideal set form— the architectural equivalent of a sonnet

or a fugue. The immediate predecessor, S Maria Formosa, is a masterpiece of another kind and not, as S Giovanni is, the ultimate resolution of a type. A unique example, though only a little apart from the mainstream, S Giovanni is perfect in itself on its own terms, an ancient form newly introduced into the Renaissance, masterfully translated into the new language, and infused with a life of its own. It is also the first fully vaulted church of its kind in Renaissance Venice, S Maria Formosa being different and atypical. The type it so fully incarnates for the first time had a long-lasting and widespread influence, easily recognizable as late as the XVIIIc and as far away as S Vlaho (Blaise) in Dubrovnik.

Both S Maria and S Giovanni are contained in squares, but the square of S Maria is more the result of putting parts together than of one generative idea controlling the whole formation. If freed in imagination of minor additions, the overall square shape of S Maria is discernible from the outside, though without rewarding effect, and it is never really sensed at all inside. S Giovanni, on the other hand, is recognized at once as a square, despite several small additions (fig. 21.1). The shape is not played up for any aesthetic effect on the outside, just for neatness; it is, however, immediately recognized as a square from anywhere one stands on the inside (approximately 49' by 45'6"), and one knows that this is a major element in the essence of the design.

Both churches obviously have a Greek cross as a core. At S Maria the long arms delay recognition of the whole cross a little, whereas in S Giovanni the moment one raises one's eyes, the cross is as clear as the square out of which it has risen. One sees a square space that crystallizes into a cross. The space is neither additive nor divisive, for at the bottom it seems simply one plain square, and at the top

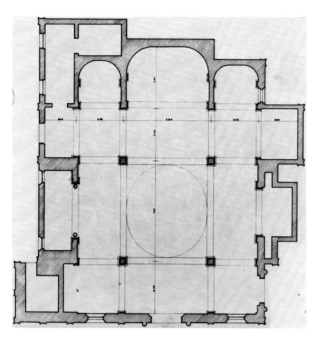

21.1 S Giovanni Griso-
stomo. Plan. The projection
at the lower left is the bottom of the campanile, added
between 1552 and 1590.
That at the upper left is also
a later addition, here of nondescript character.

a cross that has grown out of it, with
no rift between.

Most of the more or less contemporary samples of this kind of church
plan in Venice were probably replacements, literally, of Byzantine churches
on the same site, though there is little
documentary evidence in most cases,
including S Giovanni. The argument
once advanced against it here was that
the campanile was across the way until
it was pulled down in 1532, when the
Senate ordered the street widened for
the foot traffic increased by a number
of new shops (Sanudo, LV, 433, 435).
This argument wilts, however, when
confronted with such familiar isolated
bell towers as those of S Mark's, S
Maria Formosa, S Pietro di Castello,
and many more. Furthermore, old references to the new church do not mention any moving away from the old
one, but only reconstructing it (Puppi-
Puppi, 215).

One almost contemporary nine-cell
square church, S Geminiano, begun at
the west end of the Piazza in 1505, is
known to have reused old foundations
and, consequently, the old plan (*Codice
Paoletti*, 819/12; Zanotto 1838–40, I,
117; Timofiewitsch 1964, 275). S Giovanni Elemosinario, now a cross-in-
square, stands where Jacopo de' Barbari
had earlier shown one of the same
shape, surely Byzantine, lost in the
1514 Rialto fire. The probability that
the body of S Giovanni Grisostomo follows the plan of its mediaeval forerunner is strong enough to be accepted until disproved, and new documents or
excavations down to the foundations
would be needed to do that. It is the
oldest of the Renaissance versions of
this Byzantine scheme still standing in
the city. These small churches were
less adapted to the Roman rite, already
current when they were built, than to
the local variant rite, which was current when the mediaeval versions were
made, with smaller congregations and
no choirs or instrumental music.

The fact that the first church had been dedicated to a Greek little venerated in the West might lend a featherweight of probability to the idea that it had been a Greek cross, and that Codussi or the building committee had chosen the form with that in mind. The Byzantine scheme of grid with nine squares and four piers at the intersections of their boundaries was widespread then in the ex-Byzantine world (since it works well for the Eastern rites), and S Giovanni follows the same scheme. The central dome (slightly longer than wide, 20'6" by 22'0", 50'8" to the top of the dome) is on pendentives, and their four arches are carried outward centrifugally as barrel vaults (40'4" to the crown) over the nave, transepts, and chancel (fig. 21.2). The corners between these equal arms are covered by pendentive domes at a lower level, similar to those over the aisles of S Maria Formosa and, like them, now braced by tie-rods. All is handled in a spare Early Renaissance vocabulary with no Byzantine detail. Yet were a model made of the air in the church, one could not say whether it was Byzantine or of the Venetian Early Renaissance. Whether identifiable or not, it would surely be recognized as a shape beautiful in itself, compound, coherent, and indeed almost musically harmonious.

By the XIc, more or less, there were already other churches with domed cross plans in Venice: S Mark's, S Giacometto, S Lorenzo (de'Barbari map), S Maria Formosa almost surely, and probably others. The earliest Renaissance readoption of the scheme is probably here at S Giovanni Grisostomo, and thus it almost surely holds a prime place in Venetian architectural history (cf. chapter 33). Half-a-dozen Venetian churches resemble it closely, and it must have been their model (unless some completely lost church of the same type had been built earlier, but

for well-recorded Venice that is most unlikely). A few small Byzantine churches still standing in the city may have added to the familiarity of the type and helped to make it acceptable; and S Mark's was always there, in front of all eyes, towering in its prestige and in its beauty. Early Renaissance churches with Greek-cross plans outside Venice, such as Michelozzo's S Maria delle Grazie at Pistoia (ca. 1452) or Giuliano da San Gallo's Madonna delle Carceri at Prato (1485–91) are improbably related, except as cousins descended from the Alberti line (and more from his theory than his practice).

The main block of S Giovanni Grisostomo is subdivided in the ratio of 1:2:1, the center bay twice as wide as the sides, or nearly so, depending on whether the measurements include, ignore, or divide the thickness of walls or other dividing members. (No ideal ratio can work perfectly for a normal walled building.) This means that the square under the dome is as 2:2, the corner squares 1:1, and the arms 2:1. Rationalistic Renaissance idealism, Platonic belief that the highest beauty lay in pure, simple geometric figures and other such imperatives, seem to have been welcomed here (as they had been by Alberti), and Codussi demonstrated them as he had not before. The same 1:2:1 ratio affects other parts of the scheme, and must have been exploited consciously, most likely as a mystico-philosophical guarantee of harmony and, hence, beauty. Such ideas appear in some of Mauro's other works, but not in all, and it is impossible, knowing nothing of his character except as revealed by his buildings, to know whether these were instinctively his, learned somehow from Alberti or some other humanist, or pushed by the patrons of some commissions.

One important part of the chancel has been altered. A barrel vault must have covered the east arm originally, as barrel vaults covered the others, and it

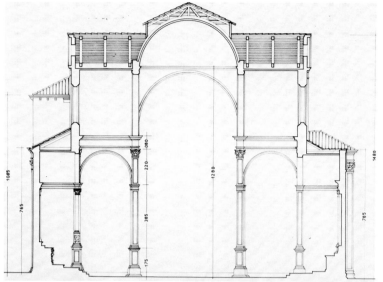

21.2 S Giovanni Grisostomo. Cross section, through Bernabò and Diletti family chapels.

21.3 S Giovanni Grisostomo. Interior looking east, toward flattened apse. Note interpolated clerestory windows in place of vault over chancel.

must have continued a short distance to extend the apse (as strips on the wall still indicate); then it shifted into the vault of the apse itself. Now there is no vault over this arm, but a flat wood ceiling, unassimilable both structurally and aesthetically (fig. 21.3). The existence of a vault here as part of Mauro's building is certain, for Sebastiano del Piombo, before he abandoned Venice in 1511, painted a fresco "on the vault of the *tribuna*" (*Cronaca* 1736, 326; Sansovino, 154). *Tribuna* means "chancel" (Masciotta, 201). A flat ceiling is not a vault; a flat ceiling is made of wood; a fresco is painted not on wood but on plaster; a vault is normally plastered. (This is another proof, incidentally, that the church had been complete before 1511.)

A barrel vault is what comes to mind at once, to match the other arms, but a barrel vault would not have let in light, which is probably what doomed it. Mauro may have used groin vaults at S Maria Formosa to admit light, and it is just possible that he might have used one here, coordinating its diameters with the others; not sacrificing all formal symmetry, yet giving in to practical and expressive considerations. But the conscious formality of the whole design is against it, and if there had been a groin vault letting in light, why would it have been replaced by the discordant flat wood ceiling? A barrel vault, then, seems certain.

The lighting seems to have been an essential adjunct of the formal design, and it is beautifully worked out except at the one most important place, the sanctuary. The arms and foot of the cross each have a 6' round window at the end, near the top. On either side of the front door, tall, graceful, arched windows of Codussi's typical Brunelleschian shape let in soft light from the street. Their arches spring from the same impost-cornice as all the lower arches of the church, and hence are concentric to those enclosing them; the windows take their place as parts of the main design, not as mere utilitarian holes in the wall. Glowing bits of light filter out of the private chapels at the ends of the transepts, from their side windows slipped in out of sight from the nave (fig. 21.4). Now, of course, there is a burst of light at the chancel from the windows under the flat ceiling, but even so the apse proper remains curiously dark.

As at S Maria Formosa, the floor was originally laid at different levels, preparing in this understated way for some of the differences that would be dramatically developed in the spaces higher up, and expressing by different levels the different functions that took place in each space below. Everything east of the crossing, for example, was raised two steps above where the congregation would be standing, and the holiest and only specially consecrated part of the building, the sanctuary, was raised up one more, the altar three more above that, and the flanking chapels only two. The aisles were raised a step above the nave (Tramontin 1968, 34), but the main body of the church has recently been repaved all on one level. The family chapels opening off the aisles were also raised because it seemed appropriate to separate them from the main square of the building where the parishioners regularly gathered; furthermore, these chapels contained consecrated altars.

The details of the interior, as at S Maria Formosa, have an Early Renaissance slightness throughout, emphasizing the space they outline rather than the masses between and behind. The four central piers, rising from their ample pedestals, are both slender and linear, basically closer to Gothic in their lack of bulk than to Roman or Byzantine. But their details, like many of those elsewhere in the church, equally simple, clear, and massless, evoke Brunelleschi (fig. 21.5).

These piers cannot escape a dilemma from which no final divorce is possible: they try to clothe their mediaeval form of a compound pier with classic detail, only a part of whose strict syntax is able to work there. Made with members carefully differentiated to carry arches at different levels, they have to have the compound differentiated core. The problem of dressing it in apt detail could easily be met with mediaeval membering, such as shafts, but not with classical parts, demanded here for the lower arches (of the corner pendentive domes) and for the higher arches (for the main vaults and the pendentives of the central dome). There is no way of using pilasters or engaged columns conjoined for two such different heights without violating their strong heritage of what they can and cannot do. There is something incompatible here that cannot be evaded.

Other architects had tried, but without success. For his lower arches at the crossing of S Lorenzo, Brunelleschi had used pilasters of the same scale as the columns of the nave arcade, of which they were the closing elements, and then for the higher arches of the crossing itself, pilasters of equivalent width but much greater height, to reach the entablature from which the crossing arches would spring. These pilasters had to be so long and so thin that they could no longer express any supporting force, and they look instead like lengths of ribbon or paper or, at best, planks. The base and capital do not work together with the shafts in the normal way because the shafts have been stretched too far to count as a connecting unit that might want a base or capital. They look more like decorative trimming held down at either end, neither one related to the whole by any structural need.

The proportions of Mauro's piers would have exaggerated this enough to become even more meaningless, for the relative height is more and the width

less. A partial reduction is made by putting the piers up on pedestals 4'8" high. The members of the compound piers expressing support for the lower arches are not pilasters here, but strips that take on a pilasterlike character by seeming to have a capital, a fascia, and a few moldings that reappear (or respond) on the opposite strip on the wall at the other end of the arch. But since the moldings then continue along the wall, like a small flattish cornice, we see that they are neither proper capitals nor a proper cornice, but just moldings marking the impost level, an all-purpose element that can substitute without trouble for a capital or a subordinate cornice. This little set of moldings, used for several purposes, manages to make a legible articulation, not with the sanction of antique usage but by the invention of a freely abridged near order. On the walls it is a sort of girdle all around the church; on the piers it becomes a substitute capital.

The lower set of arches appear adequate to carry two sides of the corner pendentive domes, though actually they have little depth and cut that little off where they meet their mates at the corners. But, as at S Maria Formosa, the width of the arches is ample enough to make up for lack of depth and for any threat of weakness; the impression, in fact, is one of easy strength.

The same small set of impost moldings has another even more surprising role: after serving as a capital for the two lesser parts of the compound piers, it runs on around the pier and crosses the two major members, those rising up for the higher arches of the cross. The effects of this cannot quite be resolved. If one thinks in the normal syntax of the classical orders, one finds that these important piers cannot be parsed. The XVIIIc architect, critic, professor, and academic crank, Antonio

21.4 S Giovanni Griso-
stomo. Crossing.

21.5 S Giovanni Grisostomo.
Pier with arches.

21.6 S Giovanni Grisostomo.
Bernabò Chapel.

Visentini, was upset by Codussi's "frivolousness" in committing the "Great Error of cutting pilasters in an unbecoming and monstrous way" (Visentini 1771, 57). There *is* an anomaly here, for below the interruption there is what starts out like a proper paneled pilaster, with its proper base set firmly on a pedestal—but suddenly the invading impost stops the panel. Above it, the panel starts again—without a new base—and runs on up like a pilaster shaft hardly more than half as high as the section of shaft below (6'5" vs. 12'6"), and it ends in a typical Early Renaissance one-leaf capital.

It is possible to read this in contradictory ways, either as one over-tall and over-narrow pilaster that has been cut across, or as two imperfect pilasters superposed, one with a base but no capital and the other with a capital but no base. As with the impost molding, different glances can give different readings. This impost molding is nonetheless able, while tying arches and wall moldings into the coalition of the ensemble, to allow the main verticals to pass through or under without enough friction to stop the upward impulse. What might have been conflict has been avoided also by the slightness of all the moldings and the sinewy strength of the lean-limbed piers. The impost interruption is less than that made by the moldings capping the pedestals at the bottom of these same piers, where their verticality has not yet picked up its full force and where— nearer the floor—horizontality is apposite.

Logically, there ought to be a paradox when the entire support of the main part of the church can be seen as a pilaster nicked in two by something clearly weaker than itself; but logic has to take second place to sensation, when the tall piers seem to work so vigorously and elegantly as supports for the vaults; only in second place does logic

allow the upper half of the pier to count as a stubby pilaster. It is not the familiar grammar of the orders that works here, but something new improvised by Codussi for the special conditions. Neither Brunelleschi nor Alberti were of help here.

The capitals of the upper pilasters are close to Roman Corinthian, though less leafy and flaring more than the standard. Above is a compressed entablature with a cornice held close to the wall as suitable for interior use. All moldings are of simple section, and slender. The parts join to make an armature for the structural and spatial schemes, the lower part with nothing that counts but verticals, and the upper developing into a concert of arches bound by simple horizontals. Codussi must have picked this up outside Venice, presumably from Alberti and Brunelleschi, taking less from local antique works in Verona or others he saw at first hand. There may even be an unconscious memory of Gothic in it. But it is not so much his sources as the synthesis he made from them that counts here, and the clarity and purity with which he achieved it. Together the pale gray-white limestone members form an airy, fine-drawn pavilion, closed in only by the papery surfaces of white plaster.

Three apses extend out to the east from the overall nine-cell square. The flanking chapels continue the direction and width of the side aisles, and begin with a short barrel-vaulted bay running on from the pendentive dome and, after passing a rib springing from strips on the walls, end in a not unexpected nearly semicylindrical apse covered with an equally not unexpected quarter-sphere or semidome.

The main apse, between them, is less normal. In 1509–11, Sebastiano del Piombo painted a large altarpiece of S John Chrysostom and six other saints for it, his last work before he left Venice. Until it was obscured by waxy soot from the inordinate number of votive candles burning in the church, it must have been the largest and richest area of color there, brighter and deeper in tone than Sebastiano's fresco on the vault above. The large flat picture fits into its space snugly because of the odd form of the apse wall, flat in the middle and curved at the ends to join the short walls separating the chancel from the accompanying chapels. The flattening comes where the church presumably had to stop because of the mediaeval houses clustered around the nearby Corte del Milion (where many of them still stand). The main apse vault is ingeniously warped above this wall to fit the curved-straight-curved plan, though it begins normally with the semicircular arch joining it to the rest of the church.

The proportional sequence of curve to straight in the main apse is 1:2:1 (curve-straight-curve), just as the proportions of the row of all three apses here are 1:2:1. This elementary harmony in the shape of the curved-straight-curved wall (which seems inherently ugly) is less sensed by anyone standing in the church than it is noticed on a drawing of the plan. The odd shape had been used in Venice before, at the Cappella Gussoni in S Lio, and would soon appear in Giovanni Bellini's *Madonna and Saints* finished in 1505 for S Zaccaria (the apse of S Giovanni must have been completed before Bellini began his altar for S Zaccaria); this has the same curved-straight-curved plan for no reason now capturable.

The chapels at the sides of the square are differently arranged; those at the ends of the north and south arms date back to the original building campaign and were designed for the most part by Codussi himself, modified perhaps by the wishes of the clients and perhaps also by those who finished the building after he died. They open from the church through arches of the same size

as those of the pendentive domes in the corner bays, arches which do not, then, fill the end walls of the transepts. The proportions of these arches to the spaces on either side of them at the back of the transepts are again 1:2:1.

The chapel at the end of the north transept must have been begun about 1499, commissioned by the wealthy Bernabò family of silk merchants recently admitted to the patriciate. They had already established a family chapel in the old church. Tullio Lombardo received two pieces of particularly fine marble for an altarpiece for it in 1500, which he completed carving in 1502 (fig. 21.6). Until then the altar had held a Gothic painting of the Madonna and Child from the old church, which was sent to the nuns of S Maria Maggiore when Tullio's relief was set up (Pope-Hennessy 1958, 55). The chapel must have been finished, or nearly finished, before a delicate relief would have been placed there. Completion by 1502 is confirmed by one of the church's twin pulpits—the mate is beside the chapel opposite—that overlaps the pilaster enframing the right side of the Bernabò Chapel. Since the pulpit is inscribed MDIII, the pilaster must have been there before that. From the end of the 1490s to 1502 are secure dates, then, for the building of the chapel. Many carvers' names are recorded as having been paid for work there during those years, and a great number of them were from Lombardy.

The interior facade of the chapel has the most elaborate design in the church. An arch of the same size as the other lower-level arches spans it and continues back into the chapel as a barrel vault. Pilasters like those on the upper piers flank the arch, run up to the main entablature, and establish a clear frame. But although the members used in the chapel are all related to those of the rest of the interior, each individual form chosen for the chapel is enriched. The archivolt is not only wider, but has carved ornament. (At the top it is tangent to the main entablature but, unsecured by a keystone, lets seesawing threaten.) The spandrels, of *paonazzo* or *calacata,* each inset with a disc tangent to all three sides, are the first colored architectural elements in the body of the achromatic church. The discs had been specially bought from Domenico Zorzi in 1500 (Puppi-Puppi, 184), making another link with the Zorzi family (though here of a different branch), old patrons of Codussi, who had already commissioned a chapel at S Michele and an important palace. The Bernabòs, unlike the Zorzis, must have wanted to make a rich effect and have asked for more carving and more color than Codussi used elsewhere.

It is the lower part where sumptuousness takes over. The severe impost running all around the church becomes richer and more correct by ending in a curvy cyma at the top; a band at the bottom serves as architrave and maybe frieze as well, completing a condensed entablature. This is supported in a new way, at the outer edge by an elegant pilaster, slimmer than the strips on the center piers and their responses on the walls. Closely coupled with this is a freestanding column with double entasis, set on a round pedestal. Pilaster and column plus cylinder stand as a pair on one rectangular pedestal more delicately detailed than equivalent pedestals anywhere else in the church. Bernabò taste is evident.

In 1501 Pietro Lombardo supplied glowing gold brown marble for these columns (Pope-Hennessy 1958, 354), but since he sold stone as a sideline, this need not involve him in their design, though they are of a general type he had used at least twice. The details seem carved by a different hand than the rest nearby, but that need not mean that the design was not by the same architect. The columns could have been supplied ready-made. There is, furthermore, some likelihood that the Cornaro

Chapel in the SS Apostoli—with similar columns and other resemblances— may have something to do with the Bernabò Chapel and with Codussi, though more probably from his influence than from any direct intervention in the design. Whatever the relation, the Bernabò can be seen as a more resolved and advanced revision of the Cornaro, which the clients may have admired and suggested as a model.

Whatever its genesis, the Bernabò Chapel shows in its details that Codussi had a great deal to do with it; it is all but certain that he designed it as a whole, but less certain that he was in charge of the execution. Tullio surely made the altarpiece, inscribed, TULLI LOMBARDI OPUS, and he could have been in charge of carrying out the surrounding architecture as well, under Codussi. It may be that this association was decisive in transforming his style from neo-Lombardo to neo-Codussi. The element which seems farthest from Mauro is the pair of columns on cylinders, and they could have been specially requested by Jacopo de Bernabò. The yoking of a column on its round pedestal with a pilaster as tall as both together is un-Roman and against what rules of Latin architectural grammar were even then current. In the XVIIIc, Antonio Visentini was again outraged here, for he believed that on no condition should pilasters be taller than columns (Visentini 1771, 55).

Marble beams run from the capitals to the back wall, where they are received by pilasters. These pilasters are shorter than the others because they are set on the top of the marble dado that runs around the wings of the chapel as backs for the marble benches fitted in there for members of the Bernabò family; the benches were reserved for the family when they attended special Masses in their chapel. To frame the relief on the altar, these smaller pilasters are forcibly paired with others not only wider but taller, because they stand not on the dado but on the back of the altar. None of all this—frame, mismatched pilasters, colored colonnettes, inlaid circles—finds a counterpart elsewhere in the chapel. Codussi was contractually in charge, but the wishes of someone else apparently dominated these last details. A XV–XVIc architect was not always free to do just what he liked.

The chapel on the right, authorized in the 1494 will of Giorgio Diletti to take the place of a family chapel in the old church, was delayed in building until 1509 or later (Puppi-Puppi, 217), after Codussi had died, though he undoubtedly had made designs for it. The chief ornament, the last altarpiece of Giovanni Bellini, signed and dated 1513, may have been started ten years earlier—Diletti died in 1503—for some other commission. It shows signs of having been planned for an arched frame, but the present frame has a straight top. There have been changes of another kind also, made by the octogenarian Bellini himself (Robertson, 128–31). The attributes of two of the three saints (S Christopher defeats changing) have been altered to shift S Louis of Toulouse to a young S Augustine (who rarely appears young) and an old S Jerome to a Chrysostom more appropriate for this site. What better example of the wishes of a client changing those of an artist? The smoke from the tiered ranks of candles, often a hundred burning at once, has so blackened the surface of the picture that it has had to be cleaned twice in the last forty years. In 1977 it was removed to the galleria of the Accademia to be cleaned and held there as a sort of hostage until there was a change in the quality of the candles sold in the church. It is now back in place as of early 1979. (The organ shutters of the church were plain sooty black until early 1978, when cleaning revealed handsome panels by Mansueti.)

The chapel is roughly a square, three steps up from the main floor (fig. 21.7). Above is a barrel vault springing from the same impost as the other arches of the lower level. The impost-cornice stops dead against the rear wall, purposely left blank to take the architecturally uncoordinated altarpiece frame, not made as foreseen at the beginning but probably only just after 1513, when the picture was finished in its present form and ready to be installed. Arched windows at the ends of the side walls of the little chapel let in a particularly pleasant light for the beautiful altarpiece, in an arrangement like that of the Cornaro Chapel in SS Apostoli (which has occasionally been attributed to Codussi). Inside, though not on the outside, the chapel is on the whole pleasant and unexceptional, and far more integrated with the design of the rest of the church than the Bernabò Chapel opposite.

Only three sides of the exterior can be seen, for the east end is built into old houses, some surely older than the church. The easiest side to see is not the most important, but the north front on the little side campo; a long flat wall butting into the campanile begun there after the street was widened in 1532, and slowly completed in the later XVIc. Pilasters and entablature, chapel and sacristy windows, a rebuilt side doorway and additions to the priest's house all go to make this an unpretentious, undistinguished, and unplanned affair.

The south wall is not flat, but breaks in and out as a result of the arrangements inside. One short break comes from a continuation of the transept (for a stairway to the pulpit and a matching storage space) soon followed by another break for the bulk of the Diletti Chapel, projecting it far enough for the side walls to have room for windows. Inexplicably, the chapel lacks the pilasters and entablature that mark all the

21.7 S Giovanni Grisostomo.
Diletti Chapel.

other breaks on this side (fig. 21.8). The only notable feature of this whole south front is the doorway at the west end, added by Domenico Codussi after his father died, almost surely following his father's wishes, perhaps enriched and made a bit more plastic (fig. 21.9).

The main interest is all on the west front, which, alas, even after the widening of the street, is still hard to see and defeatingly hard to illustrate (fig. 21.10). Essentially it is a restudy and refinement of that of S Michele, carried out more economically in baser materials, limestone and red-orange plaster, the Venetian red of pulverized overfired brick mixed into lime plaster, perhaps with some added cinnabar (natural mercuric sulphide or powdered red marble). It is more economical too in the variety of forms used for the whole composition.

Clearly a city church on a narrow street, almost necessarily kept to one plane, it still gains animation from the pattern given by the pilasters and sweeping cornices, the fastidious spotting of the windows and door and, above all, by the silhouette, Mauro's liveliest. The barrel vault of the nave is expressed outside as a slightly less than semicircular gable, and the aisles as less than quarter-circles lengthened a little horizontally (less than on S Michele or S Zaccaria), akin to the crowning curve in the middle. The curves act concertedly, without tension, but with a special bouncy zest. They seem higher and have greater lift than those at S Michele, and the cornices underlining them are less massive and more linear. The round window floats more freely in its rectangular space. And the flat lower story is in easier proportion to its openings, with more even areas of wall around them, and more in consonance with the space around the *oculus*. The proportions used at S Michele have been modified in almost every part. Everywhere, the lebensraum is easy.

The front of S Michele, facing the windswept lagoon almost alone on its small island, is properly more robust, all stone, much of it rusticated. There are stronger contrasts of light and shadow, open and solid, and of areas of different shapes—all carried out with an exquisiteness not to be expected in so bold a design. S Giovanni, deep in the city on a narrow street, hemmed in by blocks of tight-packed buildings, and in no way exposed, has no need to be so robust, and can be as effective with plainer and lower relief, and with membering that bounds areas less contrasted in size and shape.

The details have also been readjusted. The quadrants, for example, chop less violently into the upper order of pilasters (shown incorrectly as superposed pilasters in Angelini 1945, fig. 64). Visentini still thought that any cut at all "dishonors architecture" (1771, 57). Codussi achieved an equilibrated organization of ideas that he had presented earlier in different combinations with different detail and accentuation. The membering is thinner, flatter, and so minimized that with less it can effectively do more. Less interesting in itself, it leads attention to the whole, never to the parts. This is often achieved in the late works of a master who has made more effort with more material at the beginning, and has arrived at clearer, easier, and simpler statements of his ideas at the close of his career.

The facade of S Giovanni appeared so clearly to be the right resolution of this type of facade that it became the model for a number of others in the city: S Maria dei Carmini by Sebastiano Mariani, for instance, ca. 1510; or S Felice of 1531; and more extravagantly at the Madonna dei Miracoli at Motta di Livenza near Treviso of ca. 1510; not to mention about a dozen country cousins in Dalmatia, notably at Zadar and on the island of Hvar.

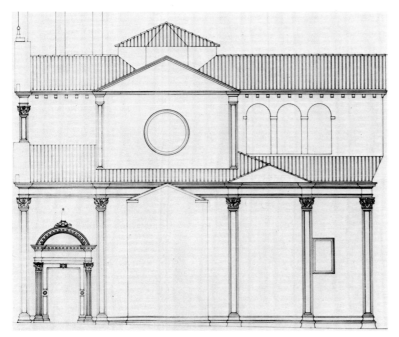

21.8 S Giovanni Grisostomo.
South flank, elevation.

21.9 S Giovanni Grisostomo.
South flank, side door.

21.10 S Giovanni Grisostomo. Front (lithograph by Moro and Kier, 1859).

Except for the campanile, set flush with the street front at the north—and doing it no harm—the ensemble has been little altered. The front doorway, like that around the south corner, must be by son Domenico, fairly close to his father's intentions; both are a bit richer and fatter, more like the work of a generation later (and also, surprisingly, rather like the doorways of the Miracoli). The most important change affecting the whole has come from the raising of the level of the street, so that the socle has been reduced to no more than a couple of moldings lying on the pavement. The overall proportions have suffered from the loss of at least a foot. The steps leading up to the main entrance, a centralizing element in the design and a suitable emphasis just there, have been entirely buried. Now one has to step down into the church, to a floor that until recently used often to be damp (until patching of the foundation walls and a new heating system were given by Save Venice, Inc.). The damage inflicted in an Austrian air raid in 1918 was slight and easily repaired, and the storm and flood of 1966 and the earthquakes of 1976 and 1977 have not—apparently—affected it seriously.

Although S Giovanni is an all but perfect example of the ideal nine-cell, five-dome, four-pier, cross-in-square scheme, that scheme is well developed only on the inside, somewhat less on the facade, and scarcely at all on the flanks. The full form, as sensed so vividly in the shape of the volume of air enclosed, invites naturally to an exterior composition—its other side, as it were—of three main levels; top, with the main dome, middle, with the corner domes, and lower, with the arms. Such a form invites dramatic and monumental exploitation, as a score of mediaeval churches of Byzantine Greece and more in southern Yugoslavia still splendidly demonstrate. The greatest number were in inland towns, in Macedonia or Serbia, unknown to more than

a handful of Venetians, but there were some on the coast and islands of Greece and Dalmatia that must have been known to more. Codussi would have been ignorant of them. Neither he nor anyone else tried anything of that nature, perhaps because it did not fit with the Venetian taste for (or habit of?) composing in planes rather than masses. All the Venetian examples of the plan have the rotundity of the vaults and domes hidden under the simple planes of tiled roofs, structurally sensible and natural. But neither Codussi nor anyone else ever tried any building up of plastic forms, not for S Giovanni or any other church or, indeed, any other building.

22 | PALAZZO ZORZI

Codussi made the first full-fledged Renaissance palace fronts in Venice, for although there had been facades with Renaissance trimming before, not one was organized throughout as a unified Renaissance composition. Although nowhere documented as by him, three palaces are now accepted as his: the Zorzi on the Rio di S Severo, the Corner-Spinelli, and the Vendramin-Calergi on the Grand Canal. They show that he was as inventive in making palaces as in making churches. Although only three, they sired a set of handsome palace fronts, more unitarily composed than any since a few late Gothic masterpieces. His plans vary little, and the facades, as generally, are almost all confined to one face only. All three palaces are faced with good stone very well laid up at a time when all stone private palace fronts were still a novel luxury. All three have a bit more applied low relief of an architectural character than those being made by his contemporaries, with a bit less decorative carved trimming, and less color. All, happily for him, were built in time of peace and prosperity, and all, apparently, for clients of wealth, power, learning, and taste.

None has a firm date. The Palazzo Zorzi and the Corner-Spinelli must have been begun first, and were probably going up at the same time for some years. Whether the first of the two or not—and it pretty surely is—the Palazzo Zorzi is so different from the others, which are closely interrelated, that it may more conveniently be looked at first. Part of its originality may come from its pioneering adaptation of a recalcitrant old type to a new vocabulary, and part from its adaptation of recalcitrant old foundations and walls to a new design.

It stands at the south end of the Rio di S Severo on part of a large plot held in the name of Marco Zorzi, who had commissioned Codussi to make the family chapel at S Michele in 1476

(Bellavitis 1976, 111). He was presumably the head of a branch of the family, and as such would have had the strongest voice in the decision for a new palace and the choice of a designer. Zorzi's early connection with Codussi of course strengthens the attribution, but the chief evidence for assigning it to him is the building itself.

The starting date of the building used to be put around 1500, but a fresh look at the front and an exceptionally thorough examination of the rest by the architect Giorgio Bellavitis, mainly in 1974 when the empty palace was waiting to be rehabilitated, has made an earlier date, such as ca. 1470–1490, seem certain. The building must have been up before 1500, for its roof, much as it is now, is shown on the Barbari bird's-eye view. A Domenico Zorzi sold some surplus marble to the Bernabòs, for whom Codussi was building a chapel in S Giovanni Grisostomo, in 1500, a fact that had been thought important for dating this palace; but it has no real connection with the building, since Domenico belonged to a branch of the family who had a different palace, still standing on the Rio di S Lorenzo near the Greek church (Bellavitis, in conversation).

The Zorzis (Venetian for Giorgio) had bought their considerable property on the Rio di S Severo at the end of the XIVc, buying or soon building the big Gothic palace now known as the Palazzo Zorzi-Bon, still standing next to where Codussi's would go a century later. Another palace stood where Codussi's now is, and money was saved by using some of its foundations and walls, of course affecting the plan. The new layout is unusual, but not unique, though unusual and unique in some of its parts. The 200' canal front is almost twice as long as the main block is deep, and the palace thus belongs in company with the Ca' Cocco-Molin, the Cappello-Memmo, and a few others

(fig. 22.1). The plot is not just a simple rectangle, for part runs deeper, and Codussi took ingenious advantage of this not only to add more spaces inside, but also to make a pleasant courtyard and probably a large garden (now the outdoor bowling alley of a popular local restaurant).

The land entrance was on the street, continuing from the bridge across the rio in front. It gave into an open portico facing the court and leading on into the body of the palace to a new kind of stairway on the left, opposite a regular but short *androne,* at right angles to the portico, running through the building to an arched water entrance in the middle of the canal facade (figs. 22.2 and 22.3). The broad L of circulation thus established is unusual, but it had some precedents in Gothic palaces, and may be based here on the layout of the Gothic palace formerly on the site.

Another arched entrance is at the left end of the facade and, matching it and the main water entrance in the center, there is a third at the extreme right (fig. 22.4). This may once have been the end of an alley that had to be preserved (though not for long) and was run through the bottom of the house like a tunnel (suggested by architect Bellavitis). A parallel alley of equivalent length and narrowness runs to the water at the far end of the adjacent Ca' Zorzi-Bon. The matching arched entrance at the left end of Codussi's facade is not easily explained by any practical need, unless it was for a *cavana,* or built-in boathouse, though *cavanas* in private palaces were rare. The archway might have been put there only for symmetry, which would have been exceptional for this time but possible for Codussi. There are even more daring concessions to symmetry that ignore logic and even truth in other parts of the front. It cannot have been an entrance for a separate branch of the family, as there are no signs of a stairway near it, any more than there are signs of a *cavana* pool. Codussi used a

22.1 Palazzo Zorzi (lithograph by Moro and Kier ca.
1845).

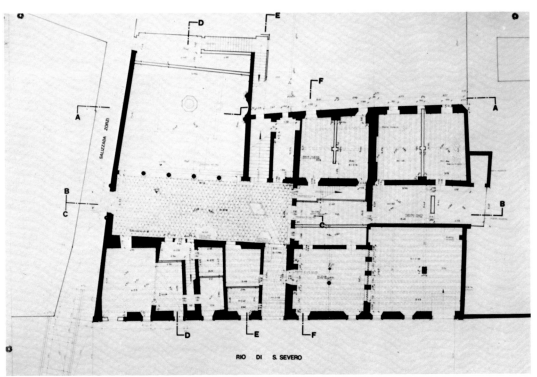

22.2 Palazzo Zorzi. Courtyard portico, leading from
land entrance (right) to *androne* and stairs (left).

22.3 Palazzo Zorzi. Plan.

22.4 Palazzo Zorzi. Canal facade.

great deal of older construction in the building, but he rejected the Gothic irregularity it might have led to, choosing instead to force classic symmetry on the unavoidable combinations of old and new. It is hard, nevertheless, to believe that the big doorways at the ends did not have some use—both of them, or at least one—but it is also hard to guess at such uses.

Two of the three identical unconventionally placed openings make unexpected accents at the ends and, despite their size, position, and prominence, exaggerated by big shadows, they are strangely independent of the stories above. The middle opening is not really in the middle, nor on the same axis as the special window above it (marking the center of the piano nobile). The pushing of the side doorways out to the edges might force a sensation of instability on the whole; where one expects legs, there are holes. But instead of malaise, the effect of such near-perversity is somehow mitigated or even balanced, and instead of perilously supported the whole front seems curiously light. Codussi must have sensed that a weighty-looking palace might be disturbing when there was nothing visible under it but lapping water, and the daringly weakened corners do make the whole seem lighter. The white *pietra d'Istria* is laid up in yard-long slabs that do not, as they easily might, imply blocks of Egyptian massiveness (though some of them do run back the full thickness of the wall), but instead play up only their weightless paper-smooth surface, thanks to the beautifully precise joints, still not ordinarily seen unless specially sought. The quality of the masonry is unsurpassed in the city.

These arched openings almost touch the pilasterlike strips running up the outside edges. Repeatedly interrupted, these verticals, taking the place of the mediaeval polelike corners on older palaces, are related to the interior strips at S Maria Formosa or S Giovanni Grisostomo. They seem about to turn into pilasters every time a panel stops and they are crossed by a horizontal molding (ten times before they reach the top cornice). Because of this and because they lack bases or capitals, they lose much of the solidity that corners can call for. On the left, what faces the canal is repeated by what faces the street, so that the strip can be seen as a three-dimensional pier, adding visual strength to the corner, which, because of the hole of the arched opening right next to it, needs all it can get (fig 22.5). These peculiar strips are another example of an original element with which Codussi experimented more than once, but never quite with complete success.

A set of moldings with Mauro's typical purity of profile marks the top of the otherwise plain socle (fig. 22.6). The next line of moldings marks both the impost of the three big openings and the sill of the eight not quite regularly spaced storeroom windows, small, nearly square, and inconspicuous. The next horizontal runs uninterrupted for the full 200' of the front, almost turning into a capital where it crosses the corner strips, and serving also as base for twenty-six dwarf pilasters, so small that most have space for only three flutes. Incidentally framing the eleven mezzanine windows, these follow one another with a controlled but complex rhythm, accented twice by being doubled, and four times by being widened enough to take six flutes.

This has an effect at once daring and subtle. One's eye runs along—as it must, since the palace has so many horizontals and is so assertive of its many layers—and cannot ever quite come to a stop, for the variations of spacing never seem to repeat or come to an end; soon, however, they reverse their scansion, reproducing one half in reverse order, like a long palindrome. Symmetry and sense become clear only when the far edge is reached. One has to take in the whole, for no part is allowed to be complete; everything is a

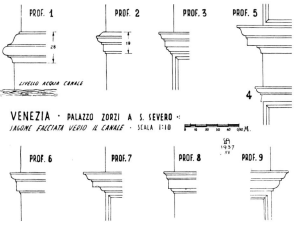

VENEZIA · PALAZZO ZORZI A S. SEVERO ·:
SAGOME FACCIATA VERSO IL CANALE · SCALA 1:10

22.5 Palazzo Zorzi. Corner pier.

22.6 Palazzo Zorzi. Profiles of horizontal moldings of facade (from Angelini, *Codussi*).

little off beat and unresolved until all has been passed in review and checked off with the matching complements on the other half. The full 200′ are held together by this reciprocating incompleteness, a principle familiar in High Baroque, unexpected here.

The same knowingly manipulated irregularity, or temporary imbalance, could become even more striking on the piano nobile if not countered by more strict, forceful, and arbitrary control. For the first time, one is made aware here of the traditional tripartite palace division, strong, and greatly extended. The wings, though far apart, act together with the long center section to assert commanding symmetry, quite dominating the rhythm of the lower story windows and pilasters, which now seem to have a relaxed, at ease quality.

The wings have about four parts of solid to three of open, arranged with the narrowest sections of wall at each end, denying any feeling of a robust corner able to bring a long, busy facade to a strong stop, but recalling in another way the weakening of the corners by the big arched openings at the bottom. The outermost and innermost of the three windows in the wings of the piano nobile now have Baroque balconies from a late alteration (to match the balconies added then to the adjacent Ca′ Zorzi-Bon). The middle windows, however, are as they were in the beginning (fig. 22.7). Their long consoles or brackets rise from the stringcourse at floor level to the sills at normal height (or hang from the latter to the former), astonishing forerunners of the same arrangement—forty or fifty years ahead of its time—that would be invented by San Gallo and Michelangelo.

The 50′ balcony of the loggia is also original, including its more conventional brackets and its svelte spindle balusters (fig. 22.8). Venice by now had more balconies than any other city in

22.7 Palazzo Zorzi. One wing.

22.8 Palazzo Zorzi. Piano
nobile. At right, two *bifore*;
at left, center window.

22.9 Palazzo Zorzi. Piano
nobile. Central window,
flanked by *bifora.*

Europe. From the XVc they are preserved on scores of palaces, and are shown often in the sketchbooks of Jacopo Bellini. Coryat (I, 205) noted in 1611, ". . . right opposite their windows, a very pleasant little terrasse, that jutteth or butteth out from the maine building: the edge whereof is decked with many pretty little turned pillers. . . . These kind of terrasses or little galleries of pleasure . . . give great grace to the whole edifice and serve only for this purpose, that people may . . . contemplate and view the parts of the City round about them in the coole evenings."

Greater rhythmic variation begins with the loggia behind the unprecedented 50' balcony, needed, perhaps, to make a strong feeling of order in front of some surprising irregularities in the openings behind. Starting from the left, first comes a pier compounded of an Ionic pilaster and a half-column carrying an arch that springs over to a free-standing column carrying a twin arch that runs on over to another compound pier. All together these make a two-light window, or *bifora*. This second pier is a bit more compound—half-column, pilaster, another half-column—and it starts the arch of another *bifora* that ends in another half-column and pilaster pier. There are, thus, four arches arranged as two *bifore*. Surprisingly, only the second arch from the left end encloses a real window, the other three being walled with big blocks of limestone set with the finest of imperceptible joints. The stones run all the way through the wall to the plaster of the room inside. The only explanation of this is that the beams of this room ran outward to the exterior wall (as they still do) and had to be carried by it, and that therefore, with the beams carrying their share of the room above and of the roof, the wall here had to be strong, and more closed than open (observed first by Bellavitis). This is not the only peculiarity behind the long balcony.

After these two *bifore* comes a short stretch of wall, about 4'6", disguised to look less by the engaged column at the end of the *bifora* and a pilaster acting as a frame for a single central window (fig. 22.9). The arrangement is unprecedented and just misses looking uncomfortably pinched, with its single window in the center, flanked by the open stretches of a pair of double windows on each side, like a near beauty whose eyes are too close together. The other jamb of the middle window has of course a matching combination of pier and wall.

The second bit of wall hides the reason behind this peculiar spacing: it was used to cover the end of a long interior wall, wider here at the outer end than way back inside the building. The long, wedgelike construction must be something left from the earlier palace on the site, and must have been abnormal even there. Surely there had been repeated alterations, and it is not clear that the Gothic palace was always one building; it may have been some sort of amalgamation.

The two succeeding *bifore* are open now (though they were walled up in the mid-XIXc) and they light the end of the normal *sala* running through the palace in the usual way. Its ceiling is framed as would be expected, with beams parallel to the front windows, and not much weight lands on the pair of fragile *bifore* there (figs. 22.10 and 22.11). Their columns are unusually tall and thin, appropriately to let light into the 110' deep *sala*. The radical rhythmic scheme of the fenestration (ignoring the walling up of some windows but counting only the pattern of columns and arches) can be most easily written out as ♫♫|♪♪|♫♫.

Thus, from the end to the middle, while all is orderly, there is no place to stop, though one may slow down or pause for a moment; the complete phrase is very long, longer than any tried before in Venice. Momentary

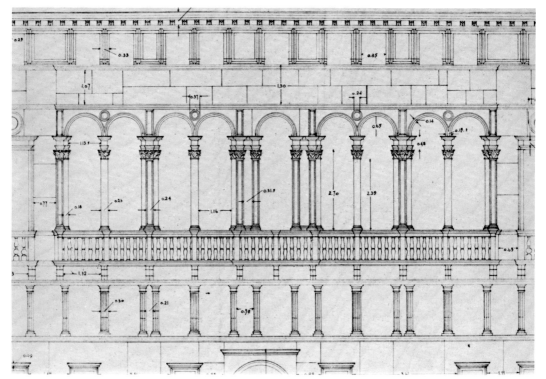

22.10 Palazzo Zorzi. Drawing of nine central windows.

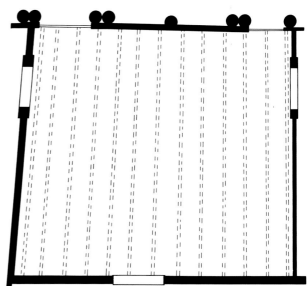

22.11 Palazzo Zorzi. Drawing of framing plan.

symmetries, which seem to appear in wing or *bifora,* turn out to be not quite complete, and our eyes are therefore gently impelled to go onward, now slower, now faster, until they reach a real resolution, which comes only at the far end.

Behind the loggia balcony, the columns stand on cylinders, those on the left almost plain, those on the right, in front of the *sala,* enlivened with low-relief garlands, the only such ornament on a front otherwise unencrusted with carved trimming, and a world removed from the rich court of the Doges' Palace going up in the same years and, by comparison, already old-fashioned (fig. 22.12). Being round, these pedestals take minimal space on a balcony where anything bigger or anything with corners would be in the way of the feet or skirts of people wanting to move from one bay of the balcony to another. The cylindrical shape here, then, has a functional as well as an aesthetic justification.

The columns and half-columns of the loggia are tall and slender, with a springy bulge (of double entasis) so delicate as to be hardly visible. Their wide-flaring Corinthian capitals carry a small block of entablature, hardly higher than the capitals. This, which seems an unaccustomed pedantry for Codussi, could have come from a reading of Vitruvius—several copies were available in Venice, and there was one in Cesena he may have known earlier (Krinsky 1967, 39, 54)—for Vitruvius did not sanction arches springing directly from capitals, and preferred complete orders with column and entablature. Codussi would not have been able to read Vitruvius for himself, for he cannot have been able to read Latin and, although he had humanist clients and perhaps friends, it is unlikely that they would have conveyed these specific bits of Vitruvius' praxis to him. More likely the entablature-block came

22.12 Palazzo Zorzi. Piano nobile. Cylindrical bases of columns on main balcony.

at second hand from a memory or sketch of Brunelleschi's S Lorenzo or S Spirito (fig. 22.13). Brunelleschi had surely been made familiar with Vitruvius in Florence.

Many of the details benefit from Mauro's originality, and though they are all worked out with the orthodox classical vocabulary, they are made to perform in it as they never had before. Almost always, too, they stay within his restricted set of geometrically pure profiles. Until the top cornice, none of the long, well-marked horizontals is made of more than one molding and a band, or of two simple but distinctively profiled moldings. They stand out with particular vividness against the large areas of smooth and shadow-catching white wall. Nowhere is there a trace of Gothic.

Over the pilasters, above their entablature-blocks, between the *bifore*, a paneled strip runs up to the next long, horizontal line of moldings. Circles of porphyry or *verde antico* are in the spandrels of the arches, already familiar in Venice and here the only color in the white cliff of the front. Over the windows in the wings are larger circles, tangent to the horizontals above and below, but their inlays of colored stone—if there ever were any—are no longer there. The circles and the strips extend the richness and activity of this principal story on upward to the blank band that stops the story and prepares for the less agitated end of the building.

A long band like a widened frieze or displaced parapet breaks forward a little over the nine windows in the center, quietly calming the nervous rippling of their arches. Then comes a long, unagitated line of nearly square windows of a "mezzanine under the roof." The scheme of the stories is like that of the Ca' Cocco-Molin of presumably similar date. This top story is capped by a small cornice, made more emphatic by sharply projecting brackets. It may

seem small for such a long facade, but the horizontal line of squarish windows and squarish panels between has readied us for the coming full stop.

Although one's eye has been invited to travel horizontally more often than vertically, by the time it reaches the top, one realizes that not only has the composition been worked out in clear layers for the main stories, and lesser lengthwise lines worked out between, but also that almost everywhere the openings have been set one above another on strong disciplinary axes, woven through the horizontals, with a few minor digressions, most of them purposeful. Where the windows of the upper mezzanine are a little closer together than those of the *bifore* below them, that serves to accentuate the quality of the subtly hitching rhythm. If one of these squarish little windows is not right over the arch below, one has to move along to recover equilibrium by seeing the reciprocating dislocation of the squarish window beside it. Nothing is extraneous, and nothing is left out.

If the long and perhaps overdetailed commentary on the sophisticated design of this facade seems too full of praise, that can be relieved by reading Ruskin's comment on the same palace (Stones, II, 262), "a Renaissance building utterly worthless in every respect."

Except for the charming main stairway in two runs, fitted in at the end of the back loggia by the court, so little is left of the original layout of the interior, now chopped, patched, chopped and patched again (mainly in the mid-XIXc), that it is impossible to be sure of more than a few walls of the original plan. Some appear to have been used again from the Gothic palace or palaces that Codussi remodeled as much as replaced. (Bellavitis examined the building at length in 1974, and has returned for verification many times since.) The great surprise is to find that the long and almost symmetrical facade does

22.13 Brunelleschi. S Lorenzo, Florence, 1421 and after. Nave columns with entablature blocks.

22.14 Palazzo Zorzi. *Bifora*
facing courtyard.

22.15 Palazzo Zorzi. En-
trance arcade, courtyard, and
fountain.

not honestly reveal or express the inner arrangements as it appears to do, but makes half-compromises with parts of its Gothic predecessor, particularly when able to use again certain principal walls. The alterations to many parts—the palace has been ruthlessly treated—are so drastic, except for the main front, that the one exposed side and the walls facing the court cannot now be accepted as original designs. Some details of beautiful quality, such as the wall fountain in the court and the two extraordinarily slender *bifore* above the back loggia, may have been finished or made entirely new after Codussi's death (figs. 22.14 and 22.15). The present owners would like to restore the building and have applied repeatedly for permission, but the municipality will allow nothing until it decides whether it would be feasible (very, very unlikely) to adapt it as a tenement for people temporarily displaced by urban renewal somewhere else in the city. This is probably an excuse to cover inertia, inefficiency, and possibly some ill-will (Rizzi, in *Gazzettino*, 10.II.78).

The long Renaissance facade, more arresting new than now, appears to have inspired others even before it was all done. The Ca' Cocco-Molin, as we have already seen, has a very long front on the Rio dei Barcaroli because the lot was longest there. The main divisions are so like those of the Ca' Zorzi in so many ways—storage floor with small square windows, mezzanine, lofty piano nobile with long arcaded loggia, topped by a low *mezzanino sotto tetto* with squarish windows, an unusual ensemble with unusual features in common—that it hints irresistibly that one may have affected the design of the other. That could mean only Zorzi to Cocco, not vice versa. The surprise comes from the Ca' Cocco's more conservative and simple vocabulary, without Codussi's freshness. The owner may have admired what the Zorzis were building or about to build on a difficult lot similar to his, but his architect, though tasteful, was old-fashioned, at least fifteen or twenty years behind the "modern" movement. It is as though a Cocco had taken a Zorzi for his bride, and when they built a new dwelling she, a head of the housekeeping, took charge of laying out the rooms on each floor, while he, as boss of the purse, hired an architect to materialize her scheme, keeping a wary eye on those new ideas. But that, alas, was not at all the way things were done then.

23 | PALAZZO CORNER-SPINELLI

Two of Codussi's three palaces, the Corner and the Vendramin, observe the three-part three-story tradition inherited from the local Gothic. Most of their other traceable sources are Florentine but, unlike his churches, less Brunelleschian than Albertian. One of his most notable feats is the fusion of borrowed, derived, and invented features into coherent ensembles, fresh as springtime, yet well rooted in the architectural pasts of both cities.

By the S Angelo boat stop on the Grand Canal stands the palazzo now known as the Corner-Spinelli, built for the Lando family, sold to the Corners in 1542, leased in 1718 to the rich Spinelli silk merchants from Castelfranco, sold to them in 1740. It is now owned and well cared for by the Salom family (fig. 23.1).

The building must have been begun in the late 1490s (though sometimes unconvincingly claimed for the 1480s or even 1470s, by Bassi 1976, 196; Carboneri, 191; Heydenreich-Lotz, 73; Hubala 1965, 769; Puppi-Puppi, 203; and others). It was finished and furnished and inhabited by 1521, for Marin Sanudo (XXIX, 567) then went to a grand party there. The interior of the *androne* was masterfully remodeled for the Cornaros by Sanmicheli in 1542, unexpectedly soon for a new palace. Other alterations came in the XVIIc, with the probable addition of a small-scale dormer; and more exterior repairs and alterations were made in the late XIXc. Finally the interiors were conscientiously restored and remodeled by Giorgio Bellavitis in 1967. The palace is now used for apartments and a showroom. The most important part of Codussi's design, the great facade on the Grand Canal is, happily, still almost intact. Temanza (125) was the first to identify it as a creation of Codussi, in 1778, and everyone since has agreed with him.

It shows the clearest integration of simple geometric proportions yet organized in Venice. The front is about 61' square, with the two upper stories of identical height, and the lower not only a third higher but also made to look stronger for apparent support (fig. 23.2). It begins with a rusticated socle stopped by the one ineffective element in the ensemble, an ill-placed, over-dainty band of garlands and roses now unpleasantly eroded (fig. 23.3). Then comes a wall of channeled ashlar of flat rustication, alternating squares and oblong blocks more suave than their rugged predecessors at the Ca' del Duca or the rio facade of the Palazzo Ducale. Codussi's network of joints in slightly chamfered channels here is very like what he had used over twenty years before on the front of S Michele and, like that, undoubtedly based on something Florentine rather than on an antique model. The two most likely candidates for rustication below flat ashlar would be either the two upper floors of Michelozzo's Palazzo Medici (after 1444) or the less well-known but equally close Palazzo Pazzi-Quaratesi (ca. 1460) in part perhaps by Giuliano da Maiano.

The windows and water entrance are round-headed, but by being enclosed in rectangular panels, they are made to fit trimly among the rectangles of the rustication. Such a way of squaring an arched opening was a North Italian practice taken over from something antique, such as the Porta dei Borsari in Verona, through which Mauro must often have passed on his way to and from Lenna. What is novel about the windows here is how they are placed in the composition. A pair is in the lower part of each half of the facade, the inner one lined up with the edge of the loggia above, and the outer one only two squares from the corner pilasters, leaving only a thin strip of wall to count as support; close beside the strong pilaster, the strip manages to seem adequate and any threat of undue stress has been avoided. The mezzanine has only one window on each side, on

the axis of the space between the pair below, and so set that its inner edge aligns with the edge of the window of the piano nobile above. The unusual high-low-high arrangement of these identical windows is seen, then, to be integrated with the others by the alignment of various edges. Even so, the subtle arrangement of lower windows deliberately off axis with those above is not only original but daring.

The two lower windows must have let light into storerooms, but the single small one above cannot have let much into the mezzanine, likely to have been used for offices, servants, or something needing more than that modicum of light. More could have come from windows facing the narrow canal on the left or the *campiello* on the right, though there is no information for either, or from windows inside, opening into the wide and high *androne* (now remodeled), then maybe in an arrangement still to be seen in other palaces, such as the Balbi-Valier on the Grand Canal at S Vio.

The two triads of windows, one on either side of the middle, bring in a triple rhythm accented on the second beat, A A A, which will recur in many variations in the design of the whole and its parts. The front is already composed in the typical 1–2–1 triptych scheme. Even the long-short-long pattern of the ashlar makes a kind of skipping triple rhythm: 2–1–2–1–2 etc.

Except for the very open window-door-window triad in the center, the arrangement of windows leaves nearly all the wall at the bottom in good-size areas, uninterrupted by openings, an effect that adds apparent strength to its important task of visual support. The only part cut away, the triad in the center, has no need to look strong, for there is nothing heavy above to want supporting, only the void of the seemingly weightless windows of the loggia. The blankness of the wall, the assertion of strength made by its rustication, and the simplicity and small scale

23.1 Palazzo Corner-Spinelli
(lithograph by Moro and
Kier).

23.2 Palazzo Corner-Spinelli.
Canal front.

23.6 Palazzo Corner-Spinelli. Piano nobile. Corinthian column at corner.

23.3 Palazzo Corner-Spinelli. Rusticated lower floors.

23.4 Palazzo Corner-Spinelli. Corner pilaster of lower floor.

23.5 Palazzo Corner-Spinelli. Piano nobile. Trilobed balcony of wing window.

of the windows are suited to the modest role of storage and lesser functions behind the bottom part of a typical Venetian palace.

One novelty on the lower story was to have a great future, the corner pilasters (fig. 23.4). Except for the exceptional, tentative, and unsuccessful experiments at the Ca' del Duca and the Ca' Gussoni (if it is really so early), no palaces in Venice had yet used orders to frame a whole story of the front. Codussi had already come near with his side strips on the Palazzo Zorzi, but they did not develop into pilasters there, staying somewhere between them and corner shafts, half-Gothic half–Early Renaissance. In Florence there was the striking example of the Palazzo Rucellai, and Codussi, ripe for it, brought the idea to the Venetian palace full-blown, systematized even to the use of superposed orders. Here on the lower story of the Corner-Spinelli, the pilasters are big, full height, and deeply paneled, like those on the front of S Michele; standing out only slightly from the walls, they catch enough light and spill enough shadow to stop the insistent net of the chiaroscuro of the ashlar channels. The fact that they cut off the horizontal lines of shadow adds to the apparent strength of the pilasters. At their tops, they develop Ionic capitals with volutes projecting at 45°, like those on the front of S Michele. Already, here on the relatively plain lower story of the palace, one can recognize details typical of the repertory of Mauro Codussi and no one else.

Above them comes what can seem to be an all-purpose combination of a sharply molded architrave, a wide frieze, and a narrow cornice, but when examined again in conjunction with what comes above it (the next order of pilasters), it works also as their paneled pedestal; then, when one finds that it runs on across the whole front of the building, it reveals itself also as a parapet-band (figs. 23.5 and 23.6). This last

breaks forward and opens into a balustrade in front of the windows, a long balcony in front of the loggia, and extraordinary trilobate balconies in front of the windows in the wings. This entablature-pedestal-parapet-balcony works so easily and is so plausible in each of its several roles that one scarcely realizes what an extraordinary coalition of standard but diverse elements it is. If each of its functions were allowed independent form, one above the other, the facade would suffer a bad rift here.

The two stories above, each a piano nobile in its own right, are linked together into more of a unit than they had ever been before (fig. 23.7). The orders at their corners, both Corinthian, continue above the Ionic of the bottom story in a sophisticated way, so systematically that it may make one wonder if it could be more than a coincidence that King Mathias Corvinus' copy of Filarete's *Treatise*, which arrived in Venice from Hungary in 1489, with its rules for superposed orders (which Codussi had not used before) showed a summary illustration not unlike the arrangement used here (Marchini, 96).

Above the pilasters of the first piano nobile there is an entablature, slightly compressed and flattened so as not to cut too potently across the front. The pilasters of the story above are shorter, with Corinthian capitals, rich for Codussi but too sober for the Lombardos. In front of a plain background, they look less forceful than those of the bottom story, which had gained force by cutting the pattern of the rustication.

More important than the pilasters and cornices, however, is the handling of the wall and windows between them (fig. 23.8). The zones of wall, the same width and height in each story, join to form something like two-story piers, lightly bound to the rest by the moldings of the entablatures and light parapet-bands. The masonry of these piers is flat; big slabs of smooth marble,

23.7 Palazzo Corner-Spinelli. Piano nobile. *Bifora* of wing.

23.8 Palazzo Corner-Spinelli. Piano nobile. Two *bifore* of loggia.

taller than wide, smoothly joined as one continuous surface. Such towering verticals had been half-anticipated in Gothic palaces on the Grand Canal, for example, the Palazzi Barbaro and Da Mula, or the Ca' Foscari, but never as fully developed as here, into almost tectonic-looking two-story supports, separated from the voids of the windows on either side (fig. 23.9). Though their origin may be Gothic, Codussi transformed them into something entirely at home in his Renaissance ensemble.

Although they may seem powerful at first glance, and almost colossal in comparison with the attenuated, small-scale stonework of the windows between, they do not in the end speak out as heavy pylons. They play their parts as flat surfaces, not as masses with appreciable thickness. There are several reasons for this: one is that they submit to an inferior role in relation to the pilasters at the corners, elements which cannot possibly be taken as very powerful; another is that they are bound to the rest of the building, including the unsturdy windows, by slender bands which could not hold in anything of much force or mass; and last, what one sees of them is a plainly atectonic surface of thin plates of marble stood unstructurally on end, arranged to make surface patterns and deliberately not revealing any depth.

The facade shows the common division into three parts more explicitly here, but not fully in the traditional way, for instead of windows cut at each edge of each wing, leaving bare wall in the middle, there is one double window in the middle, with plain walls on either side; but, since the window is double, it lets in as much light as the usual pair of singles. Small columns in its center carry arches that land at their outer ends on half-columns engaged on a slice of pier that, in its turn, carries a larger arch embracing them both. The space between the embraced and the embracer has a simple pattern of bar tracery, a Gothic feature miraculously transmuted into a Renaissance one, here more fully than in the earlier trial at S Zaccaria. A glazed circle fills the upper middle under the embracing arch or, rather, a near circle, for it has no bottom but runs down to a point like a leaf or an upside-down teardrop, filling the narrowing space between the two lower window arches. On either side of it, curvy triangles are left over and are also filled with glass. The window sash is set a foot behind all this, at the inner face of the sections of wall between the windows.

The origins of this combination lie partly in the Gothic tracery Codussi saw all about him in Venice, much of it far more elaborate, and partly in the windows of the Palazzo Rucellai in Florence (created by Alberti?) or their cousins in the Palazzo Piccolomini in Pienza (executed and perhaps designed by Bernardo Rossellino). But although derived from Gothic tracery, those models show a determination to be classical. The colonnettes, for example, carry small proper architraves straight across the whole window. This cuts the window openings in two horizontally, and the tops read no more easily as continuations sprouting out of the bottoms than they do as some new element laid on their tops. Furthermore, in the Rucellai, only the circle above the twin arches is open, and the adjacent curved triangles are not glass but stone. Codussi's version is smoother, suaver, and with an easier continuity of parts.

Venice has a few similar windows that may be a few years older: some on the mezzanine loggia of the Palazzo Manolesso-Ferro (once the Grand Hotel, now offices for the region of the Veneto); some contemporary or a little later in the imposing *sala* of the Ca' Pisani-Moretta (some enclosing sumptuously oxidized early Murano mirrors); and some in the sacristy of S Salvatore, probably a little later. Mauro

23.9 Palazzo Manolesso-
Ferro (ex-Grand Hotel).
Three *bifore* of story above
mezzanine and below true
piano nobile (lithograph by
Moro and Kier).

23.10 Palazzo Corner-Spi-
nelli. Facade (drawing from
the Visentini workshop,
British Museum, AUV II, 8).

himself had tried out the idea at S Zaccaria, on the south clerestory, but more crudely. Probably earlier, sometime between 1491 and 1494, Carpaccio, well-informed architecturally, had shown some in the S Ursula series and in the Scuola degli Schiavoni, and earlier still, Jacopo Bellini had come near in his British Museum Sketchbook (fol. 85). Those of the Corner-Spinelli are the suavest and easiest of all, with no friction between any memory of Gothic and the welcoming of the Renaissance. The arrangement was particularly successful as the classicizing equivalent of a Gothic loggia of tracery at the end of an otherwise dark *sala*, made transparent where it has to be, and with a whole new set of parts.

The doubled arches and the top of the teardrop make a trefoil, a form that reappears in plan in the curious balconies of the lower piano nobile, unique in Venice. There is a forerunner in Vicenza on the Palazzo Pigafetta (1481?) and a few other Gothic approximations there and in Padua, none necessarily related to Codussi's. The lobed pulpits in S Mark's, or in the Bellini brothers' *S Mark Preaching* or Mansueti's *S Mark Healing* from the Scuola di S Marco (Brera; storerooms of Venice Accademia), look possibly related, as may a fanciful Gothic balcony in Jacopo Bellini's sketchbook in the Louvre (Buttafava-Garbagnatti, 14). In other words, though uncommon, the form is not unique. It seems more likely to have been thought up specially for its location here than to have been borrowed by Mauro from some accidentally similar example. The main interest of the cloverleaf, now in-and-out, now up-and-down, and its echo in the up-and-down triplet of windows in the bottom story and mezzanine, and in the curves of the upper part of the upper windows, is in the way the repeated transformations of one theme in scale, rhythm, and shape, less familiar in architecture

than in music, enrich the composition. It is best described with the specific musical term *durchkomponiert*. Diagrammatically it can be shown, reading from bottom to top as A ^{A} A, A ^{a} A, A ^{a} A. Although capricious—rare for Codussi—it is still a logical and quietly powerful force in integrating the whole front into the so thoroughly *durchkomponiert* whole.

The main rhythmical scheme of the whole is enriched by the loggia, made of a pair of *bifore* like those in the wings, in other words, a pair of paired windows (fig. 23.10). Looking across this finely organized piano nobile and ignoring for the moment the subordinate ornaments, one sees first a pilaster, second a tall rectangle of smooth wall, third a *bifora*, then another tall rectangle of wall imperceptibly wider, and then another *bifora* linked on the center axis of the building to a twin *bifora*, the two together comprising the loggia, and then all the same in reverse, wall, *bifora*, wall, pilaster. The triple rhythm with alternations, seen in the windows and trefoil balconies, is played over again by the set of balconies at this level, curved-straight-curved, with their elegant slim spindles of balusters—the new form always used by Mauro instead of the old-fashioned little colonnettes.

The carved ornament on this story is integrated with the main scheme, for on each vertical plane of wall is a small rectangular panel, running crosswise, picking up the height of the zone of the capitals of the window colonnettes, and above, harmonizing with the curves of the tracery, a circle equated with the arches above the capitals. In the spandrels above the embracing arch—these windows too being set in rectangles—are smaller discs, filling the space much as the teardrops fill theirs. Everything thus fits into its place with harmonious inevitability. The discs, being of different stone, porphyry and *verde antico*, are obviously no more than

23.11 Palazzo Corner-Spinelli. Top story and cornice.

thin plaques, not cutting into the vertical stretches of flat wall whose surface they ornament.

The top story is a second piano nobile and very much the same, except for minor variations, all small, effective, and important in the total effect. For example, over the earlier reduced cornice finishing off the story below, there is another parapet-band, like the one below where it runs across the smooth sections of wall, and also turning into an open balustrade in front of the windows—but these balconies are not the same: those of the wings, above the trefoils, are straight, and where the balustrade crosses the loggia, it does not project into a balcony but stays almost flush with the wall. Again there is an A B A pattern, equivalent in rhythm to the one below, but worked out with different and simpler shapes.

Since this top floor, except in a few minor variations and one major one, repeats the floor below, and since the windows, thanks to the rectangular panels in which their embracing arches are held, fill the whole height of the story, the openings, their frames, and their balconies join those below, and together the two make one continuous two-story open curtain, contrasted with the bold, flat, two-story vertical walls on either side. Such continuity of a window and what came above and below had been partially anticipated in the Gothic (for example, on the Grand Canal, the Ca' d'Oro, the Palazzo Morosini-Brandolin, and the Pisani-Gritti, now the Gritti Hotel), and even at the beginning of the Renaissance in the Ca' Dario. But never before had there been such systematic organization of two stories of superposed piani nobili into one large-scale sequence of plane-void-plane-void etc.

The entablature at the top is importantly different, for the cornice is made to project boldly, carried on modillions and casting a deep shadow (fig. 23.11).

The cornice manages to make a successful compromise between being proportioned to the scale of the order of the story it finishes off, and to the scale of the whole building it crowns and has to finish off more vigorously. The modillions and the deep and rhythmically agitated shadow between them—deeper than other shadows because the cornice projects so much more, and agitated because the modillions interrupt it—make the top story look higher than the one just below it from some points of view, yet the height is actually the same; only the greater projection of the cornice makes the difference sometimes seem greater.

Except for the purple and green of the porphyry and *verde antico*, there is no color, and these small areas count little. Unexpectedly, the slabs facing the flat walls of the upper stories are of marble, plain, and only a little warmer in tone than the *pietra d'Istria* at the bottom and on the window frames, balustrades, pilasters, and such. Originally the two kinds of stone must have been even closer in tone, so close, in fact, that old texts regularly say that the entire front is limestone; only recently has it been clean enough to see that the marble is marble. Even when the building was new, the difference must have been subtle, with only the slightest shift in color and texture and the barely perceptible veining of the marble laid up in paired patterns like two open leaves of a book, as at S Mark's or the Miracoli. Everywhere the moldings have the simple, clear, geometric profiles that can now be recognized as one of Mauro's signatures.

Delicacy and strength come together, not in conflict but in closely woven counterpoint. The few fine-scale ornaments, such as the dentils in the top cornice, the frieze below them, or the frames for the circles and oblongs or low-relief urns applied to the surface, are kept in their places as subordinate enrichment, without affecting the stronger lines. (Only the eroded band of garlands near the water seems to confuse the clear separation.) The comparative fragility of the bar tracery of the windows in its juxtaposition to the vertical bands of wall on either side enhances the feeling of strength in the latter. Above the bottom floor the windows do not cut holes in the wall; instead they join top and bottom with the transparent balustrades to make big openwork screens, not structural, but safely sustained between the strong vertical surfaces of wall. Only the curving consoles supporting the balconies combine the two otherwise contrasted qualities. Even in the most open of Gothic palaces, no such effective contrast of open and closed had been ventured.

The few changes made since Codussi's time have little effect. The XIXc dormer of two arched windows under a pediment is small and seemingly more discreet than its predecessor (XVIIc? XVIIIc?), as shown by Carlevarijs (1703) and Canaletto (Pignatti 1958, II, 22). The bit of plastered wall facing the *campiello* by the boat stop on the right was remodeled in the XIXc, simplifying the frame around the door and adding a little curved balcony above, and, more important, extending the pilasters so that they turn the corners like piers. Nevertheless the palace still shows unhampered its fresh and wonderfully original design, with twice as much open as solid on each of the main floors, a ratio rivaling the Gothic. For the first time, tiers of superposed pilasters work easily and naturally at the corners, more integrated into the whole design than the girdle of two orders at the Miracoli, where the upper order does not touch the entablature, or Codussi's own rather fumbling tiers of columns, pilasters, and strips up and across the towering facade of S Zaccaria.

PALAZZO VENDRAMIN-CALERGI

Codussi's next palace, the Vendramin-Calergi, originally Loredan, is on the same side of the Grand Canal but nearer the other end, a little east of the Church of S Marcuola (fig. 24.1). It was hailed as the grandest private palace yet built in Venice and has been praised ever since; the first written notices, by Francesco Sansovino, in 1561 and 1581, already set the tone: "Of all the palaces on the Grand Canal, four stand out"—this, one by Sanmicheli, and two by his father—"from the artistry of their stonework, their stateliness, their size, and their cost." "The Loredan, of great bulk and height, is earlier than the others, and stands almost free on its island-like plot. It is a very noble work . . . the front all sheathed in Greek marble; . . . and the big windows with Corinthian columns everywhere . . . made according to the rules of architecture," "beautifully proportioned" (Sansovino, 387–88; Guisconi (*pseud* for same), 22). Here speaks the academic voice of an amateur of the late XVIc. Later writers were moved to outpraise one another, above all for the facade.

The interiors must have been dazzling too; an *androne* believed to have been frescoed by Giorgione, and, by 1530, Giorgione's *Tempest*, a Raphael, and one of Jacopo Bellini's sketchbooks (Okey, 131). As early as 1520, Marin Sanudo (XXVIII, 248, 256) saw plays, including a comedy by Terence, performed by a noblemen's club in the courtyard in back. In 1550 it was used officially or semi-officially for the visit of some particularly important German princes (Tassini 1970, 677).

For so prominent a building, disappointingly little is known of its beginnings. It was built for Andrea Loredan, and there had been friendly relations between Codussi and the Loredan family as far back as the early days of S Michele, when the brothers Tommaso and Bernardo Loredan had given generously to the church, as had Andrea, a cousin, who paid for much of the chancel and arranged for his wife and himself to be buried there in what was sometimes known as the Cappella Loredana. Andrea may have proposed something to Codussi for the palace site in 1481, but what, or how much may have materialized is not known, nor is it even certain that the reference is to this palace or this site. If anything was done, it could have been little beyond clearing the lot and driving a few piles, for nothing is above ground in the unobstructed view on the Barbari map of 1500. As the lot is large, readying it for building could have taken several years, but nothing like the nineteen of 1481–1500. Some exterior event could have caused a long postponement. Venetian architecture in general and Codussi in particular were developing too rapidly in these years to make it credible that plans drawn up in 1481 would still have been used in 1502, the year that work was most probably begun (Puppi-Puppi, 157, 159, 222). There is reason to believe that it was finished by 1509, before the beginning of the War of Cambrai. Once begun, work must have been pushed with unusual speed, not difficult in a work for the Loredanos, powerful, imperious, and rich, quite able to pay for large crews of laborers.

Only one element could have come from this putative early campaign, the foundations. The first part to take physical form, they would have fixed the plan. The *androne* (also the *sala* above) was not the common long rectangle, but T-shaped, with the crosswise part at the water entrance, joined to a broad stem leading back to the land entrance. This had been current in Gothic times, having evolved from the crosswise hall behind the arcades along the front of Byzantine palaces. The wings, developed in Gothic times, took away the raison d'être for such a crosswise front hall, and it gradually disappeared. Its sudden use here again may show Codussi's independence from lo-

cal tradition—he had not been brought up or trained in Venice—and his choice of an out-of-date local form, as he had done earlier at the Palazzo Zorzi, may again have been a way of taking advantage of old foundations or walls. Or, more likely here, it could have been a preference of the client, for the Loredans may have liked one of their older palaces—they had half-a-dozen—enough to want part of its scheme repeated.

The bar at the top of the T fits the layout of the front part of the palace here, being just as wide as the water entrance and its side windows taken together. The stem then makes a partly unresolved shift. If the framing pattern of the joists in the ceiling of the hall running back to the land entrance were continued forward to the facade, crossing the wider end of the hall that makes the top of the T, there would have to be girders to carry the joists here, and these girders would come to an awkward end above the windows, quite a bit off center. This would have been both elaborate and clumsy. The front section of the hall must have been framed the other way, with joists running back from the facade, as in the earlier palaces with halls running all across the front (Zuccolo, 56, fig. 52). A heavy girder now receives them at the end of the corridor-like back hall where it joins the crosswise front part.

Perhaps because it was so large, prominent, handsome, and luxurious, the palace changed hands oftener than most. In 1581 the Duke of Brunswick bought it for a huge sum, and managed to sell it in two years to the Duke of Mantua for twice as much. Some irregularity and a lawsuit made the Brunswick heirs claim it back, but in 1589 it was put up at auction and sold to Vettor Calergi, of an old Cretan Byzantine family, already accepted into the Venetian patriciate. His heir, a daughter, married a Grimani in 1608 with the

24.1 Palazzo Vendramin-Calergi. Canal front.

24.2 Palazzo Vendramin-Calergi. Facade (drawing from the Visentini work-shop, British Museum, AUV I, 52).

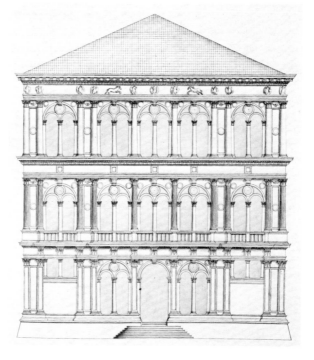

proviso that he join Calergi to his name. In 1614 they had Scamozzi add a wing behind the garden on the Grand Canal, where property values already made a garden a conspicuous extravagance. After the discovery of conspiracy and murder in 1658, the Grimani brothers, then the owners, were executed, their property confiscated, and the palace threatened with demolition. But because it was such an ornament to the city it was saved, and only the new wing was razed in symbolic humiliation and replaced by a "column of infamy" with the whole scandal engraved on it at length. Within two years, money softened the judgment, the column was pulled down, and another wing put up on the same plot.

When the male line of the Grimani-Calergi came to an end in 1739, the palace was inherited by Nicolò Vendramin, again with the proviso that he attach the name Calergi to his own. Although the Vendramin-Calergi occupied the palace for only a century, the doubled name has been used for it ever since. In 1844 it was sold to Princess Maria Carolina, Duchesse de Berry, a Neapolitan Bourbon and the widow of a son of Louis XVIII. She had many of the interiors extravagantly done over in mid-XIXc taste—many had already been done over at least once in the XVIIc and XVIIIc—and she gave refuge in the garden to the Adam and Eve from Tullio Lombardo's Vendramin tomb. Somehow she fitted in a theatre for 300 on the top floor. She was so extravagant that her pictures and other treasures had to be auctioned in Paris in 1864 and 1865. (The Adam went to a private collection and was forgotten until 1937, when it went to New York; the Eve is only a copy; the Giovanni Bellini is in Detroit.) Her oldest son, the Comte de Chambord, managed to buy some things back. She intrigued to put him on the throne of France as the last legitimate male of the main royal line, but she could not

dislodge Louis-Philippe. The palace in Venice became a little quasi-royal court, and a busy but minor center of conspiracies.

After she died the building went to her less royal heirs by her Sicilian second husband, one of whom made a typical XIXc collection of oriental objects, the remainder of which, after the cream had been skimmed and sold, has become the core of the oriental collection of the Ca' Pesaro. Wagner rented twenty rooms there and died in the garden wing in 1883. The last heirs sold the palace to Count Volpi in 1937; he arranged for badly needed restoration, and used part for one of his business ventures before ceding the palace to the municipality in 1956. They settled the gambling casino there for the winter seasons—where it continues— and rented the upper part to the National Radio Television until that found a new home in the Palazzo Labia in the 1960s. No other palace in Venice has had so busy a history.

Ever since the artistic reconstitution of Codussi by Pietro Paoletti at the end of the last century, it has been agreed that the design of the palace must originally have been his creation. He cannot have brought it to completion, for he died in 1504, but his ideas must have been respected even after his death, though of course some details reflect the taste of those subsequently in charge. Some must have come from the Lombardo atelier, and old sources randomly name Pietro, Tullio, and Sante Lombardo (who was born only the year Mauro died), or transcend stylistic and chronological possibilities by naming Serlio (who arrived in Venice only in 1527).

The most important part still preserved, the water front, shows ideas from Codussi's Palazzo Corner-Spinelli; some carried further, some repeated, and some restudied from the earlier Palazzo Zorzi, plus a number of daring new ones skilfully worked in with them (fig. 24.2). The main difference is that this is composed in layers, fewer and clearer than at the Zorzi, with only one to each story. The first impression is one of horizontality, in opposition to the contrived verticality of the upper stories of the Corner-Spinelli. Yet one can actually count more separate verticals here, for above the lower story with its ten strong pilasters, both upper stories add ten Corinthian columns; pairs flank the traceried *bifore* of the wings, and single ones stand between the *bifore* of the loggia. Together with the colonnettes in the middle of the *bifore*, this makes more verticals than on the busy front of S Zaccaria, but the effect is entirely different; the even layers, marked by long unbroken entablatures and resting on one another, bring order and serenity in place of S Zaccaria's threats of confusion and restlessness.

The lower story is very open in the center, with traceried windows on either side of the doorway, the same size as the windows of the loggia above. Even so, this story is fundamentally more a wall than are the piani nobili over it; it has flat areas of plain masonry under the pairs of small oblong windows in the wings. These are framed by pilasters so narrow that they have room for only three flutes, like those of the Palazzo Zorzi. Below the windows are inscriptions, NON NOBIS DOMINE and NON NOBIS (from Psalm 115, which continues SED NOMINI TUO DA GLORIAM), probably put there by the grateful Loredanos. The doorjambs are inscribed DOMUS PACIS. There is almost no ornament, only the capitals of the pilasters (not classically uniform but mediaevally varied), a garland on the slice of wall between the big coupled pilasters at the ends, and ordinary dentils and an egg and dart in the cornice (fig. 24.3). A grand flight of semicircular steps used to spread down into the water from the main entrance (Carlevarijs, 76).

Above the cornice, a parapet-band begins as a pedestal for the coupled columns (above the coupled pilasters) and then breaks forward to become a balcony, borne on springy brackets pushing up out of the frieze. The balcony runs the width of the wing windows, then breaks back to become a pedestal again for the next pair of columns, and then comes forward to make a new balcony the length of the loggia.

Light ornamental features such as the balconies, in no way involved with the construction of the front (except through the brackets holding them up), would have been among the last details made, particularly here low on the facade where, had they been built early, they could easily have been damaged by stones being hauled up for work on the higher stories. Small wonder, then, that they do not look like Codussi's work, for they must have come late in the building campaign, after he had died. Instead of his typical spindle balusters, there are old-fashioned dwarf colonnettes (fig. 24.4). The little piers at the end of each section have pretty reliefs, typical minor Lombardo fancies; and a little lion sits on each of them, decorative, mediaeval, and already obsolescent. These non-Codussian grace notes do not affect the main design, foreign to it though they may be. At the time, Pietro and Tullio were busy elsewhere, working for Doge Loredan on the Palazzo Ducale among others. They could have spared only a few men, not notably gifted or advanced, but probably old hands from the shop, competent to finish another man's job already well along and good enough to work for relatives of the doge.

Balconies must have been intended here by Codussi himself, for behind them are details that need the protection of a balcony, and these are unmistakably his. While the paired columns at the ends, standing on the parapet-band for a pedestal, have normal bases on a normal square plinth, the single columns behind the balcony are handled with typical originality (fig. 24.5). Below their normal flutes comes a short band of smaller flutes, standing on a cylindrical pedestal; at its bottom, where it is set on the balcony floor, it spreads into another normal torus-scotia-torus base, below which there is no square plinth. As at the Palazzo Zorzi, this corner-eliminating arrangement allows more space for free movement to anyone on the balcony, an arrangement certainly not contrived by carefree Lombardo thinking.

Except for these balconies, hidden bases, and the entablature at the top of the building, the two upper stories, both piani nobili, are alike. The basic triptych is played down almost to invisibility, marked only by the coupling of the columns between wing and loggia, like that at the corner, where discreet emphasis is added by spacing them a few inches wider. The thin bits of wall space between columns are disguised, dimmed, or even denied by the eye-catching columns themselves, two stories of them, Corinthian, fluted. Except for the coupling of the columns, the spacing is unvaried because the columns and the windows, which are what one really sees, are all alike.

The colonnettes of the windows, freestanding in the center and engaged at the jambs, are not of limestone like the more structural-seeming story-height columns but of unfluted white Greek marble delicately veined with silvery gray. Francesco Sansovino (387) was mistaken when he wrote that the front was "all sheathed in Greek marble," for it is all limestone.

The principal variation from the scheme of the windows of the Corner-Spinelli is that the teardrop has been smoothed into a circle (fig. 24.6). The moldings of the tracery are thinner, and the last touch of the saliency typical of Gothic tracery has been flattened to a profile more like a small architrave or archivolt. The result, including the taller flanking columns, is so fully

24.3 Palazzo Vendramin-Calergi. Bracket supporting balcony.

24.4 Palazzo Vendramin-Calergi. Colonnettes and pier of lower middle balcony.

24.5 Palazzo Vendramin-Calergi. Base and pedestal of columns behind balcony.

24.7 Palazzo Vendramin-Calergi. Top story entablature and cornice (drawing by Angelo Doria for Cicognara-Diedo-Selva).

24.6 Palazzo Vendramin-Calergi. Window of first piano nobile.

worked out, so inevitable-seeming, that it is surprising to realize it is an invention of Codussi's. The motif seems more like something that must always have been waiting in the storehouse of classic forms, but not yet noticed and used by anyone. The miracle is that it fitted into place without friction, as though the place had already been reserved, and was ready and waiting.

One sees a columnar screen standing in front of an arcade (the windows), with a few strips of wall (between the coupled columns); this seems to be far more a skeletal construction in front of a void than a recognizable wall with windows in it, and so to be heir to more Gothic airiness than classic solidity. The columns do not really stand free, but only seven-eighths so, with the last eighth of the shaft engaged on a pier of equivocal trefoil form or, at the sides of the wings, on a narrow strip of wall. Not only is this strip a little wider at the outer corners, but the whole corner is also strengthened by having the columnar system of the front actually turn the corner to a pilaster on the side wall; the entablature folds around to it in the same way, and thus the facade is saved from seeming to be something grand glued like paper onto a characterless block. It comes as a surprise that the strong corners, strong unbroken entablature, strong columns, and rippling row of arches all together create an effect of stable equilibrium, ease, and calm.

The top story, below its entablature, is almost the same as the middle story save for a few minor changes. The columns, here standing directly on the cornice below, are not fluted; and the carved trimming around the porphyry circles in the middle of the strips of wall between the coupled columns on the wings is more elaborate (surely executed and probably designed after Mauro's death). The entablature, 88' long and 75' above the water, executed posthumously, makes the most dramatic change. It expands as it rises,

having begun with an almost normally proportioned architrave, with inclined fascias (as on both the other stories). The frieze is stretched wider, and is ornamented with alternating reliefs of eagles and escutcheons with the six roses of the Loredanos, all precisely placed over the columns and keystones. (The frieze below was ornamented more circumspectly with squares of porphyry set flush above the keystones, and left blank above the columns, in a lively minor syncopation.) It appears to be carried on ten columns and the five sturdy keystones of the window arches between them, which complement the capitals by their emphasized potentiality as supports.

The cornice, topping what had become the tallest private palace in the city, is the most expanded of all, and brings the whole front to a dramatic end (fig. 24.7). It is taller, deeper, and richer than anything else on the building, and casts the most definite shadow. The first big-scale cornice in Venice, it set a precedent that would be followed for centuries. Codussi must have remembered the cornice of the Palazzo Medici in Florence, and have valued its decisiveness in bringing the building to a finale fortissimo. But his problem was less simple here, for the Vendramin cornice had not only to be a grand crown for the whole building, it had also to avoid overwhelming the columns that must seem to support it—if looked at in one way. His solution was both new and successful, and it goes far beyond Alberti's and Rossellino's handling of the same problem at the Palazzo Rucellai.

The three parts of the top entablature add up to more than half the height of these columns. (The classic proportions would have made it nearer a fifth.) But since it begins with an architrave not noticeably out of scale with its columns, the unclassical audacity of the whole—increasing as one's eye moves up—disturbs none but Beckmessers. It cannot be documented whether Codussi or his posthumous helpers made the final choice, but such boldness approaches the membering of the arched pediments of S Michele and S Zaccaria, and is not approached by anything in the Lombardo output. The ornaments of the frieze are more likely Lombardo, though their slightly offbeat spacing (controlled by the capitals and keystones under them) brings the Lombardos less to mind than Mauro. They are placed, nevertheless, just above a Codussian architrave. The conclusion is either that the cornice was being put up in 1504 (early for a building begun in 1502) and was begun under Codussi, who died before it could be finished, or, more likely, that Codussi's model or drawings were respected. They had little time to begin to seem old-fashioned, for the palace was done by 1509, when Priuli noted it in his diary (XXIV, 254) as a finished work; all done, then, before the restrictions that must have come with the War of Cambrai.

Some existing adjuncts may reflect lost original features, none of much importance. For example, the little dormer in the middle of the front, and another like it on the left side (maybe XIXc?), must replace something earlier, already replaced when shown by Carlevarijs in 1703 (pl. 76) or soon after by Canaletto (several times). The picturesque "Carpaccio" triple chimney pot on the right may replace something less self-consciously picturesque and more at home with the sober front. The land entrance at the back of the *androne* is post-Codussi and post-Lombardo, perhaps late XVIc, and perhaps rebuilt by the Duchesse de Berry. A loss more to be regretted is the stairway leading up from the *androne*, also thoroughly remodeled now, but still in two flights running first to and then from a large well-lit landing, roomier and grander than the plainer utilitarian

stairways in other palaces. It must have been the most monumental palace stairway in the city, eclipsing Mauro's beautiful earlier invention in the Palazzo Zorzi.

In one way the building is not at home among its Venetian contemporaries, for some of the architectural ideas it embodies look forward forty years to the palaces of Sansovino who, however, would have been unlikely to have taken heed of Codussi—to him old-fashioned and provincial—much less to have accepted that he could learn anything from him, for Sansovino grew up architecturally in Rome, under the grand Bramante and Raphael. But in this particular building (and a bit in the Corner-Spinelli) Codussi anticipated much of what would be done in the few but influential Roman palaces with engaged and coupled columns that appeared twenty years after he had worked out some of the same problems in his design for the Palazzo Vendramin-Calergi.

Unlike those of the Gothic or earlier Early Renaissance periods in Venice, this facade acts out a half-imaginary construction that is not the same as the real construction, though it draws on it and even contributes somewhat to it. Statically the pilasters, engaged columns, strips of wall, and even the window arches do contribute to the working support of the front. Almost self-sufficient, the grand scaffold of three superposed orders appears to stand independently in front of the half-hidden flat front of a building almost equally diaphanous, made of open arcades whose necessarily solid and hardworking piers show themselves only very sparely. Codussi has chosen from the various structural and semistructural elements a set of parts, developed and enhanced them, set them in relief in front of the wall, and then made them act out a dramatic structure expressive of the real structure. The front is like a relief picture of an imagined architecture, an idealized architecture in strong relief that could be imagined as freestanding; it could be called an architecture of "as if." Art here is more vivid than fact.

It is not easy to identify one basic wall plane when so much is open or cut away by windows, and so much that is dominant visually is put out in front in the form of nearly freestanding columns. But even this insistently plastic composition is all in shallow layers on parallel straight lines close together. (Codussi had tried something roughly similar, with much less success, on the much less tractable front of S Zaccaria.) Nowhere in Venice were palaces made with more relief than at the Vendramin-Calergi, nor were such features as boldly projecting wings, recessed centers, or any facade not fundamentally flat beneath the trimming, used. One begins to see this as a constant in Venetian architecture, roughly to be classified as more pictorial in nature than sculptural.

A front like this, made with superposed orders and arches, may evoke such precedents as the Colosseum, which Codussi had not seen, or the battered amphitheatre at Verona, which he had, or the remains at Vicenza and Pula, which he could have. It seems remote from the two tiers of pilasters running around the outside of the Miracoli, which do not quite add up to superposed orders, since the upper tier never comes in contact with an entablature. More to the point, Codussi's facade recalls the Palazzo Rucellai in Florence, at which he must have looked with particular interest. Alberti had made his model of the Rucellai by applying a Colosseum-like sequence of orders to a denatured version of the heavily-walled local type of stronghold-palace. It shows about one part open to thirteen solid, whereas Codussi, by eliminating all but the slimmest vestiges of visible wall, expanded the windows and arrived at one part open to only three of solid (Okey, 42), including the entablatures. He handled this so

that one senses quite the reverse of the true physical fact, and the building seems more open than walled. Nowhere else in Italy had a palace yet been made to seem so nearly diaphanous over its whole front.

The grand old monument still has its wonderfully handsome face, and the city keeps it reasonably clean. The interiors are for the most part sumptuous, with grand fireplaces of the late XVIc and XVIIc, brocade walls, stucco ceilings or beamed ones of the Sansovino type, put in mainly by the Duchesse de Berry or later, in typical XIXc *faux-bon* taste. All now serve quite appropriately as shadowy backgrounds for the gaming going on in the smoke-filled rooms, except perhaps the former chapel, ornamented with Maltese crosses by the Duchesse, who had tried to have the property entailed to the Knights of S John of Jerusalem, Rhodes, and Malta. Having a whole room for a chapel was exceptional, perhaps unique, achieved probably because many of the proprietors of the palace had great wealth, great power, and highly placed relatives and friends in both church and state. There would be no point in murmuring "sic transit" when visiting the interiors now, for, once begun, one could never stop murmuring it in XXc Venice.

25 | SCUOLA DI S MARCO

Difficulties at the Scuola di S Marco had led to the dropping of Pietro Lombardo, assisted by Giovanni Buora, in 1489 or 1490, and to the summoning of Codussi and Rizzo to make a report. Rizzo, a member of the scuola, remained briefly as adviser, and recommended that Codussi, who must already have won standing for his work at S Michele and S Zaccaria, be named chief architect and supervisor. He is early documented there also as *Moro di Martino* (among other names), Martino having been the name of his father (Temanza 1778, 93). This, then, would be a work from the end of his early period or an early work of his middle period, but, abnormal in almost every way, it fits into neither. Begun by others, it never showed Mauro's own free choice. The building was enlarged in 1523, and the rio facade was lengthened and perhaps altered in the 1530s, then partly rebuilt when found dangerously weak in the XVIIIc. The main front survived in average condition until 1832, when many individual elements were replaced. Cream-colored Verona marble was dyed green to substitute for *verde antico* (Puppi-Puppi, 203). Much deteriorated by polluted air, it has recently been partially restored.

It is not illuminating to try to find just what work on the exterior is Codussi's, for the design is clearly not the work of any one controlling mind, but of too many. Buora, who may earlier have been influential under Pietro, was kept on for some time with Mauro, but little is learned from that. Nothing stands out as typical of Codussi, for whatever is his was out of gear from the start by having to continue something half built by someone very foreign to him. The situation was like that at S Zaccaria, but far more crippling. What had been the basis of Mauro's style, the intellectual and insistently architectural works of Brunelleschi and Alberti—classical in conception and classicizing in detail—was useless here; his own artistic gestalt was irremediably hostile to what was left him to finish.

The exterior was complete by 1500 or a little before, for it shows up clearly on Jacopo de' Barbari's view and, unexpectedly, in the background of Mocetto's *Calumny of Apelles,* printed in 1500 or a year or two later. By then the campo, which had been created while the facade was building and the justly famous Colleoni statue was being put in place (1496), must already have had its present form and its paving, and already have been one of the largest in the city. Like many others, it is an irregular L, hooked around the front of the church, with the scuola at the end of the short arm, the Rio dei Mendicanti on one side and the church front on the other. The whole campo is one of those asymmetrical yet unanalyzably balanced ensembles Venice was lucky or smart enough to have educed from random odd conditions—organized without a system but with uncanny sensibility. No other scuola has a comparably impressive setting. It easily dominates the open space in front and the space added by the wide canal along the side. The unfinished church front, the irregular side chapels, and the miscellany of houses opposite can offer little competition for the extravaganza of the facade of the scuola, after S Mark's the most fanciful of any building in the city, architecturally the most extravagant in Europe.

It is not possible to be sure when the various parts of the front were built. Pietro did not stop his work in 1489–90 along a clear frontier, beyond which Codussi could go on in his own way. For Codussi, the problem was probably complicated by a model or drawings showing how the original architect had intended to finish it, and a building committee who had admired the first architect enough to have hired him. Some stones had undoubtedly been cut for not yet finished parts, and materials had certainly been gathered. Contracted workmen would not have been dismissed summarily, though Pietro may have taken a few with him, leaving room for a favored few Mauro may have brought with him.

Nothing shows his familiar hand below the second major Corinthian order of pilasters, the same size as the lower order, also Corinthian (fig. 25.1). The upper entablature is unlike the persistently ornamented Lombardo one below; it is unornamented and has the telltale Codussian sloped fascia, in contrast to the architrave below with its vertical fascias and three carved moldings. The frieze of the upper order is plain, and is followed by a correct plain cornice. This is not much, and could have been done by a couple of Codussi-trained workmen. Codussi need not have been there.

These two orders together give the main diagrammatic discipline—such as it is—to the busy lower two-thirds of the front. On the left half alone there are ten different sizes of columns and pilasters, with four sets of full entablatures, and five series of molded arches. The right, or *albergo,* half is a little simpler. None of the orders is allowed to maintain the tectonic thrust usually considered part of the essential nature of an order, though often subordinated. The two largest orders here, with their long entablatures crossing the whole building, come nearest to affirming a bit of force, but their assertiveness is made to lose a lot by all that is going on around them.

It would not be worthwhile to report on everything above this Codussian entablature, presumably put up while Codussi was supervising, for most of it is busy, overtrimmed, inconsistent, and heedless of the proprieties of structural expressions, real or feigned; and none of it is typical of Codussi when he had a free hand (fig. 25.2). Here clearly he did not. The semicircular gables are thought to have been his idea, by analogy with S Michele and S Zaccaria.

25.1 Scuola di S Marco.   25.2 Scuola di S Marco. Up-
                              per part of main wing (from
                              Cicognara-Diedo-Selva).

(They have little in common with the Miracoli.) Also, the way their arching cornices, embracing shell-like radiating flutes, projecting beyond neighboring parts, and casting disciplinary shadows, are made to stand on something that projects enough to do the same may have been his idea (fig. 25.3). Together they make a row of prominent archways on long legs, containing and half controlling the lesser decorative elements in a way that the big pilaster orders of the two lower stories cannot.

The semicircular gables appear to be carried by slim colonnettes nestled beside pilasters twice as wide and apparently twice as strong, though a close look shows that they have no more to do than support statues of allegorical females or, in the center, angels who have lost their marble wings. These pilasters and colonnettes project enough to tell as "legs" for the arching gables, giving relief and shadow to the tall archways, which count as something quite different from the competition below of busy relief, of window frames with an uneasy assemblage of pilasters, colonnettes, entablatures, segmental and pointed pediments, and yards of ruffled carved ornament. Even in these small top stories the multiformity, nervous ornament, and restless interruptions are foreign to Codussi's presumed ideals, though put up while he was *proto*. The effectiveness of the upper pilasters here is destroyed by high-relief lions' heads in their middles. Oddest of all is the set of the five smallest colonnettes working to hold up a beam, carved consoles, and a shelf of cornice (fig. 25.4) for a striding winged Lion of S Mark, now a replacement reversed in direction from the original (Cicognara-Diedo-Selva, as above).

Some of the ornament is exquisitely carved, and the rosettes and honeysuckle anthemia on the six gables are superb in silhouette, easing the arches up into the bases for the standing figures.

The colossal S Mark, patron of this scuola and of Venice, and his metaphorical lion below, are accompanied by specific allusions to his great church in the Piazza: the arched gables, the bunched columns, the slabs of varied marbles, and originally the flickering gilding. Except for scattered mediaeval churches of the Holy Sepulchre and until the XIXc revival styles, architecture —unlike sculpture—only rarely chose to include elements referring to some special meaning that had nothing to do with the immediate purely architectural context. The deliberate allusions to another building here are all but unique for Venice.

The right, or *albergo*, half of the facade lacks the attic story, and has smaller, plainer, round gables, with no mimetic supports under their ends, since the big fluted Corinthian pilasters of the main order come under freestanding little piers rather like chimneys, supporting more allegorical females or squatting genii who carry on their shoulders burdensome urns with flaming lids. The details on the gable cornices here are particularly Codussian, even more than on the other wing, but all are adrift in a foreign sea. Their only raisons d'être are to look pretty and to allude to the Church of S Mark, both accomplished successfully.

Inside the scuola there were soon exceptional treasures, chief among them the dozens of pictures commissioned for the upper halls. A series by Mansueti is still mostly in the *albergo*, but Tintoretto's miracles and episodes in the life of S Mark, miracles in their own right, are now divided between the Accademia and the Brera. Rizzo, Giovanni Bellini, Bartolomeo Vivarini, and many other artists were members of the scuola, and there was a wealth of pictures by other masters such as Palma Vecchio and Paris Bordone, as well as gilded ceilings by Pietro and Biagio da Faenza, the most acclaimed

25.3 Scuola di S Marco.
Upper part of main wing.

25.4 Scuola di S Marco. Colonnettes supporting lions on
upper part of main wing.

practitioners of that important craft. Beyond doubt, this was artistically the grandest of the scuolas until it was eclipsed by the Scuola di S Rocco.

One great treasure is now lost: the stairway, a masterwork of Codussi's. He may have begun it even before he replaced Pietro Lombardo as chief architect, and it was finished by 1495. What Mauro had created was nearly all demolished in 1815, when the scuola, the cloisters, and the monastic buildings of the Dominican Church of SS Giovanni e Paolo were made over by the Austrians, to serve as the largest hospital in the city. At first this was solely military, but in 1819 it was expanded to become the municipal hospital—which it still is. Of Codussi's work, only the indoor access portal survives and that has been tampered with. Most of what is known comes from a eulogy written by Tommaso Temanza (1778, 94–95) in the 1760s or 1770s, attributing it to a Martino di Lombardo, a misnomer that turned up several times. Since it is the best evidence we have, Temanza's praise is worth quoting.

One goes to the upper hall by spacious diverging stairways, with landings at the bottom, half-way up, and at the top. The stairs are arranged, one confronting the other, and meet in a common landing at the top, from which one can enter the upper hall through a magnificent archway. These two stairways are very grand [nobilissime] and set at an agreeable slope. But, since the arch at the bottom [of one stairway] . . . is low and pinched, on account of a little room above the landing there, whereas the arch at the top is high and wide, Martino invented a clever adjustment at the second landing . . . by using a thin cornice [and flat ceiling or flattish vault?] above the low arch [of the first run of stairs, and setting a blind arch above it, matched by three more on the other sides, the four all together bound the pendentives on which he put] a little dome, and then leaving open the arch over the next run of stairs [from the middle landing] to the top . . . so that this could be higher, and at the end match the tall arch that led into the grand upper hall.

One whole flight, and the precise form and most of the details of the rest are now lost, and the loss is a major tragedy, though the stairway has now been reconstructed by adapting Mauro's similar stair at the Scuola di S Giovanni Evangelista, begun a few years later. Both, like all the later stairways of the big scuolas, are set outside the buildings, as appendages to the main block, as though they were something perhaps too different to be easily incorporated with the simple big halls of the otherwise normal quadrangular buildings. These two, along with Codussi's stairways of a different kind in the Palazzi Zorzi and Vendramin-Calergi, were astonishing at the date, even in Venice, which led Italy in developing monumental interior stairways (with the possible exception of the Palace at Urbino, so often the first in so many categories).

The Gothic staircases in open courts were sometimes handsome but never monumental; the helix at the Contarini del Bovolo was and is an engaging freak; the Scala dei Giganti is a brilliant solution to an unprecedented problem, unique and without progeny. Neither these nor any others could be classed as monumental interior stairways—none until Codussi lifted what had been no more than a utilitarian way of going up and down indoors into the artistic repertory of major architectural elements. The double stairway, in two symmetrical runs beginning over a hundred feet apart and coming together only at the landing at the top, must be welcomed as an important invention, as it was in classicizing Temanza's intense admiration for something over 250 years old, for something made in the "inaccurate" Early Renaissance.

26 SCUOLA DI S GIOVANNI EVANGELISTA

As it is now, the stairway of the Scuola di S Marco cannot be studied as a true creation of Codussi's, but there is a splendid alternate. About three years after the S Marco stair was finished, the governors of the Scuola di S Giovanni Evangelista, perhaps prompted by envy, asked Mauro to make a stairway for their building. He was quickly inducted as a member of the scuola with exemption from the usual initiation fee. Work was begun in August 1498.

Adding a new stairway to the old building was not so simple a problem as adding a forecourt had been ca. 1481. One part of the old scuola building was a narrow Gothic oblong, originally a hospice, on the right side of the court and continuing back along the less organized space beyond it, opposite the nondescript Church of S Giovanni. To the end of this was added a longer wing, also Gothic, which contained the lower hall, of the common type with two rows of supports, like the ground floor hall of the Scuola di S Marco but probably older.

As the two blocks already contained simple, rectangular, usable rooms, filling almost all the space, and as there was no major stairway that could be demolished and replaced with a new one of adequate grandeur, this had to be put somewhere outside the building in a supplementary structure. The only possible place was along the back, the side opposite the court and church. The west end was stopped by the Rio delle Muneghette just before it ran into the Rio Marin, and the east ran over empty, grand, or inconsequential buildings. Work on something here may have begun by 1490 (Hubala 1974, 358), presumably before Codussi was called in. The long wall of the two old wings is not one straight line, but bends a little where they meet. This did not leave an easy space for a stairway in one run, but if the new stair was to be long and double like that of the Scuola di S Marco, it would have to be fitted somehow to the long bent wall. The entrances would have to be far apart, one in each of the old wings, neither near the main entrance.

Like that of the Scuola di S Marco, its model (Hubala 1974, 358, disagrees), the new stairway has two long flights, as specified in the contract (figs. 26.1 and 26.2). They rose from the far ends to meet in the middle and, like its model, begin with squarish landings, climb halfway to an intermediate landing—one uninterrupted run would have been cruelly long—and land at last at a special platform which opens out broadly to the big main *sala* 26′ by 70′. All the landings have good-size windows.

Miraculously, Mauro was able to make an advantage of the difference between the old bent wall and the new straight wall he built north of it, twice as thick, 6′, as the old bent wall. Only a need to carry exceptional weight and to buttress masonry vaults would justify this. As they climb, the stairs increase in width, from 10′ wide at the bottom landing to 12′3″ at the top. As one goes up, one senses a change in width, without realizing it intellectually. The stair is going not only upward but outward, and one's kinetic sensations are subtly multiplied, only partly through sight. This happens not in a simple mechanical way, but subliminally, and in a way which transfers invigorating animation to the architecture. This is different from the strong perspective pull of the converging walls of the Scala Regia in the Vatican, or any effect of trompe l'oeil. Here instead is a feeling of growth in the normally inanimate forms of architecture, a feeling that cannot be captured in words, but only by the stairway itself. Perhaps it can be conveyed in words by an exaggerated analogy: if Gothic soars, this sweeps itself upward.

Codussi chose to vault the entire construction. To support the stairs, he used a set of vault shapes that would fit well under them; under the slopes there are ramping half-barrel vaults, for example, and under the top landing, a flattish groin vault, acting also as cover for a small chapel at ground level. High above the steps themselves, barrel vaults run upward, with level stretches over the intermediate landings (fig. 26.3). Little domes on pendentives rise above the lower landings; a larger and higher dome crowns the landing at the top. Such a variety of vaults is rare in Venice, a city of virtuoso carpenters and carvers but not vault-raisers. So much vaulting, two heavy layers of it, and a heavy 6′ bearing wall, adequate for buttressing, all concentrated over so small an area, must have demanded extra strong foundations. Until lately, for almost five centuries, there has been little statical trouble.

The decoration is richer than in any other work by Codussi, and often might seem as rich as that of the Lombardos; it is so much more opulent than that of the courtyard that a suggestion has been made that that too is by Codussi, at an earlier period (Hubala 1974, 357). What they have in common is dissimilarity to typical contemporary work rather than similarity to one another. The court is more orderly and plain, and lacks typical Lombardo exuberance, but it also lacks anything specifically Codussian.

The lower parts of the stairway are simple, and easy to accept as Codussi's, uncontaminated by alien impact. The bottom landings are plain, with big square-headed four-light windows opposite the access, and a normal dome on pendentives on top. A barrel vault then begins its diagonal ascent to the intermediate landing, where it stops against an arch, above a break in the entablature carried by capital-like corbels, similar to those in the chancel of S Michele (fig. 26.4). A slight novelty has intruded itself into the otherwise simple entablature: hundreds of small beads on the architrave and hundreds

26.1 Scuola di S Giovanni
Evangelista. Plan of piano
nobile.

26.2 Scuola di S Giovanni
Evangelista. Stairway, longitudinal section.

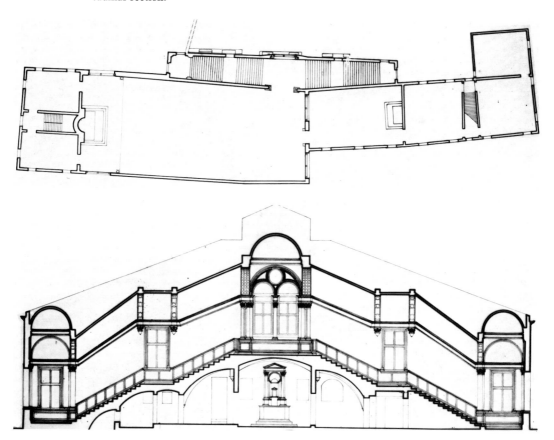

26.3 Scuola di S Giovanni
Evangelista. Stairway, first
flight on right.

26.4 Scuola di S Giovanni
Evangelista. Stairway. Corbel and rib at juncture of inclined and level barrel
vaults.

of small dentils in the bed molding. They count for little but, when noticed, look as though bought by the yard. Such decoration has not been seen in Mauro's work before.

This intermediate landing has the same kind of big four-light window, filling the wall from dado to entablature. The second run of stairs begins here, and is covered and decorated in the same way (fig. 26.5). Except for the slight shift to horizontality at the level landing, the same scheme is carried on up for what now seems a very long distance, and begins to be in danger of losing its power—never great—to hold anyone's interest. Has it been pulled out too far?

At the top there comes a sudden protean transformation. While most of the old components are still there, they have undergone changes, and along with them come spectacular new elements. The discreet little panels of the dado have been transubstantiated to a sumptuous *breccia,* and its cap has developed scores of miniature dentils. The entablature has the same narrow architrave, but now beads run endlessly along its top; the frieze has suddenly transmuted itself into mottled black marble, *lumachella;* the cornice has replaced the monotonous beads with a livelier bead and reel, and above it has pushed forward a new corona, fluted with hawk's beaks, and then above that it flares out into a plain cyma, unmatched below (fig. 26.6). There is contrast in color and texture between the marbles, limestone, and plaster.

Even more happens between the dado and the entablature; each corner of the top landing has slender freestanding marble columns with slight double entasis, common enough at this date, and flaring one-leaf capitals of a type Codussi had used before. These are combined with paneled pilasters, the panels filled with busy, slightly stiff arabesques compounded more of classical bric-a-brac than of flora (fig. 26.7). The effect is more like the *barco* at S Michele than other work of the Codussi shop; but the *barco* was made a decade after Mauro had died, and this was probably made under his supervision. The craftsmen could have been the same. Codussi may not have had much interest in the details of arabesques. A hitherto unknown hand reveals here a taste for rich trimming, as rich as that of the Lombardos; but the trimming is not like theirs, only the amount and the gusto with which it is distributed. (It is, in fact, not identifiable with anything else of the period. The closest may be in some of the carving of about the same date on the upper part of the court of the Doges' Palace, above the Scala dei Giganti.) The governors of this particular scuola might have had special access to carvers who were members of the scuola, and these carvers need not have been attached to a major atelier.

The columns come in pairs, freestanding in front of pilasters (ornamented on the sides that show beside a column, but doubled in width and kept plain where behind a pair of columns). Pairs of columns support the arch leading into the big hall; a column paired with a pilaster supports the arches at the end of the barrel vaults; and a more complicated combination is under the window arch, set in the thickness of that 6' wall (fig. 26.8).

The window is a typical traceried *bifora* on columns, and has to have a special column to receive the end of the small tracery arches where they come against the regular columns already busied in supporting the main window arch (also one of the bounders of the pendentives). The special little *bifora* column on each side of the window is also freestanding, but set away from its more important companions, for it has to be a bit more toward the center and in line with the middle member of the *bifora.* These side window columns are

26.5 Scuola di S Giovanni Evangelista. Stairway, upper flight.

26.6 Scuola di S Giovanni Evangelista. Stairway, capitals, and entablature of top landing.

26.7 Scuola di S Giovanni Evangelista. Stairway, pilaster, and column of top landing.

26.8 Scuola di S Giovanni
Evangelista. Upper landing
of stairway.

set most unclassically half in and half
out of niches (figs. 26.9 and 26.10). A
column in a niche is a peculiar conjunction, robbing both column and
niche of some of their essential functions, and at the same time gaining
compactness without hiding or cutting
anything off. The first Renaissance appearance—the Romans had tried it, as
they did everything else—is in Masac-
cio's Madonna in the National Gallery
in London (late 1420s); Rizzo tried a
version in the arcades of the Doges'
Palace; both are isolated occurrences.
Codussi may have reinvented it, and it
became a common combination in
Venice in the early XVIc, more than in
any other part of Italy.

The traceried *bifora* is like those of
the Palazzo Vendramin-Calergi with
one notable difference: the columns
carry small blocks of entablature between their capitals and the arches of
the tracery above (fig. 26.11). This intrusion is a consequence of the association with the larger arches spanning
the stairs, and their support by columns, where there is, naturally, a full
entablature between the capitals and
the springing of the arches, an inevitable continuation of that at the springing of the barrel vaults which, also naturally, has become the impost of the
arches edging the pendentives. The *bifora* is thus closely coordinated with
them by repeating the columns, entablature, and level of springing.

Since they rest on a pair of columns
or on a column paired with a pilaster,
the pendentive arches have unusually
wide soffits. These are intemperately
enlivened by three rows of twenty-
seven flat square coffers each, trimmed
in the common way with flat rosettes,
eighty-one of them on each soffit, a repetitiveness unmatched even by the
dozens flaunted on the *barco* of S
Michele (fig. 26.12). There are only two
rows on the arch embracing the *bifora*,
and altogether that makes (3 × 81) +
(2 × 27), or 297 little roses in 297 little
frames, plus 20 more in the twin

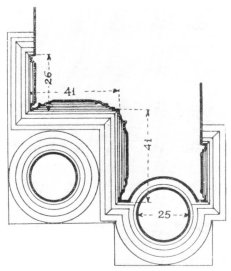

26.9 Scuola di S Giovanni
Evangelista. Plan of column
in niche and whole jamb
condition (from Angelini,
Codussi).

26.10 Scuola di S Giovanni
Evangelista. Stairway, top
landing.

26.11 Scuola di S Giovanni
Evangelista. Window on top
landing.

26.12 Scuola di S Giovanni
Evangelista. Stairway, soffit
of arch to main hall, with
egg and dart edging of pendentive, and entablature of
dome.

arches of the *bifora,* a total of 317! The architectural scheme of the domed landing is superb, with the clustering of columns, close integration of the *bifora,* its dramatic confrontation with the empty arch to the great hall, and finally the floating dome—but in some places the decoration chatters so obsessively as to seem like stuttering. This cannot be reconciled with the serene art of Codussi, and raises a question as to whether all the ornamentation can be his.

Edging these exaggerated soffits, the archivolts of the four pendentive arches, narrow like all of his, are made mainly of an egg and dart between the smallest of flat bands, so that instead of acting as an effective stop to the fancy over-rosetted soffit and firm edge for the pendentive, they make a running flicker of light and shade, decorative but somehow unarchitectural (a strange word to appear in connection with Codussi). The pendentives rise to join one another in a ring made of another entablature, with beads for an architrave, dentils in the bed molding—both at tiny scale more like furniture than architecture—and a frieze inset with niello (an engraved or lightly sunk pattern filled in with black, flush with the main surface of the stone), again less like architecture than like marquetry or metalwork. If there was a decorating assistant, perhaps he had not been trained primarily in architecture.

The underlying design is surely by Codussi, and four possible grounds for the difference from his usual spare ornamentation can be found. He could—mistakenly—have given a freer-than-usual hand to a master carver trained in another shop, different enough from the Lombardos' for its store of details to be distinguishable. Or second, the governors of the scuola, not the purely nominal grandees who were members, but the less grandly educated merchants, foremen, entrepreneurs of the crafts or such, who really ran the scuola, may have wanted a stair like that in the Scuola di S Marco but richer, and they may have insisted on lots of ornament. Or third, and less likely, Mauro himself may momentarily have wanted to show that he could, if called on, compose with the adjuncts he ordinarily eschewed, carving, color, and luxurious materials. Or perhaps he had no interest in this, and let the enrichment go by default. More probable than any one of these, however, is a combination of them, the governors asking for richness and Mauro passively willing to try it to show his skill in a new field, hence taking on some sort of decorating junior partner whom he sometimes controlled and sometimes let go (countless coffers and rosettes, beads by the gross). There must have been many ornamental carvers among the members of the scuola, some eager to help, possibly gratis.

One particularly prepossessing asset in the ensemble is the control of light. The lower landings have big windows, filling their wall space opposite the entrance. The landing at the west end has an extra window at the foot of the stair, giving on the canal. After a softer, shadowy stretch in the tunnel to the landing halfway up, comes another flare of light, definite but not as strong. Then comes another length of shadowy tunnel and, as a climax, at the top, a real outburst of light from the *bifora,* reaching 19′ up to the crown of its arch through the curves of the tracery; still more light comes from the other side, through the matching 19′ arch opening into the big hall. In musical terms one could write it forte-piano-forte-piano-fortissimo. Even the dome is included in the lighting scheme, for it looks buoyant enough to float and almost glow, 25′8″ up, and not to weigh down like a heavy, dark lid. Light comes to it by reflection from white plaster or polished marble surfaces all about, including even the marble floor (not now the original). Everywhere in the stairway light is reflected in one way or another;

there is no direct sunlight (except very late in the afternoon on the west lower landing, and even there the light is more often reflected waveringly from the canal than coming directly from the sun).

The great hall cannot now be counted as a work of Codussi, if it ever really was, for it is not clear how much, if anything, he did there. In 1727 it was drastically done over by Giorgio Massari, the leading local architect of the day. At the east end there are two *bifore* like that on the stair-landing, one a copy, the other a dummy not open to outdoors (fig. 26.13). Between them a doorway leads to the room reserved for the scuola's greatest treasure, a fragment of the True Cross, pawned and later sold by the Emperor of Byzantium, and presented in 1329 to the scuola, which had it encased in a splendid gold and jeweled late Gothic reliquary. There was also a wonderful treasure of a different kind, dating from Codussi's time, a famous set of paintings by Gentile Bellini, Carpaccio, Mansueti, and Bastiani (now in the Venice Accademia), all referring to celebrations and miracles having to do with the history of this relic after it came to Venice.

Only one important part of the exterior has a connection with Codussi, the portal and maybe the window over it. One of the two blocks of the early scuola buildings pushed out into the space between the scuola and the church, far enough beyond the other wing to offer wall space for a main entrance, conveniently facing east toward the doorway leading out of the court. Composed somewhat like a triumphal arch, the portal is, however, less Roman than Early Renaissance, less pompously triumphal than gracefully light, less Lombardo-fancy than Codussi-spare (fig. 26.14). Columns and plain paneled pilasters lead to an entablature with sharply inclined fascias, a frieze with colored circles and lozenges, and a normal cornice, with no carving anywhere. Colonnettes half as high as the main columns stand above them; the flanking pilasters have the same treatment with smaller pilasters above. The arch has an effective keystone, and it and the capitals carry yet another entablature, again with flipped fascias and no carving. The pediment above the arch is handled with learned correctness in that the cyma (derived from a temple gutter) runs up the slope but not across the floor of the tympanum—in other words, it appears only where it was in origin, at the edge of a roof. The whole arrangement projects in only moderate relief, and reads easily as one organized entity.

Something of a different nature happens above this doorway. The strip of blank wall in back of the pediment shows that a change may have taken place (fig. 26.15). On the left, over the stacked pilasters by the corner and uncomfortably not quite over the columns by the door, come two dwarfed pilasters with unclassifiable capitals (as well called unclassifiable brackets). There is not an exact correspondence on the other side, for there only one of these dwarfs appears, above the outer pilaster, and there is none above the column. Far apart, these three small elements carry, nonetheless, a cornice across the full width of the wall, a cornice that serves also as a sill for a big window, the *bifora* already noted in the big upper hall. It is flanked by pilasters gracelessly paneled with lozenges and circles, one pilaster on the right and a pair on the left—one, that is, over each of the three dwarfed elements below. The center of the window, made prominent by tracery and a column, is not in line with the center of the doorway immediately underneath, because the right jamb does not jibe with the jamb below. Having a narrower enframement at the right, the window jamb is displaced a bit to the right. The disparity—a serious one—is now half

26.13 Scuola di S Giovanni
Evangelista. Great hall,
looking east. At the right a
bifora copied from
Codussi's; at the left a
dummy *bifora*.

26.14 Scuola di S Giovanni
Evangelista. Entrance.

26.15 Scuola di S Giovanni
Evangelista. Main entrance
and *bifora* above.

masked and confused by an elaborate iron grille. The awkwardnesses are far greater and somehow deeper than any on the front of S Zaccaria, greater than on any certain work of Codussi.

It is hard to believe that Codussi or any experienced architect would have planned such an ill-assembled frontispiece from the start, particularly when one realizes that the lower doorway could easily have been placed so that it could jibe with the opening above if that opening had to be where it is. That both had to be a certain distance from the left corner is clear, since the thickness of the wall around the corner plus the chosen enframement take up some space—but the space would be equal. No imperative fixed the location of the right jamb, however, of either door or window, and they could perfectly well have been lined up, if whoever built the doorway had thought ahead enough about the window, or whoever built the window had been able to think of outside and inside at the same time.

The *bifora* is clumsy in detail, and could easily be a post-Codussian makeshift. Some work was done hereabout in 1512, eight years after Mauro died, and it may have been on this window. Or perhaps the doorway was made in 1512, posthumously, from his designs; then a follower, with no precise designs with which to continue, improvised the window without the coordination a professional would have found essential. The latter seems the more likely. The large upper hall was remodeled by Massari in the XVIIIc, when he may have altered the window, or offhandedly told an assistant to do it. Remember that right along, this scuola's roster included dozens of master masons and carvers and workmen of varying ability. If the doorway is Mauro's, as is not probable though not at all provable, whether posthumous or not, it cannot rank as an important work, nor one to

which he gave much attention. The window must be something fitted to it later or, rather, ill-fitted.

The building was badly neglected after the scuolas were closed in 1797 as potential hotbeds of dissent. Proposals were made to pull it down in 1856, but a group of concerned citizens was able to save it. A new confraternity was constituted the next year, and raised to an archconfraternity and "Society of the Building Arts" in 1929, something like a craft guild. The most urgent repairs were made—the members knew more about building than those of any other scuola in the city—in 1929 and again in 1956, and now the Venice Committee of the International Fund for Monuments has been carrying out repairs in various parts of the building since 1972.

27 TORRE DELL'OROLOGIO

One of the few utterly flat great cities of the world, Venice has only three grandly impressive sites for buildings: those of S Mark's, the Dogana (or old Customs House) on its commanding point, and the Clock Tower. There is only one great plaza, and no great avenues with striking sites at their head or foot (fig. 27.1). Fronting the Grand Canal or the lagoon (from an island, such as S Michele) can be attractive and picturesque, and the water can add a special enchantment, but such advantages do not make a grand site with monumental character; they offer no vistas leading to a climax. The lack matters particularly for public buildings, which most often seem to call for dominating settings.

The most out-of-the-ordinary of Codussi's buildings, not documented but well accepted, is the Clock Tower or Orologio. It stands on one of the three finest building sites in the city, next to S Mark's but still able to hold its own. Flush with the 500′ front wall of the Procuratie Vecchie and marking its east end, the Clock Tower faces straight across the Piazza at its widest, 265′, in front of S Mark's. This places it at the head of another strong axis that advances between the Campanile and the Porta della Carta, on into the Piazzetta to run along in front of the Doges' Palace, on between the giant red granite columns of S Theodore and the Lion of S Mark, and still onward after 315′ in the Piazzetta to dissolve over the flat waters of the *Bacino* (fig. 27.2). In the opposite direction, beginning behind the tower, another axis works its way down the long chasm of the Merceria, then as now the city's main shopping street, and then the link between the government center at the Piazza and the business center at the other end of the Rialto Bridge. The Merceria was matched in length and busy concentration only by the *Sierpes* that the Moors had threaded through the heart of

27.1 Piazza and Piazzetta.
Air view.

27.2 Orologio. Vista along axis from water, between giant granite columns.

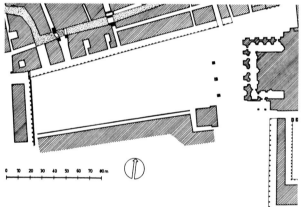

27.3 Piazza. Plan in about 1500 (from Lotz, *Italienische Plätze*).

Seville; neither one was straight for its whole length, though each had good straight stretches, yet each constituted a major axis of its city.

Francesco Sansovino (317) recognized the tower (by 1581) as "the gateway through which one goes into the city." Everything in the vicinity contributes to the emphasis focused on the spot where the tower stands. The view from the water was equally compelling when the old Gothic granaries still stood on the left, on the bank facing the *Bacino* (where the little public garden is now), and the Piazzetta made a sudden deep penetration in the wall of buildings, pulling the eye back between the giant columns, past the palace, the campanile, and S Mark's, to end in the brightly colored shaft of the tower.

Contriving the design for a building to go on such a site was not easy, particularly for an architect sensitive to the possibilities of working with the complex as a whole, with every part coordinated into one grand polyphonic composition. He would have to make something suitable for the end of the long vista through the Piazzetta (the first view seen by those arriving by ship), which would at the same time be attuned to its equally extraordinary and dissimilar neighbors—the front of S Mark's, the sweep of fifty-three arches of the original XIIc Procuratie Vecchie, and the looming campanile, some 40' square and then about 250' high. And more, for he must manage to make something that would concur with each of them, to mediate somehow in bringing their discrepant characters together in a happy relationship.

This awesome setting differed then from now in several ways. The pavement was 2' to 3' lower, and was of bright brick in herringbone pattern within a grid of white stone lines. The Piazza was as long as now and, in front of S Mark's, as wide (about two by one New York City blocks). But along the south side it became narrower after the campanile, with a mediaeval miscellany dominated by an arcaded and stuccoed brick hospital (fig. 27.3). The Procuratie Vecchie turned the northwest corner for six bays, and the Procuratie Nuove were still undreamed of. No library building flanked the Piazzetta, but just a congeries of shops and, at the end, public toilets. The government's pride in itself, unsurpassed in Europe and already incarnated in the Palazzo and the size of the Piazza, was beginning to affect both Piazza and Piazzetta, as already shown by the Procuratie Vecchie and the towering twin columns of Egyptian granite glittering with quartz crystals.

The site was finished in suitably grand style in the first years of the XVIc; the gibbet in the Piazza was taken away (Mutinelli, 328), and the three flagpoles with Leopardi's bronze bases were put up (1505) for the red and gold silk banners of the republic. (Only one flaunts the Venetian flag today, and that is blown mainly by the winds of history.) The poles, in their way a variant of the already asserted theme of the two columns at the beginning of the Piazzetta, were planted symmetrically across the axis of the main portal of S Mark's, not parallel with the facade but spread away from it at an angle equivalent to that at which the church front diverged from the axis coming out from the Orologio and running down to the giant columns. In other words, they were set in a compensating dislocation. Codussi, working on city commissions in the late 1480s, had placed the foundations (Puppi-Puppi, 165) in one of the first efforts to pull the composition at the end of the Piazza together. What had been haphazard siting began to be conciliated into an order not envisioned when most of the individual elements were given their places. Furthermore, the Campanile, flagpoles, and Clock Tower (with its soon-to-be-built wings) began to delineate a special atrium, discernible in the Piazza's immeasurable sea of space, as a prelude to the great church.

This new Clock Tower was an early and important part of a program to make the civic center impressive, with forms which might convey some of the grandeur and power of the proud republic, for at this time a big clock was counted a civic monument, something of a showpiece. Mechanical clocks had not come into general use until the late XIIIc, and hours and minutes only then began to be common measures. Earlier, the day had been divided into sections by the kinds of work common to each, or by the different activities in the churches announced by the bells in their towers (the first dozen of which had come to Venice as a gift from the Byzantine emperor in the IXc). The shorter moments were measured in Aves, the time it took to say a "Hail Mary."

The hundred-year-old clock at the north end of S Mark's having become rickety, a new one was voted in 1493. Despite the imposing scale, it was finished quickly, and must have been almost ready when, on November 3, 1495, the Senate and procurators (who were still living in the XIIc Procuratie Vecchie) decided that it should be housed in a new tower of its own beside S Mark's, at the end of the Procuratie, even though to find space for it a pair of bays would have to be pulled down where the Merceria ran into the Piazza. Work began on the site in June 1496, with the demolishing of those two bays.

Marin Sanudo (I, 205) saw this in June 1496, and wrote that the tower was going to be "the most beautiful in Italy." Yet Gentile Bellini's meticulously rendered view of the Piazza in 1496—the best record we have—with the annual Procession of the Cross, shows no trace of anything to do with

new building. He must have drawn and painted his composition a little earlier, and did not want to include any intrusion of messy scaffolding. On February 1, 1499, Sanudo saw the work uncovered for the first time, for the doge's annual march to S Maria Formosa, and found it "wrought with great art, and most beautiful." One reason for building it just then, when the doge was in disgrace and had been discovered letting Rizzo loot the till, was to show the public that the city was not without money while it was fighting Naples. Alas, though, when it was finished, Venice was suffering financial crises, chiefly bank failures (Malipiero in Longworth, 176; Puppi-Puppi, 168; Sanudo, 487). But the quality of the work was not stinted. Doge Agostino Barbarigo, the Senate, and the procurators agreed to that. The big bell was raised to the top early in December 1497, and on the tenth, the two giant woodwoses (wild men), one young, one old, were hoisted to where they could turn their bronze torsos to bang the big bell with their mallets. Soon they were christened "Moors" by the public because of the blackness of the bronze of which they had been cast (by Paolo Savin).

Jacopo de' Barbari showed the tower as it was in 1500 or just before, an independent structure, squarish but a bit deeper than wide, without the side adjuncts for the wings that would be added in a year or two (fig. 27.4). The original XIIc Procuratie, soon to be replaced, stopped against its left side, leaving the top half of the tower to rise free, more truly a tower than it is now. When it was more separate from its immediate neighbors, its verticality must have made it seem somewhat more dramatic; a fitting prelude for the vision of S Mark's. Beyond it, on the right, were three bays like those on the left, plus an extra story with Gothic windows (Gentile Bellini, *Procession . . . 1496*, Venice, Accademia; Jacopo de' Barbari, map, 1500). The effect of

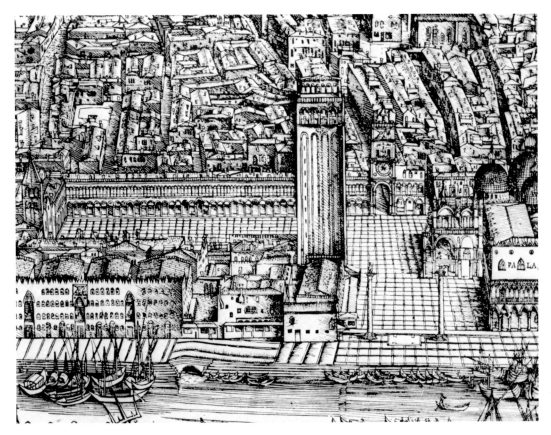

27.4 Procuratie Vecchie,
Campanile, Orologio, and S
Mark's (from the de' Barbari
map of 1500).

the new tower must have been galvanizing, for cities in the orbit of Venice began to put up lesser versions of it. The old clock tower in Padua, which may have served as a partial model (probably more to the procurators than to the architect), was altered bit by bit until it began to look more and more like its own child. The Orologio became a symbol for Venice much as the Eiffel Tower would for Paris.

Each of the well marked stories, set a few inches back from the one below, diminishes in height by about a sixth or a little more—some say only a fifth (Vio, in Samonà et al., 139). But the measurements seem nearer 18 percent than 20 percent—above the lofty ground story pedestals, though it is not now possible to see the proportions at the bottom because of the raising of the pavement.

At the bottom, high cylindrical pedestals—perhaps not quite as high as Jacopo showed them—carry columns, freestanding but so close to the corner piers that the round pedestals of one merge with square pedestals of the other, and, at the top, the panels on the piers have to be sunk to extra depth to accept the flare of the capitals close beside them (fig. 27.5). A block of unornamented entablature holds the simple archivolt of the arch spanning the Merceria. The tall piers (not pilasters—they have no capitals) then support a second entablature, also unornamented except for plain brackets. The arch swings up until tangent to this second architrave, unconnected by any keystone. Everything is simple; no ornamental carving except on the capitals, plain paneling, close-clinging and blunt moldings. (The arrangement of this arch has been seen—not very convincingly—as enough like the Cappella Bernabò in S Giovanni Grisostomo to propose Codussi as author. More is needed for a reasonable attribution—and there is a bit more.)

The dark hollow of the arch serves not only the practical need of access to the busiest street leading out of the Piazza, but makes an appropriate metaphoric reference to the shadowy hollows of the arched niches on the front of the narthex of S Mark's (figs. 27.6 and 27.7). Already here in its lowest story, the design of the tower responds to its great neighbor and begins to extend the scope of the manifold composition.

The next story is filled by the face of the clock, of the same diameter as the street arch below (fig. 27.8). Bull's-eye windows fit into the corners, framed in wreaths or chains, tangent to the rim of the clock dial and to the pilasters outside. The dial is a 16′ marble wheel in twenty-four segments, with a raised gilded bronze Roman numeral in each, legible from across the Piazza. The hour is pointed out by a blazing gold sun on a revolving arm. Another wheel placed inside this in 1498 is of blue enameled copper with emblems of the zodiac in gilded bronze relief—a bit of humanist swank of no practical use. Inside that comes a helpful wheel, blue, with accurately placed constellations of big stars, and a revolving ball, half white, half black, that turns around the heavens as it turns on itself, and thus shows the phases of the moon. This and the marking of the hours make it possible to know the times of the tides, vital for a city so largely dependent on shipping. The richness of color—gold leaf, pink marble, blue enamel—must have been a deliberate choice, to put the little facade in tune with grandly polychrome S Mark's.

The big machine that runs the clock and its adjuncts has served wonderfully well, having rarely had to be stopped for repairs; it still works better than many of the public clocks in Italy made in more recent times. The Rotary Club of Venice undertook an extraordinarily speedy, thorough, and costly restoration early in 1975, and managed to have the construction of the tower reinforced, the polychrome front

cleaned and repaired, and the clock-
work and apparatus for the moon,
Moors, and all such put in good order,
all in time to work perfectly and look
fine by Easter Sunday.

Since it contains the round clock-
face so exactly, the wall space of this
story is square, and it is bounded on
each side by strong verticals, pilasters
with capitals that have lyrelike *caulicoli* to make their volutes. The entablature above performs one unusual
duty: it swings out on a shallow horizontal curve to make a top large
enough to serve as a small stage (fig.
27.9). In plan, this curve accords with
the curves in elevation in much the
same contrapuntal way as the triple
curves of the balconies of the Corner-
Spinelli rhyme with the triple
curves of the heads of the traceried
windows there. This correspondence of
vertical and horizontal curves, rare if
not unique, suggests but does not
clinch a connection with Codussi.

The little stage is used for a special
attraction of the tower. A golden Madonna with the Child on her lap sits in
a gold and white mosaic niche inside a
central *aedicula* unlike anything else
on the tower. It may have been part of
the commission of the sculptor, once
thought to be Leopardi, now sometimes
said to be Pietro Lombardo but more
often a member of his workshop. During the annual week-long fair of the
Sensa (Ascension Day, forty days after
Easter), after the hour had been struck
by the Moors, a small door at the left
would open, and a gilded angel would
glide out, trumpeting, followed by
gilded and enameled Magi of wood,
life-size, and wearing magnificent tur-
bans and crowns. They moved forward
to the Madonna, genuflected, and went
out through a matching door at the
right. (This is still done every Ascension Week.) In the more time-pressed
XIXc, the doors were outfitted with extra machinery, hourly shifting big Roman numerals on the left, from I to

27.5 Orologio. At left, round
pedestal of column of arch
over the Merceria (the similar pedestal and column at
the right were added in the
XVIIIc).

27.6 S Mark's from the Merceria, showing the Orologio arch on its columns with double entasis and their cylindrical pedestals (from a painting by Canaletto in the Fitzwilliam Museum, Cambridge).

27.7 Orologio. Oblique view, with arch to the Merceria equaled with niches of the facade of S Mark's.

27.8 Orologio. Clock face.

27.9 Orologio. Entablature under the Madonna.

27.10 Orologio. Spandrel by clock face, with chain-ringed oculus and capital with lyrelike *caulicoli*.

XII, and Arabic figures on the right every five minutes, from 0 to 55 (fig. 27.10). The wall behind the little stage, diapered in gold and blue mosaic (now largely restored) is another reduced reference to the polychrome splendor of S Mark's, and helps assimilate some of its color into the otherwise still largely achromatic civic center.

The Fair of the Sensa soon had to be extended to two weeks, and it became the biggest commercial event of the year. The city was crowded with foreign merchants, many from the East, and also with pilgrims, many from Northern Europe, for Pope Alexander III had announced special plenary indulgences for those who visited S Mark's during the week (or weeks) and made a special contribution (Tamassia, 189-91, 203n12). The dumb-show on the tower was particularly suitable since the Magi were foreigners, Eastern, pilgrims, and, though not merchants, rich.

The entablature above this is the most normal one yet, for, although lumpish, the architrave is built up of inclined fascias and the plain marble frieze is of ordinary width. What this entablature does, however, is far from normal for, after breaking out in an ordinary way above the pilasters, the architrave and frieze break forward again for a length of 12' (the tower is only 20' wide) above five small, weak brackets put there as underpinning for a big winged Lion of S Mark (fig. 27.11). Since the smashing in 1797 of the figure of Doge Agostino Barbarigo (because he was a doge) who was kneeling before the lion, the lion has been quite a bit off center. The background is bright blue mosaic spangled with a shower of flower-like gold stars.

The heavy ledge on which the lion stands is a strange intrusion, but not unique, for near the top of the main section of the Scuola di S Marco, a zone which must have been built while Codussi was in charge, another lion stands on a similarly contrived element. Rather than inadequate visual underpinning, at the Scuola there seems to be too much: five freestanding, cigar-shaped, veined marble columns of a size and kind of marble not found anywhere else on the facade (could they be secondhand?).

Could Codussi, who was probably responsible for both—his authorship of the Orologio, proposed by Molmenti in 1911 (II, 104, 109-110), is regularly accepted—having observed the supererogatory support at the Scuola, have overreacted here and supplied too little? Here, where he did not have to coordinate with Pietro Lombardo's carefree luxuriance, temperamentally antipathetic to him, he may have fallen back into his own puritanical economy of means, prodded by a sort of backlash. In both cases the details are not strict, and probably not strictly Mauro's, though presumably he was in charge.

At S Zaccaria and the Scuola di S Marco, his least successful works perhaps, he had had to fit his design to what had already been started by others. He did not have to do that here, though one can be sure that he did have to tailor his design to a number of ideas fixed by others; the program and the wish for showiness would not have been his but imposed on him by the Senate and the procurators, or their *proto*.

Nor are the details Codussi's. The result of the combination is like those unfinished works of composers who laid out the composition, themes, and counterpoint or harmony, but not the details of the instrumentation, which were later worked out by someone else. The only reason for such a situation here would be that Mauro could not attend to all the details; he may have had to remove himself to other work, to the Scuola di S Marco, to S Maria Formosa, or for his health, or some other

27.11 Orologio. Three upper
stories.

27.12 Orologio. Platform for
Moors.

nonarchitectural cause. The working drawings or model may have had to have their final touches from the *proto* or someone in his office. The *proto* of S Mark's, under the procurators of S Mark's (the powerful *Procuratori de Supra*), in charge of the buildings in the immediate vicinity of the church and Piazza (though the money had to be voted by the *Provveditori al Sal*) was Giorgio Spavento; nothing here looks like his work. The *protos* of the state were Rizzo and Bartolomeo Bon the Younger. The execution could reflect the taste not of any specific architect, not Codussi, not Spavento, not Rizzo—Bon was out of the city at the crucial time—but that of some of the clients, ambitious procurators, or assistants of no better than indifferent merit, left to their own devices, while ignorant of the purity, clarity, and simplicity of Mauro's details.

Like the other stories, that of the lion is flanked by pilasters, again a sixth shorter than those just below, and stopped at the top by a similar entablature with the same unusual projection of architrave and pink marble frieze in the center, borne again on ineffectual brackets. This block prepares for the sculptural display of the Moors at the top, while at the same time it repeats the measure of the curved stage for the Magi and the oblong for the lion.

Instead of a roof on the tower top, there are steps rising to the platform where the Moors stand on either side of the support of the huge bell they beat, a platform setting them high enough above the edge to ensure that the angle of vision of the crowds looking up from the Piazza will not be such as to cut off their legs (fig. 27.12). The striking, jerky silhouette makes another accord with S Mark's where, at related levels, an activity of figures, wings, and crocketed pinnacles punctuates the skyline. (The sides of the tower, which now show themselves

above the Procuratie, are luxuriously sheathed in marble, pale pink and gray panels in white frames, a typical color scheme of the XVIIIc, when they were added.)

Above the last cornice, the top is fenced in. Posts mark the major and minor corners, and between them are widely-spaced colonnettes, making an openwork parapet, conceived mainly as a termination of the architecture—but today needed to keep the swarms of photographing tourists from being backed over the edge. Unless it is a later addition, this is as early a use as is known—it is never wise to say "the first"—of a balustrade to finish off the skyline of a building, a transition between solid and void, transparent against the sky. Hitherto, special crowning was done with ornamental crenellations as seen consistently in dozens of fine buildings painted by Carpaccio. Balustrades were for balconies or terraces only. Since there are colonnettes instead of spindle balusters (which Codussi always used), the detailing must have been by others; moreover, their being colonnettes argues against the later date an addition would call for. The idea for the balustrade would have originated in the railings on the terraces on the narthex of S Mark's, there functional but here nonfunctional since it is doubtful that in pretourist and precamera days anyone but workmen or carefully guided important visitors would have been allowed on the top—at least during the first years. A nonfunctional crowning balustrade appears again only with Bramante's Tempietto in Rome, after 1500 (Portoghesi 1972, 41, 53), showing itself immediately useless for anything other than the exigencies of the design.

In the first years of the Orologio, the whole upper half, the stories with the Madonna and the lion and, of course, the Moors and their bell, was a freestanding tower, rising out of a long line of pointed crenellations (like a giant

picket fence) of the old Procuratie Vecchie on one side, and an unimportant
short Gothic addition on the other,
both soon to be pulled down. In the beginning, then, it must have acted as a
small response to the Campanile,
which stood about as far south from
the axis of S Mark's as the Orologio did
to the north. Both rose flush from a
long line of buildings defining the Piazza, the Procuratie on one side and
the Orseolo Hospital, attached to the
Campanile, on the other. Together the
towers framed the church, and thus
gained an extra relation to one another,
disparate though they were in bulk and
height. The Orologio worked in many
ways to organize a wide-flung composition out of half-accidentally scattered
elements on the site, much as a spider
can relate all the diverse elements of a
periphery in one great web.

The rear of the tower, facing the narrow Merceria, was less elaborate, with
a simpler clock-face of the same size
and, of course, an equivalent arch,
again on columns on round pedestals
(fig. 27.13). The arches at each end are
a bit narrower and lower than the tunnel vault that joins them and covers
the passage from Piazza to street; thus
they give the effect of strong ribs making a strong ending. On the walls of the
passage, a pair of pilasters helps sustain
the long entablature running all the
way through. The capitals are not all
alike, and that is the only persisting
mediaevalism. Most of what one sees
now is work of the XIXc.

The tower did not long remain as it
was in 1500. If the Barbari view is to be
trusted, from 1499 to 1501 or 1502 it
was organized with a clear relation to
the adjoining two-story Procuratie (fig.
27.14). The flanking piers of the lower
story of the tower subsumed both the
stories of the Procuratie, and its top
cornice was picked up by some part of
the termination of the lower story of

the tower. One part of the Orologio,
however, is different: above their pedestals, these same lower-story piers are
cut across by the small entablature
above the freestanding columns and
under the archway across the Merceria.
This brings up a special question that
has two answers.

If the piers were uninterrupted, they
would pass muster as parts of a proportional series in the heights of the pilasters of the successive stories; ascending
6:5:4:3 (slightly different if the entablatures are included, and quite different if
the pedestals of the wall-less ground
story are counted). But now, cut by the
entablature of the arch-carrying columns beside them, neither of the resulting parts works in any clear ratio
with anything else. If Jacopo de' Barbari's record is accurate, this interruption was made after 1500; if he was
careless, Codussi was not notably logical in his proportions here. Mattia Pagan's big woodcut (31" by 66") of 1556–
59 shows it as Jacopo had, perhaps
from copying him, perhaps from correct
observation. Neither woodcut is fully
acceptable evidence.

In favor of uninterrupted piers is the
proportional sequence, bottom to top, a
rational and constructive aid to design
congenial to Codussi's intellectual
bent. But if the small entablature was
there from the beginning cutting across
the pier—which is possible since it is a
horizontal continuation from that over
the columns below the arch—it would
look like other not quite resolved instances in Codussi's oeuvre. He had
had trouble with a similar problem before because of the threatened cancella-
tion of the integrity of important supports on the front of S Michele, the
main piers inside S Maria Formosa and
S Giovanni Grisostomo. Furthermore,
if this entablature is not there, the
paneling of the lower piers (cut directly
into the stone) cannot be worked into a
rational sequence. What one can now
read of the stone-jointing is against the

27.13 Orologio. Back, seen
from the Merceria (XIXc
lithograph by Tosini-
Lazzari).

27.14 Orologio with XIIc
Procuratie Vecchie (drawing
by Silvano Boldrin from
Samonà, *Piazza*).

hypothesis of uninterrupted pilasters, but then one must remember that the lower story was extensively gone over in the XVIIIc, and that the present joints may not be the same as the first ones.

Possibly the pilasters were first planned with different paneling, or no paneling had yet been worked out, and no cutting entablature had been thought of as interfering with the harmonious scheme in which each story was proportionally shorter than the one below. Then, later, someone could have decided to make the entablature run across the pilaster, and that someone could have been one of the bossier clients, an assistant, or even Codussi himself after a last-minute change of mind. The most convincing guess is that the lower piers were first designed, on a model or drawing, without the interruption, but were then built with it. The idea was intellectually irreproachable; the execution was not.

In 1500 a decision was taken to add wings to the tower. The 350-year-old Procuratie were cracking and crumbling, and the heavy new tower must have induced new statical problems where it adjoined the lighter old foundations. This could have led to the decision to demolish enough to interpose one new house on each side of the tower, with suitably stronger underpinnings, at the cost of destroying some of the sweep of the long run of old arches. Work on these wings was begun in late 1501 or early 1502 (fig. 27.15).

Each wing is two bays wide, taking the space of three bays of the XIIc Procuratie (of which two bays had already been sacrificed for the tower). The old building must have been a bit irregular here, for the new right wing, where the end of the old arcades had been, is 2′ narrower than the apparently matching left wing, also supplanting three arches of the older building. This alteration left fifty arches from the end of the

new left wing to the end in the far corner of the Piazza, in the same spacing we still see today.

These wings have four stories, their lower two corresponding in height to the bottom story of the Orologio, and the upper two to the story of the clock-face. The ground story of the front of the wings was made of slightly compound piers carrying abnormally long spans, a continuation of the same lower entablature from which the arch over the Merceria springs. This demanded lintels more in the proportions of wood construction than of anything normal in stone. (The span was reduced by adding extra columns beside the piers in the XVIIIc.) These stand in front of a covered walk which continues directly from the long arcaded walk of the Procuratie.

The relation of the wings to the Orologio is slight, but there is no comprehensible relation at all between the front of the wings and the present Procuratie, put up only a couple of years later. The XIIc arcade had developed into a climax when it was suddenly widened and broadened into the arch over the Merceria, but the two trabeated bays of the new wings, with their uncomfortably long lintels, come as a jarring, disjunctive shift—unanticipated, unconnected, unresolved, and unassimilable.

Neither does the next story of the wings, a sort of mezzanine, fit with anything except at its top, where it is closed down by a continuation of the big entablature of the big piers of the bottom story of the Orologio. The square-headed windows are set in pairs, as are those of the Palazzo Zorzi or the lower floor of the Vendramin-Calergi, but this slight similarity can add nothing to sustain thoughts of Codussi, since paired rectangular windows had by now appeared moderately often in a variety of buildings.

The two upper stories of the wings are subsumed by the single order of pilasters of the clock-face story, pilasters

27.15 Orologio. Entrance
archway to the Merceria.

which are repeated in a thin, flat, undernourished version to mark off each bay of the wings. As they run through two stories, they could be said to act as a giant or colossal order (one that runs through more than a single story), anticipated by Alberti at S Andrea at Mantua, which Codussi (but perhaps few others in Venice) might have known from a detour on his winter trips to and from Lenna. But as the resemblance is slight, and as the upper of these two stories is only another mezzanine, this claim should not be pushed. The lower floor of this upper zone of the wings has a wholly different type of paired window, with arched heads fitted on a thin oblong panel topped by a little cornice; the window arches are not in scale with the arches of the Procuratie windows. By now, such arched *bifore* had become fairly common in Venice, and there is nothing remarkable in their appearance here—except their lack of harmony with anything else. The wing is stopped at the top by a continuation of the entablature over the clock, and a parapet-balustrade bounding the roof terrace, close in level to the narthex terrace of S Mark's, the only element in the wings that appears to have been designed with any thought of its relation to its neighbors.

It is harder to imagine the hand of Codussi in the wings than in the tower, where it seems only thinly hidden by an overlay of uncharacteristic details. Work on the wings had been delayed and was not completed until the Sensa of 1506; Mauro had died in 1504. Not only is the execution farther from his idiom than that of the Orologio, but so is the underlying design. He could have left sketches—natural to project the extensions for a tower he had already built—but the actual wings evoke him so faintly that if sketches were left, one cannot believe they were used. While Mauro was still living, the procurators charged the *Provveditori al Sal,* financially responsible for most public building, to have Pietro Lombardo provide "marble and stone" (Angelini 1945–61; Vio, in Samonà et al., 139) for the wings, but that neither solves nor complicates the problem of authorship, for Pietro sold stone for buildings he did not design. At the time he was *proto* of the Palazzo, and supplying stone for this new neighbor could have been a routine duty. Until he died in 1505, Bartolomeo Gonella was *proto* of the *Procuratia de Supra,* along with Spavento, and responsible for buildings near S Mark's; designing a municipal clock tower in the Piazza might have been a routine duty for him, since it was a substitute for a clock once on S Mark's, above the front north portal. As nothing is known of his style, there is nothing to deny his having designed these wings—but nothing based on another nothing is not much of a conclusion. The wings remain as anonymous as they are inept.

Bartolomeo Bon was *proto* of S Mark's from 1505 to 1521, and responsible to the procurators. He would have been in charge at the end of the building campaign of the wings, and possibly intermittently before, but nothing in the design can confidently be assigned to him. (On the whole, they seem to be like some modern public school or municipal office building, ordered by officials uninterested in architecture.) The Orologio can best be seen as a work designed originally by Codussi, carried out partly according to his wishes and partly not; the wings ought to be the same, by logical deduction and historical precedent, but they are not. Their design and their details are alien, and so insensitively related to their neighbors that any participation by him seems improbable. The tower no longer comes as such a dramatic climax to the infinite Procuratie; the wings interrupt and make the new and larger building, tower-and-wings, into something not clearly either vertical or horizontal; the Merceria arch no longer seems an expansion of the Procuratie arches, transitional to the greater arches of the narthex of S Mark's. The *aedicula* of the Madonna now counts for very little, when once it was a strong motif clearly related in scale to the upper arches of the Procuratie. The wings appear, in almost every respect, a bungling failure. They were finished in 1506.

To sum up the discussion of Codussi's architecture, the recorded or now well-accepted works by him are the following:

S Michele in Isola, 1468–78 or 79, with later additions
S Pietro di Castello, campanile 1482–89 or 90
S Zaccaria, 1483–ca. 1491 and later
Scuola di S Marco, 1489 or 1490–95 or later
Palazzo Zorzi, ca. 1490–1504, unfinished
Palazzo Corner-Spinelli, 1490s
S Maria Formosa, 1491 or 1492–1504, unfinished
Orologio, 1496–99
S Giovanni Grisostomo, 1497–1504, unfinished
Scuola di S Giovanni Evangelista, 1498–1504, unfinished
Palazzo Vendramin-Calergi, 1502?–04, unfinished

Except perhaps for the problematic and little-studied atrium loggia, two cloisters, and Sala Capitolare of S Zaccaria, this list can be taken as the authoritative oeuvre of Codussi. There are other works suggested as his, or foisted on him offhand, among them the atrium courtyard of S Giovanni Evangelista, the Barbarigo tomb (already discussed under Rizzo), the Cornaro Chapel in the SS Apostoli, and the

Procuratie Vecchie, to be discussed in the following chapter. Of the churches sometimes proposed, S Andrea della Certosa, S Clemente and S Felice, only the first may be close to Codussi. None of the following palaces is probable: the Contarini a S Beneto, Contarini dalle Figure, Grimani-Marcello-Giustinian, Malipiero-Trevisan, Manzoni-Angaran, Trevisan-Cappello, and the Vendramin a S Fosca. Outside Venice there is only the church at Sedrina, near Bergamo, but the evidence is insufficient to put it on the list of certain or probable works.

IV | AFTER CODUSSI

28 | THE PROCURATIE VECCHIE

After the death of Codussi in 1504 there was no *chef d'école* in Venice (though many had not recognized that there was one while he was still alive). Pietro Lombardo lived on until 1515, busy, but an accepted old master with nothing new to inspire eager men coming into their own. Major commissions went to architects of slightly lesser stature, who built a number of works of admirable quality, less often advanced than gracefully retardataire. The most important were influenced by Codussi in one way or another, and sometimes simultaneously and frictionlessly by the Lombardo shop, often for touches of trimming. Along with their works also appeared an unexpected number of fine Early Renaissance buildings that cannot now be securely attached to any designer. A handful of churches are particularly close to Codussi; most of the private palaces have a notable family resemblance, but more to one another than to their real begetter, Codussi. Perhaps he should be seen, rather, as one of their grandfathers, with Pietro the grandfather on the other side.

Of the men contemporary with Codussi's last years and continuing to work in the decade after his death, the most important is Giorgio Spavento, who died in 1507; his independent works are few, and not even all of them are surely independent. As close to Codussi as to Spavento are the mature and independent commissions carried out by his most important proselyte, Tullio Lombardo, who lived until 1532, keeping on with little change in manner but also, happily, little change in quality. Overlapping them is the hard to catch Giovanni Buora (before 1450–1513), more limited and less Codussian, although he worked side by side with him on several jobs; he may be recognizable only by details such as his refreshingly original capitals or bases. Younger, and sometimes hard to separate from two others of the same name, is the Venetian Bartolomeo Bon or Buon (1463?–1529), who is also difficult to separate from his sometimes collaborators. Last comes Antonio Abbondi, always known as Lo Scarpagnino, unmistakable in style, often delightfully inventive, and exceptionally prolific. The number of his buildings and the many records of them make it possible to assemble his oeuvre.

It is not reasonable to consider these men in the order of the dates of their birth, often no more than approximated, nor to take the individual works in strict chronological order, regardless of authorship, for that would make no sense other than chronological. Some sort of middle way has to be found for the sake of clarity and coherence. But before any development can be worked out with much satisfaction, and stated clearly, it seems essential to make a reconnaissance of one maverick masterpiece, a famous, prominently located, and thoroughly puzzling building, or group of identical buildings, never before studied except for their front—the Procuratie Vecchie.

To begin with, just as an understanding of the Clock Tower calls for an understanding of the neighboring buildings (including the older Procuratie) and the space in front, newly brought into better order by Codussi's location of the foundations of the Tower and the flagpoles, so too does an understanding of the present Procuratie demand similar considerations. These include the destroyed but still easily summoned up XIIc Procuratie and the related buildings opposite (also now lost). It is necessary to examine the whole Piazza as well, looking at its full east-west length rather than just the north-south sweep in front of the Orologio (fig. 28.1). The extraordinary new set of multiple-function buildings cannot be understood without going into the restrictions imposed by their positions, exploring what is known of the conditions under which they were built, and considering what they were built for.

The first churches of S Mark's had had open areas in front, but the developed Piazza S Marco—the only piazza in Venice since all others are *campi*—did not take form until 1173, when the doge, Sebastiano Ziani, doubled the space by buying the *morso* (or "bite") of land that had been the orchard of the nuns of S Zaccaria. According to tradition, a competition to organize the space was won by a Lombard named Nicolò Barattiero, who had raised the giant granite columns at the end of the Piazzetta (Hazlitt, II, 349; E Paoletti, II, 50). He pulled down the fortified wall around it, cleared out the trees and vines, and began paving it with a herringbone of brick in a grid of white stone lines. This was completed only in 1384, and it covered over the Badoer or Batario Canal that had cut across the middle. (Its waters still flow under the Piazza.) The old Church of S Geminiano, legendarily founded by Narses, had to be removed from its site on the canal and rebuilt at the far end of the new paved Piazza, a distant complement to S Mark's until pulled down for good by Napoleon.

It was decided to have covered walks enclose the new Piazza. Sabellico (30, written in 1489–90 while the XIIc Procuratie were still there), and Sansovino (293, written in the 1570s after they had been demolished) both remarked that this walk went all around except in front of S Mark's. The new square was to be edged not only with these but, in combination with them, with houses and shops laid out along neat, straight lines. The property all belonged to the administration of S Mark's, and the shops could be rented profitably—as they would continue to be for centuries. The houses would be assigned by the nine *Procuratori de Supra*, the officials next highest to the doge, the equivalent of a board of directors in charge of S Mark's and its properties, and they would be expected to

28.1 Giacomo Franco. *A
Procession in the Piazza*,
1571. The arcaded building
running from the Campanile
to the lower right corner is
the old Ospizio Orseolo,
opposite the Procuratie
Vecchie (Museo Correr,
Stampe Egbis).

live in these houses assigned to themselves by themselves. At the beginning of the XIVc many of the shops had been extended out into the Piazza by wooden sheds, perhaps not intended to be permanent, but they must have damaged the monumental appearance, and hence the pride of the State, and soon they began to be cleared away. A hospital-hospice of old foundation and a few smaller buildings toed the line on the opposite (south) side, continuing on west from the face of the Campanile.

Thus the largest town square in Europe, and much the most clearly organized, came quickly into being. Few of its contemporaries were anything like as clear in shape nor anywhere near as large unless rebuilt on an antique site, and none was bounded so regularly with more or less matched buildings. No longer clearly defined, the great spaces left by imperial Rome were already half-ruined, the builders of churches and family palaces having stolen hundreds of thousands of conveniently ready-cut stones or ready-made bricks. Furthermore, the squares were not so large. The great court of the Forum of Trajan, the most impressive of Rome, was only 380' long and half in ruins, while the Piazza S Marco was over 800', and beautifully kept. The Circus Maximus was longer, over 1800', but a wreck, and it had never been lined with buildings, being only a racetrack lined with seats. The Piazza Navona was as long as the Piazza S Marco and was contained between straight lines of buildings, but it was meanly narrow, like the racetrack whose form it had inherited, and the surrounding buildings were raggedly uneven in width and height—and there must have been a few missing teeth. Other mediaeval squares might incorporate a market, a town hall, or other civic building with its own colonnade facing the square, but none of any size had a covered walk all around. The

Piazza S Marco was indeed unique, approached by no rivals, not even in Constantinople.

The atria in front of the greater Early Christian churches might be colonnaded, but there were no practical and profitable buildings behind the colonnades. Quite the contrary, they had been designed to shut out the city and its worldly activities—unthinkable in mercantile Venice. Although the forecourt of a church, the Piazza S Marco was probably more like a forum (Lotz 1963, 1966, 1968, passim) than any other spatial form, public and open to all, but different enough in date, use, and form not to allow claim to direct descent. Like many things Venetian, the Piazza had no close parallels, and like the city itself, had developed its particular form from its particular conditions.

The Piazza had a variety of functions. Some were religious, the greatest of which was the Procession of Corpus Domini (since 1150), on the anniversary of the Miracle of Bolsena, combined soon with the ever more gorgeous celebration of the marriage of Venice to the sea, with the doge serving as proxy groom, and with rejoicing for the victory of Lesina. There were markets and fairs and any number of ingenious popular entertainments. Above all, the Piazza was where people gathered at all hours, particularly after horses were barred in the late XIVc (except on special occasions such as bullfights and races).

The first (or XIIc) Procuratie, facing the Piazza on its north side, was* also of a unique form, as is made clear from two reliable and uncontradicting representations made in the 1490s: Jacopo de' Barbari's bird's-eye view and map printed in 1500 (drawn and cut on

*"Were" is more strictly correct for this row of houses and shops, but the ensemble is here being considered as one building, and hence takes a singular verb.

wood blocks during several previous years), and Gentile Bellini's 30′ painting of the *Procession of the Cross in the Piazza S Marco* (Accademia), signed and dated 1496 but drawn and painted during some years before (figs. 28.2 and 28.3). From them it is possible to know the long mediaeval facade both in general aspect and in quite a few details—but nothing at all of the arrangements inside.

The front of the ground story was an arched colonnade of fifty-eight openings with five more along the west end, continuing from the corner (fig. 28.4). The arcade tended to peter out at the east until the Clock Tower and its wings were built. White columns of marble or Istrian limestone carried white capitals of plain Romanesque form—only one shows clearly between the crowded paraders in the Bellini—quite different from the typically Byzantine capitals shown on S Mark's (Arslan 1972, 16). They carry arches that are shown as semicircular by Jacopo de' Barbari, and presumably also in the different perspective recession with which Gentile had to struggle. It is clear that they were not highly stilted (which would have made drawing them in perspective much easier) like the typical contemporaries still visible on the handful of Veneto-Byzantine palaces along the Grand Canal. According to Gentile, the archivolts of the Procuratie were plain bands flush with the wall, edged with a single raised molding, seemingly of red Verona marble. (The picture is blurry just here, from wear and dirt.)

The facade of the piano nobile, above the Piazza arcade, has an extraordinary run of identical round-headed windows, more windows in a row than anything this side of Isfahan. There are two to each arch below, separated only by pipe-thin colonnettes of alternating red and white stone, pretty surely marble, not only because of the color but also because in such proportions and under

the weight of the floors and roof, limestone would be more liable to split or shear. Between the arches of the windows, running up to the molding above, are vertical strips presumably of red Verona marble, awkward to work in between highly stilted Byzantine arches, but neither difficult nor rare between round Romanesque ones. The extreme east end may have been somewhat different, a loggia with arches like the windows, but with its windows set in a bit behind—or this may look different merely because one of the Barbari engravers cut carelessly here. All was topped off with a simple molding in place of a cornice, and crowned showily with a close-set row of plain, flat, picket-sharp merlons, punctuated in back by flaring "Carpaccio" chimneys.

The XIIc Procuratie was, of course, of major importance as a huge and unique mediaeval monument in its own right, and of particular importance here as the model for the beautiful Renaissance Procuratie which would take its place early in the XVIc. The new building has remained to bound the north side of the Piazza up to our day, and is still known as the Procuratie *Vecchie* to distinguish it from the corresponding Procuratie *Nuove* on the opposite side, planned within a generation by Jacopo Sansovino.

The phenomenal early building survived for 350 years, repaired here, rebuilt there, altered from time to time, particularly in the interiors. It had become dangerously weakened by alteration and by age, and the procurators naturally wanted more modern houses, easier to keep in repair and with more space and a few modern improvements; they therefore decided to rebuild. The building had to be long and repetitious of a single small bay (and—unwittingly—like a two-story stoa); this was determined by the length of the Piazza, the need for a maximum number of rentable shops, and the need for identical houses for the procurators, each of whom was as important as any other.

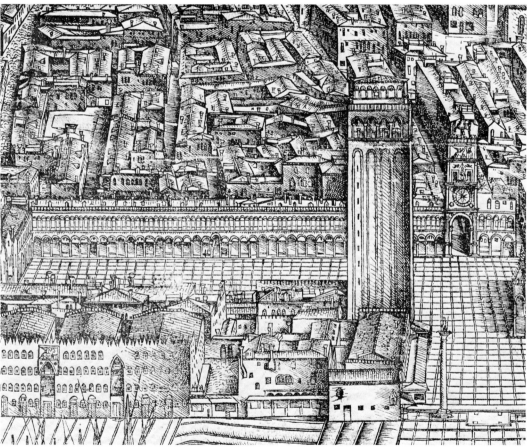

28.2 Gentile Bellini. *Procession of the Cross in the Piazza*, 1496 (Gallerie dell'Accademia, Venice.)

28.3 Procuratie Vecchie, Campanile, and Orologio in 1500 (from the de' Barbari map).

28.4 Gentile Bellini. *Procession of the Cross in the Piazza,* 1496. Detail showing the Procuratie Vecchie.

Tradition must have had extraordinary force, for the front of the new building is a copy of the old one with an extra story added, brought up to date only in details. The dates and the architect or architects are not now surely known.

Like the older one, the new Procuratie had five arches at the west end (soon made six), and fifty identical bays along the north side, running the length of the Piazza up to the wing just put up beside the Clock Tower (fig. 28.5). Instead of columns, stronger square piers of single blocks of Istrian stone carry the arches. Their pedestals are now partly buried under the stone pavement laid over the old brick one (1723 and following), but originally they stood on two continuous steps (v. M. Pagan woodcut, *Procession in the Piazza,* mid-XVIc), a stylobate like those on the newer sides of the Piazza, raising the walkway safely above the level of the pavement in the center, even then liable to occasional flooding (fig. 28.6).

The piers, 15″ square and 8′9″ tall (with approximately the same space between) are paneled with moldingless sinkages. The capitals are equally severe, a fillet, a blank band, and a projecting fascia and quarter-round (fig. 28.7). Square piers were no novelty on the Piazza, for similar ones had been used on the Ospizio Orseolo opposite, as shown by Gentile (fig. 28.8). They had lately begun to have a new vogue, having appeared on the Capitaneria del Porto in 1492, and often in paintings of the 1490s, such as Carpaccio's architecturally precocious S Ursula series. After 1500 they were common, particularly for arcades where pairs of arches could easily be fitted on square tops. The new popularity may have come with the Lombards, brought up among buildings of brick where square supports were more natural than round. For the new Procuratie they were particularly suitable, not only for bearing two arches and the greater weight from the extra story but also from the additional complication and weight of the ribless groin vaults put over the walkway. (The older Procuratie had probably not been vaulted, but simply framed in wood above the walk.)

The arches, too, have the simplest of moldings and, like the piers, are made of big blocks of *pietra d'Istria,* generally only three or four to an arch, unlike normal voussoirs. The whole lower story is designed with exceptional simplicity, not to say severity, and built with conscious emphasis on blocky sturdiness—both actually and expressively, in the consciously precise shape and placing of the few moldings or panelings which communicate that sturdiness vividly. Such a long unvaried repetition of plain forms with minimal modeling—fifty times—could easily become tiresome; only the designer's particular gift made it possible to avoid that threat.

The entablature above has an architrave which seems to be, but is not quite, tangent to the arches just under it, usually a sign of Early Renaissance date. Since it skims them fifty times, it avoids the danger of seeming to teeter, as an architrave does when balanced like a seesaw over only one arch (figs. 28.9 and 28.10). Two of the fascias are sloped, and the middle one has a soft S-curve (like the second architrave at S Zaccaria). None of the moldings is ornamentally carved; consequently parts seem to recall Codussi. Close to him also is the plain wide frieze (but not so wide as to be divisive or out of scale with the piers and arches). The cornice, with its overbusy bed molding and barely jutting corona, is not Codussian at all. Nevertheless, he could have been somewhere behind the original design—he will half appear again and again—but he could not have participated in the execution, for he had been dead for ten years when work was begun—though all those who had worked for him were not. For the last fifty years, since Venturi's first suggestion,

28.5 Procuratie Vecchie.
Forty of its fifty bays.

28.6 Mattia Pagan. *Procession in the Piazza* (woodcut, mid-XVIc). Detail showing steps.

28.7 Procuratie Vecchie. Pier of lowest arcade.

28.8 Gentile Bellini. *Procession of the Cross in the Piazza,* 1496. Detail showing Ospizio Orseolo.

28.11 Procuratie Vecchie.
Fluted column with Corin-
thian capital.

28.9 Procuratie Vecchie.
First entablature (from
Cicognara-Diedo-Selva).

28.10 Procuratie Vecchie.
Archivolt of bottom arcade
and entablature above.

most scholars have believed that a design by Codussi must somehow have been the generator of this facade. Their conviction sometimes stiffens into statement of fact—but still there is no proof.

The next two stories, identical in height (15' ceilings), are also alike in detail, with pairs of arched windows over each arch of the Piazza arcade, separated only by small columns the height of the piers below. These are the first members conceding any carved ornament; they are fluted and have pretty Corinthianesque capitals (figs. 28.11 and 28.12). The two-over-one scheme follows that of the older Procuratie. Nowhere is there anything that shows the divisions of the interior spaces of the houses, the walls separating the front rooms, or even house from house behind the facade; all the partitions are hidden by the fluted columns and the narrow stone strips they abut. Nothing new, then, save in details, and these, despite the fluting and pretty capitals, are severe.

The architraves of the two top entablatures have the most flaring fascias in Venice, a startling exaggeration of the Roman-Istrian-Codussian trick to catch more light and reduce an overhang of the architrave (fig. 28.13).

The architrave at the top of the building is, suitably, larger; and the frieze has been expanded still more, and is wide enough to be pierced repeatedly by 100 round windows, plain and trimless, one above every arched window on the floor underneath. Set low, close to the floor, these bulls'-eyes light service, servants', or storage rooms, only 5' high under the roof in front, but soon more commodious with a 10' ceiling. Cutting holes in the frieze of a classical entablature would be daring for anyone who had read his Vitruvius reverently (an occupation few builders in Venice can have indulged themselves in, for Vitruvius' *Ten Books* are addressed more to humanistic

clients than to professional builders). It was also far less daring in an age of academic innocence such as the Early Renaissance; rows of *oculi* were not rare in Venice, and had won irreproachable prominence by being adopted in the court of the Palazzo Ducale and on its rio facade. They seem perfectly at home here in the 500' frieze. Above this story is another, invisible from below, lit only by skylights probably not original, and usable only for storage.

Above a bolder cornice with blocky brackets—it had to count for the whole front and not just for its top floor—comes the wildly original crowning: stone jars or covered urns set above the bulls'-eyes, alternating with novel merlons (over the spaces between) made of flat pedestals with a slab above, swooping up to a caplike molding topped by a stone ball, 60' above the pavement of the Piazza (fig. 28.14). Fantastic merlons were familiar to the many Venetians who had been in Cairo or Aleppo, and fairly fancy ones were familiar to everyone from the Doges' Palace and the Ca' d'Oro. But nowhere yet had any like these been seen, nor any in such profusion—exotics transmogrified into an approximation of Renaissance forms—and modeled enough (mediaeval merlons were flat) to be able to catch a highlight and make an ever fresh-looking skyline, always allegro giocoso. Beginning with one sober arch on the ground floor, doubled on the two floors above, reduced in scale but kept to the same rhythm by the bulls'-eyes, this crest came as a lighter and speedier termination.

In a strict sense, the building has no front wall, for the friezes and spandrels cannot be added up to make anything like a normal roof-bearing masonry wall. Furthermore, if added together, the openings would make an area over two and nearly three times greater than the fragmentary solid zones. More

Parte di prospetto delle Procuratie Vecchie.

28.12 Procuratie Vecchie.
Elevation (drawing by Vincenzo Fatica, Museo Correr
cl III 7768/1).

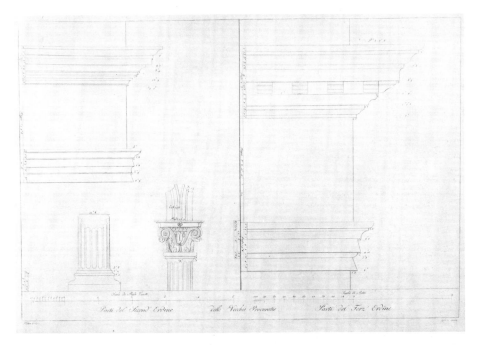

28.13 Procuratie Vecchie.
Details of colonnettes, middle entablature, and top entablature (from Cicognara-
Diedo-Selva).

28.14 Procuratie Vecchie.
Top story.

openness than solidity is usually considered a Gothic trait, for much Northern Gothic shows an aversion to visible blank wall, eliminating it where possible and disguising it where not, whereas the Renaissance commonly dealt with mass, wall, weight, and support as familiar factors in composition. Venice had long opted for openness, since the old palace plan had called for open loggias at the ends of the long center halls even before Gothic tracery was exploited to make them easier to open up. Here the building has to ignore the traditional Venetian palace plan, and substitute instead one seemingly endless loggia. It is quite possible that until Joseph Paxton's Crystal Palace of 1851 for the Exposition in Hyde Park, no such wall-less long facade as this of the Procuratie had been built anywhere.

Rearing such an enormous building, with so many identical parts so often repeated, must have brought a horde of problems. Much of the stone must have been roughed out at the quarries to reduce the quantity that would have to be carried to Venice by boat and finished at the job. There was plenty of room to fence off a workyard in the Piazza, where a crew of masons could perfect the final shape of the forty-eight monolithic square piers and the half-piers for the ends. It must have been necessary to carve 198 fluted columns and 198 capitals, not to mention archivolts, merlons, blocks of entablature and such (in addition, there was that short stretch at the west end). It would have been a noisy stoneyard, really a sort of open-air factory.

Similar semiprefabrication had been carried on for other buildings, but it could never have approached this scale even had there been the need. Few operations could have had the advantage of such space for storing materials and working them into final form. Even the Doges' Palace cannot have enjoyed so organized an operation; it took longer

to build and there was greater variety in the integral parts. Nothing from the XIIc Procuratie could have been used again except the foundations; the same number of new piers were needed as the old ones, and they were to stand where the old ones had stood. But since they would have had to bear more weight—another story and vaults—the old footings would have had to be strengthened, probably by being enlarged around the edges.

A different problem comes with the date of the design of the building, for it cannot be firmly fixed. The procurators' vote to make a bell tower in 1493 meant that two bays of the old Procuratie would have to come down. The tower was structurally complete by the end of 1497, and officially displayed to the doge for the first time early in 1499. Something must already have threatened to undermine the adjacent houses by 1500, and the procurators then voted to replace three bays on each side by new wings, or with something which eventually developed into them. Work began in late 1501 or early 1502, was interrupted for some reason, and finished only in 1506. The old Procuratie had then lost its eight easternmost bays.

In 1509 the Republic of Venice was confronted with the worst threat in her existence (until her extinction by Napoleon), the war with the League of Cambrai. For a year she had to struggle desperately for her life against the massed forces of France, Spain, Austria, and the Papacy—temporarily united by greed—all the leading European powers, except England under Henry VIII. Venice was luckily at peace with the Turks, having signed a treaty with Bajazet in 1503 that held for three decades, thanks largely to Selim I, who did not fight the Christians while he was extending his empire in other directions. Before 1509 was out, Venice had suffered near disaster at the Battle of Agnadello, the worst defeat of her history. The city had been put under interdict by Julius II, always a hater of the republic, though his strictures were not made public and were ignored.

Early in 1510 the interdict was lifted; the pope made a separate peace; Venice had one enemy less. For the next few years there followed an extraordinary series of ups and downs. To bring in more money, now always needed, the sale of civil offices was begun. In an act of vainglory to show that all was as it always had been—which it certainly was not—a particularly grand fair and Festa of the Sensa was put on in 1510. Although a number of family banks were failing, only a few families were affected, and the government only irregularly. Still there was a feeling that the city was close to a dangerous financial edge. In 1513 the Senate voted to create a magistracy of three *Provveditori* to prevent "immoderate and excessive" expenses. Confidence was gradually restored and there was sometimes really good news. At the end of 1513, for instance, negotiations were begun with the emperor; a truce was established; and the Treaty of Blois was signed, relieving Venice of most of the pressure from outside. In 1514 an alliance was contrived with France (already out of the fight) to attack and divide Lombardy.

Meanwhile a fire ravaged one of the houses by the Clock Tower. Antonio Grimani, a procurator later to become doge, persuaded his fellows to have all the others pulled down "so that they could be built new, and beautiful enough to do honor to the state" (Sanudo, XIV, 305; XV, 541; Vio, in Samonà et al., 145). This was daring in 1512 and 1513, but not as rash as the Sensa of 1510, for political maneuvering had already lessened the strains of war and, furthermore, the procurators could almost always win whatever they chose to vote themselves. A model was ordered, and presented to them in 1514 by a mysterious "Tuscan," presumably Giovanni (or Zuanne) Celestro. He may earlier have submitted a project for the Rialto Bridge, or for market buildings, now lost, and had had some brief connection with the Scuola di S Rocco (Vio, 148), but no visible works by him are known. The building was to be done under the main *proto* of the procurators, Bartolomeo Bon the Younger, soon assisted by his young kinsman (?), Guglielmo Grigi d'Alzano. A Tuscan could not be left in charge of an official Venetian building.

These recorded facts do not fit into a steady sequence. When it was known that some of the older Procuratie would have to come down for the Clock Tower, and then more for the wings, might it not have been likely that on one occasion or the other a scheme would have been envisioned for doing over the whole north side of the Piazza? By then those in authority must have realized that the row of old houses was really worn out, and that rebuilding rather than repairing was what was needed. Inasmuch as Codussi was—presumably—designing the tower, it would—presumably—have been Codussi who would have been consulted for the new building so closely related to it, since together they could make one organized design for the whole north side of the Piazza.

But "presumably" is not enough. Codussi had been inexplicably ignored when the wings were put up. Still, the possibility that a scheme for the Procuratie goes back to him has beguiled many of the most respected scholars.* And if not Codussi, then who? That is a slippery question, for we have many buildings with no names attached, and

* Arslan, Fiocco, Hubala, Lorenzetti, Mariacher, the Puppis, Venturi (who first proposed him over 50 years ago, VIII/2, 567–68), and others.

a handful of names with no buildings. Bartolomeo Gonella, of whom nothing useful is known, was *proto* until he was replaced by Bartolomeo Bon in 1505. Bon was in a very favorable position to control work of this sort, and although a considerable amount is known about him, it is of no use here. Giorgio Spavento was also a *proto de Supra* until he died in 1509, after having been ill for a couple of years, but there is no reason to connect him with the Procuratie, and it does not look at all like anything known to be his. Bartolomeo Bon, however, is documented as having worked on it, and in some part it is almost surely his—but who can say what part? Not the main scheme, not the top story, and not enough to fit it in with the rest of his oeuvre; the whole complex is best treated separately here.

What is known of Bon's work before 1514 is not consistent enough to sustain attributions. The bell chamber and peak of S Mark's Campanile, for example, are exceptional because of the special conditions forced on them and the probable requirement that they should reproduce its burned predecessor by Spavento. But for his work on the campanile, Bon had the patronage of Antonio Grimani (Lane 1973, 442; Sanudo, XIV, 20; XXX, 483; Temanza 1778, 105), who was paying for it out of his own pocket, the same Antonio Grimani who had pushed the decision to build the new Procuratie in 1513, where work was begun just as Bon's job on the campanile came to an end. Procurator Grimani was, then, associated with Bon's work twice running.

One question is whether Bon, not only a fellow-Bergamasque but also perhaps an informal pupil of Codussi, could have adapted the design of the older Procuratie, or whether he had access to a putative scheme of his putative master's. The second idea has nothing against it except the model accepted from Celestro in 1514, and as

nothing is known of Celestro's style—even if he had one—he cannot be used for or against the hypothesis. He need not have been concerned with the design of the facade. Since work was about to begin, a model would have to show more of the project than just the front; the procurators would surely have wanted to know in what kind of houses they were going to live and they would have made their criticisms heard. Celestro's model could have been mainly for the planning of the houses, and the Piazza front could have been left to Bon, as reported by Sansovino ca. 1580 and many times repeated.* Everything would be clearer if only Sanudo, on the spot from beginning to end, had named someone—Codussi, Celestro, Bon, or an unknown—but Sanudo was not interested in architects. (The only ones he bothered to name were Spavento, three times, and Pietro, once.)

Discussion so far has been of the facade only, but the Procuratie has more to it than that; there is an unprecedented, complex plan worked out to cope with conditions so abnormal that nothing from the stock Venetian *sala* with smaller rooms in the wings could be used. There are no *salas* and no wings, and the plan is not recognizably Venetian. The Procuratie of the XIIc had been built before the wing-loggia-wing *parti* had matured, and its scheme can be more easily related to the Veneto-Byzantine palaces contemporary with the Procuratie, such as the Farsetti and Loredan. The XVIc Procuratie inherited the XIIc scheme—but without inheriting Venetian palace planning.

The row of uniform shops left no spaces between that could be used as reasonably wide entrances to the houses—one might say palaces—above

*Sansovino, 363; also Cadorin, Lorenzetti, Molmenti, Moschini, Mutinelli, E Paoletti, P Paoletti, Selvatico, Temanza, Zanotto, and others.

the shops, entrances suitable to the exalted rank of the occupants. Furthermore, making arrangements for access here could have been a bit more difficult because of the mezzanines tucked in above the shops across their full width (figs. 28.15 and 28.16). Their little windows are still there today, just below the vaults of the walkway, just as shown in Mattia Pagan's mid-XVIc woodcut, *Procession in the Piazza.*

If a full-width bay of a shop were surrendered, the space could become an entryway, with a suitable door on one or both sides opening into a small hall with a stairway to the piano nobile, bypassing the mezzanine. Near the west end two such entries are preserved. Both lead to small courts: the Corte di Ca' Riva, a family which boasted a procurator as early as 1314 and continued to live here for a long time afterwards; and the Corte di Ca' Maruzzi, a family of Greek origin with many foreign connections, even at the court of Catherine the Great, known to be living here only from the XVIIIc on. Halfway back in the building, and now surrounded by rebuilt walls, these two areas may still respect the lines of the original courtyards. They appear much as they are now on Ludovico Ughi's accurate city plan of 1729 (Cassini, 116–19; Schulz 1970, 82–83; fig. 28.17).

In addition to the courts there are three covered passages, *sottoporteghi* or *sottoportici,* running through the building, one the width of a single shop-bay and the other two each taking the space of two bays (fig. 28.18). That nearest the west end, the Sottoportegho del Arco Celeste, led to a space transformed in 1863 from the Corte delle Orsoline (a home for poor old ladies from the Ospizio Orseolo) into a pool for parked gondolas, now called the Bacino Orseolo. Four bays east of this comes another double, the Sottoportego del Cavaletto, ending in a public bridge and a small private one across the Rio

del Cavaletto, which runs behind most of the Procuratie, parallel to its front. The single-width Sottoportego dei Dai and connecting Ponte dei Dai lead to the busy Calle dei Fabbri (shops of craftsmen). These public bridges connected with streets that otherwise would have to have come to a dead end at the canal, unable to debouch into the Piazza. Neighborhood traffic would have been clogged here. All in the west half of the Procuratie, these passages could also have afforded appropriate land entrances to four four-bay houses and to one of two bays, and possibly to another of four. To make these land doorways practicable, seven bays had to be surrendered from the revenue-producing shops.

Most of the plots for the houses had to end at the Rio del Cavaletto, from which, of course, there could be only water entrances. (A few may survive in the four simple, low, arched doorways still there, though their appearance today is modest and not wholly convincing.) The procurators, despite their rank, could not go everywhere by gondola, and would repeatedly have had to go and come on foot to their most important appointments at the palace and at S Mark's. Somewhere there must have been good land access for all their houses. Four or five land entrances may have been accounted for by the entries or passages just described, but the eastern half of the Procuratie must have been made up of four or five more houses, and there are no signs of more such passages or courtyards for them. The arrangement that seems to make entrances possible for what survives of the east half is strange, but nonetheless it seems the only one feasible.

For the east half of the building, a dark chasmlike street, the Calle del Cappello Nero, barely 9' wide (like the single-bay Sottoportegho dei Dai) runs between the back of the shops and a narrow block of building along the Rio del Cavaletto. On the side toward the Piazza there would have been service

28.15 Procuratie Vecchie. Present walk behind the arcades, looking east.

28.16 Matteo Pagan. *Procession in the Piazza* (woodcut, mid-XVIc). Detail showing windows above walks.

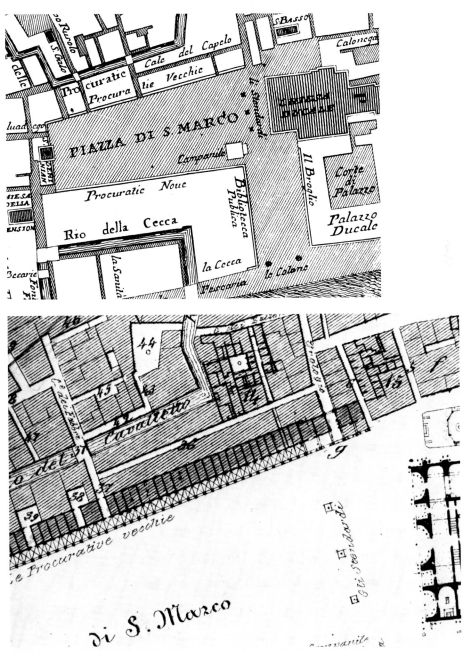

28.17 Procuratie Vecchie.
Plan of the west half (from
the Ughi map of 1729).

28.18 Procuratie Vecchie.
Plan, showing the two long
buildings and the street
(from Combatti map of
1847).

entrances for the shops, much as they are today. On the other side of the street, toward the rio, five or six monumental doorways survive—not grand, but still respectable; these could have been the main land entrances to the easternmost houses of the procurators. The stairways were (and two or three still are) close by the doors, and lead immediately up to the level of the piano nobile, and then on up but, of course, to the rooms in the back row of buildings and not to the grander rooms facing the Piazza. (There are now, and perhaps always were, a few subordinate service stairs here, and others on the other side, leading up to the mezzanines, some of which went on up to the more stately rooms on the main floor.)

This street is still crossed by several bridges of two, three, or more stories and, except for the narrow service stairs, these would have been the only access to most of the best rooms on the fronts of the houses facing the Piazza, since ample stairways were restricted to this back block. The houses were, then, wasp-waisted between the front and back rooms (fig. 28.19). The front and back sections of the building had of course to be roofed separately, each with its long east-west ridge running from end to end. In bad weather an elaborate system of gutters and downspouts kept the velvet-robed procurators from being drenched.

Nowhere else in Venice is there a similar complex of house-street-stairs-bridge-house, but nowhere else were there similar conditions, and hence nowhere else any reason to try such arrangements, both deviant and devious. The result, combined with the different scheme at the west end engendered by other conditions, makes the long body of the Procuratie into a sort of gigantic architectural chimera, assembled out of parts from different species, a fundamental peculiarity now half-obscured by endless later chopping and piecing for many different purposes, mostly

requiring spaces smaller than those of the procurators' grand houses. The old chimera had been covered with a fussy big patchwork, tucked in behind the still beautiful curtain of the facade.

All things considered, one or both halves of this scheme might have been devised by Celestro, a non-Venetian who may have worked earlier on functionally and mechanically troublesome problems at the Rialto Bridge. His solution to the planning problems of the Procuratie could have been what was accepted from the 1514 model. (Although Spavento, too, had practical engineering and planning skills, he was not named in connection with this project, which probably did not reach the planning stage before he died in 1509.) Bartolomeo Bon could have designed the Piazza facade independently, repeating—no doubt on orders—the XIIc scheme, affected or not by any modifications conceived by Codussi. This is an essentially multiple hypothesis, fitted to the few firmly graspable facts, and a few less firm, filled in with imagined possibilities, and ending with as much filling as solid matter. Convenient and engaging as they are to concoct, such hypotheses cannot always be made to coagulate into facts.

Bartolomeo Bon's name is often linked in this work with that of Guglielmo Grigi, also known as il Bergamasco, a younger countryman and a relative (b. ca.1480), who had appeared in Venice around 1515 and was recorded as working on the Procuratie in 1517, probably as little more than an assistant to Bon, already in his late 60s. Sometimes Grigi was mentioned with a Master Rocco of Padua, shadowy here and surely a subordinate. Bon was fully in charge, and had the right to dismiss him out of hand. The whole design shows variety—such as the unexpected little fluted columns and the wonderfully extravagant oscillating skyline—

28.19 Procuratie Vecchie.
Roofs of Piazza buildings
with the Corte Riva and the
Corte Maruzzi at the left,
and at the right two bridges
to the canal building.

but not enough to allow unhesitating conjectures as to what was first imagined by whom, whether Codussi, Bon, or Grigi. The only part Grigi, a sculptor and later a decorative architect, might have had any determining hand in would have to be the fanciful merlons.

Another problem, related and equally clouded, is why the wings of the tower were built with lintels in place of arches for the bottom story, uncomfortably long stone lintels that later had to be helped by adding columns under each end to shorten the span. Each pair of these new trabeated openings replaced three arches of the XIIc building, rather jerkily shifting span, height, and type of structure. The design of the wings was engendered by the tower, in indifference to the design of the early Procuratie abutting. The new Procuratie ignored it.

When the new Procuratie was put up, there was a rejection of the scheme of the wings, back to the measure and form of the older Procuratie. The front of the new building was calculated for piers standing where the old columns had been. Something became discordant between the wing and the row of houses; something signals a change of ideas. Did the two families of procurators living in the new wing houses find them unsatisfactory? Or were they already seen as discordant by some of the procurators who would, from the concern with public building entailed in their jobs, have judged such a condition with more critical eyes than those of other officeholders? Or did influential Antonio Grimani look askance at the wings and persuade the rest of the voters that the new houses should copy the old ones (conveniently enlarged), and perhaps persuade them that the commission should go to his putative protégé, Bartolomeo Bon?

For the history of the building—to sum up and repeat—all that can be said with certainty or strong probability is that the facade of the XIIc Procuratie

was replaced by an updated copy, begun in 1513 by Bartolomeo Bon, who either had some project of Codussi at hand or was himself so Codussian that some have taken his echoing of his master for the master's own work. The top story, not there in the earlier building, and the fantastic attic and cresting were largely the creation of Guglielmo Grigi il Bergamasco, a relative of Bon's working under his direction. The novel plan of the houses above the shops and in the blocks along the back may have come from a model presented by Giovanni Celestro in 1514.

The oldest picture of the "new" Procuratie Vecchie with its three stories is in a large woodcut (12" × 17") made by Giovanni Andrea Vavassore, also called Vadagnino, ca. 1525–30 (Cassini, 35–37; Schulz 1970, 42) (fig. 28.20). Once it was completed, the spectacular ensemble of Piazza and Piazzetta was, inevitably, appraised by many writing travelers. One of the earliest, William Thomas (1549), found it "fair and large, and the one side is built of hard stone [was the Ospizio stuccoed brick?] all uniformly with fair glazen windows" (66). They must still have been a novelty to him or he would not have singled them out. Fynes Moryson (I, 185) saw it filled with people (1594) and noted with hardheaded admiration the four big markets held there every week, without commenting on the scale of the Piazza or the extraordinariness of its buildings.

Architecturally the most observant of the XVIIc commentators, Thomas Coryat (1608) (216–17) was so impressed that he wrote several pages. He found it

. . . beyond all comparison the fairest of all Europe, for it hath two magnificent fronts or rowes of buildings . . . especially that on the North, that they drove me into great admiration, and so I thinke they doe all other strangers . . .

adorned with open galleries for the people to walke in, having a great multitude of faire pillars at the sides . . . built with very goodly faire white stone, or rather (as I take it) Istrian Marble, two stories high above the vaulted walke, having two faire rows of windows in it . . . the North side that for many yeares since was fully finished, hath . . . betwixt each window a pretty little piller of Istrian Marble. The pillers of the North walke are . . . square, being made of Istrian Marble . . . the walke in length is two hundred paces and fifteen in breadth. This North side doth make a singular faire show, and exceedingly grace Saint Marks place, and by so much the more beautiful it is, and by how much the more uniformity of workmanship it presenteth. For such is the symmetrie and due proportion of building . . . no part of the whole fabricke differing a lot from the other. The like uniformitie of building I observed in our Ladies street of Paris, but in a different manner and much inferior unto this.

Edward Gibbon (cited in Honour 1966, 19) felt differently in 1765: "a large square decorated with the worst architecture I ever yet saw" (directed mainly, perhaps, at S Mark's). But only two generations later, in 1834, romantic William Beckford (114) found that its architecture "impresses veneration and completes the pomp of the view." The XIXc was full of praise, much of it fulsome, and even Ruskin held his fire, for he considered the Piazza and its buildings as no more than a spacious setting for the miracle he saw as S Mark's.

Today the facade gives a perverse gratification to anyone taught the essential Beaux-Arts tenet that the only way to handle a long facade is by breaking it up with occasional projections, pavilions, porches, altered bays, or recessions, as for example on the east front of the Louvre or the garden front of Versailles; also by avoiding such improprieties as putting two arches over one, or putting the heavier over the more open, etc., etc. (fig. 28.21). Happily for the Venetians, the Doges' Palace was right there, having

denied it all triumphantly for centuries. Happily also, the very repetitiousness adds to the dramatic surprise of the overscale Campanile, the already lively Orologio and Porta della Carta, and the incredible front of S Mark's. In two ways there is more contrast than coordination with the neighboring buildings: not alone in the drawn-out repetitions but also in the complete absence of color. The chiaroscuro, however, is not like that of S Mark's, but of quite a different character.

The later history is one of piecemeal patching. General interior divisions may survive fragmentarily here or there, but not any sure details. When the Procuratie Nuove across the Piazza was finished in the XVIIc, the houses of the Procuratie Vecchie were sold to various noble families. Some of the procurators, nominally the inhabitants, were already living instead in their larger, more comfortable, and more luxurious family palaces elsewhere, and using their assigned quarters more as offices and reception rooms. Some of the shops were soon sold too, for there were now more rent-producing shops in the new Procuratie across the square. In 1797 the name was changed officially to the Galleria della Libertà, but that soon disappeared.

A major restoration was needed in the mid-XIXc, and the upper floors had to be shored up with wooden beams, while some defective stone piers were replaced and a few arches strengthened by hidden iron bars (Archives, Soprintendenza ai Monumenti, Busta A-9 Palazzi). Except for the facade, most of the west half was rebuilt early in this century, presumably retaining the form of the old courts and passages. More and more families had been selling out to business, and by the 1880s no one was left living in the Piazza. Many, however, can remember the much older husband of a widow still living in the city, who was born in the last family-occupied house a little over a

28.20 Procuratie Vecchie
when new (woodcut ca.
1525–30 by Vavassore).

28.21 Procuratie Vecchie,
looking west.

hundred years ago. The Zeno-Soranzo family had an apartment, rented out to business, which they sold only a generation ago, when the twenty-seven heirs could not agree on how to keep on maintaining it. The last noncommercial occupant was Venice's one fashionable club, the Società Unione, which moved out for larger quarters at smaller rent in 1964–65. Above the shops and cafes the building is now almost wholly occupied by an insurance company, which cares for it well. The Soprintendenza ai Monumenti has battled to protect it from intrusive signs, fancy lights, and other visual distractions for over fifty years, and has always won. Trials for cleaning the whole front were made in 1974–75, but though encouraging, the project was abandoned for the time being. The two bays then cleaned look so fine that hope keeps rising that the full row may one day be as clean and white again as when it was built.

Exceptionally handsome and well scaled iron lampposts for gaslight were set up in the Piazza in 1843, electrified in 1921, and not replaced until 1948, by electric lights in moon-white glass globes under each arch. The four floodlights now hanging high in the corners like four artificial moons, were strung up only about thirty years ago. By daylight, except on rare cold days in the dead of winter, the Piazza is still always full of people, as it has always been, though now the people look and act differently. But then, at any time people look different when in the Piazza, just as the Piazza, except in the very early morning when it may be empty, looks different without people. It is now flooded oftener than it used to be, and the floods have been not only more frequent but also deeper, for the water is higher all over the world and Venice was sinking. But now it is no longer sinking, and the shopkeepers in both Procuratie, who would be the hardest-hit victims, now know better how to avoid damage.

29 | GIORGIO SPAVENTO

The least known of the paramount masters of architecture of the Early Renaissance in Venice is Giorgio Spavento. He used to be thought the only one who was a native Venetian, but now a contract has been found that shows he came from Lake Como (Franzoi-DiStefano, 355; Fiskovic in *Venezia . . . Europe*, 185, claims he was a Dalmatian). Early in his career he was esteemed as a carpenter and mason; later he was held in still higher repute as an engineer and architect. Marin Sanudo, who did not bother with other architects, wrote of him three times (IV, 241; V, 95; VIII, 97) and when he died in 1509 called him "homo di grande inzegno" (intelligence, or levelness of head). They may have been friends.

He is little known because only people concerned with Venetian architecture of the period have more than a glancing knowledge of a couple of his buildings and so little is recorded of his activities, although he must have been busy in his last twenty years, largely on government commissions. Many works have been destroyed; many were left incomplete at his death; and many were done in collaboration with others, most often with Scarpagnino. But still, difficult as it is to entrap them, he stands out as a great figure.

By 1486 he was established enough—no one knows on what grounds—to be made one of the *protos* of the *Procuratori de Supra,* and for them he built the sacristy of S Mark's, the ante-sacristy next to it, and the small Chapel of S Theodore behind the north transept. Before Rizzo was dismissed, Spavento was already employed on the Palazzo, having probably been taken on while Rizzo was coming under suspicion in 1486, perhaps even as a precautionary measure. In 1489 he contrived a model for the bell chamber and a steep pyramidal roof for the Campanile of S Mark's. The design was accepted and construction was begun, but work must have gone slowly, and before it was finished it was so damaged by the earthquake of 1511 that it became dangerous and had to be removed. After Spavento's death, the work had been carried on by Bartolomeo Bon who, after the earthquake, put on the top still there. This is usually believed to follow Spavento's original project, but precisely how well it did so cannot be ascertained.

In 1495 Spavento was called in, as a mason, to make estimates for the Scuola di S Marco, still in budget trouble in the middle of Codussi's activity there. If the two men were not already known to one another, an acquaintance could well have begun then. From 1498, when Rizzo fled, Spavento and Bon were *protos* for the same procurators of S Mark's, either subordinated to Pietro Lombardo or already accepted as equals or near equals. Their work with him cannot be fully disentangled either from his or from each other's, or even from the work of the many others of the crew busy on the endless puzzle of the Palazzo court. In the same year, 1498, Spavento made a project for the market hall at Vicenza (the future Basilica), which was not built. In 1501 he pulled down some of the houses of the older Procuratie, presumably to make room for the wings of the tower. But if he had anything to do with the building of the wings, it cannot have been for their design, for it is in no way like his other work. In 1501 he also presented his model for a new stone Ponte di Rialto, soon rejected because of cost, and in 1502 he strengthened and half-rebuilt the old wooden one. Of all these activities of a dozen busy years, there is nothing left that can be seen and accepted convincingly as the work of Spavento except the small adjuncts to S Mark's.

In 1505 he was involved in the building of the Fondaco dei Tedeschi, but how much of it is his is not determinable. Also in 1505 he was busy with proposals for the Chapel of S Nicolò, adjacent to both S Mark's and the Palazzo. The chapel has been gutted, a characterless empty box, but its side wall, facing the Cortiletto dei Senatori at the left of the Scala dei Giganti, done in collaboration with Scarpagnino, is still well preserved. In 1506, still an engineer, he reinforced the log-gravel-and-earth dike at Malamocco. In 1507–08, still expert as a master carpenter(?), he did some work in the Palazzo, possibly ornamental woodwork but more probably construction in wood for floor beams or trusses. Along with these he was involved with construction or design at SS Filippo e Giacomo (behind S Mark's), and later with S Nicolò di Castello, both now destroyed. In 1507 he began his great masterpiece, S Salvatore, perfected the plans and saw the first stone laid, but, since he died in 1509, he did not see it built, and the work had to be erected, following his plans, by another—happily, in this case, Tullio Lombardo.

A consistent Spavento style is not easy to define, but study of what is surely his, subtracting the more easily identifiable Scarpagnino from the joint oeuvre, may make it possible to uncover an innovative and powerful designer, blessed also with simplicity and grace, in many ways the heir of many of the forms and more of the ideals of Mauro Codussi. Like Codussi, he had not been trained as a sculptor, as had most of their contemporaries, but trained in crafts closer to architecture: as a mason, a carpenter, and some sort of engineer. In consequence, he relied on architectural fundamentals and showed that reliance, excluding almost all carved ornament.

The sacristy of S Mark's (1486–91), his first work as *proto* there, shows none of the qualities that will distinguish him later (fig. 29.1). Possibly Codussi, among others, was somehow associated with the work here (P Paoletti Fr. Ed.

29.1 Sacristy of S Mark's.
Interior.

29.2 Sacristy of S Mark's
and Chapel of S Teodoro
(upper left on plan).

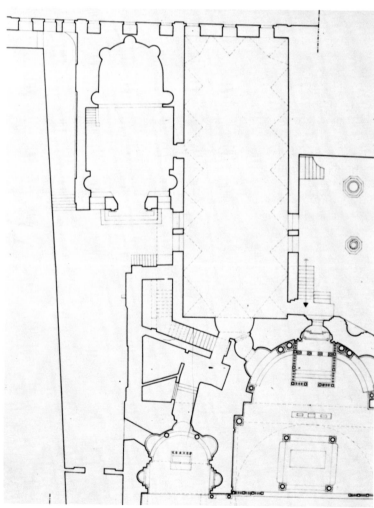

II, 265). It is no more than a typical big plain rectangular Quattrocento room with a coved ceiling with penetrations, perhaps looking a bit Florentine, with the walls sheathed in marble plaques and the vault with early XVIc mosaics, now confused by XIXc restorations. Were it not by a master later to become illustrious, it would usually and justifiably be left out of accounts of Early Renaissance architecture.

Beginning in the same year, 1486, Spavento designed (and a Master Domenico began to build) the small Chapel or Oratorio of S Teodoro, fitted in behind S Mark's as an offhand propitiation of the original patron of the city, ousted for the Apostle S Mark (figs. 29.2 and 29.3). This, too, has the simplest of rectangles for a plan—at least on the outside. The plain pedimented front is preserved, with an *oculus* and a more elaborately pedimented doorway taken from the demolished church of S Maria Nova, flanked by tall, plain, round-headed windows of a standard early type (cf. Codussi and Brunelleschi). The design is not notable for itself.

Handily adjacent to the sacristy, the inside has been adapted as a "sacristy of the canons." The space is now an unusual compound, having a short front bay just inside the door, with a deep niche in each of its side walls, making it rather monumental in spite of its small size. Sometimes called an ante-sacristy, it can rarely have been used as an entrance since it is not on any important route from anywhere to anywhere. It leads into a large, plain, groin-vaulted square, and then, unprepared-for, to a stilted semicircle pierced by five low semicircular niches in a curvilinear complex much like the apses of S Mark's (fig. 29.4). Nowhere is there any carved detail or other ornament. Clearly the result of an enthusiastic recent going-over, does it now repeat its Renaissance forms exactly? Originally frescoed, the interior, perhaps simpler then, was used as a meeting hall for the Inquisition.

Nothing in either of these reveals individuality or interest except their continuous rear elevations: a wall flush with the back of the Doges' Palace on the Rio della Canonica (fig. 29.5). Palace and church are interlayered here, since the domestic quarters of the doges are on top of these minor church adjuncts, and some of the service parts of the palace are under them, back of the crypt of S Mark's. These service necessities, kitchens, storerooms, and such, are of course accessible from inside, but also for deliveries from outside, through two low-arched *cavanas*. The bottom and some of the middle of the wall must be refacing of work already put up in the rough by Rizzo, under Doge Giovanni Mocenigo (1475–85), whose arms appear on a pilaster at the south end, where the palace proper begins. But inasmuch as the wall surfaces along the water agree fully with what Spavento put above them, and not at all with Rizzo's pugnacious rustication south of the pilaster, the top and bottom of this north stretch must all have been carried out in a single operation. And inasmuch as Spavento was responsible for the inside, sacristy and chapel, dependent on S Mark's and not on the palace, he would have been the designer of their outside facing. They must have been built concurrently, between the late 1480s and the early 1490s.

It is not their date that is their main interest, however, but their design, more severe than anything else in the Palazzo–S Marco complex, more severe than any important work yet built in Early Renaissance Venice. The entire surface, water to cornice, is divided into plain panels, regular—and orderly—yet still managing to respond to the irregular interior divisions. Windows come where the interiors demand, and floor heights fix the horizontal divisions. The same conditions that wrought havoc with the upper part

29.3 Chapel of S Teodoro.

29.4 Chapel of S Teodoro.
East end, with niche and
window on the Rio della
Canonica.

29.5 Rio facade of adjuncts
of S Mark's and Doges'
Palace.

29.6 Rio facade of adjuncts
of S Mark's and Doges' Palace. Detail.

of the courtyard appear to have become serendipitous. One reason is that a master has taken them as one of the controlling necessities of design, rather than trying to hide or disguise them with distracting trimming; another is that the area has less disorder, with uniform floor levels and less resistant window-spacing. The architect was stronger, the problem weaker.

Above an unornamented set of socle moldings, the panels and windows of the bottom story, for the most part in alternation, are approximately square. Everywhere else the windows are of a standard, tall, round-headed shape, fitted precisely between vertical oblong panels. The next zone, corresponding to the vaults of the service basements and the lower parts of the walls of the sacristies, is a row of plain panels; the windows of the sacristies, out of which no one would be expected to look, are set well above the floors here. The arched windows are set on axis with those of the basement except at the ends, where the *cavanas* temporarily vary the rhythm. These windows are coerced into working together by submitting to an all-over rhythm, powerful but not metronomically regular. For example, at the north end, the openings giving into the irregular leftover court beside S Teodoro, are close together, arrested at the outer edge by a pier equivalent to two pilasters, one lightly projected from the level of the wall, and both paneled; the next division is a similar panel, but narrower, and the last two windows have no panel at all. As these lead to an unimportant court, and are of no consequence on their inner side, they could have been arranged differently; the close arrangement must have been a free choice, a way of varying the rhythm and bringing the long composition to a well-defined end. The two with no panel between together correspond to the width of the *cavana* opening below.

Similar pilaster-like piers, lightly projected (but a little projection here counts for a lot), correspond to the walls inside and make a variation in the rhythmical beat, at once weaker because they are only half as wide as the other bays, but contradictorily stronger at the same time because they project (fig. 29.6). The windows come in groups of three—for the court, for the sacristy of the canons, for the sacristy proper—each a little differently spaced, two sets alternating with panels, those of the court set closer together. At the south end, another pilaster-like pier brings this section to a stop (before Rizzo's decorated wall begins), though it cannot run all the way down to the bottom because it is cut off by the arch of the *cavana*, an opening not quite assimilated, and perhaps unadjustably in place before Spavento's work began.

The north bays stop with a plain entablature—no trimming, no carved moldings—while the rest goes on up for two more stories; through a zone all of panels, then one with similar but lower windows, then another of even lower panels, and finally one of windows lower still (fig 29.7). These layers repeat the spacing below. At the top of everything runs a cornice with plain brackets, spaced widely and a bit irregularly to accord with the windows, panels, and projecting piers in one final Stravinskian rhythmical sequence derived from everything below but expressed with new forms (fig. 29.8). (This cornice may have been made after the death of Spavento, presumably following his intentions.)

Everything is carried out with a limited number of classical moldings, no carved ornament, nothing but plain panels, plain windows all of the same width except the odd trio at the north end, a few horizontals (stringcourses or entablatures). The only variety comes from the differences in height, the subordinated variations in spacing, but all

29.7 Rio facade of S Mark's
and Doges' Palace. Bottom
half.

29.8 Rio facade of S Mark's
and Doges' Palace. Top half.

follow a triple rhythmical figure of three figures of three. Further minor variations are slipped in by the succession of horizontals: from bold socle to modest stringcourse or supersill, to entablature, to bolder cornice and then to the crowning cornice with brackets. A sense of sequence suggests all-over control. Facing east on a wide canal made wider by the *fondamenta* (quay) opposite, the Istrian stone is swept by sun, wind, and rain often enough to stay a strong white, and the discreet modeling, without unplanned black blotches, makes its full effect. The slight sinkage of the panels and the slight protuberance of the piers and horizontal moldings all count double or triple because they have no competition. Nowhere yet in the Venetian Renaissance had more been done with less.

All this is, of course, very different from Rizzo's work nearby, on the back of the palace proper, and the two are separated visually only by a slightly more prominent pier. Happily, Rizzo's design, unaccustomedly plain here, comes with no jarring collision against Spavento's, surely begun after Rizzo's walls were well along. Perhaps this real but hardly remarked harmonization should be added to the more obvious difficulties in spacing and such, added as one of the near obstacles so triumphantly dominated by Spavento's severe mastery.

Always kept busy on work related to S Mark's and the palace, since he was one of the *protomaestri*, Spavento was engaged in 1505–06 in demolishing the crumbling old chapel or oratorio of the doges, S Nicolò, beside the south apse of S Mark's and adjacent to the Chapel of S Clemente. For Doge Leonardo Loredan (1501–21), who favored him more than once, he rebuilt the old chapel in a new way, coordinating the south side facade—the only one that showed—with Rizzo's arcades on the ground floor of the courtyard by building five more arches at right angles to

Rizzo's; thus he made a new little court, the Cortiletto dei Senatori, just north of the Scala dei Giganti. Most of the design of this little facade was done by his sometime associate, Scarpagnino, and was built later; but Spavento probably organized the interpolation of the new chapel into the irregular older parts of S Mark's, raising it up to the level of the main floor of the palace, handy to the ducal apartments and easy for the doge to slip into for a quiet meditation. Again a plain rectangular room, it soon became famous for its frescoes by young Titian, not for its architecture; yet these were surprisingly soon destroyed in some sort of alterations in 1523. The space, now gutted, is used as a workshop for the mosaicists endlessly busy keeping the precious surfaces of S Mark's in order.

Aside from Scarpagnino's deservedly famous little facade on the Cortiletto, the most interesting surviving part of S Nicolò is the roof terrace, once admired with astonishment as a hanging garden, but now used only occasionally, as part of a bar when the adjacent apartments are opened as galleries for special exhibitions. A chapel half-supported on an arcaded corridor and on its roof supporting a garden (with its necessary layer of earth) shows both the originality and structural skill of the builder. Furthermore, it is still possible to see how very pleasant a private retreat it must once have been, backed up by the tawny brick curves of the walls of S Mark's on one side, and open wide to the grandiose vista of the entire courtyard on the other, while set far enough above it to remain private and quiet.

After the Doges' Palace, the building looming largest on the Grand Canal is the former Fondaco dei Tedeschi, with its 200 rooms, once the joint warehouse and hostel of the German merchants, now the General Post Office.

For a century and a half something more than its un-Venetian bulk attracted notice, for its walls were brilliant with frescoes composed in a daring new kind of decoration created by two rising young geniuses: Giorgione, barely thirty, and Titian, not yet twenty.

Fondaco or *fondego* is the Venetian version of an Arabic word, *fonduq*, denoting an inn for travelers, a warehouse for merchants (especially Europeans), or the place where their business deals were worked out, something like the Steelyard in London or the Counter in Novgorod, and presumably even more like the compounds of the Venetian traders in Aleppo, Alexandria, or Cairo. The establishment in Venice, in operation as early as 1228, was the trade depot and market for northern copper and silver, Flemish woolen cloth, and other manufactured specialties. Here deals were made for locally manufactured Venetian exports or Venetian-imported spices, sugar, silk, and cotton from the East. It even housed its own customs office. Regulations allowed the German merchants to trade only with Venetians, never with other foreigners. There were rooms for them to stay in, men only, and sometimes other visiting Germans were put up as in a club (Dürer, for example). There were two refectories (one for summer, one for winter), a number of meeting rooms, and everything needed for an encapsulated colony of foreigners. It was at once like a monastery, a business community, and a complete village, and it was early (1587) called "a little city in the middle of ours" (Bardi, 72).

The old Fondaco, a jumble of buildings on the same site at the end of the Rialto Bridge (v. Barbari map), handy to the banking center at the other end, burned to the ground in January 1505. The next day the Senate voted to rebuild it at the city's expense, and bought adjacent land to make possible a building larger and more important in almost every practical way, because

trade with the North was so vital to the prosperity of the city. Trade was more important than possession of colonies. Though the Fondaco was city property, it was for the exclusive use of the Germans, who were to be made comfortable and kept happy. An extra benefit came from the rental of shops worked into the building complex. (The city was landlord of scores of shops, as at the Procuratie.) The good functioning of the Fondaco was held so important to Venice's well-being that it was kept operating throughout the War of Cambrai.

Nowhere is the identity of the architect made unmistakably clear, for in the only early sources different men are named. The claim for the theorist-humanist-mathematician-engineer Fra Giocondo of Verona and Rome (in Venice 1505–06 and again in 1510) is one of the weakest, depending only on a passing reference in a Latin panegyric by Pietro Contarini on the triumphant return to Venice in 1517 of Captain Andrea Gritti (later doge), "Teutonicum mirare forum spectabile fama / Nuper Jocundi nobile Fratris opus" (cited by Selvatico-Lazari, 92). This claim for authorship is not supported by other texts nor by any buildings given to Fra Giocondo, whose participation in building real buildings is in any case suspect (Brenzoni 1960, passim). Here he might have offered advice—he was employed by the city for advice on the rebuilding of the old Rialto Bridge, none of which was followed—but there is no clue for any help from him.

Tommaso Temanza (1778, 90), who wrote later and studied more documents, thought that the Senate had commissioned Pietro Lombardo. This idea, thanks to Temanza's prestige, was long accepted and repeated, though it comes from no traceable source and is contradicted by the difference between Pietro's known style and the style of the Fondaco building, which had, surprisingly, been ordered built not only "presto" but "bellissimo."

More certain are the scattered bits in official records and diaries of Sanudo—reconcilable, though not without puzzles. What is certain is that models were submitted in 1505, two by Spavento and one by "Gerolamo Tedesco," a German otherwise unknown, who as an architect has since evaporated. His scheme was preferred over either of Spavento's "for its noble and ingenious composition" (Moschini 1819, 181nl; Sanudo, VI, 120; Tassini 1886, 256). Gerolamo the German may have had a role equivalent to that proposed for Celestro the Tuscan in the Procuratie—in other words, he may have devised a general disposition of spaces. The Germans, politely consulted, naturally preferred their compatriot. As a foreigner he had to be associated with a Venetian or, rather, subordinated to one, and the Venetian chosen was Spavento, *proto* of the powerful procurators. Too busy to devote himself only to this big new project, he chose a surrogate supervisor, Scarpagnino, for whom he demanded and got double the usual pay (Brunetti-D-G, 62). This is the first record of Scarpagnino anywhere, and implies that he was recently arrived in Venice, was fairly young (he kept on working there for forty-four more years), and was launched by Spavento.

The Senate voted that the German's design should be followed because it was plain and was cheaper, though some saw little difference in probable cost (fig. 29.9). First it was specified that no changes should be made from the model—a stipulation certainly not respected—and second that no marble be used, no useless ornaments, no window tracery—a stricture that was accepted. The result is a building of downright matter-of-factness with nothing recognizably German, nor close to many Italian and to fewer

Venetian works of the time; still it is easier to see as related to Spavento than to the nebulous Gerolamo (Hitchcock, passim, makes the best case for him). More sympathetic than any Italian to the German merchants, Gerolamo (or Hieronymus) would have been well placed to work out a practical program, with the handiest disposition of rooms, their sizes and juxtapositions. Spavento, alone among his Venetian contemporaries, would not have suffered under the stringencies imposed by the Senate, and he could have found material form to embody Gerolamo's practical ideas in a harmonious whole. The references to the German's "noble and ingenious composition" are easier to accept as praise for a practical plan than for any nobility in architectural design. That, however, would not be hard to accept as Spavento's contribution—if nobility is to be found there. In any case, Spavento must fairly quickly have been put in charge.

The building is still in sound condition, though its most famous and colorful adjunct has been lost. The front on the Grand Canal is now bare and stylistically severe for Venice, but still in a sort of reduced rhythmical continuity with the many old fronts on the canal (fig 29.10). Side pavilions establish its three parts, with a wide middle loggia on the ground floor. (In most of North Italy there was a strong tradition for giving public buildings of several sorts a loggia on the ground floor.) These wings protrude from the center only 3", so little that it looks more like a defect in the alignment of the wall than a planned separation of major elements. The loggia has five arches 20' high for a landing stage for freight, and only incidentally a water entrance for the merchants, who would not be going about socially in their gondolas like their Venetian opposite numbers. Its scale is nonetheless able to make it hold its own with the porticoes of many of the grand private palaces

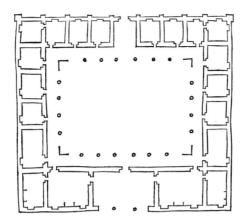

29.9 Fra Giocondo. Plan of
the Fondaco de Tedeschi.

29.10 Fondaco dei Tedeschi.
Air view.

nearby—but only in its scale, for, like the rest of the building, the arches are relentlessly plain. The square piers, early examples soon to affect important public buildings across the canal, have minimal bases and capitals between which the corners of the shafts are chamfered, not as a stylistic device but as a practical precaution against the threat of chipping from the goods continually being carried in and out.

Above a storage floor and a mezzanine, the wings are marked by 32' balconies, among the first really long ones in the city (figs. 29.11 and 29.12). They are fenced with old-fashioned colonnettes unpunctuated by piers. The refectories behind were fine rooms 20' high (the one for winter heated by a much admired iron stove from Antwerp). The floor-line of the balconies runs on across the front of the building as a stringcourse, and above it a 20' band of wall rises to an oversharp cornice which also acts as a sill for the windows of the next story. Pairs of arched windows for the piano nobile, juxtaposed but not touching, stand on single sills floating above the stringcourse. They are set oddly in syncopation with the rest, the postlike divider of each pair in the main block set over each support of the arcade below, leaving 7' of solid wall perversely over the void of each lower arch. This also makes for odd spacing in the wings, with a single window at each edge and a pair in the middle. The single window at the end of the center section joins the inner one of the wing to make a somewhat dislocated pair, with one window 3" in advance of the other and farther from it than in the other pairs.

Rising above this come two more floors of paired windows, plain and square-headed, the last a form unfamiliar still in monumental buildings on the Grand Canal. These on the Fondaco continue the axes of those below, respecting their eccentricities.

At the very top, the wings underwent an alteration, as though cut straight down the middle. The outer half continued on above the cornice, taking one of the middle pair of windows up with it along with one from the end. Thus the once familiar (but not as familiar as often claimed) *torreselle*, or corner towers, were formed (fig. 29.13). The inner half of the wing and the whole center section stop normally under the cornice. Between the low little towers ran a line of merlons, anti-functionally pierced by circles and ornamentally topped by stone balls (fig. 29.14). They are the immediate forebears of those of the Procuratie Vecchie, which, except for the hole and the alternation with pots, are like enough to be copies. A staccato row of tall "Carpaccio" chimneys used to rise behind them, with spark-trapping tops shaped like flowerpots upside down (fig. 29.15). Such a lively skyline may have been encouraged as a mitigation for the flatness that must already have been apparent on the clifflike front below. The towers were taken down in 1836, for no known reason, and more merlons strung along in their place; all are now accurate copies. Despite their fresh form, they are the only important mediaevalism persisting on the facade.

The other sides of the freestanding block, almost square, were much the same, but with no loggia and little of the balconies, towers, and merlons, only under the sides of the towers around the corner. One side of the building faced a small canal. The back faced a brick-paved street soon to be cobbled with *selci*, whence the Venetian term *salizzada* for a cobbled street (fig. 29.16). The righthand side was also on a 12' street, leading to the Rialto Bridge; opposite an intersecting street was the only doorway to the building except for the water entrance. (Another has lately been added in back.) This is a typical XVIc decorative work, far from the half-hypothetical spare style

29.11 Fondaco dei Tedeschi. Grand Canal facade.

29.12 Fondaco dei Tedeschi. Lower part of Grand Canal front showing old-fashioned colonnette balconies and unusual window spacing in relation to entrance arcade.

29.13 Fondaco dei Tedeschi. Main front as it was before 1836 (drawing by Vincenzo Fatica, Museo Correr cl III 7773/1).

29.14 Fondaco dei Tedeschi. Cresting.

29.15 Fondaco dei Tedeschi
with towers (painting by
Canaletto, Wallace Collection, London).

29.16 Fondaco dei Tedeschi.
Facade on the Salizzada del
Fondaco.

of Spavento or the unimaginable one of Gerolamo the German, but characteristic enough of Scarpagnino. With the only columns and decorative carving on the building, it seems like something brought from elsewhere.

Nineteen shops of approximately uniform size fronted on the streets, open only there, with no communication with the Germans and their carefully fostered businesses on the other side of their common back wall. A pair of special tiny shops flanked the doorway—excellent location, cramped space. Three huge monolithic square piers framed each shop window and the doorway beside it, and huge stone lintels carried the combined weight of the roof and walls and floors and whatever was on them above the ground floor. Despite the scale of the whole and of so many of its parts, such as these massive pieces of limestone, the effect was in no way monumental.

The interior of the Fondaco is unique, dominated by a square court of four tiers of plain arches, five to a side on the ground floor and ten to a side on the floors above, enclosing an impressive volume, 65' by 75', which seems almost substantial because so clearly defined, so measured out by the repetitious arches (fig. 29.17). Except for cloisters, only the Doges' Palace had a larger court, and this looks rather more like a cloister, suitable for the life of almost cloistral restrictions imposed on the merchants. The only ornaments, apart from the obsessively minimal bases, capitals, and archivolts, were a big wall clock put up in 1571, and a stone wellhead with a striking, tall, stone canopy, originally placed near the back street-side, enlivening the unyielding regularity of the whole by its form and its asymmetrical position (fig. 29.18). The position was necessary, for the canopy contained a pulley or pulleys making it possible to draw water directly to the piano nobile where the

refectories were (Brunelli-D-G, 26, 65). The canopy was demolished some time after Napoleon's alterations in 1806, and the wellhead was arbitrarily and unimaginatively moved to the center in the wilful restorations of the 1930s, typical of Mussolini's official pseudo-neoclassicism. Once many people thought this well offered the best water to be found in the city.

Two stairways led upward from the cloisterlike walk around the court, neither of them on a center axis, neither one coordinated with any of the five ground floor arches, but both still managing to fit between the corbels on the walls opposite the piers, supporting their part of the unribbed groin vaults of the corridor around the court. The edge of the vaults does not quite coincide with the open arches, and a sickle of wall is squeezed between them. In these minor instances something suggests last-minute improvisation. The absence of ornament, the clarity and purity of everything else, do not conceal the awkwardnesses here. The mixture of a grand austerity of the whole with minor carelessness in the parts makes it impossible to assess who was responsible for what. Experienced Spavento cannot have given the work continuous attention.

One element, on the other hand, shows unexpected sophistication, way ahead of its time for Venice. The corner supports are L-shaped, half a pier facing each way so that each arch in the corners can land on a piece of capital able to receive it intact (fig. 29.19). Before this, not only in Venice but everywhere else in Italy (with two distinguished exceptions, the palace at Urbino and the Cancelleria in Rome), the archivolts meeting at right angles in a corner, over a column (rarely a pier), slashed each other off, so that no more than a knife-blade point came to their support. If a pier, the support could not present a solid-looking face to the court, but only the sharp edge of its

29.17 Fondaco dei Tedeschi.
Courtyard.

29.18 Fondaco dei Tedeschi.
Plan of ground floor (drawing by Vincenzo Fatica,
early XIXc, Museo Correr).

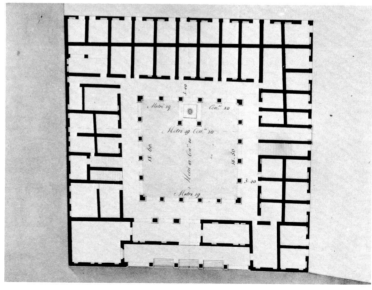

29.19 Fondaco dei Tedeschi.
Corner pier of courtyard.

corner. And as for the half-real, half-mimetic carrying role of the arches, that had to be ignored where they collided. Instead of this familiar but still uncomfortably weak "feminine ending," each side of the court of the Fondaco is brought to a strong masculine accent that stops it definitely where it ought to stop.

The height of the arches diminishes story by story. The eye does not make much effort to equate the arches of the piano nobile with those below because the sizes are so different—two small openings coming over one big one—even though they do turn out to be just half as high and half as wide (fig. 29.20). If done deliberately, this is the only occurrence of such an equation in the building. Above this, where some sort of ratio in the rate of diminution might more easily be suspected, none reveals itself. The next arches are a bit lower, but not demonstrably by a quarter, a fifth, a sixth, or any ideal amount; the top floor is unideally lower still. The successive reductions may please the eye, but they cannot be gauged by the intellect. If Fra Giocondo had had an effective voice here, there might be reason to hunt for calculated measures. As for the exterior windows, they do not even hint that any ideal geometry has affected them.

Perhaps peripheral to the architecture in the strict sense, but firmly on the border and far too important not to consider here, was the painting of the outside of the building. Hence a short excursus follows.

In what must have been a radically novel manner for 1508, the Grand Canal front was frescoed by Giorgione with large, ruddy nudes in turning, half-active poses, some standing in painted niches between the windows (figs. 29.21 and 29.22). In some of their famous cityscapes, Carpaccio and Gentile Bellini had shown older frescoed buildings with reliable clarity, most of them with abstract patterns compliant to the lines of the architecture, sometimes with a few pictorial episodes, polychrome or monochrome, even with whole figures, but always enframed and suitably firm and formal in pose. The self-effacing architecture of the front of the Fondaco gave a minimum of ready-made boundaries, with its yards of paper-flat walls pierced by rows of untrimmed openings, and subdivided only twice by shallow vertical breaks and once by a thin sill or cornice. Frescoes on outside walls were always let on a separate contract, like silk or leather hangings for interior walls, and the Fondaco may have been kept flat on purpose, waiting for them. Giorgione seems to have taken venturesome advantage of his freedom here. Along with the more than life-size lounging nudes were equestrian figures, columns in perspective, trophies, and heads in chiaroscuro, some doubtless the work of assistants. In the absence of better information, such subjects suggest easel pictures or mural decoration for interiors rather more than an organization of hundreds of feet of architectural exterior.

Certain peculiarities in Giorgione's compositional habits must be kept in mind, particularly that the space in his pictures is often equivocal. Just where are the figures in the *Tempest* in relation to one another and where in relation to the setting? Contradictions keep either from being fixed. Where is the spectator located in relation to the three figures and the throne in the *Castelfranco Madonna*? There is no answer, because different parts are seen from different points of view; optically the spectator cannot stay consistently in one place. What, then, can have been the effect of the huge miscellany spread over the front of the Fondaco? And how many of Giorgione's qualities would have been diluted or lost when able to be seen only at a great distance? The program determining the choice and placing of the figures and other items cannot be reconstructed now, nor

29.20 Fondaco dei Tedeschi.
Section through courtyard
(drawing by Vincenzo Fatica,
Museo Correr cl III 7773/1).

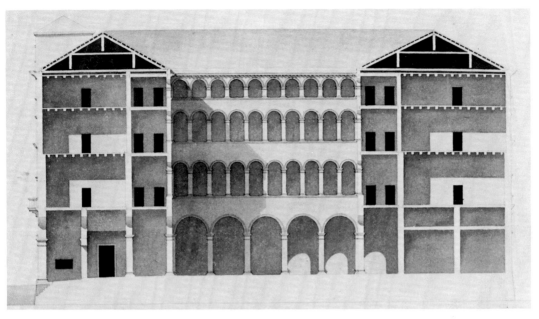

29.22 Fresco on wall of Fondaco dei Tedeschi (engraving
by A. M. Zanetti).

29.21 Fresco on wall of Fondaco dei Tedeschi (engraving
by A. M. Zanetti).

could it be only sixty or seventy years after it was painted, even to a journalist like Vasari (200) or an intellectual like Francesco Sansovino (136). Recently the program has been interpreted as political, referring to German-Venetian relations of the moment, so changed in sixty years that it was no longer intelligible (Muraro 1975, passim). While it is easy to believe that parts were superb, one is nonetheless dismayed by the ensemble. Either one has enough faith to accept the unimaginable—as one tries to do for the bright colors on the Parthenon—or one dangles in doubt.

Young Titian painted similar motifs on the side with the entrance to the building, following—one supposes—Giorgione. Inasmuch as painted fronts were popular in the Tyrol and other homelands of the German merchants, here in Venice they may well have welcomed the opportunity to have their new quarters made more like home. Venice very soon had exterior frescoes by more important painters than any other city, but the choice for the Fondaco in 1508 was the most exceptional of all. Whoever chose the two young masters for the job deserves a very high place in the hierarchy of art patrons. He was surely a senator, probably one of the procurators, and he may have been influenced by seeing the huge blank wall areas, and limited by the Senate's stipulations that the building should have no expensive finish, no marble, no fancy windows; fresco would be cheaper. But still, when everything was finished, and the building declared officially open at a sung Mass in the courtyard, the Fondaco had cost three times the original estimate (Brenzoni, 31; Brunetti-D-G, 63; Sanudo, VII, 597).

Damp and salty air attacked the frescoes, and by the XVIIc travelers had begun to complain of their deterioration; by the XVIIIc they were nearly all gone; and now in the XXc nothing is left but some XVIIIc lithographs of them, and some dismal areas of flakes of a figure in the Accademia Gallery, removed from the building only in 1936, preserved like holy relics, and even more invisible and unintelligible than most of those (fig. 29.23).

Napoleon abolished the Germans' business in 1806 and, after alterations to the inside, designated the building a customs house. More alterations fitted it for the General Post Office in 1870, as which it still functions. It was restored through the efforts of Count Ciano in the late 1930s, with a semiopaque glass ceiling over the court and under a huge roof skylight. This has repeatedly called for repairs—from broken glass, bird droppings, and bird carcasses, all-too-clearly silhouetted on the cracked glass ceiling. It was thoroughly gone over in the 1960s, and now in the late 1970s is being gone over again.

One must pause a moment and take a deep breath to prepare oneself for the contemplation of Spavento's last work: his great masterpiece, S Salvatore, surely the grandest interior built in Venice since S Mark's (fig. 29.24). Since it does not fit into the much-studied main development of Renaissance architecture, that of Florence and Rome, it is all too often omitted or slighted in general histories of architecture, its finest qualities unrecognized or ignored. But it fits easily into the less strict, less logical history of architecture in Venice, which is like a stream with less definitely bounded banks.

The largest Renaissance church yet undertaken in Venice was S Salvatore, or S Salvador in Venetian, first called La Transfigurazione del Signore, but changed in 1442 when allotted to the canons regular of S Salvatore from Bologna (Bortolan, 27; *Cronaca* 1736, 263). As with so much of Spavento's work, the exact amount of the finished design that is his cannot be isolated,

29.23 Giorgione. Fresco on wall of Fondaco dei Tedeschi before removal to Accademia in 1936.

29.24 S Salvatore.

for he fell ill when it was barely begun and soon died. Funds had been collected, and had accumulated enough to go ahead in 1506, after struggles between regulars and seculars in the local clergy. A decision was made to replace the mediaeval church, a domed Latin cross, with some sort of grilles in the floor above flowing water, believed to be like the Church of the Holy Sepulchre in Jerusalem (*Venezia e le sue Lagune*, VII, 219). Spavento's model was accepted, and some preliminary work was done the same year, 1506. For reasons not now clear, perhaps inherited from the older building with its wet near-crypt, the floor of the new nave was laid nine steps above the campo outside, though the space for the flowing water beneath—if such there still was—had been filled in.

Since the sacristy, campanile, cloister, and monastery buildings are parallel to one another and at a 30° angle to the church, which must have stood where the new one is, as shown by Jacopo de' Barbari, it may be that all of them also stand where the older ones were, although a contract of 1507 specifies that everything (presumably meaning everything above ground) must be new. Only the sacristy seems to follow Spavento's design (Hubala 1974, 337), and it has the same kind of vault with penetrations as his earlier sacristy of S Mark's (fig. 29.25). The lunettes frame pairs of arched windows, some glazed, some blind, with small *oculi* above elegant *bifore* not unlike Codussi's of only a few years before. The walls in the blind windows have recently revealed charming frescoes by Titian's brother Francesco (Boschini-Zanetti, 186), of flowering branches and playful birds. The ridges of the vaults are used for a painted pattern of long vines. Accessory rooms are on either side of the sacristy, Byzantine-looking little niched Greek crosses with domes on pendentives, one of them fitted into

the heavy masonry of the bottom of the campanile. None of these can, unfortunately, be dated, but the ellipse in the middle of the sacristy ceiling must be post-Spavento. Most of the monastery complex was put up after he had died, some under the direction of Sansovino, some still later.

His health failing, Spavento was assigned Pietro and Tullio as associates in 1507. As he died in 1509, after little more than the foundations for the main parts of the church had been laid and some few walls erected above ground at the east end (Temanza 1778, 119), he can have seen but little of it. The angle diverging from the axes of the sacristy and accessory buildings must have been a result of accommodation of the north flank of the church to the busiest street in Venice, the Merceria, and of accommodation also to the small campo in front. Since the walls probably coincide with the old church, some of the old foundations may have been used again.

Tullio continued the work on the old lines, and presumably in accord with Spavento's approved model. Part was in use by 1520 and all was vaulted by 1523, though not everything was yet all finished (Sanudo, XXIX, 89, 97). There is no record or outward sign of any intrusion by Pietro, busy elsewhere, and—one must suppose—temperamentally unsuited to working on a project by Spavento. Tullio, having exchanged his father's concepts for those of Codussi, was an ideal successor.

Except for the three semicircular apses at the east, closing the nave and aisles, everything in the plan is either a rectangle or a square (fig. 29.26). The nave is composed of three square spaces about 31' on a side, separated to the east and west and bounded on the north and south by rectangles of the same length as the squares, but only half as wide. The squares and their contiguous oblongs read as three large Greek crosses. Smaller squares are in

29.25 S Salvatore. Sacristy.
Detail showing blind win-
dows with frescoes.

the corners between their arms, with each side equal to half the side of the big squares, and therefore equal to the short side of the rectangles abutting them. To make suitable transepts, integrated into the pervasive, simple geometry of the whole, an extra rectangle is added outside the ends of each of the side arms of the easternmost cross. Repeating the rectangles of the crosses beside them, they open wide to them, but stay closed on the other three sides. Thus the richly compounded interior space of the church is brought to a definite stop where it should be, and only where it should be. The semicircular apses at the east end, as wide as the squares they adjoin, are—inevitably— just half as deep. As always, because of the inescapable interpolation of supporting piers, none of these spatial dimensions is precisely half or double, down to a centimeter (unless the measurements were perversely taken from some point inside the piers).

Protruding transepts were rare in Renaissance churches at this time. Those of Alberti at Mantua may not be part of the original scheme, and only at the Cathedral of Urbino were broad transepts projected out beyond the block of the church from the beginning (Forster, 125). Here at S Salvatore they are probably part of Spavento's definitive plan. That on the right fills the awkward space left between the block of the church and the diagonally set adjuncts, the campanile (pre-Spavento) and sacristy (old foundations?), in a way that holds them together. The back wall of the transept on the left fits along the adjacent street; it is, in fact, the only part of the church that reaches the street, with which it runs parallel.

The consequent grouping of spaces, or one might better say sequence of spaces, is a sort of concert of echoes; everything one sees is in perfect tune with everything near it, either as identical notes or as octaves (that is, 1:1 or 2:1). Codussi had anticipated this in a

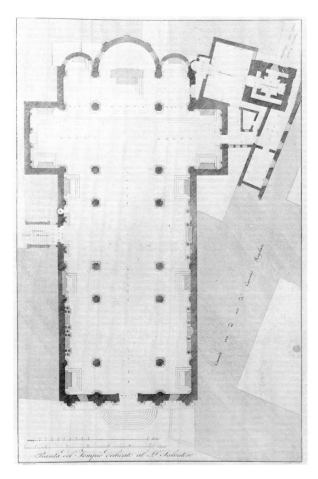

29.26 S Salvatore. Plan (from Cicognara-Diedo-Selva).

far less complicated way with his single Greek cross at S Giovanni Grisostomo, begun just ten years before. S Salvatore does not so much follow S Giovanni here as take a big step forward, to develop it further, with the grave majesty of a Handelian largo.

He has extended the nine-cell square plan into a long nave of alternating wide and narrow bays, square and oblong. The wide spaces are spread out sideways as well as lengthwise, and hence cross the main flow of space three times between the more closed-in narrower bays, making a so-called patriarchal cross. This alternation of narrow and wide openings down the nave had existed earlier in North Italian Romanesque churches, and also in the Renaissance, on a grand scale at Alberti's S Andrea at Mantua (begun around 1470) and Giuliano da Maiano's cathedral at Faenza (begun around 1474), neither one far from Venice but neither one handled the same way as at S Salvatore. There is no need, however, to look so far away for precedents, with S Mark's only a few blocks off at the other end of the Merceria, and S Giovanni Grisostomo the same distance the other way, a church Spavento may have visited often while he was working at the nearby Fondaco (if he did not want to join the Germans at S Bartolomeo). Both churches are closely related to S Salvatore, and far more likely to have been implicated in its inspiration than anything outside Venice.

A look down the nave, concentrating on the plan (but not on the polychrome marble floor, a handsome Baroque addition), shows not only an alternation of wide and narrow bays but also an alternation in the oblongs, now crosswise, then lengthwise, now in the nave and then in the aisles, and yet another alternation in the squares, now large (in the nave), then small (in the aisles), alternating thus both in size and location. Each part is close to its alternate, side by side, or corner to corner. There are equivalent alternations in height everywhere, all implicit in the plan. One cannot say that the whole is assembled by addition, that it grew only by putting elements next to one another, for it can be seen just as well as having been composed by the division of larger elements, or by interpenetration or overlapping, since the rectangles between the squares of the nave can be sensed equally as an arm of the Greek cross in front or of the Greek cross in back, or sensed as both at the same time. Consequently, one's vision is not static; the multiple alternations and the multiple readings invited keep it dynamic.

Except for the added altars and tombs, what is visible now is nearly all the work of Tullio, who was responsible for most of the execution and perhaps some indeterminable part of the organization of the elevations, particularly in the upper zones, made when the authority of Spavento would have been fading. Inasmuch as the partly finished but presumably not yet vaulted apses were almost surely by Spavento (Temanza 1778, 119), their typical Codussian tall arched windows with frames unmarked at the springing would also be his; then the compound piers on the end of the walls between the apses, and perhaps the freestanding piers in front of them might be his too. If they are—as is probable—the scheme for all the membering of the church is basically his, for the plan had already laid out an all-over system of vaults and domes with piers integral to it. The entire church could be correctly recovered from one bay and a little more, much as a High Gothic French church could be. Even though carried out by Tullio, the system must be Spavento's (Hubala 1974, 334, disagrees), and it is a development from that of S Giovanni Grisostomo, inspired as well by S Mark's. The details, richer than anything heretofore claimed for Spavento, would come in part from the nature of the commission for a big important church and in part from Tullio's responsibility for them. (Convert or not, he *was* a Lombardo.)

Just who deserves the credit for just what is even more important here than usual, for the great beauty of the church is firmly based on its extraordinarily original plan, developed logically and harmoniously into the scheme of the elevations and their compounded but not confusing vaults. All this is so unified, so fully integrated spatially—with ratios always of 1:1 and 2:1, and no others—that it must be the creation of one mind and it must have been fixed from the very first; it cannot have come from a collaborative compromise or from successive ideas of Spavento and Tullio. It must have been worked out by Spavento and largely incorporated in his winning model.

Some have lately begun to recognize it as the most beautiful of the Renaissance church interiors in the city, and from it springs Spavento's long neglected right to his place among the greatest architects of Venice. The Abbé Moschini (174) found that S Salvatore "merited all sorts of praises . . . one is not afraid to say that it is the most beautiful in the city" (1819). It was soon imitated in Padua, on a vast scale, for the Church of S Giustina, begun in 1521 or a decade later, before S Salvatore was complete, by one Matteo da Valle, who had worked under Spavento (Heydenreich-Lotz, 317; McAndrew 1974, 19). But, strangely, Spavento and his masterpiece have even in the last generations been brushed rather to one side. Pevsner (145), while calling him "otherwise little known"—alas now true—recognized the importance of the church, but others simply gave the whole to Tullio or failed to mention it at all.

Spavento's art cannot always be winnowed out from that of his helpers. The essentials of this one work, however, do stand out as his alone, and it is a masterpiece of such quality that it establishes him firmly on a level with Codussi and, in this one work, possibly higher. It is not as pretentious as it may at first sound to point out that the first stone of S Salvatore was laid in the same year as that of Bramante's S Peter's. One phenomenon sets the church aside as unique; its designer did not build it. We are able to know its beautiful form but are not able to see it physically except as someone else materialized it, much as we are able to hear Bach's *Art of the Fugue* physically only as someone else orchestrated it. Such posthumous collaborations rarely reach such synonymity. One can imagine it (but not see it) peopled by a silent congregation of figures from Piero della Francesca, from Seurat, and with the Hera of Samos.

Tullio's completion of Spavento's S Salvatore is the first full proclamation of complete independence from his father (who was still alive, and Tullio was a little under fifty), though there had been lesser indications before. The shift from a pretty and easygoing style to one of sobriety and nobility is surprising, particularly in the Renaissance when all artists underwent a long training in the workshop of a master, and usually showed traces of it to their dying days. Although it is not an early work, Tullio's contribution to S Salvatore is best taken up here, following the examination of Spavento's plan, and preceding works by Tullio that were actually carried out earlier.

Tullio was contracted in 1507 to take over from the ailing Spavento in partnership with his septuagenarian father Pietro, who left no traces, and assisted by his stonecutter and sculptor brother Giulio, whose traces—if any—are indistinguishable. Tullio may have been particularly sympathetic to the canons here, since he had been working earlier for the canons regular of S Salvatore at S Maria Maggiore in Treviso (Franzoi-DiStefano, 355), who may have recommended him to their brothers in Venice. Francesco Sansovino (121), well informed on the whole for XVIc matters, wrote seventy years later that the church had been remade or rebuilt on "the *modello* of Tullio Lombardo, the famous architect." *Modello* usually indicated a model, though occasionally a drawing or drawings. Although he mentioned Spavento's name in passing 200 years later, Temanza found the work "deserving every praise, and all by our Tullio" (1778, 119; 1963, 5). Spavento was being forgotten almost as quickly as Codussi. What could be seen and touched was what won comment, rather than anything seemingly so abstract as a plan. And what could be seen, apart from some of the chancel, was not only built but also almost surely detailed by Tullio. If a normal model, Spavento's would probably not have been large enough to show the specific forms of the details, which were in any case usually worked out as the building went up.

Since part of the church was seen in use by Sanudo (XXIX, 89, 97) in 1520, that part must have been finished all the way up, and vaulted. The rest of the vaulting was finished by 1523, probably before the plague struck. The mosaics of the small chapel to the left of the chancel were also in place by 1523, already a little old-fashioned for such a radically modern building. The Ionic capitals of the smaller pilasters and the single-leaf Corinthian of the larger, as well as the forms and sequences of the moldings were Tullio's responsibility, and perhaps to a small extent Giulio's (fig. 30.1). They are unexceptional, though the less experienced hand of Giulio may show in the Ionic, rather rich but stiff and a bit awkward, since that order was still so little used. In detail, the two entablatures would be Tullio's rather than Spavento's, and the architrave of the lower one has the Codussian oblique fascias Tullio had by now definitely adopted. None of the moldings has ornamental carvings: Spavento's abstinence still dominates, and for Tullio, already converted, that would have been no hindrance.

The first major element that could have come from an idea of Tullio's not based on Spavento is the attic above the main cornice (fig. 30.2). A step beyond Codussi, this is the first appearance of an attic between cornice and vault, an arrangement soon to become widespread. If Tullio invented it here, as well he may have, it is one of his major achievements. A quarter as high as the order below (including the pedestals), it raises the arms of the big Greek crosses, and dramatizes the difference in level between the top and the smaller square sections. The top of the arches of the great arms now rises

twice as high as the lower ones. A Roman element usually found only on exteriors, such as triumphal arches (of which there were examples accessible in Ancona, Verona, or Pula), the attic was a novelty in an interior. It bestowed two benefits: first, by raising the vaults well above the main cornice, it lessened their apparent weight—potentially crushing—and gave them instead an easy, firm, and light but not floating look; second, it allowed an extra row of windows and pushed the *oculi* in the walls at the ends of the arms higher, so that more light came into the church.

The only items of questionable scale and appropriateness in the whole church are the attic windows, discordant where they appear above the more suitably scaled windows in the apse, and worse in the tight little groups of three at the ends of the arms. Not only do they look like something taken from another building, but they fail in their one function, to give a modicum of light. The 10' *oculi* above, at the ends of the big arms, give far more (fig. 30.3). It is this dissonance and functional failure that tend to banish them from the highly integrated original scheme and categorize them as a change. If that be so, they would have to be an interpolation of Tullio's, concurrent with the attic, introduced soon after Spavento's death in 1509, and before 1520 when some of the church was already in use. Where the attic does not have windows, it fits beautifully with the rest, with its rhythm of oblong and round panels. Around 1570, even the two layers of windows were thought inadequate (more printed prayerbooks and more literate congregations?), and the tops of the domes were opened and lanterns put on them—not by Scamozzi, as so often repeated, for he would not yet have reached twenty (G G Zorzi 1957, *Arte Veneta*, 120). Thus not only was the surface of the domes lighted more, as

30.1 S Salvatore. Main Corinthian and minor Ionic
orders (from Cicognara-
Diedo-Selva).

30.2 S Salvatore. Longitudinal section (from Cicognara-
Diedo-Selva).

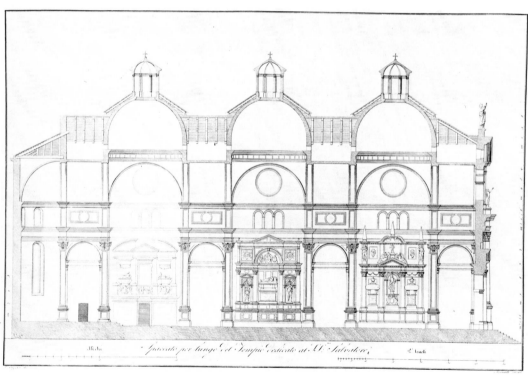

30.3 S Salvatore. Interior
looking east (print by
Tosini-Lazzari).

well as the space below, but they were made to seem less lid-like, and lighter in weight.

The membering is in pale grayish limestone, quietly contrasted with white plaster walls and vaults, adequate in its own strength to act out a lively play of possible structure (not necessarily coincident with real structure), a convincing scheme of "as if." The piers are small, and the pilasters on them are shallow and slender, the larger and the smaller being different widths and depths, which makes the piers symmetrical crosses in plan, subtly formed in accordance with what they are going to have to do higher up (fig. 30.4). The entablatures are no more than a sixth of the height of the pilasters (less than the pedestals); yet with the several cornices and arches and rings below the domes, the membering all works together as an armature able to keep the various walls, vaults, openings, and contained space in an alive but unstrained whole. The white domes are hemispheres set on pendentives rimmed by the arches at the ends of the arms and by the ring of entablature tangent to them (with an architrave with Codussian fascias). The curves of the apses in plan anticipate the curves of the arches and vaults above. Nowhere is there too much or too little except for those triple attic windows. Opulent tomb monuments, side altars, and an organ, mainly of the later XVIc, now cover most of the lower aisle walls, but are allowed to attract only secondary attention in the harmonious whole. The altar, however, is stressed spatially not only by being close to the focus of the apse but also by being raised, three steps with the whole chancel and then five more.

It would be difficult to identify specific sources for Tullio's new feeling for space, for greater scale, and greater classicism, and it would be beside the point to try; it could all have come from within himself—as an aesthetic choice, a quiet critique of what he saw all about him, including the work of his father. There is only one probable outside source: the architecture of Codussi. Tullio worked with him in 1500–02 on the Cappella Bernabò in S Giovanni Grisostomo. The extent and nature of their relationship is not known, but they did work together. When Codussi died in 1504 it was probably Tullio who was called in to finish the Palazzo Vendramin-Calergi (Hubala 1965, 65). Although little work can be attributed to Tullio with certainty, a few texts, old traditions, and respectable conjectures can be joined to lay out a calendar of his life and activities. It shows that, unlike the other Lombardeschi, who followed Pietro like dinghies, Tullio had his own craft and slowly diverged in his own direction. One would suppose that his responsibilities at S Salvatore from 1506 on would have changed his course for good, regardless of where the line is drawn between Spavento's ideas and Tullio's execution; the bare fact that he was in charge of such a building is what counts.

Tullio made an amazing journey from one trained as an ornamental sculptor in his father's famous shop (where he worked on the details of S Giobbe, the Miracoli, and tombs in SS Giovanni e Paolo) to an independent position as an architect of antithetical character. At S Salvatore he succeeded in making an organized whole unlike any earlier Lombardo work, with some complexity but with unblurred clarity. He was mainly guided by the ideas of Spavento, yet interpreted and added to them with such sympathetic understanding, except in the attic windows, that the whole is sensed as wonderfully unified, a polyphonic or even fugal composition, with a main voice and clear subordinate ones abridged from it or derived from it in some other way, guided almost everywhere by repetition or alternation.

30.4 S Salvatore. Nave,
looking east.

No one else in Venice changed styles as much or as drastically. That peculiarity can be matched—more than matched—only by the more extreme development from youth to maturity in the work of his slightly older contemporary, Donato Bramante (1444–1514)—though there is no other reason ever to think of them together.

Tullio's career is difficult to chart as a sequential development. After having begun as a helper in decorative carving in a busy shop, and having arrived as a distinguished figure sculptor by the 1490s, he went on in a way not easy to follow. The activities of his old age—he must have been born ca. 1455–60 and he died in 1532—left no certain buildings of his in Venice. He was active as a collaborator at the scuolas of the Misericordia and S Rocco, leaving little identifiable at either, and he worked for a second period at Treviso, and also at Ravenna and Belluno. Meanwhile he was still intermittently busy as a sculptor, and offhandedly in the business of selling stone (contract for S Antonio di Castello (1518), Boston, priv. coll.). He is a puzzling artist because so much of his presumed work is either insecure in attribution or based on subjective opinions that may not agree. He may not even have been as important as here claimed. Nevertheless, anyone who built S Salvatore has a claim to greatness, even though he shared it with its first designer.

It is now time to move backward a generation and look at Tullio's development as an independent artist, from minor helper to assistant to partner of his father. He had already worked under Rizzo on fireplaces and decorated doorways in the doges' apartments, but not yet in a distinguishable style of his own. With his brother Antonio he had been admitted as a master in sculpture back in 1475. In the 1480s he had worked for his father on the Scuola di S Marco and the Miracoli. Also in the middle 1480s, he must have lived for a time in Treviso, making tombs and doing some work on the cathedral. In the early 1490s he was thinking in a more architectural way than his father, with more feeling for three-dimensionality, more sense of movement in and out, and more ease in the proper classical vocabulary. His sculpture, too, was becoming antiquarianizing; he may have bought a piece of genuine antique sculpture for himself (Pope-Hennessy 1958, 111). He worked under Codussi at S Giovanni Grisostomo on the Cappella Bernabò, where his altar relief is dated 1502. And he probably completed Codussi's Ca' Vendramin-Calergi by 1509, overlapping his first labors at S Salvatore.

The first important work that shows him semi-independent is the big monument of Doge Andrea Vendramin in SS Giovanni e Paolo, of the late 1480s and early 1490s (fig. 30.5). In his will of 1477, wealthy Doge Vendramin (1476–78) had arranged with the friars of the Servi to have his tomb set up in the choir of their church. It stood there with his bones in the sarcophagus (where, according to some living friars, they may still be), until it had to be dismembered when the church was about to be pulled down in 1810 on Napoleonic orders. Space was made to put it up again in 1817, on the north side of the chancel of SS Giovanni e Paolo. Even before it was finished, Marin Sanudo admired it, claiming that it would "prove the most beautiful in the city on account of the worthy marbles in it" (Pope-Hennessy 1958, 111). A century later, the English traveler Fynes Moryson (179) found it "the fairest of all others in the city." It is still constantly admired, above all for its majesty, a quality that architecture can embody with particular aptness, and thus by suggestion impute to the occupant.

30.5 Monument of Andrea
Vendramin in SS Giovanni e
Paolo.

Andrea Vendramin, who succeeded Pietro Mocenigo and preceded Giovanni Mocenigo as doge, had done little to earn so splendid a monument. All through his twenty-sixth-month reign, Venice was neither notably prosperous nor successful in its unending war with the Turks. Rather than his slight accomplishments, it was his wealth that was memorialized in his tomb, and also his particular taste for antiquities, accumulated in a collection that was considered a museum and had called for a fourteen-volume catalogue.

With its fine white marble newly cleaned and beautifully lighted from the tiers of windows in the Gothic apse beside it, it almost always appears today at its splendid best. The evolution in less than a dozen years from the Tron to this takes us from one artistic world, of improvisation and growing awareness of the grammar of antiquity, into another, of assured classicism. It was already the most thoroughly architectural tomb in Venice. Its exceptional height and width (40' by 26'), its huge freestanding columns and deep-sunk arch, all give it extraordinary substantiality. The strong highlights and deep transparent shadows, vivid as architectural adjuncts, do what excellent recording can do for a musical composition. In addition, they provide an ideal setting for sculpture. (Figure sculpture, as a general rule, looks its best with light coming down at an angle of about 45°, and back toward it at about the same angle.)

Despite the repeated eulogies, the author of the work is nowhere named. In the XVIIIc, Temanza (1778, 114) suggested Alessandro Leopardi (intermittently in Venice from 1482 on), because some details resemble the base for Verrocchio's Colleoni, just outside the church. Often repeated, this conjecture no longer convinces. In the XIXc, Pietro Paoletti scrutinized the tomb with a fresh eye and reassigned it to the Lombardos, a conclusion accepted ever since. Much of the sculpture must be by Tullio—the Adam is signed—and the architecture, less easy to attribute, may seem close to Pietro in parts, but closer to Tullio in more (fig. 30.6). Given the probable date, late 1480s to ca. 1494, it could be here that Tullio, still in his twenties, began to leave his father and the Quattrocento behind, and to explore and even prophesy something of the High Renaissance. Tullio would have had the help of his brother Antonio and other assistants, since the whole is far too large for a single sculptor.

The seeming likeness to the Colleoni base had led to the ascription to Leopardi, but now that it is more usually given to Tullio, the relation is reversed, and Tullio's dominance in the tomb is strengthened. Moreover, what may resemble the base looks not only like it—always an important point to watch—but equally like much other Lombardo ornament. Leopardi is not established as a designer of decorative architecture in stone—he thought essentially in bronze—and his ornament, less architectural than this of the base or tomb, is more like embroidery. The lower parts of the tomb are cut in higher relief than usual, not at all like embroidery. The frieze and some of the moldings, as well as the characteristic arabesques (in their design, though less in their carving) still glint with bits of old gilding, which adds to the sparkling all-over effect already inherent in the crisp quality of the cutting. Perhaps because it is so near our eyes, every molding in the lower entablature was carved, and not just with the old Lombardo exuberance but with a new kind of richness closer to that of genuine late imperial Roman craftsmanship, and also in unusually orthodox proportions. (Was someone showing off new knowledge?) Yet it remains a sort of Lombardo product as well. Tullio is the obvious explanation.

The character of this lower entablature runs counter to that of the larger and more correct one at the top, with its plain marble frieze and carving of only two moldings (fig. 30.7). The antithesis might indicate the taste of Pietro below, and the more severe classicism of Tullio above. Another sign is that the fascias of the upper architrave are oblique, where those below are vertical. The slight double entasis of the columns might suggest old-fashioned Pietro (though this had sometimes occurred in genuine but offbeat Roman work).

One could say that Latin, nearly mastered, was dominating Tullio's natural language. The classicism is stronger than in anything since the pseudo-antique parts of the Arsenal gate, which was a copy and not, as here, an original Latin composition. The medal-like Roman profiles set in circles on the spandrels are so at home that they no longer seem like borrowings. Almost all Lombardo-style gaucheries have been put right. The general result accords with the known taste of the doge, and may follow stipulations of his. The least Roman and most Lombardo-like items are the capitals, flaring more than antique models, but with carving so crisp and undercutting so expertly managed that the sparkle of light and shade surpasses that of most genuine Roman work of the neighborhood. The only mediaevalism—probably not then recognized—is in the octagonal pedestals for the figures at the outer ends. The entablature running around them and joining them has, surprisingly, a bulging, cushioned, convex, or pulvinated frieze, an occasional Roman specialty not popularized until Palladio.

Classicizing is found not only in the general composition and details, but also in Tullio's sculpture: the icily nude Adam, with both the virtues and the faults of Roman copies of Greek work, and the two warriors in military outfits, archaeologically as correct as

Mantegna's in the same years. They are far closer to their antique forerunners than the approximations on Pietro's tomb of Pietro Mocenigo at the other end of the church, looking here less as though dressed up for a school play than as though at ease in well-researched costumes for a serious opera.

Surprisingly for Italian propriety at the height of the Neoclassic fashion, when the monument was put back together in 1817, there was objection to the nudes, particularly from one prim Dominican (fig. 30.8). It might have been thought that life-size nudes on a tomb would have made a sensation when they first appeared in the Servi, but no complaints were recorded. Later qualms had them removed and sold. The patently neo-antique Adam is now in the Metropolitan Museum in New York; the original Eve—if there ever was one—cannot be traced except in a later copy in the Palazzo Vendramin-Calergi. Did Tullio ever finish an Eve? Sanudo saw the tomb complete except for one figure in 1494; perhaps an Eve was added later by another sculptor. The naked shield-holding boys who stood on the top went to the Berlin Museum, and were smashed by bombs at the end of the last war. The two warriors, more doughty than devout, have been shifted from their posts as guards on the flanks to the niches emptied of Adam and Eve, and their old sentrylike places taken by a S Catherine and a Magdalen by Lorenzo Bregno, also salvaged from the Servi, but from a different ensemble; they are inappropriate here in scale, meaning, and style. The niches call extra attention to them by their special lining of polished slate gray marble.

The sarcophagus is surrounded by small figures of Virtues—three theological, four cardinal (fig 30.9). Above is the bier, held up by the necks and wings of eagles, with an oddly near-Egyptian winged disc at the center, a symbol of unclear meaning borrowed

30.6 Vendramin Monument.
Capital and entablature of
main order.

30.7 Vendramin Monument.
Upper entablature.

30.8 Vendramin Monument,
with original arrangement of
figures (from Cicognara-
Diedo-Selva).

30.9 Vendramin Monument.
Epitaph, bier, and effigy.

from Florence. The recumbent effigy, in sleep or death, is guarded by three young genii carrying symbolically extinguished torches. Behind them and the bier, the upper part of the niche under the entablature is empty, with nothing but three plain panels on the wall (as in several Florentine tombs), making a striking pause in the pervasive carving almost everywhere else. The main figure is thus assured of great dignity, contrasted with surrounding emptiness like a statement between two silences.

The overall design refers consciously to the Roman arch of triumph, with its monumental piling of pedestals, columns, center arch, topped by a tall attic, and flanked by narrower wings. The earlier reliance on altarpiece frames has disappeared. The wings, half as wide as the center (perhaps a deliberate ratio), are closely related yet kept subordinate to it more successfully than on any tomb so far. The big columns of the middle bay strengthen the doge-flattering allusion to a triumphal arch, and so does the setting of the arch on the columns instead of between them. This ensures a larger and more impressive central niche, which may once have loomed even more grandly in the chancel of the Servi. Also allusive to a triumphal arch are the two roundels in the side bays, quotations from the Arch of Constantine, then as now one of the prominent sights of Rome. Such a direct allusion is rare in Venetian work, for few Venetians knew Rome; but Andrea Vendramin knew it well, having served as ambassador at the court of Pope Paul II. He may have chosen the subjects of the round reliefs—the centaur Nessus and Dejanira, and Perseus and Medusa—not easy for pious laymen to decode into Christian symbols.

While the scheme follows the traditional Venetian one of three parts, at the same time it veers away from local tradition by employing fatter Renaissance forms such as Pietro had not used—nor ever would. The most arresting is the scale of the big columns, unfamiliar in Venice though not in Roman cities, and inimical to the old way of composing by an agglomeration of small parts, as in the recent Tron monument. Despite their four-leaf capitals, garland-draped shafts, and gently swelling entasis, the columns seem close to imperial Rome, closer to Tullio's taste, still growing, than to Pietro's, already set. The arabesque-filled pilasters, as high as the columns, are not foreign to Pietro or his workshop, and neither is the fancy lower entablature. To resolve these contradictions, there are two workable assumptions: first, that the tomb was a collaborative work by Pietro and Tullio; or second, that it was all by Tullio, begun under the influence of his father and master and finished nearer to his new ideal, Codussi. The second assumption is the stronger. In either case, there is some collaboration, for Pietro's presence is undeniable, though perhaps he was not physically present but just lodged in Tullio's brain. Stylistically we should read this monument from bottom to top.

The last tomb Tullio designed for Venice was that of Doge Giovanni Mocenigo (1478–85), younger brother of Doge Pietro, whose monument by Tullio's father stood at the other end of the west wall of SS Giovanni e Paolo. Under Doge Giovanni, a sixteen-year war with the Turks was settled, followed by an ineffectual war with Ferrara for which the doge was excommunicated and the city put under interdict. His term of office was also marred by two fires in the palace, in 1479 and 1483. His memorial, unlike that of his more active and successful brother and more like that of his unremarkable predecessor, Andrea Vendramin (though less grand), had to be more abstract and symbolic than historically illustrative.

In general size and scale it must have been considered from the beginning a free companion piece to Pietro's in the opposite corner. The width of both was fixed by brick piers already on the church wall (fig. 30.10). Work was not begun by Tullio for some time after the doge died in 1478—not until after 1495, though before 1500; about a decade later, then, than his grander efforts for the richer Doge Vendramin.

The architecture is completely assured, with no betrayal by Early Renaissance inexperience, experiments, or makeshifts. Except for the prone effigy and two symbolic females accompanying it, the sculpture is kept to moderately low relief and subordinated to the compositional demands of the architecture, with no gratuitous trimming, no carved detail except for the symbolic wreathing of the family arms in laurel, and the four unavoidable capitals (fig. 30.11). The last may be the first correct Composite capitals in Venice, with two rows of acanthus leaves, standard in Roman work and in the Byzantinizing XIIIc in Venice. The slender column shafts have unbulging normal entasis. Nothing betrays any Lombardo heritage. The columns at the ends stand on wide pedestals jointly with their neighbors, pedestals carved with religious scenes in medium-low relief that might—but actually does not—rob them of the robustness their position calls for. One sees more the work of an architect using some sculpture than of a sculptor contriving architectural frames for his freestanding figures and reliefs.

More than in any earlier tomb the composition is conceived in depth. The main recess, sunk over a foot into the wall, stays back in shadow, and makes a resonant setting for the jutting sarcophagus and effigy, which effectively catches the light. This was more difficult to manage here than at Pietro's tomb at the other end of the wall beside a big window (no window was possible at this end because of the contiguous monastery buildings outside). Although attached in back, the sarcophagus and its burden seem to hang

30.10 Monument of Gio-
vanni Mocenigo in SS
Giovanni e Paolo.

30.11 Mocenigo Monument.
Detail.

free. The flat bands of the two socles make the most of their pale caramel and gray marble and, by contrast, enhance the interplay of in-and-out of the several white marble forms above. (Most of the monument is of white Carrara.) One is more aware of the arrangement of masses in space than of any surface composition working in lines or flat patterns, and one begins to forget that this is still a product of the Quattrocento.

Between the two sections of pedestal under the columns, a long epitaph is set back on a different plane, an arrangement not repeated by the forms above. There each single outer column makes the entablature break forward in the usual way; then it goes back again to the wall until, above the next (or inner) column, it breaks forward but does not go back again, staying forward and running as a long lintel to bridge the recess. With *o* for "out" and *i* for "in", the pedestal could be said to go oo–iiiii–oo, while the entablature goes o–i–ooo–i–o, as does the attic it carries. This controlled reversal, contradiction, or simple sample of matched polyrhythm, works like the decoration of the scene wall of a late Roman theatre (with which it cannot have any relation), or later Renaissance work, in XVIc Rome or Florence, more than it does like the work of someone raised by Pietro Lombardo and educated by Codussi (but not yet Spavento). There may, however, have been some difference in the arrangement here in Tullio's time, making it less arbitrary at the top.

Something has been added to the top. When Giovanni Girolamo Grapiglia was commissioned to redesign the whole west wall of the church in 1574, to make it into one monument with the tomb of Doge Alvise Mocenigo above the main doorway, he took both Pietro's and Tullio's tombs in his ambitious artistic *Anschluss* and achieved the largest family monument in Ven-

ice. The older memorials were encased in arches at the ends, subordinated as wings to the grandiose new center. Since Tullio's was 5' or 6' lower than Pietro's—of no consequence when they were only distant equivalents not intended to match—Grapiglia, to force them to match, seems to have added another attic on top of the one Tullio had already put there, and finished it off with a curved pediment similar to that on Pietro's. This new attic does not go well with the one below it; its barely recessed panel is in a wide, flat frame counting less than Tullio's bolder though narrower one below. The new piece has its own cornice, as does the older one, above the cornice of the main columnar order. Could Tullio have countenanced three cornices within 8' as Grapiglia did? The new curved pediment might recall something once on the entablature spanning the center columns on Tullio's design, or have crowned his original attic. Since Grapiglia took two figures off the top of Pietro's composition to make it fit under his arch, he could have done something equally procrustean to Tullio's. If figures had been there—and they may have been—they could have given meaning to the isolation of the outer columns (on which they might have stood), columns all ready for something with their own boldly separated blocks of entablature.

Some might regard Tullio's work here as purified; others might see it as impoverished; but all would have to recognize a change, a change that will show with greater strength and quality in subsequent works. Something had happened to Tullio. He had rejected his father's style and begun to follow Mauro Codussi. Here in the main architrave of the Mocenigo tomb he again used Codussi's almost autographic flipped fascias.

Perhaps this newly developed severe and classical taste of Tullio's was innate, there from the beginning but obscured by the need to work for his father in the style he had been taught. It had shown itself a little in the Tabernacle of the Precious Blood in the sacristy of the Frari (ca. 1487), with its plain architectural forms, and a little more in the architectural backgrounds of the reliefs on the front of the Scuola di S Marco, of an architecture not typical of anyone else in Venice at the time. Perhaps it can be made out in his work, of uncertain extent, for the Cathedral of Cividale (from 1502 on, after he had worked with Codussi), a severe columnar basilica still inexperienced, provincial, and un-Venetian. (Local participation probably restricted Tullio's part in the design as carried out.) But a clear restraint, which could be Tullio's, shows in the three far from provincial domes on pendentives in front of the apse and flanking chapels. Something new is here, and it is more reminiscent of Mauro than Pietro.

S Salvatore was remarkable in many ways: for one thing, not typical of its day, it was large, while Venice is on the whole a city of small or smallish churches. Only the doges' S Mark's, the patriarchs' Cathedral of S Pietro di Castello, and a handful of churches of the monastic orders could be called large: the Frari, SS Giovanni e Paolo, S Francesco della Vigna, the Carità, the Servi, S Stefano (and S Salvatore)—and all of them have aisles. The rest of the city had small parishes with small churches, like a mediaeval Byzantine city and like many Italian ones. When a parish church was rebuilt, it would still be small, for there was usually no way of gaining extra land on Venice's limited terrain; also, new churches took advantage when they could of the foundations of their predecessors.

There is little reason to provide aisles for a small church, and when aisles are there, it is perhaps merely from tradition, or someone's personal preference, since a small church can be roofed easily without any intermediate supports inside. (Vaults, as has been said, were not often used because of their weight and what that demanded of their foundations.) The few parish churches built in the Early Renaissance were small, and generally without aisles. Against two-score earlier or monastic examples of columnar basilicas, only three of those built entirely new in this period are equipped with aisles: S Maria Maggiore, S Sofia, and S Croce on the Giudecca (both of the latter remodeled now) (McAndrew 1969, 16 n6). There were also a few important remodelings or half-remodelings or continuings of earlier schemes, such as S Michele or S Zaccaria.

Tullio had been engaged not only on the clumsy columnar Cathedral of Cividale, but perhaps also on the beautiful columnar church of the abbey at Praglia, both outside Venice, and there is a good chance that he had something to do with S Maria Maggiore in the city.* This church for Franciscan nuns, at the extreme edge of the archipelago of Venice, can never have drawn much regular attendance. Its size and its splendid paintings must have come from one or two families who took special interest in it.

The church is on a lately reclaimed island in a remote part of the city behind S Andrea della Zirada, which had been asked to cede a plot for twelve Franciscan sisters of the Strict Observance in 1497 (Cicogna, III, 417) as an inscription still attests (fig. 30.12). The gift of a miracle-working "Greek" icon of the Madonna added "S Maria dell'Assunta" to the dedication to S Vincenzo from an older oratory on the site. In March 1503 a petition to rebuild on a larger scale was accepted, and work went ahead quickly enough for the nuns to move into new quarters in a couple of years (Corner, 514; Sanudo, IV, 246). The big masonry church

* Suggested attribution later concurred in by Franzoi-DiStefano, 92.

30.12 S Maria Maggiore.
Inscription.

may have been begun about then. Another painting was accepted in 1506 (Cicognara, III, 419), and something must have been finished enough to house it, though it could have waited a while in the convent building. Pardons (granting of indulgences) to raise funds took place in the church for several years beginning in 1514. The doge paid a state visit in 1523 to what must have been a finished and furnished building (Sanudo, XVIII, 51, 67; XXV, 63; XXX, 25, 52, 62, 114; XXXIV, 261). Vavassore's map-view of ca. 1525 shows it much as it still is.

From the beginning, many gifts came from Alvise (Luigi Aloysio) Malipiero, and kept on coming until his death in 1537. The chapel on the left of the chancel was decorated for his tomb (Cicognara, III, 429; Martinelli, 423) and was long reserved for members of the Malipiero family (fig. 30.13). The equally illustrious Mocenigos endowed the corresponding chapel on the right. Both chapels, like the chancel, ended not in the curve of traditional apses, but in flat east walls, ideal for the display of painted altarpieces. The church became a favorite for the bestowal of works of art by the aristocracy, although no grand families lived in the neighborhood and it was not a parish church but a convent, of limited appeal except to families who had endowed their daughters as nuns. Soon there were a Giovanni Bellini, Titian's famous *S John the Baptist*, Tintorettos, a Palma Vecchio, Jacopo Bassano's *Noah's Ark* and, over the high altar, an *Assumption* by Paolo Veronese.

It soon came to be called S Maria Maggiore from its reputed likeness to S Maria Maggiore in Rome (Sanudo, IV, 246), a similarity not now understandable if ever seriously intended. A design must have been extant from 1503, with a nave and aisles separated by an arcade on columns, surprisingly rare in Renaissance Venice though common elsewhere in Italy. Regularly known as S Maria Maggiore, it grew, and by the XVIIc the convent was said to be sheltering 100 nuns (fig. 30.14). Given to the military in 1805, it had to serve as barracks until 1817, when all but the church building was wrecked by fire. That was soon allotted to the state tobacco monopoly by the Austrians, and its nave sliced into three low stories to gain more storage space. The ruined convent was replaced by an up-to-date jail, still in use, and repeatedly troubled by riots.

In 1961 the long-deconsecrated church was transferred to the Soprintendenza ai Monumenti. Urgent repairs were made, and the interpolated wood floors demolished (fig. 30.15). A new stone ground floor was laid 5″ or 6″ above the worn older one, changing the proportions of the pedestals of the columns. Soon after the flood and storm of 1966, major restoration came to an end. In the earthquakes of the summer of 1976 the brick barrel vault of the chancel crashed, leaving a melodramatic visual demonstration of how a wide vault only one brick thick could be kept stable by reinforcing the haunches with additional bricks and rigidifying the main span every yard or so with a rib on the outside of the web of the vault, where it would not show. The interior is now inaccessible except by special permission of the soprintendenza.

The battered Church of S Maria Maggiore is close to Tullio in its elegant elementary language of details and overall simplicity of form, and may be by him (Franzoi-DiStefano, 92), though there is no specific record. (fig. 30.16). Possible evidence may be found in the fact that the Bernabò family, when they installed his marble altarpiece, chose to give the Gothic wood panel of the Madonna from their old chapel in S Giovanni Grisostomo to the nuns of S Maria Maggiore. The gift may have been an idea of the Bernabòs or of Tullio Lombardo (Puppi-Puppi, 217).

As it stands, the building shows a rift where the vaulted chancel with its vaulted flanking chapels is joined to the flat-topped, column-flanked nave and aisles (figs. 30.17 and 30.18). The corners of the chancel are marked by tall Corinthian pilasters—only a sliver of shaft shows in the back corners—that carry an architrave with oblique fascias. The side chapels, with smaller Ionic pilasters, have a similar architrave (fig. 30.19). All these parts are characteristic of work of ca. 1480–1510 and probably come from early in the building campaign, begun in 1503. Above the arches to the chapels there are small unrelated lengths of other entablatures, once surely intended to run around the top of the aisles and the nave just under their wooden ceilings. But these entablatures are now quite unmotivated, just a few feet at the top of the wall like so much yard goods, not connected with anything. A hiatus in continuity is made uncomfortably clear.

The rift between the nave and the chancel and chapels suggests that either the two parts were built in separate campaigns or the abrupt change in design comes from an abrupt change in designer. The last arch of the nave arcade lands on a clumsy corbel, stuck to the face of the wider pilaster, that marks the front of the chancel (figs. 30.20 and 30.21). Bits of the volutes of its capital stick out unassimilated on each side of the end of the wall of the nave arcade. Obviously, something has been done that was not planned when the pilaster was put up; something was improvised later, and heedlessly. For additional proof, one can see on the outside that the east end is built of brick different from that of the nave.

A third of the way from the top, the tall pilasters on the front of the chancel facing the nave are oddly blocked by the wall carried on the arches of the nave arcade (fig. 30.22). The archivolts are narrow, but even so the outer

30.13 S Maria Maggiore.
Tomb of Alvise Malipiero
(Museo Correr, misc. draw-
ing cl III 4237).

30.14 S Maria Maggiore.
Plan (Museo Correr, mss
PD818/12).

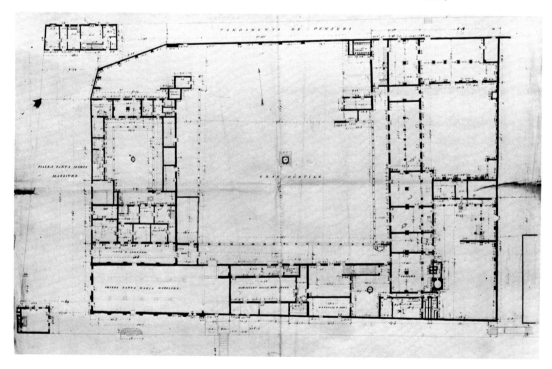

30.15 S Maria Maggiore.
Nave looking west.

30.16 S Maria Maggiore. Interior before restoration.

30.17 S Maria Maggiore.
Small unrelated entablature.
Detail.

30.19 S Maria Maggiore.
Pilaster capital of the right
side chapel.

30.18 S Maria Maggiore.
Small unrelated entablature.
Detail.

30.20 S Maria Maggiore. The rift at the joining of the chancel to the nave. Detail.

30.21 S Maria Maggiore. The rift at the joining of the chancel to the nave. Detail.

30.22 S Maria Maggiore.
Nave colonnade.

molding is pushed into the face of the pilaster and vanishes into it, there being no room for it to come down on the top of the corbel, put there solely to support it. Without cutting or jostling, however, two archivolts fit normally on each of the abaci of the elegant but unsophisticated Ionic capitals of the nave (fig. 30.23). The classical relation of volute, cushion, and echinus has not been fully observed; the voluted ends of the cushion hide the echinus, and there is little trace of the cushion between the two curled ends, no more than a thin inert strip. These capitals crown the heavy columns, which have slight but correct entasis. Proper Ionic bases stand on sturdy pedestals with more moldings than elsewhere, but they have clear and simple geometric profiles, unlike the moldings in the chancel and chapels (fig. 30.24).

By itself, this nave could as well be in Tuscany, perhaps not in Florence but in a more provincial town. The only Venetian who might have created such a pure, spare, classical design after 1503 and before 1523 would be Tullio, or possibly Spavento. It is, of course, possible that the creator of the nave was not a Venetian but a strayed Tuscan, and that would be a unique case. Surely he was no Lombard.

The exterior, even plainer than the interior, was not held important, accepting poverty perhaps as proper for Franciscans, particularly for Observants (fig. 30.25). The only parts that give away the early XVIc date are the simple stone doorways. The front doorway is correct, but has freakish Corinthianesque capitals so simplified that they are leafless, suggesting only some eccentricities of Scarpagnino (fig. 30.26). The plain frieze is inscribed in good Roman letters, DIVAE MARIAE MAIORI D. The horizontal member of the bottom of the pedimental gable at the top of the building continues the corbel table of the flanks, a surprising

30.23 S Maria Maggiore.
Nave colonnade. Detail.

30.24 S Maria Maggiore.
Nave colonnade. Detail.

30.25 S Maria Maggiore.
Exterior.

archaism occasionally matched elsewhere, for example on the backs of
S Salvatore and S Michele. The stone
quoins on the front corners now show
strikingly white against the brick of
the wall, but originally must have been
invisible under plaster. The date must
be before 1537, probably by a couple of
decades, for the Malipiero arms appear
twice, and the support of the Malipiero
family would probably have declined
after the death of Alvise, the principal
benefactor of the church.

This may seem an unduly long account of an inaccessible and half-ruined
church with no documented author;
justifiable, however, mainly if the quality of the nave be recognized as exceptional and distinguished—and also if a
kind of tolerance can be given a building to which so little attention has
been paid before.

A brief excursus may be made for the
beautiful abbey church at Praglia (south
of Padua and Abano) which has several
compelling resemblances to S Maria
Maggiore and to the oeuvre of Tullio.
Although no documents name him,
credible tradition and its marked style,
exceptionally graceful and severe, and
the probable date of ca. 1520–24 (Timofiewitsch 1963, 332), can bring it close
to his orbit. The details are thoroughly
classical, with columns on correct pedestals, elegant Ionic capitals (still rare
at this date), and unornamented moldings, like nothing in Venice save the
equally elegant and not dissimilar nave
of S Maria Maggiore (fig. 30.27). The
church could be a perfecting of the
ideas tried out at S Maria—if that too
can be claimed for him.

There is one work not by Tullio, nor
even Lombardesque (though neither
was Tullio much of the time), but by
Lorenzo Bregno (d.1523), that seems
perversely to fit here as a postscript to
Tullio better than in any other grouping. This is the monument of Admiral

30.26 S Maria Maggiore.
Inscription over main
doorway.

30.27 Abbey church at Praglia. Detail of Ionic capital.

Benedetto Pesaro in the Frari (fig. 30.28). Perhaps influenced by, and surely related to, the Vendramin and Mocenigo tombs, it is closer in date to the latter.

The monument is not wholly coherent either in its general composition or in its style—or styles. Lorenzo Bregno, a generation younger than his kinsmen Paolo and Antonio of Doge Foscari's tomb nearby, was assisted by his brother, Giovanni Battista. He showed himself bold but inexperienced, eager to pick up new ideas, but able to do little more than juxtapose them. The synthesis is meagre. Although a generation later than the so-called Transitional phase between Gothic and the developing Renaissance, this is transitional in a different sense, more like Tullio's bridging of styles, transitional between the already developed Early Renaissance and something not yet clear that was still a step beyond.

The lower part is the most overtly classical of any tomb made yet. Arranged around the doorway and developed as a monumental entrance to the sacristy as well as a memorial to a hero, it has extra reason to be an arch of triumph, with pedestals, columns, entrance arch, and attic, and even memories of the round reliefs on the Arch of Constantine (or the nearer tomb of Andrea Vendramin?). Both its general appearance and the disposition of the many details show just what it is intended to be: a testimonial to a hero. He is dressed in official regalia, with his round admiral's hat, his cloak thrown back to show off his splendid armor, and one arm holding a gilded metal banner of victory aloft. He stands on the plain lid of a sarcophagus, every inch a triumphator, with no effigy of his corpse, no acknowledgment anywhere of the possibility of the triumph of death.

The signs first giving clue to a date soon after 1500 are in the slenderness of the main columns, and their capitals made with thicker and more Roman leafage, though not yet stacked in two rows. In contrast, the flipped architrave fascias on an otherwise orthodox entablature, and the sharp near-metallic cyma are not only non-Roman but also non-Lombardesque (fig. 30.29). The decorative carving on pedestals, trophies, capitals, friezes is also alien to anything of the Lombardos.

The upper story, for which there was no Roman prototype handy, is less classicizing and more typical of the Early Renaissance at first glance—but rather less on the second. The figure of the admiral is thrust impressively forward in front of a big blank panel, effective from its unexpected scale, its blankness and power to isolate him so flashingly. This center section is flanked by fluted columns on un-Roman round pedestals, demanding unorthodox round plinths (fig. 30.30). Similar pedestals are repeated over the outer columns to carry two lounging nudes of Neptune (here making his debut on a Venetian tomb) and Mars (added later by the Florentine Baccio da Montelupo). Large, naked, and more fleshly, these pagans might have made more of a stir than Tullio's chaste Adam on the Vendramin tomb, but the Venetian Renaissance was warmer than chill Neoclassicism. On the side pedestals and on the front of the sarcophagus, set out on dark backgrounds of serpentine and porphyry, are reliefs of wonderful sailing ships, and the fortresses of Cephalonia and Leucadia, which Admiral Pesaro had captured, triumphant reminders of the victories of his lifetime without hint anywhere that he was now dead. Almost all the parts in this zone are well separated, discontinuous, almost autonomous without making a jerky composition.

The most discordant part is at the top. What is strange about the hoodlike gable is that its horizontal cornice, ordinarily the pediment floor, has been set against the back wall, already sunk behind the plane of the surrounding

30.28 Monument of Bene-
detto Pesaro in the Frari.
Elevation (from Cicognara-
Diedo-Selva).

30.29 Pesaro Monument.

church wall. This makes an extra empty space above the head of the admiral, but cramps the triangular space left for the bust of the Virgin, who therefore has to lean awkwardly forward. (She is the only religious symbol on the tomb.) The raking cornice above is not set back, and as a result hangs out like a shed roof, not only heavy but made to show off its massiveness by being deep enough to have two rows of square coffers cut into its soffit. They call attention to themselves and to the abnormal heaviness and depth by the gilded rosettes that glitter in the sinkage of each coffer. The projection and mass have one virtue: they bring the busy figures and architectural members below to a decisive stop. But that does not mean that the masses and implications of movement below have been coordinated, only that they have been stopped. On the contrary, there is an unorganized set of skirmishes there.

The pediment itself has the look of something put up more than a generation later. Possibly the monument was slow in being carried out, and the top is a score of years behind the classicizing archway at the bottom, and thus contemporary not with the Lombardos but with Baccio da Montelupo (d. 1533–35). One detail is sophisticated—the horizontal cornice of the pediment has no cyma. The cyma was properly used only where a gutter might once have been, along the edge of a roof. This was not often recognized in the Early Renaissance, but was accepted as part of the classical grammar as more of it was mastered.

It is conceivable that Lorenzo Bregno did not begin the tomb very soon after the admiral died in 1503. There had just been a bad plague, a series of bank failures, and a panic, and though most rich Venetians were still rich, some chose to hold back on conspicuous expenditures. Work may not have gone far, or just possibly may not even have begun, until after the first seasons of near disaster in the War of Cambrai

(1509 and following years), though if anyone was to be handsomely memorialized then it might well have been a victor like Pesaro. Then there was a plague in 1512, and in 1516 the Turks took Syria and Egypt, temporarily disrupting Venetian trade and its profits. There are many reasons why work might have been stopped or delayed, but there is no proof that it was. Baccio da Montelupo may have been called in after Lorenzo Bregno died in 1523 (in the plague of that year?) to complete whatever had been commenced. No matter what the cause, the pediment must have been made after the time of the dominance of the Lombardos, and probably not until 1520–25.

The whole monument was inspected, cleaned, and carefully restored and strengthened in 1907, and has needed nothing more than a little simple dusting since then.

30.30 Pesaro Monument. Detail of round pedestals and relief of ship.

31 | GIOVANNI BUORA

It must not be thought that there were opposing Lombardo and Codussi camps. There were men who worked now with one and now with the other, and there were more men who borrowed now from one, now from the other, or from both at once; rarely was there any clash in the juxtaposition. If one examines the works of these somewhat younger men in accord with the years of their birth, the important works will not follow one another in a chronological sequence; and if one examines the works chronologically, one will be forced to keep leaping from one master to another, at the same time picking up monuments that are still anonymous. The least illogical procedure is to progress by architects, pausing now and then for a short omnium gatherum of unattributed works. This means that, now that Rizzo, Gambello, Pietro Lombardo, Codussi, Spavento, and Tullio have been discussed along with a few close but not quite accepted works, Giovanni Buora (b. ca.1445–50) and Bartolomeo Bon (b. ca.1463) will follow. Stylistically the decades around 1500 were confused, and putting their products in a logical order may do them some small violence.

Long known as a name, but with an oeuvre not always distinctive or identifiable, Giovanni Buora has only now been given back part of his proper place as a charming but secondary figure sculptor (Munman 1976, 41ff). He is more notable as a specially adroit decorative carver; to a lesser extent he acted as an architect; and he also sold stone. In short, he is almost the antithesis of his contemporary, Giorgio Spavento. One might then suppose him closer to Pietro Lombardo, but the character of his sculpture is unlike and the inventiveness of his decorative work is diametrically opposed to Pietro's, being far more architectural in character. He remains an attractive sculptor, a skilful and inventive decorative carver, a reliable helper when called in to collaborate with an established master or to complete details, ready with his own small team of assistants. But as an architect he has no style deducible from the unmatching fragments where he is known to have worked, or from the out of the ordinary commission at S Giorgio Maggiore. His flair for decorative work is not as independent as that of Pietro Lombardo, but within a narrower field he could manage, to one's surprise, to be more original.

Born at Legnano or Ostenso on the Lake of Lugano ca. 1445–50, he arrived in Venice fairly young, during the first busy years of the Early Renaissance. Nothing is known of where or how he was trained. Working in Venice for the rest of his life, usually in association with better-known masters, the very best in fact, he became more personal as well as more fully Venetian in his art. He died there in 1513. Perhaps because he was unlettered and could not sign his name, it does not often appear on contracts; and when it does, it is not always connected with clearly specified duties, but usually something to do with capitals, door frames, or other decorative pieces.

Highly esteemed, Buora must have been called back and forth from one important job to another. He may have executed much of Pietro Lombardo's tomb of Nicolò Marcello (ca. 1481–85) in SS Giovanni e Paolo, and Pietro's Jacopo Marcello tomb in the Frari (imitating Rizzo). He may also have been responsible for the skilful, unoriginal, Lombardesque Surian tomb in S Stefano (Munman 1976, 41). He is known to have worked for Pietro at the Scuola di S Marco (1487–90), supposedly on the delicate doorway that seems to be so out of rhyme with the typical Lombardo work all around it. Under Codussi, he worked on the larger cloister at S Michele (beginning 1501) (Meneghin, I, 355). He must have carved some of the capitals in the church too. His most important undertaking with

Codussi was at S Zaccaria, surely on the capitals. Possibly following Codussi's designs after his death, he may have completed (or even have begun) the monumental entrance doorway and the window above it at the Scuola di S Giovanni (ca. 1512), and put some finishing touches on S Giovanni Grisostomo together with Codussi's son. He may have returned to S Michele to assist on the singing gallery, with helpers more Lombardesque than he was. The only large works now attributable to him are connected with the Benedictine Monastery of S Giorgio Maggiore.

Some works attributed to him with no documentary evidence but only on subjective opinion have become accepted as his by tradition, without fresh argument, much less any fresh discoveries. Such, for example, is the front doorway of S Zaccaria, put in place twenty years later than Gambello's chequered socle. Buora did have a contract for a carved frieze for a doorway, but it cannot have been for this one at S Zaccaria since that has a plain frieze. More arbitrary, and without even a misunderstood bit of documentation as a pretext, is the attribution to him of the Church of S Maria Mater Domini, and the abbey church and earlier cloister at Praglia. Weaker still are the claims for a few palaces, the Manzoni-Angaran-Polignac, the Grimani-Giustinian-Marcello, both on the Grand Canal, and the peculiar Palazzo Michiel on the Fondamenta della Sensa and—even more flightily—the Ca' Gussoni. These have little that could be related to him, shadowy though he be, or to one another. There are, however, two early works that deserve to be looked at and accepted as his, even though that means jumping backward here into the late XVc: the fragments of architectural decoration in S Zaccaria and the tomb of Jacopo Surian.

The nave supports in S Zaccaria and Buora's probable contributions to them have already been discussed in chapter

3 (fig. 31.1). The capitals of the nave columns ask for special notice. Highly original and easy to rank as masterpieces, they are now usually said to be by Giovanni Buora (who may, but need not, be the same as the Giovanni da Milano recorded for payments in 1470). They are datable ca. 1480 and later, but the capitals in different parts of the church must have been made a number of years apart. Buora was paid for work here in 1474, 1476, and 1481, all under Gambello. As on nearly every building where he is known to have worked, Buora dragged puzzles behind him; what he did is not always easy to identify. However, as he was a specialist in decorative sculpture, and as Gambello was busy seeing to many kinds of work all over the building and was sometimes away on other jobs, probabilities favor Buora for the capitals.

Nearly all Early Renaissance capitals, as has several times been pointed out, had a collar of only one row of leaves, like thousands of Gothic capitals made in Venice, hundreds of Byzantine, and a few score Roman examples on the nearby mainland. To a Venetian of the late XVc the word "capital" must have conjured up an image of something at the top of a column with a single ring of leaves followed by something coiling or budding under the four corners of a square lid. The unique and early capitals of the nave of S Zaccaria show more awareness of the proportions of traditional Corinthian models, but without paralyzing archaeological knowledge. Under the standard abacus flaring at the corners above a less traditional echinus carved like a collar of beads or leaves, come the corner volutes, regular spirals or neatly wrapped flowers. So far, all defer with some fealty to the antique. But just below, the bell-like body is vigorously shielded by spread-winged eagles linked by garlands of blossoms. Striking, not to say startling, they may have a meaning beyond ornamentation, referring back to

the Byzantine imperial eagle (Osella-dore, unpub. [5]), since the church had been so often favored by direct gifts from the emperors. The earlier churches on the site had capitals with imperial eagles.

These capitals are richly carved on the upper part, and left bare on the lower, which consequently can be seen as a section of the column shaft readying itself for something about to happen above. This unordinary combination had been anticipated at S Michele, made about the same time, and a few other features are similar. There is reason to think that Buora made the capitals at S Michele for Codussi (fig. 31.2). He must have come to know Codussi and could have picked up some of his attitudes; his own now seem closer to Codussi's than to those of anyone else then active. Buora's later work at S Michele, on the *barco* (1480s) is less identifiable, perhaps because a crew of miscellaneous carvers were working on it at once, and Codussi was not directing them.

In addition to the remarkable capitals in the nave of S Zaccaria, those of the ambulatory must also be carefully considered (fig. 31.3). Although carried out under Gambello, they have already shed all memories of Gothic form. The bell is divided halfway up, with fluting below, vertical or twisted, like those at S Michele made at much the same time (possibly a year or so later). The upper half manages to have leaves curling around flowers to make rosette-like volutes under the corners of the abaci. The latter are four- or six-sided, depending on which is demanded by the tight conjunction made by the arches and piers above, and to make easy coexistence with the capitals crowded in close beside them. As a result, some abaci have a six-scalloped form above six volutes, looking less Vitruvian than botanical or zoological, like some boneless sea creature.

The tomb of the physician Jacopo Surian is so lacking in a controlling concept for the design that it seems an ideal candidate for one of those composite or patchwork monuments, partly by a crew of carvers, intermittently under the direction of sculptor A, who contributed some details himself, and then partly under B, who may have done a figure or two. Although it is now established as in part by Buora, surely for some of the sculpture and hence possibly for some or most of the architecture (Munman 1976, 41–44), it cannot be explained away as an early work, for it is dated 1488–93. Who was responsible for the full architectural organization—if anyone—is not known; probably there was more than one person.

It was planned for the Frari, but put instead beside the main door of S Stefano. The tomb was long associated with the *bottega* of the Lombardos (and its sculpture even with Pietro himself), but it is now known to be a work by Buora, though much of it was patterned on Pietro's Nicolò Marcello tomb of a decade earlier, shorn of wings, roof, redundant sarcophagus, and bracket supports. Some details were copied outright, such as the entablature above the columns with its architrave overwhelmed by an outsize egg and dart, and its cornice with a fluted corona and shelf-like cyma (fig. 31.4). Such direct copying does not establish common authorship for, while a master might restudy best, he would be less likely to repeat perfunctory weaknesses, as an ex-underling might. There are other awkwardnesses; the frieze pushes the entablature apart, overemphatic because so wide and so plain amid such fanciness and because it is slate black marble amid limestone. The lower parts, an overlarge limestone relief of swags of fruit, a squall of fluttering crinkly ribbons, and two inset marble skulls, have no connection with the Marcello tomb. The framing piers serve

31.1 S Zaccaria. Pedestal of nave column.

31.2 S Michele in Isola.
Capitals of nave columns,
barco in background.

31.3 S Zaccaria. Capitals of
ambulatory.

31.4 Tomb of Doctor Jacopo
Surian in S Stefano.

as pedestals for the undersized columns, though over half as high as what they purport to support.

The fluted columns are so slender, delicate, and small in scale—the whole tomb is only 22′6″ by 9′6″—that they look inadequate for the superposed arch and load. The deep antae or piers behind do not show enough to lend apparent strength here where it seems needed. The arch suffers triply, for in addition to its unsatisfying support and its pinched or sliced beginning, it is made to look weak in contrast to the big scale and bold relief of what it encloses, the lunette of the Madonna, donor, and saints.

Small and weak though they are, the columns yet manage to jostle the sarcophagus and effigy instead of enframing them protectively and allowing them enough space for a sense of repose. The sarcophagus supports a sleeping effigy and is held uncomfortably high by gryphons, their claws busy clutching scrolls tightly but unstably. In the shadow between, two baby genii hold a long inscription, unreadable because of the shadow, the small letters, and the shallow incising. The fine low relief on the bottom of the sarcophagus is even harder to see, but that is no surprise since the whole tomb is not easy to see, set as it is in form-destroying light right under a window.

In other words, many of the separate parts, though handsome in themselves, suffer from the way they have been handled. There is an air of flimsiness and lack of coordination, brought about by the lack of architectural authority. The work must come from someone innocent of much architectural experience—or criticism. Some parts are so different from the rest that they seem intruders from some other monument; some seem properly made to order. The cornice is, for example, suitably proportioned, thoroughly architectural, but somewhat bold. On top of it, at an incompatible scale, comes something that begins like a "Florentine" pediment, but stops short in the middle to curl back above a huge pair of feathery wings, themselves at still another scale.

In the tombs closer to the Lombardos, there are innocent violations of classic syntax, slights to the discipline of structural integrity, but rarely such indifference to scale and overall coherence. Yet, except for the heraldic reliefs on the spandrels and the scrolls at the top, every part of the monument could have come—separately—from the Lombardo repertory. *Bottega* workmen could have done most of the carving, and one of the masters might have helped with the figures, but the basic design must have been produced by a weak follower.

Some tomb monuments are known that no longer have physical existence, for example that of Venetian Pope Eugenius IV Condulmer (1431–47), once in the monastery church on the island of S Giorgio in Alga, northwest of the city (fig. 31.5). Much was destroyed in a bad fire in 1717, but the buildings were somehow soon restored, only to be handed over to the new municipal authorities in 1799 for a political prison, and then for the storage of gunpowder. They have been repeatedly vandalized, and almost nothing remains (Piamonte 1975, 145–47). There is no information as to the date of the making or the destruction of the monument, but it still has a ghostly existence in one of Grevenbroeck's drawings of ca.1754, which shows it to be thoroughly Lombardesque, reminiscent of several surviving tombs, familiar in every part except for the mammoth shell swooping over the top. Though the pope had died a generation before, his tomb cannot have been made before the late XVc, possibly on commission or from a bequest of his nephew, the next Venetian pope, Paul II Barbo (1464–71), who had always particularly venerated him.

495 | GIOVANNI BUORA

31.5 Monument to the
Venetian Pope Eugenius IV
(drawing by Jan II van Grevenbroeck, Museo Correr,
Cod. Gradenigo 228, I/73).

More than anyone else, Buora must have been responsible for the most extraordinary of the early elements at S Giorgio Maggiore, the dormitory wing known as the *Manica Lunga* ("long sleeve"). Although work had been started perhaps as early as 1449, surely by ca. 1460, probably by his father Antonio, the effective campaign got under way only in 1488 or 1494, presumably under the direction of Giovanni, with help from his now old father. The early work went slowly. The wing was not yet roofed ca. 1500 (Barbari map) and after Giovanni's death in 1513, work was still dragging on, now under his son Andrea (figs. 31.6 and 31.7). Vavassore showed the *manica* as it now appears ca. 1525, but something was still being finished somewhere inside in 1533, and the building was not considered complete until 1540 (fig. 31.8). It is hard to guess why it took so long, for even throughout its dinosaurian 415′ length, it was utterly plain in structure and decoration. Fire ruined a large part in 1569, and repairs ran on until 1604. Alterations were made for the military in the XIXc, and extensive undoing of them plus approximate rebuilding were needed in 1951–53 to transform the hulk into a vocational school for 600 boys as part of the Giorgio Cini Foundation.

The corridor runs the length of the building between rows of 17′ by 17′ cells on the upper floor, luxurious dimensions for Benedictines. A lightweight barrel vault covers it, penetrated over each cell door by a scoop, with a wall lunette for a window, a sort of clerestory since the corridor is higher than the roofs of the cells. The repeated interruptions by the scoops make what is technically a barrel vault look instead like one long groin vault. All has now been virtually rebuilt, probably much as it was in the beginning. Since one cannot often see down such a sweep of tunnel-like interior, the effect is astonishing—astonishing,

however, only from its extent, not from any happy architectural ideas. Fundamentally it is no more than an outlandish exaggeration of the old palace *portego* or *sala* scheme, with rooms opening off each side. Suitably severe for monks, it is nowhere relieved by any of what Buora was best at, decorative inventions. Unless documented, it would never have been attributed to him.

The little facade at the south end, begun in 1508, is of quite a different nature (fig. 31.9). Though plain, it makes a perky effect rising abruptly out of the big, flat, wet Basin of S Mark's. Its pinkish plaster is divided by white limestone bands like those of the Capitaneria across the water (before that was painted over). The usual Venetian triptych is made up of wings reflecting the cells and a center for the corridor, all the same height regardless of the roofs behind. The arched windows and *oculus* are not noteworthy, but the skyline is: three stilted semicircles pulled up into quasi-oriental ogees in a diluted iteration of Codussi's silhouette on the Scuola di S Marco, where Buora had worked earlier. (The scalloped skyline of the scuola had come from S Mark's, where it was a XIVc embellishment emulating recent churches in Constantinople and other Byzantine cities; the *Manica* emulates only the scuola.) The simple cornice has an architrave with two sloped fascias, a souvenir of Codussi (fig. 31.10). Everything in the building has counterparts elsewhere; nothing exemplifies pure Buora.

From this and the varied earlier carving already noted (almost all done under some superior master architect) or more independent works (almost all of uncertain authorship), no clearly defined artistic personality emerges for Giovanni Buora. His most original contribution appears to have been in his ornamental carving, nowhere of greater

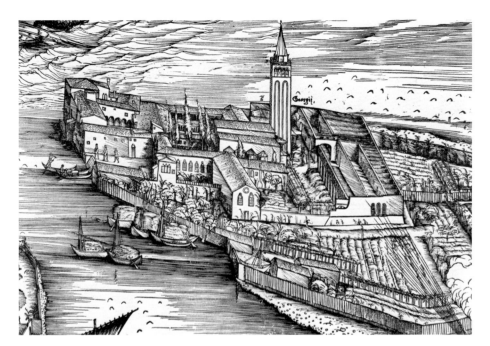

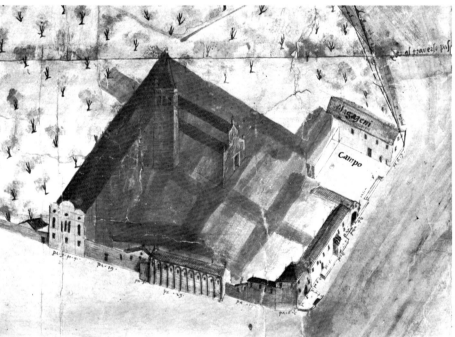

31.6 S Giorgio Maggiore. The Manica Lunga without a roof (from the de' Barbari map of 1500).

31.7 S Giorgio Maggiore. The Manica Lunga. (Drawing said to be ca. 1470 but, because the Manica is roofed and already has its facade, more likely of ca. 1510–15, Archivio di Stato, Miscellanea Mappe, 39.)

31.8 S Giorgio Maggiore.
The Manica Lunga, ca. 1535
(from the Vavassore map).

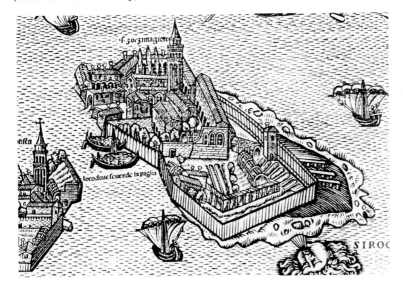

31.10 S Giorgio Maggiore.
The Manica Lunga. Detail of
cornice.

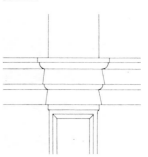

31.9 S Giorgio Maggiore.
The Manica Lunga. Facade.

31.11 S Giorgio Maggiore.
Cloister of the Cypresses.

quality or more inventiveness than in the capitals and pedestals for the columns of S Zaccaria. These are not close to the other items associated with his name, nor with anything else in Early Renaissance Venice; they seem to be beautiful orphans of uncertain parentage.

The earlier of the two cloisters at S Giorgio, the so-called "Cloister of the Cypresses," may have been planned by Giovanni Buora before he died in 1513, along with the adjacent *Manica Lunga*, as parts of a grand scheme for rebuilding the whole establishment. But the cloister was not begun until 1516, by his son Andrea, and was not fully finished until ca. 1540 (fig. 31.11). In other words, cloister and dormitory were being built largely at the same time. Andrea was involved with the cloister from the first, for he was contracted to supply twenty columns in 1514, presumably just the shafts, which were often prefabricated. He had probably been helping in his father's stone business and took it on when his father died. The undertaking at S Giorgio had been unusually big; the cloister, for example, was abnormally large, eleven bays by thirteen. There must have been a very considerable population of monks to justify this and the huge dormitory, or else an abbot with grandiose hopes.

The Ionic columns on a low parapet, separating the cloister walk from the now green but bare garden, have normal bases, variously tumescent shafts with double entasis, and Ionic capitals of typical Early Renaissance shape (figs. 31.12 to 31.17). A collar, either fluted or with fish-scale imbrication, leads with a sophisticated apophyge to a fish-scale echinus. Most of the volutes of the cushion are joined by a lifeless, thin strip below the flaring abacus as often in early Ionic, for example at Praglia or S Maria Maggiore. The variations from capital to capital impart a fresh, homemade look. The columns in the corners make no concession to the usual imperative to face both ways in order to be attuned to the capitals of both adjacent arcades, necessarily at right angles; they are, instead, just like the others, facing the right way for one side and the wrong way for the adjacent side. Above these corner columns the robustly molded archivolts come to grief, destroying one another completely. Over all the unexceptional other columns, where the archivolts threaten to collide, a limp, drooping, keystone-like bracket of fish scales acts as a figleaf and hides all. Below it, a compromise merger of moldings runs straight down (stilted) to the top of the capital. The fact that the collision could have occurred shows an early date; the fact that it was hidden shows a later stage of sophistication; both are quite possible ca. 1516, the presumed date of the design.

Chapter rooms had been a regular element in the composition of monasteries for centuries. The meetings held there, always most formal, could be for instruction, for business having to do with the day-to-day running of the whole establishment, or exceptional immediate problems, or relations with the head house of the order. Some were attended by all the monks; those in the larger houses by a select governing committee. They were, in their way, the administrative offices of their establishments.

The chapter room, with its handsome entrance, in the middle of the north side of the cloister at S Giorgio, built a little later than the cloister but, like nearly all Benedictine chapter rooms, traditionally open wide to it, was later sequestered to some other use, and the entrance walled in. The door to the chapter room and a pair of *bifore* were discovered, opened up, and restored in 1951 (figs. 31.18 and 31.19). For some reason, perhaps having to do with the terrain or with older buildings on the site, the chapter room floor is

31.12 Cloister of the Cy-
presses. Ionic columns on a
low parapet.

31.13 Cloister of the Cy-
presses. Normal bases, variously tumescent shafts
with double entasis.

31.16 Cloister of the Cypresses. Fish-scale bracket.

31.14 Cloister of the Cypresses. Ionic capitals of typical Early Renaissance shape with fluted collars.

31.15 Cloister of the Cypresses. Corner column.

31.17 Cloister of the Cypresses. Base of column, north side of cloister.

31.18 S Giorgio Maggiore.
Chapter house. Door.

lower than the cloister walk, and one
has to walk down into it. The doorway
and the windows, too rich in moldings
and ornaments for the Early Renaissance, were made only in 1524–33.
These and the windows in the story
above must, then, stem entirely from
Andrea, and not from his father. But
the cloister itself, markedly different in
detail and in date, could more likely be
from a design of the father's executed
by the son.

Besides a share of the cloister, and
the whole chapter room, only one other
work can be given to Andrea Buora,
and this authorship has only recently
been discovered by Philip Rylands,
in Mercati (*Rendiconti . . . Atti . . .
Pont.Accad. di Archaeologia*), XV, 22–
25. It is the first chapel on the left at
the Madonna dell'Orto, the Cappella
Valier. Vincenzo Valier made a will in
1520 to assure himself a family chapel
here, and his widow completed it in
1526 (Cicogna 1824–53, II, 276). It is so
close to "early" Early Renaissance
chapels and chancels that one might
misdate it by half a century. The admirable restoration of the church by the
English Venice-in-Peril Fund, 1968–71,
has put it back in beautiful order,
above all by reopening the original
slow curve of the apse with its windows at each edge (one now a door),
which must have given ideal light to
the altarpiece (not that now there).

Save for a few details, its domed cube
could be coeval with such other domed
cubes as the Cornaro chapel at the
SS Apostoli, Codussi's chancel at
S Michele or Pietro's at the Miracoli.
(The archway leading in from the
church is the only element now fully
betraying the late date.) Unornamented
sobriety, purity, and clarity (as well as
phototropically sloped fascias) confirm
its place in the Codussi family, by direct and legitimate descent from Mauro
to Giovanni to Andrea Buora (assisted

31.19 S Giorgio Maggiore. Chapter house. Window.

31.20 S Giorgio Maggiore. Window of wing facing cloister.

here by his brother Antonio). Ultimately it goes back to Brunelleschi and, though retardataire by at least two generations and of no originality, it is, nevertheless, a work of high quality. The combination is rare—it is chronologically backward but aesthetically winning.

In time, the cloister fell into such disrepair that some of the arches had to be propped up with brick piers. The reconditioning of everything on the island for the Cini Foundation in the 1950s called for considerable rebuilding here, both for restoration and adaptation to new uses, and the whole has now happily recovered its original appearance, or something close to it.

32 | BARTOLOMEO BON

Bartolomeo Bon, Buon or, in his native Bergamo, Bono or Buono, sometimes called Bon il Bergamasco, was a follower, possibly a pupil, and perhaps a relative of Codussi. He is not to be confused with the earlier Venetian-born Bartolomeo Buon of the Ca' del Duca. The first notice of this later Bon Bergamasco in Venice is of 1485, but it does not refer to him surely enough to fix him there that early, or to approximate his age. By 1489 he was mature enough to be awarded the commission for the Church of S Rocco, and by 1492 important enough to be named *protomaestro* of the Salt Office, a post not given to tyros, since it had an important voice in the allotting of funds for public buildings. He had to give this up in 1496, when he was sent to the East as consultant to Admiral Trevisan (as military engineer?). On his return in 1498 he resumed the post, and was soon made Captain of the *Provveditori* of the all-powerful Council of Ten. He was indeed an important personage, but we are not sure why. In 1505, on the death of Bartolomeo Gonella, he was raised to the top, *proto* of the *Procuratori di S Marco de Supra*, responsible for government buildings in the Piazza and Piazzetta. For thirty-one years, until he died in 1529, he was in one way or another concerned with all the important city buildings, as what might now be called city architect. Busy with supervising, and away from 1496–98, he cannot have had as much uninterrupted time as some of his contemporaries to cogitate what he had to build. Nevertheless, his work is always beautifully finished, without signs of haste or cut corners.

Save for the halt in building called for by the War of Cambrai, the years of his activity saw a special flowering of architecture in Venice, sometimes moderate in quantity but still a springtime, brought to an end only with the change of season following the arrival of Sansovino and Sanmicheli, with their new and compelling Roman-Florentine High Renaissance ideas. The change follows Sansovino's succession as *proto* of the procurators of S Mark's on Bon's death in 1529, though of course samples of the old manner—some of great distinction—kept blooming for a score of years. Bon's work was all in the old native ways. Like Buora and a number of others, he more often contributed parts of buildings designed by someone else; for example, the Campanile of S Mark's (1511-, following Spavento), the Scuola di S Rocco (1516-24, finished by Scarpagnino), and most of the Procuratie Vecchie. His individual architectural character is not easy to isolate.

His first works show how much he followed, though never completely, the lessons early learned from Codussi. Slowly he tempered his severe training by a discreet taste for the idiosyncratic Venetian display familiar from the work of the Lombardos. But although he may have been a sculptor like them, he tended to avoid ornamental carved moldings and other such trimming. Except in one special late case, such ornament was not an essential of his architecture, nothing in its very bones, but just something added to its surface. He showed enough originality to allow him to profit from the examples of his predecessors without becoming their rote-repeating follower. What is identifiable as surely his, however, does not have enough particular characteristics to allow additional attributions ever to be more than half-passable guesses. He had no telltale quirks, nor did he repeat favorite motives. The posts he was given show that he was held worthy of trust, but none of his prominent buildings and positions was mentioned by Marin Sanudo in his interminable diary, written in almost the same years (1496-1533). Marin mentioned Bon once (miscalling him Beneto)—not in connection with building, but with

money (XIV, 20). For such an important and hardworking artist, surviving information about Bon is slim.

His first traceable work in Venice is the Church of S Rocco, according to Sansovino, writing a century later (185) and often repeated by others. It was on land that belonged to the Franciscans of the Frari, who had already allowed the Confraternity of S Rocco a little building (still there) for a small scuola and church. In 1489 friendly dealings worked out a transfer of this and more land for a new church. Work was begun that year, after the relics of the much-venerated plague-saint had been obtained, some said by theft from his birthplace, Montpellier, others said from a castle in Lombardy. The enthusiasm roused by many reported miracles, mostly of recovery from the plague—there were eleven plagues between 1478 and 1528, mostly bubonic —brought intensified devotions to this potential deliverer. There had been a bad epidemic in 1485 (diphtheria or influenza?, Pullan 1968, 151), just as the confraternity was enlarging itself and considering a new building. Elevation to a scuola grande, also in 1489, speeded the accumulation of funds to start a church and keep work going more quickly than usual. The east end was done in less than a year, and the facade went up in 1494-95. An old bell tower was pulled down in 1508 so that the dome could be successfully constructed. By the middle of the XVIIIc, the hurriedly built nave had to be replaced, and only Bon's east end was preserved; his front portal was saved by moving it around to serve as a humbler north side door.

What is left shows that the loss was a minor misfortune (fig. 32.1). Bon's east end has three semicircular apses, the side ones half as wide as the center. They are set behind lengths of barrel vaults, while the main apse follows a square chancel with pendentives carrying a drum with windows and a stilted hemispherical dome. Apse and chancel

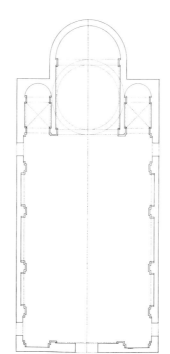

32.1 Church of S Rocco.
Plan (drawing from the Visentini Workshop; RIBA).

32.2 Church of S Rocco.
Facade (engraving from
Coronelli, *Chiese*).

together took up a third of the length of the interior. As so often, they were raised three steps above the common floor for the laity, or rather the 500 members of the scuola, the maximum allowed. Everything is executed in a plain but elegant way, with sober ornament, all clearly in what will soon be recognized as the Codussi tradition, though in 1489 that was not fully formed. S Maria Formosa was still being built, and S Giovanni Grisostomo had not been begun. The scheme of S Rocco must be based on S Michele in Isola, even to setting the narrow apse windows high enough to allow for a big altarpiece below them. Only the little side domes are missing. Bon early took his place as half-pioneer, half-follower. Possibly he had come to know Codussi through family or local Bergamasque connections, and it must not be forgotten that two Camaldolesians were said to have stolen the relics of the saint from Montpellier, which could have led to relations between his new church and the monks of S Michele and their architect.

Of Bon's nave we know nothing more than that it was boxlike, without columns, and had either a flat ceiling or the exposed rafters of a shed roof. The facade was of Codussian type, in a variation hard to believe successful (Barbari view; Coronelli 1703; fig. 32.2). Although not in front of an aisled interior, it was marked as though it was by painfully tall, thin pilasters, framing the usual tall arched windows on either side, and a small, low door in the middle, emphasized somewhat by three concentric steps below (like S Michele) and a semicircular lunette above. Its remains can be seen in its new location on the north side of the building (figs. 32.3 and 32.4). Higher up came a big *oculus* in a garlanded frame, and then across the whole front a heavy entablature. The side sections did not have the Codussian quadrant, but a complete semicircular gable with

32.3 Church of S Rocco. North door.

32.4 Church of S Rocco. North door. Detail.

a belfry perched on top, elements calling attention to themselves and contributing less than nothing to a sense of unity (as quadrants do). In the center, a little story bounded by dwarf pilasters ended in a low pediment, uncomfortable between the insistently bouncy sides. This had a smaller *oculus*, perhaps above, perhaps below the nave ceiling—if there was one. It is impossible to believe that this odd composition rivaled the east end and its high altar in quality. It was destroyed when the nave was rebuilt in the XVIIIc.

The high altar is a later work, made in 1520 (fig 32.5). Set up on three additional steps, it provides a more emphatic setting for the celebration of the Mass. Perhaps in accord with the richer tastes of the richer members of the scuola, Bon's manner here was less Codussian, more opulent in its marquetry of porphyry and *verde antico*, by now a favorite deep color chord (inherited from Byzantium). Like a number of Early Renaissance tombs, it is based partly on the Roman triumphal arch, with a particularly disciplined and coherent arrangement of parts, even to the setting of the main columns in shallow niches, emphasizing their correlation with the wall. The altar block, or *mensa*, comes to the same height as the pedestal of the main order, which is carried as a dado around the entire east end, binding it into one multisegmented composition. At the ends of the altar, short cheeks of wall of the same height run forward to set it physically apart, to enshrine it as it were by separating it and the celebrants from its less sacred immediate surroundings.

The center bay is arched above its sumptuous mottled marble columns, and the niche they combine to form enframes a *cassone*-like sarcophagus for the relics, with a painted panel for a front (fig. 32.6). On the sarcophagus stands a bronze figure of the saint, carrying his traveler's staff and, in the traditional iconographic gesture, raising

his tunic to show the plague sore on his leg. (He had become infected while nursing the stricken, was miraculously cured in a forest retreat, and was thenceforth better able to cure others.) Beyond the arch, lesser columns do their part, supporting the top entablature, which, like the lower, has an architrave with inclined fascias. The architectural framework is strong-looking, the sculpture comfortably set in its niches, and the polychromy a triumph of discreet sumptuosity. No moldings are carved. Venturino Fantoni is said to have been entrusted with most of the execution in 1520 (Martinelli, 352), with some of the sculpture made by Bon himself.

Bon's professional connection with the Clock Tower has already been mentioned. The facades of the wings now visible must have been finished after he became *proto* of the *Procuratori de Supra* in 1505, and as they had power, enjoyed using it, and almost always got their way, Bon may have been seeing to it that some of the procurators' ideas were carried out here as well as in the Procuratie half-a-dozen years later. Any association of Bon with the design of the wings can be only conjectural, and not very convincing.

Like everyone else's, Bon's relations to the Procuratie are enigmatic, though it was he who had the contract to build (or rebuild) them. The best guess is that the facade on the Piazza is essentially his, or more his than anyone else's. He was the *proto* in charge, and he is named in the oldest (but not contemporary) texts. He was also close to Antonio Grimani, a particularly important procurator (who became doge in 1521) and the principal proponent of the project, who managed to have many of the old houses demolished after fortuitous fires in 1512 and 1513 (Da Mosto, 282; Sanudo, XIV, 305; XV, 541). There is nothing in the facade that is necessarily incompatible with

Altare Maggiore della Chiesa di S. Rocco

32.5 Church of S Rocco
(from Cicognara-Diedo-
Selva).

32.6 Church of S Rocco.
High altar.

the not too personal style of his more certain works (though there is nothing so compatible either that it calls for the rejection of everyone else). What is really novel and daring is the repetitiveness, and here that was inherited, not invented. Bon may have had some earlier scheme of Codussi's to follow, which many have long accepted, or he may have had to accept something of the mysterious Tuscan Celestro's model of 1514, as well as quite a lot of suggestions from various insistent procurators. All that is firmly established is that Guglielmo Grigi carried out the top story (though he need not have designed it). The whole is best kept somewhere between limbo and Bartolomeo Bon, nearer the latter.

After quite a lot of political and financial maneuvering, work must have begun in 1514, and at first have gone ahead quickly, for soon there were discussions of how to decide which house should go to whom. By 1518 or soon after, several were occupied, and Procurator Andrea Gritti (to become doge after Grimani in 1523) was able to give a great wedding party for his daughter in his new house on the Piazza (Sanudo, XXV, 248; XXVIII, 317–25; XXIX, 399; XXX, 483; XXXI, 41).

It matters little who designed the ground story arcades, for they follow their forerunners and those of the Ospizio across the way with little more than restyling, no deeper than the changes we now see every few years in automobile bodies. But something really new began with the sophisticated piani nobili, with their elegant fluted colonnettes, their sharp light-catching archivolts, their simple entablatures with oblique fascias on the architraves, plain friezes and unornamented cornices held close to the wall (fig. 32.7). (One remembers S Maria Formosa.) The only decorative carving is on the capitals (how avoid it there?), which appear to be all alike as in antique colonnades, but in fact are almost imperceptibly varied. Except for these near trifles, the general plainness makes clear which party had the designer's loyalty, and even the capitals are not foreign to the plain-speaking tenets of the Codussi-Spavento-Tullio-Bon believers.

In 1517 much of the work was turned over to Bon's kinsman Guglielmo de' Grigi (also called il Bergamasco), known in Venice only from 1515. He must have been younger than Bon, though they died only a year apart, in 1529 and 1530. Although nominally in charge, he was directly under Bon and responsible to him. Bon retained the right to dismiss him out of hand, without consulting others. There is now no way of knowing whether the topmost frieze, with its *oculi*, and the animated skyline of fancy merlons alternating with vases is his invention (as is often assumed), or an adaptation of something of Bon's, or a definite design of Bon's. The vases or urns are not unlike those Codussi (?) put on the *albergo* wing of the Scuola di S Marco in the 1490s, but not of a type confined to these two; and while they might add a featherweight of evidence for some relation to Codussi, they need not, for the relation is not unique. In any case, the top of the building is a tour de force. There are 450 apertures on that long facade (counting the mezzanine windows); controlling them and keeping the all-but-unbelievable rows of them alive enough to catch and hold the interest is the work of a true master (or two? or three?).

Bon was commissioned in 1510, thanks again to Antonio Grimani who found the funds, to put a new top on the Campanile of S Mark's. The old one had been struck by lightning in 1489 with such intensity that the beams from which the bells were hung burned through, and they crashed 200' to the ground. The top had been hit before and would be hit again, but never so devastatingly after 1776, when a

32.7 Procuratie Vecchie.
Upper floors.

Franklinian lightning rod was installed, one of the first in Europe (Lane 1973, 443). After the 1489 disaster, a new top had been projected by Spavento. Jacopo de' Barbari showed the Campanile in 1500 in his first edition with only a temporary wood cover (fig. 32.8). Bon may have taken over all or some of Spavento's scheme. The War of Cambrai had delayed all civil work in 1509 and a bad quake in 1511 stopped it again. After serious checking and reconsideration, the top was finally finished in 1514.

Reuwich's summary woodcut of 1486 and Foresti Bergomense's of 1490 give versions—not necessarily accurate—of the pre-Spavento top, fairly close to that now existing. It seems likely that successive designers did little but change details. The only evidence for Spavento's scheme is the part of the bell chamber that showed in the first edition of Barbari's view. In his second edition, in or just after 1514, and in Montalboddo's crude woodcut of 1517, and Vavassore's clearer one of ca. 1525 (Cassini, 32–37), the top is shown as finished by Bon in 1514, as it still appears today, and probably more or less as it had always looked (figs. 32.9 and 32.10).

The shaft of the XIIc–XIVc tower is typical of mediaeval campanili in all respects but one, its size. Soaring above everything, it acts like a giant axle to the spreading islets and canals of the city. The 39' square brick shaft tapers 160' up to a 34' square, stiffened and visually vitalized by five vertical strips in relief. Inside, there is another separate brick shaft, bound to the outer one by the many runs continuing up each side as one endless stairway. The weight, and the foundations it demanded and got, are astonishing for the XIIc. Spavento or Bon used limestone arches to link the tops of the long exterior strips, and Bon used limestone again for most of his bell chamber above them. Above it comes a brick attic, under a 60' pyramidal spire

sheathed in coppery bronze plates, once gilded. If it were lower, the pyramid could appear to weigh down, like many Romanesque tower tops, and reduce the seeming force of the upward thrust of the shaft; if steeper, it would act the other way, and imply a movement on up beyond the top, like many Gothic spires. This does neither, but remains quietly static, without pulling down or pushing up.

At the tip, 320' from the pavement of the Piazza, a gilded 16' angel with flaring wings veers with the wind and gives information to ships coming and going. After having been tried on a wood scaffold in 1513, this was finally set on a swivel at the top of the masonry construction before 1517. The figure has had to be repaired or replaced several times after lightning and minor fires, and the present one is wholly new. The gold-faced plates of the spire and the flashing facets of the turning angel shone as a daytime beacon for distant ships. (No one, of course, would try to come in at night.) The bell chamber was found ideal as a lookout for firespotters, day and night. Here Galileo demonstrated in 1609, to a select group of the Signoria, the virtues of the telescope he had just invented, showing them the satellites of Jupiter and the mountains of the moon (Doglioni, pseud for Sansovino-Bardi, 9; McNeill, 195).

In time the tower was seriously weakened, less from any deterioration of the original masonry or foundations than from the many unwise cuttings made in the inner shaft, and a chimney flue channeled up through the outer one (for a fireplace for the watchman). On the morning of Bastille Day 1902, it collapsed straight down on itself, harming no one, "like a gentleman," said a popular quip (fig. 32.11). Miraculously, the biggest, heaviest, and most sonorous of the five bells, *La Marangona*, plummeted 200' without cracking. The mayor, Count Grimani, perhaps with

32.8 Campanile of S Mark's
in 1500 (from the de' Barbari
map).

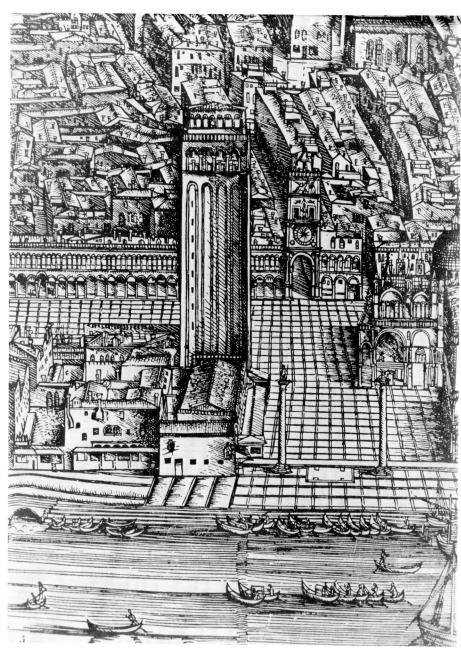

32.9 Campanile of S Mark's.

32.10 Campanile of S
Mark's. Later XVIc views
(from G Keller, 1607).

32.11 Campanile of S
Mark's. Afternoon of July
14, 1902.

the extra inspiration of knowing that Procurator Grimani had paid for the new top with Grimani money augmented by the sale of a few unused items in the treasure of S Mark's (Lane 1973, 442), ordered it immediately rebuilt, "dov'era e com'era." Faithfully reconstituted, it was blessed by the patriarch on S Mark's Day 1912, and has given no trouble since, even when the top swayed all too visibly in the spring and fall earthquakes of 1976.

The most exceptional feature is in the design of the arcades (fig. 32.12). Slender colonnettes play their part on the visible outside face, and similar ones on the inside face, while between them—little seen but giving essential strength—oblong piers have been ingeniously fitted in a way suited to the particular needs here: resistance to weight and to the vibration of the bells. The resulting scheme is probably unique, and may have been conceived by either Spavento or Bon.

The middle colonnettes on three faces of the outside are of *verde antico*, not nearly as strong as their limestone neighbors (the one on the other face is of polished granite). These colored shafts appear to have been appropriated from something else. Perhaps they had been made for Spavento's unlucky project or, since they lack the apophyge and fillet of the newer neighbors, they may come from something earlier, cut down for new use. Such shifting of color in an arcade had been common in mediaeval work, as so sumptuously displayed on S Mark's below, but it was far less common in antique practice, and perhaps not connected with antiquity at all by the architect here, since the touch of color could easily occur to anyone who saw the advantages of relating the crown of the tower to the polychromy of S Mark's, and also to the more restrained Clock Tower across the way. An unexpected and little-seen elegance comes from the

balustrade above the bell chamber, with its marble sill upheld by colonnettes of bronze.

The colonnettes of the bell chamber have no capitals. The oblong pier, after a fillet and quarter-round corresponding to the moldings at the tops of the column shafts, flares outward to a strongly molded block into which the tops of the cylindrical shafts disappear (fig. 32.13). It is a flight from classical syntax, suitable for the detailing of small parts above normal eye level. Important guests were invited to the bell chamber on occasion, but to admire the view, not the refinements of carved capitals. (What they saw instead—if they looked—would have been curiously like English Gothic "nook" capitals.) They seem more akin to the simplifications and abbreviations of Spavento than to the somewhat richer ornamentation sometimes associated with Bon, but in truth they are not typical of either.

In the Procuratie and the Campanile, the ideas of Bon—if any are there, as is probable—cannot be entirely extricated from those of the gifted men who worked on those buildings before him. Where his work came first and was altered or augmented later by others, sometimes deliberately, sometimes accidentally, it is easier to convince oneself of what is the work of his hand, as in the lower part of the Scuola di S Rocco. Any other attributions—and several have been not very convincingly proposed—must stand on guesswork.

The Scuola di S Rocco moved out of the "scuoletta" still standing beside the back of the Frari, into what soon became the largest and grandest of all the scuolas. It was begun on some scheme about which almost nothing is known, probably a model worked out by interested members. A cornerstone was laid in 1515, a year before the permit to build was issued in 1516. Then, when it had become legal to go ahead, the

32.12 Campanile of S
Mark's. Bell chamber.

32.13 Campanile of S
Mark's. Detail of bell chamber capitals.

proto Bartolomeo Bon was invited to be
the architect (Cicognara-Diedo-Selva, II,
81n2; Mazzucato, 6; Temanza 1778,
101; Venturi, IX, 816). It is not clear
whether he then made his own model,
followed the older one, or adapted it.
The question is important, because deviation from the model (or from *a*
model) led to troubles later.

The scuola had its full complement
of 500 members, with the Doge Leonardo Loredan (1501–21) and a few patricians honorarily at the top, but not
allowed to hold office and with no
voice in the decisions about the building. There had been more plagues; before the building was finished, there
occurred one of the worst in Venetian
history, a plague plus typhus, in 1527–
29. It was said (doubtfully) to have cut
the population of the city, then about
120,000, by a fifth. Many of those who
could, moved to the country. But still
there was plenty of money to go ahead
with the building. Bon would presumably have been responsible for the
foundations (except whatever had been
put in to make ready for the cornerstone of 1515), responsible for the resulting plan, and for any new parts. He
is the author of nearly all the lower
story, surely of the lower half of the
main front, most of the left side, and
most of the finish of the big groundfloor hall within. How much free
choice the model and the ideas of the
building committee of the confraternity
would have left him is unknowable.

The lower story of the front sets the
style for the whole exterior. As at the
Scuola di S Marco, it is not symmetrical, for the two bays at the right (one of
them with a door) front the *albergo*,
and the three at the left, the main halls
(fig. 32.14). The columns framing the
bays in front of the great hall are reduced to pilasters on the *albergo*. The
whole is more unified than the hybrid
Scuola di S Marco for several reasons:
first, except at the doors, the front is
set on a continuous pedestal; second,

32.14 Scuola di S Rocco.
Main front.

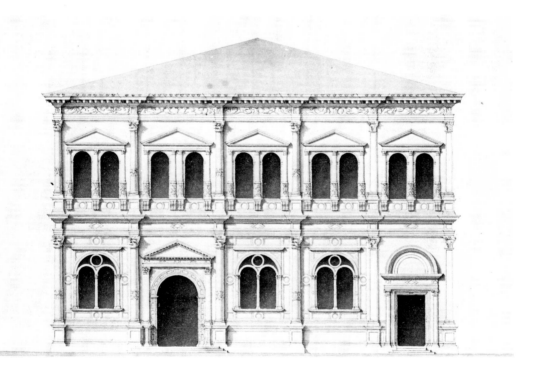

the front is metered into almost even bays by a common order; and third, the story comes to a quiet end with a strong entablature, projected a little above each column or pilaster but never broken upward or stopped.

Bon's ground floor windows follow Codussi's palace type, traceried *bifore* with slender stonework (fig. 32.15). The open circle and triangles above are now more closely enframed in rectangles, fitted precisely into the limits of the bay. The circle is repeated above and below by blind round panels, and again at impost level on either side. Everything fits together neatly, with a clear sense of conformity of parts. The same scheme, reduced, runs down the left side of the building, with pilasters at the ends only, and the four windows spaced almost regularly. (The rear and north side depend on later work.)

The main doorway is larger and richer, up on four semicircular steps, with octagonal pedestals for its own lesser order, and a low pediment contained below the main entablature that marks the level of the upper floor, and between the freestanding columns of the major order (fig. 32.16). The architraves of the entablatures both have Codussian inclined fascias, another sign—if one be needed—of Codussian descent. The design is a simple scheme, with no carved moldings and no arabesque, but here elaborately costumed in medium to small architectural members and fine marbles, with no carved decoration of surfaces anywhere. Codussi and not any Lombardo is behind it, but second generation Codussi, less severe than the first.

The larger columns, embracing the whole floor, are curiously wreathed a quarter of the way up with clipped vines, thorns, laurel, and a few flowers. The capitals, still exaggeratedly flaring, have figures tucked in under the volutes, and are not identical. The *griffes* on the otherwise classical bases, the

octagonal pedestals of the lesser order, the chamfered jambs and archivolt, as well as the tracery in the windows nearby, all show random memories of the Middle Ages, but quietly mutated into something that can pass almost unnoticed in the crowd of Renaissance details round about. The *albergo* door is smaller and less novel. It must have been the many marbles rather than anything in the architectural composition that Sanudo, already in 1523, found "among the most beautiful things in the world" (Sanudo, XXXIX, Aug 23, 1523), high praise from him who so rarely noticed buildings. Sansovino (228), son of an architect, but a son who did not think like an architect, remarked only on the "incredible expense."

The great hall of the ground floor follows the regular three-aisled scheme, like that of the Scuola di S Marco (fig. 32.17). Unclassical octagonal pedestals like those of the doorway outside carry the slender columns, with flutes twisting diagonally the first third of the way up and then straightening out. (This decorative fantasy has now been used often enough not to make it worth a genealogical search for a single distinguished ancestor, say the Cornaro Chapel or the Nicolò Marcello tomb.) The capitals are so expansively flaring that the abacus, three times as wide as the top of the shaft, is enabled to offer a good broad base for the wood brackets that carry the beams running the length of the hall (fig. 32.18). Unclassically "off" in proportion, the capitals take advantage of it, and start out with necking bands with a mixture of leaves, flowers, and heads. The spreading acanthus under the volutes all but swallows the egg and dart of the echinus. Instead of a flower in the middle of the concave sides of the abacus, there is a tiny Lion of S Mark with his book. Like much else here, this fantasy is by some carver not traceable elsewhere.

32.15 Scuola di S Rocco.
Front windows.

32.16 Scuola di S Rocco.
Main doorway.

The general richness would seem to be, as at the Scuola di S Marco, a response to the taste of the rich middle-class members of the confraternity, or at least of those who worked themselves onto the committee in charge of the building. As at the Scuola di S Marco, they seem to have been a cranky lot, and suddenly, in 1524, Bon was dismissed, on the pretext that with four days warning he had not supplied the exact dimensions of the door or doorways of the stairway, and that he was deviating from the model. The mysterious and now sinister Tuscan Giovanni Celestro was paid for "correcting" some of Bon's "errors." He may even have submitted a new model (Angelini 1961, 17; Cicognara-Diedo-Selva, II, 81n1). In a really capricious mood, the committee appointed Sante Lombardo, Tullio's son, who was barely twenty. He lasted three years, and accomplished almost nothing before being dismissed again on the charge of "making changes." Then in 1527 Scarpagnino was appointed, and he finished the building in harmony with Bon's beginning. It is really Bon's and Scarpagnino's. Not close to anything in the city of the time (just as the Scuola di S Marco had not been) it has, curiously, mistakenly, and perversely long been held up as a sample or even a paradigm of the early XVIc in the architecture of Venice.

Bartolomeo Bon did not pursue just one consistent style throughout his half-obscure career, as did Pietro Lombardo or Mauro Codussi or even Giovanni Buora when left a reasonably free hand. He did not repeat favorite motives which could be collected as clues. As might be expected of a later artist, he is more an eclectic than his great models. Consequently attributions are few and sometimes deceiving. Beyond those just considered, there are no other extant works documented as his, nor any which ask acceptance into his

32.17 Scuola di S Rocco.
Main groundfloor hall.

32.18 Scuola di S Rocco.
Capital of main ground floor
hall.

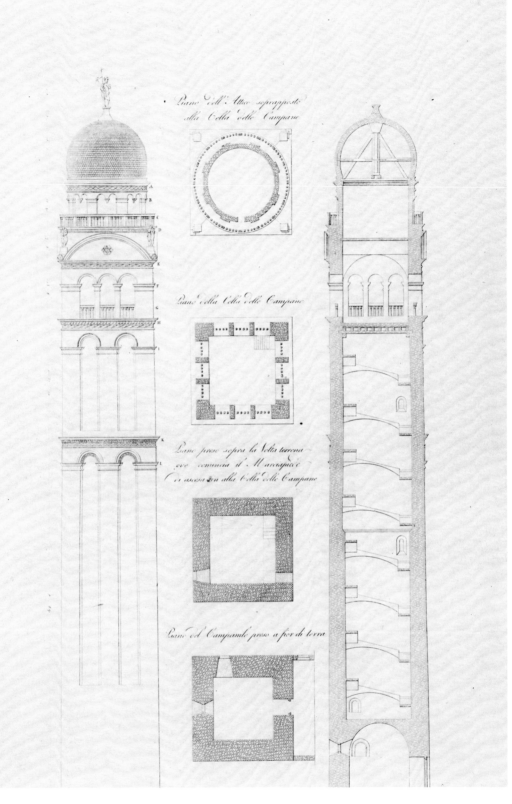

Piano dell' Attico sopra posto
alla Cella delle Campane

Piano della Cella delle Campane

Piano preso sopra la Volta terrena
ove comincia il M arcuplo è
Per ascesa sin alla Cella delle Campane

Piano del Campanile preso a fior di terra

32.19 Madonna dell'Orto.
Elevation and plan.

oeuvre. The Palazzo Cappello-Trevisan, behind S Mark's, used often to be given to him, sometimes with reference to "obscure" documents (D'Ancona-Gengaro, 753). True, he did travel for two years with Admiral Trevisan, for part of whose family it was built; thus there is some claim. But the exceptionally handsome building looks more like the work of his hard-to-catch putative kinsman Guglielmo Grigi, though not enough so to be drawn out of the large company of anonymous works. Both Bon and Grigi may have had something to do with it. As for the campanile of the Madonna dell'Orto, an early mélange of sections built at different times and with extensive XIXc restorations, remarkable for its unique, unattributable, pseudo-oriental, ultra-hemispherical or onion dome, shown on reputable views from Vavassore ca. 1525 onward, the occasional attributions to Bon do not convince at all (figs. 32.19 and 32.20). He is an insecure eclectic, but surely never this exotic. (Onion domes, pretty surely fanciful, had been shown now and then on other towers or even on the crossings of churches, as by Vavassore ca. 1525 for S Pietro di Castello and SS Giovanni e Paolo—neither to be believed.)

32.20 Madonna dell'Orto. Dome.

33 | MISCELLANEOUS CHURCHES AND LATER PALACES

Although more uniform in function than palaces, churches were built in more varieties of form. Many were of the usual types, like those on the mainland, plain naves, usually without aisles, almost all ending in an apse. They would ordinarily be tricked out with Venetian trimming or given unmistakable local character in some other way. A typical example would be Bon's Church of S Rocco, if only more of it were left. A better example is S Maria della Visitazione (also called S Gerolamo), near the big Dominican "Gesuati" on the Zattere. One group of churches from the late XVc and early XVIc stands apart, unmatched by any similar group on the mainland. An important example has already been considered, S Giovanni Grisostomo. Like the others in the group, it has a thoroughly Byzantine plan and vaulting scheme, and its details are all of the Early Renaissance.

Independent as she had become, Venice was still officially an entity within the Byzantine Empire, self-governing with what might today be called "commonwealth status" (Norwich, 49)—until the empire fell to the Turks in 1453. As far back as the XIc, masonry churches of Byzantine conformation had been built in Venice. The church, however, had not depended on Constantinople—most ecclesiastical officers were Venetian nobles—for officially it was under Rome, through the somewhat insecure Patriarchate of Grado, permanently transferred to Venice in 1451. The liturgical language was Latin, not Greek; the local rite was close to the Roman, which was officially accepted in 1456, but, like many others at the time, as often idiosyncratic as standardized. The local church managed to be more independent of the pope than in any Catholic city of comparable size and accessibility. The pope was regarded as a foreign power, and not always a friendly one, rather than as the supreme ecclesiastical authority.

The real head was the patriarch archbishop. The doge had the final authority in the appointment of the patriarch and the bishops, chosen from names proposed by the Senate. Confirmation or even approval by Rome was a formality not always remembered.

There is a handful of churches built after the fall of Constantinople that are still more Byzantine than Latin in their basic scheme. Some, such as S Giacometto di Rialto (reputed the oldest in the city, but actually a work of the XIc–XIIc), went back to times when ties to Byzantium were closer. With its Greek-cross plan and Byzantine details, it must—before several remodelings— have shown plainly what it really was, a minor Byzantine provincial work.

When new churches were built above the foundations of old Greek-cross churches, often they economically followed the old lines, as one can guess from the form of half-a-dozen surviving, or from the views of the others with domed Greek-cross roofs on the Barbari bird's-eye view. There are even specific notices of one old bottom used for a new top at S Geminiano. Byzantine buildings already remote in time seem to have served as inspiration along with the Renaissance revival of antique forms, much as the XIIc Proto-Renaissance served as inspiration for Brunelleschi (Ackerman, 1977, in letter). Although not part of the group under discussion, the most prominent of all, inescapably, was the great Greek cross of S Mark's, traditionally begun in 1063 on the site of an earlier Greek-cross church, on the specific model of yet another built still earlier in Constantinople, the Apostoleion or Church of the Holy Apostles. S Mark's was large, while the churches of the new group were not; and S Mark's cross stood free, with a dome in the middle and on each arm, while those of the new group had their crosses enclosed

within squares and never had domes on the arms, like S Giovanni Grisostomo and Byzantine examples of the Second Golden Age.

All were vaulted, and they make up the only important group of vaulted buildings in Venice, where weight and foundations all but banned everything but small isolated vaults—with very few exceptions (most notably S Salvatore). The central domes, none in the group spanning more than 35', stood on pendentives borne on slender piers, making small three by three checkered plans of nine cells. The Greek cross, formed by the nave and transept, rose above the corner squares, which might or might not also be domed, but at a lower level. The pendentives, like those of Codussi and unlike those of Pietro Lombardo, were kept plain, without sculpture, without even roundels.

The family likenesses within the group are striking. While domes on pendentives had already been successfully contrived at S Giobbe, S Michele, and the Miracoli, in the dozen years after ca. 1475, the central features of the new churches are more like one another than like the domed cubes of S Giobbe or the Miracoli. There may be more similarity to Codussi, but not enough for any of them to claim direct connection. Although he may have had more to do with adapting an older Byzantine church of similar plan, S Maria Formosa—nothing proves or disproves it—the first Renaissance church of this Byzantinizing type still standing in Venice is S Giovanni Grisostomo, his last church, begun in 1497 (inscription). It *may* have been the model for S Geminiano (begun 1505) and S Giovanni Elemosinario (begun 1527), and others now destroyed, of which less is known, such as S Giovanni in Oleo, S Margherita, S Tomà, and the forechurch of S Andrea della Certosa (McAndrew 1969, 15–18). While the scheme of the last is recoverable to a great extent, its date is not. All these merit study in some detail, when any is available, and deserve an effort to be lined up chronologically, when that is possible.

For convenience, one complete church may be set apart to lead the group, S Nicolò di Castello or di Bari, built at the east end of the city and pulled down ca. 1810 for Napoleon's public gardens. In 1471 the Senate had begun to deliberate what to do about the poor old men, many of them infirm ex-sailors, who had been sleeping under the arcades of the Ducal Palace, and in 1474 a vote was taken to provide land for a hospital and old sailors' home, with a church of its own. In 1476 the first stone was laid jointly by the patriarch, Matteo Gerardi, and the doge, wealthy Andrea Vendramin (1476–78). Vendramin had been ambassador in Rome and a friend of Pius II, Paul II, and Sixtus IV, who not only gave him the Golden Rose but also, exceptionally for Venice, funds for the new building (Cornaro 1749, XII, 405). Both the patriarch and the doge had strong connections with modern art—works of the Early Renaissance—and they may have had to do with the choice of an architect. It is unlikely that the doge would have urged Tullio Lombardo for this commission, for although Tullio designed most of his grandiose tomb, that choice was probably made by the doge's heirs.

Mark, George, and Nicholas were the trio of saints most often called on for help by sailors, and their churches, shrines, and altars were given special devotion. Nicholas, in particular, was a sort of Christian Poseidon to them, and the new church in Venice was appropriately dedicated to him. He was especially venerated for his calming of a tempest that seemed about to annihilate both the crew and the ship taking him on one of his benevolent voyages. Relics of S Nicholas had been brought back from the First Crusade, and were kept in another Church of S Nicolò,

near the end of the Lido, opposite S Elena; but these were not fully credited since his tomb at Myra, in Asia Minor, where he had been bishop, had already been emptied and its contents, including his body, taken in triumph to Bari, where it is still treasured in one of the finest of all Romanesque churches.

Marco Antonio Coccio, a teacher of Latin rhetoric in the provinces, who chose to call himself Sabellicus when writing in Latin, and who became Sabellico in Italian or Venetian, declared that in 1489 or 1490 he had seen a wooden church by the naval Ospedale di Gesù (Sabellico 1957, 26). Yet in 1500 a complete masonry church appeared by the hospital on the Barbari bird's-eye view, and it must have been this that was consecrated in 1503. The wooden building may have been a small oratorio to serve the old sailors until their new church, being both richly and rapidly built, should be ready for them. Sabellico could have seen wood scaffolding for truing the walls and framing the vaults, and taken them for a wooden church—he was not sharp-eyed. But it would have been difficult for an unfinished masonry shell to look like a wooden church to anyone, even careless Sabellico. The only major construction in wood in a masonry building at this time would have been for the centering of the vaults, a light wood framework for light vaults, if put up in the regular Byzantine way, which is most probable, rather than in the more wood-demanding, heavier Roman way, which is not at all probable. This could suggest that little or none of the monumental masonry of S Nicolò was visible above ground when Sabellico visited the site in 1489–90; surely none of it was advanced enough to be in use. Surprisingly, Sanudo, who went everywhere and noted everything in his Diaries, never mentioned this church until 1524 (Sanudo, XXXVII, 123).

Knowledge of the destroyed church comes chiefly from four measured drawings made in the workshop of Antonio Visentini, from among the hundreds prepared there in the 1740s and 1750s for sale to English grand tourists gathered around Consul Joseph Smith. For convenience, many are dimensioned in English, not Venetian, feet. (The variable Venetian foot was usually a shade over 13".) Most of this trove of informative drawings is now in the Royal Institute of British Architects or in the British Museum (henceforth indicated as RIBA or BM). In the case of S Nicolò, the RIBA drawings are more to be trusted than those in the BM, having been made by the best of Visentini's team of draftsmen.

The plan is based on a perfect Greek cross, with a nave twice wider than the aisles, producing oblong spaces proportioned as 1:2 for the nave, west and east of the crossing, and the same for the transepts north and south (fig. 33.1). A domed square is in the center, and lesser domed squares in the corners, all fitting into an enclosing square about 60' on a side. A second large dome covers a square chancel, an additional but well-integrated space echoing the crossing, and in front of a semicircular apse with five narrow windows. Altogether, it is a perfect exemplar of this distinct Byzantinizing Venetian Renaissance type—if the RIBA plan is to be trusted, as it probably is. The scheme is closely related to other churches in the group, and also in a way to S Salvatore, which could be formed by overlapping the big square three times in a row.

The individual shapes of the domes are shown clearly in the RIBA drawing of the long section (fig. 33.2). That over the chancel was flattened, saucerlike, to less than 6' high, easy to slip under the roof; it does not show at all from the outside. The dome at the crossing was dramatized, inside and out, by its loftier hemispherical shape set on a drum (without windows), rising inside altogether to 65' from the floor. Several prints show consistently that it had a ribbed metal sheath that rose a bit higher than the real dome, and that it carried a little lantern on top, with a wonderful ornament like a tree with twenty-four golden apples, recalling the unforgettable little trees crowning S Mark's.

The church walls are tall, taller than wide, and the dome and gleaming finial give it still greater lift, made even more vivid by the long, low lines of the hospital building beside it. The banding on the front, shown in the prints (Carlevarijs, Canaletto, Coronelli, Giampiccolo, Lovisa, Marieschi, and on the letter "N" in Visentini's alphabet set) must be for the bonding of the intended but never executed masonry face (fig. 33.3). Pedestals by the doorways suggest applied pilasters, perhaps in two stories, and probably not columns as arbitrarily shown on the BM Visentini plan; the upper parts would never have been able to accept these—at least not gracefully. Sinkages beside the four-light facade window cannot have been intended to be developed into windows, as might at first appear, for they would have cut into the small corner domes inside (fig. 33.4). The gable seems to be awaiting a pediment.

From the thin evidence, one does not now see a facade nearly as coherent as the interior. But, successful or not, the facade enjoyed a uniquely enviable location, fronting the main deep-water passage from the Adriatic to the lagoon out of which the city rose. Every ship coming in to Venice in the normal way would have passed it. The church was the first of the sights a traveler was granted, the Island of the Certosa nearby having typically and deliberately hidden its church from profane eyes by interposing lesser buildings and opulent clusters of trees.

But S Nicolò is not utterly a ghost; one element is still to be seen. The main doorway had never been finished,

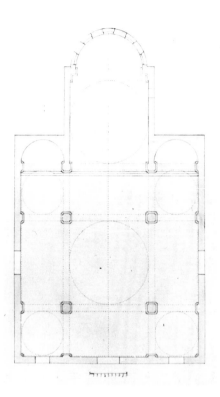

33.1 S Nicolò di Castello or di Bari. Ground plan (drawing from the Visentini workshop; RIBA).

33.2 S Nicolò di Castello. Longitudinal section (drawing from the Visentini workshop; RIBA). The ideal arrangement of barrel vaults (43′6″ to the top) and domes on pendentives as in S Giovanni Grisostomo and S Salvatore; of windows, with big oculi set between the pendentives of the main dome; and of some of the lesser domes. There are more *oculi* over the arched windows of the apse. The piers are slender and paneled and crossed —Codussi-fashion—by the main horizontals. The top cornice and the archivolts are also kept slender, with one appropriate exception for the more robust arch emphasizing the beginning of the apse.

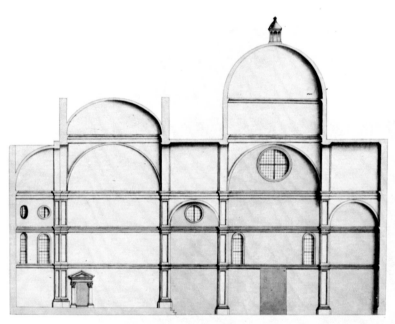

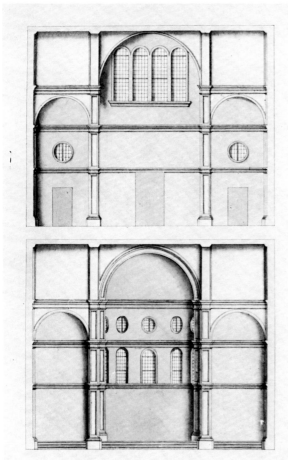

33.3 S Nicolò di Castello.
Painting by Canaletto (private collection, Milan).

33.4 S Nicolò di Castello.
Cross-sections (drawings
from the Visentini workshop; RIBA). More round
windows are over the side
doors of the facade, and it
comes as a major surprise to
find that instead of a large
round window above the
main doorway, there is an
uncomfortable loggia-like
compound of four arched
lights, crowded up against
the last pendentive arch in
the one amateurish touch in
an otherwise sophisticated
and thoroughly harmonious
interior.

33.5 S Nicolò di Castello.
Main doorway, now on side
wall of Accademia.

never given its cornice, but happily its
frieze and flanking pilasters were re-
trieved just in time and in 1824 (inscription) set into the side wall of an
addition to the newly arranged picture
galleries of the Accademia (fig. 33.5).
Although as rich as any Lombardo
composition, it does not have the character of the output of the Lombardo
shop. The pilaster arabesques are superb, unsurpassed, but they appear to
have been made a little later than the
Lombardo heyday, though their individual virtues make them hard to date
closely. The graceful capitals, with
smiling children's heads between the
volutes, may not be far from those on
the Palace of the Camerlenghi by Scarpagnino, not rebuilt until into the
1520s. The arabesques, beautifully
carved in small masses of high and
rounded relief that never jostle one another, are prodigal with flowers, nubbly
garlands, grapes, other fruits, birds, little marine monsters, masks, and many
more conceits all dexterously choreo-
graphed into distinctive patterns with
ease and grace, unlike any others. The
scheme of the interior of course removes the whole church from the immediate circle of the Lombardos, while
the doorway alone removes it from the
circle of Codussi, where the general
scheme might have placed it. Possibly
the portal shows a change of mind on
the part of those in charge; it may have
been one of the last parts to be finished, after the consecration in 1503
and the death of Codussi in 1504. Tullio had been working for the doge's
heirs, and could combine Lombardo
and Codussi, but neither the general
scheme nor the portal goes with his
style.

If S Nicolò was not carried ahead
after the laying of the first stone in
1476 (which may have been the beginning of the hospital only), and if there
were delays as a result of the plague of
1478, and if money was sent from
Rome in 1487, and if Sabellico saw
some sort of wooden church there in

1489–90, it is reasonable to think that the main work was done mainly in the 1490s. This would pull the group of quincunx churches together in the period of one generation. The forechurch of the Certosa would easily be included if it was built after the main church, which has been thought to be a work of the 1480s. S Giovanni Grisostomo is known to have been begun in 1497. In modern times, one would suppose that one contractor, a specialist in vaulted four-column, five-dome, nine-cell churches, moved his crew of specially trained masons from one job to another successively.

More substantial is what is known of another lost church, S Geminiano, once in the center of the west end of the Piazza, an understated complement to S Marco. A church dedicated to SS Geminiano and Menna had stood originally in the middle of the present Piazza, then half its present size, but when Doge Ziani bought the orchard of the nuns of S Zaccaria, a new building was built at the far end of the new space. (Characteristically, no one asked the pope for the proper permit to do this.) When this XIIc church had deteriorated, the Senate voted a whole new building as part of the still emerging grand scheme for a more monumental Piazza. The architect is recorded as Cristoforo del Legname, but nothing else is known about him except that he was also a sculptor. (A portrait bust by him is in storage in the Ca' d'Oro.) Work was begun in 1505, actively encouraged by Doge Leonardo Loredan.

Work went slowly much of the time, first interrupted by the War of Cambrai in 1509, and later by lack of funds. Nevertheless, the church must soon have been usable, for there was some sort of function there in 1512 and a burial in it in 1517 (Sanudo, XIV, 121; XXIII, 445), followed in the next few years by a miscellany of important functions. It still lacked a facade, and this was supplied only in the 1550s by

Sansovino, on a design still well known from having been reproduced so often in various *vedute* of the Piazza.

The plan and scheme of the interior, which is all that is relevant here, are known only from unreliable drawings from the Visentini atelier, now in the BM, and from some distorted but informative prints of sections by eccentric Father Coronelli, 1650–1718 (fig. 33.6). They are also known from the presumably accurate drawings and the illustrations made from them for the two volumes of Cicognara, Diedo, and Selva's invaluable *Fabbriche più cospicue di Venezia*, published in 1815–20 from meticulous drawings made earlier; in this case, before the church was pulled down on Napoleon's orders to make way for a grand stairway and ballroom he felt would be needed for the palace of his stepson, Viceroy Eugène Beauharnais (fig. 33.7). There are a few disagreements among these diverse sources of information about the church, but they are minor.

Count Zaguri, who lived nearby, became alarmed by the deterioration of his parish church of S Maurizio, built in 1495, and then enraged by the threatened destruction of beautiful S Geminiano. He and some helpers prepared a full set of drawings of the latter, and arranged for the rebuilding of San Maurizio as a copy of the church about to disappear. Most of the work, carried out after his death with funds he left, was directed by the well-known architect Antonio Diedo and finished in 1806, with a chill Neoclassic temple-front facade by Giovanni Antonio Selva (fig. 33.8). Much can be learned from this replica, remembering always that it is only a cold copy, a dulled transcription, only as faithful to the original as frozen fruit is to fresh.

The plan of S Geminiano was a squarish four-pier, five-dome, nine-cell quincunx church, with a rectangular apse about the same size as the rectangular bays of the nave and transepts. Unreliable Coronelli, and Cicognara's

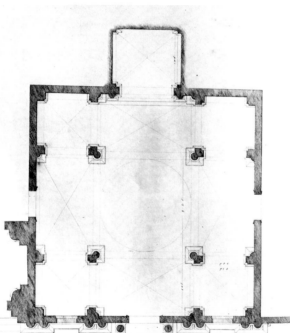

33.6 S Geminiano. Plan (in-accurate) by Coronelli.

33.7 S Geminiano. Plan (accurate) by Cicognara-Diedo-Selva.

33.8 S Maurizio. Interior.

reliable draftsmen show this as the only apse, fairly surely all by Cristoforo del Legname (Selvatico, 243; Temanza 1778, 252). Other drawings show this flanked by twin semicircular apses that were surely there when the church was pulled down (Correr C1, III, 8047) and probably earlier, for they are identical to smaller chapels at the ends of the side aisles of many other related contemporary churches (fig. 33.9). Also, texts through the XVIIc speak of three altars. These lesser apses could, however, be part of lesser changes made to the interior by Sansovino in the middle of the XVIc.

The membering of the interior parts shows considerable sophistication (figs. 33.10 and 33.11). The four piers, sometimes criticized for their height, showed mainly as tall, fluted Corinthian columns, set high on 6' pedestals, that carried an entablature and the main arches of the barrel-vaulted arms and pendentives of the main hemispherical dome (as on the S Maurizio copy). These columns were three-quarters free, but attached in back to two lower pilasters without pedestals so that they ran down to the floor and kept within classic proportions. They were set at right angles to one another, each carrying the lesser arches of the lower vaults of the corner squares. The prints, drawings, and copy do not agree whether full domes, pendentive domes, or groined vaults were in these squares. Pilaster responds on the walls received the other ends of these arches. The main dome may have been on a drum with windows, and it may have been put up by Sansovino. These differences matter little, for the church fits the type entirely whichever way was chosen, and it was not the first or influential in any particular way as far as we know.

The general scheme, the thoroughgoing classicism, and the inclined fascias of the architraves recall Codussi, and suggest that Cristoforo del Legname

may have had some particular relation to him. There was a more certain relation directly to Byzantine building, for, as has already been mentioned, the piers almost surely stood on XIIc footings. If they did, the walls of the square probably did also. The same text that tells of seeing the old foundations and the piers exposed in 1807 goes on to say that the church was "renewed" (*rinnovata*) by Cristoforo (Codice Paoletti, Correr MS O D C 819/ 13; also Cicognara-Diedo-Selva and Zanotto, I, 529). The pavement was 1'9" below the present pavement of the Piazza, laid in the XVIIIc, and 3' above that of the early XIIc church on the site or above the old brick pavement of the XIIc, though the exact differences in level are disputable.

The church was constantly being praised, most often for Jacopo Sansovino's tactful facade, singularly happy with its strangely diverse neighbors, and for the chapel he added and in which he chose to be buried. But it was praised also for Cristoforo's interior. Francesco Sansovino (109), just before 1581, found that, "although small, it may be the best adorned that you could wish in the whole City, being sheathed inside with marbles and Istrian stone, and being of elaborate and skilful construction." His follower, Girolamo Bardi (60), soon after 1587, saw it as "charming and graceful . . . and judged by all almost like a ruby among many pearls." Such praise is typical of the age and place, in its dwelling on material richness as the ultimate good.

Less is known of the other churches in the group, and they cannot be definitely dated. Three are perfect squares. Of the forechurch of S Andrea della Certosa only the plan is certain, from two drawings in the Venetian Archives, probably of the XVIIc and XVIIIc (Archivio di Stato, Fondo S Andrea, busta 36, Timofiewitsch, 282 illus 153, and McAndrew 1969, fig 13). This fore-

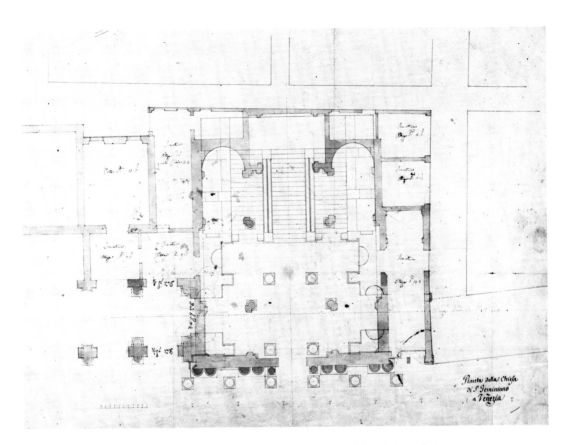

33.9 S Geminiano. Later
drawing with three apses
(Museo Correr, cl III 8047).

33.10 S Geminiano. Interior, cross section (engraving from Coronelli, *Chiese*, 1708–09).

33.11 S Geminiano. Interior (from Coronelli, *Chiese*).

church is an ideally perfect four-column, five-dome, nine-cell quincunx specimen. There is no evidence for the date of construction, though sometime in the 1490s seems probable. Equally undatable, more unreliable, and furthermore quite unidentifiable are two Visentini plans in the RIBA (McAndrew 1969, fig 3, fig 4; 1974, 17). Unless more about them is discovered, they can add nothing to our knowledge except the doubtful possibility that the group was larger.

Even less is known and much less is left of the other two early XVIc three-aisled churches. (S Maria Maggiore has been discussed under Tullio, chapter 30.) The larger, or average-size S Croce, on the Giudecca, has been reduced to an adjunct of a jail.

A single-nave, aisle-less Gothic building was deteriorating badly, and discussions for a replacement began in the late XVc. Preliminary work may have been started, but the real building began in 1508 (inscription), and must have gone rapidly, being completed or nearly so in 1511, and consecrated in 1515. It could go quickly because most of the side walls and apse were saved and used in the new construction (Franzoi-DiStefano, 264). Mediaeval corbel tables and vertical steps are still there (fig. 33.12). XVIc views of the city regularly show it with aisles lower than a presumed nave, often with clerestory, but by the end of the XVIIc, many of them (when not copying earlier ones) show a single gable roof. The conclusion is that in resuscitating and restyling the old building, the scheme was changed to a church with aisles. The facade, with a pediment flanked by lower half-pediments, reinforces this (fig. 33.13). Its uncommonly large round window, uncomfortably placed with the new cornices, gives evidence of remodeling rather than rebuilding. Sometime in the XVIc it was transferred from Franciscan Observants to Benedictine nuns. Sometime in the XVIIc, perhaps in 1699 or more likely 1669 (date on ceiling and *Cronica*, 448) the church was remodeled again back to an aisleless arrangement with a plain gable roof—following the lines of the half-pediments, and leaving the higher pediment in the middle as a sort of false front. The XVIc capitals from the nave columns were saved and used on piers against the walls under a XVIc cornice, still in place (figs. 33.14 and 33.15). Big semicircular windows were cut near the top, to let in more light. Traces of the old windows can be made out in the brickwork.

The Gothic church had a big choir balcony at the west end, and some similar arrangement was repeated in the remodeling. Had it not been, the new nave, limited in width because of the space taken by the aisles, would have been freakishly long and narrow. The chancel and flanking chapels are still vaulted (fig. 33.16). The Gothic screen across the middle of the nave (Franzoi-DiStefano, 265) has vanished, as has the large XVIc arched front portal. The huge inlaid cross of red Verona marble remains, and also the aisle windows of the main front (fig. 33.17).

The poor church has lost all its pictures and relics, both once famous, and, though neatly kept, is not a rewarding example of ecclesiastical architecture of the early XVIc. It serves on Sundays for the inmates of the old nunnery buildings, now a house of correction, with tailor and printing shops for instruction, a TV room, cinema, and sports field.

The Church of S Sofia, dedicated to Divine Wisdom, and not to S Sophie, martyr, went back to the XIc and was rebuilt in XIIIc Gothic with nave and aisles despite its small size. As far back as 1500 (Barbari) it was half shut off from its own campo by a house, and was entered only through a vestibule. It was drastically remodeled in 1568 (inscription) but there must have been

33.12 S Croce, Giudecca.
Apse with corbel tables.

33.13 S Croce, Giudecca.
Facade.

33.14 S Croce, Giudecca.
XVIc capitals reused.

33.15 S Croce, Giudecca.
XVIc capitals reused.

33.16 S Croce, Giudecca.
Chancel and chapel.

33.17 S Croce, Giudecca.
Inlaid cross of facade.

work done earlier in the XVIc, which has left a side door, and shallow niches for altars with Ionic pilasters decorated with panels with discs, carrying architraves with flipped fascias. The column shafts and a pair of capitals may also come from this time. There was a flat wood ceiling (Niero 1972, 30, 61). In 1698 there was another remodeling, by Antonio Gaspari (Bassi 1963, passim), less drastic than he had projected, but altering the capitals of the nave arcade and everything above them. It was closed in 1810, emptied, used for storage of sand, and then reopened as an oratorio in 1836. Little is known of the early XVIc aisled state, except that it existed.

Note: The churches of S Maria della Visitazione (or S Gerolamo), S Maria Mater Domini, and S Felice were also to have been discussed. Illustrations of these three churches follow (figs. 33.18 through 33.20).

The pages after the general discussion of palaces would have taken up some specific examples. The two last planned but unwritten chapters were to have been on Guglielmo Grigi and Antonio Scarpagnino, and finally more on cloisters was to have been included.

From the 1490s into the 1520s and 30s builders in Venice preferred one type of church, based on Codussi's S Giovanni Grisostomo, and continued with the old established type of palace, with new-style windows and doorways and quite often with some application of the orders, as inaugurated by Codussi, but without his traceried *bifore*, which may have seemed unclassical to the new generation of clients. These clients could make a pretense of knowing about classical architecture, thanks to the publication of books, of prints of ancient buildings, and the new works in Rome and Florence, and undoubtedly from the greater and greater circulation of drawings. This phase reached a high development in the work of Scarpagnino (in Venice 1505–49).

In addition to the few palaces built around 1500 or before, and the three masterpieces by Codussi, there is of course a variety of others. Most important is a group affected by those of Codussi. As many as one quarter of the palaces in the city may have been more or less remodeled (Pignatti 1971, 135). The changes, as usual, were no more than skin-deep. There was no change in plan or construction. On the whole more were faced with white stone, and more made more of their balconies. Horizontal divisions were more regularly stressed by flattish cornices with little projection. Ground floors became more and more differentiated, treated as a plain base to the arches of piani nobili. The mezzanine came into much more use, and also the low story below the roof, "mezzanino sotto tetto."

In the grander palaces now the stories were divided vertically and horizontally by the orders and the old three-story triptych. They were faced with stone, some of it marble, and the blank areas of wall on the wings were often trimmed with oblongs and circles of purple and green, framed and embellished with sprays, garlands, and trophies, as though held together and held up by ribbons with bowknots. These, and a few friezes and arabesques in pilaster panels, were the heritage of the Lombards, whereas the division by orders came, of course, from Codussi.

33.18 S Maria della Visitazione.

33.19 S Maria Mater Domini.   33.20 S Maria Mater Domini. Detail.

33.21 S Felice.

Appendix A

BUILDING METHODS AND MATERIALS

All building materials had to be brought in by boat, loaded at the mainland and unloaded at the building site, doubling the cost of labor. Uniquely, much of the material was secondhand or even thirdhand, for it was much easier to pick up ready-made bricks or ready-cut stones from abandoned buildings on Torcello, other islands, or the mainland, than to bake or cut new ones. Luckily there were seemingly endless quantities of such material. Clay suitable for new bricks of good quality was also plentiful—near Padua and Treviso—and brick was regularly preferred to stone because it weighed less. Walls were commonly three bricks thick, five for walls in the largest buildings that had to carry more weight. New bricks were larger than those in common use today, about 10" by 5" by 1½"; old brick pilfered from mediaeval or Roman buildings was even larger, about 10" to 20" by 5" to 10" by 2" to 3". So many bricks were taken from the once large Roman port city of Altinum (twelve miles from Treviso, destroyed by Attila) that new bricks like them were called "altinelle," no matter where they came from. These became standardized at about 8" by 4" by 2".

Pietra d'Istria is of a compact granular structure tending toward marble (but coarser), salt white when quarried and smoothed, but dimmed to tones of neutral gray as airborne dirt lodges in its sugar-like surface. Where it is well washed by rain or faces south in direct sunlight, it can stay fairly white but, sheltered or shadowed under a cornice or balcony or on the sunless north side of a building, it blackens from corrosive layers of accumulated soot and sometimes a dead microscopic moss once nourished by damp sea air. In the last half-century the increasing pollution of Venetian air has damaged this beautiful and much-used stone more than in the total of eight centuries before—as the oldest buildings in the city tragically testify.

The great virtue of the stone, beside the unending supply, the proximity of the quarries, and the consequent low cost, is that its dense structure rejects capillary action, making it ideal for the lower parts of buildings that have to be now wet, now dry. Also, it resists the damage by normal amounts of salt in water or air that affect other stones. Freshly quarried, it can be carved more easily than marble, and once cut and left in the air, it slowly becomes harder. As a building stone for the peculiar conditions in Venice, it is still unsurpassed and still much used.

Truly pure marble is white; the purest and whitest used in Venice came most often from Carrara in Tuscany or, less often, from Greece, that from the Island of Paros being particularly prized. Much was taken from old monuments, pilfering being easier and cheaper than quarrying. Although it came from veins dug close to the sea, white Carrara—there are other kinds—was not always easily had in Venice, and transportation could make it cost more than colored varieties from Verona or Vicenza, sometimes even more than exotics from Greece or Egypt brought back in the regular mercantile fleets. At the time of the Latin Kingdom in Constantinople, every boat sailing back to Venice had to bring marbles or other prized stones, or carving, most of which went to S Mark's.

To show at its best, marble must be polished, for a rough lump fresh from the quarry shows little color or pattern of veining. Marbles exposed on exteriors have lost much of the color that led to their choice, like the pretty pebbles picked up at tide-edge when unpocketed later at home—dry, dull, and not worth keeping. The crystalline grains of true marble are somewhat translucent, and through them light enters into the stone and illumines the color, as in no other stone used in building. But alas, the essential polished surface is delicate, and polluted

air can destroy the glossy finish, form a skin or scab, then penetrate that and force it to flake off, leaving a duller surface underneath, with less color and vulnerable to new corruption, and so on and so on. *Pietra d'Istria* also forms a skin, but it is a more protective one, and more durable.

The colored stones that change least are polished porphyry and polished green serpentine (sometimes called *verde antico*, which is also the common name of a spotted and streaked spinach green marble; the names are loosely interchangeable). Both porphyry and true serpentine are so hard they can keep their glossy surfaces and color even in adverse weather and noxious air. Both are enlivened by glittering flurries of feldspar, like snowflakes. Polished granite, more mottled in color, also has a durable surface and hence durable color. Pinkish Egyptian granite was particularly prized in Venice.

The favorite among the many marbles from nearby Verona was a rusty red or pink orange, mottled with pebbles or chips of harder stone, set close like islands in an archipelago and separated by meandering channels of softer and darker stone. This marble, often called *brocatello*, can look perversely edible. Left outdoors, it bleaches, and the softer channels erode, sinking below the surface of the harder islets, rather like a little relief map of Venice. The handsome *breccias* (gravel), richest and most varied of all in color, and sometimes mortadella-like in pattern, are affected the same way, so much so that they were rarely exposed on exteriors. (Their use for the Scala dei Giganti is exceptional.) Left outdoors, most variegated marbles fade and flake more than plain ones. The bundles of shafts across the front of S Mark's make a set of samples that any geological museum or stone merchant would envy, though only the hard polished porphyry and granite can still show their true colors; their once brilliant neighbors are now like lustreless tallow. Much of the Miracoli has suffered a similar fate.

Porphyry was used in Venice most commonly in thin-cut circles, made from slices of antique column shafts from Altinum or some other Roman city on the near mainland, or brought in ships sailing back from the East. All of it had come originally from Egypt, from a mountain near the Red Sea, but as no more was being quarried, all of it had to be secondhand. Except for such slices from old columns, the Renaissance used less secondhand or third-hand material than the Gothic and Byzantine periods; but in those earlier times there had been many more antique fragments handily scattered in the ex-Roman vicinity or to be picked up in the East, often by Crusaders, tradesmen, or sailors who sold them. Inlaid circles of colored marbles, porphyry, or green serpentine have true Venetian ancestry. They were in use by the XIIc, but by the XVc their use had spread so far afield as no longer to be a sure sign of Venetian parentage. Alberti, for example, used them handsomely at Rimini.

The foundations of all but very small buildings were made in one of two ways, depending on what was underneath. When the ground was solid, on the main islands of the archipelago where the city had been founded—Dorsoduro for example, hence its name—the stones of the socle or some sort of stone platform below them could be laid directly on the firm earth (as at the Frari, or the Scuola di S Rocco).

On newer land, made of piled mud dredged from the small natural channels to make them wider and deeper for boat traffic, different support was needed. Stone blocks had to be carried down below the lowest tide levels, not much of a problem since normal tide in Venice was less than 2'. (It is now about 2'6".) Such base walls were made

wider toward the bottom, doubled or tripled, to spread out the accumulated weight of roof, walls, floors and whatever might be on them over a large area, and so to assure fewer pounds per square foot (fig. A1). Although this was best done with stone, brick was sometimes used, where it would always be below the lowest tide, and never change from wet to dry. If exposed at the waterline, it did not last as long as stone. The foundation was one of the main controls on a building's height.

These masonry footings rested on a submerged raft of touching logs. Below one such layer came another, its logs at right angles to the first, and below that sometimes a third, crosswise to the second, parallel to the first. The wood was usually oak, the best from the Dolomites or Yugoslavia, occasionally a hard white poplar or elm, or later, larch from the great forests near Cadore. None of these would rot if kept under water, but if used anywhere that was now wet and now dry, they would slowly disintegrate (as they recently have under canalsides in Copenhagen). The procedures for foundations and their materials have changed little today.

The log mat lay on top of wood piles 7" or 8" thick and generally no more than 8' to 12' deep, though sometimes as much as 20'. They did not go down far enough to reach bedrock for support—under Venice no one knew where that might be—but only into a layer of hard clay between 10' and 16' below the water and soft mud. Usually there were about nine piles to the square yard, one every foot, and rubble was rammed between them, but where weight was going to be concentrated they might be driven closer together to compress the clay between and make an almost solid layer of clay and wood acting together, with broken stone, brick, and sherds tightly rammed into the interstices, sometimes consolidated with a kind of waterproof mortar. Since it did not reach anything to stand on at the bottom, this kind of construction made what would now be called a "floating foundation," surprisingly like that reinvented ca.1880 in Chicago for skyscrapers on mud and clay.

The oldest description of typical Venetian foundations, written by Thomas Coryat in 1608, is still valid, and one of the clearest.

The foundations of their houses are made after a very strange manner. For, whereas many of them are situate in the water, whensoever they lay the foundation of any house they remove the water by certaine devices from the place where they lay the first funda-mentall matter. Most commonly they drive long stakes into the ground. . . . Then they ramme in great piles of woode, which they lay very deepe, upon the which they place their bricks or stone, and so frame the other parts of the building. These foundations are made so exceeding deep, and contrived with so great labour, that I have heard they cost them very neare the third part of the charge of the whole edifice (Coryat II, 205-6).

Because of this cost, old foundations were commonly used over and over, for a succession of new buildings on the same site.

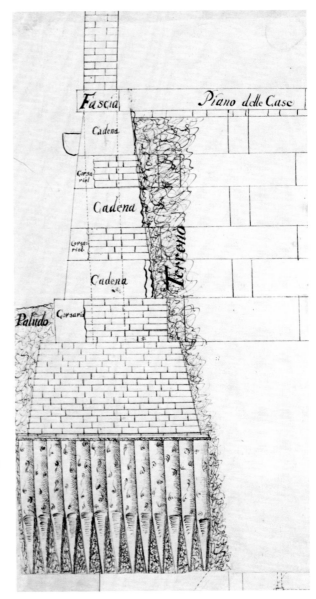

A1 Typical foundation: brick wall, alternating bonds of stone and brick, flaring brick footing above wooden piles (Museo Correr, Raccolta Grimani).

Appendix B

S MARIA DEI MIRACOLI AND THE CHAPEL AT URBINO

The author was not sure whether these two pages at the end of chapter 12 (S Maria dei Miracoli) were really relevant. He had verbally decided shortly before his death not to include them, but they had not yet been removed from the original text. Therefore it seemed best to put them in the appendix.

Along with the clear signs of the descent from S Mark's, some relation to the small and slightly earlier (ca.1480) chapel of the Palace at Urbino keeps suggesting itself (fig. B1). Its architect, the Dalmatian Luciano Laurana (d1479), had had some of his training in Venice, and although he had left the Palace in 1474 for work at Gubbio, he would have left designs behind in Urbino that would have been followed by the assistants he had trained. He may have kept in touch. The two palaces, Urbino and Gubbio, were being built for the same Duke, Federico da Montefeltro, a man keenly interested in architecture and in Laurana, and he would have seen to it that Laurana's designs were respected in both places. Important models and drawings were essential, and must have been well known. At the Miracoli, one of the principal carvers was Ambrogio d'Antonio da Urbino, who had worked earlier for Pietro Lombardo at S Giobbe, and he still may have had connections with Urbino. Furthermore, it may be important that when the Duke died in 1482, work on his palaces came to an almost complete stop. Highly skilled workmen, no longer employed there, may have come up the coast to busy and prosperous Venice to look for new jobs (Lieberman, 363). It is only in the later phases of the decoration of the Miracoli that a connection with Urbino seems to become apparent—*after* the death of the Duke.

Like the Miracoli, the interior of the Urbino Chapel is arranged in two stories of polychrome paneling, with ornaments of colored stone circles and fine carving of a character not remote from Pietro's, though somewhat more restrained. Uncommon or unknown else-

B1 Urbino. Ducal Palace chapel.

where, some of the ornament is identical, such as the flaming cannonballs (like plum puddings), an Urbino peculiarity repeated at the Miracoli in less than a decade (Heydenreich-Lotz, 89). Either Pietro himself, or someone in Venice connected with the Miracoli, must have been familiar with this exquisite chapel, tiny, but so engaging that it would surely be remembered by anyone who had seen it. But the similarity is limited to such literal superficialities as marble facing and relief ornament. Laurana and Lombardo are miles apart in temperament and style. Urbino or no Urbino behind it, the Miracoli would be a remarkable building anywhere, and in Venice it stands out particularly as *sui generis*.

Appendix C

THE CLOISTERS OF S ZACCARIA

The two cloisters of the convent of San Zaccaria are among the least known architectural monuments of the Renaissance in Venice, primarily because the employment of the convent as military barracks since the mid- or late nineteenth century kept them inaccessible to the public, and because even before that time they were partially immured in the process of conversion to governmental functions. Scholars who might have gained entrance seem to have been unaware of their existence. Indeed, oblivion was their fate from the start: the cloisters are not distinguishable in the plan of Venice by Jacopo de Barbari of 1500, or on any of the dozens of bird's-eye plans of later centuries. They appear first on the cadastral survey plans of the Napoleonic regime and are mentioned as extant by a few nineteenth-century authors, but are not described or represented in published graphic or photographic images. A thorough and able campaign of restoration carried out in the early 1960s provided the first opportunity in modern times to assess properly the architectural conception, but adequate photographs, apart from those taken to document the restoration, have yet to be made available.

THE FIRST CLOISTER

The convent is entered today through a portal that gives onto the southernmost end of Campo San Zaccaria (fig. C1). A string of cellular spaces, partly open to the sky, gives access to the cloister and, at its farther end, to the watergate on the Rio dei Greci. The cloister, a rectangle of 5 × 7 double-arched bays, has a cistern for the collection of fresh water beneath the pavement of the open area and a characteristic *vera da*

This account has been written by James S. Ackerman using the virtually complete research and field notes left by John McAndrew. While the opinions expressed are those of the writer, they appear to be in harmony with those adumbrated in the notes.

pozzo in the center (fig. C2). On the inner face of the corridor in the center of the northern side (left in fig. C1), four arches open into a hall that originally was the chapter house (the interior has been entirely rebuilt).

Each bay of the cloister on the ground floor has a groin vault supported on square piers on the arcaded side and by corbels on the inner wall. As each bay has two arches, a column is placed between each pair of piers to support them. Modern (nineteenth-century) tie rods used to reinforce the vaults are held on the exterior by round iron plates over each pier that inject a decisive but inauthentic design feature.

Around the cloister a low brick parapet with a stone upper surface supports the piers and all of the columns except those of the central bay of each side, which is open for access. In these central bays the columns are supported on pedestals the height of the parapet.

There is no entablature or course between the groundfloor arcade and that of the upper story. The simple stucco wall extends from the lower arches to a thin stone slab on which the upper arcade rests. The unusually great distance (about 14') between the two levels distinguishes the cloister from others of its time. The upper arcade (which is fully open only on the west and north sides) has only columns, of the same design as those below. The timber-roofed corridor has beams that extend out in the traditional Venetian style from the surface of the wall to support the eaves.

Perhaps to suggest that the columns do not have a significant structural role, the outer archivolt fascias of both the lower and upper arcades merge well above the abaci of the capitals (see the similar device in cloister II), while over the piers, where there is more room for lateral spread, they merge right on top of the abacus in the usual fashion (a device not followed in cloister II). This

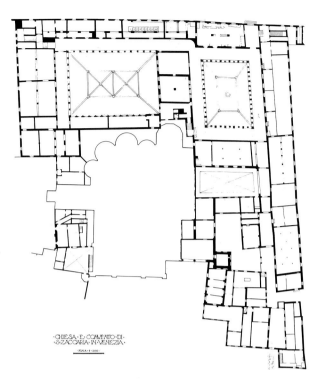

·CHIESA·E·CONVENTO·DI·
·S·ZACCARIA·IN·VENEZIA·
·SCALA·1·200·

C1 S Zaccaria. Plan of convent.

C2 S Zaccaria. First cloister.

C3 S Zaccaria. First cloister.
Detail.

C4 S Zaccaria. Chapter
house portico.

C5 S Zaccaria. Chapter
house portico. Detail.

is an ingenious refinement that contrasts with the inelegant conception and execution of the capitals and shafts. The capitals are an awkward version of the Ionic order in which doughy leaves at the four corners are pressed against volutes that spring from the necking torus. The center of each face reveals a bare bell. There are minor variations in execution: a few capitals are without volutes and some have more complex cutting. The pier capitals are blocks of the simple Tuscan type, and the shafts have the paneling on each face found in the works of Codussi and his school, but less refined in carving (fig. C3).

The surviving portion of the chapter house is the open entrance arcade of four arches supported on a central column and two lateral piers (fig. C4). Passage is through the two central bays; those at the side have a parapet. The arcade is distinguished from that of the cloister by its greater ornateness of detail (fig. C5). The archivolts are accented with bead- and egg-and-dart moldings, and there are foliated roundels on the intradosses of the arches and panels of the piers; the latter closely resemble those of the portals of San Giovanni Grisostomo in Venice.

On the northwest corner of the cloister corridor an elegant Renaissance stair leads to the upper level. Its portal, with an inscription of 1496, is only partly contemporary with the cloister.

THE SECOND CLOISTER

The second cloister is reached today through a passage in the northeast corner of cloister I that probably was built after the suppression of the convent in 1810. Its main axis runs north/south, perpendicular to that of cloister I. It also has 5 × 7 double-arched bays but, as the arches are substantially wider, the overall size is greater (fig. C6). Only the west side has arcades on two levels; on the east and north there is no upper arcade and the southern tract is modern.

The design conception is the same as that of the first cloister, but the effect is quite different because the increased bay width alters the proportions and increases the horizontality; the impression is that of a more mature work of an early sixteen-century amplitude. There are other innovations as against the predecessor; over the central bay of the west side, where the parapet stops to permit passage from the court, the motif is repeated in the upper story, giving access from the upper arcade to a balcony overlooking the court (the railing—and the balcony?—is modern). In addition, the upper corridor is open on both sides, providing a full view of the rear of the church. On the church side the arcade is supported only on piers, without intervening columns.

Also in contrast to cloister I, there is a thin stone cornice supported on simple modillions of cyma profile characteristic of the work of Codussi. The merging of the outer archivolt fascias above the column abaci noted in cloister I occurs here, also above the piers, reducing the effect of the separation of bays (fig. C7).

All the alterations seem to be refinements over cloister I and reinforce the impression that cloister II was executed after the first was well underway or complete, though details such as the capitals are of the same design and generally of the same unrefined execution.

HISTORY

The building of two almost contiguous and roughly contemporaneous cloisters in the same convent is unusual in Quattrocento Venice and might be attributed to the accommodation of two conventual groups. Bozzoni (*Il silentio de S Zaccaria snodato* 1678, p. 88) mentions that there were at one time both monks and nuns in residence, but he also speaks of a division of the nuns themselves into Osservante and Conventuale (the latter being lax in rule

C6 S Zaccaria. Second
cloister, west wing.

C7 S Zaccaria. Second
cloister. Detail.

prior to the Counter Reformation) between which there were sufficient differences "che sembrava in certa maniera un doppio Monasterio." This, together with the exclusive appearance of abbesses as chief officers in the documents and in the building records, suggests that the latter alternative is the better explanation for the duplication of cloisters. The abbesses, and presumably many of the nuns, came from the wealthiest and most powerful families in Venice, and their convent was extremely rich.

The building of the cloisters is undocumented apart from the inscription on the frieze of the stair portal of cloister I, 1496 in roman numerals (the final "I" is almost eradicated). The portal, however, is a pastiche of elements from different parts of the cloister. The frieze is not contemporary with the arch, which is inscribed "ABATISSA MARIA ELECTA VENIERA"; that abbess is recorded in 1632 (Cicogna II, 107). The 1496 inscription, however, may accurately record the foundation date of the cloister. Sabellico, writing in 1489/90 (ed. Meneghetti, p. 27; published in 1502) speaks of the "monastero opera antica" in contrast to the new church, which suggests that work had not yet begun. A starting date in the 1490s would conform with the style of cloister I.

The building records of the church of S Zaccaria do not survive for the period 1491–1555. (The most intensive phase of construction is recorded in the "Libro della fabrica della giexia de scto. Zacharia," ASV, Conventi Soppressi, S Zaccaria, carta B. 31, Fabbriche I, covering 1457–84.) Mauro Codussi appears in the records up to 1491, when they cease, but by that time the church was largely completed and he must have turned his attention to other tasks (Puppi-Puppi, 194).

Although the details of the cloisters are dim reflections of the vocabulary of Codussi and (in the arcade of the chapter house) of the Lombardo family, and could have been produced at any time after the early 1470s, the overall conception is original and quite free of the mediaeval echoes that characterize most work by minor masters at the end of the fifteenth century. The change in proportions between cloisters I and II is characteristic of the evolution of vernacular architecture over the period 1490–1520: a date of around 1510 would be plausible for the second cloister. The work closest in spirit to the cloisters is the Procuratie Vecchie in Piazza San Marco, of 1513–14. Because Codussi was architect in charge of S Zaccaria in the preceding decade, his name has been proposed as the designer (first by P. Paoletti in Thieme-Becker, *Kunstlexikon,* "Codussi," with the date ca. 1483–90). That is plausible only if we suppose that he left rough sketches or a model in the hands of workmen not trained or supervised by him.

Palazzo Vendramin-Calergi
and the Grand Canal (en-
graving by Visentini after
Canaletto).

GLOSSARY

abacus the upper part of a capital, consisting of a thin, four-sided block

absidiole a curved wall niche or minor apse

altana a light wooden superstructure on a roof, used as a kind of summer-house

anta a projecting wall end treated as a columnar element

apophyge the slight swelling at the top and bottom of a column shaft

caulicoli the stem or stalk-like elements linking the foliage of a capital with its volutes

cavetto a concave molding, usually quarter round in profile

chamfer a diagonal cut along the edge of a square corner

console a projecting bracket used as a support point, often of S-shaped profile

corona the vertical-faced projecting part of a cornice

cyma a molding, S-shaped in profile; a cyma recta is concave in its projecting part, while a cyma reversa is convex

echinus the annular molding at the bottom of a Doric or Ionic capital

entasis the gradual taper of a column; referred to as double entasis when it occurs at both top and bottom

fascia the subdivisions of the face of an Ionic or Corinthian architrave, traditionally into parallel vertical planes

fillet a narrow, flat, raised band, run as a continuous molding

griffe an ornament at the base of a column, tying the round base to a polygonal pedestal and usually of leaf- or tongue-like form

guilloche an interlace pattern used as a running molding

lesena a pilaster-like strip, but without base or capital

loggiato a semi-enclosed space, open on one or more sides through a colonnade

modillion a small bracket used to support the projecting part of a cornice

muntin a glazing bar dividing one pane of glass from the next

rail a horizontal bar in a framework, as of a window or a paneling system

rinceaux a rich but stylized vine or vegetation pattern used as a molding

rustication texturing of a wall surface, usually by roughening or quarry-facing the stones but sometimes by sinking channels between them

socle a base or pedestal, usually for a column or wall

soffit the underside or inside of an architectural element, as a window or an arch

style a vertical bar in a framework, as of a window or a paneling system

trabeation the relationship, sometimes only a visual one, between column or other support and beam or lintel carried, the whole forming a horizontal-vertical grid system

voussoir a wedge-shaped component part of an arch

BIBLIOGRAPHY

Ackerman, James S. "Architectural Practice in the Italian Renaissance." *Journal of the Society of Architectural Historians* XIII, 1954.

Ackerman, James S. *Palladio.* Harmondsworth, 1966.

Ackerman, James S., and Lotz, Wolfgang. "Vignoliana." In *Essays in Memory of Karl Lehman.* New York, 1964.

Alazard, Jean. *La Venise de la Renaissance.* Paris, 1956.

Alberti, Alberto. *La chiesa di S Maria del Riposo in Barbaria delle Tole a Venezia.* Venice, 1964.

Alberti, Leon Battista. *De re aedificatoria.* Florence, 1485 (Paris, 1512, and Strassburg, 1541).

Alberti, Leon Battista. *I dieci libri de l'architettura.* Translated by Pietro Lauro. Venice, 1546.

Il Sant'Andrea di Mantova e Leon Battista Alberti. Atti del convegno di studi organizzato dalla citta di Mantova con la collaborazione della Accademia Virgiliana nel quinto centenario della basilica di Sant' Andrea e della morte dell'Alberti. Mantua, 1972.

Albrizzi, Giovanni Battista di Girolamo. *Il forestiero illuminato intorno alle cose più rare e curiose antiche e moderne della Città di Venezia e delle isole Circonvicine.* Venice, 1740.

Algarotti, Francesco. *Saggi, a cura di Giovanni da Pozzo.* Bari, 1963.

D'Ancona, Paolo, and Gengaro, Maria Luisa. *Umanesimo e Rinascimento. Storia dell'arte classica e italiana,* vol. III, 3d ed. Turin, 1953.

Anderson, William J. *The Architecture of the Renaissance in Italy.* London, 1896 (London and New York, 1909).

Andreis, G. *Memorie sulla chiesa di S Giovanni in Bragora.* Venice, 1848.

Angelini, Luigi. *Un artista ignoto per secoli.* Bergamo, 1962.

Angelini, Luigi. *Bartolomeo Bono e Gugliemo d'Alzano, architetti bergamaschi in Venezia.* Bergamo, 1961.

Angelini, Luigi. *Le opere in Venezia di Mauro Codussi.* Milan, 1945.

De Angelis d'Ossat, Gugliemo. "Un palazzo veneziano progettato dal Palladio." *Palladio* IV, 1956.

De Angelis d'Ossat, Gugliemo. "Venezia e l'architettura del primo rinascimento." In *Umanesimo europeo e umanesimo veneziano*. Florence, 1963.

De Angelis d'Ossat, Gugliemo. "I Sangallo e Palladio." *Bolletino del Centro Internazionale di Studi di Architettura 'Andrea Palladio'* VIII, 1966.

Annales Camaldulenses. 9 vols. Edited by G. B. Mittarelli and A. Costadoni. Venice, 1755–1773.

Aretino, Pietro. *Lettere sull'arte, commentate da Fidenzio Pertile, a cura di Ettore Camesasca.* Milan, 1957–1960.

Argan, Giulio Carlo. *L'architettura barocca in Italia.* Milan, 1957.

Argan, Giulio Carlo. *L'arte italiana dal Seicento all'Ottocento.* Rome, 1938.

Argan, Giulio Carlo. "Andrea Palladio e la critica neoclassica." *L'Arte,* July 1930.

Argan, Giulio Carlo. "L'importanza del Sanmichele nella formazione del Palladio in Venezia e l'Europa." In *Venezia e l'Europa.* Venice, 1955.

Argan, Giulio Carlo. *The Renaissance City.* New York, 1970.

Argan, Giulio Claudio. "Sebastiano Serlio." *L'Arte* XXXV, 1932.

Argan, Giulio Claudio. "Tipologia, simbologia, allegorismo delle forme architettoniche." *Bolletino del Centro Internazionale di Studi di Architettura 'Andrea Palladio'* I, 1959.

Armao, Ermanno. *Vincenzo Coronelli. Cenni sull'uomo e sulla vita.* Florence, 1944.

Arslan, Edoardo. "Un documento del Sansovino a Giangiacomo de'Grigi." In *Studi in onore di Mons. Carlo Castiglioni.* Milan, 1957.

Arslan, Edoardo. *Gothic Architecture in Venice.* Translated by Anne Engel. London and New York, 1972.

Ashby, Thomas. "Sixteenth-century Drawings of Roman Buildings Attributed to Andreas Coner." *Papers of the British School at Rome,* vol. II, 1904, and vol. VI, 1913.

Avena, A. "Commemorazione 'A Michele Sanmicheli.'" *Vita Veronese,* December 1959.

Averlino, Antonio. See Filarete.

Azevedo, Emmanuele de. *Venetae Urbis descriptio a Nicandro Jasseo P. A. concinnata anno MDCCLX, edita anno MDCCLXXX.* Venice, 1780.

Bailly, Auguste. *Le serenissime republique de Venise.* Paris, 1946.

Bandeloni, Enzo. "Pietro Lombardo, architetto nella critica d'arte." *Bolletino del Museo Civico di Padova* LI, 1962.

Barban, Bernardino. "La chiesa di San Michele in Isola." In *San Michele in Isola 1829–1929.* Venice, 1929.

Barbaro, Daniele. *La pratica della perspettiva di Monsignor Barbaro eletto patriarca d'Aquileia opera molto utile a pittori, a scultori et ad architetti.* Venice, 1569.

Barbieri, Franco. "Un architetto italiano del '500 alla scoperta del 'Gotico' da un tacuino manoscritto inedito di Vincenzo Scamozzi presso il Museo di Vicenza." *Palladio* V, 1955.

Barbieri, Franco. *La Basilica palladiana.* Corpus Palladianum II, Vicenza, 1968.

Barbieri, Franco. *Vincenzo Scamozzi.* Verona and Vicenza, 1952.

Barbieri, Franco. "Vincenzo Scamozzi studioso e artista." *La Critica d'Arte,* 1949.

Bardi, Girolamo. *Delle cose notabili della Citta di Venetia, Libri II . . . con l'aggiunta della dichiaratione delle istorie, che sono state dipinte nei quadri delle Sale dello Scrutinio, & del Gran Consiglio del Palagio Ducale.* Venice, 1587.

Barocco europeo e barocco veneziano. See Branca, Vittore, ed.

Barocchi, P. *Trattati d'arte del Cinquecento, fra manierismo e contrariforma.* Bari, 1960.

Baron, Hans. *The Crisis of the Early Renaissance.* 2d ed., rev. Princeton, 1966.

Barres, Maurice. *Amori et dolori sacrum—la mort de Venise.* Paris, 1902.

Baschet, Armand. *Souvenirs d'une mission—les archives de la Serenissime Republique de Venise.* Paris, 1857.

Bassi, Elena. *Appunti per la storia del Palazzo Ducale di Venezia.* Vicenza, 1962.

Bassi, Elena. *Architettura del sei e settecento a Venezia.* Naples, 1962.

Bassi, Elena. *Il convento della Carità.* Corpus Palladianum VI, Vicenza, 1971.

Bassi, Elena. "I disegni dell'Accademia di Belle Arti di Venezia." *Atti e memorie dell'Accademia di Belle Arti di Venezia.* Venice, 1959.

Bassi, Elena. "Episodi dell'architettura veneta nell'opera di Antonio Gaspari." *Saggi e memorie di storia dell'arte* III, 1964.

Bassi, Elena. "Episodi dell'edilizia veneziana nei secoli XVII e XVIII." *Critica d'Arte* VI, 1959.

Bassi, Elena. *Gianantonio Selva, architetto veneziano.* Padua, 1936.

Bassi, Elena. "Introduzione a uno studio dell'architettura barocca veneziana." In *Venezia e l'Europa.* Venice, 1956.

Bassi, Elena. "I palazzi Zane a San Stin." *Arte Veneta* XIII, 1959.

Bassi, Elena. "Palazzo Pesaro." *Critica d'Arte* VI, 1959.

Bassi, Elena. *Palazzi di Venezia, Admiranda Urbis Venetae.* Venice, 1976.

Bassi, Elena. "Il restauro dei palazzi." *Critica d'Arte,* 1951.

Bassi, Elena. "Il Sansovino per l'Ospizio degli Incurabili." *Critica d'Arte* no. 57-68, 1963.

Bassi, Elena, and Trincanato, Egle Renata. *Guide for Visitors to the Ducal Palace in Venice.* Milan, 1972.

Basso, L. *Le XV siècle venetien.* Turin, 1960.

Battagia, Giuseppe. *Cenni storici e statistici sopra l'isola della Giudecca.* Venice, 1832.

Battistella, A. *La repubblica di Venezia.* Venice, 1921.

Battisti, Eugenio. *L'antirinascimento.* Florence, n.d.

Battisti, Eugenio. *Rinascimento e barocco.* Turin, 1960.

Battisti, Eugenio. "Proposte per una storia di Manierismo in architettura." *Odeo Olimpico* VII, 1968-1970.

Battisti, Giovanni Antonio. *Raccolta d'istruzioni d'architettura civile parte inedite, e parte infedelmente sin'ora impresse, ed in parte rovinose, da celebri architetti de' migliori tempi innalzate, disegnate ed incise con tutta l'accuratezza.* Venice, 1786.

Beatiano, G. C. *L'Araldo Veneto, overo universale armerista mettodico di tutta la scienza araldica.* Venice, 1680.

Becherucci, Luisa. *L'architettura italiana del cinquecento.* Florence, 1936.

Bellavitis, Giorgio. "La condizione spaziale di Venezia nell'opera prima di Mauro Coducci." *Psicon,* III, no. 6, January–March 1976.

Beloch, K. J. "La populazione di Venezia nei secoli XVI-XVIII." *Nuovo archivio veneto,* n.s. III, 1902.

Beltrami, Daniele. *Storia della popolazione di Venezia dalla fine del secolo XVI alla caduta della Repubblica.* Padua, 1954.

Beltrami, Luca. *La "Ca' del Duca" sul canal grande.* Milan, 1900.

Beltrami, Luca; Boni, Giacomo; Fradeletto, Antonio; Molmenti, Pompeo; Mondolfo, Anita; and Moretti, Gaetano. *Il campanile di S Marco riedificato; studi, ricerche, relazioni.* Venice, 1912.

Bembo, Pietro. *Opera.* Venice, 1729.

Benese, Giovanni Botero. *Relatione della repubblica venetiana.* Venice, 1605.

Benevolo, Leonardo. *La città italiana del Rinascimento.* Milan, 1969.

Benzoni, G. *Venezia nell'età della Contrariforma.* Milan, 1973.

Berchiet, F. "Contributo alla storia dell'edificio della Veneta Zecca." *Atti del Istituto Veneto di Scienze, Lettere ed Arti,* 1909-1910.

Berengo, Marino. *La società veneta alla fine del settecento; ricerche storiche.* Florence, 1956.

Bernardi, Jacopo. *Il santuario della Beata Vergine dei Miracoli in Venezia.* Venice, 1887.

Bertanza, Enrico. *Documenti per la storia della cultura in Venezia.* Venice, 1907.

Berti, Giovan-Battista. *Nuova guida per Venezia ossia memorie storico-critico descrittive di questa regia città.* Padua, 1830.

Berti, Giuseppe. *L'architettura a Venezia e la scultura attraverso i secoli: il rinascimento.* Turin, n.d.

Bertini Calosso, A. "Andrea Palladio e il tempietto di Clitumno." *Atti del III Congresso di Storia dell'Architettura.* Florence, 1938.

Bertotti Scamozzi, Ottavio. *Le fabbriche e i disegni di Andrea Palladio raccolti ed illustrati.* Vicenza, 1776–1783.

Bertotti Scamozzi, Ottavio. *Il forestiere istruito delle cose più rare di architettura.* Vicenza, 1761.

Bertotti Scamozzi, Ottavio. *Le terme dei romani disegnate di A Palladio e ripubblicate con la giunta di alcune osservazioni da Ottavio Scamozzi.* Vicenza, 1797.

Bessone Aureli, Antonietta Maria. *Dizionario degli scultori ed architetti italiani.* Città di Castello, 1947.

Bettanini, Giuseppe. *La chiesa di S Nicolo dei Mendicoli in Venezia.* Noale, 1935.

Bettini, Sergio. "La critica dell'architettura e l'arte del Palladio." *Arte Veneta* III, 1949.

Bettini, Sergio. "Palladio urbanista." *Arte Veneta* XVI, 1961.

Bettini, Sergio, et al. *Venezia e Bisanzio.* Catalogue. Venice, 1974.

Bettini, Sergio. *Venezia e la sua laguna.* Novara, 1953.

Bianchi, Feliciano. *Isole della laguna.* Bergamo, 1938.

Bianchini, Giuseppe. *La chiesa di S Maria Assunta de' Gesuiti in Venezia.* Venice, 1891.

Bianchini, Giuseppe. *La chiesa di S Maria Formosa in Venezia.* Venice, 1892.

Bianchini, Giuseppe. *La chiesa di S Maria Mater Domini in Venezia.* Venice, 1893.

Bianchini, Giuseppe. *La chiesa di S Maria in Nazareth detta degli Scalzi in Venezia.* Venice, 1894.

Bianchini, Giuseppe. *La chiesa di S Maria della Pietà in Venezia.* Verona and Padua, 1896.

Bianchini, Giuseppe. *La chiesa di S Maria del Rosario vulgo i Gesuati.* Venice, 1889.

Bianchini, Giuseppe. *La chiesa di S Maria Zobenigo.* Venice, 1895.

Bianconi, O. "Palladio e Veronese." *Svizzera italiana*, October–December 1955.

Bima, Carlo. *Giorgio da Sebenico. La sua cattedrale e l'attività in Dalmatia e in Italia.* Milan, 1954.

Bisacco, D. Alfonso. *La chiesa di S Pantaleon in Venezia.* Venice, 1933.

Biscario, G. "Pietro Lombardo e la cattedrale di Treviso." *Archivio Storico d'Arte* II, 1897.

Bittanti, Ernesta, ed. *Venezia descritta da un pellegrino per Terra Santa del secolo XV.* Florence, 1895.

Blunt, Anthony. *Artistic Theory in Italy.* Oxford, 1940.

Blunt, Anthony. "A Neo-Palladian Programme Executed by Visentini and Zuccarelli for Consul Smith." *Burlington Magazine* C, 1958.

Blunt, Anthony. *Some Uses and Misuses of the Terms Baroque and Rococo as Applied to Architecture.* London, 1973.

Blunt, Anthony, and Croft-Murray, Edward. *Venetian Drawings of the XVII and XVIII Centuries in the Collection of Her Majesty the Queen at Windsor Castle.* London, 1957.

Bolognini Amorini, (Marchese) Antonio. *Elogio di Sebastiano Serlio, architetto bolognese.* Bologna, 1823.

Bonelli, Renato. *Da Bramante a Michelangelo. Profilo dell'architettura del Cinquecento.* Venice, 1960.

Bonelli, Renato. "Prospettiva del Cinquecento." *L'Architettura*, 1958.

Bonfanti, S. *La Giudecca nella storia, nell'arte, nella vita.* Venice, 1930.

Boni, Giacomo. "S Maria dei Miracoli in Venezia." *Archivio Veneto* XXXIII, 1887.

Bonicatti, Maurizio. *Aspetti dell'umanesimo nella pittura veneta dal 1455 al 1515.* Rome, 1964.

Bordiga, Giovanni. "Jacopo Sansovino a Venezia." *Rivista mensile della Città di Venezia* VII, no. 6, 1929.

Boriosi Crucianti, M. "Il giardino veneto." *Antichità Viva*, no. 2, 1966.

Borromeo, S. Carlo. *Instructionum et Supellectilis Ecclesiasticae libri duo.* Translated by C. Castiglione and C. Marcora in Arte Sacra, de Fabrica Ecclesiae. Milan, 1952.

Bortolan, Mons. Gino. *Le Chiese del Patriarcato di Venezia.* Venice, 1975.

Boschieri, Giacomo. "Il palazzo Grimani a S Luca." *Rivista di Venezia,* 1931.

Boschini, Marco. *La carta del navigar pittoresco. Dialogo tra un senator venetian deletante e un profesor de pitture.* Venice, 1660. Reprint. Venice, 1965.

Boschini, Marco. *L'arcipelago con tutte le isole, scogli, secche, e lassi fondi, con i mari, golfi, seni, porti, città e castelli; nella forma che si vedono al tempo presente . . .* Venice, 1658.

Boschini, Marco. *I gioielli pittoreschi, virtuoso ornamento della città di Venezia.* Venice, 1676.

Boschini, Marco. *Le minere della pittura veneziana.* Venice, 1664. Later editions, with additions, in 1675, 1682, and 1704.

Boschini, Marco, and Zanetti, Anton Maria. *Descrizione di tutte le pubbliche pitture della Città di Venezia e isole circonvicine o sia rinnovazione delle Ricche Minere di Marco Boschini, colla aggiunta di tutte le opere che uscirono dal 1674 sino al presente 1733.* Venice, 1733.

Bosisio, Achille. *La chiesa di S Maria del Rosario o dei Gesuati.* Venice, 1943. Reprint. 1951.

Botero Benese, Giovanni, *Relatione della repubblica venetiana.* Venice, 1608.

Bottari, Giovanni, and Ticozzi, Stefano. *Raccolta di lettere sulla pittura, scultura ed architettura scritte da' più celebri personaggi dei secoli XV, XVI e XVII pubblicata da M Gio. Bottari, e continuata fino ai nostri giorni da Stefano Ticozzi.* Milan, 1822–1825.

Bottari, Stefano. *Storia dell'arte italiana,* vol. II, *Il rinascimento, l'arte del quattrocento,* and vol. III, *Dal cinquecento ai nostri giorni.* Milan, 1955–1957.

Bouwsma, William J. *Venice and the Defense of Republican Liberty.* Berkeley, 1968.

Bozzoni, Domenico. *Il silentio di S Zaccaria snodato.* Venice, 1678.

Bracaloni, P Leone. *L'arte franciscana nella vita e nella storia di settecento anni.* Todi, 1924.

Branca, Vittore, ed. *Barocco europeo e barocco veneziano.* Florence, 1962.

Brandi, Cesare. "Perchè il Palladio non fu neo-classico." In *Essays in the History of Architecture Presented to Rudolf Wittkower.* London, 1967.

Branzi, S. "Andrea Palladio e i disegni delle antichità." *Il Gazzettino,* July 1, 1959.

Bratti, (Daniele) Ricciotti. "Notizie d'arte e di artisti." *Miscellanea Storia Veneta* IV, 1930.

Bratti, (Daniele) Ricciotti. "L'ultima ala delle Procuratie." *Rivista di Venezia,* 1930.

Bratti, (Daniele) Ricciotti. *Vecchie isole veneziane.* Venice, 1913.

Bratti, (Daniele) Ricciotti. *Venezia scomparsa.* Venice, 1911.

Braudel, Fernand. *La Méditeranée et le Monde Méditerranéen à l'Époque de Philippe II,* 2d enlarged edition. Paris, 1966.

Brenzoni, Raffaello, *Dizionario di artisti veneti: Pittori, scultori, architetti dal XIII al XVIII secolo.* Florence, 1972.

Brenzoni, Raffaello, "Un documento sanmicheliano." *Bollettino d'Arte* III, 1959.

Brenzoni, Raffaello. *Fra Giovanni Giocondo veronese.* Florence, 1960.

Breve cenni intorno la basilica di S Pietro Apostolo in Venezia. Venice, 1842.

Brosses, Charles de. *Lettres familières sur l'Italie publiés d'aprés les manuscrits.* Introduction and notes by Yvonne Bézard, Paris, 1931.

Brown, Horatio F. *In and Around Venice.* London, 1905.

Brown, Horatio F. *Life on the Lagoons.* London, 1904.

Brown, Horatio F. *Studies in the History of Venice.* London, 1907.

Brunetti, Mario. *S Maria del Giglio vulgo Zobenigo nell'arte e nella storia.* Venice, 1952.

Brunetti, Mario. *La Scuola Grande Arciconfraternità di S Maria del Carmelo ieri e oggi.* Turin, 1962.

Brunetti, Mario, et al. *Venice.* Translated by James Emmons, New York, 1956.

Brunetti, Mario, and Lorenzetti, Giulio. *Venezia nella storia e nell'arte*. Venice, 1950.

Brunetti, Mario. *Venice and Its History*. Venice, 1964.

Brunetti, Mario; Dazzi, Manlio; and Gerbino, Guido. *Il Fondaco nostro dei Tedeschi*. Venice, 1941.

Burckhardt, Jacob. *Briefe an einen Architekten 1870-1889*. Munich, 1913.

Burckhardt, Jacob. *The Cicerone*. Translated by Mrs. A. H. Clough. London, 1873.

Burckhardt, Jacob. *Die Cultur der Renaissance in Italien*. Basel, 1860.

Burke, Peter. *Culture and Society in Renaissance Italy 1420-1540*. London, 1972.

Burke, Peter. *Venice and Amsterdam: A Study of Seventeenth-century Elites*. London, 1974.

Buttafava, Claudio, and Garbagnati, E. *Architecttura nel segno dei maestri*. Bergamo, 1962.

Caccin, Angelo M. *S Maria Gloriosa, die Frari-Basilika in Venedig*. Venice, 1964.

Caccin, Angelo M. *The Church of Sts. John and Paul in Venice*, 2d rev. ed. Translated by Maria Luisa Beffagna. Venice, 1961.

Cadorin, G. *Pareri di quindici architetti, e notizie istoriche intorno al Palazzo Ducale di Venezia*. Venice, 1838.

Caffi, Michele. "Guglielmo Bergamasco ossia Vielmo di Alzano." *Archivio Veneto* XXVIII, 1884.

Calabri, D. "Sistemazione dell'ex-convento dei Tolentini a Venezia." *Architettura*, April 1968.

Canal, Bernardo. "Il collegio, l'ufficio e l'archivio dei Dieci Savi alle Decime in Rialto." *Nuovo Archivio Veneto* XVI (1908): 115-150, 279-310.

Il canal grande di Venezia. Venice, 1931.

Candiani, C.; Musolino, G.; Niero, Don Antonio; and Tramontin, Silvio. *Culto dei santi a Venezia*. Venice, 1965.

Cantalamessa, Giulio. "Cappella Grimani in S Francesco della Vigna." *Rassegna d'arte*, 1902.

Cantalamessa, Giulio. "La Loggetta del Sansovino." *Rassegna d'arte*, 1902.

Cantimori, D. "L'età barocca." In *Manierismo Barocco Rococò, Concetti e termini, Convegno dell'accademia dei Lincei, 1960*. Rome, 1962.

Dal Canton, Giuseppina. "Architettura del Filarete ed architettura veneziana." *Arte Lombarda* XVIII, 1973.

Cappelletti, Giuseppe. *Le chiese d'Italia dalla loro origine sino ai nostri giorni*. 21 vols. Venice, 1844-1870. Volume IX (on Venice) 1851.

Cappelletti, Giuseppe. *Storia della chiesa di Venezia dalla sua fondazione sino ai nostri giorni*. Veice, 1849-1855.

Carboneri, Nino. "Mauro Codussi." *Bollettino del Centro Internazionale di Studi di Architettura 'Andrea Palladio'* VI, pt. 2, 1964.

Carraro, G., and Manoli, P. *Venezia deve vivere*. Venice, 1969.

Casaburi, S., and Longhetto, O. "Il ponte di Rialto." *L'Architettura*, June 1958.

Casola, Pietro. *Canon Pietro Casola's Pilgrimage to Jerusalem in the Year 1494*, by M. Margaret Newett, Manchester, 1907.

Casoni, Giovanni. *Guida per l'Arsenale di Venezia*. Venice, 1820.

Cassini, Giocondo. *Piante e vedute prospettiche di Venezia (1479-1855)*. Venice, 1971.

Cataneo, Pietro. *I Quattro primi libri di architettura...* Venice, 1554. First four parts only; full eight parts Venice, 1567 as *L'Architettura*. Reprinted by Gregg Press 1964.

Cattaneo, Raffaele. *L'architettura a Venezia*. Venice, 1861.

Cavizago, Giovanni. *Olivolo e la sua Cattedrale*. Venice, 1943.

Cessi, Francesco. *Allesandro Vittoria, architetto e stuccatore (1525-1608)*. Trent, 1961.

Cessi, Francesco. "Fortuna di Andrea Palladio." *Padova* III, 1960.

Cessi, Francesco. *Mattia Carneri, architetto e scultore, 1592-1673*. Trent, 1964.

Cessi, Roberto. *Storia della repubblica di Venezia*. Milan and Messena, 1944-1946.

Cessi, Roberto. *Un millennio di storia veneziana*. Venice, 1964.

Cessi, Roberto, and Alberti, Annibale. *Rialto, l'isola, il ponte, il mercato.* Bologna, 1934.

Cessi, Roberto; Bratti, (Daniele) Ricciotti; and Brunetti, Mario. *La laguna di Venezia.* Venice, 1934.

Cevese, Renato. "Licenze nell'arte di Andrea Palladio." *Bollettino del Centro Internazionale di Studi di Architettura 'Andrea Palladio'* VII, 1968-1969.

Chambers, D. S. *The Imperial Age of Venice, 1380-1580.* History of European Civilization Library. Edited by Geoffrey Barraclough. New York and London, 1970.

Charvet, L. *Sebastiano Serlio 1475-1554.* Lyon, 1869.

Chastel, André. *Art et religion dans la Renaissance italienne.* Paris, 1945.

Chastel, Andre. *L'art italien.* Paris, 1956.

Checchi, Marcello; Gaudenzio, Luigi; Grossato, Luigi; et al. *Padova, Guida ai monumenti e alle opere d'arte.* Venice, 1961.

Checchia, Pietro. *Croniche dell'origine e fondazione del monastero e chiesa della B Vergine dei Miracoli.* enice, 1742.

Cheke, Sir Marcus, *The Cardinal de Bernis.* London, 1958.

Chierici, Gino. *Il palazzo italiano dal secolo XI al secolo XIX.* Milan, 1954-1957.

Chierici, Gino. *Palladio.* Florence, 1949.

Chiminelli, Caterina. "Le scale scoperte nei palazzi veneziani." *Ateneo Veneto* XXXV, 1912, vol. 1 fasc 3, 209ff.

Cian, Vittorio. *La cultura e l'italianità di Venezia nel rinascimento.* Bologna, 1905.

Ciartoso Lorenzetti, Maria. See Lorenzetti, Maria Ciartoso.

Cicogna, Emmanuele Antonio. *Breve notizia alla origine della confraternita di S Giovanni Evangelista in Venezia.* Venice, 1855.

Cicogna, Emmanuele Antonio. *Cenni intorno la chiesa di S Maria Formosa di Venezia e gli ultimi restauri.* Venice, 1843.

Cicogna, Emmanuele Antonio. *Il forestiero guidato nel cospicuo appartamento in cui risedieva il gabinetto della Repubblica Veneta ed ora l'Imperiale Regio Tribunale Generale di Appello.* Venice, 1817.

Cicogna, Emmanuele Antonio. *Delle iscrizioni veneziane; raccolte ed illustrate.* 6 vols. Venice, 1824-1953.

Cicogna, Emmanuele Antonio. *Saggio di bibliografia veneziana.* Venice, 1847.

Cicognara, Leopoldo. *Catalogo ragionato dei libri d'arte e d'antichità possedute dal Conte Cicognara.* Pisa, 1821.

Cicognara, Leopoldo; Diedo, Antonio; and Selva, Giovanni Antonio. *Le fabbriche più cospicui di Venezia misurate, illustrate, ed intagliate dai membri della Veneta Reale Accademia di Belle Arti.* Venice, 1815-1820.

Cicognara, Leopoldo; Diedo, Antonio; and Selva, Giovanni Antonio. *Le fabbriche e i monumenti più cospicue di Venezia. Seconda edizione con notabile aggiunte e note* (by Zanotto). Venice, 1838-1840.

La civiltà veneziana del rinascimento. Essays by Valeri, Chabod, Barblan, Braudel, Jedin, Elwert, Fiocco, Marozzo della Rocca, and Tiepolo. Florence, 1958.

La civiltà veneziana nell'età barocca. Essays by Malraux, Sestan, Salvatorelli, Sella, Ronga, Getto, Ivanoff, de Luca, Polvani, Marozzo della Rocca, and Tiepolo. Florence, 1959.

La civiltà veneziana del settecento. Essays by Valeri, Fanfani, Berengo, Damerini, Vecchi, della Corte, Marcazzan, Chastel, Marozzo della Rocca, and Tiepolo. Florence, 1960.

Clarke, Sir Ashley, and Rylands, Philip. *The Church of the Madonna dell'Orto.* London, 1977.

Cochin, Charles Nicolas. *Voyage d'Italie, ou recueil des notes sur les ouvrages de peinture et de sculpture qu'on voit dans les principales villes d'Italie,* Paris, 1758 and 1769.

Cochrane, Eric, ed. *The Late Italian Renaissance 1525-1630.* London, 1970.

Cocteau, Jean, and Leiss, Ferruccio. *Venise.* Milan, 1953.

Coleti, Nicola. *Monumenta Ecclesiae Venetae Sancti Moysis.* Venice, 1758.

Collins, P. "Philosophy of Architectural Criticism." *Journal of the American Institute of Architects.* January 1968.

Colonna, Francesco. *Hypnerotomachia Poliphili.* Venice, 1499.

Comolli, Angelo. *Bibliografia storico-critica dell'architettura civile ed arti subalterna.* Rome, 1787–1792. Facsimile, Milan, 1965.

Constable, W. S. *Canaletto, Giovanni Antonio Canal, 1697–1768.* Oxford, 1962.

Contarini, Gasparo. *The Commonwealth and Government of Venice.* Translated by Lewis Lewkenor. London, 1599.

Contarini, Nicolò. *Degli istorici degli cose veneziane i quali hanno scritto per pubblico decreto.* Venice, 1718.

Contin, Bernardino. *La prospettiva pratica di Bernardino Contino.* Venice, 1684.

Cope, Maurice. "The Venetian Chapel of the Sacrament in the 16th Century." Ph.D. dissertation, University of Chicago, 1965.

Le Corbusier. *Perspectives humaines. Propos d'urbanisme.* Paris, 1946.

Cornaro, Alvise. *Trattato sull'architettura.* Fragment published by Schlosser in 1952.

Corner (or Cornaro or Cornelius), Flaminio. *Ecclesiae venetae et torcellanae antiquis monumentis illustratae.* Venice, 1749.

Corner, Flaminio. *Notizie storiche delle chiese e monasteri di Venezia e di Torcello.* Padua, 1758.

Coronelli, Marco Vincenzo. *Arme, blasoni o insegne gentilitie delle famiglie patritie esistenti nella republica di Venetia dedicata dal P cosmografo Coronelli.* Venice, 1694.

Coronelli, Marco Vincenzo. *Atlante veneto. Singolarità di Venezia.* Venice, 1692–1697.

Coronelli, Vincenzo. *Biblioteca universale sacro-profano antico-moderno.* Venice, 1707–1716.

Coronelli, Vincenzo. *Cronologia universale.* Venice, 1707.

Coronelli, Vincenzo. *Isolario ovvero Atlante veneto.* Venice, 1696–1697.

Il P. Vincenzo Coronelli dei Frati Minori conventuali, 1650–1718. Rome, 1951.

Coronelli, Vincenzo Maria the younger. *Guida de'forestieri o sia epitome diaria perpetua sacra-profana per la Città di Venezia.* Venice, 1744.

Coryate, Thomas. *Coryate's Crudities.* Reprint of the 1611 edition. Glasgow, 1905.

Costa, F. *Le delizie del fiume Brenta.* Venice, 1770.

Costadoni, Anselmo. *Annales Camaldolensis Ordinis Sancti Benedictini.* Venice, 1755–1773.

Cozzi, Gaetano. *Il Doge Nicolò Contarini. Ricerche sul patriziato veneziano agli inizi del Seicento.* Venice, 1958.

della Croce, Marsilio. *Historia pubblica e famosa entrata in Venetia del Serenissimo Enrico III.* Venice, 1574.

Cronaca Veneta sacra e profana. Venice, 1736.

Cucchini. *La laguna di Venezia e i suoi porti.* Venice, 1912.

Cueva, Alfonso de la. *Relation de l'etat, des forces et du gouvernement de la Republique faite au Roi Catholique Philippe d'Autriche.* N.p., 1603.

Ćurčić, Slobodan. "Architectural Significance of Subsidiary Chapels in Middle Byzantine Churches." *Journal of the Society of Architectural Historians,* XXXVI, 1977.

Damerini, Gino. *La Ca' Grande dei Capello e dei Malipiero di S Samuele ora Barnabo.* Venice, 1962.

Damerini, Gino. *La Ca' Moro.* Venice, n.d.

Damerini, Gino. *I giardini sulla laguna.* Bologna, 1927.

Damerini, Gino. *I giardini di Venezia.* Bologna, 1931.

Damerini, Gino. *L'isola e il cenobio di S Giorgio Maggiore.* Venice, 1956.

Damerini, Gino. *Il palazzo Balbi in volta di canal.* Venice, n.d.

Daud, Diana. *Juste Le Court and his Circle.* Ph.D. dissertation, Columbia University, n.d.

Davey, Norman. *A History of Building Materials.* London, 1961.

Davis, James C. *The Decline of the Venetian Nobility as a Ruling Class.* Baltimore, 1962.

Dazzi, Manlio. "Sull'architetto del Fondaco dei Tedeschi." *Atti del Istituto Veneto di Scienze, Lettere ed Arti* XCIX, no. II, 1939–1940.

"Death of a Monument; the Fall of the Campanile in the Piazza of S Marco." *Architectural Review* CXXIV, November 1958.

Dellwing, Herbert. "Die Kirchen S Zaccaria in Venedig." *Zeitschrift für Kunstgeschichte* nos. 3-4, 1974.

Dianoux, Lucien. *Les monuments civils, religieux et militaires de Michele Sanmicheli.* Genoa, 1878.

Dickens, A. G. *Reformation and Society in Sixteenth-century Europe.* London, 1966.

Diehl, Charles. *La république de Venise.* Paris, 1915.

Diehl, Charles. *Une république patricienne.* Paris, 1915.

Dinsmoor, William Bell. "The Literary Remains of Sebastiano Serlio." *Art Bulletin* XXIV, 1942.

Direction du Palais des Doges. *Le Palais des doges—guide historique-artistique.* Venice, 1959.

Dixon, George Campbell. *Venice, Vicenza, and Verona.* Fair Lawn, N.J., 1959.

Dizionario biografico degli Italiani. Edited by Alberto M. Ghisaberti. Rome, 1960–.

Dizionario enciclopedico di architettura e urbanistica. Edited by Paolo Portoghesi. Rome, 1968-1969.

Doglioni, Giovanni Nicolò. *Delle cose notabili della città di Venezia.* Venice, 1641.

Doglioni, Giovanni Nicolò. *Le cose notabili della città di Venezia di Nicolò Doglioni ampliate da Zuane Zitio.* Venice, 1666.

Doglioni, Giovanni Nicolò. *Historia veneziana scritta brevemente da Gio Nicolò Doglioni delle sucesse dalla prima fondatione de Venetia sino all'anno de Christo MDXCVIII.* Venice, 1598.

Doglioni, Giovanni Nicolò. *Veneta trionfante e sempre libera, dove per ordine de'tempi si legge la sua origine, & augmento; la potenza in soccorrer altri Principi; le vittorie ottenute; le Città soggiogate per forza, e di suo volere.* Venice, 1613.

Dogo, L. *Questa strana Venezia.* Novara, 1965.

Dolcetti, Giovanni. *Il libro d'argento delle famiglie venete, nobili, cittadini e popolari.* Venice, 1922-25.

Donati, Ugo. *Artisti ticinese a Venezia.* Lugano, 1961.

Donin, Richard Kurt. *Venedig und die Baukunst von Wien und Niederösterreich.* Vienna, 1963.

Donin, Richard Kurt. *Vincenzo Scamozzi und der Einfluss Venedigs auf die Salzburger Architektur.* Innsbruck, 1948.

Douglas, Hugh A. *Venice on Foot.* London, 1907.

Durandus, William (Gulielmus). *The Symbolism of Churches and Church Ornaments. A Translation of the First Book of the Rationale Divinorum Officinorum.* Edited by Neale and Webb. Leeds, 1843.

Elenco degli edifici monumentali e dei frammenti storici ed artistici della città di Venezia. Venice, 1905.

Enciclopedia italiana. Rome, 1949-1952.

Erizzo, Nicolò. *Relazione storico-critica sulla Torre dell' Orologio di S Marco in Venezia.* Venice, 1860.

Escher, Konrad. "Die grossen Gemäldefolgen im Dogenpalast in Venedig und ihre inhaltliche Bedeutung für den Barock." *Repertorium für Kunstwissenschaft* XLI, 1918.

Essays in Honor of Erwin Panofsky. New York, 1961.

Evelyn, John. *Diary.* London, 1959.

Evenett, H. "The New Orders." In *The New Cambridge Modern History II.* Cambridge, 1958.

Fabri, (Frate) Felice. *Venezia nel MCDLXXXVIII, descrizione di Felice Fabri da Ulma.* Translated by Vincenzo Lazari, edited by Domenico Zasso. Venice, 1881.

Fabri, Felix. *Wanderings in the Holy Land.* Edited by Aubrey Stewart. London, 1892-1893.

Fanello, Vincenzo. *Della chiesa di S Pantaleone e S Giuliana.* Venice, 1698.

Fantasia composta in laude di Venezia. Venice, 1582.

Fasolo, F. "Opere monumentali e problemi nuovi. S Maria della Salute—Venezia." *Fede e Arte,* April-June 1967.

Fasolo, G. "Il Ponte di Rialto e gli architetti vicentini." *Vicenza.* 1933.

Fassetti, Antonio Francesco. *L'architettura di Andrea Palladio divisa in quattro libri di nuovo ristampata ed abbellita coll'impressione delle figure in rame non più usata con l'aggiunta del quinto libro che tratta delle antichità di Roma dell'autore medemo* [sic] *non più veduto.* Venice, 1711.

Fedalto, Giorgio. *Ricerche storiche sulla posizione giuridica ed ecclesiastica dei greci a Venezia nei secoli XV e XVI.* Florence, 1967.

Ferguson, Wallace K. *The Renaissance in Historical Thought.* Cambridge, Mass., 1948.

Ferrari, L. *I Carmeliti Scalzi a Venezia, cenni storici.* Venice, 1882.

Ferri, Pasquale Nerino. *Catalogo riassuntivo della raccolta di disegni antiche e moderne posseduta dalla R Galleria degli Uffizi di Firenze.* Florence, 1890–1897.

Ferri, Pasquale Nerino. *Indici e cataloghi III: Disegni di architettura esistenti nella Galleria degli Uffizi in Firenze.* Rome, 1885.

Festschrift V Fasolo: Saggi di storia dell'architettura. Quaderni d'Istituto di Storia dell'Architettura VI-VIII. Rome, 1961.

Festschrift Wolf Schubert. Weimar, 1967.

Filarete (Antonio Averlino) *Treatise on Architecture.* Translated by John R. Spencer. New Haven, Conn., 1965.

Filiasi, Conte Giacomo. *Memorie storiche dei veneti primi e secondi.* Venice, 1796–1798.

Filosi, Giuseppe. *Relazione istorica del campanile di S Marco.* Venice, 1745.

Finotto, P Ferdinando, *S Giobbe, la chiesa dei Santi Giobbe e Bernardino in Venezia.* Venice, 1971.

Fiocco, Giuseppe. *Alvise Cornaro, il suo tempo e le sue opere.* Vicenza, 1965.

Fiocco, Giuseppe. "Andrea Palladio, padovano." *Annuario della R Università di Padova, 1932–33.* Padua, 1933.

Fiocco, Giuseppe. "L'architettura di G M Falconetto." *Dedalo,* October 1931.

Fiocco, Giuseppe. "Un capolavoro ignorato di Jacopo Sansovino a Venezia." *Mitteilungen des Kunsthistorischen Instituts in Florenz* XI, 1964.

Fiocco, Giuseppe. "La casa di Alvise Cornaro." In *Miscellanea in onore di Roberto Cessi.* Rome, 1958.

Fiocco, Giuseppe. "La chiesa di SS Giovanni e Paolo e il suo convento." *Rivista della città di Venezia,* 1932.

Fiocco, Giuseppe. "Fortune e sfortune del Palladio." *Padova* IX, no. 2, 1935.

Fiocco, Giuseppe. "L'ingresso del rinascimento nel Veneto." *Atti del XVIII Congresso Internazionale Storia dell'Arte,* 1955.

Fiocco, Giuseppe. *Palazzo Pesaro.* Venice, 1925.

Fiocco, Giuseppe. "Palazzo Pesaro." *Rivista della città di Venezia,* November 1925.

Fiocco, Giuseppe. "Palladio vivo." *Primato,* no. 20, 1942.

Fiocco, Giuseppe. "Prelusio ad Andrea Palladio." *Bolletino del Centro Internazionale di studi di Architettura 'Andrea Palladio'* I, 1959.

Fiocco, Giuseppe. "Sebastiano Mazzoni." *Dedalo,* 1928–1929.

Fiocco, Giuseppe. *Veronese.* Rome, 1934.

Fogaccia, Piero. *Cosimo Fanzaga.* Bergamo, 1945.

Fogolari, Gino. "L'Accademia Veneziana di pittura e scultura nel settecento." *L'Arte* XVI, 1913.

Fogolari, Gino. *Carità.* N.p., 1924.

Fogolari, Gino. *I Frari e i SS Giovanni e Paolo a Venezia.* Milan, 1931.

Folnesics, Hans. *Bau- und Kunstdenkmale des Künstlenlandes.* Vienna, 1916.

Folnesics, Hans. *Studien zur Entwicklungsgeschichte der Architektur und Plastik des XV Jahrhunderts in Dalmatien.* Vienna, 1914.

Fondazione Giorgio Cini. *Restauri all'isola di S Giorgio Maggiore.* Venice, 1964.

Fontana, Gian Jacopo. *Manuale ad uso del forestiero in Venezia.* Venice, 1847.

Fontana, Gian Jacopo. *Cento palazzi fra i piu celebri di Venezia sul Canal grande e sulle vie interne dei sestieri.* Venice, 1865.

Il forestiere istruito nelle cose più pregevoli e curiose antiche e moderne della Città di Venezia e delle isole circonvicine. Venice, 1819.

Forlati, Ferdinando. "Il Fondaco dei Tedeschi." *Palladio* IV, 1940.

Forlati, Ferdinando, *S Giorgio Maggiore.* Padua, 1977.

Forlati, Ferdinando. "Lavori di restauro del monastero di S Giorgio all'isola." *Arte Veneta* VI, 1952.

Forlati, Ferdinando. "Da Rialto a S Ilario." *Storia di Venezia.* Venice, 1958.

Forlati, Ferdinando. "Storia e restauri del S Marco di Venezia." *Palladio,* n.s. XV, 1965.

Forssmann, Erik. "Palladio e la pittura a fresco." *Arte Veneta* XXI, 1967.

Forssmann, Erik. *Palladios Lehrgebäude, Studien über den Zusammenhang von Architektur und Architekturtheorie bei Andrea Palladio.* Stockholm, 1965.

Forssmann, Erik. "Über Architekturen in der venezianischen Malerei des Cinquecento." *Wallraf-Richartz Jahrbuch* XXIX, 1967.

Fortescue, Adrian. *The Uniate Eastern Churches.* London, 1923.

Fortis, Umberto. *Jews and Synagogues; Venice, Florence, Rome, Leghorn.* Venice, 1973.

Foscari, Lodovico. *Affreschi esterni a Venezia.* Milan, 1936.

Foscari, Lodovico. *Segreti veneziani.* Venice, 1941.

Fossati, Giorgio. *Storia dell'architettura.* Venice, 1740.

Francastel, Galienne. "De Giorgione au Titien: L'artiste, le public et la commercialisme de l'oeuvre d'art." *Annales* XVI, no. 6, 1960.

Franceschi, Domenico. *Dialogo di tutte le cose notabili che sono in Venezia, tra un veneziano ed un forestiero.* Venice, 1568.

Franco, Fausto. "I disegni delle antichità del Palladio." *Arte Veneta* XII, 1958.

Franco, Fausto. "Le interpolazione del Filarete trattista fra gli artefici del Rinascimento architettonico a Venezia." In *Atti del IV Congresso Nazionale di Storia dell'Architettura,* 1939.

Franco, Fausto. "F Muttoni, l'architetto di Vicenza." *Bollettino del Centro Internazionale di Studi di Architettura 'Andrea Palladio'* IV, 1962.

Franco, Fausto. "Il Palladio di Roberto Pane." *Arte Veneta* XVI, 1962.

Franco, Fausto. "Piccola e grande urbanistica palladiana." *Bollettino del Centro Internazionale di Studi di Architettura 'Andrea Palladio'* I, 1959.

Franco, Fausto; Honour, Hugh; Medea, Alba; Ojetti, Paola; and Pallucchini, Rodolfo. *Palladio, Veronese e Vittoria a Maser.* Milan, 1960.

Frankl, Paul. *Principles of Architectural History: The Four Phases of Architectural Style 1420-1900.* Translated by James F. O'Gorman. Cambridge, Mass., 1968.

Frankl, Paul. *Die Renaissancearchitektur in Italien.* Leipzig, 1912.

Franzoi, Umberto. "La Scala dei Giganti." *Bolletino dei Musei civici veneziani* IV, 1965.

Franzoi, Umberto, and di Stefano, Dina. *Le chiese di Venezia.* Venice, 1976.

Franzoi, Umberto, and Trincanato, Egle Renata. *Venice au fils du temps.* Boulogne-Billancourt, 1971.

Freschot, Casimir. *Nouvelle relation de la ville et république de Venise.* Utrecht, 1709.

Fuga, Emilio. *Guida di Murano.* Venice, 1953.

Fugagnollo, Ugo. *La Piazza S Marco.* Venice, 1965.

Fulin, Rinaldo. *Breve sommario di storia veneta.* Venice, 1963.

De Fusco, R. *Il codice dell'architettura.* Naples, 1968.

Gabrielli, A. M. "L'Algarotti e la critica d'arte." *Critica d'Arte* I, 1929.

Gabrielli, A. M. "La teoria architettonica di Carlo Lodoli." *Arte Figurativa* III, 1945.

Gallacini, Teofilo. *Trattato . . . sopra gli errori degli architetti.* Venice, 1767.

Gallimberti, N. "La tradizione architettonica religiosa tra Venezia e Padova." *Bollettino del Museo Civico di Padova* LII, 1963.

Gallo, Luigi. *Lido di Venezia—Abbazia di S Nicolò.* Venice, 1964.

Gallo, Rodolfo. "Andrea Palladio e Venezia (Di alcuni edifici del Palladio ignoti o mal noti)." *Rivista di Venezia* I, 1955.

Gallo, Rodolfo. "L'architettura di trasizione dal gotico al Rinascimento e Bartolommeo Bon." *Atti dell'Istituto Veneto di Scienze, Lettere ed Arti* CXX, 1961-1962.

Gallo, Rodolfo. "Contributi su Jacopo Sansovino." *Saggi e memorie di storia dell'arte* I, 1957.

Gallo, Rodolfo. "Corte, Colonne a Castello e la Casa della Marinarezza veneziana." *Ateneo veneto*, 1938.

Gallo, Rodolfo. "Per la datazione delle opere del Veronese." *Emporium*, March 1939.

Gallo, Rodolfo. "Una famiglia patrizia: i Pisani ed i palazzi di S Stefano e di Strà." *Archivio Veneto*, 1944.

Gallo, Rodolfo. "L'architettura di trasizione dal gotico al Rinascimento e Bartolommeo Bon." *Atti dell'Instituto Veneto di Scienze, Lettere ed Arti* CXX, 1961-1962.

Gallo, Rodolfo. "Jacopo Sansovino a Pola." *Rivista di Venezia*, 1926.

Gallo, Rodolfo. "La loggia e la facciata della chiesa di S Basso di Baldassare Longhena." *Atti dell'Istituto Veneto di Scienze, Lettere ed Arti* CXVII, 1958-1959.

Gallo, Rodolfo. "Michele Sanmicheli a Venezia." In *Michele Sanmicheli: Studi raccolti*. Verona, 1960.

Gallo, Rodolfo. "Le ricerche della tomba di Marco Polo." *Rivista mensile della Città di Venezia*, September 1924.

Gallo, Rodolfo. "Vincenzo Scamozzi e la chiesa di S Nicolò da Tolentino di Venezia." *Atti dell'Istituto Veneto di Scienze, Lettere ed Arti* CXVII, 1958-1959.

Gamba, Bartolommeo. *Gli edifici, i monumenti e gli ornamenti più insigni della città di Venezia*. Venice, 1822.

Gambier, Henri. *Histoire de la Règublique de Venise et ses 120 Doges*. Venice, 1959.

Gardani, Dante Luigi. *La chiesa di S Giacomo di Rialto*. Venezia Sacra VI, Venice, 1966.

Gardani, Dante Luigi. *La chiesa di S Maria della Presentazione (detta Zitelle) in Venezia*. Venice, 1961.

Gattinoni, Gregorio. *Il campanile de S Marco, monografia storica*. Venice, 1910.

Gattinoni, Gregorio. *Inventario di una casa veneziana del secolo XVII, degli eredi di P Veronese*. Mastre, 1914.

Gaye, G. *Processo ed atti per il crollo della Libreria*. Venice, 1855.

Gazzola, Piero. "Appunti per quattro lezioni su Michele Sanmicheli." *Bollettino del Centro Internazionale di Studi di Architettura 'Andrea Palladio'* I, 1959.

Gazzola, Piero. *Michele Sanmicheli—catalogo e schede della mostra a Palazzo Canossa*. Venice, 1960.

Geanakoplos, Deno John. *Byzantine East and Latin West: Two Worlds of Christendom in Middle Ages and Renaissance*. Oxford, 1966.

Geanakoplos, Deno John. *Greek Scholars in Venice*. Cambridge, Mass., 1962.

Gerola, Giuseppe. *Monumenti dell'isola di Creta*. Venice, 1905-1932.

Gerola, Giuseppe. *I monumenti medioevali delle tredici Sporadi*. Athens, 1914.

von Geymuller, Heinrich. *Cento disegni di architettura d'ornato e di figure di Fra Giovanni Giocondo sconosciuti e descritti*. Florence, 1882.

Gianotti, Donato. *Libro de la republica de vinitiani*. Rome, 1542.

Gilbert, Creighton, ed. *Renaissance Art*. New York, Evanston and London, 1970.

Gille, Bertrand. *The Renaissance Engineers*. London, 1966.

Gilles de la Tourette, F. *L'orient et les peintres de Venise*. Paris, 1924.

Gilmore, Myron F. *The World of Humanism*. New York, 1952.

Giovanni degli Agostini. *Istoria degli scrittori veneziani del padre Giovanni degli Agostini*. Venice, 1754.

Giovannoni, G. *Saggi sull'architettura del rinascimento*. Milan, 1931.

Giovannoni, G. "L'urbanistica del Rinascimento." In *L'urbanistica dall'antichità ad oggi*. Florence, 1943.

Giovio, Paolo. *La prima (e seconda) parte dell'istorie del suo tempo, tradotto per M Ludovico Domenichi con un supplimento sopra le medesime istorie, fatto da Girolamo Ruscelli*. Venice, 1560.

de Gobbi, E. *Cronistoria del monastero e guida della chiesa di S Zaccaria in Venezia*. Venice, 1950.

Golzio, Vincenzo. *L'architettura romana: il Palladio*. Rome, 1937.

Golzio, Vincenzo. "Seicento e settecento." In *Storia dell'arte classica e italiana* IV. Turin, 1950.

Gombrich, Ernst H. "Celebrations in Venice of the Holy League and the Victory of Lepanto." In *Studies in Renaissance and Baroque Art Presented to Anthony Blunt.* London, 1967.

Gombrich, Ernst H. *Norm and Form: Studies in the Art of the Renaissance.* London, 1966.

Gombrich, Ernst H. "Zum Werke Giulio Romanos." *Jahrbuch der Kunsthistorischen Sammlungen in Wien.* Vienna, 1934–1935.

Grabar, André. "Byzance et Venise." In *Venezia e l'Europa.* Venice, 1955.

Gradenigo, Pietro. *Notizie d'arte tratte dai notatori e dagli annali.* Venice, 1942.

Grassi, Candido. *La villa Manin di Passariano.* Udine, 1961.

Gualandi, Michelangelo, ed. *Memorie originali italiane risguardanti le belle arti.* Bologna, 1840–45.

Gualdi, Paolo. "Vita di Andrea Palladio." *Saggi e memorie di storia dell'arte* II, 1958–1959.

Guicciardini, Francesco. *Della istoria d'Italia, libri XX.* Venice, 1738–1740.

Guida artistica della chiesa di S Michele in Isola di Venezia. Venice, 1889.

Guildford, Sir Richard. *The pylgrymage of Sir Richard Guyldforde to the Holy Land AD 1506.* London, 1851.

Guisconi, Anselmo (Francesco Sansovino). *Tutte le cose notabili e belle che sono in Venetia.* Venice, 1556.

Gusman, Pierre. *Venise* (Les Villes d'Art célèbres). Paris, 1902.

Gutkind, E. A. *International History of City Development.* London, 1964–1969.

Hadeln, Detlev, Freiherr von. "A Drawing After an Important Lost Work by Pordenone." *Burlington Magazine* LXVI, 1924.

Hager, Werner. "Zur Raumstruktur des Manierismus." In *Festschrift Martin Wackernagel.* Cologne, 1958.

Hale, John R. "Quattrocento Venice." In *Cities of Destiny,* edited by Arnold Toynbee, London, 1967.

Hale, John R., ed. *Renaissance Venice.* London, 1973.

Hare, Augustus. *Venice.* 3d ed. London, 1891.

Harris, John. "Three Unrecorded Palladio Designs from Inigo Jones's Collection." *Burlington Magazine* CXIII, 1971.

Haskell, Francis, and Levey, Michael. "Art Exhibitions in 18th-century Venice." *Arte Veneta* XII, 1958.

Hausenstein, Wilhelm. *Venedig—Venezianische Augenblicke.* Dresden, 1925.

Hay, Denys. *The Italian Renaissance in Its Historical Background.* Cambridge, England, 1961.

Haydn, H. *The Counter-Renaissance.* New York, 1950.

Haynes, Alan. "Daniele Barbaro: a Venetian Patron." *History Today* XXV, no. 12, December 1975.

Hazlitt, W. Carew. *The Venetian Republic, Its Rise, Its Growth, and Its Fall, 421–1797.* London, 1900.

Heckner, Georg. *Pracktisches Handbuch der kirchlichen Kunst.* Freiburg, 1886.

Heitz, C. *Recherches sur le rapport entre architecture et liturgie.* Paris, 1963.

Hellmann, Mario. *San Nicolò del Lido nella storia, nella cronaca, nell'arte.* Venice, 1968.

Hellmann, Mario. *Venezia mia.* Venice, 1970.

Henze, A. "Das venezianische Stadtlabenbild des 18 Jahrhunderts." *Kunstwerk,* October 1967.

Heydenreich, Ludwig H. "Il bugnato rustico nel Quattro- e nel Cinquecento." *Bolletino del Centro Internazionale di Studi di Architettura 'Andrea Palladio'* II, 1960.

Heydenreich, Ludwig H., and Lotz, Wolfgang. *Architecture in Italy 1400–1600.* Harmondsworth, 1974.

Hoffman, Hans. *Hochrenaissance, Manierismus, Frühbarock.* Zurich, 1938.

Holmes, George. *The Florentine Enlightenment 1400–50.* London, 1969.

Honour, Hugh. *The Companion Guide to Venice.* New York, 1966.

Howard, Deborah. *Jacopo Sansovino: Architecture and Patronage in Renaissance Venice.* New Haven and London, 1975.

Howard, Deborah. "Sebastiano Serlio's Venetian Copywrights." *Burlington Magazine* CXV, 1973.

Howell, James. *SQPV: A Survey of the Signorie of Venice.* London, 1651.

Hubala, Erich. "Die Baukunst der venezianischen Renaissance (1460–1550)." Habilitationsschrift, Munich, 1958.

Hubala, Erich. "Palladio und die Baukunst in Berlin und Munchen, 1740–1820." *Bollettino del Centro Internazionale di Studi di Architettura 'Andrea Palladio'* III, 1961.

Hubala, Erich. "Palladio und die Baukunst in Deutschland in 17 Jahrhundert." *Bollettino del Centro Internazionale di Studi di Architettura 'Andrea Palladio'* III, 1961.

Hubala, Erich. "Venedig." *Reclams Kunstführer Italien* II, no. 1, 1974.

Huse, Norbert. "Über ein Hauptwerk der Venezianischen Plastik im 13 Jahrhundert." *Pantheon* XXVI, no. 2, March–April 1968.

Hyma, A. *Italian Renaissance Studies.* Edited by E. F. Jacob. London, 1960.

Ivanoff, Nicola. "Alcune lettere inedite di Tommaso Temanza a Pierre Jean Mariette." *Atti del Istituto Veneto di Scienze, Lettere ed Arti* CXVII, 1959–1960.

Ivanoff, Nicola. "Il concetto dello stile nella letteratura artistica del '500." *Istituto di Storia dell'Arte di Trieste* IV, 1955.

Ivanoff, Nicola. "Un ignota opera del Longhena." *Ateneo Veneto,* 1945.

Ivanoff, Nicola. "Ignote opere di Sebastiano Mazzoni." *Emporium,* June 1948.

Ivanoff, Nicola. "Monsù Giusto ed altri collaboratori del Longhena." *Arte Veneta* II, 1948.

Ivanoff, Nicola. "Il motivo architettonico della Basilica della Salute." *Gazzettino Sera,* 20 November 1952.

Ivanoff, Nicola. "La Scala d'Oro del Palazzo Ducale." *Critica d'Arte,* no. 47, 1961.

Ivanoff, Nicola. "Stile e maniera." *Saggi e memorie di storia dell'arte* I, 1957.

Ivanoff, Nicola. "Venezia: S Giorgio Maggiore." *Tesori d'Arte Cristiana,* no. 74, Bologna, 1967.

Jacob, Henriette Eugenie. *Idealism and Realism: a Study of Sepulchral Symbolism.* Leyden, 1954.

Jannacco, C. "Barocco e razionalismo nel Tratto di architettura di Vincenzo Scamozzi." *Studi Seicenteschi* II, 1961.

Jedin, Hubert. "Gasparo Contarini e il contributo veneziano alla Riforma Cattolica." In *La civiltà veneziana del Rinascimento.* Venice, 1958.

Johnson, Eugene J. *S Andrea in Mantua, The Building History.* University Park, Pennsylvania, and London, 1975.

Kahnemann, M. *Michele Sanmicheli.* Venice, 1960.

Kaufmann, Emil. *Architecture in the Age of Reason: Baroque and Post-baroque in England, Italy and France.* Cambridge, Mass., 1955.

Kaufmann, Emil. "Piranesi, Algarotti and Lodoli [A Controversy in XVIII-century Venice]." In *Essays in Honor of Hans Tietze.* Paris, 1958.

Klauser, Theodor. *A Short History of the Western Liturgy: An Account and Some Reflections.* Translated by John Halliburton, London, 1969.

Koenigsberger, H. G. "Decadence or Shift? Changes in the Civilization of Italy and Europe in the Sixteenth and Seventeenth Centuries." *Transactions of the Royal Society,* series 5, X, 1960.

Kostof, Spiro, ed. *The Architect: Chapters in the History of the Profession.* New York, 1977.

Krautheimer, Richard. "Alberti and Vitruvius." In *Studies in Early Christian, Mediaeval, and Renaissance Art.* New York and London, 1969.

Krinsky, Carol Herselle. "Cesare Cesariano and the Como Vitruvius Edition of 1521." Ph.D. dissertation, New York University, 1965.

Krinsky, Carol Herselle. "Seventy-eight Vitruvius Manuscripts." *Journal of the Warburg and Courtauld Institutes* XXX, 1967.

Kristeller, Paul Oskar. *Studies in Renaissance Thought and Letters.* Rome, 1956.

Kunert, Silvio de. "Affreschi decorativi veneziani." *Rivista della Città di Venezia,* 1930.

Labacco, Antonio. *Libro appartenente all'architettura nel qual si figurano alcune notabili antiquità di Roma.* Venice, 1552.

Labalme, Patricia Hochschild. *Bernardo Giustinian: A Venetian of the Quattrocento.* Rome, 1969.

Lacchin, E. "Artisti che lavorano per la chiesa di S Maria della Salute." In *Tempio della Salute.* Venice, 1930.

Lampertico, F. "Su Andrea Palladio. Discorso tenuto in occasione del III centenario della morte nel Settembre 1880." *Scritti storici e letterarie.* Florence, 1882.

Lane, Frederic C. *Andrea Barbaro Merchant of Venice 1418–1449.* Baltimore, 1944.

Lane, Frederic C. *Venetian Ships and Shipbuilders of the Renaissance.* Baltimore, 1934.

Lane, Frederic C. *Venice and History.* Baltimore, 1966.

Lane, Frederic C. *Venice, A Mritime Republic.* Baltimore, 1973.

Lang, Susanna "Visentini Drawings." *Architectural Review* CXIII, 1953.

Langenskiold, Eric. *Michele Sanmicheli, the Architect of Verona, His Life and Works.* Uppsala, 1938.

Larsen, Sven Sinding. "Some Functional and Iconographical Aspects of the Centralized Church in the Italian Renaissance." *Acta ad archaeologiam et artium historiam pertinentia* II, 1965.

Lavagnino, Emilio. "Architetti neopalladiani veneti del XVIII e XIX secolo." In *Venezia e l'Europa.* Venice, 1955.

Lavagnino, Emilio. *S Spirito in Sassia.* Turin, 1962.

Laven, Peter. "Daniele Barbaro, patriarch elect of Aquileia, with special reference to his circle of scholars and to his literary achievement." Ph.D. dissertation, University of London, 1957.

Laven, Peter. *Renaissance Italy 1464–1534.* London, 1966.

Lazari, V. *Scritture di Jacopo Sansovino e parti riguardanti le fabbriche della Zecca.* Venice, 1850.

Lazzari, Antonio. *Itinerario interno e delle isole della città di Venezia.* Venice, 1831.

Lazzari, Francesco. *Il convento della Carità.* Venice, 1835.

Lazzari, Francesco. *Notizie di G. Benoni architetto ed ingegnere della Veneta Repubblica.* Venice, 1840.

Leclerc, Helène. *Les origines italiennes de l'architecture théatrale moderne.* Paris, 1946.

Lees-Milne, James. *Baroque in Italy.* London, 1959.

Levey, Michael. "An English Commission to Guardi." *Burlington Magazine* CII, 1960.

Levey, Michael. *Painting in Eighteenth-century Venice.* London, 1959.

Levi, Cesare Augusto. *I campanili di Venezia: Notizie storiche.* Venice, 1890.

Levi, Cesare Augusto. *Notizie storiche di alcune scuole d'arte e mestieri scomparse o esistenti ancora in Venezia.* 2d ed. Venice, 1893.

Lewis, C. Douglas. "The Late Baroque Churches of Venice." Ph.D. dissertation, Yale University, n.d.

Lewis, C. Douglas. "Two Lost Renascences of Venetian Architecture: New Plans by Bon and Sanmicheli for the Site of the Ca' del Duca." Master's thesis, Yale University, n.d.

Lewis, C. Douglas, "Notes on XVIII century Venetian Architecture." *Bolletino dei Musei Civici Veneziani* XII, 1967.

Licini, Antonio. *Siti pittoreschi e prospettivi delle lagune venete.* Venice, 1838.

Lieberman, Ralph E. "The Church of S Maria dei Miracoli in Venice," Ph.D. dissertation, New York University, 1972.

Livi, C.; Selia, D.; and Tucci, U. "Un probleme d'histoire: La décadence économique de Venise." In *Aspetti e cause della decadenza economica veneziana nel secolo XVII.* Venice, 1961.

Logan, Oliver. *Culture and Society in Venice 1470–1790.* London, 1972.

de Logu, Giuseppe. *L'architettura italiana del seicento e del settecento.* Florence, 1935.

de Logu, Giuseppe. *Italienische Baukunst, eine Anthologie vom 11 bis 19 Jahrhundert.* Zurich, 1946.

Longhurst, Margaret Helen. *Notes on Italian Monuments of the 12th to 16th Centuries.* Unfinished. Compiled by Jan Lowe and published in photostat by the Victoria and Albert Museum. London, ca. 1931.

Longo, A. *Origine e provenienza a Venezia dei cittadini originari.* Venice, 1817.

Longworth, Philip. *The Rise and Fall of Venice.* London, 1974.

Lopez, Robert S. *The Three Ages of the Italian Renaissance.* Charlottesville, Va., 1970.

Lopez, Robert S., and Miskimin, H. "The Economic Depression of the Renaissance." *Economic History Review* n.s. XIV, 1962.

Lorenzetti, Giulio. "Gli affreschi della facciata di Palazzo Trevisan a Murano." In *Miscellanea di studi storici in onore di Camillo Manfroni.* Padua, 1925.

Lorenzetti, Giulio. *Ca' Rezzonico.* Venice, 1938.

Lorenzetti, Giulio. *Le feste e le maschere veneziane.* Venice, 1937.

Lorenzetti, Giulio. *Itinerario sansoviniano a Venezia.* Venice, 1929.

Lorenzetti, Giulio. "Jacopo Sansovino scultore, note ed appunti." *Nuovo Archivio Veneto,* n.s., XXX, no. 2.

Lorenzetti, Giulio. "La libreria sanoviniana di Venezia." *Accademie e biblioteche d'Italia* II fasc. 6; III fasc. 1, 1929–1930.

Lorenzetti, Giulio. "La loggetta al Campanile di S Marco." *L'Arte,* 1910.

Lorenzetti, Giulio. "La loggetta sansoviniana in un disegno del '700." *Il Marzocco,* 28 April 1912.

Lorenzetti, Giulio. *Mostra delle tre scuole.* Venice, 1947.

Lorenzetti, Giulio. "Note su Alessandro Vittoria." *L'Arte,* 1909.

Lorenzetti, Giulio. *La scuola grande di S Giovanni Evangelista a Venezia.* Venice, 1929.

Lorenzetti, Giulio. *Venezia e il suo estuario.* Rome, 1926.

Lorenzetti, Giulio. *Venezia nascosta. Palazzo Merlati e i suoi stucchi.* Venice, 1931.

Lorenzetti, Maria Ciartoso. "Stucchi veneziani del settecento." *Le Tre Venezie* VII, 1929.

Lorenzi, Giambattista, ed. *Monumenti per servire alla storia del Palazzo Ducale di Venezia.* Venice, 1868.

Lorenzoni, Giovanni. *Giorgio Fossati, le cosidette opere inedite palladiane di Padova e l'idea di Palladio.* Padua, 1963.

Lorenzoni, Giovanni. *Lorenzo da Bologna.* Venice, 1963.

The Lost Chapter of Cochin's Voyage d'italie by Pompeo Usiglio (pseud). Edited by Paul Hyland and Cornelius VerHeyden de Lancey. Privately printed. Cambridge, Mass., 1933.

Lotz, Wolfgang. "Architecture in the Later Sixteenth Century." *College Art Journal* XVIII, 1958.

Lotz, Wolfgang. "Italienische Plätze der 16 Jahrhunderts." In *Jahrbuch 1968 der Max-Planck-Gesellschaft zur Förderung der Wissenschaften,* 1968.

Lotz, Wolfgang. "La Libreria di S Marco e l'urbanistica del Rinascimento." *Bollettino del Centro Internazionale di Studi di Architettura 'Andrea Palladio'* III, 1961.

Lotz, Wolfgang. "Mannerism in Architecture, Changing Aspects." In *Acts of the Twentieth International Congress of the History of Art.* Princeton, N.J., 1963.

Lotz, Wolfgang. "Notizien zum kirchlichen Zentralbau der Renaissance." In *Studien zur toskanischen Kunst (Festschrift L. H. Heydenreich).* Munich, 1964.

Lotz, Wolfgang. "Die ovale Kirchenraume des Cinquecento." *Römisches Jahrbuch für Kunstgeschichte VII,* 1955.

Lotz, Wolfgang. "Das Raumbild in der italienischen Architekturzeichnung der Renaissance." *Mitteilungen des Kunsthistorischen Instituts in Florenz* VII, 1956.

Lotz, Wolfgang. "Redefinitions of Style: Architecture in the Later 16th Century." *College Art Journal* XVIII, 1958.

Lotz, Wolfgang. "Riflessioni sul tema 'Palladio urbanista.'" *Bollettino del Centro Internazionale di Studi di Architettura 'Andrea Palladio'* VII, 1966.

Lotz, Wolfgang. "The Roman Legacy in Sansovino's Venetian Buildings." *Journal of the Society of Architectural Historians* XXII, 1963.

Lotz, Wolfgang. "Sansovinos Bibliothek von S Marco und die Stadtbaukunst der Renaissance." In *Festschrift Wolf Schubert.* Weimar, 1967.

Lotz, Wolfgang. "La transformazione sansoviniana di Piazza S Marco e l'urbanistica del cinquecento." *Bollettino del Centro Internazionale di Studi di Architettura 'Andrea Palladio'* VIII, 1966.

Luciolli, Gerolamo, and Ronzani, Francesco. *Le fabbriche civili, ecclesiastiche e militare di Michele Sanmicheli.* N.p., 1823.

Luxoro, Maria. *La biblioteca di S Marco nella sua storia.* Florence, 1954.

Luxoro, Maria. *Il palazzo Vendramin-Calergi (Non Nobis Domine...)* Florence, 1957.

Luzzatto, Gino. *An Economic History of Italy to the Beginning of the Sixteenth Century.* London and New York, 1961.

Luzzatto, Gino. *Storia economica di Venezia dall XI al XVI secolo.* Venice, 1961.

Mack, Charles R. "The Rucellai Palace: Some New Proposals." *Art Bulletin* DVI, 1974.

Magagnato, Licisco. *Commento e note alla vita di Michele Sanmicheli di Giorgio Vasari.* Verona, 1960.

Magagnato, Licisco. "In margine alla mostra veronese di Sanmicheli." *Arte Veneta* XIII–XIV, 1959–1960.

Magagnato, Licisco. "La mostra dei disegni del Palladio a Vicenza." *Emporium,* March 1950.

Magagnato, Licisco. *Teatri italiani del cinquecento.* Venice, 1954.

Magagnato, Licisco, ed. *Ville del Brenta nelle vedute di Vincenzo Coronelli e Gianfrancesco Costa.* Milan, 1960.

Magagnato, Licisco, and Riva, F. *Michele Sanmicheli architetto veronese.* Verona, 1960.

Magrini, (abate) Antonio. *Memorie intorno la vita e le opere di Andrea Palladio pubblicate nell'inaugurazione del suo monumento in Vicenza 19 agosto 1845.* Padua, 1845.

Magrini, Giovanni, ed. *La laguna di Venezia, monografia coordinata da Giovanni Magrini. Delegazione italiana della Commissione per l'Esplorazione scientifica del Mediterraneo.* Venice, 1925.

Maiers, Johann Christoph. *Beschreibung von Venedig.* Leipzig, 1795.

Maimeri, M. "Cronologia Sanmicheliana." *Vita Veronese,* March 1959.

Maimeri, M. "Curiosità Sanmicheliana." *Vita Veronese,* September 1959.

Maimeri, M. "Onoranze a Sanmicheli." *Vita Veronese,* April 1959.

Maimeri, M. "Sommario di bibliografia Sanmicheliana." *Vita Veronese,* December 1959.

Malipiero, Domenico. *Annali venete dall'anno 1457 al 1500.* (2 vols., as Archivio Storico Italiano VII) Florence, 1843–44.

Manfredi, [Fra] Fulgentio. *La vera e reale descendenza de Venetiani.* Venice, 1598.

Manierismo, Barocco, Rococò: concetti e termini. Convegno internazionale dell'Accademia Nazionale dei Lincei. Rome, 1962.

Marcello, Pietro. *Vite de prencipi di Vinegia. Tradotte in volgare da Lodovico Domenichi con le vite di quei prencipi, che furono dopo il Barbarigo, fin al Doge Priuli.* Venice, 1557.

Marchini, G. "Aggiunto a Michelozzo." *La Rinascità* VII, 1944.

Marchini, G. "Per Giorgio da Sebenico." *Commentari* XIX, 1969.

Marchiori, G.; Perocco, G.; and Zanotto, S. *Immagine di Venezia. Fotografie di Gianni Berengo Gardin.* Milan, 1970.

Mariacher, Giovanni. "Antonio da Righeggio e Antonio Rizzo." *Le Arti* II, 1941.

Mariacher, Giovanni. "Il continuatore del Longhena a Palazzo Pesaro ed altre notizie inedite." *Ateneo Veneto,* January–June 1951.

Mariacher, Giovanni. *The Ducal Palace of Venice.* Rome, 1956.

Mariacher, Giovanni. "La facciata dell'Ateneo e un'opera ritrovata di Andrea dell'Aquila." *Ateneo Veneto,* 1953.

Mariacher, Giovanni. "S Maria dei Miracoli." *Tesori d'Arte Cristiana* IV, il rinascimento. Bologna, 1967.

Mariacher, Giovanni. "New Light on Antonio Bregno." *Burlington Magazine* XCII, 1950.

Mariacher, Giovanni. "Le opere di Mauro Codussi in Venezia." *Ateneo Veneto*, 1945.

Mariacher, Giovanni. *Il Palazzo Ducale di Venezia*. Florence, 1950.

Mariacher, Giovanni. *Il Palazzo Vendramin-Calergi a Venezia*. Venice, 1965.

Mariacher, Giovanni. "Pietro Lombardo a Venezia." *Arte Veneta* IX, 1955.

Mariacher, Giovanni. "Profilo di Antonio Rizzo." *Arte Veneta* II, 1948.

Mariacher, Giovanni. *Ca' Rezzonico, An Illustrated Guide*. Venice, 1967.

Mariacher, Giovanni. "Il restauro della facciata di Ca' Rezzonico." *Bollettino dei Musei Civici Veneziani* no. 3, 1964.

Mariacher, Giovanni. *Il Sansovino*. Verona, 1962.

Mariacher, Giovanni. "La scuola del Carmine e la sua conservazione." *Rivista di Venezia* XIII, 1934.

Mariacher, Giovanni. "Tempio del Santissimo Redentore." *Tesori d'Arte Cristiana* XII. Bologna, 1967.

Mariacher, Giovanni. "Tullio Lombardo Studies." *Burlington Magazine* XCVI, 1954.

Marozzo della Rocca, R. and Tiepolo, F. "Cronologia veneziana del seicento." In *La civiltà veneziana dell'età barocca*. Venice, 1959.

Martegani, Ugo; Della Corte, Carlo; and Puppi, Giampietro. *Un punto chiamato Venezia*. Milan, 1971.

Martinelli, Domenico. *Il ritratto di Venezia, diviso in due parti*. Venice, 1684.

Martinioni, Giustiniano. *La Venezia del Sansovino con aggiunte le cose notabili dall'anno 1580 all'anno 1663*. Venice, 1663.

Masciotta, Michelangelo. *Dizionario di termini artistici*. Florence, 1967.

Masséna, Victor, Duc de Rivoli, Prince d'Esseling. *Les livres à figures vénétiens de la fin du xve siècle et de commencement du xvie*. Paris and Florence, 1914.

Masson, Georgina. *Giardini d'Italia*. Milan, 1961.

Masson, Georgina. *Italian Villas and Palaces*. New York, 1959.

Mauroner, Fabio. *Luca Carlevarijs*. Padua, 1945.

Mauroner, Fabio. *I veneziani del settecento visti da Luca Carlevarijs*. Padua, 1945.

Mayor, A. Hyatt. *Venice, Impressions drawn by Fritz Busse*. New York, 1960.

Mazzariol, Giuseppe, and Pignatti, Teresio. *La pianta prospettica de Venezia del 1500 disegnata da Jacopo de'Barbari*. Venice, 1963.

Mazzoni, S. *Il tempo perduto*. Venice, 1661.

Mazzucato, Alessandro. *The Great School and the Church of S Rocco in Venice*. Venice, 1957.

Mazzuchelli, G. M. *Gli scrittori d'Italia*. Brescia, 1758.

McAndrew, John. *Catalogue of the Drawings Collection of the RIBA: Antonio Visentini*. Farnborough, Hants, 1974.

McAndrew, John. "Sant'Andrea della Certosa." *Art Bulletin* LI, 1969.

McCarthy, Mary. *Venice Observed*. Paris and New York, 1956.

McNeill, William H. *Venice, the Hinge of Europe 1081–1797*. Chicago, 1974.

Meeks, Carroll L. V. *Italian Architecture 1750–1914*. New Haven and London, 1966.

Meiss, Millard. "Reports on Scholarship in the Renaissance. Florence and Venice a Year Later." *Renaissance Quarterly* XXI, no. 1, 1968.

Melani, Alfredo. *Palladio 1508–1580. La sua vita, la sua arte, la sua influenza*. Milan, 1928.

Memmo, Andrea. *Elementi di architettura lodoliana o sia l'arte del fabbricare con solidità scientifica e con eleganza non capricciosa*. Rome, 1786.

Memorie intorno agli architetti e i pittori che operarono nel secolo XVI nella Scuola di S Rocco di Venezia. Venice, 1814.

Meneghin, Vittorino. *S Michele in Isola di Venezia*. Venice, 1962.

Meyer, Alfred G. *Das Venezianische Grabdenkmal der Frührenaissance*. N.p., 1899.

Miari, F. *Il nuovo patriziato veneto*. Venice, 1891.

Michalsky, E. "Das Problem des Manierismus in der italienischen Architektur." *Zeitschrift für Kunstgeschichte* II, 1933.

Middeldorf, Ulrich. "Two Sansovino Drawings." *Burlington Magazine* LXIV, 1934.

Middeldorf, Ulrich. "Unknown Drawings of the Two Sansovinos." *Burlington Magazine* LX, 1932.

Milesio, Giovanni Bartolomeo. "G. B. Milesio's Beschreibung des Deutschen Hauses in Venedig—Aus einer Handschrift in Venedig." *Abhandlungen der K Bayer Akademie des Wissenschafts*, 1881.

Milizia, Francesco. *Memorie degli architetti.* Bassano, 1785.

Milizia, Francesco. *Le vite de'più celebri architetti d'ogni nazione e d'ogni tempo precedute da un saggio sopra l'architettura.* Rome, 1768.

Minotto, Tommaso. *Notizie della chiesa e dell'ex-convento di S Maria dei Miracoli.* Venice, 1855.

Miozzi, Eugenio. "Il forte di S Andrea del Sanmicheli ed il ponte di S Nicolò del Malacreda." In *Rapporti preliminari della Comissione di studio per la conservazione difesa della laguna.* Venice, 1961.

Miozzi, Eugenio. *Venezia nei secoli—la città.* Venice, 1957.

Molinier, Emile. *Venise, ses arts décoratifs, ses musées et ses collections.* Paris, 1889.

Molmenti, Pompeo. *La storia di Venezia nella vita privata dalle origini alla caduta della repubblica.* Bergamo, 1922–1925.

Molmenti, Pompeo. *Venezia, nuovi studi di storia e d'arte.* Florence, 1897.

Molmenti, Pompeo. *Venice, Its Individual Growth from the Earliest Beginnings to the Fall of the Republic.* Translated by H. F. Brown. London, 1906–1908.

Molmenti, Pompeo, and Fulin, Rinaldo. *Guida artistica e storica di Venezia e delle isole circonvicine.* Venice, 1881.

Molmenti, Pompeo, and Mantovani, D. *Calli e canali in Venezia.* Venice, 1893.

Molmenti, Pompeo, and Mantovani, D. *Le isole della laguna veneta.* Bergamo, 1904

Mondini, Francesco. *Il Carmelo favorito.* Venice, 1675.

Monnier, Philippe. *Venise au XVIIIe siècle.* Paris, 1908.

Montibiller, C. "La pianta originale inedita della chiesa dei padri Carmelitani Scalzi di Baldassare Longhena." *Arte Veneta* VIII, 1954.

Monumenti veneti intorno a Padri Gesuiti. Venice, 1762.

Mora, Antonio. *Descrizione delle isole che circondano la città di Venezia.* Venice, 1754.

Moro Lin, G. *Scene di Venezia.* Venice, 1841.

Morris, James. *The World of Venice.* London, 1960.

Moryson, Fynes. *An Itinerary containing his ten Yeeres Travell.* 1617. Reprint. Glasgow, 1907.

Moscheni, Giovanni Battista. *Monumenta ecclesiae venetae Sancti Moysis, ex ejus tabulario potissimum, atque alionde ac secundum Antistitum seriem, de prompta digesta hodiernoque illius praesuli Joanni Baptistae Moscheni sicata.* Venice, 1758.

Moschetti, Andrea. *I danni ai monumenti e alle opere d'arte delle Venezie nella guerra mondiale MCMXV–MCMXVIII.* Venice, 1932.

Moschetti, Andrea. "Di un quadrennio di Pietro Lombardo a Padova." *Bollettino del Museo Civico di Padova* XVI, 1913–1914.

Moschini, (abate) Giannantonio. *La chiesa e il seminario di S Maria della Salute.* 1819. Reprint. Venice, 1942.

Moschini, (abate) Giannantonio. *Description de l'eglise des saints Jean et Paul.* Venice, 1819.

Moschini, (abate) Giannantonio. *Discorso sopra il tempio di S Giorgio Maggiore nell'incontro che ne fu fatta la nuova solenne benedizione il giorno tredici del marzo dell'anno 1808 da sua Eccellenza Nicola-Saverio Gamboni Patriarca di Venezia.* Venice, 1808.

Moschini, (abate) Giannantonio. *Guida per la città di Venezia all'amico delle belle arti.* Venice, 1815.

Moschini, (abate) Giannantonio. *Guida per l'isola di Murano.* Venice, 1808.

Moschini, (abate) Giannantonio. *Itinéraire de la ville de Venise et des îles circonvoisines.* Venice, 1819.

Moschini, (abate) Giannantonio. *Nuova guida per Venezia... e un compendio della istoria veneziana.* Venice, 1828.

Moschini, (abate) Giannantonio. *Nuova Guida per Venezia con XLVIII oggetti di arti incisi e con un compendio della istoria veneziana.* Venice, 1834.

Moschini, (abate) Giannantonio. *Ragguaglio delle cose notabili nella Chiesa e nel Seminario Patriarchale di S Maria della Salute.* Venice, 1819.

Moschini, (abate) Giannantonio. *Stato delle belle arti in Venezia nel secolo XVIII.* Venice, 1807.

Moschini, Vittorio. "Giorgio Massari, architetto veneto." Dedalo XII, 1932.

Moschini, Vittorio. "Di un progetto del Meyring e d'altro ancora." *Arte Veneta* XIX, 1965.

Moschini, Vittorio. "La villa Garzoni del Sansovino." *L'Arte,* n. s., I, 1930.

Moschini Marconi, Sandra. *Gallerie dell'Accademia di Venezia.* Venice, 1945.

Da Mosto, Andrea. *I dogi di Venezia nella vita pubblica e privata.* Milan, 1960.

Da Mosto, Andrea. "La facciata della chiesa di S Nicolò da Tolentino." In *Raccolta di scritti storici in memoria di Monticolo.* Venice, 1914.

Da Mosto, Andrea. "Interni seicenteschi di palazzi veneziani." *Rivista della Città di Venezia,* 1932.

Mothes, Oscar. *Geschichte des Baukunst und Bildhauerei Venedigs.* Leipzig, 1859–1860.

Mugnone, Giuseppe. "Antonio Visentini usurpatore della fama di Andrea Urbani." *Il Gazzetino,* 22 October 1963.

Munman, Robert. "The Monument to Vittore Cappello of Antonio Rizzo." *Burlington Magazine* CXIII, March 1971.

Munman, Robert. "Two Lost Venetian Statues." *Burlington Magazine* CXLL, June 1970.

Munman, Robert. "Venetian Renaissance Tomb Monuments." Ph.D. dissertation, Harvard University, 1968.

Muraro, Michelangelo. "The Political Interpretation of Giorgione's Frescoes on the Fondaco dei Tedeschi." *Gazette des Beaux-Arts* LXXXVI, December 1975.

Muraro, Michelangelo. "La scala senza giganti." In *Essays in Honor of Erwin Panofsky.* NEW York, 1961.

Muraro, Michelangelo. *Les villas de la Vénétie.* Venice, 1954.

Muratori, Saverio. *Studi per una operante storia urbana di Venezia.* Rome, 1959.

Murray, Peter J. *The Architecture of the Italian Renaissance.* London, 1963.

Murray, Peter J. "Palladio's Churches." In *Arte in Europa. Scritti di storia d'arte in onore di Edoardo Arslan,* 1966.

Musatti, E. *Guida storica di Venezia.* Padua and Venice, 1890.

Musatti, E. *I monumenti di Venezia, guida sinottica.* Venice, 1893.

Musolino, G. *La beata Giuliana di Collalto, chiesa e monastero dei SS Biagio e Cataldo alla Giudecca.* Venice, 1962.

Mutinelli, Fabio. *Annali urbani di Venezia dall'anno 810 al 12 maggio 1797.* Venice, 1838.

Mutinelli, Fabio. *Guida del Forestiero per Venezia antica. Passeggiate quattro.* Venice, 1842.

Muttoni, Francesco. *L'architettura di Andrea Palladio vicentino di nuovo ristampata e di figure in rame diligentemente intagliate arricchiata, corretta, e accresciuta da moltissime fabbriche inedite.* Venice, 1760–1768.

Nani, Battista. *The History of the Affairs of Europe in this present Age, but more particularly of the Republic of Venice. Englished by Sir Robert Knoeywood, Knight.* London, 1673.

Nani, Battista. *Historia della Republica Veneta.* 4th ed. Venice, 1686.

Nani Mocenigo, M. "L'Arsenale di Venezia." *Rivista marittima,* 1927.

Negri, F. *Notizia intorno alla persona e alle opere di Tommaso Temanza.* Venice, 1830.

The New Cambridge Modern History, vol. I, *The Renaissance,* ed. G. R. Potter. Cambridge, 1957.

Nicoletti, G. *Illustrazioni della chiesa e scuola di S Rocco.* Venice, 1885.

Niero, Don Antonio. *La basilica della Salute in Venezia.* Venice, 1957.

Niero, Don Antonio. *La chiesa dei Carmini.* Venezia Sacra no. 5. Venice, 1965.

Niero, Don Antonio. *La chiesa di S Sofia in Venezia: Storia ed arte.* Venice, 1972.

Niero, Don Antonio. *I patriarchi di Venezia.* Venice, 1961.

Niero, Don Antonio. *La scuola grande dei Carmini, storia e arte.* Venice, 1963.

Niero, Don Antonio; Scarpa, Gigi; and Tramontin, Silvio. *L'isola della Salute nella storia, nell'arte e nella pietà veneziana.* Venice, 1958.

Notizie interessanti che servono a far conoscere in tutti i suoi sestieri l'inclita città di Venezia. Belluno, 1779.

Okey, Thomas. *The Old Venetian Palaces and the Old Venetian Folk.* London, 1907.

(Ongania, Ferdinando.) *Calli e canali in Venezia.* Venice, 1900.

Ongania, Ferdinando. *Le vere da pozzo in Venezia.* Venice, 1911.

Ongaro, Max. *Il palazzo ducale di Venezia.* Venice, 1927.

Onians, J. B. "Style and Decorum in Italian Sixteenth-Century Art." Ph.D. dissertation, Warburg Institute, 1968.

Onofri, Fedele. *Cronologia veneta nella quale fedelmente e con brevità si descrivano le cose più notabili di questa famosissima città di Venetia.* Venice, 1691.

Orlandi, Fra Pellegrino Antonio. *L'abecedario pittorico.* Naples, 1733.

Orlandini, Giovanni. *Sullo origini delle denominazioni stradali veneziane.* Venice, 1912.

Oselladore, Dino. *La chiesa di S Zaccaria, seconda gemma della pietà veneziana.* Venice, 1964.

Pacifico, Pietro (Pier) Antonio. *Cronaca veneta, ovvero succinto racconto di tutte le cose più cospicue & antiche della città di Venezia.* Venice, 1697.

Pacifico, Pietro (Pier) Antonio. *Cronaca veneta sacra e profana, o sia un compendio di tutte le cose più illustri ed antiche della città di Venezia. Rinnovata in questa ultima edizione.* Venice, 1793.

Padoan Urban, Lina. "Teatri e 'teatri del mondo' nella Venezia del cinquecento." *Arte Veneta* XX, 1967.

Paganuzzi, Giovanni Battista. *Iconografia delle trenta parrocchie di Venezia.* Venice, 1821.

Palladio, Andrea. *L'antichità di Roma.* Rome, 1554.

Palladio, Andrea. *I cinque ordini di architettura...esposti per un'esatta istruzione di chi ama e coltiva questa bella utilissima arte.* Venice, 1784.

Palladio, Andrea. *Fabbriche antiche disegnate da Andrea Palladio e date in luce da Riccardo Conte di Burlington.* London, 1730.

Palladio, Andrea. *I quattro libri dell'architettura.* Venice, 1570.

Palladio. Catalogo della mostra. Texts by Forssman, Lotz, Cevese, Murray, Burns, Puppi, and Pallucchini. Venice and Vicenza, 1973.

Pallucchini, Rodolfo. "Andrea Palladio e Giulio Romano." *Bolletino del Centro Internazionale di Studi di Architettura 'Andrea Palladio'* I, 1959.

Pallucchini, Rodolfo. "L'arte veneziana del quattrocento." In *La civiltà veneziana del quattrocento.* Venice, 1957.

Pallucchini, Rodolfo. *Carlevarijs—Marieschi—Canaletto. Meraviglie di Venezia.* Milan, 1964.

Pallucchini, Rodolfo. *Catalogo, mostra degli incisori veneti del settecento.* Venice, 1941.

Pallucchini, Rodolfo. "Giulio Romano e Palladio." *Arte Veneta* XII, 1958.

Pallucchini, Rodolfo. "Vincenzo Scamozzi e l'architettura veneta." *L'Arte* XXXIX, 1936.

Pane, Roberto. *Andrea Palladio.* Turin, 1948. Revised ed. Turin, 1961.

Pane, Roberto. "Andrea Palladio e la interpretazione dell'architettura rinascimentale." In *Venezia e l'Europa.* Venice, 1955.

Pane, Roberto. "Palladio artista e trattatista." *Palladio* VI, 1942.

Pane, Roberto. "Palladio e la critica." *Comunità* XVII, January 1963.

Pane, Roberto. "I quattro libri dell'architettura." *Bollettino del Centro Internazionale di Studi di Architettura 'Andrea Palladio'* I, 1959.

Paoletti, Ermolao. *Il fiore de Venezia, ossia i quadri, i monumenti, le vedute ed i costumi veneziani.* Venice, 1837–1840.

Paoletti, O. *Raccolta di documenti inediti per servir alla storia della pittura veneziana.* Venice, 1894.

Paoletti, Piero. *L'architettura e la scultura del rinascimento in Venezia, ricerche storico-artistiche.* Venice, 1893–1897.

Paoletti, Piero. *L'architecture et la sculpture de la renaissance à Venice, recherches historico-artistiques traduit par M. M^{ie} Le-Monnier.* Venice, 1897–1898.

Paoletti, Piero. *La Scuola Grande di S Marco.* Venice, 1929.

Paolillo, D. R. and Dalla Santa, C. *Il Palazzo Dolfin-Manin a Rialto.* Venice, 1970.

Parks, George B., ed. *The English Traveler to Italy—The Middle Ages.* Stanford, Calif., 1954.

Paruta, Paolo. *Historia vinetiana.* Venice, 1605.

Paschini, Pio. "Daniele Barbaro letterato e prelato veneziano del Cinquecento." *Rivista di Storia della Chiesa in Italia* XVI, 1962.

Paschini, Pio. *Domenico Grimani Cardinale di S. Maria.* Rome, 1943.

Paschini, Pio. "Il mecenatismo artistico del cardinale Marino Grimani." In *Miscellanea in onore di R. Cessi.* Rome, 1958.

Paschini, Pio. "Il mecenatismo artistico del patriarca Giovanni Grimani." In *Studi in onore di A. Calderini e R. Paribeni.* Milan, 1956.

Pasinetti, Francesco. *Guida di Venezia.* Venice, 1949.

Pavanello, Giuseppe. *La chiesa di S Maria Formosa nella VI sua ricostruzione (659–1921).* Venice, 1921.

Pavanello, Giuseppe. "La scuola di San Fantin ora Ateneo Veneto." *Ateneo Veneto* I, 1914.

Pee, H. *Die Palastbauten des Andrea Palladio.* Wurzburg, 1941.

De'Pellegrini, G. *Armerista dei cittadini veneziani.* Venice, 1890–1891.

Penrose, Boies. *Travel and Discovery in the Renaissance, 1420–1620.* Cambridge, Massachusetts, 1952.

Perocco, Guido. *Guide to the School of S Giorgio degli Schiavoni.* Venice, 1959.

Perocco, Guido. "Umanesmo veneziano e umanesmo europeo." *La Fiera Litteraria,* 1960.

Perocco, Guido, and Salvadori, Antonio. *Civiltà di Venezia, Il Rinascimento.* Venice, 1974.

Pevsner, Nikolaus. *An Outline of European Architecture.* 6th ed. Harmondsworth, 1960.

Pevsner, Nikolaus. "Palladio and Europe." In *Venezia e l'Europa.* Venice, 1955.

Piamonte, Giannina. *Litorali ed isole. Guida della Laguna veneta.* Venice, 1975.

Piamonte, Giannina. *Venezia vista dall'aqua.* Venice, 1967.

Piel, Friedrich. *Die Ornament-Grotteske in der italienischen Renaissance. Zu ihrer kategorialen Striktur und Entstehung.* Berlin, 1962.

Pignatti, Terisio. *Canaletto, disegni scelti e annotati.* Florence, 1969.

Pignatti, Terisio. *Canaletto, Selected Drawings.* London, 1970.

Pignatti, Terisio. *Palazzo Ducale.* Novara, 1964.

Pignatti, Terisio. *Piazza S Marco.* Novara, 1958.

Pignatti, Terisio. "Il ponte di Rialto del Palladio e un disegno guardesco del Correr." *Bollettino dei Musei Civici Veneziani,* 1958.

Pignatti, Terisio. *Il quaderno del Canaletto alle gallerie di Venezia.* Milan, 1958.

Pignatti, Terisio. *Das venezianische Skizzenbuch von Canaletto.* Translated by Erich Steingräber. Munich, 1958.

Pignatti, Terisio. *Venezianische Veduten des 18 Jahrhunderts.* Nuremberg, 1964.

Pignatti, Terisio. *Venice.* London, 1971.

Pillati, F. "G Zorzi, I disegni delle antichità di Andrea Palladio." *Bollettino d'Arte* III, 1959.

Pilo Casagranda, F. "Un sconosciuto architetto d'altari Jacopo Antonio Pozzo (1645–1721)." *Palladio* VIII, 1958.

Pincus, Debra Dienstfrey. "A Hand by Antonio Rizzo and the Double Caritas Scheme of the Tron Tomb." *Art Bulletin* LI, 1969.

Piovene, Guido. "Anacronismo della Venezia quattrocentesca." In *La civiltà veneziana del quattrocento*. Venice, 1957.

Pittoni, Laura Coggiola. *Jacopo Sansovino, scultore*. Venice, 1909.

Pittoni, Laura Coggiola. "Note d'arte settecentesca veneziana." *Rivista della città di Venezia*, 1927.

Pivoto, Giannantonio. *Vetera ac nova ecclesiae sancti Thomae Monumenta editio secunda auctior et correctior*. Venice, 1758.

Planiscig, Leo. *Venezianische Bildhauer der Renaissance*. Vienna, 1921.

Pommer, Richard. "Italian Architectural Drawings on Tour in the USA." *Burlington Magazine* CIX, 1967.

Pompei, Alessandro. *Le cinque ordini dell'architettura civile di Michele Sanmicheli rilevati dalle sue fabriche e descritti e publicati con quelli di Vitruvio, Alberti, Palladio, Scamozzi, Serlio, e Vignola*. Verona, 1735.

Pope-Hennessy, Sir John. "The Evangelist Roundels in the Pazzi Chapel." *Apollo* CVI, no. 188, 1977.

Pope-Hennessy, Sir John. *Italian Renaissance Sculpture*. New York, 1958.

da Portogruaro, Davide. "Un'opera ignota di Baldassare Longhena." *Rivista di Venezia*, January 1933.

da Portogruaro, Davide. "Il tempio e il convento del Redentore." *Rivista mensile della città di Venezia* IV–V, 1930.

Della Pozza, A. *Palladiana*. Vicenza, 1941.

Della Pozza, A. *Palladio*. Vicenza, 1943.

Dal Pozzo, Bartolommeo. *Le vite de' pittori, degli scultori ed architetti veronesi*. Verona, 1718.

Prandi, A. *Trattati di architettura dal Vitruvio al secolo XVI*. Rome, 1949.

Prescott, Hilda Frances Margaret. *Friar Felix at Large*. New Haven, Conn., 1950.

Price, Lake. *Interiors and Exteriors in Venice by Lake Price, Lithographed by Joseph Nash from the Original Drawings*. London, 1843.

Prijatelli, K. "Opere poco note di architetti veneziani del seicento e settecento." *Arte Veneta* XV, 1961.

Priuli, Girolamo. *I diarii, 1494–1512*. Edited by Roberto Cessi. Bologna, 1912–1938.

Pullan, Brian, ed. *Crisis and Change in the Venetian Economy*. London, 1968.

Pullan, Brian. *Rich and Poor in Renaissance Venice*. Oxford, 1971.

Puppi, Lionello. *Andrea Palladio*. Milan, 1973.

Puppi, Lionello. "Filarete in Gondola." *Arte Lombarda* XVIII, 1973.

Puppi, Lionello. *Michele Sanmicheli, architetto di Verona*. Padua, 1971.

Puppi, Lionello. *Palladio*. Florence, 1966.

Puppi, Lionello. "Il 'Sesto libro' del Serlio." *Arte Veneta* XXI, 1967.

Puppi, Lionello, and Puppi, Loredana Olivato. *Mauro Codussi*. Milan, 1977.

Quadri, Antonio, and Moretti, Dionisio. *Il Canal Grande di Venezia descritto da Antonio Quadri rilevato ed inciso da Dionisio Moretti*. Venice, 1828.

Quadri, Antonio. *Descrizione topografica di Venezia e delle adiacente lagune*. Venice, 1840–1941.

Quadri, Antonio. *Otto giorni a Venezia*. Venice, 1821–1922.

Quadri, Antonio. *Tempio d'SS Giovanni e Paolo in Venezia descritto ed illustrato*. Venice, 1835.

Quadri, Antonio. *Venezia descritta*. Venice, 1828.

Rambaldi, Pier Liberali. *La chiesa dei SS Giovanni e Paolo e la cappella del Rosario*. Venice, 1913.

Rambaldi, Pier Liberali. *La Scala dei Giganti in Palazzo Ducale, Memorie storiche e documenti del restauro del 1728*. Venice, 1910.

Rambaldi, Pier Liberali; Dal Zotto, Antonio; Savini, Marco; and Marangoni, Luigi. *Per il restauro della cappella del Rosario nella chiesa dei SS Giovanni e Paolo in Venezia*. Venice, 1910.

Ravà, Aldo. "Appartamenti e arredi veneziani del '700. Il ridotto della Procuratessa Venier e il mezzanino del Palazzo Vendramin ai Carmini." *Dedalo*, 1920.

Ravà, Béatrix. *Venise dans la littérature francaise depuis les origines jusqu'à la mort de Henri IV.* Paris, 1916.

Raymond, J. *An itinerary contayning a voyage made through Italy in the years 1646 and 1647. Illustrated with divers figures of antiquities. Never before published.* London, 1648.

Régnier, Henri de. *La vie vénetienne (1899–1924).* Paris, 1963.

Relatione della Città e Republica di Venetia. Nella quale sono descritti li principali di sua edificatione, avanzamenti, acquisti, e perdite fatte, governo, riti, costumi, dominio, forze, erario, adherenze con prencipi, e differenze con gl'elettori dell'Impero per causa di precedenza. Cologne, 1672.

The Renaissance, a Reconsideration of the Theories and Interpretations of the Age. Edited by Tinsley Helton. Madison, Wisc., 1961.

Renier-Michiel, Giustina. *Origine delle feste veneziane. Nuova ristampata dell'edizione del MDCCCXXIX con una introduzione di Federico Pellegrini.* Venice, 1916.

Restauri all'isola di S Giorgio Maggiore. Venice, 1964.

Ricci, Amico. *Storia dell'architettura in Italia dal secolo IV al XVIII.* 3 vols., 1857–1859. Reprint. Bologna, 1967.

Riccioti Bratti. See Bratti.

Richard, (Abbé) Jerome. *Description historique et critique de l'Italie, ou nouveaux mémoires sur l'état actuel de son gouvernement, des sciences, des arts, du commerce, de la population & de l'histoire naturelle.* Dijon and Paris, 1766.

Ridolfi, Carlo. *Le maraviglie dell'arte o vero le vite degl'illustri pittori veneti e dello stato.* 1648. Reprint, edited by Detlef Freiherr von Hadeln. Berlin, 1914–1924.

Ridolfi, Ottaviano. *Li cinque ordini di architettura et aggiunta de l'opere del ecc. M Giacomo Barocio da Vignola con un ragionamento di M Ottaviano Ridolfi.* Venice, 1603.

Rizzi, Aldo. *Luca Carlevarijs.* Venice, 1967.

Rizzi, Paolo. "Così la 'macchina' impedisce un restauro da un miliardo." *Il Gazzettino,* 10 February 1978.

Robb, Brian. *Tintoretto's S Rocco Crucifixion.* London, 1969.

Robertson, Giles. *Giovanni Bellini.* Oxford, 1968.

Rodolico, Francesco. *Le pietre dure delle città d'Italia.* Florence, 1953.

Rodriguez Canevari, Bruna. "La casa de Pietro Liberi sul Canal Grande a Venezia." *Saggi e memorie di storia dell'arte* IX, 1974.

Rogers, Ernesto N. "Palladio e noi." *Bollettino del Centro Internazionale di Studi di Architettura 'Andrea Palladio'* I, 1959.

Rogissart, Sieur de, and Havard, Abbé. *Les délices d'Italie contenant une description exacte du pais, des principales villes, de toutes les antiquités, & des toutes les raretez qui s'y trouvent.* Paris, 1707.

Romanin, Samuele. *Storia documentata di Venezia.* Venice, 1912.

Rosci, Marco. *Il trattato di architettura di Sebastiano Serlio.* Milan, 1967.

Rosenfeld, Myra Nan. "Sebastiano Serlio's Late Style in the Avery Library Version of the Sixth Book on Domestic Architecture." *Journal of the Society of Architectural Historians* XXVIII, 1969.

Rossi, Paola. *Girolamo Campagna.* Verona, 1968.

Rowdon, Maurice. *The Fall of Venice.* London, 1970.

Rusconi, Giovantonio. *Dell'architettura di Gio Antonio Rusconi con centosessanta figure dissegnate dal medesimo, secondo i precetti di Vitruvio, e con chiarezza e brevità dichiarate libri dieci.* Venice, 1590.

Rusconi, Giovanni Antonio. *I dieci libri di architettura di Gio: Antonio Rusconi. Secondo i precetti di Vitruvio, nuovamente ristampati & accresciuti della prattica degl'horologi solari.* Venice, 1660.

Ruskin, John. *Examples of the Architecture of Venice.* London, 1887.

Ruskin, John. *St Mark's Rest.* New York, 1879.

Ruskin, John. *The Stones of Venice.* London, 1851–1858.

Saalman, Howard. "Early Italian Architecture." *Burlington Magazine* CXX, 1978.

Saalman, Howard. "Early Renaissance Theory and Practice in Antonio Filarete's Trattato di Architettura." *Art Bulletin* XLI, 1959.

Sabellico, Marco Antonio Coccio, called. *Chroniche che tractano de la origine de Veneti e del principio de la cita o de tutte le guere da mare e terra facte in Italia: Dalmatia: Grecia: e contra tuti di infedeli composto per lo excelentissimo mesere Marco Antonio Sabellico e volgarizato per Matheo Vesconte da Sancto Canciano.* Milan, 1508.

Sabellico, Marco Antonio. *Historiae rerum Venetarum ab urbe condita libri XXXIII.* Basel, 1556.

Sabellico, Marco Antonio. *Le historie vinitiane divise in tre Deche con tre libri della quarta Deca. Nuovamente ricorrette & in diverse parte accresciute di molte cose, che nell'esemplare Latino mancauano.* Venice, 1554.

Sabellici, Marci Ant. *De Venetae Urbis situ* (in Opera Omnia). Venice, 1494.

Sacchi, F. *Venezia.* Novara, 1941.

Sagredo, Agostino. *Degli edifici consacrati al culto divino in Venezia o distrutti o mutati d'uso nella prima metà del secolo XIX, note storiche tratte da un catalogo inedito di don Sante della Valentina.* Venice, 1852.

Sagredo, Agostino. *Sulle consorterie delle arti edificatorie in Venezia.* Venice, 1856.

Saint-Didier, Linajon de. *La ville et la République de Venise.* Paris, 1680.

Salvadori, Antonio. *101 Buildings to See in Venice.* Translated by Brenda Balich. Venice, 1969.

Sajanello, Giovanni Battista. *Historica monumenta ordinis sancti Heironymi congregationis B Petri de Pisis.* Venice, 1742–1758.

Samonà, Giuseppe, et al. *Piazza S Marco: l'architettura, la storia, le funzioni.* Padua, 1976.

Sandri, Maria Grazia, and Alazraki, Paolo. *Arte e vita ebraica a Venezia 1516–1797.* Florence, 1971.

Michele Sanmicheli, 1484–1559, Studi raccolti dall'Accademia di Agricoltura, Scienze e Lettere di Verona per le celebrazioni del quarto centenario della morte dell'architetto veronese. Verona, 1960.

Sansovino, Francesco. *Delle cose notabili che sono in Venezia.* Venice, 1561.

Sansovino, Francesco. *Delle cose notabili della città di Venetia, libri II, nuovamente riformati, accresciuti et abeliti con l'aggiunta della dichiarazione delle istorie che sono state dipinte nella sala dello Scrutinio e del Gran Consiglio Ducale, fatta da Girolamo Bardi fiorentino.* Venice, 1587.

Sansovino, Francesco. *Venetia città nobilissima et singolare descritta in XIII libri.* Venice, 1581.

Sansovino, Francesco, and Stringa, Giovanni. *Venetia città nobilissima...con molta diligenza corretta, commentata.* Venice, 1604.

Sansovino, Francesco; Stringa, Giovanni; and Martinioni, D Giustiniano. *Venetia città nobilissima et singolare descritta in XIIII libri da M Francesco Sansovino...con aggiunta da D Giustiniano Martinioni.* Venice, 1663.

Sanuto, Marin. *Cronachetta (1493).* Edited by R. Fulin. Venice, 1880.

Sanuto, Marin. *I diarii, 1496–1533.* Edited by R. Fulin, F. Stefani, N. Barozzi, G. Berchet, and M. Allegri. Venice, 1879–1903.

Sanuto, Marin. *Vite dei dogi.* Città di Castello, 1906.

Sapori, Francesco. *Jacopo Tatti detto il Sansovino.* Rome, 1928.

Sardella, Pierre. *Nouvelles et spéculations à Venise au début du XVIe siècle.* Paris, 1948.

Sartori, Fra. *S Maria Gloriosa dei Frari.* Venice, 1956.

Scamozzi, Vincenzo. *L'idea della Architettura universale.* Venice, 1615.

Scamozzi, Vincenzo. *Taccuino di viaggio da Parigi a Venezia.* Edited by Franco Barbieri. Venice and Rome, 1959.

Scattolin, Angelo. *I "casoni" veneti.* Venice, 1936.

Scattolin, Angelo, and Rotondi, Pasquale. *Palazzo Labia in Venezia.* Venice, 1969.

Scattolin, Giorgia. *La scuola grande di S Teodoro.* Venice, 1961.

Schlosser, Julius von. *Zwei Kapitel aus der Biografie einer Stadt.* Darmstadt, 1958.

Festschrift Wolf Schubert. Weimar, 1967.

Schubring, Paul. *Die Architektur der Italienischen Hochrenaissance.* Munich, 1924.

Schudt, Ludwig. *Italienreisen im 17 und 18 Jahrhundert.* Vienna, 1959.

Schulz, Juergen. "The Printed Plans and Panoramic Views of Venice, 1486–1797." *Saggi e memorie di storia dell'arte* VII, 1970.

Schulz, Juergen. "Vasari at Venice." *Burlington Magazine* CIII, 1961.

Schulz, Juergen. *Venetian Painted Ceilings of the Renaissance.* Berkeley, California, 1968.

Scolari, Filippo. *La chiesa di S Maria del Pianto in Venezia ridonata al culto publico.* Venice, 1851.

Scolari, Filippo. *Commentario sulla vita e sulle opere di Scamozzi.* Treviso, 1837.

Scott, Geoffrey. *The Architecture of Humanism.* 2d ed. 1924. Reprint, Gloucester, Mass., 1965.

Seguso, L. *La chiesa di S Cassiano ed il restauro di una chiesetta annessata.* Venice, 1886.

Selva, Giovanni Antonio. *Petit ouvrage posthume de Jean Antoine Selva redigé par M Gamba.* Venice, 1819.

Selvatico, Pietro. *Guida di Padova e dei suoi principali contorni.* Padua, 1869.

Selvatico, Pietro. *Storia estetico-critica delle arti del disegno.* Venice, 1856.

Selvatico, Pietro. *Sulla architettura e sulla scultura in Venezia dal medioevo sino ai nostri giorni.* Venice, 1847.

Selvatico, Pietro, and Lazari, V. *Guida di Venezia e delle isole circonvicine.* Venice, 1852.

Semenzato, Camillo. "Classicità e classicismo di M Sanmicheli." *Vita Veronese,* December 1959.

Semenzato, Camillo. "Elogio del Falconetto." *Padova* IV, 1958.

Semenzato, Camillo. "Pietro e Tullio Lombardo architetti." *Bollettino del Centro di Studi di Architettura 'Andrea Palladio'* VI, 1964.

Semenzato, Camillo. "Problemi di architettura veneta: Giorgio Massari." *Arte Veneta* XI, 1957.

Semenzato, Camillo. "Il viaggio dello Scamozzi da Parigi a Venezia." *Arte Veneta* XIII–XIV, 1959–1960.

Serlio, Sebastiano. *Libro Primo d'architettura di Sebastiano Serlio... secondo...terzo...quarto...quinto.* Venice, 1559.

Serlio, Sebastiano. *Tutte le opere d'architettura, di nuovo aggiunto (oltre il libro delle porte) gran numero di case private...raccolto di Gio Dom Scamozzi.* Venice, 1584.

Serra, Luigi. *A Vittoria.* Rome, 1921.

Serra, Luigi. *The Doge's Palace.* Rome, 1956.

Setton, Kenneth M. "The Byzantine Background to the Italian Renaissance." *Proceedings of the American Philosophical Society* C, no. 1, 1956.

Simonsfeld, Heinrich. *Der Fondaco dei Tedeschi in Venedig und der deutsch-venezianischen Handelsbezeihungen.* Stuttgart, 1887.

Sinding-Larsen, Staale. "Some Functional and Iconographical Aspects of the Centralized Church in the Italian Renaissance." *Institutum Romanum Norvegiae Acta* II, 1965.

Sirigatti, Lorenzo. *La pratica di prospettiva.* Venice, 1596.

Smart, Alastair. *The Renaissance and Mannerism in Italy.* London, 1971.

A Catalogue of the Capital & Valuable Cabinet of Prints, Books of Prints, & Drawings of Joseph Smith, Esq., His Majesty's Consul at Venice (lately deceased). London, 1776.

Sommi Picenardi, G. *Del gran priorato dell'Ordine Gerosolimitano detto di Malta in Venezia.* Venice, privately printed ca. 1965.

Soravia, G. B. *Le chiese di Venezia descritte e illustrate.* Venice, 1822–1824.

Spencer, John. "The Ca' del Duca in Venice and Benedetto Ferrini." *Journal of the Society of Architectural Historians* XXIX, 1970.

Spezzati, Gastone. *Le ville venete della riviera del Brenta.* Venice, 1962.

Spielmann, Heinz. *Andrea Palladio und die Antike, Untersuchung und Katalog der Zeichnungen aus seinem Nachlass.* Munich, 1966.

Sprigge, Sylvia. *The Lagoon of Venice, Its Islands and Communications.* London, 1961.

Stedman, Wendy. "The Tomb of Andrea Vendramin in SS Giovanni e Paolo, Venice, by Tullio Lombardo." Ph.D. dissertation, Yale University, n.d.

Stefanutti, Ugo. *La scuola grande di S Marco.* Venice, 1960.

Stella, A. "La crisi economica della seconda metà del secolo XVI." *Archivio veneto,* series 5a, LVIII-LIX, 1959.

Stokes, Adrian. *Venice, an Aspect of Art.* London, 1945.

Stringa Giovanni. *La Venezia già descritta da Messer Francesco Sansovino ed hora con molta diligenza ampliata da Giovanni Stringa.* Venice, 1604.

Strong, D. E. "Drawings by Palladio from the Antique." *Burlington Magazine* CII, 1960.

Studi in onore di Mons, Carlo Castiglioni. Milan, 1957.

Tafuri, Manfredo. *L'architettura del manierismo nel cinquecento italiano.* Rome, 1966.

Tafuri, Manfredo. *L'architettura dell'umanesimo.* Bari, 1969.

Tafuri, Manfredo. *Jacopo Sansovino e l'architettura del '500 a Venezia.* Vicenza, 1969.

Tassini, Giuseppe. *Alcuni palazzi ed antichi edifici di Venezia storicamente illustrati.* Venice, 1879.

Tassini, Giuseppe. *Curiosità veneziane, ovvero origini delle denominazioni stradali di Venezia.* 4th ed., 1887. Reprint, with an introduction by Lino Moretti. Venice, 1964.

Tassini, Giuseppe. *Edifici di Venezia distrutti o volti ad altro uso da quello cui furono in origini destinati.* Reprint, Venice, 1885.

Tea, M. "M Sanmicheli; la vita e le opere." *Vita Veronese,* December 1959.

(Temanza, Tommaso.) *Delle antichità di Rimini.* Venice, 1741.

Temanza, Tommaso. *Dissertazione sopra un'antica pianta dell'inclita città di Venezia delineata circa la metà del XII secolo.* Venice, 1781.

Temanza, Tommaso. *Vite dei più celebri architetti e scultori veneziani che fiorirono nel secolo decimosesto.* Venice, 1778.

Temanza, Tommaso. *Zibaldon.* Edited by Nicola Ivanoff. Venice and Rome, 1963.

Teneti, Alberto. *Piracy and the Decline of Venice.* London, 1967.

Tenenti, Alberto. "Studi di storia veneziana." *Rivista Storica Italiana* LXXVI, no. 2, 1963.

Thieme, Ulrich, and Becker, Felix, editors. *Allgemeines Lexikon der bildenden Künstler.* 34 vols. Leipzig, 1907-1940.

Tietze, Hans, and Tietze-Conrat, Erica. "The Artist of the 1486 View of Venice." *Gazette des Beaux-Arts* XXIII, 1943.

Tietze, Hans, and Tietze-Conrat, Erica. "The Iconography of Michele Sanmicheli." *Gazette des Beaux-Arts* XXIX, 1946.

Timofiewitsch, Wladimir. "Der Altar der Scuola degli Orefici in S Giacometto in Venedig." *Mitteilungen der Kunsthistorischen Instituts in Florenz* IV, 1963-1965.

Timofiewitsch, Wladimir. "Ein Beitrag zur Baugeschichte der Procuratie Nuove." *Arte Veneta* XVIII, 1964.

Timofiewitsch, Wladimir. "Fassadenentwürfe Andrea Palladios für S Petronio in Bologna." *Arte Veneta* XVI, 1962.

Timofiewitsch, Wladimir. "Genesi e struttura della chiesa del Rinascimento veneziano." *Bollettino del Centro Internazionale di Studi di Architettura 'Andrea Palladio'* VI, 1964.

Timofiewitsch, Wladimir. "Ein Gutachten Sebastiano Serlios für die Scuola di S Rocco." *Arte Veneta* XVII, 1963.

Timofiewitsch, Wladimir. "Literaturberecht: Die Palladioforschung in den Jahren 1940-1960." *Zeitschrift für Kunstgeschichte* XXIII, 1960.

Timofiewitsch, Wladimir. *Die sakrale Architektur Palladios.* Munich, 1968.

Timofiewitsch, Wladimir. "Ein unbekannte Kirchenentwurf Palladios." *Arte Veneta* XIII-XIV, 1959-1960.

Timofiewitsch, Wladimir. "Eine Zeichnung Andrea Palladios für die Klosteranlage von S Giorgio." *Arte Veneta* XVI, 1962.

Toniolo, Anna. "The Gardens of Venice." *Apollo* XC, 1969.

Toscanella, Orazio. *I nomi antichi e moderni delle provincie.* Venice, 1567.

Toynbee, Arnold. *A Study of History.* London, 1954.

Toynbee, Arnold, ed. *Cities of Destiny.* London, 1967.

Tramontin, Silvio, and Corrao, B. *S Canciano, la Chiesa e la Parrocchia.* Venice, 1970.

Tramontin, Silvio. *S Giovanni Grisostomo* (Venezia Sacra 7). Venice, 1968.

Tramontin, Silvio. *S Maria Mater Domini* (Venezia Sacra 3). Venice, 1962.

Tramontin, Silvio. *La chiesa di S Maria dei Miracoli* (Venezia Sacra 1). Venice, 1959.

Tramontin, Silvio. *S Stae, la chiesa e la parrocchia* (Venezia Sacra 2). Venice, 1961.

Trevisano, Bernardo. *Della laguna di Venezia.* 2d ed. Venice, 1718.

Trevisano, Bernardo. *Descrizione delle isole che circondono la città di Venezia.* Venice, 1754.

Trincanato, Egle Renata. *Appunti per una conoscenza urbanistica di Venezia.* Venice, 1954.

Trincanato, Egle Renata. *Palazzo Ducale, Venezia.* Novara, 1969.

Trincanato, Egle Renata. *Venezia minore, con un capitolo di Agnoldomenico Pica.* Milan, 1948.

Un Turchio architetto. Riflessioni sopra alcuni equivoci sensi espressi dall'autore dell'orazione recitata in Venezia dell'Accademia di Belle Arti l'anno 1787 in difesa del fu F Carlo Lodoli. Padua, 1788.

Umanesimo europeo e umanesimo veneziano. Florence, 1963.

UNESCO. *Rapporto su Venezia.* Milan, 1969.

Ungaro, Giuseppe. *The Basilica of the Frari.* Padua, 1972.

Urbani de Gheltof, Giuseppe Marino. *I camini.* Venice, 1892.

Urbani de Gheltof, Giuseppe Marino. *Conservazione dei monumenti in Venezia.* Venice, 1879.

Urbani de Gheltof, Giuseppe Marino. *Guida storico-artistica della Scuola di S Giovanni Evangelista.* Venice, 1895.

Urbani de Gheltof, Giuseppe Marino. *Il palazzo di Camillo Trevisan a Murano.* Venice, 1890.

Valeri, Diego. *Venise.* Notes by Rodolfo Pallucchini. Paris, 1957.

Valeri, Nino. *L'Italia nell'età dei principati del 1343 al 1516.* Verona, 1950.

Vardanega, A. Le chiese di Venezia dedicate alla Vergine "S Maria Mater Domini." *Mater Dei* I, 1929.

Vasari, Giorgio. *The Lives of the Painters, Sculptors and Architects.* Translated by A. B. Hinds. London, 1963.

Vasari, Giorgio. *Vita di Jacopo Tatti detto il Sansovino.* Edited by Giulio Lorenzetti. Florence, 1913.

Vaughn, Dorothy. *Europe and the Turk: A Pattern of Alliances 1350–1700.* Liverpool, 1954.

Vaussard, Maurice. *Daily Life in Eighteenth-century Italy.* Translated by Michael Heron. London, 1962.

Veludo, Tommaso. *Venezia e le sue lagune.* Venice, 1847.

Venezia e l'Europa. Atti del XVIII Congresso Internazionale di Storia dell'Arte. Venice, 1955.

Venice. Museo Civico Correr. "Compendio dell'ordine e progresso del Monastero illmo. di S Lorenzo" (by Tomaso Fuggazoni).

Venice, Museo Civico Correr. "Raccolta di disegni originali dell'ingegnere Cesare Fustinelli di Provenienza Cicogna-Casoni."

Venice. Museo Civico Correr. Antonio Gaspari papers.

Venice. Museo Civico Correr. "Monumenta veneta ex antiquis rederibus templorum, aliarumque aedium vetustate collapsarum collecta, studio et cura Pietri Gradonici Jacobi Den F, Anno MDCCLIX." Ms. Gradenigo 228 (by Jan van Grevenbroeck).

Venice. Correr Library. C D C 819 1500/10. Codice Paoletti.

Venice. Museo Civico Correr. "Il Contra Rusconi o Sia l'Esame Sopra l'Architettura di Giovanni Rusconi. Trattato architettonico preparato per la stampa e illustrato con disegni del Visentini ma mai pubblicato" (by Antonio Visentini).

Venturi, Adolfo. *Storia dell'arte italiana.* Milan, 1901–1940.

Vianello, Riccardo. *La Giudecca, una gemma di Venezia.* Venice, 1966.

Visentini, Antonio. *Isolario veneto, ovvero prospettive de XX isole situate intorno alla città di Venezia disegnate con esatezza con nobile varietà di ornati.* Venice, 1777.

Visentini, Antonio. *Osservazioni di Antonio Visentini architetto veneto che servono di continuazione al trattato di Teofilo Gallaccini sopra gli errori degli architetti.* Venice, 1771.

Vittoria, Eugenio. *Venice, the Ducal Palace.* Translated by Margaret Forsman Shor. Venice, 1974.

Vivian, Frances. "Joseph Smith and the Cult of Palladianism." *Burlington Magazine* CV, 1963.

Vivian, Frances. "Joseph Smith, Antonio Visentini, e il movimento neoclassico." *Bollettino del Centro Internazionale di Studi di Architettura 'Andrea Palladio'* V, 1963.

Vivian, Frances. "Joseph Smith, Giovanni Poleni and Antonio Visentini." *Italian Studies* XVIII, 1963.

Vucetich, A. *Elenco degli edifici monumentali.* Venice, 1905.

Watson, Francis John Bagott. "Notes on Canaletto and his Engravers." *Burlington Magazine* XCII, 1950.

Watson, Francis John Bagott. "Un nuovo libro di disegni del Carlevarijs." *Arte Veneta* IV, 1950.

Weise, Georg. "Vitalismo, animismo e panpsichismo e la decorazione del cinquecento e seicento." *Critica d'Arte* VI, 1959.

West, Thomas Wilson. *A History of Architecture in Italy.* London, 1968.

Willich, Hans, and Zurcher, Paul. *Die Baukunst der Renaissance in Italien.* Wildpark and Potsdam, 1929.

Wischnitzer, Rachel. *The Architecture of the European Synagogue.* Philadelphia, 1964.

Wittkower, Rudolph. *Architectural Principles in the Age of Humanism.* 2d rev. ed. London, 1960.

Wittkower, Rudolph. *Art and Architecture in Italy 1600–1750.* London, 1958.

Wittkower, Rudolph. "S Maria della Salute: Scenographic Architecture and the Venetian Baroque." *Journal of the Society of Architectural Historians* XVI, 1957.

Wittkower, Rudolph. "S Maria della Salute." *Saggi e memorie di storia dell'arte* III, 1966.

Wittkower, Rudolph. "Sviluppo stilistico dell'architettura palladiana." *Bollettino del Centro Internazionale di Studi di Architettura 'Andrea Palladio'* I, 1959.

Wolters, Wolfgang. "Casino Mocenigo." *Antichità Viva* V, 1966.

Würtenberger, Franzsepp. *Der Manierismus.* Vienna and Munich, 1961.

Yriarte, Charles. *Venise, histoire, art, industrie, la ville, la vie.* Paris, 1876.

Yriarte, Charles. *La vie d'un patricien de Venise au XVIe siècle.* Paris, 1874.

Zanella, Giacomo. *Vita di Andrea Palladio.* Milan, 1880.

Zanetti, Vincenzo. *Guida di Murano.* Venice, 1866.

Zangirolami, Cesare. *Indicatori anagrafici.* Venice, 1921.

Zangirolami, Cesare. *Storia delle chiese, dei monasteri, delle scuole di Venezia, rapinate e distrutte da Napoleone Bonaparte.* Venice, 1962.

Zanini, Gioseffe Viola. *Della architettura di Gioseffe Viola Zanini, padovano, pittore, et architetto, libre due.* Padua, 1629.

Zanotte, Francesco. *Guida Massima della città di Venezia.* Venice, 1852.

Zanotto, Francesco. *Il Palazzo Ducale di Venezia.* Venice, 1853–1861.

Zanotto, Francesco. *Nuovissima guida di Venezia e delle isole della sua laguna, nella quale si sono coretti da oltre 200 errori che s'incontrono nelle altre guide.* Venice, 1856.

(Zanotto, Francesco.) "Pittura, architettura, scultura, e calcografia." In *Venezia e le sue lagune,* vol. VII. Venice, 1847.

Zanotto, Francesco. *Venezia prospettica monumentale storica ed artistica.* Venice, 1856.

Zarlino, Gioseffo. *Istitutioni harmoniche del rev. messere Gioseffo Zarlino da Chioggia.* Venice, 1573.

Zava Boccazzi, Franca. *La Basilica dei SS Giovanni e Paolo in Venezia.* Venice, 1965.

(Zeno, Niccolò.) *Dell'origine di Venetia et antiquissime memorie de i barbari, che distrussero per tutto'l mondo l'imperio di Roma onde hebbe principio la città di Venetia.* Venice, 1558.

Zevi, Bruno. "Attualità culturale di Michèle Sanmicheli." *Bollettino del Centro Internazionale di Studi di Architettura 'Andrea Palladio'* I, 1959.

Zevi, Bruno. "Problemi di interpretazione critica dell'architettura veneta." *Bollettino del Centro Internazionale di Studi di Architettura 'Andrea Palladio'* I, 1959.

Zilotti, G. M. *Il tempio della Pace innalzato alla gloria di Maria nel chiostro esteriore dei Padri Predicatori dei SS Giovanni e Paolo di Venezia.* Venice, 1675.

Zompini, Gaetano Gherardo. *Le arti che vanno per via nella Città di Venezia inventate ed intagliate da Gaetano Zompini.* Venice, 1753.

Dalla Zorza, A. *Palladio.* Vicenza, 1943.

Zorzi, Alvise. *Venezia scomparsa.* Venice, 1971.

Zorzi, E. *Venezia.* Milan, 1942.

Zorzi, Giangiorgio. "Altri disegni di vari artisti riguardanti monumenti antichi nelle raccolte palladiane di Vicenza e Londra. *Palladio* I–II, 1956.

Zorzi, Giangiorgio. "Ancora della vera origine e della giovinezza di Andrea Palladio secondo nuovi documenti." *Arte Veneta* III, 1949.

Zorzi, Giangiorgio. *Le chiese e i ponti di Andrea Palladio.* Venice, 1967.

Zorzi, Giangiorgio. "Il contribuito di Andrea Palladio e di Francesco Zamberlan al restauro del Palazzo Ducale di Venezia dopo l'incendio del 20 dicembre 1577." *Atti dell'Istituto Veneto di Scienze, Lettere ed Arti* CXV, no. 2, 1956–1957.

Zorzi, Giangiorgio. "Contribuzione alla datazione di alcune opere palladiane." *Arte Veneta* IX, 1955.

Zorzi, Giangiorgio. *I disegni delle antichità di Andrea Palladio.* Venice, 1959.

Zorzi, Giangiorgio. "Due rivendicazioni palladiani." *Arte Veneta* VI, 1952.

Zorzi, Giangiorgio. "Nuove rivelazioni sulla ricostruzione delle sale al piano nobile del Palazzo Ducale di Venezia dopo l'incendio dell' 11 maggio 1574." *Arte Veneta* VII, 1953.

Zorzi, Giangiorgio. *Le opere pubbliche e i palazzi privati di Andrea Palladio.* Venice, 1965.

Zorzi, Giangiorgio. "Progetti giovanili di Andrea Palladio per palazzi e case in Venezia e in terraferma." *Palladio* IV, 1954.

Zorzi, Giangiorgio. "Quattro monumenti sepolcrali disegnati da Andrea Palladio." *Arte Veneta* XVII, 1962.

Zorzi, Giangiorgio. "La vera origine e la giovinezza di Andrea Palladio." *Archivio Veneto Tridentino* II, 1922.

Zorzi, Giangiorgio. *Le ville e i teatri di Andrea Palladio.* Venice, 1968.

Zorzi, Ludovico. "Elementi per la visualizzazione della scena veneta prima del Palladio." In *Studi sul teatro veneto fra Rinascimento ed età barocca,* edited by Maria Teresa Muraro. Florence, 1971.

Zucchini, Tommaso Arcangelo. *Nuova cronaca veneta, ossia Descrizione di tutte le pubbliche architetture sculture e pitture nella città di Venezia divisa in sei sestieri.* Venice, 1784.

Zuccolo, Giovanni. *Il restauro statico dell'architettura di Venezia.* Venice, 1975.

Zurcher, Richard. *Stilprobleme der italienischen Baukunst des Cinquecento.* Basel, 1947.

De Zurko, Edward Robert. "Alberti's Theory of Form and Function." *Art Bulletin* XXXIX, 1957.

SOURCES AND CREDITS FOR ILLUSTRATIONS

INDEX